POLITICS
and the
NOVEL DURING
the
COLD WAR

By David Caute
Non-Fiction

Politics and the Novel during the Cold War
Marechera and the Colonel: A Zimbabwean Writer & the
  Claims of the State
The Dancer Defects: The Struggle for Cultural Supremacy
  During the Cold War
Joseph Losey: A Revenge on Life
The Fellow-Travellers: Intellectual Friends of Communism
Sixty-Eight: The Year of the Barricades
The Espionage of the Saints
Under the Skin: The Death of White Rhodesia
The Great Fear: The Anti-Communist Purge under Truman and
  Eisenhower
The Fellow-Travellers: A Postscript to the Enlightenment
The Illusion: Politics, Theatre & the Novel
Frantz Fanon
The Left in Europe since 1789
Essential Writings of Karl Marx
Communism and the French Intellectuals

Fiction

Fatima's Scarf
Dr Orwell and Mr Blair
The Women's Hour
Veronica and the Two Nations
News from Nowhere
The K-Factor
The Occupation
The Decline of the West
Comrade Jacob
At Fever Pitch

POLITICS
and the
NOVEL DURING
the
COLD WAR

David Caute

Transaction Publishers
New Brunswick (U.S.A.) and London (U.K.)

Library of Congress Catalog Number: 2009044440
ISBN: 978-1-4128-1161-3
Printed in the United States of America

Library of Congress Cataloging-in-Publication Data

Caute, David.
    Politics and the novel during the Cold War / David Caute.
        p. cm.
    Includes bibliographical references and index.
    ISBN 978-1-4128-1161-3 (alk. paper)
        1. Fiction--20th century--History and criticism. 2. Political fiction--History and criticism. 3. Cold War in literature. 4. War and literature. 5. Politics and literature. I. Title.

PN3448.P6C38 2009
809.3'935809045--dc22

                                                        2009044440

FOR MARTHA

Contents

Introduction

In these pages I set out to examine how politically engaged novelists of the Cold War era, Western and Soviet, conveyed their understanding of recent and contemporary history through works of fiction.

The Cold War is normally pasted into history books post-1945, with the rapid cooling of the wartime military alliance against Nazi Germany; yet hostility between the major capitalist states and Bolshevik Russia extends back to the October Revolution of 1917, resulting in a separate peace ceding Russian territory to Germany signed at Brest-Litovsk (March 1918). This hostility becomes fiercer with the armed intervention of America, France and Britain in the Civil War on the side of the tsarist ('White') generals. The founding of the Communist International (also known as the Third International or Comintern), following social insurrections in Germany, posed a clear threat to carry the Bolshevik Revolution to the West. Large Communist parties in Germany and France announced allegiance to Moscow. Diplomatic recognition of the Soviet Union, a pariah state, was long delayed, in America's case until 1933. Hostility to Bolshevism and the Communist International prevented the formation of an effective diplomatic and military coalition to resist Hitler's grotesquely rapid aggressions against Austria, Czechoslovakia and Poland. That London and Paris preferred appeasement to Moscow's embrace, became evident when a coalition of monarchists, falangists and other conservative forces rose in revolt against the Spanish Popular Front Government constitutionally elected in 1936.

A prime aim of the present study is to compare Soviet and Western fictional responses to the Cold War, bearing in mind that the geographical and linguistic divide in American and European universities between 'Russian Studies' and 'Cold War Studies,' now reinforced by a noticeable ideological divide, has tended to impede a comparative approach.

In the United States and Western Europe, the 'political' novel, the urgent, morally committed depiction of recent tragedies and disasters, flourished spontaneously in the 1930s and 1940s, the crisis years of economic depression, fascism, the Spanish Civil War, the rise of Stalinism, and the Second World War. The thirties and forties spawned arguably the greatest era of political fiction and playwriting we have known: Feuchtwanger, Heinrich Mann, Brecht, Malraux, Koestler, Orwell, Hemingway, Dos Passos, Sinclair Lewis, James T. Farrell,

1

Steinbeck, Sartre, Camus were all at work. Almost all of the cardinal political dramas of those twenty years are to be found in literary fiction or reportage by creative writers. But by mid-century, with the return of peace and an American-led prosperity, the heyday of *une litterature engagée* was over and the political novel temporarily fell into disrepute. The macro-climate had changed, the god had failed. Newspapers, airwaves, government propaganda almost with one voice condemned Soviet Communism and Soviet actions in Eastern Europe. America was heading into the public hysteria and witch-hunting era known (inaccurately) as 'McCarthyism.'

The dominant Western media now associated 'propaganda' and 'ideology' with 'brainwashing' – all regarded as fatal to 'art' and all flourishing on the empty steppes of Russia and among the human anthills of Mao's China. Western culture had discovered that political commitment is virtually incompatible with genuine art. Social 'messages' were anathema. Exceptions were made for such loaded themes as 'The Unknown Political Prisoner' (a sculpture competition), but on the whole literature and politics were permitted intercourse only when it was time to laud the civic courage or liberal vision of a Pasternak, a Solzhenit-syn, an Akhmatova – in short, Soviet dissidents were granted a special license to conflate art and justice.

The Russians themselves were keen to help – the virulence of Zhdanovist fulminations on the cultural front accelerated Western literature's fastidious withdrawal from politics (like the hem of a taffeta gown being lifted from the slaughterhouse mud). The Soviet campaign against 'decadent formalism,' modernism and experimentation, 'the art of a dying class,' and the anathemas delivered against such 'jackals' as T. S. Eliot – all this prompted shudders of revulsion. Hitler's skull now sat, so to speak, on Stalin's desk. In East Berlin, Brecht commented, 'The campaign against the formalism of decaying bour-geois art has turned into a campaign against the sense of form.... *It is only boots that can be made to measure.*'[1] Yet Soviet official culture continued to choke on modernism, formalism, satire, and subversive allegory right through to the *glasnost'* era of the 1980s.

Cold War culture has, of course, not confined its attention to diplomatic and military history. Novelists have devoted more attention to the life experiences of populations living under the Soviet and Western political and socio-economic systems. The angry collision of conflicting perceptions forms the bedrock of the literary Cold War – likewise the persecution of dissident Soviet voices. Worth noting at the outset is that while dissenting Soviet novelists may have shared the general Western view of the Stalin terror and the cult of personality, most of them were less impressed by standard Western versions of international relations before, during and after the second world war. None lauded Western armed intervention in Russia's Civil War. None regarded the Munich agreement of 1938 as justifiable; few if any doubted that the Western powers had hoped to appease Hitler while sending the German legions east. No Soviet novelist (including Solzhenitsyn, the most outspoken critic of Stalin) came forward to condemn the Nazi-Soviet Pact in full-frontal mode. Solzhenitsyn gave the Yalta settlement a twist unique among his compatriots by denouncing Roosevelt and Churchill as cowards scheming to abandon Eastern Europe to Tsar Stalin.

Most (not all) of the novels discussed in these pages were written within the 'Aristotelian' or 'realist' code, providing a common theme and a chronologically coherent sequence of events joined by causal links. This genre of writing tends to leave unexamined the author's relationship to the narrative. It assumes the reality of the characters and events as described, and it assumes that language – available vocabularies and established literary forms—can mirror reality. By this view words 'fit' things, if properly chosen, because language is the product of life, the servant of mimesis. Authorial authority passes unquestioned, the illusion is secure and empathy follows. The elements of prose 'art' –syntax, rhythm, composition, narrative, chronology, point-of-view, colloquial speech, reiteration and portraiture –pass largely unexplained as part of a concealed craft. As with the conjuror/magician in a theatre, we pay to be taken in. There is no point in asking, 'How many children had Lady Macbeth?' No archive can reveal the true extent of Shylock's wealth.[2]

Of course, the 'realist' mode was itself a novelistic convention – a kind of time-bound contract between writer and reader –burdened by many 'unreal' features. Authors did not invite questions concerning the godlike status they assumed from the first page. They not only knew everything their characters knew but could contentedly observe that 'X did not know' or 'if only X had known.' The reader colluded in the suspension of disbelief. Admittedly the late nineteenth-century novel displayed a certain discomfort (or wriggling); for example Rider Haggard may begin an adventure novel with the author meeting an acquaintance in a London club, who tells him a story he has heard from someone else. By this device Rider Haggard may hope to sidestep the burden of authorial omniscience, of having been everywhere and known everything, by implanting the certainties in a previous act of alchemic storytelling.

At the core of the realist novel since the eighteenth century has been the autonomous individual and the belief that individual characteristics can be faithfully captured by way of literary transcription. Although realist novelists normally pay close attention to milieu, to the social setting and seminal family ties, the individual's ultimate responsibility for his or her actions is the bedrock of 'character.' Hence 'Cast of Characters.'

Perhaps paradoxically, this has been as true of socialist or Soviet fictional chronicles of collective endeavour. The individual hero and heroine, villain and traitor, each driven by free will, are preferred to an updated Greek chorus – whereas in Eisenstein's films we encounter the masses as a choreographed collective bonded by class struggle. Bourgeois or socialist, the novel's virtues and limitations dictate an almost inescapable emphasis on the 'character' and moral quality of the individual. Hemingway's *For Whom the Bell Tolls* offers a prime example.

Art, commented Sartre, is a permanent revolution. Yet the political and aesthetic revolutions appeared to be deadlocked in mutual distrust. The Soviet-led Communist movement demanded a traditional 'realist' form and content, while the artistic avant-garde, surrealists and absurdists, had abandoned the outer world as false or meaningless. Sartre could not admire the archaic romanticism of Communist socialist realism, yet he frequently expressed hostility towards the ivory tower avant-garde, rejecting the surrealist doctrine that authentic revolt takes place not so much in factories, warships and streets as by means of anarchy of the soul (*esprit*), scandalous gestures and surrender to the logic of dreams. Art for art's sake is depicted by Sartre as a diversionary manoeuvre patronized by a bourgeoisie who prefer to hear themselves mocked as philistines rather than denounced as exploiters.

As viewed by Sartre, Stalinism demanded a servile reproduction of official values – operas, oratorios and cantatas whose function was religious rather than imaginative. He (like Malraux) regarded Picasso – who joined the PCF in 1944 and remained loyal to it, but whose art was reviled by Soviet curators and critics—as the very image of this contradiction. The communists resembled a boa constrictor suffering an acute bout of nausea: Picasso was the cow they could neither digest nor vomit up.

In *What is Literature?* (1947) Sartre argued that it is the writer's duty to dispel ignorance, prejudice, inertia, false emotion while refusing to place himself at the service of any temporal power, dogma or mystification. The exercise of the imagination is simultaneously an affirmation of freedom and a 'stepping back' from reality in order to create a new one. Literature emerges as (potentially) a form of secondary action, action by disclosure. Here Sartre takes a long swipe at 'bourgeois' literature. Having acted as the bad conscience of the nobility in the eighteenth century, the French writer had come perilously close to serving as the good conscience of the bourgeoisie in the nineteenth. But in Sartre's own case, his novels and plays revealed an innate reluctance to embrace a crucial dimension of socialist realism – the leading role of the Party.

But the modernist movement, broadly taken, has presented a more fundamental challenge to the entire 'realist' idiom. To eradicate doubt from their messages, socialist realist writers had of necessity to eradicate doubt from the envelopes of conveyance. Following his emigration from Communist Czechoslovakia to France, Milan Kundera's writing has increasingly detached itself from the realist tradition. In *Les testaments trahis*, he offers an illuminating general comment: 'The greatest novelists of the period since Proust, I am thinking notably of Kafka, of Musil, Broch, of Gombrowicz or, from my generation, of Fuentes, have been extremely sensitive to the half-forgotten aesthetics of the pre-nineteenth-century novel; they have integrated the essayist's reflections in the art of the novel; they have rendered composition freer; reconquered the right to digress...renounced the dogma of psychological realism...and above all they have set themselves against the obligation to suggest the illusion of reality to the reader...'[3]

In his essay 'The Truth of Lies' (1989), Mario Vargas Llosa employs a different idiom to make essentially the same point as Kundera when he asserts that the separation of fiction and history flourishes in the 'open society' as defined by Karl Popper. Only in the open society does each remain 'autonomous and different, without invading or usurping each other's domains and functions.' In a closed society, by contrast, 'fiction and history are no longer different things and have started to become confused and to supplant each other, changing identities as in a masked ball.'[4] In other words authentic fiction must always signal its own inauthenticity, its own nature as manipulative invention.

Political passion returned to the Western novel with the break-up of the Cold War consensus. The Vietnam War and the eruption of the New Left worldwide released new political energies among creative writers. The choices had of course altered. Communism on the Soviet model was no longer a viable option. The problem of fashioning an authentic literary form to convey a political position was compounded by a loss of confidence in realism—and to some extent modernism – under assault from postmodernism. In academic corridors a new literary priesthood emerged, the devotees of a fiction rooted in myth, fable, fantasy, 'modern magic' – and the supposed impossibility of language.

Part 1

The Spanish Civil War

1

Commentary: The Spanish Labyrinth

'I remember saying once to Arthur Koestler,
"History stopped in 1936," at which he nodded in
immediate understanding. We were both thinking of
totalitarianism in general, but more particularly of
the Spanish Civil War.'[1]

The Spanish Civil War began in the summer of 1936 with a revolt of right-wing army commanders resentful of the growing socialist and anti-clerical stance of the Republican government recently elected by popular vote. Francisco Franco became the best-known leader of the 'nationalist' (sometimes 'falangist') revolt. Cadiz, Saragossa, Seville and Burgos declared for the insurgents, while Madrid, Barcelona, Valencia and Bilbao remained under the control of the legal government. On 7 October 1936 the Soviet government lifted the arms embargo to which it had subscribed in August and which the fascist powers had ignored from day one. Franco's forces received active military assistance from the German air force and from Mussolini. On 22 October the International Brigades were founded, 90 per cent of the officers being Communists operating under the directives of the Comintern, even though the Spanish CP was miniscule (35,000) compared to the socialist UGT (over 1 million) and the anarcho-syndicalists (2 million). Stalin sent materiel and personnel to shore up Republican defences, gradually bringing the Republican government and army under covert Soviet control. The British, French and American governments are held to have 'betrayed' Spanish democracy by refusing to intervene and by imposing an arms embargo which hurt only the Republic and which Hitler and Mussolini happily ignored. On this issue the Communists walked out of the Popular Front government in France.

Meanwhile foreign volunteers arrived, trade unionists, idealists and intellectuals, the majority enlisting in the Communist-controlled International Brigades—Americans of the Abraham Lincoln Brigade alongside German and Italian refugees from fascism. A minority of volunteers (like Orwell) headed

9

for the anarchist and much smaller Trotsykist (POUM) militias operating out of Barcelona, where anarchists were dominant in the trade union federation, the Confederación nacionale del Trabajo (CNT). Ideological tensions within Barcelona, exacerbated by a tradition of Catalan semi-autonomy, led to the fighting witnessed by Orwell in May 1937, followed by a brutal, Soviet-led, purge of the Trotskyists.

Not a few writers made that journey, among them Malraux, Hemingway, Dos Passos, Auden, as well as writers whose international literary fame lay ahead, notably Orwell and Koestler. The writers who went to Spain duly reported back by way of fiction, or direct reportage, or in many cases both. Most of them arrived determined to fight one enemy, fascism, but a minority came away, if they survived the Civil War, obsessed by a new enemy – Stalinism. In some cases the rage showed itself immediately, as with Dos Passos and Orwell; in other cases it surfaced after a 'strategic pause,' as with Koestler and Malraux.

Here we find the roots of cold war culture, of the schism within the Left, of 'the god that failed' which reached rampant proportions post-1945. This was what Orwell meant when he remarked to Koestler that 'history stopped' in 1936 – he meant history perceived as unsteady progress towards socialism. The primal contest between left and right, socialists and reactionaries, was superseded in the course of the Spanish Civil War by the desperate conflict between democracy and totalitarianism.

Malraux and Hemingway accepted the necessity of Communist leadership because wars are wars, not utopias: both these writers reckoned they understood military discipline and strategy, the need for a chain of command, so get it into your head who you're fighting for, and who against, and then take a break from family bickering. Don't expect perfect democratic behaviour, perfect tolerance, when fear descends along with death. Here Koestler's judgment on the two writers unsurprisingly reflected a Continental bias: 'Their art is so different that it can be said to occupy two opposite poles within the novelist's range...[the] same values are expressed in contrasting attitudes and idioms. Courage, in Hemingway's world, has an embarrassingly exhibitionist, adolescent, dumb-hero quality. Courage, in Malraux's world, is lucid and intelligent bravado, with a discursive Gallic flourish.'[2] Koestler regarded the film of Malraux's *L'Espoir* (*Days of Hope*, 1937) as 'one of the greatest films ever made,' a reminder that the novel reads in part like an expressionist film script in search of an Eisenstein.

Neither Malraux (a combatant of sorts) nor Hemingway (an engaged observer) witnessed the events in Barcelona which shook Orwell, who fought on the Aragon front in the POUM militia, although this Old Etonian and former colonial policeman believed in military discipline and a proper chain of command, and was appalled to see militia boys enlisting with no clue how to fire a rifle (and with no rifle). Orwell came away from the front-line trenches with a bullet in the neck, a permanent hatred of Stalinists, and a famous sequence of anti-Soviet books germinating in his head. Arthur Koestler was a very different kettle of fish. *Spanish Testament* marks Koestler's last stand as a clandestine Communist wearing the mask of the Popular Front.

Many major writers of the 1930s moved freely between fiction, opinion-laden essays and journalism. Their vocabularies and mind-sets remained broadly constant from one genre to the next, even when fiction obviously demanded a shift in literary convention. Good reportage in fact is close cousin to 'literature' not only in its descriptive powers but in its narrative strategies. Among the American novelists who went to Spain, Hemingway and Dos Passos had produced a significant journalistic output in advance of their 'imaginative' work.[3] The political novels of Orwell and Koestler published in the 1940s, can be fully understood only in the light of previous experiences reported autobiographically, not least from the Spanish Civil War.

Front-line reportage often served as a rehearsal, a test-track, for the more complex work of fiction. The level of description, evocation and insight may match one another in the two genres. Koestler's time in Room 41 of Seville prison, and his largely unsuccessful attempts to remain true to his beliefs and affiliations under interrogation, clearly lead on to Rubashov's fictional ordeal in *Darkness at Noon*. Koestler's tactical accommodations with the truth while in Spain and writing *Spanish Testament*, his Marxian Machiavellianism, opened the way for interrogator Gletkin's tactical trial of strength with defendant Rubashov in the novel.

In Orwell's case, the link between *Homage to Catalonia* and *Animal Farm* may seem less obvious; from war-torn, ideology-riven Catalonia to a somnambulant English farm, there is almost no resemblance in setting, tone and style – yet both books are about political integrity, personal honesty, the catastrophic betrayal of the revolution, and the inevitably tragic fate of the oppressed. Both books are about 'power corrupts'; about the imposition of crippling orthodoxy, about mendacious propaganda and lies, about 'progress' hideously deformed. Orwell learned these grim truths from different sources, not least the press of the late 1930s, but they were etched into his soul by the acid personal experience recounted in *Homage to Catalonia*.

Homage to Catalonia is non-fictional autobiographical reportage, nothing invented or imagined – a genre already explored by Orwell's foray in *Down and Out in Paris and London* and into the lives of Lancashire miners during the Depression in *The Road to Wigan Pier*. But *Homage* marks his first confrontation with international politics on the basis of first-hand experience, as distinct from occasional essays and book reviews. Orwell's novels published before the war also convey the same acute power of social observation and analysis but, in the convention of the time, by means of invented action and implication, avoiding explicit authorial intervention. An Orwell novel obeys the convention of authorial self-effacement; his works of reportage thrust him to the highest platform of the observation tower. Orwell regarded himself as a better reporter and essayist than novelist, and few would disagree – though in *Animal Farm* he achieved, just once, his much admired Swift's gift for imaginative allegory.

Some French reviewers used the word 'reportage' to describe the form Malraux adopted in *L'Espoir*. Gabriel Marcel, writing in *Vendémiaire* (12 January) compared it to 'une sorte de reportage hybride entrecoupé de dialogues inventés.' Louis Gallet expressed reservations about 'its incoherent jerky manner, the tough, wild characterisations, the gallopade of jostling images, as on a cinema screen...'[4] Curtis Cate complains of the 'exasperating intermingling of the concrete and abstract, the complex imagery...left deliberately tangled and obscure, leaving the reader to unravel the elements, as in a Cubist painting... this is how a Robert Delaunay or a Juan Gris might have recorded nocturnal impressions of Madrid if either had chosen to live there.'[5]

2

Malraux: *Days of Hope*

Among France's politically committed writers of the interwar years, André Malraux had no equal. Sartre called him 'a weight of hot blood in the age's heart.' This intense young man, 'nerveux, rapide, au visage un peu allongé,' whose literary style took on board the Swedish and German expressionist filmmakers, the ethos of Mallarmé, Apollinaire, Picasso, Braque and Léger, went in search of the art treasures of the Far East, became politically involved, and joined the Kuomintang. Out of this came his celebrated political novels, *The Conquerors* (*Les Conquérants*, 1928) and the sublime *Man's Fate* (*La Condition humaine*, 1933) – the latter widely regarded as Malraux's classic, most perfectly shaped novel.

Here he portrays two different species of revolutionaries: the Moscow-led Comintern's professionals, disciplined bureaucrats, competent, dedicated, even idealistic, but utterly lacking in imagination (Borodin, Katov); and the questing existential fictional heroes like Garine and Kyo, for whom the revolution provides an algebra of personal fulfilment and sacrifice. It was they who captivated young readers, particularly in post-1945 France when Malraux himself had, paradoxically, moved on from communism to Gaullism.[1]

The exiled Trotsky welcomed the deviations in *The Conquerors*, although he regretted that the novel was marred by excessive individualism, aesthetic caprices, '*une petite note de supériorité blasée.*' He praised Malraux for showing how the opportunism of Stalin and his agent Borodin prepared the ground for counter-revolutionary terror in China. Malraux politely rebuffed Trotsky's embrace, but in *Man's Fate* the conflict between the revolutionary militants and the cautious Comintern is revealed as more acute than ever – the revolutionaries must take on not only the bourgeoisie and the French financiers, but also the Comintern leaders at Hankow. The fictional hero Chen's single-handed attempt to assassinate Chiang Kai-Shek, in defiance of the orders of the Comintern, is not presented as damnable.[2] Even the cosmopolitan Ilya Ehrenburg complained that in *Man's Fate*, Malraux had transformed a revolution into the story of a group of conspirators – indeed among Communists of the 1930s Malraux was a rare bird, bored by the petty manoeuvres of party politics under the Third Republic, a compulsive itinerant cavalier, admiring solo-adventurers like Saint-Exupéry and T. E. Lawrence – and rarely out of touch with his own celebrity status. Like Sartre, he rejected the prevailing French literary culture: 'The history of artistic sensibility in France for the past fifty years might be called the death-agony of the brotherhood of man.'[3] Louis Aragon recalled how everyone crowded round Malraux when a group of French writers visited Moscow in 1934 to attend the first Congress of the Soviet Writers' Union – and this despite the fact that he had not yet written a novel granted free circulation in the USSR. (Later *Days of Wrath* [*Le Temps du mépris*, 1935] proved more acceptable in Moscow.)

Set in Hitler's Germany, *Days of Wrath* is dedicated to the Communist resistance. Kassner, a miner's son and organiser of a proletarian theatre, with a formidable record as a party 'delegate' in China and Mongolia, returns to Nazi Germany to prepare strikes in the Ruhr and to organise an illegal intelligence service. Arrested, Kassner suffers the brutality of the SA and the Gestapo. The novel projects Malraux's vision of communism as communionalism, a quasi-mystical fraternity, the rebirth of the hero, the man transfigured by a seismic spiritual awakening.

Both *Days of Wrath* and *Days of Hope* (*L'Espoir*, 1937) join the epic to the lyric, stretching their wings beyond the conventions of the 'well-made novel.' The heroes of the Spanish Civil War share Kassner's values: 'Communism restores to the individual all the creative possibilities of his nature.'[4] Clearly in evidence is what Irving Howe called the obsessive need to shift the direction of history, an impulse already observable in Garine, hero of *Les Conquérants*, and again with Kyo and Chen in *La Condition humaine*. Howe commented further: 'It is central to Malraux's vision of heroism in our time that the moment of trial, the gesture which defines and embodies the heroic, should come into being primarily in anticipation of defeat.'[5] Malraux's conception of shifting the direction of history is existential, a matter of individual will(s) rather than an inscription discovered by Marx, writ large by Lenin, and brought to fulfilment by Stalin. Dialectical materialism –along with every other determinist 'law' of history – was of little interest. In *The Conquerors* it is said of the Swiss revolutionary Garine: 'While the expert knowledge of the Bolsheviks and their passion for revolution filled him with admiration, the doctrinal trash which accompanied it exasperated him.' The prototype of Malraux's later fictional heroes, blending action with culture and lucidity, Garine complains about the Roman mentality of Borodin: 'He wants to manufacture revolutions as Ford manufactures cars.' In this Borodin is held to be typical of Moscow-trained cadres. In *La Condition humaine* Kyo remarks, 'But Marxism contains both the idea of inevitability and a worship of the power of the will. And whenever I see the first being allowed to predominate over the second, I am ill at ease.'

Two days after the Civil War broke out in Spain Malraux crossed the frontier, arrived in Madrid with raised fist, 'Salud!' – then went on to Barcelona, where he met the admired anarchist Durruti (the 'Negus' of *Days of Hope*) at the airport, and witnessed the four days of fighting described early in the novel. He promptly threw himself into organizing an auxiliary air force staffed by foreigners. The Republic had suffered a crushing blow when half of the fifty planes at the disposal of General Emilio Herrera, the Air Force commander-in-chief and one of the few generals (fifteen out of two hundred) to remain loyal to the government, flew from Morocco to Seville unaware that the city had fallen to the fascist General Queipo de Llano – who seized the planes and shot the pilots.[6]

Returning to Paris, 'the Byron of the age' (as he certainly was – or Lafayette, Garibaldi), Malraux hectically bought up twenty Petez 540s, ten Bosch 200s, and some Bréguets 'at the flea-market.' Granted permission to form a squadron, the España, at Barajas (Madrid's airport), he was granted the rank of colonel – he liked to wear the insignia, plus a flat cap and gold braid. Malraux's biographer Jean Lacouture describes him 'a very amateur airman, unsuited to piloting, with virtually no knowledge of bombing or navigation...' but his 'incredible physical courage,' fraternal spirit and sense of humour ensured his authority over the squadron. A subsequent biographer, Curtis Cate, puts it more bluntly: Malraux never learned to drive a car let alone pilot a plane. When he bought a Ford for his mistress Josette Clotis, she could drive it, he couldn't. When he applied to join the French Air Force in 1940 he got nowhere: 'Nor did Malraux's "exploits" with the escuadrilla España cut any ice with the Air Ministry professionals he talked to. Unlike Edouard Corniglion-Molinier or Antoine de Saint-Exupéry, Malraux never learned to fly an aeroplane, still less a fighter or a bomber.'[7]

Even so, Lacouture reports that 'his ready flow of words, his kindness and the sense of humour...endeared him to pilots and mechanics.' On top of that his fame as a writer, the tokens of recognition shown him by Spanish leaders like Largo Caballero and Negrin, by the Soviet ambassador Rozenberg, by Ehrenburg and Koltzov, made an impression. However, it did not make an impression on the Republican Air Force's Colonel Ignacio Hidalgo de Cisneros, who held that 'Malraux did not have the faintest idea what an aeroplane was' and that the men he gathered were mainly mercenaries, over whom he exercised no authority. (Freelance pilots were ultimately lured by payments of 50,000 francs a month, 150 times the pay of a Spanish Air Force second lieutenant.) Cisneros demanded that the squadron be disbanded but the government was afraid of making a bad impression in France. Historians point out that the International Squadron was of enormous service while the government's bomber command was non-existent.[8]

For two months Malraux inhabited the Hotel Florida on Gran Via, until the squadron was relocated at Albacete then Valencia. In the Florida gathered the legendary tower of Babel, the Russians, John Dos Passos, the poets Pablo

Neruda and Rafaël Alberti. Georges Soria, correspondent of *l'Humanité* recalled that Malraux spoke English and German badly, and neither Spanish nor Italian. He spoke in syntactically complex French, with 'a vocabulary that was never impoverished by a desire to be understood.' Soria recalled conversations between Malraux and Hemingway during which 'Ernie,' staring at his glass and obviously turned off, waited for Malraux to finish one of his breathless improvisations in order to get in a word. Hemingway, who distrusted theorizing about politics or literature, called Malraux 'Comrade Malreux,' a bad pun on 'malheureux, unhappy.'[9]

The first important engagement was the Medellin operation. The Squadron never had more than six planes in the air at a time, never more than nine in working order. Bombs had to be thrown out of windows and other orifices. On Christmas Eve he was ordered to attack Teruel and the Saragossa road. The plane overturned on take-off and was wrecked, but he was only 'slightly bruised.' Malraux himself did not take part in the squadron's operation of 11 February 1937 when it bombed Cadiz harbour, where Italians were disembarking. After the fall of Malaga, 100,000 refugees were pursued by the Italians. The España Squadron intervened, its last action.[10]

He made the trip to America, speaking at Harvard on 8 March 1937, to raise funds and awareness for the Loyalist cause. (His month-long speaking tour, promoted by the *Nation* magazine, at that time edited by Louis Fischer, ranged from New York to Washington, Harvard, Los Angeles and Hollywood, where he was a 'must' for a few days, San Francisco, Berkeley, Toronto and Montreal. Any explicit appeal for war materiel could have led to his arrest or expulsion by the FBI. He described in graphic detail the lack of medical supplies, the plight of the wounded, the need for x-ray plates and anaesthetics. Aware of his audience, he adopted something of a 'take it or leave' stance on communism and 'economic democracy,' no word about class struggle. 'For Communists what has to be conquered is not other men but nature.' In words to be passionately repeated by a character in *Days of Hope*, the American reporter Slade (modelled on Herbert Matthews of the *New York Times*), Malraux challenged his American audiences to rouse themselves before the battle was lost. Slade reflects bitterly in *Days of Hope*: 'If a fascist state or a communist state disposed of the combined strength of the United States, the British Empire, and France, we should be struck with terror.'[11] Malraux again met up with Hemingway in New York. For Hemingway, 'comrade Malreux' was something of a poseur; the return compliment from Malraux was *'un faux dur'* and *'un fou qui a la folie de la simplicité'* – roughly 'a bogus hard man' and 'an idiot with the stupidity of simplicity.' During Malraux's trip to Spain in July 1937, he handed over the American takings to President Azaña in person.

Days of Hope, written from May to October 1937, describes the Spanish Civil War from its outbreak up till the battle of Guadaljara, close to Madrid, in March 1937—a defeat of the Italian armoured legions despatched by Mussolini. The action begins with the fascist uprising in Barcelona, then follows its suppression during fierce street fighting by anarchist militias and loyal sections of the Civil Guard. Malraux moves on to the siege of the Alcazar in Toledo, then on to the defence of Madrid, saved by the arrival of Russian equipment. The action switches between Republican ground forces and an air squadron of bomber planes. The cast of characters is huge, the structure of the novel is epic, like the war itself, and much less tightly plotted around a few protagonists than *Man's Fate*.

Malraux attributed barbarism to the fascists, Hemingway to Man. In Toledo, fascists and Republican *milcianos* warily circle each other in the plaza, during the periodic truces, the *milicianos* offering cigarettes to the tobacco-starved occupants of the besieged Alcazar fortress. Malraux depicts the passage of insults:

"'...because we, anyhow, are fighting for an ideal, you bastards!" they heard a fascist shouting as they came up.'

One of the *milicianos* shouts back: "'Ours is a finer one than yours, seeing it's for everyone on earth!'"

"'To hell with an ideal that's for everyone! It's only the highest ideal that counts, don't you know that much, you ignoramus?'"

A moment later the milciano remembers his next lines:

"'Say, call that an ideal, dropping gas on the Abyssinians? And shutting the German workers in concentration camps? And paying farm labourers a peseta a day? Do you call the massacre at Badajoz an ideal, you bloody butcher's boy?'"

"'Russia – call that an ideal?'"

Soon they get on to the burning of churches.

The American journalist Slade, strongly pro-Republican, has been listening to these exchanges. He was 'reminded of the futile altercations of Paris taximen and Italian cab-drivers.'[12] But the exchange, if authentic, makes Malraux's central point that what separated the two sides in Spain, the Frente Popular (Popular Front) and Franco's forces, was the desire for fraternity versus the attachment to hierarchy. The revolution is an anguished response to centuries of humiliation. A character states that under the Republic wages have tripled; as a result the peasants have been able to buy themselves shirts; the fascists have restored the old wages and the new shirt shops have had to close.[13]

Malraux's forte is the one found in Eisenstein's films, the ability to choreograph mass action, whether military or civilian. But the reader's ability to maintain concentration may depend on his appetite for non-stop bang-crash-smash (as in Homer's *Iliad*), backed up by high-flying verbal artillery about revolution, art, courage, death. Much of it reads like a treatment for a film (and indeed Malraux threw himself with zest into the making of a film version called *Sierra de Teruel*, which he directed himself with the collaboration of the Republican government). The narrative of *Days of Hope* frequently employs cinematic comparisons or metaphors: '*Moreno a un visage de cinéma*'; Scali '*un air de comique américain dans un film d'aviation*'; the Poles in the International Brigades have 'mugs [*gueules*] out of Soviet films.'[14]

Characters like Garcia, Manuel, Magnin, Hernandez, Scali are real enough, but their identities tend to merge in a composite Communist hero dedicated to discipline, efficiency, victory. They all tend to sound alike, despite intermittent efforts at characterisation.[15] A lot of it is breathless stuff:

"'We've got to rush some of the young troops to Toledo," Heinrich said. "Let's dash off to Madrid. As things are it will be an easy task evacuating Toledo."

"'Too late," Hernandez replied.

"'Let's try anyhow.'"[16]

Yet what follows is an impressive account of Hernandez taken prisoner in Toledo jail and the subsequent executions of prisoners in groups of three, like an amateur theatre production, improving and speeding up as each side learns its part. A bus conductor, a puny little man with a complexion the colour of black olives, lifts his fist in the Frente Popular salute. 'The firing squad hesitated, not because they were impressed, but waiting for the prisoner to be called to order...'[17]

They are all obsessed, as Malraux himself, by powers of command, by giving orders and being obeyed by militiamen with no schooling in military discipline, often associating it with class rule, often exhausted and frightened. Communists must always take command if qualified, and obey senior commanders. And in this respect *Days of Hope* fully reflects the non-revolutionary policy of the Comintern – although nowhere does Malraux show repression of the revolution. His is a Spain with the occasional Soviet newspaperman but no NKVD agents (see reference note here on Soviet state security acronyms)[18] and no sinister commissars like André Marty, whom Hemingway was to depict with such loathing. Yet Malraux knew how Marty had arrested Gustave Regler, despatched to International Brigade headquarters by *Deutsche Zeitung*, published in Moscow. Marty wrote suspicious reports about Malraux himself, whom he accused of having taken part in an anarchist plot,[19] but Malraux's novel is strikingly friendly towards all Republican factions including the anarchists.

In Barcelona, for example, the Catholic Civil Guard commander Colonel Ximénès decides to remain loyal to the Republican government and fights alongside his old enemies the anarchists. He and the anarchist Puig share citizenship of the fatherland of courage. The fighting in Barcelona is wonderfully vivid, the reckless disregard for life and limb, but courage is not a word they like to use or hear; they say 'luck' instead. The colonel had crossed the Plaza, limping, under a hail of fascist bullets. "'You had luck, too, when you crossed the Plaza.'" Puig compliments Ximénès. The colonel in turn congratulates Puig on having had luck while storming a fascist position while equipped only with a Cadillac and machine gun.

The Communist Magnin – largely modelled on Malraux himself –regards innate courage or innate cowardice as rare – one or two men in twenty may come into that category. 'Courage is a thing that has to be organized; you've got to keep it in condition, like a rifle.' Malraux's view of anarchism is anticipated by his portrait of the terrorist Hong in *Man's Fate*. Hong is devoted to a poem he has learned by heart: 'I fight alone and win or lose/I need no one to win my freedom for me/I need no Jesus Christ to think he died for me.' In the Spanish novel, the Republican officer Garcia – another stand-in for the author –regards the trade union experience among anarcho-syndicalists of the CNT as their positive quality, their ideology as the downside. The novel pursues the political evolution of le Négus, an anarcho-syndicalist transport worker from Barcelona who believes in the revolution as apocalypse. By December 1936, six months into the Civil War, he no longer believes this – only in the struggle against fascism.

Le Négus tells Manuel there are too many bureaucrats in the CP. Manuel's answer speaks for Malraux himself: 'But you know as well as I do that Dimitrov's no bureaucrat.'[20] (Indeed in 1934 Malraux had travelled to Berlin with André Gide in an abortive and humiliating effort to negotiate the release of Dimitrov, defendant in the Nazi Reichstag Fire Trial, and of the imprisoned German Communist Party [KPD] leader Thälmann. After the Second World War Malraux was to change his view, associating Dimitrov with the shameful East European show trials of 1948-49.) In *Days of Hope*, Malraux's alter egos reject the anarchist ethos: by contrast the Communists form a disciplined cell within each military unit; they obey their cell secretaries; they are the dependable core and their loyalty is profound, almost physiological, as within a family.[21] In different ways and voices, Malraux, Koestler and Hemingway all saw the Communists as the only disciplined force capable of saving Spain. 'Apocalyptic fervour is ingrained in every one of us,' says Garcia, 'and there's the danger. For that fervour spells certain defeat.... Our humble task...is to organize the Apocalypse.'[22]

Malraux either sidesteps the ingrained dictatorial outlook of Stalinism – or did not yet allow himself to perceive it. At a banquet given him by the *Nation* during his speaking tour of the U.S. in 1937, Malraux declared, 'Trotsky is a great moral force in the world, but Stalin has lent dignity to mankind; and just as the Inquisition did not detract from the fundamental dignity of Christianity, so the Moscow trials do not detract from the fundamental dignity [of Communism].'[23] Irving Howe argued that in *Days of Hope* the cult of physical action for action's sake leads to 'a contrived and shabby rationale for the brutalities of Stalinism in Loyalist Spain, an exaltation of efficiency in a context that makes it both inhuman, and, finally, inefficient.'[24] This verdict is aberrational; these were the only words Howe accorded to *Days of Hope* in the course of a long chapter on Malraux's fiction.

Unlike Hemingway, Malraux does not attempt, does not wish to attempt, to take us inside the mind of a fascist officer operating in the field. What is fascism? The Communist Manuel answers, 'The cynical outlook plus a taste for action makes a man a fascist, or a potential fascist.... It's second nature with the fascists to look up to their leaders as beings of a superior race.'[25] Malraux made much of the fact that Franco deprived Miguel de Unamuno, arguably Spain's leading writer, of his post as rector of Salamanca University. Unamuno, who had initially sided with the Nationalists, although an opponent of the death penalty, had made a speech insisting that the University must be the servant of truth, regardless of politics. He also remarked that even the humblest women who had taken up arms and risked their lives for the Republic were less contemptible than those ladies who cannot do without flowers and fine linen, and watch Marxists being executed. Unamuno was heckled and insulted – indeed, this was the occasion when General Millán Astray notoriously leapt up with a defiant cry: 'Death to intelligence! Long live death!' Two characters in *Days of Hope* excitedly discuss the event.

Air battles against Heinkels and Junkers are described with boyish zest, but defeat is always on the devil's agenda. Frequent juxtapositions and constant use of the ironic trompe l'oeil or double-take undermine any notion of absolute victory. Manuel sees his men running towards the fascist tanks which evidently don't fire, since no one falls. The fascists must have surrendered. He refocuses his glasses: his own men are going over to the enemy.

The reception of *L'Espoir* in France largely followed ideological lines. The fascist Robert Brasillach, writing in *Action française*, was vitriolic in his mockery of Malraux's exposure of deep fissures between communists and anarchists: 'Just between ourselves, if this novel had been composed by a Hitlero-Japanese, a lubricous viper, a Trotskyist dog...it certainly could not be more harmful to the cause it wishes to defend.'[26] From the left bank communist commentators were ritually adulatory. Reviewing *L'Espoir* in Louis Aragon's Communist paper *Ce Soir* (13 January 1938), Paul Nizan called it 'a great book' which achieved a synthesis of two forms of action – military and literary. (*Ce Soir* had published long extracts from the novel in serial form, *en feuilleton*, during November 1937.) Marcel Arland, writing in *Nouvelle revue française* (February 1938) compared it to Victor Hugo's *Les Misérables* –other flattering comparisons included Stendhal's description of military chaos at Waterloo in *The Charterhouse of Parma*.[27]

Several critics remarked – some not without sarcasm –on the absence from the novel of the Spanish masses and ordinary 'base militants.' Arland regretted the absence of popular Spanish life. John Charpentier, critic of *Mercure de France* (March 1938), noted that 'the happiness of the flock seems to preoccupy [Malraux] less than the joy [jouissance] of the pastors.' René Vincent, writing in *Civilisation* (April 1938) mocked artists who style themselves 'friends of the people' yet find ordinary people uninteresting, and are capable of being just as 'egoist' as right-wing writers like Barrès or Montherlant. Writing in *Esprit*, Jacques Madaule reckoned that Malraux's constant calls for sacrifice, and his cult of force, had much in common with fascism.[28]

For the exiled Leon Trotsky, Malraux's embrace of Stalinist leadership in Spain, was too much. His scornful overview, sent to André Breton, was published by *Partisan Review*:[29] 'His pretentiously cold studies of heroism in other lands often made one uneasy. But it was impossible to deny him talent.... But what in fact happened? The artist became a reporter for the GPU,[30] a purveyor of bureaucratic heroism in prudently proportioned slices...' Malraux was guilty of 'lying reports from the fields of battle (Germany, Spain, etc.)...symbolic for a whole stratum of writers, almost for a generation...who lie from pretended "friendship" for the October Revolution.'[31]

Shooting of the film of the novel, *Sierra de Teruel*, began on 20 July 1938 shortly after the battle of the Ebro. Malraux's dollar-raising in America and his personal contacts with Aza a, Negrin and Alvarez del Vayo, the Republican eminences, secured the required vehicles, planes, actors, studios, hotels. Barcelona had been bombed by the Italians for five months and in January 1939 the film team had to evacuate. The final scenes were shot at Joinveille. The film was first screened at a private showing attended by the exiled Premier Negrin at the Palais de Chaillot shortly before the outbreak of the second world war – in September it was banned by the Daladier government and then disappeared, resurfacing only after the Liberation.[32]

Disgusted by the Nazi-Soviet Pact, Malraux enlisted as a private in the tank corps. His adventures as a prisoner of war and Resistance leader, together with his distinguished career postwar as art historian, anti-Communist, '*atlanticiste*,' Gaullist and minister of the Fifth Republic, are another story.

3

Hemingway: *For Whom the Bell Tolls*

Ernest Hemingway[1] began work on his Spanish Civil War novel in March 1939, virtually at the moment of the Republic's final collapse, having sent some thirty syndicated news despatches from Spain for the North American News Agency (NANA). The novel was in galley proof by August 1940, using a title taken from John Donne's 'Devotion': 'And therefore never send to know for whom the bell tolls, it tolls for thee.' The book had sold 491,000 copies by 4 April 1941 –Hemingway's most commercially successful book and a Book of the Month Club selection (a further 200,000 copies).

Graham Greene was impressed: 'It stands with Malraux's magnificent novel of the Republican air force as a record more truthful than history, because it deals with the emotions of men, with the ugliness of their idealism, with the cynicism and jealousy that are mixed up in the best causes – as we now know.'[2] Edmund Wilson, too, was enthusiastic: 'Hemingway the artist is with us again, and it is like having an old friend back.' The *New York Times* hailed what it called his best book, 'the fullest, deepest, truest,' while Dorothy Parker in *PM* guessed that it might come to rank alongside Thackeray's *Vanity Fair* or *Uncle Tom's Cabin*.[3]

No doubt the war in Europe assisted; Hemingway's epic now looked like an ominous prelude telling and tolling of things yet to come. When he spoke to the Second American Writers Congress in Carnegie Hall, New York City, on 4 June 1937, he had recently returned from two months' reporting the Spanish Civil War. Hearing this famous writer, still in his thirties, denouncing the native and foreign fascists operating in Spain – 'Fascism is a lie told by bullies. A writer who will not lie cannot live under fascism' –some in the audience interpreted his remarks as full-blooded commitment to the People's Front. It is certainly the case that Hemingway's NANA dispatches convey none of the ambivalence revealed eventually in *For Whom the Bell Tolls*.[4] His reports from Madrid, Valencia, Teruel, Tortosa and other locations between March 1937 and September 1938, like his soundtrack commentary to Joris Ivens's partisan documentary film *The Spanish Earth* (sponsored by 'Contemporary Historians,' including Hemingway, Dos Passos, Lillian Hellman, Archibald MacLeish), were frankly partisan, though they tell us less about the basic issues of the war than about enemy airpower, bombs, shells, death and the cowardice or bravery of a succession of Spanish chauffeurs. The virtue of the Republican camp is simply assumed never argued.

By the time he wrote *For Whom the Bell Tolls* it was all over. Franco had destroyed the Republic. Fascism ruled. The Civil War was already a tragic history. Hemingway chose as his focal point a group of partisans living under primitive conditions in a cave on the high forested slopes of the Sierra de Guadarramas, sixty miles northwest of besieged Madrid and therefore behind the Nationalist lines. Carlos Baker reckons the action takes place during a sixty-eight hour period in the last week of May 1937.[5] This was the time of the Republican offensive against La Granja and Segovia.[6] One odd feature of the time-set, late May, is that as the eyewitness Orwell reminds us in *Homage to Catalonia*, the Trotskyist POUM was not suppressed and its leader Andreas Nin arrested until 15 June 1937 –yet these events are referred to in Hemingway's novel[7] (see below).

Hemingway invented the cave and the bridge to be blown up, indeed his fictional guerrillas themselves had no actual counterparts in that sector. They were sculpted out of the primordial Spain described in *The Sun Also Rises* and *Death in the Afternoon*: Pilar the gypsy seer with more than a touch of Falstaff, her husband Pablo the anarchistic horse trader, El Sordo the guerrilla leader.

The hero-protagonist Robert Jordan, a young and idealistic American professor who loves Spain, dominates the narrative but he does not monopolise it. We will discover his fate at the end of a somewhat bloated narrative in which his characteristic compression yields to a more expansive, leisurely fullness of detail, a syntactical loosening up that did not impress every reviewer. Mark Schorer recalled a Hemingway aphorism from *Death in the Afternoon*: the dignity of movement of an iceberg is due to only one-eighth of it being above water.[8]

Robert Jordan has already shown his mettle by mercy killing a comrade, another dynamiter, because the man, a Russian called Kashkin, was fatally wounded and had begged Jordan never to let him fall into enemy hands alive. But Robert Jordan will not mention this unless someone asks him, indeed he inclines to reticence, sometimes silence. He feels strongly about the Loyalist cause, the Republic, the people, the decencies, but he has not taken on board class struggle and does not pin his heart to his sleeve: 'What were his politics then. He had none, he told himself. But do not tell anyone else that, he thought. And don't ever admit that. And what are you going to do afterwards. I am going back and earn my living teaching Spanish as before, and I am going to write a true book.'

Hemingway knows that a good cause does not make a good man. The supreme value of independent thought is brought out in Jordan's searching conversation with the naturally decent partisan Anselmo, who detests 'this-too-much killing'

–the necessity of it in time of war, and the regrets. "'That we should win the war and shoot nobody,'" says Anselmo. He hopes he will be forgiven for the killing he has done.

Forgiven by whom? the American asks.

"'Who knows? Since we do not have God here any more, neither His Son nor the Holy Ghost, who forgives? I do not know.'"

"'You have not God any more?'"

"'No. Man. Certainly not. If there were God, never would He have permitted what I have seen with my eyes. Let them have God.'"

"'They claim Him.'"

"'Clearly I miss Him, having been brought up in religion. But now a man must be responsible to himself.'"

"'Then it is thyself who will forgive thee for killing.'"

"'I believe so,' Anselmo said. "Since you put it clearly in that way I believe that must be it. But with or without God, I think it is a sin to kill.'"[9]

Anselmo might instead have answered, 'A man forgives himself twice over when he says God forgives him.'

Similarly a wrong cause does not inevitably make a bad man. Hemingway's honourable Nationalist lieutenant Paco Berrendo—though not loyal to the elected Republican government, a sincere Carlist and red-hater – protests when an arrogant captain orders a sniper to go up to the top of hill to confirm that there are no Reds still alive there. The sniper says yes but doesn't move out of fear. The devout Catholic Berrendo intercedes urging caution. To prove his point, Captain Mora stands up on a boulder and shouts, 'Red canaille. Shoot me. Kill me.' Nothing happens.

"'Now do you believe me, Paco?" he questioned Lieutenant Berrendo.'

"No," said Lieutenant Berrendo.'

The historian Robert Payne comments that Jordan, if a real historical figure, 'would have been working for [Aleksandr] Orlov and the NKVD,' who were in charge of guerrilla operations behind the Nationalist lines. Orlov (who later defected) claimed that by July 1937 he was training 1,600 guerrilleros in six schools and that 14,000 (probably an exaggeration) were already operating behind enemy lines.[10] We learn early on that Jordan has been assigned his dangerous and delicate mission by the Soviet General Golz (said to be modelled on the Polish General 'Walter') to coincide with an imminent Republican offensive; by blowing the bridge Jordan will cut off the fascists' line of reinforcements. It will take the reader over 400 pages to discover whether he pulls it off, survives or dies. On the bent back of that question mark Hemingway invites the reader to stay with him. The story-line carries multiple digressions in the manner of a Bildungsroman. The love affair of Robert Jordan and Maria –she has been raped and her head shaven by fascists, then rescued by Pablo's band –is for entertainment and sales; 'headed for Hollywood' complained the *New Republic*'s Edmund Wilson, who thought the love affair had 'the too-perfect felicity of a youthful erotic dream.'[11] But the stories of Pablo, Pilar and other Spaniards involved are essentially instructive, informative. Here the novel is engaged in 'history-painting.'

The politics of the novel are clearly pro-Republican, no question about that, but when it comes to the Soviet role there is a kind of admiring ambiguity. Golz is a gifted soldier and the genuine article: 'I am générale soviétique,' he says. 'I never think. Do not try to trap me into thinking.'[12] Someone growls at him in Russian or Polish, though Hemingway prefers to express it as 'in the language Robert Jordan did not understand.' Golz responds in English: 'Shut up, I joke if I want. I am so serious is why I can joke.' On occasion Robert Jordan thinks about the ruthless discipline exacted by the Communist General Lister. 'In few armies since the Tartar's first invasion of the West were men executed summarily for as little reason as they were under his command.' Some 160 pages into the book Hemingway sets up an extended passage in which he explains his politics through the mind of Robert Jordan:

> And what about a planned society and the rest of it? That was for the others to do. He had something else to do after this war. He fought now in this war because it had started in a country that he loved and he believed in the Republic and that if it were destroyed life would be unbearable for all those people who believed in it. He was under Communist discipline for the duration of the war. Here in Spain the Communists offered the best discipline and the soundest and sanest for the prosecution of the war...the only party whose programme and discipline he could respect.

As for fighters like Pablo (a local guerrilla leader who has turned cautious or cowardly to the point of betrayal when he steals Jordan's detonator, but who is also a symbol for the canker of defeatism gnawing at Republican morale): 'They all had the politics of horse thieves...the Republic would have to get rid of all that bunch of horse thieves that brought it to the pass it was in when the rebellion started. Was there ever a people whose leaders were as truly their enemies as this one?' But: 'Enemies of the people. That was a phrase he might omit. That was a catch phrase he would skip.... Any sort of clichés both revolutionary and patriotic. His mind employed them without criticism.' Here Jordan's thoughts spread out a bit to why the Communists 'were always cracking down on Bohemianism.... Down with Bohemanism, the sin of Mayakovsky. But Mayakovsky was a saint again. That was because he was safely dead.'[13]

Jordan is certainly not a naïve believer. He has no great faith in any of the known Republican leaders. 'I remember when I thought Largo was OK Durruti was good and his own people shot him there at the Puente de los Franceses. Shot him because he wanted them to attack.... Oh muck them all to hell and be damned. And that Pablo that just mucked off with my exploder and my box of detonators.'[14]

When in Madrid Hemingway resided at the Hotel Florida (scene of his bad play, *The Fifth Column*) and visited Gaylord's. Robert Jordan reflects that Gaylord's is the place to find out things. 'At one time he had thought that Gaylord's had been bad for him. It was the opposite of the puritanical, religious communism of Velazquez 63, the Madrid palace that had been turned into the International Brigade headquarters in the capital.... At either of these places you felt that you were taking part in a crusade...in spite of all bureaucracy and inefficiency and party strife, something that was like the feeling you expected to have and did not have when you made your first communion.' Hemingway goes on from the fragile analogy to describe this feeling. 'It was a feeling of consecration to a duty toward all of the oppressed of the world which would be as difficult and embarrassing to speak about as religious experience and yet it was authentic as the feeling you had when you heard Bach, or stood in Chartres Cathedral or the Cathedral at Léon and saw the light coming through the great windows; or when you saw Mantegna and Greco and Brueghel in the Prado.'[15] Thus Hemingway unzips his reticent hero. That the author is describing his own sentiments is not in doubt –he never disagrees with his protagonist and for that reason is the Western novelist closest in approach to the Russian tradition of indirect monologue.

Passages alluding to Soviet secretiveness abound. The *Pravda* journalist 'Karkov,' we are told, 'had three wounded Russians in the Palace Hotel for whom he was responsible...two tank drivers and a flyer.... In the event the city should be abandoned, Karkov was to poison them to destroy all evidence of their identity before leaving the Palace Hotel.' Karkov – in real life the ill-fated *Pravda* journalist Mikhail Koltzov –explains to Robert Jordan that he always carries poison for his own use. (Apparently Koltzov had come to dinner with Hemingway and Martha Gellhorn [his companion and future wife] in Gaylord's and told a story about being given poison to administer in case Madrid fell.)[16] Hemingway's character Karkov is nicely sardonic: 'We detest with horror the duplicity and villainy of the murderous hyenas of Bukharinite wreckers and such dregs of humanity as Zinoviev, Kamenev, Rykov and their henchmen,' Then he says, 'And because I make jokes sometimes: and you know how dangerous it is to make jokes even in joke?'[17]

Now we come to the Barcelona business, the problem of the anarchists and the Trotskyist Workers' Party of Marxist Unification (the unforgettable POUM). The *Pravda* correspondent describes Barcelona: 'It is all still comic opera. First it was the paradise of the crackpots and the romantic revolutionists. Now it is the paradise of the fake soldier. The soldiers who like to wear uniforms, who like to strut and swagger and wear red-and-black scarves. Who like everything about war except to fight.' Is this Hemingway's own view? Robert Jordan asks Karkov about the POUM. 'What about the P.O.U.M. putsch?' (according to Orwell, an eyewitness, there never was any such thing – in putting such a phrase into his hero's mouth Hemingway adopts it as his own).

'The P.O.U.M. was never serious,' Karkov replies. 'It was a heresy of crackpots and wild men and it was really just an infantilism. There were some honest misguided people. There was one fairly good brain and there was a little fascist money. Not much. The poor P.O.U.M. They were very silly people.'

On the evidence, yes, 'Karkov' does speak for Jordan/Hemingway, too. Hemingway had presumably not read Orwell's *Homage to Catalonia* (few had), or heard of Orwell, though they were to meet in liberated Paris in August 1944. At one juncture a character in the novel, encountering some anarcho-syndical-ists, thinks of them as 'the crazies, the ones with black-and-red scarves.' They yell 'Viva la libertad' and 'Viva la FAI. Viva la CNT.'

Jordan asks Karkov (as Hemingway may have asked Koltzov):

'But were many killed in the putsch?'

'Not so many as were shot afterwards or will be shot.... They never did kill anybody. Not at the front nor anywhere else. A few in Barcelona, yes.'

And what about Nin, leader of the POUM?

'"Nin was their only man. We had him but he escaped from our hands."

'"Where is he now?"

'"In Paris. We say he is in Paris. He was a very pleasant fellow but with bad political aberrations."'[18]

In reality, after intense fighting in the streets the POUM had been outlawed, Nin tortured and killed, followed by attacks on anarchists and Catalan separat-ists. Hemingway knew that Andrés Nin had been murdered. Karkov's 'in Paris' is immediately qualified by 'We say he is in Paris.' Then Karkov shifts to the past tense: 'He [Nin] was...' As earlier mentioned, Hemingway seems to have confused what was knowable within the time-set of the novel, late May 1937, when Nin had not yet been seized, with what he had learned about Nin's fate two years later. Passages comparing useful Communist 'discipline' to the dis-ruptive romanticism of the POUM and the anarchists ('crazies') drew the most intelligent and sustained political attack on the novel, that of Dwight Macdonald in *Partisan Review* (January 1941). Macdonald's outlook was close to Orwell's: only by embracing the revolutionary demands of the Spanish peasantry could the Republic hope to win the war. Hemingway gave so little sense of these concrete aspirations that 'it seems little more than chance that they are Loyalists rather than Rebels...' Macdonald argued that, despite rejecting Stalinist catchwords, Hemingway was still in the grip of Stalinist values – as when he had the simple peasant lad Andries improbably describe anarchists as 'dangerous children; dirty, foul, undisciplined, kind, loving, silly and ignorant but armed.'[19]

Certain points may be made about these 'Karkov-Jordan' passages. The bal-ance of conversation is almost master-disciple. The young American earnestly inquires, the ace Soviet journalist has the knowledge and the perspectives. Yet the fictional Robert Jordan is a rather modest figure to merit such high-level Soviet attention. Karkov, after all, is said to be 'in direct communication with Stalin...[and] at this moment one of the three most important men in Spain.' Hemingway evidently sensed the problem and offered a rather long-winded solution, Karkov's professed admiration for Jordan's book of Spanish travels:

'It's why I bother with you. I think you write absolutely truly and that is very rare.'[20]

(By way of footnote: Martha Gellhorn later met up with Koltzov on a wooden bench in the Hradcany Castle Prague. He explained that he was bringing Eduard Beneš a message from Stalin: if the Czechs would fight, the Soviet army would back them against Hitler. Koltzov had been kept waiting for four days; Beneš declined to see either him or Gellhorn. Koltzov took Gellhorn to dinner in a workers' restaurant and told her what he thought would happen next.[21] By the time Hemingway wrote *For Whom the Bell Tolls*, he knew that Koltzov had perished [shot]).

Perhaps the episode most offensive to Communists is the portrait of the French Communist André Marty, a hero of the Black Sea Fleet revolt of 1919, depicted in the novel as the crackpot, paranoid 'Comrade Massart.' Marty, a Communist deputy in the French National Assembly, boasted of executing some 500 brigaders. He was known as Le Boucher d'Albacete (the NKVD headquarters where the Servicio Investigaciòn Militar [SIM] operated a prison).[22] The pathological distrustful Marty preferred to shoot an innocent man rather than let a real spy go free. Hemingway not only describes Comrade Massart's destructive actions, he takes us inside his head and memories of the Russian Civil War. We track Massart's interlocking suspicions of the Soviet General Golz: 'That Golz should be in such obvious communication with the fascists.... Golz that he had known for nearly twenty years....Golz who had fought against Kolchak and in Poland.... But he had been close to Tukhachevsky. To Voroshilov, yes, too. But to Tukhachevsky. And to who else. Here to Karkov, of course...' And so Massart's fevered mind roams on: Marshal Tukhachevsky had perhaps already been executed by firing squad, Karkov's day was to come.[23] Massart's 'thoughts' move conveniently and compactly among the human and historical landmarks the author wants to bring to our attention.

In a notable scene the partisan woman Pilar, wife of Pablo, tells Robert Jordan about the brutal, degraded massacre of a town's bourgeoisie, falangists and priest carried out by Pablo and an increasingly drunken mob. Pilar, a mentor and leader of the guerrilla band, is fearsome; she can detect the 'odour of death' on a doomed man (as in a bullfight). The victims are brought out one by one, from the doorway of the Ayuntiamento, like released bulls – except that 'released' conveys the innocent, surging energy of the bull, in contrast to the dark knowledge of the humans doomed to a degraded and degrading end.[24] Pablo had them beaten to death with flails, then thrown from a cliff into a river. To begin with there is inhibition; by the end of the day drunken bloodlust prevails. Don Ricardo Montalvo, a landowner, defiantly cries, 'Arriba España! I obscenity in the milk of your fathers.' The politics of this powerful scene, the painstaking individualisation of brutal collective conflict, are a triumph for the novel as history-teller.

Hemingway's description of the incidental, almost casual, cruelties inflicted by men debased by civil war in some respects echoes Isaac Babel's collection of stories *Red Cavalry*, written in 1920 when Babel, although a Jew, served with an anti-Semitic Cossack regiment of Budyonny's Red Army during the war against Poland. The echo is again found in Italo Calvino's story of partisan fighting in northern Italy during the closing months of the Second World War, *The Path to the Spiders' Nests* (*Il sentiero dei nidi di ragno* [1947]). Calvino later recalled, 'Almost as soon as I had stopped being a partisan I discovered...*For Whom the Bell Tolls*. It was the first book with which I as an ex-partisan could identify: it was from reading that novel I began to transform into narrative motifs and phrases what I had seen an experienced, the detachment of Pablo and Pilar was "our" detachment.' Calvino adds: 'The kind of literature we liked was that which contained a sense of seething humanity, of ruthlessness, and also of nature. We also felt that the Russian writers of the Civil War period – that is, before Soviet literature was purged, and became idealized – were our contemporaries. In particular, Isaac Babel: his *Red Cavalry*...also sprang from an intellectual's encounter with revolutionary violence.' Calvino called *Red Cavalry* 'one of the masterpieces of twentieth-century realism,'[25] probably employing the term 'realism' as meaning true-to-life, unvarnished by revolutionary romanticism, even though Babel's staccato style and abrupt disjunctures may seem closer to the expressionist aesthetic prevalent in literature, art and cinema after the first world war; this rather brutal sensibility emerges again in the output of the Italian 'neo-realist' movement, including Calvino's *The Path to the Spiders' Nests*. Like Hemingway in his Pablo-Pilar scenes, Calvino was determined to show that individual ignorance, ideological confusion, rage and base motives were alive and well within the ranks of the anti-fascist partisans. Calvino goes further than Hemingway in highlighting how many desperados jumped ship during the chaotic years after 1940: now Black Shirts, now carabinieri, now red partisans, now robbers and rapists.

When Carlos Baker wrote (with italicized emphasis) of Hemingway 'as an artist,' and described the novel as 'partisanship in the cause of humanity' (following Goethe, always a solid precedent), he subscribed to a belief which achieved almost canonical status in Western literary criticism during the Cold War: when the genuine artist abandons journalism for 'art,' the truth about humankind takes over from narrow partisanship.

Through Robert Jordan, Hemingway distances himself from the narrow partisanship he associates with Marxism. Robert Jordan reflects that he is in love with Maria, even though 'there isn't supposed to be any such thing as love in a purely materialist conception of society.' But then he remembers that he is not a 'materialist.' He tells himself, 'Never. And you never could have. You're not a real Marxist and you know it. You believe in Liberty, Equality, and Fraternity. You believe in Life, Liberty, and the Pursuit of Happiness. Don't ever kid yourself with too much dialectics. They are for some but not for you. You have to know them not to be a sucker.'[26] This soliloquy occurs as Robert Jordan is positioned below the hilltop battle in which El Sordo's partisans lose their lives. Carlos

Baker comments: 'But where the communist dialectic runs contrary to the older dialectics of the French and American Revolutions, Jordan will remain an essential nonconformist, a free man not taken in...'[27] For Baker, religious sentiment is the real thing, not least as death approaches, whereas slogans uttered by the Communist heroine La Pasionaria are merely tools of the trade 'for bringing passionately inspired news of Marxist victories.' When young Joaquín, one of El Sordo's partisans under attack from enemy planes, shifts suddenly into 'Hail Mary, full of grace...,' Baker celebrates 'the conflict between the Catholic faith and the secular pseudo-religion of the communists.'[28]

Following the publication of *For Whom the Bell Tolls* in 1941, Hemingway remained officially out of favour in the Soviet Union, although no foreign prose writer was more admired and emulated in Russia than he – Akhmatova praised him, and Konstantin Simonov clearly owed a debt. Winner of the 1954 Nobel Prize, Hemingway was accorded a Russian translation of *The Old Man and the Sea* and a two-volume edition of his work in 300,000 copies. *For Whom the Bell Tolls* remained proscribed. But Ehrenburg's praise obviously could not extend (in public) to Hemingway's negative portrait of Soviet policy in Spain.

4

Dos Passos: Betrayal

John Dos Passos, too, came to Spain, and experienced an agony not entirely personal to himself. The resulting novel, *Adventures of a Young Man* (1939), was by his own or any standards second rate, but Dos Passos commands our attention not only because he knew Spain well but because he had been paramount among American social novelists of the interwar years; indeed his influence on other radical writers—structural, stylistic, political—persisted into the 1960s and 1970s, long after Dos Passos himself had enlisted with 'the god that failed' and adopted an ultra-conservativism no less crusaderly than the progressive outlook which made his name.

Like Hemingway, Edmund Wilson, Malcolm Cowley and his friend E. E. Cummings, Dos Passos belonged to the First World War 'ambulance corps' generation. A Harvard graduate, the son of a Portuguese American, it was in the Party's cultural journal *New Masses* that he first produced tightly knit, vivid biographies of famous people, many of whom later surfaced in the fictional trilogy *USA* (in the style of the time, *U.S.A.*) His talent as an 'imaginative' writer was most evident when he returned to subjects first explored as a journalist, confirming the deceptive nature of such standard categories as 'imaginative,' 'creative,' and 'invented.'[1] His epic trilogy, *USA*, while incorporating a host of new literary devices, was basically an extension of the naturalist tradition: subordination of art and rhetoric to 'life'; colloquial language, not only found in dialogue but woven into the narrative; emphasis on the environment, on the force of 'things'; characters who are shaped by, governed by, the environment rather than autonomous heroes who mould the world to their will. A tone of moral neutrality, of 'scientific objectivity' about money, sex and milieu, never concealed an underlying passion for justice and an admiration for the champions of the underdog, radicals like Big Bill Hayward, John Reed and Emma Goldman, labour leaders working to organize the poor and the unemployed in the face of police brutality, corrupt local officials, brainwashed juries of the inter-war years. But his collages of fiction, newspaper reports, biographies and

33

newsreels proved to be unacceptable to Soviet orthodoxy. In 1934, Karl Radek told the first Soviet Writers' Congress that Dos Passos had succumbed to the decadent influence of James Joyce – the creator of 'a dunghill swarming with worms seen through a microscope held upside down.' (Dos Passos himself played down any debt to Joyce: 'Cutting through Paris I bought an early copy of Ulysses and even shook the limp hand of a pale uninterested man in dark glasses sitting beside the stove in the back room of Shakespeare and Company whom Miss Beach claimed was James Joyce.'[2])

After the outbreak of the Spanish Civil War, Dos Passos himself joined a group of radical writers calling themselves Contemporary Historians, including Hemingway, Lillian Hellman, Dorothy Parker, Archibald MacLeish, to subsidize and promote Joris Ivens's film, *The Spanish Earth*, narrated by Hemingway. Dos Passos – whose face had adorned the cover of *Time* magazine—knew Spain and the Spanish language better than most – indeed he was granted an interview with Azaña when he became *el señor presidente* of the Republic's Council of Ministers. His former secretary, José Robles, who taught Spanish literature at Johns Hopkins University, had been on a visit to his native land when the Civil War broke out but had then disappeared. Reaching the Republic's seat of government, Valencia, on 7 April 1937, Dos Passos presented himself to Foreign Minister Julio Alvárez del Vayo, who professed ignorance about Robles—as did everyone else. Dos Passos seems to have heard of José Robles's fate – shot without trial as a fascist spy—from Hemingway, who broke the news at the duke of Tovar's castle during a Thälmann Day ceremony. His long-standing friendship with Hemingway was over. An angry Dos Passos travelled to Barcelona, rubbed shoulders with anarchists and Trotskyists, and obtained an interview with Andrès Nin a week before the POUM leader was arrested and vanished. In Barcelona, he apparently ran into Orwell. He admired the revolutionary idealism of the POUM, but 'the popular movement in Catalonia [seems] doomed, hemmed in by ruthless forces of world politics too big for it.'[3] Reaching America, Dos Passos cemented his break with Stalinism by lending his support to the Trotsky Defense Committee.

Oddly, *The Adventures of a Young Man* contains no 'José Robles,' no anguished search for a vanished Spanish friend. The central character, Glenn Spotiswood, is a union organizer involved in providing soup kitchens for striking miners of the Slade County minefields, meets up with a friend of his youth, Paul, recently back from working in Russia. Dos Passos here uses dialogue in a crudely instrumental way to expose Bolshevik practice: 'They paid me in gold.... They gave me everything in the world but as soon as I'd get a station started the goddam party line would come in and they'd shoot my best guys or put 'em on forced labor and send me off somewhere else...' Paul is now converted to the New Deal; the president is succeeding in feeding the workers whereas 'In Russia they've starved 'em deliberately. There's no way to explain it to anyone who hasn't seen it...trainloads of 'em being shipped to Siberia.'

'You mean collectivization?' asks Glenn naively.

But a curious mutation was in the pipeline: while Glenn will always remain as American as apple pie, the individual American Communists depicted in the novel begin to emerge as darkly foreign – for example, the bandy legged Dr. Blumenthal 'with his silly English giggle,' whose accent veers suspiciously between 'a slight cockney twang' and 'very Oxonian.' 'I never believe in telling anybody the truth, least of all the masses,' he confides.[4] Other Communist activists in the frame whom our hero Glenn will again encounter in Spain include Irving Silverstone (obviously Jewish), found imparting the line to a gathering of well-dressed radicals; and Bernard Morton from Pittsburgh 'and a town on the Baltic,' who speaks in a drawl but then his voice 'was suddenly as hard as a traffic cop's.'[5] Intent on enlisting for service in Spain, Glenn heads for a mysterious tenement building, where the first question put to him is 'Volunteer or mercenary?'

'Then Glenn is led into a room, and his guide calls out: "Dr. Wiseman...here's another customer..."' Dr. Wiseman, clearly yet another Jew, chuckles, 'Haha – more cannon fodder.' Having cursorily checked Glenn's medical condition, and given several rasping chuckles, Dr. Wiseman pronounces Glenn 'sound as a dollar...or ought I to say sound as a Soviet ruble?' Reaching Spain, Glenn meets Saul Chemnitz, who has a 'jewishlooking nose.'

But true comrades (non-Jews) can still be found. Glenn runs into Frankie Perez among a medley of militiamen, *milicianos*. Frankie (who had helped him organize a pecan shellers' strike in Horton some years back) asks Glenn whether he has joined the Brigada Internationale. Glenn nods and says he's no longer in the CP, at which Frankie smiles and slaps him on the shoulder. Until recently working as a barber in Barcelona, he had fought for three days in the streets, been twice wounded, and lost an arm.

'Here several different kinds of war,' he explains. 'We fight Franco but we also fight Moscow...if you go to the Brigada you must not let them fight us. They want to destroy our collectives. They want to institute dictatorship of secret police just like Franco. We have to fight both sides to protect the revolution.'

After further adventures among Communist volunteers, Glenn is arrested and brought before a panel of two bespectacled Germans and the 'Baltic' American already known to Glenn, Bernard Morton. One of the Germans, Peter, speaking 'in slow precise British English,' accuses Glenn of working for the Trotskyist counter-revolutionary party involved in organising the Barcelona uprising. He accuses Glenn of using his meeting with the Barcelona barber Frankie Perez to establish contact with wreckers and spies. Perez, he announces with satisfaction, has been shot.[6]

Locked up again, Glenn hears enemy artillery and machine gun fire approaching. Finally, in a desperate situation, he is offered a suicide mission carrying water to a machine gun post beleaguered in a pill box near hill 14, covering the evacuation. Glenn accepts the mission and is killed by enemy fire when halfway up the hill. (This may be why Edmund Wilson reckoned that Hemingway's Robert Jordan ended up 'not fundamentally so much different' from the hero of *Aventures of a Young Man*.[7]) The novel received a hammering from old friends. Malcolm Cowley called it Dos Passos's weakest novel in eighteen years (*New Republic*, 14 June 1939): 'Technically it is rather conventional, perhaps because Dos Passos was trying to answer some of the criticisms made against *USA*. People had said that he used too many tricks of narration, like the Newsreels and the Camera Eye; now he tells a straight story. People had said that his characters were presented only from the outside; now he also tries to tell what happened in a man's head.' This was a fair comment at the literary level, but Cowley's animosity was clearly political (in April 1938 he had been one of 150 American intellectuals publicly endorsing the Moscow trials.) Dos Passos was 'wrong' about the CP's role in the Harlan strike of 1932, and wrong again about the Spanish Civil War— although Cowley conceded that 'a great many Communists are merely bureaucrats of the revolution, clinging to their positions and careless about the liberty of others.'[8] Cowley attributed Dos Passos's recent embitterment to the José Robles affair. Robles had been 'a young man whom almost everybody knew and liked,' but 'People who ought to know tell me that the evidence against him was absolutely damning. Hemingway, who interceded for him with the highest officials of the Spanish government, became convinced of his guilt.' Cowley also dragged Malraux into the fray: '...at least it is likely that some passages in *Man's Hope* [*Days of Hope*] were written with Dos Passos in mind...' Which passages? Malraux's novel was completed a couple of years before *Adventures of a Young Man* appeared and never touches on anything, even by fictional indirection, resembling the Robles affair.

The violent animosities of 'the god that failed' era were clearly alive and well fully ten years before the famous book of that name reached the public. Reviewing Dos Passos's novel in the Stalinist *New Masses* (4 July 1939), Sillen described Sinclair Lewis and Dos Passos as 'inconceivably rotten' writers, building their stories 'out of palpable lies.' 'They had once written progressive books; now they were writing contemptible slanders, nasty, ill-tempered and hysterical slanders about everything decent and hopeful in American life. Once upon a time they had been concerned about their craft; but now they were turning out sloppy writing, hollow characters, machine-made dialogue, editorial rubber stamps.'[9] More specifically, in *Adventures of a Young Man*, 'Dos Passos fails to tell his readers that the POUM were more successful in fighting against the side of the republic because that is what they were out do with fascist help.'

Rallying to Dos Passos in the pages of *American Mercury* (August 1939), the gifted novelist James T. Farrell (some years later a leading figure in the American Congress for Cultural Freedom) hit out at the Stalinists. Author of the vivid *Studs Lonigan* trilogy, written at a young age and comparable to *USA* as an indictment of social and economic inequalities, Farrell drew a parallel between *Adventures of a Young Man* and a celebrated novel by a disaffected Italian

Communist, Ignazio Silone's *Bread and Wine* – how is integrity to be preserved in revolutionary politics? According to Farrell, Dos Passos's protagonist Glenn Spotiswood begins to sense that the revolutionary party of Lenin has become the counter-revolutionary party of Stalin. 'He is describing a dead end of a historic movement – the Communist Party.' Farrell wound up with the warning that the general critical reception accorded to *Adventures of a Young Man*, particularly Malcolm Cowley's, 'reads like a warning to writers not to stray off the reservations of the Stalinist-controlled League of American Writers...'[10]

The postwar years were to demonstrate Dos Passos's sustained passion for engagement – but in the form of a conversion to conservatism carried to the extreme of McCarthyism. After a visit to Britain in July 1947, he reported for *Life* ('Britain's Dim Dictatorship' and 'The Failure of Marxism', 19 January 1948). The Labour Party's socialist agenda, he argued, now threatened to extinguish the hard-won liberties of a gallant, stoical island people. But Dos Passos's jeremiad lost itself in confusion. On the one hand he interpreted Stalinism largely in terms of the Russian tradition of despotism and 'serfdom,' analogous to that of Ottoman Turks; and yet—he warned—the conceit of British socialists was to imagine that their policies could escape the 'ultimate implications' of the Russian experience. 'Now public ownership, planned economy...have become words heavy with virtue, while profits, free enterprise, investments and even dividends have taken on an evil context... An apologist for the profit system [today] often finds it hard to hold his job.' But which job? No examples are given, most probably because none could be found.

During the 1940s Dos Passos took on board the weight of a certain melancholy. Like Whittaker Chambers he appeared to derive a morbid satisfaction from having converted from the 'winning' to the 'losing' side (which he called democracy): 'When some of us, still applying the standards we had learned in trying to defend Sacco and Vanzetti and the Harlan miners, the Spanish republicans, started looking with a critical but not necessarily unfriendly eye at the new institutions [of the New Deal and Labour Britain], we got a good shellacking...[because we] pointed out that the Communist Party was a greater danger to individual liberty than all the old power mad bankers and industrialists from hell to breakfast...' America's Press, radio and educational system were now controlled by liberals who had 'crawled under the yoke of the Communist Party.' Or so he enjoyed believing. He had no quarrel with McCarthyism. Indeed those who opposed the 'housecleaning' of the fifties were guilty of a 'lynching' solidarity in defence of entrenched positions of power. 'Lynching' had become a favoured term—for example the liberals had engineered 'the moral lynching of Whittaker Chambers' – perhaps the most headlined postwar namer of names.[11]

5

Orwell: *Homage to Catalonia*

*'I know that it is the fashion to say that most of
recorded history is lies anyway. I am willing to
believe that history is for the most part inaccurate
and biased, but what is peculiar to our age is the
abandonment of the idea that history could be
truthfully written.' –Orwell, Homage to Catalonia.*[1]

The English writer George Orwell[2] had tried to enlist in the International
Brigade but failed to get the necessary endorsement from Harry Pollitt, secretary
of the British CP, during a brief interview. *Faute de mieux*, he went out to Spain
under the auspices of the Independent Labour Party (ILP) which, under a system
of rather arbitrary 'twinning,' brought him into the militia ranks of the POUM
(Partido Obrero de Unificación Marxista)—although he never actually joined
the POUM.) 'The Lenin Barracks,' he recalled, 'was a block of splendid stone
buildings with a riding-school and enormous cobbled courtyards; it had been
a cavalry barracks and had been captured during the July fighting... I was at
the barracks about a week. Chiefly I remember the horsy smells, the quavering
bugle-calls...the long morning parades in the wintry sunshine, the wild games
of football, fifty a side, in the gravelled riding-school. There were perhaps a
thousand men at the barracks...'[3]

When he arrived in late December 1936 his sympathies were very much with
the Communists. 'The Russian arms and the magnificent defence of Madrid by
troops mainly under Communist control had made the Communists the heroes
of Spain. As someone put it, every Russian plane that flew over our heads was
Communist propaganda. The revolutionary purism of the POUM, though I saw
its logic, seemed to me rather futile. After all, the one thing that mattered was
to win the war.'[4]

He was to change his view radically. Actually he says very little about Russia
and the Russians in *Homage to Catalonia* and seems scarcely to have set eyes
on one while in Spain. The book contains no portraits of Soviet officers, jour-

nalists, or highly placed Comintern commissars to compare with Hemingway's offering in *For Whom the Bell Tolls.*

Orwell was appalled by the military training he encountered at the Lenin Barracks: a lot of useless marching and no weapons training because no weapons. A 'mob of eager children,' a 'complete rabble by any ordinary standards,' about to be thrown into the front line not knowing how to sight a rifle or how to throw a 'bomb' (his term for a hand grenade, which is tossed at the enemy by hand after releasing a metal pin; and which if not tossed in time, or far enough, will kill the owner.) He was equally impatient with the propaganda he found in the POUM papers, *La Battalla* and *Adelante*, the 'ceaseless carping' against the 'counter-revolutionary' Communist Party (PSUC). It 'struck me as priggish and tiresome.' He could understand the argument that this was dividing and weakening the Republican forces. But what soon most disgusted him was Communist propaganda accusing POUM of deliberate sabotage, of being disguised fascists, a Fifth Column, 'traitors, murderers, cowards, spies, and so forth.' This was never said by PSUC militiamen or Communists from the International Brigade, only by 'sleek persons in London and Paris.'[5] ('Sleek' was a favourite Orwell term of condemnation, presumably the opposite of 'rugged.')

Towards the end of January 1937 he was transferred from his largely Spanish group to join several English volunteers who had come out from the ILP under the leadership of Robert 'Bob' Edwards. Some twenty-five ILP volunteers were assigned to 3rd Regiment, Division Lenin, POUM, on the Aragon front at Alcubierre. Years later Edwards remembered Orwell in battle dress: 'corduroy riding breeches, khaki puttees, huge boots caked with mud, a yellow pigskin jerkin, a chocolate-coloured balaclava helmet with a knitted khaki scarf of immeasurable length wrapped round his neck and face up his ears.' Orwell himself recalled, 'This period which seemed so futile and eventless is now of great importance to me. It is so different from the rest of my life that it has already taken on the magic quality which, as a rule, belongs only to memories which are years old... the winter cold, the ragged uniforms of militiamen, the oval Spanish faces, the Morse-like tapping of machine-guns, the smells of urine and rotting bread, the tinny taste of bean-stews wolfed hurriedly out of unclean pannikins.'

Homage to Catalonia is written in the form of alternate sections of personal experience and political-historical analysis. They are co-exist as if happening together, or, 'as filtering through the same sensibility and in the same evocative process.'[6] Features of style included multiple hyphens and no shyness about the word 'I.' He relishes the physical life even when recording the sensations of being almost mortally wounded. The physical life extends to nature and buildings. He freely uses English moral terms which may sound incongruous, though by no means anachronistic: decency, humbug, spilling the beans. He steers clear of sex and theory (where Koestler will head doglike for either or both).

When he first arrived in Barcelona class differences seemed to have disappeared, no one took tips, 'waiters and flower-women and bootblacks looked you in the eye and called you "comrade."' But now, returning from the front on leave, the smart hotels and restaurants were full of rich people consuming expensive meals, while the poor faced rising prices and shortages. The beggars were back: 'Outside the delicatessen shops at the top of the Ramblas gangs of barefooted children were always waiting to swarm round...' The familiar form of tú and camarada was now rarely used among strangers. Cabaret shows and brothels previously closed by the workers' patrols had re-opened. Foreign cigarettes were smuggled in for the wealthy. A confectioner's shop displayed a window full of elegant pastries and bon-bons at 'staggering prices.'[7]

Orwell-Blair was back to playing the double life earlier described in *Down and Out in Paris and London*. He was the volunteer tramp who could put on collar and tie 'at the drop of a hat,' the gamekeeper with a poacher's snare in his tweed pocket, the egalitarian who had special combat boots custom-made in Barcelona because his feet were so large, the man who took his wife (who had joined him) to a smart hosiery shop on the Ramblas and was appalled when the shopkeeper bowed and rubbed his hands 'as they do not do even in England nowadays.' By local standards the Blairs seem not to have been short of money. 'After several months of discomfort I had a ravenous desire for decent food and wine, cocktails, American cigarettes and so forth, and I admit to having wallowed in every luxury that I had money to buy.'[8]

Unlike Malraux and Hemingway he no longer believed that the war could be won by purely military means, deferring the land question. The Civil War had to promote a social revolution or perish. 'The thing for which the Communists were working was not to postpone the Spanish Revolution till a more suitable time, but to make sure that it never happened.' Later, in 'Spilling the Spanish Beans,' he put it more strongly: the Spanish government, like the Catalan government, 'is far more afraid of the revolution than of the Fascists.'[9] But what did he mean by 'the Spanish Revolution'? Was Orwell a revolutionary in the British context? And if not, why support a revolution in Spain? Not surprisingly, we find that Orwell's line of thinking was as strong on pragmatism as on ethics. He soon realised that the 'defence of democracy' (the Communist line in Spain) was not only hypocritical (the Comintern had until 1934 denounced bourgeois democracy as the handmaiden of fascism) but also meaningless to the peasants and workers he encountered in Catalonia and Aragon. When Franco's rebellion attempted to seize power throughout Spain, the poor had taken up arms not in defence of ballot boxes and vote counting and the liberal constitution – they took up arms to seize the land and the factories and to pulverise that great landowner and oppressor, the Catholic Church. Indeed, the seizure of property including the private dwellings of the rich had been going on before Franco's rebellion and was one of its precipitating causes.

In Orwell's view, the Communists were determined not merely to postpone the social revolution on the 'first things first' principle, but actually to put into reverse the gains already won by workers and peasants. This was not a freezing or postponement of the revolution but a counter-revolution. Orwell used the word 'undo.'[10] Then why should the ordinary people continue to fight and die in the militia and the new People's Army? For what? He made the point that only the revolution could persuade the people to take up arms in the areas controlled by the military rebellion, in the rear. (Hemingway's *For Whom the Bell Tolls* takes place behind fascist lines – one reason why the author is so unclear what his Spanish peasants are fighting for.)

For Orwell socialism was about equality or it was about nothing – witness *Animal Farm*. In the strip of Aragon controlled by anarchist and POUM militia, 'The revolutionary atmosphere remained as I had first known it. General and private, peasant and militiaman, still met as equals; everyone drew the same pay, wore the same clothes, ate the same food and called everyone else "them" and "comrade"; there was no boss-class, no menial-class, no beggars, no prostitutes, no lawyers, no priests, no boot-licking, no cap-touching. I was breathing the air of equality, and I was simple enough to imagine that it existed all over Spain. I did not realise that more or less by chance I was isolated among the most revolutionary section of the Spanish working class.'[11]

His affection for them grew:

> How easy it is to make friends in Spain! Embarrassing generosity, ordinary decency, extraordinarily friendly to foreigners. Many of the normal motives of civilised life—snobbishness, money-grubbing, fear of the boss, etc. – had simply ceased to exist. The ordinary class-division of society had disappeared to an extent that is almost unthinkable in the money-tainted air of England...a community where hope was more normal than apathy or cynicism, where the word 'comrade' stood for comradeship, and not, as in most countries, for humbug... I am well aware that that it is now the fashion to deny that Socialism has anything to do with equality. In every country in the world a huge tribe of party hacks and sleek little professors are busy proving that Socialism means no more than a planned state-capitalism with the grab-motive left intact... to the vast majority of people Socialism means a classless society, or it means nothing at all.[12]

From his own observations Orwell could not accept that events in Barcelona after 3 May amounted to anarchists and the POUM stabbing the government in the back. He saw no attempt at a putsch, no attempt to storm buildings held by the PSUC, by Civil Guards and Assault Guards, by the government of Catalonia, the Generalidad. The tactics of the militia and armed workers were defensive, hence the barricades built out of cobblestones. 'Barcelona is a town with a long history of street-fighting. In such places things happen quickly, the factions are ready-made, everyone knows the local geography...people take their places almost as in a fire-drill.'[13]

What set Orwell on his famously escalating hostility to Soviet Communism and its Western advocates had as much to do with their mendacious reporting of events, the 'lies,' as with the events themselves. An honest use of words mattered to him as much as an honest use of the gun. In *Animal Farm* and *Nineteen*

Eighty-Four, contempt for manipulative propaganda runs in tandem with the disgust at the physical perversions of power. Returning to London from Spain, his blood boiled as he caught up with the Communist press and the following report in the *Daily Worker* (11 May 1937): 'The German and Italian agents, who poured into Barcelona ostensibly to "prepare" the notorious "Congress of the Fourth International", had one big task. It was this: They were – in co-operation with the local Trotskyists – to prepare a situation of disorder and bloodshed... in which the German and Italian Governments could land troops or marines quite openly on the Catalan coasts, declaring that they were doing so "in order to preserve order".... The POUM, acting in co-operation with well-known criminal elements, and with certain other deluded persons in the Anarchist organisations, planned, organised and led the attack in the rear-guard...'[14] Even an on the spot report from Barcelona by John Langdon-Davies of the liberal *News Chronicle* [no date given] disappointed him: 'This has not been an Anarchist uprising. It is a frustrated putsch of the "Trotskyist" POUM, working through their controlled organisations, "Friends of Durruti" and "'Libertarian Youth"...'[15] In fact much of Langdon-Davies's report seems to survive Orwell's critique. Orwell does not deny the existence of a document inciting the murder of Republican and Socialist leaders, he merely insists that it was a leaflet not a poster – in which case he must have seen it. And if Langdon-Davies says all the walls were plastered with the murderous poster, he must either have seen it for himself or be lying in the crudest, most unforgivable manner—yet Orwell tells us 'I am not attacking Mr Langdon-Davies's good faith.' He does not deny that the leaflet was signed by 'Friends of Durruti,' he merely insists that this was an anarchist group with no affection for the POUM. He does not comment on Langdon-Davies's claim that the leaflet was reprinted in the POUM paper *La Battalla* 'with the highest praise.'[16] If that is so, Orwell's entire moral position – many pages of narrative and argument – may appear rather one-sided: for example his disgust on seeing a cartoon widely distributed by the PSUC showing the POUM as a sinister figure slipping off the hammer-and-sickle mask to reveal a hideous, maniacal features marked by a swastika.

Orwell points out that before, during and after the suppression of the POUM in May-June 1937, its militia continued to fight loyally at the front, many serving four to five months at a stretch; several thousand died during an attack to the east of Huesca shortly after POUM was suppressed as a political party. Yet in Barcelona the crackdown he witnessed, and from which he was a fugitive, forced to sleep rough at night, affected not just arrested leaders like Nin (until recently minister of justice in the Catalan government, translator of Russian classics into Catalan, and a figure in Catalonia's literary revival), but anyone ever connected with the POUM, including wounded militiamen, hospital nurses, wives. Such was Orwell's disgust that he withdrew his application to join the International Brigades.

In his novel *The Case of Comrade Tulayev* (to which we shall return), Victor Serge devotes a chapter to the Spanish Civil War, supportive of the suppressed left opposition. An upright man of principle who deplores the bloodshed of the ongoing purge, his Soviet hero Ivan Kondratiev observes the military situation in Madrid—with the Russians Orlov and Gorev actually in command, teams of inquisitors, secret prisons and an atmosphere of intrigue, blackmail, fear. Serge uses the Spanish chapter to argue that it was a fatal mistake to try to 'win the war first, and have the revolution after,' 'because if people are to fight they need something to fight for'[17] – Orwell's point. Serge also highlights Stalinist brutality towards the POUM. (At the time of Serge's own arrest in the USSR in 1933, his correspondence with Andrés Nin, then in jail at Algeciras, was one of the accusations levelled against him in the Lubianka.)

Orwell kept a diary at the front which was confiscated during the July crackdown when the police raided the room in the Continental Hotel occupied by Mr and Mrs Blair. Orwell had been out of town trying to get his medical discharge certificate, without which he could not leave the country. As soon as he reached the hotel he found his wife Eileen waiting on tenterhooks in the lobby. 'Get out! Get out of here at once!' she hissed in his ear. 'They had seized every scrap of paper we possessed, except, fortunately, our passports and cheque book. They had taken all my diaries, all our books, the press cuttings...all my souvenirs and all our letters...' But the copious diary details in *Homage to Catalonia* suggest that all was not lost. John McNair of the ILP, for whom Eileen Blair worked as a secretary, later reported how he preserved the notes and early 'manuscript versions' of what became *Homage* by placing them on the sill outside the window when the police arrived to search his office in Barcelona.[18]

One perhaps manipulative feature of Orwell's narrative is its indiscriminate use of the word 'fascist.' His future friend Arthur Koestler was more discriminating. Strolling through the streets of the rebel-held port of Vigo, Koestler found it 'chock-full of troops – Legionaires, Carlists, Phalangists, but no Moors...' He put the backbone of Franco's infantry at 80,000 Moors, 100,000 Italians, and the Foreign Legion, supported by the Falange Española, the Requetes and, finally, segments of the regular army.[19] In short, the Nationalist forces were extremely heterogeneous and by no means composed exclusively of volunteers. Many were conscripted. But Orwell does not seem interested in such distinctions. He lumps them all together, referring to the 'the Fascist ex-owners' of the country houses and farm buildings of lime-washed stone with rounded arches and roof beams, 'noble places' he much admired. Monarchists, Carlists, Nationalists, Catholics, Falangists, are all 'Fascists.' The enemy soldiers a few hundred yards away behind their parapets and redoubts are simply 'the Fascists.' On one occasion he did not shoot at an enemy soldier running along the top of a parapet, because he was holding up his trousers with both hands: 'I had come here to shoot at "Fascists"; but a man who is holding up his trousers isn't a "Fascist", he is visibly a fellow-creature, similar to yourself, and you don't feel like shooting at him.'[20]

This passage has been cited as evidence of Orwell's humanity. That may be so, but our point is that by wrapping the word 'Fascist' in quotation marks on this single occasion, but not on hundreds of other occasions, he inadvertently draws attention to a powerful manipulative feature of his narrative. One is reminded of the scornful phrase 'Los Rojos,' the Reds, used by Franco's people to describe anyone fighting for the Republican government. By contrast, when Hemingway brings his fictional enemy officer into focus, he is careful to sketch in the man's precise allegiance and credo: Lieutenant Berrendo is a devout Catholic Carlist from Navarre and a red-hater. Orwell does say that the Spaniards hopefully would not make very 'good' fascists if Franco won the war, but most of the people he was shooting at were not precisely convinced fascists. Indeed on one occasion Orwell found himself assailed as a 'fascist.' At the time he was an acting *cabo*, or corporal, in command of twelve men. When a feeble fellow refused to take up a particular sentry post because exposed to enemy fire, Orwell began physically to drag the man along and was surrounded by a ring of shouting men: '"Fascist! Fascist! Let that man go! This isn't a bourgeois army! Fascist!" Etc. etc.'[21]

Admittedly, Malraux follows much the same path. Whether describing fighting in Toledo or Madrid, he settles in to the convenient shorthand term 'fascists.' In Toledo, for example: 'Confronted by the empty square, they hesitated. *Milicianos* and fascists stared at each other, unmoving.'[22]

Ten days after Orwell returned to the front with the POUM militia, now an acting *teniente* (junior officer) in charge of thirty men, he narrowly escaped death. At five in the morning, with the dawn light dangerously behind them, this very tall man imprudently raised his head above the parapet while talking to two sentries – and got a bullet clean through the neck. The world almost lost its subsequently most influential English writer at the age of thirty-four. His description of what the bullet felt like demonstrates the true writer's willingness to die in order to get up a few good sentences about dying. 'There must have been two minutes during which I assumed that I was killed. And that too was interesting – I mean it is interesting to know what your thoughts would be at such a time. My first thought, conventionally enough, was for my wife. My second was a violent resentment at having to leave this world which, when all is said and done, suits me so well. I had time to feel this very vividly.'[23]

He came back, after hospitalisation, to Barcelona again, now a 'nightmare,' a 'peculiar feeling of evil in the air – an atmosphere of suspicion, fear, uncertainty and veiled hatred.' The government of Largo Caballero had fallen. The Communists had taken over the reins of internal security. The prisons were groaning. In streets and corridors one offered only the faintest of winks to fellow-fugitives one knew from the front. Although in pain because of his wound, Orwell dared not spend a night with his wife or in any hotel – all guests had to be reported to the police. He had to sleep rough in long grass at the edge of a derelict housing lot: 'I had five days of tiresome journeys, sleeping in impossible places.... I did not make any of the correct political reflections. I never do when things are happening.' Filling in time by visiting the new Gaudi cathedral, he came upon 'one of the most hideous buildings in the world' with its 'four crenellated spires exactly the shape of hock bottles'—which (he concluded) the anarchists had been wrong to spare.[24]

In the middle of all this sleeping rough, he and Eileen took the immense risk of visiting the imprisoned Belgian POUM comrade, George Kopp, in prison, and trying to get him out. He managed to see an officer who was polite, concerned, but guarded.

'"This Major Kopp – what force was he serving in?"

'The terrible word had to come out: "In the POUM militia."'

'"POUM!"'

Soon came the obvious question:

'"And you say you were with him at the front. Then you were serving in the POUM militia yourself!"

'"Yes."[25]

Orwell's propulsion into passionate anti-Communism was stimulated not only by the 'lies' he read on returning to London, but by the refusal of left-wing publishers and periodicals to print his own testimony. In July 1937, soon after his return from Spain, the first article he wrote for the *New Statesman*, 'Spilling the Spanish Beans,' was rejected. In it he told of the current reign of terror and argued that the main struggle was now within the Government camp. The piece appeared in *New English Weekly*, on 29 July and 2 September.

As a softener the *New Statesman* sent him a book to review, Franz Borkenau's *The Spanish Cockpit*, but on 29 July the editor, Kingsley Martin, added injury to injury when he rejected the review on the ground that 'it too far controverts the political policy of the paper. It is very uncompromisingly said and implies that our Spanish correspondents are all wrong.' By the end of July, Orwell's publisher Victor Gollancz, aware of his association with POUM, had adopted the same position as Kingsley Martin – he declined to publish *Homage to Catalonia* (as yet unwritten). Orwell told Rayner Heppenstall that Gollancz was part of the 'Communism racket.'[26]

Homage to Catalonia was published by Secker and Warburg on 25 April 1938, price 10s 6d (not cheap). Fredric Warburg printed 1,500 copies. The advance was £150 but was not earned by sales. According to Warburg, the book 'caused barely a ripple on the political pond. It was ignored or hectored into failure.' Raymond Mortimer chose V. S. Pritchett to review the book in the *New Statesman* (30 April) alongside Geoffrey Brereton's *Inside Spain*. Pritchett uttered conciliatory sighs for the (alas) late Spanish Revolution, praised Orwell's sincerity and gifts with the pen, and patted him on the head for his well-meaning impracticality. 'Tall and bony, the face lined with pain, eyes that stared out of their caves, he looked far away over one's head, as if seeking more discomfort and new indignations.'[27] Pritchett's opening sentence, though ironic by intent, reinforced an English literary prejudice: 'There are many strong arguments for keeping creative writers out of politics and Mr George Orwell is one of them.'[28]

Orwell (Pritchett discerned) was the 'typical English anarchist.' Mr Orwell was simply wrong-headed when he carried the defence of POUM 'into the field of high politics and strategy.' Had not Russian arms saved the Republic?[29]

On 21 October 1938, Orwell wrote to Raymond Postgate noting that the much postponed trial of the executive committee of the POUM by the Spanish government had just begun, 'only a byproduct of the Russian Trotskyist trials.' He was particularly troubled by the accusation that the 29th division (POUM), with which he himself had served from 30 December 1936 to 20 May 1937, deserted from the Aragon front. He complained that the left-wing press was reluctant to publish refutations, 'held back by a desire not to embarrass the Spanish Government.'

Discovered in 1989 in the National Archive, Madrid, a security police report to the Tribunal for Espionage and High Treason, dated 13 July 1937 (three weeks after the Blairs escaped across the frontier into France) describes Eric and Eileen Blair as 'Known Trotskyists' and 'linking agents of the ILP and POUM.'[30] Discovered in Moscow's State Military Archive, an unsigned document, dated 11 May 1937, relays the demand for 'energetic and merciless repression' by means of a 'military tribunal for the Trotskyists.' Eric Blair and his wife are named as 'pronounced Trotskyists' operating in Barcelona with clandestine credentials and maintaining contact with opposition circles in Moscow.[31]

Homage to Catalonia did not appear in America until 1952, in France until 1955.[32] Yvonne Davet, for many years secretary to André Gide, translated several of Orwell's books in the vain hope of finding a French publisher.[33] During the postwar years, when the debate about 'the god that failed' was at its most intense, Orwell passed more or less unsighted in France.

6

Koestler: Sentence of Death

Arthur Koestler's enduring literary legacy is *Darkness at Noon* (1940). In this short novel Koestler enlists fiction's imaginative freedom of manoeuvre to penetrate the historical catastrophe of the Moscow purge trials. An intellectual whose partisan passage from Stalinism to passionate anti-Communism incarnated 'the god that failed' phenomenon, Koestler sets out to solve a conundrum which baffled foreign observers of Stalin's purges: why did the Old Bolsheviks, fathers of the Revolution, Lenin's companions, finally confess to crimes of which they were utterly innocent?

Koestler's dramatic experiences of the Spanish Civil War clearly have a bearing on his conversion – but how clearly? Koestler is a devious writer, addicted to intrigue and inclined to subordinate the truth to the party line. Whereas Orwell in the main addressed himself when writing, receiving in return an unflinching gaze, Koestler tended to look over his shoulder with slanting eyes, at the readers who must not learn the whole truth, at colleagues or informants whose existence must be concealed; then later, as an anti-Communist, at the rivals and enemies he must ridicule, at the need to dispel the inherent myopia of Anglo-Saxons. Even when operating in full freedom, without Nazis at his heels, Koestler was instinctively a 'clandestine' writer.

Hungarian by birth,[1] he had been working as a journalist for the Ullstein newspaper chain at the time he was recruited into the German Communist Party. From 1931 to 1938 he remained loyal to the Party, working outside Germany after Hitler's seizure of power. During 1932-33, he travelled widely in the USSR on assignment, never confusing the papers in his left pocket with those in the right: 'I was careful never to show my bourgeois, NARKOMINDYEL documents at the Party offices and factories that I visited.... On the other hand I never showed my Comintern letter to hotel managers...it would have deprived me of the preferential treatment for bourgeois tourists who have to be humoured for reasons of propaganda.'[2] He added: 'But euphemisms and camouflage are part of the ever-present conspiratorial ritual of the Communist world.'[3] Witnessing

49

the cruelties of collectivization in the Ukraine, he remained silent on the details. Painfully revealing is the story of his love affair with the beautiful Nadeshda, a woman of Baku, and how his own intimacy with the GPU led him first to deceive her when inviting her to meet a German comrade working for GPU, then to denounce her to the same comrade (she was already under surveillance as too upper class) for maybe – or maybe not – having taken a note from his pocket.[4] 'If I were a Catholic,' he concludes this episode, 'I would detect in my betrayal of Nadeshda the dialectics of Providence, and derive comfort from it. But I am not.'[5]

After the National Socialists took power in Germany, Koestler moved to Paris, where he worked for Willi Münzenberg's International Workers Aid (IWA). Founded in 1921, financed from Moscow, IWA produced newspapers (*Berlin am Morgen, Arbeiter Illustrierte Zeitung*), films (*Storm over Asia*), plays.[6] Koestler's boss Willy Münzenberg, who had known Lenin during his exile in Switzerland (he makes a brief appearance in Solzhenitsyn's *Lenin in Zurich*), could whip up left-liberal front organizations as effortlessly as a chef tosses an omelette. In short, the West Comintern propaganda operation run by Münzenberg, Otto Katz and Koestler was simultaneously principled, sincere, cynical, unscrupulous. Koestler possessed all of these qualities in abundance. *Spanish Testament* is a testimony to his own addiction to conspiracy and camouflage.

During the first month of the Civil War Koestler made his first trip to Spain as a Comintern agent under cover of representing both the liberal *News Chronicle* of London and the conservative *Pester Lloyd* of Budapest – but that latter ac-creditation was forged, in his own words 'a confidence trick,' and *Pester Lloyd* had no idea he was their man in Spain.[7] He reached Nationalist-held Seville via Lisbon, where the Portuguese authorities were openly pro-Franco and visas to rebel-held territory could be obtained if one cultivated the right Spanish con-tacts. Koestler did just that. Armed with a s*alvo conducto*, he left for Seville after only thirty-six hours in Lisbon. Now able to study rebel headquarters at close quarters, he interviewed the flamboyant commander-in-chief of the Southern Forces, General Queipo de Llano, who loved the sound of his own voice on the radio making extravagant threats. 'When we are victorious,' he told Koestler, 'Spain will be governed by a military cabinet; we shall sweep away all the parties and their representatives.' None of these gentlemen [conserva-tives like Gil Robles] will be members of the Government.' The Marxists, he added, make it a habit to slit open the stomachs of pregnant women and spear the foetuses. 'This went on and on, unceasingly, one story following another – a perfect clinical demonstration in sexual psychopathology. Spittle oozed from the corners of the General's mouth...'[8] But how accurate was Koestler's report? He later admitted that he had written up the interview with a 'poison pen.'[9] His published reports and reminiscences from Spain furnish a maze of evasions and contradictions.

Willi Münzenberg and his assistant Otto Katz had sent Koestler to Spain in the hope of repeating their success with the Reichstag Counter-Trial. The upshot was *L'Espagne ensanglantée* ('bloodied Spain'), Koestler's exposure of Nationalist atrocities, duly presented in London to a 'Commission of Inquiry' administered by Communists but fronted by liberals. Koestler made two subsequent visits but *Spanish Testament* fails to come clean about his second mission in the autumn of 1936; to have done so would have blown his cover as a liberal correspondent.

Koestler's second visit to war-torn Spain was by his own admission some years later a Münzenberg Comintern operation instigated by Alvarez del Vayo, the Republic's foreign minister, the mission being to search the private archives of right-wing politicians who had fled from Madrid after Franco's rising, and to produce evidence of Nazi Germany's direct hand in the military revolt. On this occasion he was provided with a Spanish passport, a huge Italian Isotta Fraschini, a chauffeur and a translator. 'I stayed in Madrid for three or four weeks until the search was completed.'[10] But all this was admitted only later—not a whisper of it can be found in *Spanish Testament*.

In the first days of 1937 he paid his third and last visit to Republican Spain, once again presenting himself as a correspondent for the *News Chronicle*. Conscious of his English audience, Koestler's calls himself 'an incorrigible Left-wing liberal' and disguises Marxism as 'the classic theory of Socialism,' according to which a transitional stage of pedagogic rule on the part of the most highly developed section of the community must intervene after the downfall of the old system...until the transitory régime itself gradually withers away...'[11] Marxism-Leninism ('the classic theory') comfortingly embodies the dictatorship of the pedagogues—this would surely sound to Left Book Club ears like the 'dictatorship of the Left Book Club.'

On the positive side, Koestler got straight to the social roots of the class war in Spain, the appalling rural wages, seasonal unemployment, the despotic nature of village power, the role of the Church, 'the largest landowner in Spain' as well as the owner of the Madrid tramway system, and of the Banco Espiritu Sancto (The Bank of the Holy Ghost), which according to Koestler, 'largely helped to finance Franco's insurrection.'[12] No mercy for the Church. However, having stressed cruel social poverty and the role of the Church as exploiter, Koestler adroitly slides the argument away from peasant land seizures and social strife towards traditional English icons, Oliver Cromwell, John Stuart Mill, and 'the age of enlightenment.' 'The anti-clerical demands of the Spanish Popular Front in the year 1936 were not a whit more radical or "red" than those of the age of enlightenment: separation of church and state, distribution of Church lands among the landless peasants, secular education, freedom of religious worship, freedom of speech and freedom of the pen.' Distribution of land was happening in Spain wherever the peasant masses got the upper hand, but Koestler offers reassurance: 'The truth is that the Spanish Popular Front was not striving towards a Soviet State or a Bakunin Utopia, but towards one goal alone: the raising of the Spanish State, which had never yet succeeded in emerging from the clerical, feudal stage, to the constitutional, material and spiritual level of the great European democracies.'[13]

Reaching the doomed city of Malaga, he was arrested and imprisoned in grim conditions after the Italian legions disembarked. Transfer to a more modern prison in Seville followed, but there was no relief from constant fear and uncertainty, the executions at night, Koestler constantly expecting the shuffle of the greasy priest to stop outside his own cell, No. 41. Clearly his own experience of a potential death sentence by Spain's fascists fed his depiction of Rubashov's nightmare imprisonment under Stalin in *Darkness at Noon.*

Although not a British subject, Koestler kept demanding to see the British consul – he knew the card to play.[14] But how would Franco's justice operate with regard to the correspondent of an English newspaper? After a week or two Koestler was intrigued by the arrival of a smiling young lady called Helena wearing 'a well-fitting Phalangist uniform,' accompanied by two elegant young officers. Helena, who worked on the side for the Hearst Press, asked him whether he was a Communist. (He was.)

'To this I had to reply in the negative.'

'"But you are a Red, aren't you?"'

'I said that I was in sympathy with the Valencia [Republican] Government, but did not belong to any party.'

(This deception is directed not only against the Phalangist Helena, but also against readers of *Spanish Testament.*)

Helena tells him the consequences of his activities are death. He asks why. She says he is condemned as a spy. 'She spoke with an American twang, drawling out the vowel sound in "death" so that it sounded like "dea-ea-h-th", and watched the effect.' She tells him that General Franco has been asked by the *News Chronicle* and by Mr Hearst of New York to spare his life. She does not know whether General Franco will or will not spare his life.

'The young lady on my bed asked me in charming conversational tones if I would like to make a statement to her paper with regard to my feelings towards General Franco.'

He tells us that he began a statement, crossed it out, dictated another, ending with the words: 'But I believe in the Socialist conception of the future of humanity, and shall never cease to believe in it.' Miss Helena asks him what exactly he means by that. Impatient, she then suggests a formula brief enough for an American audience to understand: 'Believes in Socialism to give workers chance.'[15] What really shames him is something he said with feigned casualness to one of the prison warders, one of the 'Dons,' in the hope that it would be passed on (and up): 'I am no longer a Red (a Rojo).'[16]

Following this inconclusive interview, the governor of the Seville prison now allows him a piece of soap, a face towel, a shirt, a stump of pencil and five sheets of white paper strictly for 'composing' but not for writing letters. 'My diary dates from this day onwards.' He learned the pattern of executions: 'True, not a single man had been shot without trial.... In the case of every single prisoner of war, without exception, the charge was one of "rebelión militar".... The proceedings lasted two to three minutes. The so-called Prosecutor demanded the death sentence: always and without exception. The so-called Defending Officer – always and without exception – asked for a life sentence in view of mitigating circumstances. Then the prisoner was marched off. He was never informed of his sentence, which was passed the moment he was out of the door; it was one of death; always and without exception. The record of the sentence was passed on to the commander-in-chief of the Southern Forces, General Queipo de Llano (of whom, as we have seen, Koestler had drawn an unflattering portrait after the first of his three visits to Spain.) Koestler tells us that, 'Twenty to twenty-five per cent of the prisoners – according to Queipo's mood or the situation at the front – were reprieved. The rest were shot.'

The British Consul eventually showed up, bringing a somewhat coded letter from Koestler's wife. Although he and Dorothea Ascher were estranged, and she had never set foot in England previously, he describes her assiduous campaigning and lobbying in London for his release, heroically concealing that the *News Chronicle*'s correspondent was a member of the Kommunistiche Partei Deutschlands. In *Spanish Testament* Koestler does not tell the full truth about the British consul's prison visit, and fails to report that the consul asked hesitantly whether he had proof of all the atrocity allegations in *L'Espagne ensanglantée* – the real reason for Koestler's imprisonment as a Communist spy. Koestler replied humbly that some of the atrocity material was 'doubtful.' (He knew it was false.) The consul left soon afterwards with a murmured encouragement and a limp handshake.[17] On another day Koestler was led to an office. There sat the military examiner, with a thick pile of documents. Koestler managed to read the inscription on the cover: *Auxilio de rebelión militar* – affording aid to armed rebellion. The examination lasted two hours. Half the time the examiner was trying to get him to admit that the *News Chronicle* was a Communist paper. He asked where Koestler had got the material for his first book – as noted earlier, a good question. Koestler attributed the material to the League for the Rights of Man, etc.[18]

Suddenly he is released. The governor hands him over into the custody of a stranger in a black shirt (no tie), who bows with exaggerated formality then whips him up into the sky in an open Baby Douglas, tiny and fragile. The pilot yells: 'When the Reds shoot our people, their last cry is our cry of *Viva Espa a.* I have seen Reds being shot and they too cried *Viva Espa a.*' The small plane tosses perilously in the wind above the mountains. They arrive at La Linea, the frontier town adjoining Gibraltar. A. Koestler is still alive. 'For my eventual release I have to thank those "kind friends" whom my wife found and of whom she wrote me in her letters...among them were fifty-eight English Members of Parliament, twenty-two of them Conservatives.'[19] *Spanish Testament* carried a preface by the Duchess of Atholl – a conservative fellow-traveller of the Spanish Republic (whom Orwell thoroughly distrusted and despised.) Koestler later recorded how the duchess asked him point-blank whether he was a Communist before granting her *imprimatur*. He said no. She said: 'Your word is good enough for me.' The Koestlers even went to the length of resuming their marital cohabitation in London for the sake of appearances. Koestler comments: 'A deception, once started, has the compelling momentum of a rolling stone.'[20]

Orwell's review of *Spanish Testament* appeared in *Time and Tide* on 5 February 1938, shortly before the publication of *Homage to Catalonia*. Given that Koestler's book came out under the same Victor Gollancz-Left Book Club imprint that had rejected Orwell's book, and given Koestler's standardized denigration of the POUM (along with the Catalonian anarchists),[21] Orwell's verdict was astonishingly friendly, although he did note that, 'The earlier part... looks rather as though it had been "edited" for the benefit of the Left Book Club.' Some six years later, in an essay on Koestler's work in general, Orwell's view of *Spanish Testament* had not altered. He then (1944) added a far-reaching comment: 'The sin of nearly all left-wingers from 1933 onwards is that they have wanted to be anti-Fascist without being anti-totalitarian. In 1937, Koestler already knew this, but did not feel free to say so. He put on a mask to say it in [his novel] *The Gladiators*.'[22]

Koestler reports that after his return from Spain he retained some hope that 'the first workers' state' could recover from the Stalinist terror. He still thought of Soviet Russia as 'our last and only hope on a planet in rapid decay.' This was evidently his state of mind when he began writing *Darkness at Noon* at the time of Munich. He clung to this schizophrenic attitude until (he says) the Nazi-Soviet Pact.[23]

While Koestler's incarceration in Cell 41 of Seville prison undoubtedly fed into his account of Rubashov's final days in the Lubyanka in *Darkness at Noon*, the parallel is tenuous if only because Koestler underwent little serious interrogation by the 'fascists' – and because he was in any case the Red Spy they took him for. By contrast the fictional Old Bolshevik Rubashov has to be persuaded to manufacture the case against himself. What most intimately links the Spanish experience with *Darkness at Noon* (as we shall see) is the odyssey round the archipelago of 'objective truth,' the dominant notion that what serves the party line and destiny is true even when, at a trivial bourgeois level, not true. Rubashov's fictional 'trial of faith' affords Koestler a spectacular display of his own intellectual ingenuity.

Part 2

The God That Failed

7

Commentary: The Soviet Trials

Briefly, the sequence of events. A series of trials had been accompanied by purges: the Shakhty trial of 1928, the Industrial Party trial of 1930, the Menshevik trial of 1931, the Metro-Vickers trial of 1933. By the early 1930s the GPU had become a state within the state; Party members, far from being immune as tended to be the case in the days of the Cheka, were now prime targets. On 1 December 1934 the popular Leningrad communist leader and Politburo member Sergei Kirov was assassinated, possibly on Stalin's instructions. The leading old Bolsheviks Zinoviev, Kamanev and other 'Zinovievites' were accused of indirectly instigating Kirov's assassination by contaminating the ideological atmosphere. By the time they were brought to trial in August 1936 the charges had become more specific; they were accused or organizing a terrorist cell under Trotsky's guidance. All except one of the accused confessed their guilt in court. All were shot. A second show trial followed in January 1937, with Radek and Piatakov the principal accused. The charges included a plot to dismember the USSR with the connivance of Germany and Japan. In June the press announced the arrest and execution of a number of military commanders, notably Marshal Tukachevsky, on similar charges. The last act out was played out in March 1938 when Bukharin, Rykov, Krestinsky and sixteen others faced sentence. Among the accused was Yagoda, until recently the head of the GPU and therefore the engineer if not the architect of the earlier trials. He was now accused of poisoning Soviet Russia's most honoured writer, Maxim Gorky, on Trotsky's instructions.

The wider world followed these events, amazed. What was going on? Orwell commented: 'From our point of view the whole thing is not merely incredible as a genuine conspiracy, it is next door to incredible as a frame-up. It is simply a dark mystery, of which the only seizable fact – sinister enough in its way – is that Communists over here regard it as a good advertisement for Communism.'[1] Perhaps the most puzzling, and spectacular, dimension was the prosecution's use of elaborate and mutually corroborative confessions. Only rarely did the charade wobble. Krestinsky, for example, retracted his confession that he had been a Polish spy since 1921, but next day reverted to his plea of guilty.

Most sceptical or hostile foreign observers concluded that the accused had been beaten to their knees by protracted interrogation, torture, deprivation, threats and promises regarding their families. This was to be the main explanation offered by Khrushchev in 1956: 'application of physical methods of pressuring him [the prisoner], tortures, bringing him to a state of unconsciousness, deprivation of his judgment, taking away of his human dignity. In this manner "confessions" were acquired.' Mass arrests, deportations and executions without trial, added Khrushchev, 'created insecurity, fear and even desperation.' Khrushchev did not specify which leaders and which trials his formula applied to, but in 1957 the new official history of the CPSU described Zinoviev, Kamenev, Rykov and Bukharin as having been 'mistaken' and therefore 'objectively' anti-Soviet. This effectively undermines the vividly dramatic specific charges on which their trials were based.

The trials had their supporters beyond the ranks of the Western Communist parties. The noted Russia expert, Sir Bernard Pares, reported after a visit to Moscow that the guilt of the accused was established beyond doubt. Another respected scholar, Sir John Maynard, who had already been taken for a conducted ride over collectivization, explained that the accused had simply made a 'clean breast' of their sins. With the exception of André Gide, the French fellow-travellers spoke with one voice: guilty. Kingsley Martin, editor of the *New Statesman*, later recalled that while he refused to suspend his disbelief, to express doubts about the Moscow trials was to incur immediate odium as a kind of Gestapo agent, witting or unwitting, and as an assassin of Republican Spain. The Webbs reaffirmed their admiration for Soviet justice on the ground that the Soviet leaders *must* be right, they *must* know. Upton Sinclair was quite sure that proven Bolshevik revolutionaries, who had withstood the worst that the tsar's police could throw at them, would never confess to crimes they had not committed. Sinclair believed that Tukhachevsky and the other generals summarily shot in 1937 had got only what they deserved: 'If the medicine they had to swallow is bitter, the answer is that they got their own medicine.' In April 1938, some 150 American intellectuals issued a statement linking support for the Moscow verdicts with the cause of progressive democracy in the United States.

Of course there were still awkward questions for the faithful to answer. Why did the defendants appear in court without counsel? The British lawyer D. N. Pritt, a devoted fellow-traveller and frequent visitor to Moscow, explained that the defendants had specifically renounced counsel because they now saw the error of their ways and wanted only to reveal the truth. All these friendly observers stressed how healthy and alert the defendants appeared in court. Admittedly it was bizarre if not byzantine to see the main engineers of the earlier purges and confessions, successive heads of the GPU chosen by Stalin, Yagoda then Yezhov himself, confessing to the most fantastic range of crimes.

No defence of the trials was more exploited by the Communists than that of the popular German novelist, Lion Feuchtwanger. He later recalled how, viewed from France, the Zinoviev trials had seemed to him ludicrous, but as soon as he reached Moscow and attended the Radek trial 'my doubts melted away as naturally as salt dissolves in water. If that was lying or prearranged, then I don't know what the truth is.' When Feuchtwanger was granted a personal interview by Stalin, he discovered that 'for many years he has been striving to win over competent Trotskyists rather than destroy them.' It was truly 'affecting to see how doggedly he is endeavouring to use them for his work.' Alas, to no avail: either Trotskyism would be stamped out or there would be war. By contrast, as each new trial hit the headlines, André Gide exposed it as a sham and a fix. He was duly accused of serving the composite beast 'Trotsky-Gestapo.'

Apparently invisible to observers like Feuchtwanger was Stalin's determination to purge the party and the country of all Bolshevik veterans whose histories and records afforded them power, prestige and judgment independent of his own. Stalin wanted a party of young Stalinists utterly beholden to him, and he got it.

The U.S. ambassador to Russia, Joseph E. Davies, attended the Radek trial and concluded that the Soviet state had uncovered a real conspiracy: 'To have assumed that this proceeding was invented and staged...would be to presuppose the creative genius of Shakespeare and the creative genius of Belasco in stage production.' In March 1939, a further strain was thrown on the ambassador's credulity, for there, a few feet away in the court room, sat Krestinsky, undersecretary of state, 'to whom I had presented my credentials just a year ago'; there sat Rosengoltz, former Commissar of Trade, 'with whom I lunched just a year ago...at his country home'; there sat Dr Pletnov, 'the heart specialist who had treated me professionally...' All traitors to the motherland? Yes, yes, concluded the U.S. ambassador. Later, after Hitler's invasion of the Soviet Union, Davies's best-selling memoir, *Mission to Moscow*, propagated the myth that the Russians had effectively eliminated the fifth column. Thomas Mann wrote to his brother Heinrich describing the book as 'extraordinarily interesting': '*ich empfehle es Dir sehr* – I strongly recommend it to you.' Heinrich Mann himself was impressed by the trials as 'evidence of an intellectuality unique in the world.' This *Intellektualiät* manifested itself in the Dostoyevskyan manner in which prosecutor and accused worked together to clarify the truth.

When the Germans invaded the USSR in June 1941, some apologists for the trials were quick to argue that Russia's capacity to resist proved the efficacy of the eradication of the fifth column. This was Heinrich Mann's conviction and even his nephew Klaus Mann, by no means a fellow-traveller, began to wonder whether his earlier doubts had been ill-founded. (In reality, Russia's disastrous military performance against Finland in 1940, then against the Wehrmacht's onslaught, reflected the decimation of the senior officer corps by firing squad, including veterans of the Civil War of 1918-1920. This, however, was not the only factor.)

In the novel *Life and Fate*, Vasily Grossman introduces his readers to a fictional hero, Krymov, for twenty-five years a devoted Communist, who had led a soldiers' mutiny in 1917, fought in the Civil War, and brought his encircled detachment to safety in 1941 – the full curriculum of heroism. Commissar Krymov has been sent to Stalingrad to curb tendencies towards *partisanshchina* within the Red Army – the creation of new war aims, including the end of the kolkhoz (collective farms), independently of the Party. Krymov himself is arrested, interrogated in the Lubyanka, and accused of fantastical collusion with Trotsky, the Germans, etc. Everything he has ever said has been reported, it's all in his file, his minor love affairs, the nicknames of foreign comrades, every triviality.

As if echoing Koestler (had Grossman, one asks more than once, got hold of a copy of *Darkness at Noon*?), the interrogator says to Krymov: "'If you are genuinely capable of sincere repentance, if you still feel any love at all for the Party, then help the Party with your confession.'" Later, after a sleepless night, Krymov tells the interrogator: "'I can allow that, in spite of myself, I may have given expression to views hostile to the Party... But espionage, sabotage...'" A moment later, Krymov jumps up, grabs the investigator's tie, and bangs his fist on the table. "'You son of a bitch, you swine," he cried out in a piercing howl, "where were you when I led people into battle in the Ukraine and the Bryansk forests?... Were you ever in Stalingrad, you bastard?... I suppose you were defending our Motherland here in the Lubyanka, you Tsarist gendarme!...Were you ever nearly executed in Shanghai? Were you shot in the left shoulder by one of Kolchak's soldiers in 1917?'" In consequence of this outburst Krymov is systematically beaten up, very seriously, then injected with camphor by a doctor.[2]

8

Beyond *Darkness at Noon*

Darkness at Noon was written and published under extraordinarily taxing conditions. Begun in the autumn of 1938 at the time of the Munich agreement, surviving Koestler's arrest in Paris, internment and flight across France after the outbreak of war (described in his brilliant report, *Scum of the Earth*), the German text was lost but an English translation was smuggled to London before Koestler's escape to England via North Africa and Portugal. Koestler corrected the page proofs during his five weeks in Pentonville prison; he was still incarcerated on the day of publication in December 1940.

A prefatory note declares, 'The characters in this book are fictitious. The historical circumstances which determined their actions are real. The life of the man N. S. Rubashov is a synthesis of the lives of a number of men who were victims of the so-called Moscow Trials. Several of them were personally known to the author. This book is dedicated to their memory.' (Koestler later explained that Rubashov derives his personality and appearance—the pince-nez, wispy beard, the incisive gestures—from Trotsky and Karl Radek. Rubashov's intellectual sophistication belongs to Bukharin.)

Koestler mentions a crucial encounter with a lifelong Austrian friend, Eva Weissberg. Her husband, the physicist Alex Weissberg, had been employed by the Ukrainian Institute for Physics and Technology. The Weissbergs, now divorced, had each been arrested (separately) in Russia some years after Koestler had visited them in 1933. Koestler says that Eva, a ceramicist, had been accused of inserting swastikas into the pattern on the teacups she designed for mass production. 'She spent eighteen months in in the Lubyanka, where the GPU tried to brief her as a repentant sinner for the Bukharin show-trial.' She attempted suicide.[1] Finally released and expelled from Russia, in the spring of 1938 Eva Weissberg was able to brief Koestler on 'the GPU's method of obtaining confessions.' This 'provided me with part of the material for *Darkness at Noon*.'[2] This begs a range of questions regarding the pressures applied to Eva Weissberg as distinct from the fictional pressures applied to Rubashov. A recent (2003) account by her sister-in-law, Mrs Barbara Striker, who heard Eva's account of her Russian imprisonment first-hand, does not mention the Bukharin trial: 'At the time [in the Lubyanka] her investigator pressured her to sign an untrue statement by threatening her [that] she will rot in prison all her life without trial.' She then slashed her wrists but was saved by a wardress. This may imply that she was threatened with prolonged incarceration rather than subjected to the 'mindwash' techniques that Koestler implies she passed on to him.[3]

The mindwash psychological approach is absolutely central and distinctive to *Darkness at Noon*, but Koestler only confuses the issue with his prefatory quotes from Machiavelli's Discorsi and Dietrich von Nieheim, Bishop of Verden, both advocating ruthless raison d'état where the existence of the state (or church) is threatened. Neither Machiavelli nor the Bishop expected the victims to sign up by way of elaborate confessions to the tyrant's version. Did Joan of Arc plead guilty when brought to the stake? In *The Gulag Archipelago*, Solzhenitsyn praises *Darkness at Noon* as a 'talented inquiry' which more than any other document helped to clarify the 'riddle' of the trials. Solzhenitsyn believes Bukharin confessed out of total devotion to the Party: 'They had to stick together. Even if they made mistakes, they had to stick together on that, too.'[4] But Solzhenitsyn's general approach to the false confessions of the old Bolshheviks veers more towards mundane factors, fear and cowardice. He is contemptuous of Bukharin's cowardice. Individuals always have a choice: 'If you study in detail the whole history of the arrests and trials of 1936 to 1938, the principal revulsion you feel is not against Stalin and his accomplices, but against the humiliatingly repulsive defendants – nausea at their spiritual baseness after their former pride and implacability.'[5]

Unusual among novelists, Koestler is less concerned with personal courage and integrity than with the perverse geometry of ideological fanaticism. The early pages are full of ironic references to the Party being by definition infallible because of its role in capital H History. Rubashov himself is said to have subscribed to this belief (though it is not found in Marx). History itself is mockingly hypostasized as an entity that 'makes no mistakes' – yet Stalinist language in the purge era was mainly about patriotism, foreign enemies, spies and sabotage – not about Marxist theory or what Isaiah Berlin was to term 'historical inevitability.'

Koestler invents a powerful force called (awkwardly) 'the grammatical fiction'—but what is it? It is a shadow, a Doppelganger, which reverses Rubashov's normal thought processes; it can also be taken as an ironic description of the first person singular, the self, the 'I,' which the Party holds to be of no account. Koestler knows all about the 'grammatical fiction' but his hero does not: 'Of its nature or its mode of being, its ontological status or its psychological or intellectual procedures he knows nothing.' Gradually Koestler allows Rubashov to become aware that he has betrayed himself and millions of others by his failure to recognise the existence of the 'grammatical fiction.' 'I must pay.'[6]

The narrative begins with Rubashov's arrest in Moscow, poignantly described. By this time there have been three trials of the so-called 'opposition.' A former Civil War commander, Rubashov is fatally compromised: only six months have passed since he made a new public statement affirming his devotion to the 'Leadership' and the criminality of the opposition.[7] Worse than that: under ultimatum he had made a public declaration which sealed the fate of the faithful Arlova, his secretary and mistress, after she called on him to be the chief witness in her defence because she had done what she had done in good faith, taking her cue from him, her trusted boss, when he headed a mission abroad. Rubashov had let down the faithful Arlova, lying to save his own neck, abandoning her to her fate. This admission risks pretty well killing off our sustained interest in the fate of Rubashov. (Koestler himself had likewise abominably betrayed the beautiful Nadeshda, a woman of Baku, while working as a journalist in the USSR.)

The huge beehive of a Soviet prison with its two thousand prisoners is conveyed with economy of detail: the long corridors where the lights forever burn nakedly and dimly, the silence broken only by the shuffling of a jailer's shoes, the clanging of cell gates, the screams of those tortured at night. 'The infirmary was small and the air stuffy; it smelled of carbolic and tobacco. A bucket and two pans were filled to the brim with cotton-wool swabs and dirty bandages. The doctor sat at a table with his back to them, reading the newspaper and chewing bread and dripping. The newspaper lay on a heap of instruments, pincers, and syringes. When the warder had shut the door, the doctor turned slowly round. He was bald and had an unusually small skull, covered with white fluff, which reminded Rubashov of an ostrich.'[8]

Rubashov has not only been capable of base treachery towards a female subordinate, he also embodies the most ruthless and senseless aspects of Stalin's foreign policy before, during and after Hitler's coming to power and the crushing of the Communist movement. His activities in Germany, Holland and Western Europe, the smashing of the Party and the 'Movement,' are recounted in flashback as he sits in his cell, longing for cigarettes, and tapping messages on the wall to the half-mad, sex-starved Monarchist in the next cell. (SERVES YOU RIGHT, the Monarchist had responded when Rubashov revealed who he was.)

Koestler introduces minor fictional characters (as remembered by Rubashov) to emphasise the long-standing mendacity of the Party line. The West European character Richard, one of the few faithful members to have survived the Nazi purge, complains how the local Party's clandestine press constantly presents a smashing defeat as a victory, as a necessary clarification of the real nature of capitalism. Rubashov hears Richard's pleas but the Party line is louder. The recalled conversation with Richard takes place in a European gallery in the presence of two paintings, a Last Judgement and a Pietà. The latter offers a silent commentary on the pitiless totalitarian speech of Rubashov as he drives

Richard towards destruction. The same logic follows soon afterwards with the story of Little Loewy. The Party line must override the alternative logic of humanitarian considerations. Little Loewy's eventual suicide is the result of years of betrayal by his political masters.[9]

These two flashbacks or analepses recalling Rubashov's meetings with Richard and Little Loewy provide rare disruptions of the sequential momentum. But they contribute to the advancement of a textual argument; the story has to move into reverse—reculer pour mieux sauter. Koestler also uses these episodes to establish historical points – for example, how the 'the Country of the Revolution' had violated the naval embargo on trading with fascist states and how the local Party had used the argument that if the USSR did not benefit from such trade the capitalists would; after all, strengthening the USSR was the prime objective during the phase of fascist crudescence—until the next revolutionary wave.

Rubashov ponders in his cramped cell: 'But how can the present decide what will be judged truth in the future? We are doing the work of prophets without their gift. We replaced vision by logical deduction, but although we all started from the same point of departure, we came to divergent results.'[10] 'Vision' and 'logic' are Koestlerian categories. According to Philip Sturgess, the word 'logic' and its variants does not crop up during the first third of the novel but then makes forty-eight variant appearances. The phrases in which 'logic' appears carry both a totalitarian resonance (there can be no appeal against 'logic') and – on the contrary—convey the mental armoury of any intelligent individual.

Rubashov's early interrogations are conducted by the sympathetic NKVD officer Ivanov, more in sorrow than in anger. The Rubashov-Ivanov dialogues carry a constant inference that the two men, interrogator and prisoner, belong to the same generation, share the same mentality, and could easily exchange roles. Examining Magistrate Ivanov explains the divisions of cases into categories. A (Administrative) cases are summarily tried by a Board in secret. If category A, Rubashov will be finished off by the 'confession' of a colleague. Category P means public trial. For that, Ivanov suggests a partial confession: the prisoner got involved with opposition but drew back from the dastardly plot to murder No. 1 (Stalin). Likely sentence is twenty years but in reality two or three years followed by an amnesty, 'and in five years you will be back in the ring again.'[11] It is not clear why Ivanov should make such an improbable promise to Rubashov, who must have known that no disgraced Bolshevik leader ever broke back into 'the ring.'

Ivanov's fictional role is to remind Rubashov of his past career, while Rubashov keeps saying, 'Stop this.... For God's sake stop this comedy.' Ivanov of course continues since he is in effect passing background information to the reader. Koestler has the habit in his novels of getting his characters to smile, particularly if they are playing a consciously Machiavellian role like Ivanov the interrogator. Ivanov smiles too often but Rubashov begins to confide in him

– which may remind us that since the era of Crime and Punishment the Russian prosecutor has been recognised as the personification of an inner voice, a conscience, whereas in the West, by a parallel process, psychoanalysis assumed the role of secret policeman. Rubashov confides that for some time he has not believed that 'the leadership' enjoys the support of the masses, the proles. (For some reason he calls them the Plebs, a pre-industrial category.)

One hundred pages into the novel we leave Rubashov for the first time, to find Ivanov conversing with his deputy in the canteen after dinner. Here we meet Gletkin, the almost robotic interrogator who is to be Rubashov's nemesis. Gletkin is critical of his superior, Ivanov, who has allowed Rubashov to have paper, pencil, cigarettes, confident that he will capitulate once the logic of the situation has sunk in. Gletkin favours torture, the short route: 'Human beings able to resist any amount of physical pressure do not exist.'[12] As interrogating officials, Ivanov and Gletkin exert the awe and mystery of arbitrary State Power but, discovered arguing in the canteen, they forfeit the mystique of byzantine power. (In Kafka's *The Trial*, senior officials of the court may allow K. to engage them in conversation – but they are never found talking to one another.) Koestler later explained that the superficial models for Ivanov and Gletkin were two GPU officers he ran into in Baku in 1933; afterwards he realised that they had deliberately set themselves up in reverse roles, the No. 1 pretending to be the subordinate bringing documents to his nachal'nik (chief).

Ivanov abruptly vanishes. Rubashov learns that he is under arrest because (Gletkin coldly explains), he has conducted the case negligently and 'in a private conversation expressed cynical doubts as to the well-foundedness of the accusation.' Gletkin then discloses that Ivanov has been shot 'in execution of an administrative decision.'[13] Gletkin is said to be in his late thirties, the generation just old enough to have fought in the Civil War but without any historical or cultural background. He carries a scar on his clean-shaven head and wears a stiff uniform with a revolver holster. Rubashov thinks of Gletkin's generation as the mental 'Neanderthalers.'

Later he asks Gletkin why he has not tortured him; after all, Gletkin is known to favour 'the so-called "hard method"'. Gletkin routinely replies that torture is forbidden by 'our criminal code' then adds that a certain type of accused confesses under physical pressure then recants at the public trial. 'You belong to that tenacious kind. The political utility of your confession at the trial will lie in its voluntary character.'[14] Oddly, this virtually brings him back to Ivanov's position.

Rubashov's confession is spelled out over two pages.[15] The language, dichotomies and above all ironies employed are surely Koestler's own – not the language used in Russia, one of whose persistent qualities was its refusal to admit dual values and valid choices. Soviet language (and therefore confessions) never admitted dialectics, contradictions, paradoxes. It was a language of the catechism, unitary, denunciatory, moralistic, humanistic, 'lofty,' censorious. There are no real precedents among Stalin's victims when Rubashov writes: 'I plead guilty to not having understood the fatal compulsion behind the policy of the Government...to having followed sentimental impulses, and in so doing to have been led into contradiction with historical necessity. I have lent my ear to the laments of the sacrificed, and thus became deaf to the arguments which proved the necessity to sacrifice them.' [The word 'sacrifice' is inconceivable.] 'I plead guilty to having rated the question of guilt and innocence higher than that of utility and harmfulness. Finally, I plead guilty of having placed the idea of man above the idea of mankind....'

A secretary has been taking this down. 'He believed he saw an ironic smile on her pointed profile.' (She may know that she is taking down Koestler's version of a confession not Rubashov's.) Rubashov continues. What he had wanted was 'a liberal reform of the dictatorship' (but 'liberal' was not a word ever uttered by a Bolshevik, and by the time of the 1936 Constitution the USSR was notionally the 'most democratic' country in the world). While conceding that 'Humanitarian weakness and liberal democracy, when the masses are not mature, is suicide for the Revolution,' he admits that he advocates 'the abolition of the Terror,' which he calls 'counter-revolutionary' (but Bolsheviks never spoke of their official actions as Terror).

Virtually every word of Rubashov's fictional confession violated the regime's vocabulary. It is utterly inauthentic as history, if useful as irony.

Confronted by the main witness against him, young Kieffer (known as Hare-Lip), Rubashov signs a more practical confession exactly as demanded by Gletkin—that he had incited Hare-Lip to murder the leader of the Party. He is then given only an hour of sleep before a protracted examination in which he and Gletkin both go without sleep – no one is allowed to replace Gletkin, no relays, and he does not smoke or eat in front of Rubashov. The accusation consists of seven points.

Rubashov stubbornly refuses to admit to industrial sabotage of the aluminium industry. He expresses irritation at the universal allegations of sabotage, the 'epic of denunciations.' Gletkin asks him to explain why state industries are currently in so unsatisfactory a condition if there is no sabotage. Rubashov replies: 'Too low piece-work tariffs, slave-driving and barbaric disciplinary measures.' Gletkin responds defensively by pointing out that Rubashov had received the present of a watch as a boy, whereas Gletkin came from a peasant milieu without watches. He was sixteen before he learned that the hour is divided into minutes. The peasants now operating the new industries have no sense of time: 'If we didn't sack them and shoot them for every trifle, the whole country would come to a standstill...' Rubashov tells him that the term 'scapegoat' originated in a Hebrew custom of annually sacrificing a goat laden with all the sins of humans. Gletkin replies: 'According to what I know of history, I see that mankind could never do without scapegoats...'[16]

But Gletkin here once again becomes Koestler's cipher rather than a real GPU /NKVD official. The word 'scapegoats' is unknown to the official Soviet vocabulary of the purges. 'If we don't sack them and shoot them for every trifle' could conceivably lodge in an apparatchiks' brain, but not come to life on his tongue. Next, Gletkin shames Rubashov by quoting from the condemned prisoner's own writings: 'It is necessary to hammer every sentence into the masses by repetition and simplification.... For consumption by the masses, the political processes must be coloured like ginger-bread figures at a fair.' Rubashov may have thought as much, but if he is said to have written it down, where did he publish it? No Bolshevik would have written in that idiom. It is Koestler we overhear.[17] Koestler is denying Bolsheviks the right to self-righteous deception and false consciousness.

Gletkin shuts the cover of the dossier. He bends forward a bit, settles his cuffs, and makes the remarks on which commentators – and Koestler himself in *The Invisible Writing*—have based their analysis of Koestler's historical overview of the Moscow show trials: "'Your testimony at the trial will be the last service you can do the Party.'"[18] But Rubashov is exceptional in terms of biography, intellect, character. 'To you, Comrade Rubashov, we propose no bargain and we promise nothing.' He addresses Rubashov in terms of historical justification:

"'For the first time in history a Revolution has not only conquered power but kept it, becoming a bastion of the new era, one tenth of the world's population. As the leader has made clear, the task is tenaciously to survive the period of reaction, not to engage in adventures. The bulwark must be held, at any price and with any sacrifice.... Whole sets of our best functionaries in Europe had to be physically liquidated.... We did not recoil from co-operation with the police of reactionary countries in order to suppress revolutionary movements which came at the wrong moment.... But the leader of the Revolution understood that all depended on one thing: to be the better stayer.'" Gletkin concludes his oration: "'The Party promises only one thing: after the victory, one day when it can do no more harm, the material of the secret archives will be published.'"[19]

But how does Gletkin's frank objectivity, his candid admission about the elimination of 'our best functionaries in Europe,' of rival 'revolutionary movements which came at the wrong moment' stand up against the real adversarial language employed not only by Pravda but also by the Münzenberg propaganda outfit in the West, which Koestler himself loyally served throughout the 1930s? We may compare Gletkin's 'parole' and 'langue' to Central Committee documents (now available) from that era. For example:

Strictly Secret [*Strogo Sekretno*]. All Union Communist Party (Bolshevik) Central Committee, 4 December 1937. (Signed by Stalin.) 'On the basis of incontrovertible evidence' [*na osnovanim neoproverzhimykh dannykh*] the Politburo deems it necessary to remove from membership of the Central Committee and to subject to arrest seven named 'enemies of the people' [kak vragov naroda] and four who it turns out [okazavshikhsia] are German spies and one named as both a German spy and agent of the Tsarist Okhrana, linked to the counter-revolutionary work of two others named. All these persons admit their guilt [*priznali sebia vinovnymi*]. The Politburo asks the Central Committee to sanction the expulsion and arrest of the above mentioned.[20]

This is the actual language used and it had little to do with Marxism. The indictment refers to 'rogues' [*merzavtsi*], using such terms as 'deficiencies,' 'intolerable,' 'abysmally' [iz ryk von plocho], to describe the functioning of the NKVD abroad. Or take the first page of Yezhov's letter of resignation to Tov. *Stalinu* (Comrade Stalin), dated 23 November 1938 (Document 191). Yezhov asks the Central Committee to relieve him of his work as Commissar for Internal Affairs for the following reasons: he had ignored warnings contained in a statement to the Politburo on 19 November by the head of the NKVD for Ivanovsky province, Zhuravlev, entirely corroborated by the evidence he set out. Yezhov also takes responsibility for ignoring what was signalled to him about the suspicious conduct [*podozritel'nii povedenia*] of Litvin and other NKVD officials 'some of whom pretended to be putting a stop to [*zamiat'*] enemies of the people, while themselves being linked to anti-Soviet activities conspiracies [*buduchi sami sviazany s nimi po zagovorshchicheskoi antisovetskoi deiatel'nosti*].' Yezhov's letter of resignation ends with the reflection that the main 'lever of intelligence,' 'intelligence gathering by agents' operating abroad, had come under the control [podstavlennoi] of foreign intelligence agents. These documents may tell us little about reality or the causes of the purges, but what they do confirm is that the language used at the highest level, addressed to Koestler's 'No.1,' had little ideological content and remained anchored in the language of personal responsibility, unexplained conspiracy, and treachery. Thirty years later, the transcripts of the Brezhnev-era Praesidium discussions concerning the dissident Solzhenitsyn, and what to do about him, reveal the Soviet leaders still speaking among themselves as if addressing the world.

Rubashov's trial is conveyed through a newspaper report read to Vassilij, concierge of his apartment block. Rubashov's own experience of the trial is beyond the frame. Levene comments: 'He [Rubashov] has, in essence, relinquished both the ethical and aesthetic right to speak for himself.'[21] In fact, Rubashov's grip on the narrative has been previously removed by his author; the trial scene may be treated as a simple alienation effect, a relegation of the individual from empathetic close-up to the status of another newspaper headline. At the very last, at the hour of Rubashov's execution, Prisoner 402, the unseen tsarist in the next cell, advises Rubashov by tapping to empty his bladder. Rubashov goes obediently to the bucket. Koestler will report his experience of dying, of being shot in the back of his head.

Postwar, Koestler's novel gained horrendous vindication when the process of bogus confession repeated itself in a series of East European trials. At the 1952 trial of Rudolf Slansky, general secretary of the Czechoslovak Party, Vlado Clementis, foreign minister, and twelve other defendants all confessed to 'Trotskyist-Titoist-Zionist' crimes of which they were innocent. Eleven of the fourteen were Jews. Among the victims was Koestler's old, pre-war colleague and patron Otto Katz, otherwise known as André Simon, editor in chief of *Rude Pravo*, whose last words belong entirely to fiction: 'I... belong to the gallows.

The only service I can still render is to serve as a warning example...'[22] Simon had of course read *Darkness at Noon*.

Scum of the Earth (1941), Koestler's report of his flight across France from the Nazis, demonstrates that his natural talent resided in acute personal observation, vivid description, head-on portraits, unvarnished self-scrutiny, and sardonic penetration of mentalités, attitudes, ideologies. Koestler's intelligence, international experience, and multilingual gifts made him one of the great anti-totalitarian commentators of the mid-century.

Darkness at Noon was published in December 1940. Orwell reviewed it in the New Statesman (4 January 1941), greeting a brilliant novel and an exceptional interpretation of the trials and confessions – in that respect Orwell saw it as an expansion of Boris Souvarine's pamphlet 'Cauchemar en URSS.' Orwell reflected that 'the worst thing' had been the eagerness of left-wing intellectuals in the West to justify the Moscow trials.

During the autumn of 1944 Orwell published an extended appreciation of *Koestler* in Polemic, in which he commented that 'no Englishman could have written *Darkness at Noon*.' The novel 'reaches the stature of tragedy whereas an English or American writer would have turned it into a political tract.'[23] Orwell arrived at a strikingly important general statement about the status of politically driven writing in the era of Hitler and Stalin:

> I mean by this the special class of literature that has arisen out of the European political struggle since the rise of Fascism. Under this heading novels, autobiographies, books of 'reportage', sociological treatises and plain pamphlets can all be lumped together, all of them having a common origin and to a great extent the same emotional atmosphere. Some of the outstanding figures in this school of writers are Silone, Malraux, Salvemini, Borkenau, Victor Serge and Koestler himself. Some of these are imaginative writers, some are not, but they are all alike in that they are trying to write contemporary history, the kind that is ignored in the text books and lied about in the newspapers. Also they are all alike in being continental Europeans.... The special world created by secret-police forces, censorship of opinion, torture and frame-up trials is, of course, known about [in England] and to some extent disapproved of, but it has made very little emotional impact.

Prophetically, on the eve of the god that failed era, Orwell called for an English 'literature of disillusionment about the Soviet Union,' as distinct from 'ignorant disapproval' and 'uncritical admiration.'[24]

But with *Arrival and Departure* (1943), his first book to be written in English,[25] Koestler had moved to an anti-revolutionary position disturbing to Orwell. An uneasy blend of allegory and realism, the novel is said to be set in 'Neutralia' in the spring of 1941. There are interesting passages (plus one of Koestler's statutory rapes), including a chilling description of Nazi deportation trains operating by night across Europe, and a monologue about the similarities between the two great totalitarian systems now locked in mortal combat. In Orwell's opinion, and it is hard to disagree, the novel was really 'a tract purporting to show that revolutionary creeds are rationalisations of neurotic impulses.' He admonished Koestler for seeming to have lost any vision of the future; and for forgetting that the aim of socialism was not to make the world perfect but better.[26] Paradoxically, this foreshadowed the indictment later to be brought against Orwell himself by Isaac Deutscher, E. P. Thompson and Raymond Williams.

9

Serge: *The Case of Comrade Tulayev*

Victor Serge, with whom Koestler can fruitfully be compared, wrote at least[1] two novels about the purges, *Midnight in the Century* (1936-38) and *The Case of Comrade Tulayev* (1940-42). The latter displays a breadth and depth of knowledge about Stalin's Russia unequalled by any other Western writer, Koestler included – and there can be no doubt that the term 'Western' applies to Serge despite familial and emotional ties to Russia. Born Victor Lvovich Kibalchich in Belgium in 1890 (four years before Koestler), Serge first set foot in Russia in 1919, by that time a seasoned anarchist who had already served two prison terms and joined in the failed Spanish insurrection of 1917. In May 1919, he embraced the Bolsheviks, took part in the first three congresses of the Comintern, and supported (with misgivings) the suppression of the Kronstadt sailors' rebellion in February-March 1921 – which he later regretted. After working for the Comintern in Europe, he returned to the Soviet Union in 1925 and joined the Left Opposition. Expelled from the Party in December 1927, he was arrested and held for eight weeks. During the next five years of precarious liberty within the USSR he wrote and published abroad five books, including three novels – but nothing of his saw the light of day in the Soviet Union until 1989.

In *Memoirs of a Revolutionary, 1901-1941*, Serge describes the atmosphere before his second arrest: 'I felt more and more that I was a hunted man.... Acquaintances avoided me in the street. Bukharin, whom I ran into outside the Lux Hotel, slipped by with a furtive "How's things?" – eyes right, eyes left, then off sharp.'[2] This image is later supplanted by one of Bukharin on trial, 'his ravaged face, still able to smile, questioning himself before the microphone of the Supreme Tribunal, a few days before his death...'[3] In 1933, Serge was duly arrested as an Oppositionist unwilling to sign up the mandatory 'General Line' and interrogated on the basis of accusations – no doubt extracted by terror – made by his sister-in-law and secretary, Anita Russakova. He was then deported under guard by train to Orenburg on the Ural River. In this poverty-stricken Kazhak town, mainly inhabited by the Kirghiz, exiles could only get

71

paid work by collaborating with the GPU, always engaged in elaborate games of divide and rule. For three years he and his son Vladimir (Vlady), aged thirteen in 1933, almost starved to death. He was in Orenburg when the shock waves of Kirov's assassination spread across the USSR.

All four books Serge wrote in the small wooden house in Orenburg were confiscated by the GPU when he was expelled from the country in April 1936 following an international defence campaign conducted by prominent French intellectuals, spearheaded by Magdeleine Paz's Révolution prolétarienne, and including André Gide.

Stateless, he was given permission to live in Belgium. After he protested loudly against the first Moscow trial, the Soviet legation in Brussels withdrew his passport and citizenship. The emergence of the popular fronts, signalling a new fraternity between Communist and Socialist parties throughout Europe, left neo-Trotskyists[4] like Serge short of allies. Moscow also used its influence to keep his work out of the mainstream press. In June 1940, he fled from Paris with his family on foot, spent a frantic year in Marseille, and was finally able to escape to Mexico, where he lived out his few remaining years, writing for the drawer. *The Case of Comrade Tulayev* was written during this period of flight, in Paris, Agen, Marseille, and Ciudad Trujillo, Mexico. The novel was published in Paris in 1948 as *L'Affaire Tulaév*, a year after Serge died in poverty. By the time it appeared in the U.S. in 1950, and in Britain a year later, *The Case of Comrade Tulayev* inescapably took its place alongside Koestler's *Darkness at Noon* as a Cold War novel – although Koestler's rejection of the entire Marxist heritage contrasted with Serge's view of a revolution fatally 'betrayed' by Stalin and the party. What political stance Serge himself would have adopted by the early fifties one cannot be sure. It is known that six days before his death he wrote to Malraux, apparently endorsing his commitment to the Gaullist RPF, which he described as 'courageous and probably reasonable.' This letter caused consternation on the Left when published in the Gaullist *Rassemblement* on 31 January 1948; it may have been a desperate attempt to regain French soil thus escaping his Mexican poverty and surveillance by the FBI,[5] but scholars anxious to protect Serge's reputation as a revolutionary socialist are up against a widely observable law: you cannot face two ways at once. The protracted bitterness of Serge's relations with the Soviet regime and mutual recriminations with Western Communists must have led him inexorably to 'the god that failed.' We cannot be sure.

Tulayev is written in the realist-panoramic idiom widely practised in France and the USSR: the narrative is apportioned between the authorial voice and what the characters do or say. Serge has no inhibition about rapid changes of 'points of view,' jumping from one mind to the next, even where this fractures empathy. An abundance of explicit dialogue ensures that little is left to the imagination. Implication is rare. The author is not shy of standing in judgment on his characters: 'Coward that he [Popov] was, what he most wanted to know was whether it was serious for himself.'[6]

Although Serge somewhat blurs the chronology, the assassination of his fictitious Comrade Tulayev obviously occurs some three or more years after the (unsolved) murder of Kirov in Leningrad in December 1934. Serge's central purpose is to show how an almost random assassination of a leading Bolshevik, unplanned and uncoordinated, must inevitably lead to yet another wave of arrests on the basis of fabricated evidence or no evidence at all.

On a freezing day a stout man in a short fur-lined coat and an astrakhan cap gets out of a powerful black car and says something to his chauffeur, who is overheard to answer deferentially: 'Very good, Comrade Tulayev.' The character Kostia, a quite ordinary citizen whom we have already got to know (he works in the office of a subway construction yard), and who happens by chance to be walking along, instantly associates the name Tulayev with the mass deportations in the Vorogen district, with university purges, and other acts of repression. On impulse, or reflex, Kostia shoots him dead with the Colt he happens to be carrying. Amazed by his own action, he flees over the snow through small quiet streets and reckons 'I acted without thinking.'[7] Kostia longs for a pair of good shoes, but endures soleless ones, sour soup, icy winds, acute hunger. If Kostia can stay at liberty he has no regrets. The authorities will indeed fail to find the culprit – there are no clues.

Before the assassination, Serge describes an intriguing but elusive episode. At this juncture the Colt, with its short barrel and black cylinder, still belongs to Kostia's neighbour Romachkin, who likes to walk in the public gardens that border the outer walls of the Kremlin facing towards the city. Romachkin is eating a sandwich when he encounters a man in uniform striding along followed by two others. The man is 'tall, almost gaunt...bristlingly moustached...the man stepped out of the portraits published in the papers, displayed four storeys high on buildings... There was no doubt: it was He.'[8] The oddest part of this is 'tall, almost gaunt' – Stalin was famously short of stature and thickset. Yet: 'As in final proof of his identity, the Chief drew a short pipe from his pocket, put it between his teeth, and walked on.' What happens next is that Romachkin's hand 'flew into his coat pocket, groping for the butt of the Colt.' Just six feet from Romachkin now, the Chief stopped, 'daring him; his cat eyes shot a little cruel gleam in Romachkin's direction. His mocking eyes muttered something like, "You abject worm, Romachkin", with devastating scorn.' Romachkin is left bitterly lamenting his own cowardice. This scene is described perfectly realistically (apart from the tall, gaunt Stalin), yet it carries a surreal quality – was it a dream?—particularly when the Colt passes to Romachkin's neighbour Kostia as a gift, a kind of Excalibur; Serge surely implies that every ordinary, humble Muscovite yearned to assassinate Stalin and his henchmen given an opportunity.

Following the assassination of the hated Comrade Tulayev, Serge widens his canvas to explore Stalin's security apparatus. The fictional Maksim Erchov, appointed 'High Commissar for Security,' initially displays liberal instincts: ten thousand dossiers are reconsidered – industrial administrators (Communists), technicians (non-party), officers (both), making possible 6,727 releases of which 47.5 per cent resulted in rehabilitations. The press announces that during the time of Ershov's executed predecessor over 50 per cent of persons sentenced were innocent. Serge clearly has in mind the successive OGPU chiefs Yagoda (executed) and Yezhov (same fate). Subsequently the Central Committee statisticians and the press director are dismissed when an émigré paper in Paris capitalizes on this information. Many of those released are once more denounced, their innocence redefined as hideous guilt all over again.[9]

When Erchov delivers his opinion about the Tulayev case to Stalin – Erchov believes that the assassination was the act of an isolated individual—he receives a sarcastic response. Erchov immediately and supinely responds with a list of twenty-five 'culprits' together with suggested sentences for each. On receiving a further sarcastic response, Erchov increases the proposed sentences. Meanwhile his suave assistant Gordeyev has drawn up a list of 'all persons whose antecedents might make them suspect of terrorism. So far we have found seventeen hundred names of persons still at liberty.'[10]

The long, aching tongue of the permanent purge now reaches out for Maksim Erchov himself. He is abruptly relieved of office by the Organization Bureau. Stalin no longer trusts him. Erchov will be relentlessly interrogated and required to confess his own part in the 'plot' against Tulayev. Outraged, he refuses to collaborate, though himself the orchestrator of many such false charges. As with Koestler, the interrogations described by Serge are generally free of torture, bright lights in dead of night, physical torments, beatings. Erchov's prison cell is comfortable, the lighting soft. 'Cot, bedclothes, pillows, a swivel chair. Nothing else, nothing.... He asked for a daily shower and was granted it...' The word 'shot' keeps passing through his head. Weeks pass during which he is not allowed a glimpse of the sky. Then comes interrogation after interrogation. 'Men who were of a high rank, but whom he did not know, questioned him with a mixture of deference and harsh insolence.' Many of the questions asked about his conduct as High Commissar have no direct or obvious bearing on the Tulayev case. '"When you signed the appointment of Camp Commandant Illenkov, did you know the past record of that enemy of the people?"' Other subjects include his wife Valia's contraband furs and perfumes. Questions relating to two other leading characters in the novel are repeatedly pressed: 'What did you do to prevent the arrest of your accomplice Kiril Rublev? What did you do to conceal the past of the 'Trotskyist' Kondratiev on the eve of his mission to Spain? What messages did you give him for the Spanish Trotskyists?'[11]

Meanwhile the imprisoned Erchov is urged to confess to the 'plot' to murder Tulayev. 'You must see, nevertheless, that the Party cannot admit that it is impotent before a revolver shot fired from no one knows where, perhaps from the depths of the people's soul... [The Chief] knows that when somebody shoots Tulayev, it is himself that was aimed at. Because it can't be otherwise, there is no one but himself that anyone can either hate or has to hate...'[12] The fictional Ricciotti offers a powerful image remarkably similar to the frank pragmatism expressed by Koestler's Gletkin: 'We are performing a surgical operation with an axe. Our government holds the fort in situations that are catastrophic, and sacrifices its best divisions one after the other because it doesn't know anything else to do. Our turn has come.'[13]

Serge's character Gordeyev, Erchov's deputy and his nemesis, represents the conforming Stalinist mentality at its most unctuous when interpreting the Chief's general directive: 'In short: we have lived at the heart of an immense and ramified plot, which we have succeeded in liquidating. Three fourths of the leaders of the previous periods of the revolution had ended by becoming corrupt; they had sold themselves to the enemy, or if not, it was the same thing, in the objective meaning of the word.... Henceforward no one must be considered above suspicion except for the entirely new men whom history and the genius of the chief have summoned up for the salvation of the country...' So it goes on, enemies, plots, sabotage: Trotskyism in Spain, deals between Warsaw and Berlin, Japanese concentrating troops in Jehol while building new forts in Korea, their agents having manoeuvred a breakdown of turbines at Krasnoyarsk... [14]

Sabotage mania. An industrially backward nation unable to confront its own inefficiency, a nation in the grip of scapegoating paranoia led from the top. In prison 'Kot-the-Tomcat, the Pimp—face tilted up, mouth open, showing carnivorous teeth – studied Ryzhik benevolently and almost guessed: '"Uncle, you an engineer or an enemy of the people?"' Ryzhik asks him: '"And what do you call an enemy of the people?"' 'Answers began coming out of an embar- rassed silence. '"Men that derail trains... The Mikado's agents... The people that start fires underground in the Donetz...Kirov's assassins...They poisoned Maxim Gorki... I knew one once – president of a kolkhoz, he killed the horses by putting spells on them... He knew a trick to bring drought..."' [15]

Serge's chosen few are invariably distinguished by intelligence rather than raw courage: 'Ryzhik clearly deciphered the hieroglyphics...which had been branded with red-hot iron into the very flesh of the country. He knew, almost by heart, the falsified reports of the three great trials...of the minor trials in Kharkov, Sverdlosk, Novosibirsk, Tashkent, Krasnoyarsk, trials of which the world had never heard...'[16]

In the Butyrky prison, Ryzhik recognises Zvyeryeva, whom he had known for twenty years. 'Hysterical, crooked to the marrow, devoured by unsatisfied desires, how had she outlived so many valiant men?'[17] The character Zvyerevya occurs in several of Serge's novels and was based on a woman official he loathed. When he was enduring the elaborate required formalities before his expulsion from the USSR, in 1936, it was this woman Zvyereva who took his manuscript novels from him at Glavlit and did not return them. 'Huh! Viktor Lvovich [Serge], so you're leaving – in order to betray...you are betraying us!'[18] In *Tulayev* she appears as the sexually frustrated examiner in charge of Ryzhik

(Serge). Serge accords this woman special treatment, the authorial punishment of catching her masturbating: 'Because her breasts were ageing she slept in a black lace brassiere.... She admired herself. "My belly is tight and cruel..." On the mount of Venus there was only an arid tuft; below, the secret folds were sad and taut, like a forsaken mouth. Towards those folds her hand glided, while her body arched.... Above her, in a loathsome emptiness, floated the forms of men mingled with the forms of very young women brutally possessed.' And more.[19]

Panic sets in throughout the state apparatus when they realise, too late, that Ryzhik is dying; he has rejected food and water without the prison warders noticing. The message that prisoner 4 is dying goes up to the Chief— Ryzhik's death will scuttle 50 per cent of the 'evidence' set up for the trial.

In prison, Rublev demands books and paper. He foreshadows a frequent theme in Solzhenitsyn's work when he declares: 'I do not wish to be treated worse in a Socialist prison than in a prison under the old regime.... After all, citizen, I am one of the founders of the Soviet state.' Meanwhile, the sickly Popov of the Control Commission, a former Chekist – Serge's portrait of this man conveys the nausea he arouses—tells Rublev: 'You will say whatever they want you to say, because you know the situation...because you have no choice: obey or betray.... Or we will call upon you to stand in front of the same microphone and dishonour the Supreme Tribunal, the Party, the Chief, the USSR...and what a pretty spectacle your innocence will make at that moment.' Rublev consents to this logic: 'That if I must perish, crushed by my Party, I consent.... But I warn the villains who are killing us that they are killing the Party.'[20]

The thoroughly honourable veteran Bolshevik Ivan Nicolayevich Kondratiev is invited to make a major speech as a deputy member of the Central Committee. He reflects that 16-17 million horses were lost during collectivization, about 50 per cent. Serge uses Kondratiev's thoughts to convey his own historical knowledge – indeed here is one of the earliest fictional interventions in the historians' long debate, extending to the present day, about the statistics of the purges. Kondratiev reflects: 'According to the no longer up-to-date statistics of the C.C. Bulletins, we have eliminated to date between sixty-two and seventy per cent of Communist officials, administrators and officers – and that is in less than three years...between 124,000 and 140,000 Bolsheviks. It is impossible, on the basis of the published data to determine the proportion between men executed and men interned in concentration camps...'[21]

Kondratiev reaches the white colonnade of the Red Army House, where he is to deliver his speech. Secretaries come running to greet him, dressed in new, polished uniforms, with yellow knee leathers, shining holsters, shining faces, and 'obsequious handshakes.' Young officers throw out their chests to salute him – Kondratiev feels 'as if he were surrounded by perfectly constructed manikins.' On the walls hang portraits of Voroshilov on a horse and the Chief as if made of painted wood, his smile a grimace, 'the Chief like a Caucasian waiter saying, in his pungent accent, "Nothing left, citizen...'" The buffet carries caviar, Volga sturgeons, smoked salmon, glazed eels, fruits from the Crimea and Turkestan.[22] (Serge leaves nothing to chance.)

The speech Kondratiev is to deliver has been written for him, its mechanical phrases and sentiments well known to him from editorials, 'the sort of words which Trotsky once said that when you spoke them you felt as if you were chewing cotton batting...' (Would Kondratiev quote Trotsky, even to himself?) But suddenly Kondratiev departs from his speech and brings dismay to his audience, talking of errors, liquidations, Barcelona, the Aragon front, the arms which did not arrive, the heroism of the Spanish anarchists. 'Your elders have nearly all perished servilely.... I urge you to feel that you are free men under your armour of discipline...'[23] He ends with contradictory comments on the Chief (backward country, innate suspicion, yet also 'the inspired guide,' 'continuer of Lenin'). Kondratiev is now doomed, of course. He is promptly summoned by the Chief: 'So you are a traitor, too?' Kondratiev stands his ground, expressing deep regret for the generation of Old Bolsheviks purged and executed. 'What men! History takes millenniums to produce men so great!' The Chief says, 'Not another word on this subject, Kondratiev. What had to be had to be. The Party and the country have followed me... It is not for you to judge.' He calls Kondratiev an 'intellectual.'[24]

Having got out of Russia by the skin of his teeth before the 1936-1938 wave of trials, Serge viewed the new confessions—complicity with the Gestapo or plotting to kill Kirov – as differing only in degree from earlier capitulations by Oppositionists. 'The confessions were made out of utter devotion.' Obviously there are striking affinities between Koestler and Serge, both cosmopolitan linguists, both political prisoners (Serge in Russia. Koestler in Spain), both fugitives-on-foot from the Nazi invasion of France. Both wrote their 'show trial' novels, their fictional portraits of the Stalinist purges, at approximately the same time, the same perilous juncture. Serge's fictional approach is more polymorphous than Koestler's; he spreads his canvas wider, providing the richer, more variegated picture of Stalin's Russia. 'Terror and suffering were everywhere mingled with an inexplicable triumph tirelessly proclaimed by the newspapers.' Serge describes the Armenian theatre: the spectator pushes his head through a hole in the box into a world of magic – 'the Mysteries of Samarkand in ten scenes with thirty actors in real colours'. Most striking is that Koestler and Serge arrive at similar, sometimes identical, conclusions about how the confessions were obtained and paraded at show trials.[25]

10

Orwell: From Big Pig to Big Brother

Orwell's animosity towards Soviet Communism, while much strengthened by his own experiences in Spain, was reinforced by wide reading. To take one example, reviewing Eugene Lyons's *Assignment in Utopia* (1938) Orwell broadly accepted the veteran American reporter's negative portrait of the Soviet Union—if not his tendency towards strident sensationalism. The proletariat, theoretically the masters, had been robbed of the right to strike; internal passports had reduced the people to a 'status resembling serfdom'; the USSR was a police state: 'The GPU are everywhere, everyone lives in constant terror of denunciation, freedom of speech and of the press are obliterated to an extent we can hardly imagine...sometimes some monstrous state trial at which people who have been in prison for months or years are suddenly dragged forth to make incredible confessions.... Meanwhile the invisible Stalin is worshipped in terms that would have made Nero blush.'[1]

In April 1944, the publisher Victor Gollancz received the typescript of a very short work of fiction destined to sell in huge quantities from that day to this. He turned it down (having earlier rejected *Homage to Catalonia*)—he could not bring himself to publish what he construed to be a general attack on Stalin and the Soviet system. Gollancz was not alone in his refusal of Orwell's *Animal Farm*. T. S. Eliot, a director of Faber & Faber, also concluded that the moment was not opportune. Jonathan Cape, having spoken to 'an important official in the Ministry of Information,' decided that it would be 'highly ill-advised to publish at the present time.' The 'important official' was Peter Smollett, alias Smolka, a Soviet agent.

A few days after Hiroshima and Nagasaki, Fredric Warburg, publisher of *Homage to Catalonia*, finally published Orwell's fictional masterpiece. '*Animal Farm*,' Orwell later explained, 'was the first book in which I tried, with full consciousness of what I was doing, to fuse political purpose and artistic purpose into one whole.' He had been brooding about exposing 'the Soviet myth in a story that could easily be understood by almost anyone...' One day he saw a young boy driving a huge cart-horse along a narrow path and whipping it whenever it tried to turn. 'It struck me that if only animals became aware of their strength we should have no power over them...' The upshot was the 'fairy story' (as he called it), which continues to enthral not only adult readers but also children unaware that they are reading an allegory about Stalin's Russia transcribed to an English farm normal in every respect but one: the animals have risen in rebellion and chased out Farmer Jones. Written with subtle, unobtrusive clarity—indeed the style vanishes into a clear pane of glass—Orwell's fable of an animal rebellion on Manor Farm achieves an immaculate fusion of political message and artistry, right up to arguably the most stunning single sentence in twentieth-century literature (daubed on the wall of the big barn): ALL ANIMALS ARE EQUAL BUT SOME ANIMALS ARE MORE EQUAL THAN OTHERS.

The farm animals gather one night in the barn to hear the patriarch of the pigs, Old Major (standing in for Karl Marx as well as Moses), recount his vision of liberation and issue seven of animal Commandments. Heartened and inspired, the animals sing the Blakean song 'Beasts of England' before rebelling, chasing out the drunken farmer, and taking over the farm.

> Soon or late the day is coming,
> Tyrant man shall be o'erthrown
> And the fruitful fields of England
> Shall be trod by beasts alone
>
> Rings shall vanish from our noses
> And the harness from our back
> Bit and spur shall rust forever
> Cruel whips no more shall crack.

In terms of Soviet history, Orwell elided the February and October revolutions. The boar Napoleon, heir to the primacy of the deceased Old Major, obviously represents Stalin, Snowball is Trotsky, the carthorse Boxer is the honest Stakhanovite worker of Soviet legend. The frisky little acolyte pig Squealer, always whisking his tail, is any Soviet commissar of propaganda. There is no separate role for Lenin. Elsewhere Orwell commented that both Lenin and Trotsky bore some responsibility for Stalinism.

In *Animal Farm* the manipulation of history by the dominant pigs centres on the gradual mothballing of 'Beasts of England,' the erosion of the original slogans proclaiming animal rights and animal freedom. Napoleon and Squealer persecute Snowball out of the revolution (the treatment meted out to Trotsky, Bukharin, Zinoviev and the other Old Bolsheviks). Within the metaphor of life on the farm, Orwell provides parallels for a succession of historical events from the suppression of the Kronstadt rebellion by Lenin and Trotsky, to collectivization, the purge trials, and the Nazi-Soviet Pact. Following Jonathan Swift's allegorical tradition, the real counterpart events reside between the lines of the animal story and are visible only to the well informed reader. Few children would catch a glimpse of this other narrative.

Soon corruption and power hunger produce a new class system, led by the pigs. Napoleon begins to walk on two legs, to wear clothes, to sleep in the farmer's bed and slurp down his beer. Human nature is fallible; power corrupts; revolutions produce a new ruling class. Breaking the rule that no animal shall ever again be sent for slaughter, Napoleon begins to wheel and deal with local human farmers and traders. The slogans continually change:

'All animals are equal'

becomes

'All animals are equal but some animals are more equal than others.'

Orwell never sermonises or draws authorial conclusions. Indeed, there is no overt authorial voice. The story simply unfolds, revealing the human face of animals and the animal face of humans.

Was Orwell indicating that power hunger will always prevent human beings from achieving a truly just and democratic society? Rejecting the book for publication by Faber, T. S. Eliot believed that he had discerned a basic inconsistency in Orwell's egalitarianism: by endowing the pigs with superior species powers – they learn to read and write the English language—had Orwell perhaps contradicted himself by falling into the Conservative view that human beings are inherently unequal by natural endowment? The pigs are from the start cleverer, more capable, than the other animals and therefore surely destined to rule the roost. So the Seventh Commandment—ALL ANIMALS ARE EQUAL—means what? Clearly equality was for Orwell a matter of rights and decencies, not of innate capacities.

Orwell achieves one dramatic coup after another as the pig-potentates descend to new levels of indecency. We know that the boar Napoleon has taken selected canine puppies from their mothers and locked them away somewhere, but we are shocked when they suddenly burst out as 'nine enormous dogs wearing brass-studded collars.' Exit Napoleon's rival, Snowball (Trotsky). Orwell explained to Dwight Macdonald: 'The turning point of the story was supposed to be when the pigs kept the milk and apples for themselves. (The Bolsheviks' suppression of the Kronstadt sailors's rebellion.) 'If the other animals had had the sense to put their foot down, it would have been all right.' (Solzhenitsyn was later to imagine the power of a popular rejection of the arbitrary power of the GPU/NKVD.) He added: 'What I was trying to say was, "You can't have a revolution unless you make it yourself". There is no such thing as a benevolent dictatorship.'

Few readers will forget the scene when the faithful carthorse Boxer, twelve years old and worn to the bone, is callously sold for glue and bonemeal. Rising ever earlier, toiling ever later, determined to put his last ounce of strength at the service of the Rebellion and Comrade Napoleon, the loyal 'Stakhanovite' toiler Boxer is finally packed into an 'ambulance. Too late does the old stallion's

faithful mate Clover spot the fateful words on the side of the van: 'Alfred Sim-
monds, Horse Slaughterer and Glue Boiler.' The sound of Boxer's drumming
hoofs inside the van grows fainter. Two days later the pig Squealer—in effect
Napoleon's Commissar for Propaganda—announces that Boxer has died 'in
hospital.'

Lies! The beasts of *Animal Farm* witness the deliberate distortion of each of
the original Seven Commandments of the Rebellion. Even the song which first
inspired their revolt is finally banned because—as Squealer explains—'The
purpose of "Beasts of England" was to express our longing for a better society in days to come. But that society has now been established. Obviously,
therefore, the song has lost its meaning.' He who controls the past, controls
the future. When Orwell's animals cease to believe in their own memories,
they are helpless in the face of the ultimate betrayal, 'Four legs good, two
legs better!' Decked out in absurd human garb, the big boar Napoleon finally
waddles out of the farmhouse on two legs with a whip clasped in his trotter.
The animals are offered new odes to Napoleon: 'Lord of the swill-bucket...
Thou art the giver...'

Later, in *Nineteen Eighty-Four*, the same theme is pursued through the
Party's motto coldly logical motto: 'Who controls the past controls the future;
who controls the present controls the past.' In a strictly human setting Orwell
again describes the murder of language and memory, the obliteration of history
through the 'memory hole,' the vaporization of people into unpeople.

In short, progress had fouled itself.

Orwell commented elsewhere that 'men exploit animals in much the same
way as the rich exploit the proletariat. I proceed to analyse Marx's theory from
the animals' point of view...' Yet this parallel is fragile, not to say sentimental.
How can a mixed farm like Manor Farm survive unless the ruling livestock
themselves resort to the basic rule of farming—slaughter? Why does Orwell
seem to approve when the pig Snowball loses no time in organizing an Egg
Production Committee? When subsequently Orwell condemns Napoleon for
selling 400 eggs a week to the slimy Mr Whymper, he leaves us with a nagging
question: if every egg laid since the Rebellion had been hatched, and every
cockerel born had been granted life, what then, comrades? One also notes that
those animal sub-proles found on farms but generally exterminated as a menace
to production as vermin (flies, fleas, tics, squirrels, rats, mice, bugs, vipers) are
not included among the 'Beasts of England.'

In *Animal Farm* Orwell seems to be saying that 'the central problem of
revolution' is power and power-hunger. The majority of ordinary animals of
Manor Farm, the 'common people' are loyal, hard working, idealistic, trusting;
their virtues are exemplified by the carthorse Boxer and his mate Clover; their
sober common sense is represented by Benjamin the Donkey. The clever pigs
are the culprits, destroying every sacred principle of equality and decency in
their lust for power and its material rewards.

Time and again in his essays and critical work Orwell exonerated 'the people,' the Spanish people and the English people, blaming 'them' for rapacity—our rulers, priests, landlords, intellectuals, the fellow-travellers, always the oppressive minority. The truth consistently missed (or consciously bypassed?) in Orwell's two great works of political fiction is that revolutions fail, then succumb to 'Thermidor,' largely because the raw clay is inadequate, not because the sculptor is a crazed fanatic. The seminal failing of revolutionary theory from Rousseau to Marx, Bakunin and Lenin, has been the failure to recognise that seizing the Tower of London, the Bastille, the Peter and Paul Fortress; seizing and executing the king or tsar; seizing the telegraph office; expropriating the 'means of production,' the banks, factories and the land itself; taking control of the army, the police and the secret police; setting up parliaments of saints (the Cromwell era), committees of public safety (the Robespierre era), or workers' and peasants' soviets (the Lenin era) – none of this can of itself secure the success of the revolution's real and ultimate aim: liberty-equality-fraternity. In the course of every revolution considered relevant by Marxists – principally the English, French and Russian revolutions—old habits of violence, greed and prejudice immediately resurfaced under the new institutions. The people learn from their oppressors, just as brutalized sons learn from their fathers – and lose no time in handing out the same treatment when they inherit the whip hand.

Animal Farm was published in August 1945, eleven days after the Hiroshima bomb, the signal for the atomic cloud hanging over Orwell's next venture into cosmic pessimism, *Nineteen Eighty-Four*. On 24 August, the *Manchester Guardian* reviewed the book anonymously under the rubric 'Books of the Day.' Describing it as 'a delightfully humorous and caustic satire on the rule of the many by the few...a very amusing and intrinsically wise book,' the reviewer managed not to mention Stalin, the USSR or communism in the brief space (about 130 words) allotted.

Meanwhile the French Communist Party had emerged powerful enough from the Resistance to command portfolios in de Gaulle's first postwar government. On 10 January 1946, Orwell reported to Koestler: 'The French publisher who signed a contract to translate *Animal Farm* has got cold feet and says it is impossible for "political reasons". It's really sad to think of a thing like that happening in France, of all countries in the world.'[2] Possibly, the French may have been unresponsive to the Swiftian tradition of animal allegory, despite the success of Anatole France's political satire *L'Ile des pingouins*. Perhaps the 'little England' element in Orwell's sensibility may have been offputting – after all, the animals of Manor Farm sing 'Beasts of England' rather than 'Animals of the World, Unite!' And the villain of the piece carries the name Napoleon. Koestler's equally provocative *Darkness at Noon* came out in France in the same year under the title *Le Zéro et l'Infini*. In postwar France, Orwell remained little known. Camus's biographer Olivier Todd mentions briefly that Camus 'appreciated' *Animal Farm* but never met Orwell.[3] The major biographies of Sartre contain not a single index reference to Orwell. One finds a solitary reference to Orwell in a letter, written in English in May 1950, from Simone de Beauvoir to Nelson Algren: 'Speaking of equality, do you know this joke by George Orwell, who wrote a bad book against USSR but was some witty (sic). After the Big Revolution, the republic of beasts decide "All animals are equal...but...Some animals are more equal than the others."'[4] But had she read this bad book?

Enthusiasm was no greater in the opposite direction. Only a single reference to Sartre is discovered in Orwell's collected essays and journalism. On 22 October 1948, he wrote to his publisher Fredric Warburg: 'Dear Fred... I have just had Sartre's book on anti-Semitism [*Portrait of an Antisemite*], which you published, to review. I think Sartre is a bag of wind and I am going to give him a good boot.'[5]

The Foreign Office's new, semi-clandestine weapon of cold war propaganda, the so-called Independent Research Department (IRD), was not slow to recognise George Orwell as a major weapon in Britain's anti-Communist armoury. (The Foreign Office internally admitted that IRD was a name designed to disguise 'the true nature of its work.')[6] Documents show the IRD making efforts to maximise the international impact of his work.[7] The IRD's Ralph Murray hoped to get *Animal Farm* released in Russian and requested assistance in raising 2,000 marks. On 24 June 1948, the IRD contacted Orwell on behalf of the German-based Russian émigré magazine *Possev*, a weekly political review based in Limburg. V. Puachev wrote to Orwell in appreciative terms (24 June 1949), thanking him for granting translation rights without charge, with the translator Gleb Struve as intermediary. The book has made what Puachev rather grandiosely called 'a great impression on the Russian reading public' – in reality those living in the West. Now he approached Orwell for advice on potential investors in a Russian-language edition to be distributed in Berlin, Vienna and other cities under Soviet occupation, 'the other side of the iron curtain.' Two thousand Germans marks was needed for an edition of 5,000 copies. Orwell passed the letter on to the IRD; Celia Kirwan forwarded it to Charles Thayer, director of the Voice of America, in November 1949. (However, there is no evidence that IRD did raise the money.)[8] Foreign Office documents released in July 1996 show British embassies eager to receive copies and translations. '"I have been so taken with the relevance of Orwell's fairy-story," wrote Ernest Mair, our man in Cairo. "The idea is particularly good for Arabic, in view of the fact that both pigs and dogs are unclean animals to Muslims."'[9]

In April 1946 Orwell had received a letter from a Ukrainian stateless refugee, Igor Szewczenko, (later professor of Byzantine studies at Harvard), who was working among ex-POWs and 'displaced persons' scattered in camps across Germany. He reported how he had translated passages of *Animal Farm* 'ex abrupto' for Soviet refugees, who were profoundly affected by concordances between the tale and the reality they knew. Szewczenko hoped Orwell would consent to a Ukrainian edition for the benefit of survivors of the famine and purges. As a result, Orwell wrote his only preface to the novel specifically for this Ukrainian edition and was besieged by offers to translate it into Latvian, Serbian, etc. On 24 September 1947, Orwell wrote to Arthur Koestler on behalf of a refugee who wanted to translate 'some of your stuff into Ukrainian, without payment of course' for dissemination among Ukrainian DPs in the American zone of Germany. As for the 'more or less illicit' Ukrainian edition of *Animal Farm*: 'I have just heard from them that the American authorities [Military Government] in Munich have seized 1,500 copies of it and handed them over to the Soviet repatriation people [Repatriation Commission], but it appears about 2,000 copies got distributed among the DPs first... I am sure we ought to help these people all we can...'[10]

The American seizures can be explained in terms of Law No. 191 which, in harness with Control Regulation No. 1, forbade the circulation within Germany of publications which 'discredited' any of the Four Powers. Orwell's specially written preface fell squarely into this offence: 'Nothing,' he wrote, 'has contributed so much to the corruption of the original idea of Socialism as the belief that Russia is a Socialist country and every act of its rulers must be excused, if not imitated.'[11] A few months later, as the Cold War sharpened, the Ukrainian edition was freely published in Munich. Further: in August-September 1948 Orwell's satire was dramatized on American zone radio. OMGUS Report, Information, No. 39, described it as 'of noteworthy political import.' In December 1948 *Der Monat*, edited by Melvin Lasky, began serialization.[12]

Writing in the 1980s, the editor of *Commentary*, Norman Podhoretz, attempted to expropriate Orwell into the camp of neo-conservativism, citing Orwell's anti-anti Americanism: '"To be anti-American nowadays," Orwell had written, "is to shout with the mob. Of course it is only a minor mob, but it is a vocal one.... I do not believe that the mass of the people in this country are anti-American politically, and certainly they are not so culturally."'[13] Alfred Kazin challenged Podhoretz's argument, pointing out that in *Nineteen Eighty-Four* England is Oceania Airstrip I. 'We know whose airstrip it is.' By 1948, he added, Orwell was 'maddened' by 'England's dependency on America.'[14] This is dubious. On 2 January 1948 Orwell wrote: 'I particularly hate that trick of sucking up to the Left cliques by perpetually attacking America while relying on America to feed & protect us.'[15]

'It was a bright cold day in April and the clocks were striking thirteen.' So begins Orwell's next and most famous novel. A vile wind, swirls of gritty dust, the smell of boiled cabbage, a huge poster of Big Brother, no electricity during the day, and Hate Week rapidly establish the nightmare world surrounding our hero, Winston Smith. During the remaining, illness-plagued months of his life Orwell had laboured on a work – eventually titled *Nineteen Eighty-Four*, originally 'The Last Man'—in which two nightmares merged: (1) a world subjected to permanent war between three super-powers; (2) the strikingly 'human' autocracy of the pig Napoleon yielded to the totalitarian technology of Big Brother, to Thought Crime monitored by the Thought Police. 'You might dodge successfully for a while, even for years, but sooner of later they were bound to get you.'[16]

Nineteen Eighty-Four conveyed the history of the future, rooted naturally in the history of the recent past, allowing Orwell unbridled release of his personal fears and phobias about modern manipulation of the media through 'Ingsoc' and 'Newspeak' ('the only language in the world whose vocabulary gets smaller every year'). Orwell proceeds into the novel by means of a stunning array of arresting slogans: 'Big Brother is Watching You,' 'Freedom is Slavery,' 'War is Peace.' The Party has rid itself of any vestige of social idealism; the proles are treated as contemptible; power and power alone is the motive. One recent commentator has suggested that the novel amounts to a *summa* of what Orwell had learned about terror and conformism in Spain, about servility and sadism at school and in the Burma police, about squalor and degradation in *The Road to Wigan Pier*, about propaganda and falsity during decades of polemics. Christopher Hitchens adds, 'It contains absolutely no jokes. It is the first and only time that his efforts as a novelist rise to the level of his essays.'[17]

If this had been so it would have been because *Nineteen Eighty-Four* is a thinly fictionalized essay. In *Animal Farm*, much is left to the imagination: the reader is invited to complete a crossword puzzle by means of verbal connections, while simultaneously making a series of identity 'fits' in a jigsaw puzzle. In *Nineteen Eighty-Four*, virtually everything, including the constant remoulding of history, is explicitly spelled out. Every motion of the fictional action is designed to illustrate the 'facts' about Oceania. The genius of the book resides in its frightening intensity of focus, its determination to take the reader by the throat, largely through empathy with one ordinary Englishman, Winston Smith, still capable of loving Shakespeare, remembering true beer and old-fashioned sexual love, and believing that $2 + 2 = 4$ regardless of what the Government may have to say about it. But whereas *Animal Farm* offers a narrative which is short, honed-down, exquisitely composed, the perfect novella, *Nineteen Eighty-Four* reads like an attempt to stuff a rucksack of notebooks into a medium-sized envelope.

The action always focuses on this one hero, Winston. Other characters, cursorily sketched in without much conviction, sometimes mere cardboard cut-outs, are barely allowed lives of their own. Although it is an entire global system which is under scrutiny, our tickets as time travellers remain restricted to Winston's second-class compartment. His (cleverly chosen) job in the Ministry of Truth, rewriting the newspapers, rewriting the past, allows Orwell to lean over his shoulder and pack in page after page of nightmarish exposition. Through Winston Orwell informs us, 'Oceania was at war with Eastasia; Oceania had always been at war with Eastasia. A large part of the political literature of five years was now completely obsolete. Reports and records of all kinds, newspapers, books, pamphlets, films, sound tracks, photographs—all had to be rectified at lightning speed.'[18]

Although the *dramatis personae* of the novel are supposedly inhabiting a totalitarian future, in which the English language itself is being incinerated, most of them sound like average Londoners grumbling away about the scarcity of razor blades during the Blitz. Many of them – Symes, Parsons, the man who keeps the antique shop, Winston's former wife—are inserted to illustrate a point about conformity, cowardice or courage. They tend to look, smell and sound like leftovers from Orwell's fiction of the thirties, taken out of mothballs. One can't exactly believe in any of them, not even the Identikit hero Winston Smith. Even the Inner Party's O'Brien, torturer and brainwasher extraordinary, resembles a fruity Hampstead intellectual of the 1940s who likes a glass of wine served by a white-coated butler while gloating over the current day's batch of engineered lies in *The Times*. Orwell's totalitarian 1984 keeps relapsing into the England of the 1930s and 1940s.

Much of the invented cargo of 'facts' in the novel proves to be inconsistent in one way or another. Why has 'Airstrip One' (Oceania's British province) been converted to the 24-hour clock and to metric measures and distances when (as we learn) it almost exclusively Anglo-American and includes no part of Continental Europe?[19] Orwell, who had regarded himself as an advocate of a socialist federation of Europe, introduces the metric systems as symbols of tyranny: the clocks strike thirteen; an old prole asks in vain for a pint of beer in a pub that measures only in litres. Airstrip One is also measured in kilometres, a sure sign of oppression; presumably Orwell stopped short of having Londoners forced to drive on the right side of the road because that was what Americans did anyway.

Take Orwell's handling of nuclear warfare. It is said of the late 1950s: 'At that time hundreds of bombs were dropped on industrial centres, chiefly in European Russia, Western Europe and North America.' Nuclear warfare had ceased because 'the ruling groups' came to fear 'that a few more atomic bombs would mean the end of organised society, and hence of their own power.'[20] When describing London prole children emaciated by malnutrition, he simply overlooks the horrors of fallout; the citizens of 1984 carry no evidence of the deformations and radiation sickness inevitable from nuclear contamination, even though this aspect of Hiroshima and Nagasaki cannot have been unknown to a writer of Orwell's acuity.

Orwell's depiction of sex and love in this ghastly future is muddled and lacking in confidence. In *Brave New World* (1932), Aldous Huxley presented a genetically engineered future, some six hundred years hence, in which eroticism was encouraged among children and extreme sexual promiscuity among young adults. Fanny rebukes her friend Lenina Crowne in the women's locker room for not having had more than one man in four months: 'After all,' she repeats the slogan, 'everyone belongs to everyone else.'[21] What is discouraged in Huxley's dystopia is love and monogamy. Although Orwell had read *Brave New World*, he takes it as axiomatically logical that sex as well as love should be actively discouraged among party members (the proles are free to shag themselves senseless). The Party women in Orwell wear odious scarlet sashes, symbols of chastity, and there is even a Junior Anti-Sex League alongside the Spies (obviously updates of the Soviet Pioneers). 'The women of the Party were all alike. Chastity was as deeply ingrained in them as Party loyalty.' They had been indoctrinated from their earliest years: 'The sexual act, successfully performed, was rebellion.'[22] (Yet Winston Smith's former wife, while hating sex, insisted on regular weekly copulation because having a child was 'our duty to the party'.[23]) Later we are told that 'sexual privation induced hysteria, which was desirable because it could be transformed into war fever and Leader worship.' Julia explains to Winston: 'All this marching up and down and cheering wand waving flags is simply sex gone sour.'[24] Yet the Inner Party official O'Brien predicts: 'The sex instinct will be eradicated. Procreation will be an annual formality like that of renewal of a ration card. We shall abolish the orgasm. Our neurologists are at work upon it now.'[25]

Were such trends observable within existing totalitarian dictatorships? Surely not. Hitler set German women of pure race to redouble their efforts. Soviet culture was certainly rather shy and prudish in the Victorian sense, yet it also embraced romance; nowhere is there a hint that young women of the Komsomol should suppress sexual instincts.

Orwell describes in detail the Inner Party's systematic assault on language, memory and history. All the examples we are given are in English because English is the main language used in Oceania. Orwell tells us that the prevailing philosophies and social systems of the three empires, Oceania, Eurasia and Eastasia, carry different names (Ingsoc, Neo-Bolshevism, Death-worship) but are in essence indistinguishable.[26] So what form does thought control take in Eurasia, which is said to reach to the Channel Coast, presumably embracing Frenchmen, Germans, Portuguese, Italians, Poles and millions of Russians – are they all simultaneously going through parallel submission to Big Brother – and if so in what languages?

In the end, the strain of stuffing it all in drives Orwell to insert an unashamedly intellectual essay into the flesh of his fiction, Emmanuel Goldstein's 'Principles of Oligarchical Collectivism.' (The American Book of the Month Club wanted to cut the essay and offered more money if Orwell consented, but our man was up to the challenge.) Julia falls asleep while Winston reads Goldstein to her – well she might snooze. Goldstein's essay is one hundred per cent Orwell's. So anxious is he to find a direct outlet for his own version of history and political sociology, that he does not allow the Trotsky figure Goldstein even a touch of idiosyncrasy, obsessiveness or personal conceit. Goldtsein, too, is just a cipher, not quite alive, not quite dead, who engages in a welter of geopolitical detail about the past wars between Oceania, Eurasia and Eastasia. Several atlases are required. For good measure, Orwell shoves in 'The Principles of Newspeak' as an appendix. In general, a good novelist will know more about the world he describes than he tells his readers. He must make sure of that. Orwell had already demonstrated in *Animal Farm* that an authorial reserve of unfired ammunition will not be wasted if his art feeds off implication.

But how are spirited solitary dissidents like Winston Smith subdued, crushed, converted? Orwell's answer is 'by every means you can think of'—physical violence, executions, torture, and police beatings, operate alongside psychological brainwashing, media manipulation, mind control. When O'Brien supervises Winston's torture on the rack, and with electric shocks, and finally by showing him the caged rats, we are left with a puzzle: O'Brien is demanding more than mere obedience, more than submission, he insists on genuine, sincere conversion. 'You must love Big Brother' and: 'There will be no love, except love of Big Brother.' This resembles physics without particles.

Orwell's own historical experience up to the time of writing the novel confirmed the immense motivating and unifying force of naked nationalism within the major totalitarian movements. Yet O'Brien despises Nazis and Bolsheviks for failing to recognise their own motivation, for muddling the issue by justifying their power in the name of the Nation or the Working Class. In practice, totalitarian regimes harnessed, enlisted, time-honoured human emotions, qualities and aspirations to the cause. Yet the Inner Party's ideologue O'Brien warns Winston how he will emerge from the horrors of Room 101: 'Never again will you be capable of human feeling. Everything will be dead inside you. Never again will you be capable of love, or friendship, or joy of living, or laughter, or curiosity, or courage, or integrity. You will be hollow. We shall squeeze you empty, then we shall fill you with ourselves.'[27] This resembles algebra or calculus without arithmetic. As for his promise that, 'There will be no art, no literature, no science,' we are up against Hitler's passion for opera, art and architecture (Speer tells that the Führer had to be reminded there was a war going on); and Stalin's devotion to the arts was never doubted by the writers, film directors and composers he bullied, censored, imprisoned, executed.

Perhaps the most compelling intellectual influence on *Nineteen Eighty-Four* was the prominent polemicist James Burnham, professor of philosophy at New York University. In 1940 Burnham had made his break with socialism *tout court*, and almost immediately began to predict a god-that-failed apocalypse: the presidential election of 1940, he warned, might be the last in America. In his influential book, *The Managerial Revolution* (1941), a massive wartime bestseller, Burnham argued that Nazism, Stalinism and the New Deal, despite their apparent ideological conflicts, really represented phases in a single, coherent motion—the overthrow of the old capitalist class by a new elite of managers who controlled the technical process of production. In his essay, 'James Burnham and the Managerial Revolution,' Orwell follows Burnham when he refers to the new ruling class 'shaped and brought together by the barren world of monopoly industry and centralized government.' These bureaucrats, scientists, technicians, trade union organizers, sociologists, teachers, journalists, and professional politicians 'look towards the USSR and see in it, or think they see, a system which eliminates the upper class, keeps the working class in its place, and hands unlimited power to people very similar to themselves.'[28]

A year after publication, *Nineteen Eighty-Four* had sold 49,917 copies in the U.K., 170,000 in America, plus a further 190,000 through the Book of the Month Club. From his hospital bed, Orwell issued statements of partial reassurance to a thoroughly alarmed world: his new novel was merely a warning, not a prophecy—it was (he said) up to each of us to make sure that the nightmare dystopia of permanent atomic war between super-powers and the total eradication of liberty did not happen. Many regarded Orwell's term 'Ingsoc' as referring to the Labour Party—Orwell felt obliged to issue a disclaimer. He had naturally voted Labour in 1945 and continued to trust the Labour government to defend civil liberties and 'decency.' Even so, Orwell's publisher Fredric Warburg commented of the novel, 'It is worth a cool million votes to the Conservative Party; it is imaginable that it might have a preface by Winston Churchill after whom its hero is named.'

The book was reviewed as an anti-Communist polemic by the *Economist*, the *Wall Street Journal*, *Time* and *Life*. James Hilton wrote in the *Herald Tribune* (12 June 1949): 'It is as timely as the label on a poison bottle.'[29] An editorial in *Life*, reprinted along with a condensed version of the book in *Reader's Digest* (September 1949), identified Big Brother as a 'mating' of Hitler and Stalin. But was he? The British Foreign Office was not too concerned about such debates: on 4 November 1949, the FO's semi-clandestine IRD informed Charles Thayer, director of the Voice of America, that the IRD was sponsoring the translation of *Nineteen Eighty-Four* into fourteen listed languages.[30]

Orwell's death at the age of forty-six was a tragedy, rekindled by the death of Camus at a similar age ten years later. The proprietor of the Sunday *Observer*, David Astor, rang Koestler in Paris and invited him to write 900 to 1,000 words by way of an obituary – Koestler wanted more words; who wouldn't? 'He was the only one whom his grim integrity kept immune against the spurious mystique of the "Movement", who never became a fellow-traveller and never believed in Moses the Raven's Sugarcandy Mountain – either in heaven or on earth.' Koestler singled out for praise the opening section of 'The Lion and the Unicorn,' 'England Your England,' as well as *Animal Farm*, which he rated the best parable since Swift – and *Nineteen Eighty-Four* as equal in logical horror to Kafka's *In the Penal Colony*.[31]

The global impact of Orwell's *Nineteen Eighty-Four* was without precedent. Arguably it exercised a greater impact on the culture of the Cold War than any work of history, political science or reportage. The Voice of America lost no time in serializing the novel. Film and cartoon versions received CIA support. The U.S. Information Agency sponsored the translation and distribution of Orwell's last two novels in thirty languages.

The Communist camp instinctively resorted to what Orwell had called, in 'The Prevention of Literature' (1946), 'prefabricated phrases bolted together like the pieces of a child's Meccano set.' In the CPUSA's cultural organ *Masses and Mainstream*, Samuel Sillen – who had savaged Dos Passos's *Adventures of a Young Man* ten years earlier— accused Orwell of a 'diatribe against the human race.' In England, the Marxist historian A. L. Morton agreed: 'His object is not to argue a case but to induce an irrational conviction...that any attempt to realise socialism must lead to a world of corruption, torture and insecurity. To accomplish this no slander is too gross, no device too filthy; *Nineteen Eighty-Four* is, for this country at least, the last word to date in counter-revolutionary apologetics.'[32] On 12 May 1950, *Pravda*'s I. Anisimov denounced Orwell's 'filthy book...slobbering with poisonous spittle' and written at the instigation of Wall Street. The Russians inevitably deployed some of the terms which Orwell himself had famously associated with the Soviet school: hyena, hangman, cannibal, petty bourgeois, lackey, flunkey, mad dog.[33]

More interesting were the complaints of Isaac Deutscher, biographer of Trotsky and Stalin. Writing in December 1954, Deutscher noted that the Orwellian terms 'Thought Police,' 'Crimethink,' 'Hateweek' now regularly occurred in newspaper articles and political speeches. Big Brother had appeared on cinema and television screens on both sides of the Atlantic.[34] Orwell had failed to understand Stalin's purges because as a provincial English rationalist without Marxist education, he could not analyse the real motivation behind the seemingly irrational (an uncanny echo of Maurice Merleau-Ponty's critique of Koestler's *Darkness at Noon*). Deutscher's conclusion was bleak: '*1984* [sic] has taught millions to look at the conflict between East and West in terms of black and white, and it has shown them a monster bogy and a monster scapegoat for all the ills that plague mankind.'[35]

As the New Left emerged in Britain, the ex-Communist historian E. P. Thompson renewed Deutscher's attack—although his target was Orwell's essays rather than his novels. Thompson's 'Outside the Whale' (1960), which takes its title from an inversion of Orwell's influential essay 'Inside the Whale' (1940), focused on the dire impact of Orwell's work, which had been absorbed into 'Natopolitan' culture and sowed a deep self-distrust on the Left. Socialism, Thompson complained, was explained away by Orwell as a product of middle-class guilt, frustration and ennui, a projection of the personal neuroses of maladjusted intellectuals. The cumulative impact of Orwell's journalism '... must appear like an endless football game in which one side (Fascism, Reaction) is invisible, while the other side (Anti-Fascism, Communism, Progress) spend their whole time fouling each other or driving the ball into their own goal. Orwell is like a man who is raw all down one side and numb on the other'. Thompson chided Orwell for failing to distinguish between 'the deformities' of the Communist movement and 'the nature and function of the movement itself' (in essence the distinction advanced by Deutscher and by Khrushchev himself in 1956). Orwell was guilty of blinding a later generation 'to the forces within Communism making for its transformation.'[36]

In May 1961, Conor Cruise O'Brien (not to be confused with the villain of *Nineteen Eighty-Four!*) offered some reflections on Orwell in the *New Statesman*. Orwell, he conceded, 'kept scoring direct hits. You knew that certain things he said were true, because you winced when you heard them.' O'Brien likened Orwell's impact on the English Left to that of Voltaire on the French nobility, leaving them self-critical and defenceless. But Orwell brooded about sandals, beards, vegetarians and psychologists; he loved roast beef, the English countryside, Kipling, decency. The sum total of these 'Tory growls' added up to 'an English conservative eccentric'. O'Brien identified Orwell, like Camus, as reluctant anti-imperialist: 'although he condemns imperialism he dislikes its victims even more.' O'Brien suggested that the inhabitants of *Animal Farm* had points in common with Orwell's natives in *Burmese Days*, who, 'once the relative decencies of the Raj are gone, must inevitably fall under the obscene domination of their own kind'.[37]

The attacks from the left continued into the (real) year 1984, when Orwell's novel was massively re-examined in numerous seminars and essays. Salman Rushdie announced that '...the Orwell of "Inside the Whale" and *Nineteen Eighty-Four* is advocating ideas that can only be of service to our masters.'[38] (Had he lived, would Orwell, like Sir Salman, have accepted a knighthood?) Raymond Williams complained that Orwell had laid the foundations for the orthodox political beliefs of a generation by means of a 'successful impersonation of the plain man who bumps into experience in an unmediated way, and is simply telling the truth about it'.[39] A whole human project had falsely been presented as fraudulent and in its consequences cruel.[40] Williams had co-authored a pamphlet with Eric Hobsbawm defending the Soviet invasion of Finland in 1939; forty years later he provided a form of apology for Pol Pot and the Khmer Rouge, plus Mao's cultural revolution.[41] By the year 1984, *Nineteen Eighty-Four* had been translated into twenty-three languages, with worldwide sales of 15 million. The British Penguin edition, first published in 1954, had sold 3 million.[42] Five years later Soviet Communism began its disintegration.

Mention should be made, finally, of Orwell's notorious 'list.' His reputation as the St George of English letters came under strain when, in July 1996, Foreign Office papers for 1949 became available to the public. The damage was compounded in June 2003 when the FO released what may be described as 'Orwell's list,' previously kept under the wraps of 'Section 3 (4)' – and indeed Orwell himself had stipulated absolute confidentiality and anonymity when supplying thirty-eight names of political 'unreliables' to the IRD. In metaphorical terms, Orwell's fingerprints are all over FO files 1110/221 and 1110/189. 'Orwell is revealed in role of state informer,' announced the *Daily Telegraph* (12 July 1996) adding: 'To some, it was as if Winston Smith had willingly cooperated with the Thought Police in *Nineteen Eighty-Four*.' Orwell regarded himself as a strong defender of civil liberties, having urged the Freedom Defence Committee (FDC) to take a stand against the Labour government's proposal to purge Communists from certain jobs in the civil service without providing an open hearing and a defence lawyer to cross-examine hostile witnesses.[43] Yet the thirty-eight names on Orwell's list, sent to the IRD in May 1949, had no clue that they had been listed, let alone a chance to defend their reputations. On 4 March 1949, the IRD circulated British information officers across the world: 'In our work of weaning people away from Communism, considerable attention must clearly be concentrated on those elements which have "advanced" views...perhaps the most likely is "Tribune"...it combines the resolute exposure of Communism and its methods with [Left-wing views].'[44]

Orwell's list as sent to the IRD appears to have been somewhat modified, or self-censored, when compared with the parallel entries among the full 135 names found in the writer's quarto notebook from which he made his selection—and which the IRD never saw.[45] In the list of thirty-eight the comment on Tom Driberg is: 'Usually named as "crypto" but in my opinion is NOT reliably pro CP.' Yet in the notebook Tom Driberg is not only 'Homosexual' and 'English Jew' but 'Commonly thought to be underground member.' The list posted to the IRD had been largely purged of racial comments – although Deutscher was 'Polish Jew' and Cedric Dover was 'Eurasian.' The nature and extent of Orwell's anti-Semitism is open to debate, but he was certainly sceptical about Zionism. A private letter to Celia Kirwan (1949) advises that anti-anti-Semitism was not a 'strong card' to play against the Russians, not merely because of the presence of Jewish figures like Kaganovich and Anna Pauker in the Communist leadership but because 'I also think it is bad policy to try to curry favour with your enemies. The Zionist Jews everywhere hate us and regard Britain as *the* enemy, more even than Germany.' Reading this, Adam Watson of the Foreign Office commented internally: 'we are not anti-semitic'.[46] Elsewhere Orwell found Sartre's argument in *Portrait of an Antisemite* schematic and laughed at the idea that anti-Semitism was found mainly among the bourgeoisie 'and that goat upon whom all our sins are laid, the "petty bourgeois."' Orwell insisted that anti-Semitism 'is extremely widespread, is not confined to any one class, and, above all, in any but the worst cases, is intermittent'. The first step towards a serious study of it would be 'to stop regarding it as a crime.'[47]

Perhaps the most disquieting dimension of Orwell's list is its fingering of people he knew, or against whom he had a burning personal grievance, most notably Kingsley Martin, editor of the *New Statesman*, who is described in the list given to the IRD as: '??Too dishonest to be outright "crypto" or fellow-traveller, but reliably pro-Russian on all major issues.' Martin had threatened to sue *Tribune* after Orwell wrote, 'Don't imagine that for years you can make yourself the boot-licking propagandist of the Soviet regime or any other regime, and then suddenly return to mental decency. Once a whore, always a whore.'[48] In failing to signal his personal grievance against Martin to the IRD, Orwell was guilty of malevolent whispering in a time of trial. His thumbnail sketches, the spots with which he damned his 'unreliables,' resemble English variants of the prejudiced popular evidence harvested in America by the FBI: anti-American, pro-Russian, Wallace supporter, anti-white, homosexual, Jew/Jewish. It is surely significant that Orwell cut out and pasted into his notebook a list of alleged Communist-front organisations in the U.S. taken from the magazine the *New Leader* (14 June 1946).[49] Orwell constantly used the term 'crypto' as if it was an objective category of secret Party member, 'Underground member' likewise. In several cases, names supplied to the IRD were accompanied by no more than '?' or '??.' Not included in the list he sent to the IRD was the editor of *The God that Failed*, Richard Crossman, MP, and one of its contributors, Stephen Spender, who might have thought of Orwell as a friend. Spender is described as "Sentimental sympathiser and very unreliable. Easily influenced. Tendency to homosexuality."

A case can be made in mitigation: for many British and American intellectuals in the late 1940s, working with or for an Allied government against the 'Soviet threat' was entirely consistent with having worked with or for an Allied government against Hitler. Clandestine operations were considered inevitable rather than disreputable. Sergeant Eric Blair of the St John's Wood Home Guard was now enlisting against the orchestrator of the Prague coup of February 1948, the Berlin blockade, the rising Stalinist terror in Eastern Europe.

11

Commentary: Totalitarianism, Ideology, Power

The notion of 'totalitarianism,' so seminal to Western Cold War culture, with its built-in equation of the Hitler and Stalin regimes, was certainly familiar to Orwell's generation in the 1930s, but it did not assume dominance in the media and public opinion until the late 1940s. Orwell used the term freely in his essays and letters. 'Totalitarianism has abolished freedom of thought to an extent unheard of in any previous age.... It not only forbids you to express –even think – certain thoughts, but it dictates what you *shall* think, it creates an ideology for you...' In *Nineteen Eighty-Four*, the Party-controlled mass media oversees a systematic perversion of language and reason, instilling a final public acceptance of blatant contradictions: 'War is Peace,' 'Freedom is Slavery,' and 'Ignorance is Strength'—in short, 'doublethink.' 'A totalitarian state is in effect a theocracy,' Orwell had written in June 1941, 'and its ruling caste, in order to keep its position, has to be thought of as infallible.... Totalitarianism demands, in fact, the continuous alteration of the past, and in the long run probably demands a disbelief in the very existence of objective truth.'[1]

Orwell's pessimism was all-pervasive: 'Since about 1930, the world has given no reason for optimism whatever. Nothing is in sight except a welter of lies, hatred, cruelty and ignorance, and beyond our present troubles loom vaster ones which are only now entering into the European consciousness.'

In general the term 'totalitarian' remained foreign to Soviet dissident writers. Few drew direct parallels between Stalin's Russia and Hitler's Germany. In all probability, the devastating experience of the war and the Nazi occupation put such comparisons beyond the pale. Vasily Grossman was the only Soviet novelist to emerge with a full-fledged model of totalitarianism. In the novel *Life and Fate*, he speaks of 'totalitarian countries, where society as such no longer exists.'[2] Under Stalin and Hitler the party or the state was held to be the only legitimate interpreter of society. 'The violence of a totalitarian State is so great as to be no longer a means to an end: it becomes the object of mystical worship and adoration.'[3] In both *Life and Fate* and *Everything Flows*, Grossman dares to equate Hitler's final solution with Stalin's massacre of peasants: '...the identical creaking of the barbed wire stretched around the Siberian taiga and around Auschwitz'.[4] In *Everything Flows*, Grossman draws the parallel between the German refusal to treat Jews as human beings and the Soviet refusal to see Ukrainian kulaks as such. The urban workers were given ration cards entitling them to 800 grams of bread, but not a gram was allocated to the children of peasants.[5] The Nazi attribution of 'non-human' status to racial or national enemies found its sinister echo in the Bolsheviks' similar contempt for the 'class enemy,' domestic or foreign, fit only for extermination. Grossman inexorably draws the parallel between Nazism and Stalinism. When people are to be slaughtered en masse, a special campaign is required 'to stir up feelings of real hatred and revulsion. It was in such an atmosphere that the Germans carried out the extermination of the Ukrainian and Byelorussian Jews. And at an earlier date, in the same regions, Stalin himself had mobilized the fury of the masses...to liquidate the kulaks as a class and during the extermination of the Trotskyist-Bukharinite degenerates and saboteurs.'[6]

In his invented episodes, Grossman does not invariably find it easy to press history into fictive convention, as when in the German concentration camp, Mostovskoy, an old Bolshevik, is interrogated by a subtle, serpentine Gestapo officer, Liss, a Russian-speaking native of Riga with a keen interest in political theory, who keeps suggesting that Nazis and Bolsheviks, despite their war to the death, are two sides of the same coin. Says Liss somewhat improbably: 'In essence we are the same—both one-Party states. Our capitalists [in Germany] are not the masters. The State gives them their plan... Your State also outlines a plan and takes what is produced for itself. And the people you call masters—the workers—also receive a salary from your one-Party state.'[7] Gestapo officer Liss clearly does Grossman's work for him when he conflates Hitler's purge of Röhm and the Brownshirts (SA) in 1934, the 'night of the long knives,' with Stalin's purges of 1937; Stalin's liquidation of 'millions of peasants' with Hitler's 'millions of Jews.' But would a Gestapo man high on Aryan superiority liken Germans to the Russians they regarded as primitives? Such sophisticated interrogators as Grossman's Gestapo officer Liss – one is reminded of Koestler's Gletkin – tend to surface more often in fiction than in reality. 'Mostovskoy watched Liss and thought to himself: "Did this vile nonsense really confuse me for a moment? Was I really choking in this stream of poisonous, stinking dirt?"'[8] Here Grossman resorts to Swiftian irony: 'Where would these men ever find people stupid enough to believe that there was the faintest shadow of resemblance between a Socialist State and the Fascist Reich?' Although this ironic mode is within reach of history-writing, it is more commonly found in fiction and allegory.

No other writer – until Solzhenitsyn surfaced—went so far as Grossman in depicting an almost complete symbiosis of the Hitler and Stalin regimes.

Hannah Arendt maintained that *The First Circle* ought to be required reading for students of totalitarianism.[9]

'Totalitarianism creates an ideology for you,' said Orwell. This loaded use of the word 'ideology' was to become popular, indeed prevalent, among the 'god that failed' generation of intellectuals (for whom a belief in the virtues of pluralism and liberal capitalism was the opposite of 'ideology.' Nationalising the coal mines was 'ideological,' keeping them in private hands wasn't). Alexander Schmemann argues that what Solzhenitsyn wants to show is not the daily experience of prison life but the reality behind it, 'a radical reduction of man, in the name of abstract ideas, i.e. of ideology...by depicting, as only an artist can, what happens to a man and to the world when man and life are reduced to ideology.'[10] This demonic 'ideology' was indeed an obsession with Solzhenitsyn himself, witness the following remarkable passage: 'Macbeth's self-justifications were feeble – and his conscience devoured him. Yes, even Iago was a little lamb too. The imagination and the spiritual strength of Shakespeare's evildoers stopped short at a dozen corpses. Because they had no ideology. Ideology – that is what gives evildoing its long-sought justification.... That is the social theory which helps to make his acts seem good instead of bad.... That was how the agents of the Inquisition fortified their wills: by invoking Christianity; the conquerors of foreign lands, by extolling the grandeur of the Motherland; the colonizers, by civilization; the Nazis, by race; the Jacobins (early and late), by equality, brotherhood and the happiness of future generations. Thanks to ideology, the twentieth century was fated to experience evildoing on a scale calculated in the millions.'[11] This passage has the distinct advantage of universalising 'ideology,' religious as well as secular, back across frontiers, class divisions and the centuries.

For Orwell, the roots of modern totalitarian ideology could be found in the lust for power transferred from traditional ruling castes to the upstarts of the twentieth century. In September 1944, Orwell summed up what he saw as Koestler's main theme, and main failing, in his novel *The Gladiators* (1938). After the slaves have established their City of the Sun – no slavery, no hunger, no injustice, no floggings, no executions – things go wrong. Even the cross, symbol of slavery, has to be revived to punish malefactors. Spartacus finds himself obliged to crucify twenty of his most faithful followers. Orwell objected that the slaves' republic, Sun City, is 'wrecked rather by hedonism than for the struggle for power...the more turbulent and less civilized slaves, chiefly Gauls and Germans, continue to behave like bandits after the Republic has been established...by allowing the City to be destroyed because Crixus the Gaul cannot be prevented from looting and raping, Koestler has faltered between allegory and history. If Spartacus is the prototype of the modern revolutionary – and obviously he is intended as that – he should have gone astray because of the impossibility of combining power with righteousness.... The story partly fails because the central problem of revolution has been avoided or, at least, has not been solved.'[12]

And that 'central problem' was power and power-lust.

This critique is interesting but doubtful. The story of Soviet Russia is not simply down to inherent power hunger among the elite, the Party. The upsurge of liberational fervour in the years following 1917 could not make up for the country's massive under-development and illiteracy, for a huge peasantry's attachment to private property and religious superstition, for the instinctive intolerance and unforgiving partisanship of a people who had never benefited from democracy and liberal institutions. Having defeated the ancient regime and its White armies, the revolutionary leadership then encounters the harsh reality of governing human nature in its most intractable forms—not forgetting foreign enemies. Power hunger is invariably linked to inequality, scarcity of resources, the imbalance between supply and demand. Orwell's ruling elites in *Animal Farm* and *Nineteen Eighty-Four* do not forget to hog the material privileges. Marx's anticipation of the replacement of 'the government of the people' by 'the administration of things' has remained as utopian as pie in the sky.

This said, *Animal Farm*—like William Golding's *The Lord of the Flies* – nevertheless presses the sharpest question mark into the flesh of human nature itself. Only abolish class rule and its whispering acolyte, religion – Marx insisted—and the serpent would become redundant. But Marx, it was clear to Orwell, had gravely underestimated the power of egoism and self-aggrandisement in human nature. In *Nineteen Eighty-Four*, the Inner Party's O'Brien gives Winston Smith a clear explanation of the Party's motivation: power for power's sake: 'Power is not a means; it is an end. One does not establish a dictatorship in order to safeguard a revolution; one makes the revolution in order to establish the dictatorship.' (Isaac Deutscher indignantly responded that every historian knows this is not true.) O'Brien gloatingly tells Winston: 'But always – do not forget this, Winston – always there will be the intoxication of power...the thrill of victory.... If you want a picture of the future, imagine a boot stamping on a human face – forever.'[13] Deutscher remonstrated that Orwell should have paid attention to the explanation of Stalinism provided by Trotsky in *The Revolution Betrayed*, but had preferred 'to cling to the oldest, the most banal, the most abstract, the most metaphysical, and the most barren of all generalisations... "sadistic power-hunger"'.

The political empiricism recommended by Orwell was, according to the historian E. P. Thompson, the 'inscape' of the doctrine of original sin, the confined space in which you could still make minor motions inside the whale, within the narrow confines of human nature. The problem confronting Deutscher, E. P. Thompson and the advocates of a revived, humanistic Marxism was that Marx had offered no theory of power or of the individual ego. Although he constantly denounced his contemporaries, whether Louis Bonaparte or rival socialists, in vividly psychological and moral terms as scoundrels and sell-outs, he insisted that class struggle was the primary, self-propelling, force of history. Governments were merely the executive committee of the ruling class. Tyranny was to be understood in terms of historical structures rather than in terms of monomaniacal tyrants and their satraps. Yet Big Brother is the ultimate expert in mass psychology. As Alfred Kazin pointed out in an essay on Orwell, 'the tyrants deconstruct human consciousness, emptying it of everything that does not lend itself to the authority of the monolith'.[14]

Boris Pasternak's *Doctor Zhivago* offers several illuminating passages on what may happen when power passes to the powerless. During the 1918 fighting in Moscow, the Zhivago family shelter in their rooms amid scenes of semi-starvation, intense cold, the search for fuel, the terrible typhus epidemic. Bolsheviks and Mensheviks and Social Revolutionaries are somewhere off-stage arguing about the timetable of history, or about Lenin's *The State and Revolution*. One evening during a blizzard, Zhivago reads a late extra paper printed on one side only, announcing that a Soviet of People's Commissars had been formed and that the Dictatorship of the Proletariat was thus established.[15] As he squats to poke the logs of his stove, Zhivago's thoughts descend into irony: 'What splendid surgery! You take a knife and cut out all the old stinking sores. Quite simply, without any nonsense, you take the monster of injustice which has been accustomed for centuries to being bowed and scraped and curtsyed to, and you sentence it to death'. Zhivago senses in this ruthless motion an authentic Russian literary heritage, 'Pushkin's blazing directness' and 'Tolstoy's bold attachment to the facts'.[16] But what, Zhivago muses, were these 'facts' in reality? Commissars were being appointed to run housing, trade, industry, municipal services—'men in black leather jerkins, with unlimited powers and an iron will, armed with means of intimidation and revolvers, who shaved little and slept less. They knew the slinking bourgeois breed, the average holders of cheap government stocks, and they spoke to them without the slightest pity and with Mephistopholean smiles, as to petty thieves caught in the act.'[17] Bolsheviks, Mensheviks, Right SRs, Left SRs, and anarchists—they were all dangerous when they got the upper hand, scum, Reds, rampaging peasants wearing the uniforms of sailors and militiamen, capable of using their guns on you for any reason or whim.

Solzhenitsyn's reflections on power-hunger largely echo Pasternak's and replicate Orwell's. In *The Gulag Archipelago*, he writes about the NKVD: 'Excluded by the nature of their work and by deliberate choice from the higher sphere of human existence, the serviteurs of the Blue Institution lived in their lower sphere with all the greater intensity and avidity. And they were possessed and directed by the two strongest instincts of the lower sphere, other than hunger and sex: greed for power and greed for gain. (Particularly for power. In recent decades it has turned out to be more important than money. Power is a poison well known for thousands of years.... For those, however, who are unaware of any higher sphere, it is a deadly poison. For them there is no antidote.)'[18] What was the NKVD mentality? How did they treat people under their control? Solzhenitsyn cites the case of Esfir R., 1947, a Russian woman who was also a foreigner's girlfriend. '"Come on now, does an American have a special kind of—? Is that it? Weren't there enough Russian ones for you?"' The interrogators demanded from the young woman details of sexual intercourse, despite her tears.[19]

Solzhenitsyn confesses how badly power affected him as a young officer in the army. 'In the intoxication of youthful successes I had felt myself to be infallible, and I was therefore cruel.... In my most evil moment I was convinced I was doing good, and I was well supplied with systematic arguments. And it was only when I lay there on rotting prison straw that I sensed within myself the first stirrings of good. Gradually it was disclosed to me that the line separating good and evil passes not through states, not between classes, nor between political parties either – but right through every human heart...' He adds: '... no camp can corrupt those who have a stable nucleus.... Those people became corrupted in camp who before camp had not been enriched by any morality at all or by any spiritual upbringing'.[20]

Meanwhile, Thought Control increasingly prevailed in university departments, academic curricula and graduate degrees. Kow-towing became the norm. Viktor Shtrum, the central character in Vasily Grossman's novels *For a Just Cause* and *Life and Fate*, makes a discovery of genius but falls into disgrace and waits to be arrested. He ponders a new questionnaire everyone must fill in, probing origins, antecedents, past events. 'Have you or your closest relative ever been the subject of a judicial inquiry or trial? Have you been arrested? Have you been given a judicial or administrative sentence? When? Where? Precisely what for?'[21] Shtrum ponders the questions he would like to ask potential staff for his laboratory: 'It was all the same to him whether his future colleague was a Russian, a Jew, a Ukrainian or an Armenian, whether his grandfather had been a worker, a factory-owner or a kulak...whether or not his brother has been arrested by the organs of the NKVD...whether his future colleague's sister lived in Geneva or Kostroma.'[22] But it wasn't all the same to the NKVD.

In *The First Circle*, Solzhenitsyn mentions how in the late Stalin years all foreign and 'cosmopolitan' references had to be excised from graduate theses, leading to endless revisions, as in the case of Nerzhin's wife, Nadya, writing a graduate thesis at Moscow University (so long as she can keep secret her marriage to a political prisoner):

'"Weeding out the foreigners" meant going through the thesis and throwing out every reference to a foreigner: "As Lowe has shown" for instance, would have to read, "As scientists have shown"... On the other hand, if a Russian, or a russified Dane or German had done anything at all to distinguish himself, then you had to give his full name and duly bring out his great patriotism and immortal services to science.'[23]

In Solzhenitsyn's *Cancer Ward*, Shulubin, a former lecturer, describes the devastation of Soviet academic life in his time. '"But then the oak-trees began to topple. There was the fall of Muratov at the agricultural academy. Professors were being arrested by the dozen. We were supposed to confess our 'mistakes'! I confessed them!... I withdrew into the study of pure biology, I found myself a quiet haven. But then the purge began there as well.... They suggested we reshape anatomy, microbiology and neuro-pathology to fit in with the doctrines of an ignorant agronomist and an expert in horticulture."' (Solzhenitsyn is referring to Trofim Lysenko.) Shulubin gave up teaching, became a librarian. "'But then librarians receive secret instructions from the authorities: for the destruction of books by this or that author... Into the stove with all your genetics, leftist aesthetics, ethics, cybernetics, arithmetic...'"[24]

12

Sartre: History, Fiction and the Party

Jean-Paul Sartre[1] was the most influential writer of the postwar years to keep the Communists at arm's length while resisting, adamantly, the prevailing 'god that failed' syndrome. Subjected to furious diatribes both from Moscow and the PCF at home in France, regularly denigrated as an agent of Wall Street, Sartre replied in *Qu'est-ce que la littérature?* (*What is Literature?* 1947): 'The politics of Stalinist Communism is incompatible with the honest practice of the literary craft.' What was demanded was unreserved allegiance. Sartre refused to subscribe to Party-driven literature or Andrei Zhdanov's Politburo blueprint for 'socialist realism.' As a philosopher, he resisted any deterministic view of history. *L'Humanité* (7 April 1948) described him as 'nauseous,' as a 'demagogue,' and as 'Koestler's double.'

For twenty years after the war his audience was vast: novelist, playwright, philosopher, essayist – the sheer versatility of his literary gifts, set beside his prodigious output, filled bookshops and theatres. Existentialist or Marxist, or both? His aphorisms excited attention: 'Hell is other people'; 'the French masses have fallen outside of history.' He became the consciousness and the conscience of a generation pitched into a state of shock as the wartime alliance rapidly gave way to the Cold War. Sartre's work is a progression from one breaking point to the next.

By his own account, Sartre emerged from the war convinced that existentialism provided the only viable account of human experience, historical materialism the only viable account of history. The dominant notion at this juncture is found in his comment that *l'homme n'est rien d'autre que ce qu'il se fait* – man is nothing other than what he makes of himself. He refused to subordinate the individual's capacity for choice to any force greater than his own freedom. Likewise a collective, the working class, was free to choose between acquiescent reformism and revolutionary praxis (a term favoured by Sartre).

In the immediate postwar years, he confidently believed in his ability to coherently combine his work as a writer and as a political activist. In her novel

The Mandarins, Simone de Beauvoir describes her fear that too many committee meetings and platform speeches would sap his energies. Robert Dubreuilh (Sartre) insists that now (1945) is the time for a new political initiative following the 'negative' collaboration of the vigilance committees, the Resistance. Overriding her objections, he comments that one book more or less won't make much difference—at certain moments other forms of action are more urgent. She replies, 'But I find your books very important...what they bring to people is something unique. Whereas with your political work, you aren't alone in the undertaking.' Later she presses the point again. 'You are first and foremost a writer.' 'What counts for me is the revolution,' he replies.[2] Sartre became a leading voice in what was known as the 'third force,' the Rassemblement démocratique révolutionnaire, owing allegiance to neither the Communists nor the pro-American Socialists.

By 1950-51, his rising detestation of American global influence, of France's colonialist wars in defence of a defunct empire, and of mounting persecution of the PCF in France, drove him, briefly but not so briefly, from 1951 to 1956, to yield almost unconditional public allegiance to the Soviet Union. He never joined the Party, a step too far, but he did come to regard his expressed choices and priorities as essentially strategic. He would no longer give voice to his misgivings if they brought 'comfort to the bourgeoisie.' He became a politician of the pen. Convinced that Washington, not Moscow, was itching for a military solution, by 1951 he had assumed the public profile of a fellow-traveller. He even ordered the cancellation of a scheduled production of his play, *Les mains sales*, in Vienna.

Roads to Freedom (*Les Chemins de la Liberté*) was Sartre's major enterprise as a novelist, a three-volume sequence followed by an unfinished fourth. The challenge embraced is historical, philosophical and literary. (But is 'Roads to Freedom' the most appropriate translation of *Les Chemins de la liberté*? A no doubt less commercially attractive rendering, 'The Ways of Freedom,' would better convey Sartre's conception of 'freedom' as an inescapable ontological condition, a permanent field of possibilities, an odyssey. With 'ways' goes 'waysides,' the places where we sometimes fall or effectively drop out.) The main action is condensed into a period of roughly two years, from the summer of 1938 to the summer of 1940, when the Nazi armies occupied France. At a global level, his subject is the political crisis of the late 1930s, the spectre of fascism, the creation of the Popular Front, the Spanish Civil War, the diplomatic appeasement of Hitler by Chamberlain and Daladier at the expense of Czechoslovakia (the Munich agreement), the impact of the Nazi-Soviet Pact. This historical background provides the proscenium arch within which carefully chosen individual characters confront (or evade) the rival claims of political commitment or private life. Throughout the descent into the Second World War, Sartre's protagonists wrestle with what the author clearly regards as 'the Communist temptation.'

The petty compromises of political life in the last years of the Third Republic held no attraction for Sartre and his companion Simone de Beauvoir. She recalls how Raymond Aron's membership of the Socialist Party in the 1930s had disgusted Sartre and herself. In their view, '*la société ne pouvait changer que globalement, d'un seul coup, par une convulsion violente*—society could only change in its entirety, from a single blow [or all at once], by a violent convulsion.'[3] Reformist pragmatists like Aron dismissed this as the latent romanticism of the cynic. It was military conscription and the war, including a spell in captivity, which brought Sartre into contact with *la France réelle*, ordinary French workers, peasants and clerks, the *poilus*, whose lot was to endure rather than shape events. This encounter called into question Sartre's fastidious recoil from the compromises and demagogic slogans of politics, setting in motion a dialogue between the 'pure' claims of the intelligence and the cruder choices offered by collective action.

Thereafter, as novelist, playwright and journalist, Sartre wrestled with the dilemma of 'dirty hands' (the title of his play, *Les Mains sales*): an efficacious pig farmer will smell of pig. Yet what is involved when an intellectual decides to join the Communist Party: is it a step towards changing the world – or is it yet another version of escape from 'freedom,' of losing one's identity in a comforting patriarchal embrace? Sartre's fictional narrative seems to imply that to join the party and not to join it represent alternative versions of escapism. The two central characters who represent these options, Brunet and Mathieu Delarue, are thus the protagonists of a specifically modern tragedy. Both are middle-class – indeed whatever Sartre's beliefs about the proletariat as the true subject of a literature of praxis,' whatever he may have argued about literature coming to full fruition only in a classless society, the fact is that the vast majority of characters in his novels and plays, including the militant Communists, are middle-class intellectuals or *déraciné* bohemians.

The literary structure of the trilogy reflects a deliberate shift from private relationships to the public domain. The characters of the first volume, The *Age of Reason* (*L'Age de raison*, 1945), are only dimly aware of what lies beyond their personal ambitions, love affairs and existential pains. Indeed, the first ten chapters are the work of an artful miniaturist, not unlike the tableaux of an intimate stage play, as we discover what each member of a small circle of acquaintances needs and fears from the other(s). Dialogue is the crucial instrument of both action and characterization, although Sartre also uses the resources of prose to describe the resistant opacity of the material universe and the hidden adventures of perception. *The Age of Reason* evidently carries a double meaning: first, from the eighteenth-century Enlightenment, when God yielded to reason (Sartre's characters discover no meaning in human existence beyond or above the projects they fashion out the blank page of existential philosophy). But Sartre also points to a radically variant type of 'Reason,' that of middle-aged accommodation – Be reasonable! Sartre's protagonist and alter ego Mathieu is reminded by his conformist brother that he should have reached, in his mid-thirties, the 'age of reason.' Mathieu retorts scornfully, 'You mean the age of Reconciliation, the time to capitulate to bourgeois marriage, property and prudence' – in short to what Sartre called '*mauvaise foi*.'[4]

At the outset (the summer of 1938) history lies just off-stage, in the wings of a stage flickering with half-lights. Mathieu worries about Hitler and about France's non-intervention in the Spanish Civil War; he watches the artist Gomez depart for besieged Madrid – yet he cannot stir himself to action. The political anger he feels, as a man of the Left, remains other people's anger, an indignation 'in the air,' *au courant*. He would like to exchange his hollow freedom 'for a good sound certainty...it would take me out of myself.' But Mathieu is preoccupied by the urgent search for four thousand francs to procure a safe abortion for his mistress, Marcelle. She would rather marry and have the child but that does not suit him, he confines their relationship to regular visits four times a week, removing his shoes at the door in order not to disturb her old mother, never inviting Marcelle out to meet his friends in his natural milieu, the bars, cafés and thé dansants of Montparnasse, selfishly compartmentalizing his life, splashing money he can ill afford on taxis (habitually) and champagne (a single extravagance) in order to impress Ivich, the attractive, spoiled, sulky and deeply unhappy daughter of a Russian émigré. Sartre conveys the self-aware alienation of his bookworm hero: '...everywhere I go I bear my shell with me, I remain at home in my room, among my books.' Even his professorial duties never seem to intrude on his day as he pursues his various private rendez-vous, a fact unremarked by the author.

But Communist discipline is no solution and Mathieu rejects the erect, clear-eyed Brunet's invitation to join the party. 'Oh yes,' he responds, 'go down on your knees and you will believe.... But I want to believe first.'[5] Brunet calls him a grown-up child. In *The Age of Reason* the Communist temptation is a mere speck on the lens; by the close of the third volume in the trilogy, *Iron in the Soul* (*La Mort dans l'âme*), it dominates almost the entire field of vision.

The second volume, *The Reprieve* (*Le Sursis*, 1945,) takes its title from the false reprieve apparently granted by the Munich agreement of September 1938. Here Sartre provides a panoramic and synoptic overview of Europe paralysed by the approach of war. The action takes place during eight days, culminating in Munich and the abandonment of Czechoslovakia to Hitler. Mathieu is now one of the French reservists possessing a white mobilization order, waiting to be conscripted by the Minister of National Defence. The Popular Front which had come to power in 1936 had already fragmented, the Communists having broken with their Socialist and Radical partners in protest against the government's policy of non-intervention in Spain. Unable to hold his coalition together, the Socialist premier Léon Blum had resigned in favour of the anti-Communist Radical, Edouard Daladier, who now depended on the support of conservative elements for his parliamentary majority.

Sartre shows us Chamberlain and Daladier in action, depicting the French leader as a crumpled figure with a dead cigarette hanging from his lips: 'Daladier sank back and blurted out "Go on", with a limp wave of his hand.' Chamberlain is the sentimental 'old gentleman,' equally ill-suited to the task of the hour, curbing Hitler. Meanwhile the Czechoslovak leaders, Masaryk and Beneš, protest bitterly as their country, carved out of the dismembered Austria-Hungary by the Treaty of Versailles, is now itself dismembered with the loss of vital military fortifications, the equivalent of France's Maginot Line. The Czechs would like to bring the Russians into an anti-Nazi alliance but neither Chamberlain nor Daladier will have it. All of Europe gathers round radio sets to hear Hitler's final ultimatum to Czechoslovakia: 'Today I march at the head of my people as their first soldier...' In some 'collage' passages the headlined giants rub shoulders with humble fictional characters in the same sentence, the same breath. When Mathieu's flame, Ivich, falls asleep, so does Neville Chamberlain the other side of the Channel.

. Does Europe care about Munich? Do the fictional characters of *The Reprieve* really care? They are not sure. The higher diplomacy takes place on Olympus. Hitler must be halted (perhaps) but of Sartre's characters only the Spanish artist Gomez has volunteered to fight in Spain. A mood of helpless resignation is followed by euphoria when Munich brings its apparent reprieve. (The second edition of the *Great Soviet Encyclopaedia* (1955) described Sartre's fictional depiction of the Munich agreement and the fall of France as 'what comes to a doomed and insuperably divided people'.)[6]

Mathieu Delarue is discovered holidaying by the seaside with his pompous brother Jacques and his wife Odette (who had brought him a fat dowry). Jacques has refused to lend Mathieu the money for Marcelle's abortion, urging him to marry her. 'A man must have the courage to act like everyone else', he has declared, 'in order not to be like anybody.' Jacques accuses Mathieu of enjoying bourgeois privileges while affecting to despise capitalism. 'You display an abstract sympathy with the Communists, but you take care not to commit yourself, you have never voted.'[7] (De Beauvoir recalled that Sartre likewise did not vote when the Popular Front was elected.) Jacques is an appeaser with a soft spot for fascism and the 'New Europe.' As usual he plays back Mathieu's professed beliefs to discomfort him. You were always so exact, cynical and analytical, he remarks: 'Then comes war...and my rebel, my plate-smasher, goes off politely, without any hesitation.' Later, after the fall of France, Jacques is found with his wife on the road heading south from Paris. 'Had there been any danger,' he tells his wife, 'I would have stayed.' Insisting that he left the city for her sake, to be with her, because she had been frightened, he also recalls how he had been turned down for military service by an M.O. 'Don't you remember how angry I was?' Odette, a non-smoker, is so disgusted that she steals one of his cigarettes as he snores over the wheel of the car.

As war approaches, Mathieu is found loitering at the seaside. 'He contemplated those twenty years, like an expanse of sunlit sea, and he now saw them as they had been: a finite number of days compressed between two high, helpless walls, a period duly catalogued, with a prelude and an end, which would figure in the history manuals under the heading: Between the two wars.' But would Mathieu's thoughts have assumed so prescient a form in the summer of 1938, or is Sartre injecting authorial hindsight? Either way, Sartre takes care to limit our affection for his hero. At the end of *The Reprieve*, Mathieu's nemesis, Ivich, reappears as he is about to leave his Paris apartment for the army depot. He gives her his apartment and some money but won't let her accompany him to the station because he is due to say goodbye to another woman with whom he has just spent the night. Boarding the train, he reluctantly tells the other woman his name.

Iron in the Soul takes place in June 1940, the fall of France. Mathieu has been in uniform since September 1938. (Sartre himself was not conscripted until a year later, his job being to send up balloons, observe them through field-glasses, and then telephone the local artillery battery with news of wind changes.) The curtain had come down on the phoney war (*drôle de guerre*), the long period of attrition described in Sartre's *War Diaries*: 'The men nowadays no longer have that religious trust in their generals. To tell the truth, they have no trust of any kind.'[8] Despite occasional cross-cutting and symbiotic fusions, we follow the story of the fall of France through a succession of clearly defined scenes which pay due respect to transitions of time, geography and action. The outer world is restored to its own conveyor belt. As Sartre extends the range of his narrative to encompass the ordinary *poilus*, the short-legged, demoralized khaki citizens of the Third Republic, he increasingly resorts to the naturalistic tradition whose great French precursor was Emile Zola. His mastery of the argot and patois of war-stranded workers and peasants marks a triumph of the ear and the imagination. But, himself briefly a prisoner of war, Sartre's fictional depiction of a German POW camp allows no illusions. The odour of collaboration, of Marshal Pétain's New Order, of Vichy, soon pervades the camp. The French prisoners display an alarming gratitude for every small concession – food, a visit from relatives – offered by the conquerors. Abandoned by their own officers – but was that the case? – they need to believe that the Germans are reasonable, fair, efficient. In Germany, says one, 'You pay your taxes but at least you know where the money goes.' Willingly they set their watches in German time. The voices of priests are heard, denouncing materialism: 'And I say unto you, rejoice, my brothers, rejoice in the dark place of your suffering, for where there has been sin, there, too, is there expiation, there, too, is there redemption.'

Although Sartre does not explicitly equate sexual 'normality' with courage and patriotism, two of his characters, Daniel and the youth Phillipe, suggest an equation between homosexuality and the kind of pacifism that Sartre had come to despise as 'bad faith.' The homosexual Daniel exults in the defeat and degradation of France. Paris is now a ghost city as it awaits the conquerors: 'They are running and crawling. I, the criminal, reign over the city in their stead.' Awe and joy overwhelm him as at last he sees 'them'; boldly he returns their gaze, looking into 'sun-tanned faces in which eyes showed like glacier lakes'. He longs to be a woman so that he might load the victors with flowers. But soon he will find distraction and solace in the seduction of the bourgeois boy pacifist Philippe, who did in the end serve with his unit in the Nord but then ran away with everyone else.

And Mathieu? Among fellow-soldiers demoralized by disaster, he is alone with his education and self-possession: 'In the darkness they all looked alike.... He sat down on the edge of the road because there was nowhere else for him to go. Night entered him through mouth and eyes, through nose and ears.' Secure against physical victimisation because he can throw a punch as well as any Hemingway hero if strictly necessary, he tries to get drunk with the lads out of solidarity but can't – then feels ashamed. Besieged in a church tower, he achieves catharsis through the barrel of his gun, by killing, a savage atonement for years of vacillation. 'Each one of his shots avenged some ancient scruple.... He was free.'[9] His ultimate fate is not described, but Brunet, passing through the same village, sees the church tower collapse before he is taken prisoner. Whether or not Sartre intended Mathieu to die in the church, he reappears in the unfinished (and untranslated)[10] *Drôle d'amitié* (1949), joins the Resistance, is tortured and dies.

In the final section of *Iron in the Soul*, Sartre reflects on the attitude of the Communist Party, which had been declared illegal after the Nazi-Soviet Pact and the desertion of its leader, Thorez, from the ranks of the army. We are now with the Communist militant Brunet in a prisoner-of-war camp. We learn that he had written the leading, two-page article in *l'Humanité* justifying the Pact. To seal us hermetically into Brunet's PV, Sartre reverts to the long, unbroken paragraphs – a tunnel of words and sensations – inside which dialogue runs on continuously, one speaker after another, like rain on the roof. Sartre introduces a mysterious figure, Schneider, who clearly knows a good deal about the Communist Party yet is not a member. In conversation with him, Brunet insists that the solidarity between the European proletariat and the 'workers' state,' the Soviet Union, is rooted in inexorable historical laws; on the other hand he angrily rejects Schneider's suggestion that the clandestine PCF could ever condemn resistance to Nazi occupation (as it soon did, following the Comintern line, until Hitler invaded the Soviet Union.)Thus Sartre conveys the flagrantly schizophrenic outlook imposed on Party militants. *Drôle d'amitié*, will reveal that Schneider's real name is Vicarios, an intellectual who broke with the Party over the Nazi-Soviet Pact. Brunet is destined for disillusionment. He discovers that, while a prisoner, the Party line has changed making nonsense of everything he has dutifully done. Brunet's patriotism is now equated by his erstwhile comrades with Gaullism and the imperialism of the bourgeois states—he should have praised the masses' love of peace.[11] In his play *Les Mains sales* (*Dirty Hands*),Sartre was to torment the Communists again about the devastating impact of abrupt changes in the global Party line, the lynching reversal of allegiance demanded.

Most precious to Sartre is the individual's ultimate responsibility to others, to society. A recurring theme in his fiction and drama is the pseudo-revolt of the wealthy boy who affects to love avant-garde poetry and regards himself as a privileged spirit, above the common herd. Such a character is Lucien in the early short story, *Childhood of a Leader*; another example is Philippe, who first appears in *The Reprieve* and surfaces again in *Iron in the Soul*. When the hesitant bourgeois adolescent, Lucien, falls in with a surrealist who chatters about Rimbaud while pursuing a bohemian existence, the boy's entrepreneurial family offers no objection. In a desperate effort to discover his own identity, Lucien embraces anti-Semitic chauvinism; in the final paragraph he is found gazing at himself in a mirror with no finer project than the cultivation of a moustache.

Or, to reverse the proposition about public and private responsibility, take the case of Sartre's Gomez, the Spanish artist whose bold political choices serve as a counterpoint to the cautious, introspective Mathieu. While Mathieu agonises about raising funds to pay for his mistress's abortion, Gomez walks out on wife and son, Sarah and Pablo, to fight for the Republican forces in Spain, rising to the rank of general. He buys Pablo a soldier's outfit: 'He must learn to fight, otherwise he'll become a mouse, like the French.' But (once again) a good cause does not make a good man. 'You are evil, my poor Gomez,' Sarah tells him, 'very evil.'[12] Bored by a week's leave with his family, he makes contact with Mathieu, travelling first class while reading *l'Humanité*. He shows Mathieu a photograph of his Spanish mistress; she is fifteen. 'But war matures them,' he comments. 'Here's one of me in action.' Unlovable Gomez may be as he seeks out a nightclub with 'music and women,' but his political vision is steady; he knows that Hitler wants not just Vienna, Prague or Danzig, but all of Europe.

In the first chapter of *Iron in the Soul* we find Gomez, now a refugee from Franco's victory in Spain, in heat-soaked New York. Bitterly Gomez rejoices at news of the fall of Paris; he has not forgotten that, 'When Franco entered Barcelona, the French shook their heads and said it was a pity...' The narrative then cuts to his deserted wife and son fleeing south from Paris in a column of refugees.[13] Their taxi runs out of petrol, the driver nevertheless demands his full 200 francs, a harrowing scene reminiscent of the intensely moving episode in *The Reprieve* when Sarah blindly drags Pablo behind her through city streets after Gomez's unaffectionate return to the Spanish war and other women. Nor does Gomez in New York give them much thought; he's more interested in shapely legs traversing the sidewalks of Fifth Avenue. Sartre does allow him good artistic taste: visiting the New York Museum of Modern Art, he singles out Klee, Rouault and Picasso as the artists who ask 'awkward questions.'[14]

In *What is Literature?* Sartre embraces the necessity of literary commitment, *une literature engagée*, while clarifying in uncompromising terms his objections to fiction on the Stalinist model. While the fate of literature was bound up with that of the working class, the French proletariat was separated from writers like himself by an iron curtain, strait-jacketed by propaganda. Socialist realist theory insisted on reducing literature to an immediate political function, according to the priority or tactic of the moment. Sartre preferred what he called a literature of *praxis*, capable of inducing reflective consciousness and showing the reader his powers of self-determination.[15] Man is defined by the distinctive faculty for fashioning a free life out of free will. Sartre's fictional approach to individual responsibility and freedom of choice reflects a debt to Malraux's – although in *Days of Hope* characters are swept along by the wind of destiny; they do not make history, merely define themselves as they climb its unscaleable rock face. With Sartre, man's initial sense of 'otherness' and estrangement from everything, human or inanimate, that he encounters, provides him with the space in which he encounters anguish, alienation – but also the grim challenge of 'freedom.' Sartre's fictional characters illustrate our typical strategies of evasion as we attempt to annihilate our freedom by way of inertia, passivity and cynicism – a syndrome strikingly similar to the one described in George Orwell's essay 'Inside the Whale.' A master cartographer of the landscape of evasion, the flight from responsibility, Sartre rejected all determinisms, whether Marxian, Freudian or behaviourist.

Only two chapters of the intended fourth volume, *Drôle d'amitié*, appeared in 1949 before the project was abandoned. Sartre, as it turned out, had abandoned prose fiction for good; his appetite for writing recent history as fiction yielded to the urgencies of journalism, biography and political theory.

The line dividing 'reportage' from fiction became increasingly hazy towards mid-century. Memoirs and autobiographies—Simone de Beauvoir's for example—straddled the divide. Her non-fiction contains passages of continuous dialogue which betoken either a prodigious memory or a relaxed attitude to invention. In some respects, her autobiographical *La Force des choses* (*Force of Circumstances*, 1963) reads like a rewrite or make-over of her novel *The Mandarins* (1954). Here she explains her motive in writing the novel: 'I have already explained what is for me one of the essential purposes of literature: to make manifest the equivocal, separate, contradictory truths that no one moment represents in their totality, either inside or outside myself; in certain cases one can only succeed in grouping them all together by inscribing them within the unity of an imaginary object. Only a novel, it seemed to me, could reveal the multiple and intricately spun meanings of that changed world to which I awoke in August 1944 [the Liberation]; a changing world that had not come to rest since then.'[16]

The Mandarins provides rich insights into the political divide separating Sartre and Camus, hitherto close friends, which by 1950 had widened into a final and fatal rift. However, by setting the novel in 1945, in the immediate aftermath of the Liberation, de Beauvoir[17] obscures the essentially gradual, cumulative, nature of the quarrel. She also gives the impression that the issue of Soviet labour camps was decisive; in fact it was merely instrumental. What brought on Sartre's final anathema was the publication in October 1951 of Camus's extended essay, *L'Homme révolté* (*The Rebel*), which targeted Utopia and the determinist metaphysics which would stop at nothing to impose Utopia. 'In this New Jerusalem, echoing with the roar of miraculous machinery, who will still remember the cry of the victims.'[18] According to Sartre, Camus had now made his 'Thermidor' (counter-revolution) by attempting to stand outside or above history; his fastidious emphasis on means would merely gratify the consciences of those who preferred to criticize the status quo rather than abolish it. Again, Sartre was obsessed by not giving comfort to the bourgeoisie. Olivier Todd comments that Sartre's hatred of the bourgeoisie seems 'more theological and psychological than sociological.' His quintessential bourgeois (like Mathieu's brother Jacques in *The Age of Reason*), is a lying swine, exploiter, philistine parvenu, a theoretical partisan of the rights of man who yet practised colonialism. In finally denouncing Camus as a bourgeois, he accused him of objective complicity in all these sins—plus a kind of ignorant frivolity and posturing. Talented as an artist, certainly, but no kind of thinker.[19]

Problems of chronology apart, how faithful are de Beauvoir's fictional characters, Dubreuilh and Henri, to the real Sartre and Camus? She herself later played down the correspondences, denied she had written a *roman à clef*, and affected to despise the 'gossips': 'The extent and the manner of the fiction's dependence upon real life is of small importance; the fiction is built only by pulverizing all these sources and then allowing a new existence to be reborn from them. The gossips who poke about among the ashes let the work that is offered them escape, and the shards they rout out are worth nothing...'[20] Yet De Beauvoir proceeds immediately to play the 'gossip' and 'poke around' her own novel. Was the character Anne really de Beauvoir? A full (interesting) paragraph on that. Was the character Henri really Camus (as many had assumed)? Is the Dubreuilh character really Sartre? A great deal more 'poking around' follows, highly illuminating but seemingly in flat contradiction of her stricture about small gossipy minds pursuing trivial questions.

Sartre and his circle detested 'the god that failed' syndrome which dominated the Western media by the late 1940s. Simone de Beauvoir recalled how the American journalist Louis Fischer, once a fellow-traveller and later a contributor to *The God that Failed*, took Sartre into a corner 'and explained the horrors of the Soviet regime.... Eyes burning with an aberrant fanaticism, he related breathlessly stories of disappearances, treason, liquidiation, doubtless true, but neither the meaning (*sens*) nor the implication (*portée*) of which one understood.'[21] Mounting his campaign to expose the reality of Soviet forced labour camps in *The Mandarins*, de Beauvoir's Koestler-figure, Scriassine, produces unseemly characters like the American journalist 'Bennet' who, we are told, has spent 'fifteen years' as a correspondent in Moscow – here de Beauvoir displays ignorance of the realities governing Soviet visas for the American press. She has Bennet supporting Scriassine's anti-Soviet stance while pleading that State Department imperialism does not represent the American people or the left-wing American unions. De Beauvoir stuffs her American characters into the most improbable moulds; they emerge with bizarre contours and are easily reduced to mincemeat.

Following the Liberation the bourgeoisie – as viewed by de Beauvoir— showed its true, philistine colours by oozing gratitude to the Americans – all those silk-stocking tarts—whereas de Beauvoir's circle were convinced that the battle of the French beaches had taken place at Stalingrad, not in Normandy. Finding herself seated opposite some Red Army soldiers in the Paris Metro, she almost fainted with pleasure until her companion, a woman friend of Russian origin, attempted to speak to the young Ivans in fluent Russian, whereupon suspicion darkened their fair brows and they glowered.

Anti-Americanism within the French intellectual Left was almost as much a matter of culture, of style, as of politics. Light is shed on this by de Beauvoir's unlikely love affair with the Chicago-based writer Nelson Algren – to whom *The Mandarins* is dedicated. Algren was an ex-Communist, pro-Wallace leftist whose passport remained withdrawn by the State Department throughout the 1950s, but this accident-prone, heavy-drinking, gambling macho male of the Chicago street scene frequently failed the political tests of the Left Bank. By letter she berated him (in English) as 'a very arrogant, narrow-minded American man.... Yea, you have got dollars and atomic bomb, but French is a good language, too, and you could try to learn it'.[22]

Koestler described Sartre as a 'malevolent goblin or gargoyle' and de Beauvoir as 'a planet shining with reflected light.' De Beauvoir saw Koestler as a tumultuous newcomer, an interesting man who took himself appallingly seriously when drunk, and who made toes curl by constantly referring to his own publications. He was vain and self-important but also full of warmth, life, curiosity—yet cut off from others by his personal obsessions. 'One night I got so drunk I let him come home with me. We slept together. It wasn't any good. It didn't mean anything. He was too drunk, so was I. It never happened again... I really detested him, that arrogant fool.'[23] This seems to have been the night of 23 October 1946. Several days after their one-night stand Koestler recorded in his diary: '...two nightmare hours with Simone.'

De Beauvoir's portrait of Koestler is complex and perceptive—far from his venomous and implausible caricature of her in *The Age of Longing*. Venomous caricatures were his speciality, not hers. De Beauvoir's character Scriassine's first name is Victor but she hardly ever uses it, even in bed. His most famous publication is said to be *Le Paradis rouge*. He smiles a lot, plays chess, and does not conceal his contempt for the myopic French Left: 'In France you have never felt the pressure of history in all its urgency.' The country of Diderot, Hugo, and Jaurès imagines that culture and politics go hand in hand. Paris has long taken itself for Athens. But Athens, says Scriassine, no longer exists. He (unlike the real Koestler) freely admits the existence of 'American imperialism' and equates its expansionism with that of Russian totalitarianism. One or the other must carry the day – Dubreuilh's dream of an independent, socialist Europe is a chimera. The disaster for Europe will be incomparably greater if Soviet Communism wins. Anne's response is passionate: 'Don't tell me that in the case of a conflict you would hope for an American victory!'[24]

Novelists develop mannerisms of which they are probably not aware. They resemble nervous ticks. In Koestler's novels characters do a lot of smiling. Smiles come thick and fast as nouns and verbs. 'He smiled' may substitute for 'he said.' De Beauvoir's comparable tick, doubtless unconscious, is to have characters frequently shrugging their shoulders. '*Il haussa les epaules.*' Virtually everyone shrugs regardless of sex or political orientation. Yet by an odd playback, she endows her character Scriassine with the habit of smiling. Paradoxically the fictional de Beauvoir, as depicted in Koestler's *The Age of Longing*, is never seen to smile. She is, after all, a Soviet agent.

De Beauvoir's alter ego Anne nevertheless finds Scriassine fascinating and perhaps entertains a womanly desire to get behind the cynical exterior. She accepts his invitation to dinner. They meet in the bar of the Ritz. She enjoys the novelty of drinking whisky. She does not feel like sleeping with anyone, but he has a room in the hotel paid for by the Franco-American review he works for. Scriassine does not proposition Anne 'point blank' (*de but en blanc*), instead he asks what she would answer if a man for whom she had some sympathy were to proposition her point blank. She says that would depend. He cannot abide the prevarication: 'How can we talk about politics or psychology with this question gnawing at us (*qui nous rôdera tans la tête?*') As soon as she consents—'*Soit, ce sera oui*—he invites her up to his room. 'Straight away?' 'Why not? You can see that we have nothing more to say to one another.'

Taken in his embrace, Anne closes her eyes and hears disturbing words: 'It seems as if the young girl is afraid (*intimidée*). We won't harm the young girl; we will deflower her but without harming her.' She is shocked: 'I had not come here to play the violated little thing (*pucelle*), or any other game.'

In bed, he fires a 'brutal' question: '*Tu n'es pas bouchée?* (literally, 'blocked' as the neck of a wine bottle is blocked by a cork.) She says no but does not discuss with him (or us) the arguments for diaphragms, condoms or coitus interruptus. Soon he says imperiously, 'Open your eyes.' Then he puts his penis in her hand 'with authority,' senses her lack of enthusiasm, reproaches her: '*Tu n'as pas un vrai amour pour le sexe de l'homme.*' She thinks to herself: 'How can one love this piece of flesh if one does not love the whole man?' As soon as he enters her he begins to talk. 'Tell me what you feel. Tell me.' She tells him not to worry about her, to let her be. He speaks with anger: 'You're not cold. It's your head resisting. But I will force you.' (This sounds very like Koestler, whether his novels or his life.) She sees a 'veritable hatred' in his eyes. Then comes the violence: '"So you don't want it," he said. "You don't want to! Stubborn mule [*tête de mule*]"! He struck me lightly on the cheek. I was too tired to escape into anger; I began to tremble: a fist descending; a thousand fists.... "Violence is everywhere," I thought; I trembled and tears began to flow.' She doesn't regret the sexual encounter: 'One learns so many things about a man in bed! Much more than by obliging him to ramble (*divaguer*) for weeks on a divan.'

Next day she meets Scriassine in a coffee bar and tells him that he had seemed hostile in bed. He shrugs (as de Beauvoir's characters do) and suggests that a certain hostility was inevitable since she does not fully embrace his politics.[25] Then he adds: 'In bed, to detest a little is not a bad thing.' This she finds horrible. The portrait of Scriassine-Koestler is more than a revenge for his of her in *The Age of Longing*; it sticks.

13

Commentary: Soviet Forced Labour Camps

Progressive Western intellectuals agonised over the truth or falsity of press reports of Soviet forced labour on a massive scale. The Webbs, Laski and many others were taken in by the showcase, GPU-run prison at Bolchevo, with its model factories, libraries and educational facilities. They began by lauding humanitarian prison reform and ended by ignoring or condoning the creation of a new hell on earth. They rejoiced over the abolition of capital punishment in a country where a human life was often not worth a death certificate. Harold Laski lauded Soviet justice; by bringing judges, social workers and trade union officials into close collaboration, it was now a model for the world. At Bolchevo, he was told that all punishments were in the hands of the prisoners themselves. Bernard Shaw observed that whereas an English delinquent entered prison an ordinary man and emerged a criminal, in Russia it was the reverse – 'but for the difficulty of inducing him to come out at all'. He had observed Soviet prisoners taking the greatest delight in making tennis rackets. An affirmation by Gorky stirred the Webbs: 'Out of the ranks of the lawbreakers of fifteen years there were salvaged, in the colonies and communes of the OGPU, thousands of highly qualified workers and more than 100 agronomists, engineers, physicians and technicians. In the bourgeois countries such a thing is impossible...' At Bolchevo, wrote Ella Winter, one sees no walls, no guards, no convict uniforms, 'no bent heads.'

In Simone de Beauvoir's fictional account, *The Mandarins*, what brings the political divide between Dubreuilh (Sartre) and Henri (Camus) to a point of irredeemable bitterness is the fraught issue of Soviet forced labour camps. Later de Beauvoir recalled how, in *The Mandarins*, she had given the impression that French intellectuals had discovered the full facts about Soviet camps as early as 1946 although in reality it came to a head only in 1949. By 1946 the documentary evidence existed; only by 1949 (she claims) was the evidence fully understood.[1] Fully understood by whom? De Beauvoir implicitly depicts her own Left Bank circle as the avant-garde of perception. The French Left had long discounted reliable reports of forced labour in the USSR. Orwell commented in *Partisan Review* (winter 1945) that if it could be proven that 'Russian concentration camps in the Arctic actually exist and that they contain eighteen million prisoners as some observers claim, I doubt whether this would make much impression on the russophile section of the public'.[2]

Albert Camus's[3] attitude had more in common with Orwell's, empirical rather than 'dialectical,' common decency rather than proletarian morality—except that Camus emerged from the Resistance on broadly friendly terms with the fellow-travellers whom Orwell detested. In October 1944 Camus had written that 'Anti-Communism is the beginning of dictatorship'.[4] By the end of 1946 he was less sure; De Beauvoir herself recalls how, in December of that year, at a party, Camus accused Maurice Merleau-Ponty of trying to justify the Moscow trials in 'Le Yogi et le Prolétarien,' his riposte to Koestler's 'The Yogi and the Commissar.' Sartre joined in the argument, supporting Merleau-Ponty; Camus walked out, slamming the door. Sartre pursued him into the street but he refused to come back.[5] The following year the Party ideologist Jean Kanapa announced that Camus had taken his place among the 'bourgeois fascisants'—a much favoured word at that time, falling short of 'fascist,' or even 'neo-fascist,' but suggesting 'on the way to fascism.'[6]

In October 1948, Camus commented that Soviet camps were no more acceptable than Nazi ones.[7] De Beauvoir was to some degree minimising Camus's antipathy to the USSR when, in *The Mandarins*, she has Henri Perron seeming to share Dubreuilh's total attachment to the USSR as the beacon of the future. There would be 'no hope on earth' (thinks Henri) if the Soviet Union stood no chance of 'becoming what she ought to be.'[8] In one of her many uses of indirect narrative, de Beauvoir grants Henri a long mental soliloquy: silence about the Soviet camps would be a defeat and a misuse of his own carefully guarded independence. And yet, good chap that he is, Henri still prefers the USSR to the U.S. Dubreuilh and his consort Anne admit that in the Soviet Union 'on traitait les travailleurs en criminals pour s'autoriser à les exploiter.'[9] But the admission is a private one, confined to comrades – it is not for publication.

The character Scriassine (Koestler) solicits the collaboration of Dubreuilh and Henri in exposing the full facts about Soviet forced labour. They are all united in the left independent SRL, Dubreuilh's brainchild, but Dubreuilh believes it is not the time to publicly condemn the Soviet camps because the American-led anti-communist crusade is now the main enemy. The crunch comes on pages 370-380, when Scriassine and the Soviet émigré Peltov try to poison Henri's mind against Dubreuilh: why has he not been attacked in 'la presse coco' for three months? Surely he had secretly joined the PC at the end of June? When Henri later challenges Dubreuilh about this point-blank, but without citing his sources, the author puts us inside Henri's head as he hears Dubreuilh's indignant denial: 'he looked sincere but it was the air of sincerity he would have had if he had been lying.'[10]

Dubreuilh has entered politics; his head is full of realpolitik. At the onset of the Cold War the need not to 'give comfort to the enemy' was as pervasive as during the Spanish Civil War and the run-up to the Second World War. Writers and intellectuals took up positions as 'strategists of the truth' – who was the ultimate enemy? 'Think about it,' Dubreuilh says to Henri. 'If the referendum and the elections are not a triumph for the left, we risk a Gaullist dictatorship. It is not the moment to support anti-Communist propaganda.' To do so would be 'criminal.' Henri replies that the right-wing paper *Le Figaro* already possessed the new documents on Soviet forced labour. Why let the Right seize the moral issue? To force any real change in the USSR the European Left must speak out. 'In any case we will be forced to declare our position.' In response Dubreuilh argues that although the Soviet camps exist, and are deplorable, they are not an integral necessity of the Soviet system.[11] Moreover, the Parti communiste remains the sole hope of the French proletariat. Dubreuilh's face and hands have turned white as he realises that a break between himself and Henri is imminent.

Henri goes ahead, writes and publishes in the newspaper *L'Espoir* his denunciation of the Soviet camps, while meeting Dubreuilh more than half way: the existence of the camps does not call into question the whole Soviet system; he also emphasises the crimes of capitalism. But a furious Dubreuilh immediately has Henri expelled from the SRL, which henceforward severs its ties with *L'Espoir*.

In de Beauvoir's novel it is therefore the issue of silence about Soviet forced labour camps rather than the problem of interpretation which fatally divides Robert and Henri; in reality, when Camus's *The Rebel* (*L'Homme révolté*, 1951) came under attack in Sartre's journal, *Les Temps modernes*, it was because of Camus's broad, historical interpretation of Soviet ideology as fatally and irredeemably totalitarian. Indeed Sartre and Merleau-Ponty had already publicly acknowledged, in *Les Temps modernes*, the existence of ten million prisoners incarcerated in the forced-labour camps of the USSR.[12] The key events in persuading Sartre to voice this admission were two libel trials held in Paris in 1949. For Simone de Beauvoir it was the Kravchenko trial which established beyond doubt the existence of the camps. The crucially convincing witness was a former German Communist of cosmopolitan outlook, a well-connected intellectual, Margarete Buber-Neumann. Her grimly authentic story, *Under Two Dictators*, was published in the same year she gave evidence in Paris. Exiled in Moscow, Buber-Neumann had been caught up in the terror. In April 1937, her husband Heinz Neumann was arrested by the NKVD in the Lux Hotel, where many foreigners resided. The search commando leader announced: 'Sixty books of Trotskyite, Zinovievite, Kamenevite, and Bukharinite content confiscated...' She never saw him again. Margarete's turn came in June 1938. One after another of her friends had been seized. 'Every room in this wing [of the Lux Hotel] held a similar tragedy. Mothers and wives spent their days going from one prison to the other in the hope of finding out the whereabouts of husband or son.... At night they waited for their own arrest. For weeks and months the bag which was to accompany them to Siberia stood ready packed in a corner.'[13]

She found herself with other German women, all anti-Nazis, in Birma concentration camp in the Karanganda complex. She was 'No. 174,475. Margarete Genrichovna Buber-Neumann. Socially dangerous element. Five years.' 'On one occasion my work consisted of carrying sacks of grain from a cleansing machine up into a barn along a narrow plank. The sacks were heavy and many of the women groaned and grunted under the burden.'[14] She fell ill. Some time after the Nazi-Soviet Pact these women were suddenly transported back to Moscow, their legs wrapped in lice-infested rags to keep out the cold. Returning to the Butyrki prison, she found herself with twenty-three German women, some of them famous 'politicals' or the wives of prominent Communists. The prisoners were suddenly well treated and none could fathom why: two boiled eggs for breakfast and lunch even better, a good borshch with a slice of meat in it, then goulash with mashed potatoes, followed by kissel or stewed apples.

Among her fellow-prisoners she came across Brecht's friend the actress Carola Neher, who had played Polly in the film of the Brecht-Weill *Threepenny Opera*. After the Nazi seizure of power, Neher had fled to Prague, where she married a German engineer. Arriving in Moscow with him, she began to work in films and radio but was arrested in 1936 and sentenced to ten years' hard labour. She had never again seen her son, one year old at the time of her arrest. Invited to act as an NKVD spy in prison, she had refused; in reprisal she was put in solitary confinement without heating or a bed or food. Now Neher had been brought back to Moscow from a hard labour camp with a shorn head. During the Cold War, Brecht's Western detractors, notably Koestler, were to allege that he had done nothing to help his former mistress when he visited the Soviet Union in 1936.

Margarete Buber-Neumann resumed her story: 'Another pleasant surprise was in store for us. One day we were taken out of our cell into a room full of women's clothing...shoes, hats, coats, gloves. They were second-hand and rather old-fashioned, but...another proof, almost indisputable, that we were a step nearer to freedom.' In reality she was a step nearer the SS, to whom she was handed over at Brest-Litovsk with thirty other German anti-Nazis. 'The SS commandant and the GPU officer saluted each other.... We went over the bridge... I looked back. The GPU officials still stood there in a group watching us go. Behind them was Soviet Russia. Bitterly I recalled the Communist litany: Fatherland of the Toilers; Bulwark of Socialism; Haven of the Persecuted...'

She was to endure the next five years in Ravensbruck. In 1940, Himmler introduced corporal punishment in the camp—even women were flogged. As the end of the war approached, Margarete's rising fear was that the Russians would reach Ravensbrück before the Americans or British. The Swedish Red Cross arrived and negotiated with the SS the release of 300 French women. Margarete herself got aboard a train carrying German soldiers westward. Finally, she and a companion came upon the Americans. 'They stood there silently spread out in open order.... We came up to the nearest man. He had a round, red, friendly face and he looked at us curiously.' In broken English, she explained the coloured patches on her miserable clothes and her fear of the Russians. '"OK, sister. Go through." And he made a gesture of invitation with his hand. I never heard such a beautiful arrangement of words before in my life.'[15]

Sartre and de Beauvoir absorbed Margarete Buber-Neumann's testimony during the Kravchenko libel trial, but of course the German woman was in no position to provide a comprehensive map of the Gulag. Hot on the heels of the Kravchenko case came another libel action, brought by David Rousset against the same defendants, the Communist literary periodical *Les Lettres françaises*. Sartre's erstwhile colleague in the RDR, David Rousset had visited the U.S. in pursuit of documentary evidence on Soviet camps. 'A fat ex-Trotskyite with several missing teeth and a black patch over one eye,' Rousset was the author of *L'univers concentrationnaire*, an impressive book about survival in Nazi camps.[16] De Beauvoir recalled that he had returned from captivity in Germany a frail skeleton weighing 40 kilos. Now he denounced the Soviet government as representing 'the fiercest social reaction since the disappearance of Nazism.' Writing in *Le Figaro littéraire* (November 1949), Rousset pointed out that a Special Board (OSSO) of the NKVD had been empowered in 1934 to sentence all 'socially dangerous' persons to forced labour for terms up to five years—indeed the 52nd volume of the *Great Soviet Encylopaedia* (1947) confirmed OSSO's powers. Rousset appealed to all former deportees to provide evidence to a commission of inquiry. Meanwhile, throughout October 1949, *Le Figaro* published an extended series of eyewitness testimonies on forced labour. Jules Margoline's 'Cinq Ans dans les camps de concentration soviétiques' was serialized in ten parts.[17]

The PCF responded in predictably fierce terms. *Les Lettres françaises* (17 November) came out with a long polemic by its editor Pierre Daix, accusing Rousset of being a 'menteur éhonté' intent on diverting attention from the crimes of the capitalist world, and of fomenting a new, Hitlerian war against the USSR. Daix denied the existence of forced labour imposed by administrative decision; corrective labour (he said) was limited to a maximum of one month, and could be imposed only by a tribunal of judges elected and revocable by the people.

Perhaps encouraged by the outcome of the Kravchenko affair, Rousset brought a libel action against Daix and *Les Lettres françaises*. Rousset's prime witness was the Austrian physicist Alex Weissberg, once director of the Kharkov Institute of Physics. Arrested in March 1937, Weissburg spent three years in Russian and Ukrainian prisons before being handed over to the Gestapo in 1940, under a secret clause of the Molotov-Ribbentrop Pact – the same fate as Buber-Neumann. Weissberg staged a coup when he produced a testimonial on his behalf, addressed to Stalin himself, written in 1937 by the French Communist scientists Frédéric Joliot-Curie and Jean Perrin. The effect on the court, according to Arthur Koestler, 'was that of a bombshell.'

A number of Communist intellectuals who had been interned in Nazi concentration camps stoutly supported the defendants. Marie-Claude Vaillant-Couturier, a prosecution witness at the Nuremberg trial who had narrowly survived in Auschwitz, declared that Rousset's investigations were 'contrary to the interests of France.'[18] The defence witnesses constantly reverted to the patriotic-chauvinistic leitmotivs of the Second World War. Claude Morgan, editor of *Les Lettres françaises*, stood up to protest against a 'German' (Weissberg) testifying in the German language in a French court against the USSR. Maître Théo Bernard, representing Rousset, asked Jean Laffitte, secretary general of the World Peace Council, whether he would condemn such camps if they did exist. The reply was this: 'You might as well ask me whether I would condemn my mother if she was an assassin. My mother is my mother and not an assassin.'[19]

The legal upshot was similar to that in the Kravchenko case: nominal damages (100,000 francs) were awarded to Rousset. The PCF prolonged the judicial appeals until 1953, without success.[20] A letter to the *New York Times* signed by a group of prominent liberal anti-Communists, declared the Paris trial to have been 'nothing less than a full-dress indictment of the entire system of slave labour...comparable in moral significance and surpassing in human scope the Dreyfus trial of a half-century ago'.[21] Yet Sartre and Merleau-Ponty questioned Rousset's motives for revealing the truth about Soviet labour camps. Why had he refused to take part in parallel inquiries into conditions in the French colonial empire, in Franco's Spain, and in Greece? Rousset was promoting the unacceptable theory of Enemy Number One—the Soviet Union.[22] What about the recent crimes committed in the name of freedom, including forced labour conditions in the colonies? This dire logic repeated itself when the Communist press responded angrily to the acknowledgment by Sartre and Merleau-Ponty that forced labour was operated on a massive scale in the USSR, involving between ten and fifteen million detainees. Utterly ignoring their evidence, Pierre Daix posed the familiar question: 'With whom are you? With the people of the Soviet Union, who are building a new society, or with their enemies?' (Later Daix was to disown the PCF line on everything.)[23]

14

Koestler and the Little Flirts

Although less well known (deservedly) than his earlier fiction, Koestler's *The Age of Longing* (1951) deserves some attention as an often frenetic assertion that the god had indeed failed. The rampant sarcasm and scorn speak so loud as to produce a form of satire sometimes verging on blatant cartoon. This is certainly a *roman à clef* to the extent that the reader is meant to identify the characters with some cardinal quality in their real-life models – but here again Koestler's appetite for sarcastic parody often blurs the outlines. The novel confirms Koestler's addiction to neo-Freudian theories of political maladjustment.

The Age of Longing was squeezed out of a life of political activism, essay writing, and frenetic hedonism well described in the diary kept by his future wife, Mamaine Paget. The entry for 17 October 1946 reads: 'Paris by air. Met by Arthur, very depressed. We had some calvados in various cafés and later a wonderful evening dining in Montmartre, going to cafés and bals musettes, then to the Lapin Agile [a chansonnier where traditional songs were sung]...and finally we ate oysters and drank Alsatian wine in a bistro called Victor on the Bd. de Montmartre at 4.30 A.M.'[1] By 1948 *Darkness at Noon* had sold half a million copies in the U.S. Published in France after the war as *Le Zéro et l'Infini*, it sold 420,000 copies and was fiercely denigrated by the Communists. By Koestler's account they bought up entire stocks from provincial bookshops in order to destroy them. Koestler clearly relished his provocative, indeed pariah, presence in left-wing Paris. On 6 August 1950, the Party's weekly paper, *L'Action*, revealed that Koestler's villa at Fontaine Le Port was the 'headquarters of the Cold War' and that Koestler was training 'Fascist thugs to form a terrorist militia'.[2]

Clearly *The Age of Longing* is an act of reprisal against French intellectuals critical of *Darkness at Noon* and *The Yogi and the Commissar*, notably Sartre, de Beauvoir and their colleague Maurice Merleau-Ponty, author of *Humanisme et Terreur* (1947) and co-founder with Sartre of *Les Temps modernes*.[3] Another target is Louis Aragon, an unconditional apologist for the Moscow trials. Writing in *Commune* (1937), Aragon had insisted that to cast doubt on this or that detail of the indictments was to imply that it was not Hitler who set fire to the Reichstag, to exonerate the role of Hitler and the Gestapo in Spain...*en fait, ils sont les avocats d'Hitler et de la Gestapo.*[4]

By contrast, Merleau-Ponty's *Humanisme et Terreur* dismissed the Moscow prosecutors' allegations as unfounded in hard fact, and as 'crimes' only from a Stalinist historical perspective. According to Merleau-Ponty, Koestler's analysis of the Bukharin trial in *Darkness at Noon* was wide of the mark because Bukharin really did understand the historical motive for his condemnation, the objective link between the Right Opposition and the kulaks' resistance to collectivization.[5] Merleau-Ponty speculated that the condemned Bolsheviks might in the future be rehabilitated when a new phase of history had altered the significance of their conduct. He insisted that there is no such thing as objective justice divorced from politics: the same French magistrates had condemned the Communist Resistance, then condemned the anti-Communist collaborators. Violence exists, Merleau-Ponty explained, and the only question is whether some violence is progressive and tends in the long run to suppress violence by eradicating its causes. This was the only valid 'dialectical' approach. Koestler was put down as an ex-Communist, sadly ignorant of Marxism, striving to purge himself of guilt. In his new-found sympathy for the 'yogis' of capitalist democracy, Koestler had forgotten that such 'yogis' fostered poverty, created wars and oppressed colonial peoples.[6] Although Orwell's opinion of Merleau-Ponty's argument is not discovered, it can readily be imagined. Paradoxically, the handsome French philosopher became the lover of Orwell's future wife, Sonia Brownell.

Koestler had succeeded Orwell as London correspondent of the New York magazine, *Partisan Review*. Early in March 1948, acting on a recommendation from the U.S. embassy in Paris, the State Department advised the attorney general that, although a former Communist barred under the regulations, Koestler's entry into the U.S. was 'highly desirable in the national interest.' On 12 March, Koestler embarked on the *Queen Mary*, following a meeting in Paris with Malraux and U.S. ambassador Chip Bohlen.[7] On board ship he discussed psychological warfare with John Foster Dulles; on arrival he did the same with General Bill Donovan, wartime head of OSS and one of the architects of the CIA. He lunched with Henry and Clare Luce and with Cyrus Sulzberger. All contacts were at the top level. He addressed a packed Carnegie Hall, with prominent East European exiles arranged behind him on the platform. The 'Babbits of the Left,' he told his audience, had to get 'seven deadly fallacies' out of their heads, among them the confusion of 'socialism' with the USSR, the guilt-ridden refusal to prefer American 'imperialism' to Soviet totalitarianism, and the refusal to believe that twice two is four even if the Hearst press and the witch-hunters said the same.

Richard Crossman, an intellectual Labour MP and editor of *The God that Failed* (1949), a collection of six essays of disenchantment, recalled the heated argument with Koestler out of which the book (in France *Le Dieu des ténèbres*) was born. "'Either you can't or you won't understand," said Koestler. "It's the same with all you comfortable, insular, Anglo-Saxon anti-Communists. You hate our Cassandra cries and resent us as allies—but, when all is said, we ex-Communists are the only people on your side who know what it's all about.'" [8] Wartime head of the German section of the Psychological Warfare Executive, Crossman developed *The God that Failed* project with the publisher Hamish Hamilton in London and with Cass Canfield (of Harper) in New York. The project epitomised the ongoing collaboration of intellectuals and intelligence agencies. Crossman sent each of the six essays for publication in *Der Monat*, a monthly sponsored by the U.S. High Commission in Germany. The Foreign Office, meanwhile, obtained permission to distribute Koestler's contribution in the British Zone of Germany.[9]

While writing *The Age of Longing*, Koestler became a founding activist of the Congress for Cultural Freedom (CCF).[10] Paradoxically, when he and Mamaine set off for Berlin in June 1950 on 'a kind of intellectual airlift,' as he later put it, they found Sartre in the next sleeper at the Gare de l'Est—their first meeting since relations were broken off eighteen months earlier. Koestler may not have mentioned to Sartre that he had been cruelly satirising him and Simone de Beauvoir as 'Professor and Madame Pontieux' in *The Age of Longing*.

The Age of Longing is anticipated in two polemics, 'The Little Flirts of St. Germain des Prés,' first published in *Le Figaro Littéraire* (July 1949), and 'Les Temps héroïques' (a caustic allusion to *Les Temps modernes*), describing a Paris ravaged and poverty stricken after a 'second liberation' (Soviet occupation). De Beauvoir appears as Sinaida Bovarovna at the publishing house Gallimardov, a frigid woman of letters who engages in blood-curdling revolutionary rhetoric and works on 'dialectical language'—liberty becomes 'the right to vote for the unanimous list of the unanimous people.' The Paris press is Soviet-controlled and censorship is rife. Bovarovna's Committee for Vigilance over Liberty and Press denounces Malraux and Camus as 'agents of the Vatican'.[11]

Koestler had long since adopted the psychoanalytical approach to political radicalism which became in the 1950s a key component of Western Cold War culture. According to his caustic analysis in 'The Little Flirts,' the 'loyalty' displayed by the anti-anti-Communists is not simply devotion to the Soviet Union but also 'loyalty to the world of adolescence, the revolt against family and convention, the nausea of puberty, translated into the idiom of the class struggle...loyalty to that urge for self-castigation, inherent in the artist's condition, which, among the intellectuals of the Left, expresses itself in an abject prostration before the "proletariat" – not, to be sure, before the real victim of social injustice, but before a legendary and apocryphal figure, half Messiah, half Buffalo Bill'.[12]

Ignoring the concrete issues one might find discussed in the left-wing press, whether in France or Britain—McCarthyism, colonial rearguard wars or West

German re-armament, for example—Koestler continued his giddy ride across an archipelago of mixed metaphors when discussing 'the little flirts': 'With them it is always Yes and No – or rather "Oh no, please don't"... They are only happy doing a verbal pirouette on the tightrope over the No Man's Land, suspended between heaven and earth.'[13] So: semi-virgins, Peeping Toms, tricoteuses, fallen angels, Paradise, little flirts, tightrope, No Man's Land, heaven and earth.

Koestler was a prominent subscriber to the dominant interpretive trend in mid-century Western political science, the alchemic mutation of neurosis and self-hatred into political radicalism. In his essay, 'A Guide to Political Neuroses' (1953), he writes of a 'political libido,' a 'political unconscious,' and its 'repressed memories,' adding: 'For nearly every aberration of the sexual drive we can find a corresponding type of disturbance in the political libido.'[14] Awkward facts are censored and become repressed complexes. This scheme 'will be seen to cover the whole range of political pathology, from the "controlled schizophrenia" of [the atom spy] Klaus Fuchs, through the wish-dream world of the Stockholm peace campaigner, to the flight from reality of the "neutralist"... generally speaking, the Left is politically over-sexed.' The busybody whose name is on every progressive committee and who has embraced every good cause 'is the political equivalent of a nymphomaniac.'[15] As for the despised 'political masochist,' 'The slightest injustice in his own country wrings from him cries of despair, but he finds excuses for the most heinous crimes committed in the opposite camp...' For example: 'When a coloured tennis-player is refused a room in a London luxury hotel, [he] quivers with spontaneous indignation...'[16]

Completed at Fontaine le Port in July 1950, *The Age of Longing* appeared in March 1951 and went into the American bestseller lists. The preface explains that the events described 'have not yet taken place,' the time setting being the imminent future, 'the middle 1950s.' A lethargic, decadent Western elite is shown rolling over with its feet in the air as the Red Army prepares to dine out along the banks of the Seine. Koestler reverts to the thinly allegorical approach employed eight years earlier in his novel *Arrival and Departure*. The USSR, never referred to by name, is re-styled the Commonwealth of Freedomloving People (or 'Peoples'?) – but henceforward we shall say 'Soviet' to avoid tedium. The Father of Peoples (sometimes the Father of the People) dies during the course of the novel. The French Communist Party and its satellites are called The Movement—a term likewise anticipated in *Arrival and Departure* but on that occasion given to pro-Nazis.

And so to his fictional characters. Professor Pontieux, 'the famous French philosopher,' must be Sartre although Koestler endows him with wrong physical characteristics, 'tall and gawky,' and misleading biographical details: Pontieux is old enough to have lost his only son during war. Quite probably Merleau-Ponty is grafted on to the Pontieux figure. 'He can prove everything he believes, and he believes everything he can prove.'[17] Pontieux has launched a philosophy called 'neo-nihilism' in his famous work 'Negation and Position,' which had been the fashionable craze after the war (clearly Sartre's *Being and Nothingness*). During a lecture Pontieux gets lost in his text, upsets a water glass, and declares, 'Man is only true to himself when he surpasses the limitations inherent in his nature.' Here Koestler's jibe at Merleau-Ponty (as well as Sartre) is by no means wide of the mark: 'Pontieux went on to explain that only in a planned society could man surpass his own limitations through the voluntary acceptance of the necessary curtailments of his freedom. As often as not, history realised its aims by the negation of its own negations. Thus in certain circumstances democracy may manifest itself under the outward form of a dictatorship, whereas in another situation dictatorship may appear under the guise of democracy.'[18]

The figure of Madame Mathilda Pontieux must be aimed at Simone de Beauvoir—her hair is 'done up in a classic bun,' she has 'classic if wilting features,' and a deep, 'slow, insulting voice.' She sneers at Koestler's ficitious Soviet writer Leontiev because he is on the brink of defection to the West: 'Don't forget to learn to like chewing gum and to spit at a Negro when you see one. Otherwise you can't become a Hero of Culture in New York.' And more: 'You think you have come to a free country [France], and you don't seem to realise that you have come to a country under foreign occupation, in the process of being transformed into a colony.... You cannot enter a café or a restaurant without finding it full of Americans who behave as if the place belonged to them. They tip the waiters fantastic sums, so they get all the attention and French customers are treated like dirt.'

Koestler places his own vocabulary on the tongue of Madame Pontieux, although de Beauvoir's writings never approach political commitment in Freudian terms. Discussing Soviet aims, she declares, 'The point is that if you know you are going to be raped you might as well...convince yourself that your ravisher is the man of your dreams.'[19] (In *The Mandarins* the heroine discerns the sadistic side of Scriassine/Koestler, the illusion that 'loneliness can be cured by force.') At the end of *The Age of Longing*, with a pro-Soviet putsch imminent, we are told that Pontieux has been arrested by the French government but not his wife, though she is the real Soviet agent 'which poor Pontieux never guessed'.[20] He is 'just a clever imbecile' according to Koestler's alter ego, Julien Delattre.

We have mentioned Koetler's character Leontiev, an honoured Soviet writer about to defect while visiting France. Here, even given the persecutorial climate of Zhdanovism, Koestler cannot resist gross exaggeration: Leontiev 'presided at the periodical courts-martial at which those convicted of formalism, neo-Kantianism, titroskism, veritism and whatnotism were given their deserved punishment'.[21] Koestler's invented vocabularies, unlike Orwell's in *Nineteen Eighty-Four*, arrive with a slapdash sneer. The most influential intellectual in the PCF, the imperial poet and novelist Louis Aragon (wose favoured pen name was simply Aragon), is wheeled in as 'Emile Navarin.' Chairing a Peace Rally, Navarin warmly introduces Comrade Leontiev—although in last Friday's issue of the Soviet magazine 'Freedom and Culture,' Leontiev had called Navarin 'a decadent vermin who had wormed his way into the Movement by systematic double-dealing and deception'. (In reality, Aragon was always honoured in the Soviet press, 'vermin,' incidentally, were invariably plural, never singular). Koestler tells us that 'Navarin' (Aragon) started his speech with a demand 'that the teaching of History in the schools should start with 1917 and all that went before should be written off as rubbish'. This is stupefying nonsense given the PCF's devotion to the French Revolution classical-humanist heritage. No Marx? As usual, Koestler took his Anglo-American readers for simpletons.

Koestler was addicted to sexual metaphors – 'prostitute,' 'the old whore,' 'virginity' – all in political contexts.[22] The Sartre-character, Pontieux, is a 'syphilitic spider.' Soviet spokesmen call reactionaries 'syphilitic flunkeys.' The young Soviet Party man, Fedya Nikitin, working in the Paris embassy as a cultural attaché, compares living abroad to inhabiting 'a colony of syphilitics.'[23] The word 'syphilitic' was inconceivable on the Soviet official tongue.

In *The Age of Longing*, the liberal, anti-Communist intellectual, Julien De-lattre, stands in for Koestler. 'Read more history,' he commands the American heroine Hydie angrily. 'Its caravan-routes are strewn with the skeletons of people who were thirsting for faith – and their faith made them drink salt water and eat the sand, believing it was the Lord's supper.' Julien further explains to Hydie: 'Now I happen to believe that Europe is doomed, a chapter in history which is drawing to its finish. That is so to speak my contemplative truth.... But I also happen to believe in the ethical imperative of fighting evil, even if the fight is hopeless...'

None of the main characters is positioned to monopolise our attention. The narrative moves back and forth between various points of view and thoughts and biographies, including that of the young Bolshevik cultural attaché Fyodor (Fedya) Grigorievich Nikitin. Viewed as the real enemy, a potential Gletkin, Fedya has the effect of arresting Koestler's self-destructive sarcasm about the 'French 'flu' and 'little flirts'; indeed Koestler invariably raises the level of his writing when describing the commissars—respect turns to empathy and a more imaginative presentation. Fedya Nikitin is physically unblemished, fit, virile, threatening; Western man cowers, sick, doomed. Now working in mid-fifties Paris, Nikitin explains his Bolshevik commitment to his new mistress, the American girl Hydie, in effect describing himself as a member of Stalin's new class. 'My father was a member of the revolutionary proletariat and was killed by the counter-revolution... I joined the Youth Movement and later the Party. When the rich peasants opposed the collectivization to sabotage the Five Year Plan, I was mobilised by the Party and sent back to the Kaukasus to help with bringing in the harvest.... When that was finished the Party sent me to the University... [to study] history, literature, diamat and culture in general.'[24]

Descended from Irish landowners on her mother's side and from West Point soldiers on her father's side, Hydie nervously asks Fedya what 'diamat' means.

Koestler's portrait of Malraux (Georges de St. Hilaire) is generous and admiring. St Hilaire is already forming a new Resistance group, partly out of nostalgia for the last one, partly because he believes that 'in the gesture alone, regardless of purpose, can the dignity of man find its ultimate fulfilment'.[25] What we know of Koestler's own meetings with Malraux verges on comedy. On 29 October 1946, they all met at Malraux's flat—Koestler, Sartre, Camus, Sperber. Koestler's mistress Mamaine Paget sent a vivid portrait of Malraux to her sister: 'He is very rich and has an enormous flashy flat...horrible and very bare and *ungemütlich*. The walls are hung with large modern paintings and reproductions of Piero della Francesca.... We were given some whisky but not invited to sit down.... Malraux obviously has an ex-ophthalmic goitre, for his eyes protrude and he talks non-stop to the accompaniment of curious sounds at the back of his nose and throat.... K[oestler] unusually humble and hardly able to get a word in edgeways...'[26] In October 1947, she and Koestler dined with Malraux and his wife, meeting up in the Pallas-Athénée, 'an enormous luxurious bar full of glamorous demi-mondaines in extravagant clothes'. Malraux 'got very tight' but she gathered that his subject was the gamble he was taking in backing de Gaulle: 'When K[oestler] said "What about the General's entourage?", Malraux replied "*L'entourage du Général, c'est moi*"...after a bit he said '*Je suis le plus grand philosophe du monde*'...[27]

Koestler's fictional Soviet cultural attaché Fyodor Nikitin has been keeping a notebook containing lists of cultural figures, Malraux included, to be interned or liquidated when the time comes. It will come soon – a military invasion of Europe is imminent, assisted by the fifth column and a lack of physical and mental resistance. Julien explains to Hydie how the clean-up will be conducted, the task being to eliminate all possible centres of resistance, the foci of all independent thought and action.[28] 'Needless to point out that if the French intellectuals working for this outfit had their way, nine out of ten of their colleagues and competitors would be shipped to the Arctic, including their dearest Party comrades.'[29]

At page 232, between books one and two, comes thirteen pages of 'Interlude,' printed in italics and described by the author as 'a chapter from an as yet unwritten history book on the fall of pre-Pubertarian man.' Beginning with an unexplained X-bomb explosion in the Ural Mountains, this disastrously awkward Interlude confirms that for Koestler fiction had become a dead form – yet still the ideal one for carrying his inevitable AK rape scene between Fedya Nikitin and Hydie. She 'had put up a gallant resistance, so that he had been obliged to take her virtually by force'. An essential part of his enjoyment was to conquer the female's resistance – and she has never had it so good![30]

Informed by Julien Delattre what the Soviet rapist-lover's secret mission amounts to, Hydie carries the report to her father, then to a police commissioner. Having broken with Fedya (who already has a new mistress), Hydie goes to his apartment and shoots him, though not fatally as it turns out. The incident is hushed up. She and her father leave for America, whereas Fedya must now face the Arctic Circle, as guard or prisoner, by way of punishment for a bourgeois liaison which went wrong. 'He could almost feel in his nostrils the biting, cold clean air spiced with the smell of firs, snow and timber...'

Reviewing *The Age of Longing*, even as dedicated an anti-Communist as Edward Crankshaw found Koestler's fervour repellent. James Burnham and Koestler 'now try to whip us up into an active crusade against Communism, using Communism's weapons... they seek to plunge the world into a militant crusade, for one reason alone: to recover their own lost faith.'[31] Writing for *Commentary* (April 1951), Alfred Kazin called *The Age of Longing* an 'exasperated farce' basically contemptuous and weary of human beings in general. Koestler was 'one of those quick-witted ideologues whom our age has raised to prominence not because of their sensibility or depth of moral insight, but because we are grateful to them for their candor and have learned from their sufferings'.[32]

In the preface to his book of essays, *Trail of the Dinosaur*, (1955), Koestler declared his literary-political career to be over.

15

Commentary: Fellow-Travellers

In his regular 'London Letter' for the American journal *Partisan Review* (May 1943), Orwell commented, 'The English left-wing intelligentsia worship Stalin because they have lost their patriotism and their religious belief without losing their need for a god and a fatherland.'[1] Orwell took very seriously three international conferences of intellectuals orchestrated by Moscow in 1948-49: Wroclaw, Paris and New York. Any English or American participant who rebelled against the Moscow line was crossed out of more than one hundred names of suspects listed in his (now notorious) notebook. The historian A. J. P. Taylor, not included in the IRD list, is crossed out of the notebook, reprieved, with the heavily underlined remark, 'Took anti-CP line at Wroclaw Conference [1948].'

In the fictional *Age of Longing* and the essays in *The Trail of the Dinosaur*, Koestler lashes out at 'The pink intellectuals of St. Germain des Prés... the semi-virgins of totalitarian flirtations; the Peeping Toms who watch History's debauches through a hole in the wall; the tricoteuses diligently knitting their novels and editorials in the shadow of the Lubianka. And when we, fallen angels, out of a Paradise transformed into a dark and immense torture-chamber, try to tell them what it was like, the semi-virgins who have never fallen from anywhere, look at us with their innocent, myopic little smile and explain to us that we exaggerate...'[2]

In Victor Serge's *Comrade Tulyaev* we move from Russia's purges to Paris, where Xenia, daughter of the stammering apparatchik Popov, is now desperately trying to rouse opinion against the trial of the distinguished historian Rublev. In a scene which serves as a prototype for mockery of French fellow-travellers (not least Koestler's in *The Age of Longing*), Xenia meets Professor Passereau, 'famous in two hemispheres, President of the Congress for the Defence of Culture, corresponding member of the Moscow Academy of Sciences.' Xenia begs him to intervene on behalf of the distinguished historian Rublev. Passereau expresses sympathy, sighs about revolutions devouring their children, smoothly assures her that if Rublev is innocent he will be reprieved by the 'magnanimity of the Chief of your Party.' 'Furthermore, the League has, properly speaking, but one object – to fight fascism.'[3] Anything which might complicate that cannot be countenanced.

Solzhenitsyn (like Shostakovich privately) mocks Western progressives for being taken in by Soviet propaganda and for laying their personal prestige at the feet of tyranny—Steffens, Dreiser, Shaw, Wells, Rolland, Feuchtwanger, Bloch, the Webbs, Laski and many others may come to mind. The fellow-traveller, in Solzhenitsyn's view, believes what he chooses to believe. In a satirical account[4] of a mythical visit to Butyrki prison by Mrs R[oosevelt], Solzhenitsyn invents a fictitious story about a real person, coyly giving the date as 'the blazing hot summer of 19—.' The setting is clearly postwar (Mrs R is a widow) and in the era of the UN and UNRRA – but presumably it takes place before the Cold War hardened, otherwise she would not have been invited. In short, a chronological never-never land. The distinguished American visitor is greeted by rapidly refurbished cells, prisoners wearing special clothes and enjoying special food—a general whitewash worthy of comic opera. The anguished cries of the prisoners she inspects are translated for her benefit as a unanimous protest against the oppression of blacks in the United States. New regulations are posted on the prison walls: 'You are now permitted...to lie on your bunks day or night... to write your memoirs.' Likewise the sudden arrival of library books by St Augustine and St Thomas Aquinas, a white statue of the Catholic Madonna, plus the Bible, Koran, Talmud, 'and a small dark statuette of the Buddha'. The ingredients of this comical pudding—satire, farce, slapstick—do not blend well. Solzhenitsyn is not a Brecht (*The Rise of Arturo Ui*) or a Chaplin. Much more effective, and moving, is the concluding page of *The First Circle*. The Moscow correspondent of the Paris paper *Libération* is travelling by car to a hockey match, when he catches sight of an impressively spotless van bearing the inscription 'MöCO-Fleisch-Vande-Meat' in four languages. He will duly report how neat and hygienic are Moscow's food delivery vans. In fact, prisoners from Mavrino are within, Gleb Nerzhin among them, on their way to the hell camps of the Gulag.

In *The Unbearable Lightness of Being* (1984), the Czech émigré writer Milan Kundera describes a futile circus of Western intellectuals, celebrities and attendant media who plan to march to the Cambodian frontier to protest the Vietnamese refusal to allow entry to an international medical committee. In the ballroom of a large hotel in Bangkok, the Americans have hijacked a French project and the French protest furiously against the use of English. They reach the Cambodian border by bus. Photographers and cameramen swarm around them. A famous American actress rushes to the front. A Frenchwoman, a professor of linguistics, grabs her by the wrist. 'This is a parade for doctors who have come to care for mortally ill Cambodians, not a publicity stunt for movie stars!' A well-known American photographer then steps back a few paces into a rice field and is blown to pieces by a mine. When the interpreter calls out in Khmer through a megaphone that these people are doctors requesting entry for humanitarian reasons, she is met by a 'stunning silence...a boundless and endlessly indifferent silence.'[5]

Kundera also ventilates an obsession with 'kitsch'. 'What repelled [Sabina] was not nearly so much the ugliness of the Communist world (ruined castles transformed into cow sheds) as the mask of beauty it tried to wear—in other words, Communist kitsch.' Postwar Soviet films gushed kitsch. 'The model of Communist kitsch is the ceremony called May Day. Since the time of the French Revolution, 'What makes a leftist a leftist is not this or that theory but his ability to integrate any theory into the kitsch called the Grand March.' Kundera adds ironically, 'The brotherhood of man on earth will be possible only on a base of kitsch.'[6]

16

Greene: *The Quiet American*

For the long decade that followed victory over Hitler, British (and French) Cold War policy was intimately linked to the colonial rearguard action in Africa and Asia. In British Malaya and French Indochina the linkage between guerrilla insurgency and the influence of Moscow-Peking was real enough. In Kenya, the Canal Zone of Egypt and Algeria, the spectre of Communist influence was artificially propagated to secure American support and neutralise principled opposition at home. Early in 1951, Graham Greene first visited Hanoi. At the time the British press had only one correspondent covering all of Indochina. General de Lattre put a small plane at the famous novelist's disposal, enabling him to visit the Cao Dai, an extraordinarily eclectic political-religious sect with its own pope and its own army. Greene recalled, 'Perhaps there is more direct *reportage* in *The Quiet American* than in any other novel I have written.' 'The press conference is not the only example of direct reporting. I was in the dive bomber...which attacked the Vietminh post and I was on the patrol of the Foreign Legion paras outside Phat Diem. I still retain the sharp image of the dead child crouched in the ditch beside his dead mother.'[1]

When Greene returned to Vietnam in October 1951, he found that after his son's death in combat De Lattre had blamed Catholics espionage; Greene was suspect, a likely British agent not least because he was known to have visited his brother Hugh in Malaya, where he was directing government propaganda. Accordingly, Greene was now put under the supervision of an engagingly cultured inspector of the Sûreté.

Greene describes the genesis of *The Quiet American*. While visiting a self-dramatizing officer of mixed race, Colonel Leroy, he shared a room with an American attached to the economic aid mission. The two drove back to Saigon together (like Greene's fictional Fowler and Pyle): 'My companion bore no resemblance at all to Pyle, the quiet American of my story – he was a man of greater intelligence and less innocence, but he lectured me all the long drive back to Saigon on the necessity of finding "a third force in Vietnam".[2] I had never before come so close to the great American dream which was to bedevil affairs in the East as it was to do in Algeria.'[3] So the subject of *The Quiet American* came to Greene on the road through the delta, 'and my characters quickly followed, all but one of them from the unconscious'.[4]

Greene's was the acceptable face of colonialism – no blimp, he – and throughout *The Quiet American* the Francophile Greene conveys his soft spot for colonial rule. He himself had served in Sierra Leone during the war; his marvellous novel *The Heart of the Matter* (1948) reflects a form of affection for the sheer hopeless weariness of colonial administrators trying to make something right out of what – sooner or later – must be wrong. As for *The Quiet American*, Greene was obviously more at home in portraying an urbane, well-read police inspector than the communist insurgents whom Greene generally kept well out of sight. When Fowler and Pyle find themselves hiding in the marshes from the Vietminh, the guerrillas are 'them,' insuperably alien and hostile, menacing *our* lives. Even when Fowler makes contact with a Vietminh agent in Saigon, Mr Heng turns out to be straightforward but without personal characteristics or discernable vices, a sure sign of 'otherness' in Greeneland. It may be that repeated visits to Vietnam and grants of privileged access which ordinary journalists must have envied (dinner with General de Lattre, special flights, a subsequent meeting with Ho Chi Minh in Hanoi), led Greene to feel almost as intimately at home there as he did with the British farmers of Kenya: 'When the revolt came, it was to the English colonist like a revolt of the domestic staff. The Kikuyu were not savage, they made good clerks and stewards. It was as though Jeeves had taken to the jungle. Even worse, Jeeves had been seen crawling through an arch to drink on his knees from a banana-trough of blood...Jeeves had sworn, however unwillingly, to kill Bertie Wooster "or this oath will kill me and all my seed will die".'[5]

Observing the French at war, he is observant yet indulgent. Their superior culture does not justify their use of the hideous weapon napalm, but their style of mind allows for a tragic dimension. Their military press conferences – one military victory is claimed after another even though the Vietminh regularly cut the road fifty miles south of Hanoi—are depicted as tragic as well as frankly farcical. Although the fictional American correspondent Granger is only doing his professional duty in pressing for hard casualty figures, Greene cannot help sympathising with the evasiveness of French military spokesmen. At one point, an elegant colonel, unable to bear more, breaks into fluent English as if descending in shame into the language of 'allies' eager only to humiliate France. None of the supplies promised by the Americans have arrived; they are down to one serviceable helicopter; any man seriously wounded in the field can expect to die. Granger is keen to report this but the colonel slaps a veto on what he has revealed: the Communists would make capital in Paris—and still he would be without helicopters.[6]

An example of Greene's ambivalence is found in the episode where Fowler (in reality Greene himself) flies in a dive bomber of the Gascogne Squadron in a series of vertical strikes at a Vietminh position (the agony of the dives is wonderfully described). While flying home, the pilot casually destroys a lone sampan found heading along the Red River. After casually accomplishing this little slaughter Captain Trouin says, "'We will make a little detour. The sunset is wonderful on the *calcaire*. You must not miss it.'" Fowler is disgusted. Later, in the officers' mess, he asks the pilot why he felt he had to destroy the sampan. Trouin replies drily, "'Who knows? In those reaches of the river we have orders to shoot up anything in sight.'" But then he opens up his conscience—he loathes releasing napalm from 3,000 feet in complete safety. He goes further: "'I'm not fighting a colonial war. Do you think I'd do these things for the planters of Terre Rouge? I'd rather be court-martialled. We are fighting all of your wars, but you leave us the guilt.'" He adds, "'You know we lose one class of St Cyr every year'" (St Cyr being the French military academy producing the young officers; by 4 July 1951 France had lost 35,000 men including eight hundred graduates of St Cyr). The pilot Trouin suffers troubled moods but "'The rest of the time I think I am defending Europe.'" Of course France cannot win this war. One day the politicians will do a deal 'making nonsense of all these years.' Captain Trouin's ugly face 'wore a kind of professional brutality like a Christmas mask from which a child's eyes peer through the holes in the paper. "You would not understand this nonsense, Fowler. You are not one of us.'"[7]

Greene shed tears for the dying British and French empires with dry eyes. The regret he experienced was cultural rather than political or military. Born in 1904, he had grown up in an Oxbridge-educated class which could not predict the dying of the flag, the recolouring of the globe – he had blithely joined in strike-breaking during the General Strike of 1926. In *Paris Match* he wrote, 'The United States is exaggeratedly distrustful of empires, but we Europeans retain the memory of what we owe to Rome, just as Latin America knows that it owes to Spain. When the hour of evacuation sounds there will be many Vietnamese who will regret the loss of the language which put them in contact with the art and faith of the West. The injustices committed by men who were harassed, exhausted and ignorant will be forgotten and the names of a good number of Frenchmen, priests, soldiers and administrators, will remain engraved in the memory of the Vietnamese...'[8]

Greene enjoyed his two-room bachelor flat at in St James's Street or Albany, shopping at Fortnum's, sojourning on Alexander Korda's (producer of *The Third Man*) luxury yacht in the Mediterranean. The Cold War colonial battles in Malaya and Vietnam – one could add Kenya – were for him necessary 'ways of escape.' He needed those crisis situations like his fictional Thomas Fowler (and he himself) needed opium pipes.[9] He was happy to turn the sunset of the French and British empires into best-selling novels and well-paid journalism

(*Life*, *Paris-Match*). What he could not abide was brash, clumsy, hygienic Americans trying to turn the clock forward.

The time-set of the main action in *The Quiet American* is the Chinese New Year, 1952, with a subsidiary sequence following Pyle's death some time later. The narrator, Fowler, a world-weary English journalist guiltily married to a Catholic wife far away, enjoys the services of a beautiful Vietnamese girl, Phuong, with whom he communicates in French, and who unfortunately wants marriage, vigorously supported by her English-speaking sister, who works in a secretarial capacity for the American Legation. If Fowler represents the weariness of imperial Europe, his friendly adversary, the young American agent Alden Pyle, Boston-raised and Harvard educated, nominally working for economic and medical aid, incarnates the brash certainties of the New World: '...with his gangly legs and his crew-cut and his wide campus gaze he seemed incapable of harm'.[10] Pyle admires the three books of a certain York Harding, advocate of a 'Third Force' for democracy and author of *The Role of the West*, *The Challenge of Democracy*, *The Advance of Red China*.

Pyle is also sexually naïve and inexperienced (for Greene an almost criminal offence), dancing badly and reacting like an overgrown boy scout when female impersonators appear on stage at a Saigon cabaret: '"Fowler," he said, "let's go. We've had enough, haven't we? This isn't a bit suitable for *her*."' 'Her' is Fowler's sophisticated mistress Phuong. In Greeneland those parading superficial puritan morality invariably turn out to be the real sinners. Men incapable of venial sin—Fowler tells Pyle he's had more than forty women, if Pyle really needs to know—are condemned to Greene's heterodox 'Catholic' version of Freudian repression. Pyle does not smoke opium or drink spirits – a bad sign. His mother sends him Vit-Health sandwich spread from Boston. 'I like to know what I'm eating.'[11]

Pyle is in Indochina on a secret mission, financing a 'Third Force' led by General Thé operating in the shadowy terrain between the French and the Communists. Arguing fiercely with Fowler, Pyle warns: '...if this country goes...' Meanwhile he declares himself in competition for Phuong while politely apologising to Fowler for the intrusion. Unlike Fowler, Pyle can offer the girl marriage. Torn between possessiveness and guilt, Fowler helps out Pyle by translating his declaration of love and his marriage proposal from English into French. 'I translated for him with meticulous care—it sounded worse that way.' Fowler smokes an opium pipe but Pyle refuses—the Service he serves has 'strict rules.'[12]

Fowler learns that Pyle has been 'importing plastics for toys'—but not in reality for toys. 'That day all over Saigon innocent bicycle pumps had proved to be plastic bombs and gone off at the stroke of eleven.' The Communists are blamed for the civilian deaths, but Pyle is responsible. Fowler believes that Pyle is deluding himself by running General Thé, who is 'only a bandit with a few thousand men; he's not a national democracy'. Pyle's bloodshed continues and grows worse. 'He was impregnably armoured by his good intentions and his ignorance.'[13]

When Pyle tells Fowler, 'You have to fight for liberty,' Fowler's riposte is close to a sneer: 'I haven't seen any American fighting round here.'[14] Although by no means a fellow-traveller of the Vietminh, Fowler displays a blend of guilt and veiled superiority: 'they'—these peasants here in Russia, China, Vietnam—do not demand from life and society what 'we' demand.

'"You and your like are trying to make a war with the help of people who just aren't interested."

'"They don't want Communism."

'"They want enough rice," I said. "They don't want to be shot at. They want one day to be much the same as another. They don't want our white skins around telling them what they want."

'"If Indo-China goes..."'

Later Pyle predicts what life would be like under Communist rule:

'"They'll be forced to believe what they are told, they won't be allowed to think for themselves."

'"Thought's a luxury. Do you think the peasant sits and thinks of God and Democracy when he gets inside his mud hut at night?"

'"You talk as if the whole country were peasant. What about the educated? Are they going to be happy?"

'"Oh no," I said, "we've brought them up in *our* ideas. We've taught them dangerous games..."'[15]

There is no guarantee that Fowler's viewpoint exactly expresses Greene's, but the first-person narrative, which allows for no ironies at Fowler's expense, beyond those to which he readily exposes himself, strongly suggests that Fowler speaks for the author: 'It's very dangerous writing in the first person. Everybody thinks I am Fowler – well, I share some of his views about the Americans. But I'm not as bitter about them as he is. I didn't have my girl stolen by an American.'[16] Fowler constantly objects to Pyle's familiar use of his Christian name—even when the American is saving his life at the risk of his own in the swamps surrounded by Vietminh in for the kill. Greene's anti-Americanism was clearly visceral as well as political, and by no means confined to Pyle. The American journalist Granger is crude, often vile. He writes of things he has not seen: 'Stephen Crane can describe a war without seeing one. Why shouldn't I? It's only a damned colonial war anyway. Get me another drink. And then let's go and find a girl. You've got a piece of tail [Phuong]. I want a piece of tail too.'[17] What Greene (himself a prodigious patron of prostitutes worldwide) objected to in Granger was the use of 'a piece of tail' instead of 'a girl.' Greene's fellow-travelling sinologist cousin Felix Greene told Norman Sherry that during Graham's trip to China in 1957, he shocked Chinese officials by announcing, 'in every place he went,' that '"There are two things I want, a pretty girl to sleep with, and to know where I can get some opium."')[18] When it becomes clear that Granger is not going to get Phuong, he heads for 'The House of Five Hundred Girls,' in reality Le Parc aux Buffles, the soldiers' brothel, where Greene had availed himself soon after his arrival, emerging in disarray.[19] In *The Quiet American*, Greene describes the immense courtyard of the brothel but transfers his own experience to the loud-mouthed Granger, who is proud to be the centre of a scrimmage of competing pieces of tail. Even the innocent Pyle, too, has been led into the mêlée by Granger but Fowler gallantly pursues him, gets hold of his sleeve and leads him out to safety, 'with the girl hanging on to his other arm like a hooked fish'. In short, Greene the novelist sends his two principal American characters, rather than his English surrogate, Fowler, in clumsy search of flesh at the House of Five Hundred Girls.

Fowler reports taking to his mistress Phuong after he suspected she was meeting the hated Alden Pyle at her English-speaking sister's. 'I began – almost unconsciously – to run down everything that was American...the poverty of American literature, the scandals of American politics, the beastliness of American children. It was as though she was being taken from me by a nation rather than a man.'[20] Greene's Americans, including the bluff, hearty economic attaché, belong to a species of uniformly clean and superficially friendly hypocrites – that is to say, they mistake their own commercial and geopolitical interests for global values, for 'democracy.' And yet Alden Pyle is a subtly depicted and complex character, brave, principled, resourceful—loyal. Greene's endows the villain of the piece with many admirable qualities and, conversely, Fowler with many shabby manoeuvres in his private life. Pyle says with utmost sincerity to Fowler, '"Oh, but I know you're straight, absolutely straight, and we both have her [Phuong's] interests at heart.' Fowler replies: '"I don't care for her interests. You can have her interests. I only want her body. I want her in bed with me."'[21] Later Fowler deceives the sweet-natured, trusting Phuong when he tells her that his wife in England has agreed to a divorce. Pyle also lies about his plastic bombs, but he lies for The Cause, never to get his leg over the girl. Pyle is brave and ingenious; when he could leave his rival to die in the marshes he doesn't.

How consistent was Greene's anti-Americanism? When he first visited America in 1938 on his way to Mexico he saw rampant materialism, lack of tradition, naivety, destructive altruism. Yet *The Heart of the Matter* (1948) was the choice of the Book of the Month Club; he wrote for American magazines and sold the dramatic rights to the novel to Rogers and Hammerstein, indeed he complained in *The Times* (31 June 1949) because the Bank of England had refused him a currency allowance of £10 a day to work on the script in America. He sold the film rights to *The Quiet American* to a Hollywood producer, well knowing that the book's political message would very likely emerge reversed. Obviously Greene's own experiences of 'McCarthyism' affected his judgment, hence his 'Open letter on Chaplin' in the *New Statesman* (27 May 1952) after the great comedian was denied automatic re-entry to the United States and threatened with detention for questioning after attending the London premiere of *Limelight*. Earlier that year, Greene had become a victim of the same McCarran Act, after telling *Time* about his four weeks in the Oxford CP when a nineteen-year-old student. For years afterwards his visits to America were restricted in duration and subject to permission. In 1954 he was detained in Puerto Rico while in transit from Haiti to London.

In *The Quiet American*, Pyle and other Americans acting in league with the maverick General Thé plant bombs in Saigon hoping that the Communists will take the blame. Greene was taken to task in the *New Yorker* for blaming the Americans for the great explosion in the main square of Saigon when many people lost their lives.[22] Challenged, he produced further evidence of contacts between American services and Thé, citing two incidents involving the killing of American personnel which were 'hushed up for diplomatic reasons.' In one, 'An American consul was arrested late at night on the bridge to Dakow (where Pyle in my novel lost his life) carrying plastic bombs in his car.'[23] Greene's suspicions undoubtedly emanated from the Sûreté and French officials known to Greene – but he turned suspicion into fact.[24] *The Quiet American* novel plays down the fact that the Vietminh had already engaged in fierce urban terrorism, including suicide assassinations.

Further fictional scenes indicate Pyle's complicity until he finally admits it. He has warned Phuong (now his mistress rather than Fowler's) not to go to her habitual morning milk bar on the morning when there is an explosion in the Place Garnier, causing horrible mutilations. Shocked by the resulting bloodshed, Pyle admits involvement: 'There was to have been a [French] parade,' he explains to Fowler, his denials at an end. He had not known the parade had been cancelled. But even this does not divert him. He turns up at Fowler's apartment and says he has reprimanded Thé but won't give him up: 'In the long run he's the only hope we have. If he came to power with our help, we could rely on him...' It is at this point that Fowler decides to have Pyle murdered by his Communist contacts, even though Pyle had saved his life in the marshes after they ran out of petrol at dusk.

The film version (1958) was (as Greene had anticipated) a travesty. He had already told an interviewer (14 August 1956): 'I don't suppose they can film it the way it is written. They'll probably make it so that it looks as if the American was being bamboozled all the time by the Communists or somebody.' Written, directed and produced by Joseph L. Mankiewicz, filmed on location in Saigon by Robert Krasker (cinematographer of Greene's *The Third Man*), the film was released as the Eisenhower administration was preparing to take up the burden, abandoned by the French, of containing Communism in Southeast Asia. In Mankiewicz's version, Fowler's anti-Americanism is carefully doctored to appear as naïve stupidity; Alden Pyle's third-force idealism is less noxious than in the novel, more wholesome and totally sincere; he is acting entirely on his own initiative, for an independent aid agency, not for the CIA. In the film it is not the bright-eyed Pyle (played by Audie Murphy) who is responsible for bombs, explosions and deaths in Saigon; indeed the sophisticated Fowler (Michael Redgrave) is exposed as woefully naïve. Greene later condemned Mankiewicz's film as 'a complete travesty' and 'a real piece of political dishonesty.'[25]

The Cold War cutting edge of the novel became doubly apparent when it rapidly appeared in Russian translation in 1956. *Newsweek* (1 October) returned to the attack ('When Greene is Red') on the basis of a five-column article in *Pravda* calling the novel 'the most remarkable event' of recent British literary history. Soviet admiration for Fowler and denunciation of Pyle, and Soviet admiration for Fowler's decision to have Pyle murdered, confirmed for *Newsweek* Greene's 'dreary stereotyping of his American characters': 'All the leading characters turn out to be cut-and-dried political symbols, rather than the complete fragments of humanity which Greene intended (but hardly achieved).'[26]

In fact, as became clear after a debate at the Soviet Writers' Union,[27] Greene's political line came too close to neutralism for Soviet taste. The noted critic A. Anikst praised his 'humanism' and artistry but regretted his 'pacifist' attitude to the war in Indochina. 'This is a great pity, for the author affirms by the very logic of his novel that the North Vietnam army waged war for the liberation of the country from the colonisers, and for bringing the desired peace to the people of Vietnam.' A. Elistratov commented that although Greene had acknowledged the influence of Fielding, James, Conrad and Joyce, and must be reckoned part of the 'decadent' school in English fiction, happily his attitude towards ethical and aesthetic questions was more serious than that of his contemporaries. *The Quiet American* was an advance on *The Heart of the Matter*, which released the hero only through suicide. By contrast, A. Startsev, commented that until recently Greene had been part of the reactionary literary 'group' which included Koestler, Dos Passos and Aldous Huxley – sadly his new novel merely reflected the political bankruptcy of this 'coterie.' B. Isakov disagreed: 'I have not come across a parallel unmasking of Catholicism, written with such power. Some Catholic!' The author had come to a parting of the ways—hence the attacks on him in the 'American bourgeois press.' T. Lanin regarded the figure of Pyle as a considerable literary achievement—here was a character who might be subjectively sincere yet whose activities caused untold damage.

None of the Soviet critics ventured into 'the heart of the matter,' Greene's partly masked conviction that men need a faith but faiths care little for men. Man is bad because fallen; he wishes to be good; the more ardently he attaches himself to any exclusive recipe for salvation, whether the church's or the party's, the worse his actions are likely to become. Likewise all wars tend to destroy the values in whose name they are fought. These were not notions that Soviet culture, still devoted to primary colours as defined by ideology, could take on board.[28]

In the years ahead, Greene's attitude towards the Cold War, and towards the perceived quality of life under the two systems, was to undergo many shifts of gear, some so dramatic (and faintly perverse) as to suggest a degree of showman-ship—as when he proposed that his Soviet royalties should be paid to the wives of Daniel and Sinyavsky, and as when he responded to Anatoly Kuznetsov's defection with a public vow to allow no more of his books to be published in Russia. Commentators—including Greene's authorized biographer Norman Sherry—have been drawn into hothouse speculation by Greene's continued admiration for his old MI6 colleague Kim Philby, despite his defection to the Soviet Union in 1963 after thirty years of spying and treachery (sending his own agents to their deaths in Albania by shopping them to the Russians, for example). When Norman Sherry chided Greene about this during an interview in August 1962, 'Greene became highly flushed – the only occasion I remember the edge of his wrath.' Sherry writes, 'Greene's answer sounded as if he had been briefed by Philby: "They [the agents sent to Albania] were going into their country armed to do damage to that country. They were killed instead of killing."'[29] Greene visited the Soviet Union three times in 1987 alone, once to receive an honorary degree from Moscow State University, and met Philby on four occasions. Philby's last wife, a Russian, had taught herself English by reading *The Heart of the Matter.*

Part 3

History and Fiction in the Soviet Orbit

17

Commentary: The Socialist Realist Novel from War to Cold War

The classical voices of Marxism, from Marx and Engels to Lenin, Stalin and Mao Tse-tung, were unanimous in their insistence that a 'progressive' literature must be 'realist' in form. Marx likened realism to 'strong Rembrandtian colours, in all their living qualities...'[1] In 1888, Engels described realism as truthful in detail but also in representing 'typical characters under typical circumstances.' This declaration coincided with a sharp swing among avant-garde writers towards subjectivity, introspection, impressionism, formal experimentation and, indeed, contempt for the claims and tastes of the working people. Indeed the term 'avant-garde' was rapidly inverted: previously associated with writers and artists committed to radical political solutions, it became associated with an elite contemptuous of politics.

A long cultural war was on the horizon. By the time Lenin came to power, a host of avant-garde movements, unpredicted by Marx and Engels, had mushroomed in Russia and the West. Lenin, who regarded even Vladimir Mayakovsky's revolutionary poetry as 'tricky and affected,' told Clara Zetkin: 'I am unable to consider the productions of Futurism, Cubism, and other isms the highest manifestations of artistic genius. I do not understand them. I experience no joy from them.' By the late 1920s, they had been firmly suppressed in the Soviet Union.[2]

The insistence on 'realism,' mainly on the nineteenth-century model (Dickens, Balzac, Tolstoy), went hand-in-glove with a determination that fiction should be programmed to promote the Party line. Art was a tool and a weapon. The term 'socialist realism' was first coined in May 1932 and immediately declared to be the mandatory method for Soviet culture. To reinforce the diktat the Politburo abolished all independent writers' organisations and founded a single Union of Writers with obligatory membership for professionals. The First All-Union Congress of Soviet Writers, held in 1934, attempted a definition:

'Socialist realism is the basic method of Soviet literature and literary criticism. It demands of the artist the truthful, historically concrete representation of reality in its revolutionary development...linked with the task of ideological transformation and education of workers in the spirit of socialism.' Reiterating that Soviet literary principles were based on Lenin's *Party Organization and Party Literature* (1905), and quoting Stalin's profound definition of Soviet writers as 'engineers of the soul,' the Party's senior spokesman on literature and the arts, Andrei Zhdanov, demanded a totally didactic literature: 'At the same time as we select Soviet man's finest feelings and qualities and reveal his future to him, we must show our people what they should not be like and castigate the survivals from yesterday that are hindering the Soviet people's progress.'[3] Among the key requirements were patriotism or *narodnost'* in its various meanings, above all devotion to the socialist motherland.

Stalin was demanding a new version of 'praise poetry': it laid claim to the future as well as the present. The Soviet writer must not only accurately portray in Leninist terms the class struggle, past or present, but must also inject inspirational solutions and exemplary, heroic behaviour, as required by the Five Year Plans: in factories and fields, virgin lands and power stations. The Bolsheviks had long since abandoned the duality at the heart of Marx's philosophy, the tension between 'life' and 'leadership,' between the experience of the proletariat and the scientific analysis of that experience, as the prime determinant of consciousness. With the arrival of Lenin, leadership assumes the total burden and absolute power; the Russian peasant-proletarian masses are viewed as the recalcitrant clay out of which the Party vanguard will mould 'socialist consciousness'.

The Stalin Prizes, initiated in 1939 to honour his sixtieth birthday, rewarded writers in good odour with the Party. In June 1947 the Council of Ministers announced 157 prizes—those in the first-class category were worth 200,000 rubles, or £9,000. The title 'People's Artist' had been introduced in August 1936—sixty-four people, writers included, held the title in 1947.[4]

By and large, Soviet fiction, whether orthodox socialist realism or the dissident works applauded in the West, focused on events inside the Soviet Union: collectivisation, industrialisation, the purges, the terror, the trials, the onset of war and the ghastly experience of Nazi occupation. The Stalin described by Soviet novelists was the dictator who destroyed Russians rather than the expansionist ogre feared in the West. What brought Pasternak and Solzhenitsyn to the forefront of the cultural Cold War was their fictional reading of Russia's internal history since the Revolution. The figure of Stalin – particularly his imagined mindset, his stream of consciousness – intrigued novelists, admirers and detractors alike. Stalin's internal critics became fascinated, even obsessed, by the enigma of his personal responsibility for the military collapse of 1941, with its catastrophic consequences not only for the Red Army and Air Force but for the 70 million Soviet citizens who fell into the hell of Nazi rule. But here again the literary focus among the dissidents tended to be domestic and internal rather than international. The often melodramatic portrayal of Russia's fraught wartime alliance remained the jealously guarded province of officially approved novelists, dramatist and cineastes.

In the post-Stalin era, and particularly following Nikita Khrushchev's sensational speech to the 20th Congress of the Party in 1956, the compelling historical subject for Soviet dissident writers can be summed up as 'the Party versus the people.' A generation began to reexamine its own catastrophic experiences; revisionist analysis was ventilated by long-suppressed memories of the forced collectivisation of agriculture; of the brutal treatment of so-called 'kulaks' and the ensuing famine; of the terror of the 1930s, whose cruel depredations touched virtually every Soviet family; of slave labour and slave deaths in the Gulag.

Solzhenitsyn was by no means the only Soviet writer approaching fiction as what Geoffrey Hosking calls 'a kind of moral chronicle or "literary investigation,"' uncovering the truth about Soviet society and 'using the material thus brought forth to illuminate man's moral and spiritual nature.'[5] Russian writers had always tended to regard themselves as truth-tellers, as holy fools, even legislators, 'the other government,' during centuries of autocracy. Writing in the nineteenth century, Alexander Herzen had called Russian literature the '"second government", the true authority in society'. 'For lack of democratic institutions, the Russian writer has never just been an artist, but a spokesman for the truth and a public conscience as well.'[6]

In the main attempts at an honest history of the USSR's national disasters came from novelists, playwrights, and poets rather than historians, political scientists and sociologists. Without the often heroic contribution of novelists very little plausible history would have been written in the Soviet Union. Since the late 1920s if not earlier Soviet professional historians had been muzzled by censorship and physical repression; prevented from entering the secret archives, they must tow the Party line down to the latest blink of the ideological eye. Many relevant archives were closed; within the university faculties and the history institutes every doctoral thesis was closely monitored. Many were aborted in the womb (itself a history waiting to be written).

On the other hand, the dissident Soviet novelist also worked within the confines of the Party line as interpreted by the Union of Writers and the Soviet censor, Glavlit. Novels challenging the conventional wisdom might gather dust for years while editors and Party functionaries played 'pass the parcel.' The new Soviet working class, inflated by wave after wave of new recruits, peasants hastily imported into the new towns and industrial projects, had to be converted, convinced, cajoled, moulded by exemplary stories of courage and virtue. Soviet Communism resembled a kind of secular Calvinism preaching that God's 'elect,' while guaranteed Eternal Salvation, would reveal themselves only by their pious deeds on this earth. Socialist realism can be viewed as a systematic adaptation of fiction, drama, and poetry to the didactic imperative of History as interpreted by the Party. Many writers gleaned the Party line from *Voprosy istorii* (*Questions of History*) and other mainstream historical journals. Literary magazines like *Novyi mir* (*New World*) and *Literaturnaia gazeta* published historical material.

Outright defiance of the Party line and the official orthodoxy did not surface until the 1960s, when the use of samizdat – a chain of underground typists—became increasingly widespread. In Stalin's time and during the thaw associated with Khrushchev, dissident status was more often imposed than sought – Pasternak and Vasily Grossman are conspicuous examples. The term 'dissident' itself can be deceptive. The Party, after all, encouraged criticism of Soviet reality in fictional form – provided the perspective was ultimately 'positive' – and much depended on the random vagaries of reviews and high-level interventions following publication. Had Vladimir Dudintsev not come under fire for his novel, *Not by Bread Alone*, had apologies not been demanded from him, he would not have been so lauded in the West or even associated with the 'thaw.'

Soviet realist fiction has tended to employ traditional narrative devices and models, inherited from pre-revolutionary storytelling—the dean of Marxist critics, Georg Lukács, stamped the *licet* of 'realism' on this method, whereby the writer-artist teased out a huge underlying, dialectical truth about class society by means of entertaining, page-turning, artifices. The central fault line in Lukács's commentaries is to be found where the method applied to the 'bourgeois era' (Scott-Goethe-Balzac) is transferred mechanically to Soviet writers working under Party prescription— tasks to be achieved! After 1917, the socialist novelist's indispensable 'innocence' was taken from him by the commissars. He was enlisted as an engineer of souls. He was no longer wholly 'himself.' Official socialist realism was no longer 'realism.'

The socialist realist fiction relentlessly promoted by the Soviet Party amounts to a kind of Bunyanesque allegory of virtue and frailty. Packed with heroes, heroines, villains, journeys to and from, tests of character and moral dilemmas, cruel choices, ancient sentiments, lessons learned, the model Zhdanovist novel tells of self-sacrificing service pitted against Corruption, Greed, Sloth, and (sometimes) the seductive bright lights of the West. The conservatism of Soviet ideology resides not so much in its unchanging determinism as in its inflexible moralism. Paradoxically, an ideology subscribing to a determinist philosophy of history yet insisted that individuals were completely responsible for their own behaviour.

Reporting from Moscow early in 1946, Isaiah Berlin took a dim view of the new fiction he had been reading. 'As for fiction the commonest path is that taken by such steady, irretrievably second-rate novelists as Fedin, Kataev, Gladkov, Leonov, Sergeev-Tsensky, Fadeyev, and such playwrights as Pogodin...in general produce work of high mediocrity modeled on late-nineteenth-century archetypes, written with professional craftsmanship, long, competent, politically *bien pensant*...' Among the younger generation, the journalist, playwright and poet Konstantin Simonov 'has poured out a flood of work of inferior quality but impeccably orthodox sentiment, acclaiming the right type of Soviet hero, brave, puritanical, simple, noble, altruistic, entirely devoted to the service of his country'. Berlin commented that there were many authors of the same genre as Simonov; authors of novels dealing with exploits in kolkhozes, factories, or at the front; writers of patriotic doggerel or of plays which guy the capitalist world or the old and discredited liberal culture of Russia itself, in contrast with the simple, now wholly standardized, type of tough, hearty, capable, resolute, single-minded young engineers or political commissars ('engineers of human souls'), or army commanders, shy and manly lovers, sparing of words, doers of mighty deeds, 'Stalin's eagles,' flanked by passionately patriotic, utterly fearless, morally pure, heroic young women, upon whom the success of the five-year plans ultimately depends.[7]

At the core of the realist novel since the eighteenth century has been the autonomous individual and the belief that individual characteristics can be faithfully captured by way of literary transcription. Although realist novelists normally pay close attention to milieu, to the social setting and seminal family ties, the individual's ultimate responsibility for his or her actions is the bedrock of 'character.' Hence 'Cast of Characters.'

Perhaps paradoxically, this has been as true of socialist or Soviet fictional chronicles of collective endeavour. The individual hero and heroine, villain and traitor, each driven by free will, are preferred to an updated Greek chorus – whereas in Eisenstein's films we encounter the masses as a choreographed collective bonded by class struggle. Bourgeois or socialist, the novel's virtues and limitations dictate an almost inescapable emphasis on the 'character' and moral quality of the individual. In the socialist realist novel individual idealism, self-sacrifice and courage are almost invariably the prerogatives of Bolsheviks and 'patriots' – hence the offence caused by Pasternak's portraits of gallant White officers in *Doctor Zhivago*. In the Stalinist novel, the cause assumes a transcendence akin to Christian idealism. In Pyotr Pavlenko's *Happiness* (*Schast'e*, 1947), Colonel Alexei Voropayev boards a boat on the Black Sea. A war hero burdened by an artificial leg, he intends to start a new life in a backward stretch of countryside. Despite his physical disability, the widower Voropayev is almost neurotically active. His attitudes and actions are exemplary – though he tends to forget his young son, still in Moscow. A much decorated veteran of many campaigns (Third Ukrainian Front, Fourth Guards Army), he incarnates the new equation of ideal Soviet man and soldier. When he finds kolkhozes in decay, his instinct is to rally all the war veterans and impose iron discipline on 'slackers, shirkers, boozers, and ne'er-do-wells' who have allowed the farms to lapse into rack and ruin. Sick leave is reserved for the dead. Pavlenko takes care to sketch in the colonel's personal failings – he is forgetful of his young son and remains beyond the reach of the local woman who loves him, Lena, while sublimating his love for the military surgeon Goreva, failing to answer her letters from Europe, until the resolute victrix sweeps down to the Black Sea on the last page and takes him by storm.

A good cause did not make a good man out of Sartre's character Gomez. Whereas the Stalinist hero's personal defects are rooted excusably in service and self-sacrifice, Sartre allows his military hero Gomez no alibis for his treatment of his wife and child—only good artistic taste: visiting the New York Museum of Modern Art, he singles out Klee, Rouault and Picasso as the artists who ask 'awkward questions.'[8]

The Great Patriotic War occupies centre-stage in Soviet fiction, but the novels and short stories which survived an overbearing censorship by no means reflected the sentiments of many leading authors. In July 1943 the People's Commissariat for State Security issued a secret report quoting a long list of 'hostile, defeatist' opinions – yet providing no sources or references and no doubt relying on informers and intercepted mail or telephone calls. Several writers describe the Anglo-Americans as 'the masters now,' and not necessarily from a hostile perspective. Kornei Chukovsky, the prestigious children's poet, translator of Walt Whitman and close friend of Pasternak, is quoted as saying 'Our fate is in their hands. I'm glas a sensible new era is beginning. They will teach us culture...' Chukovsky spoke of art flourishing in 'democratic countries,' whereas 'in conditions of despotic rule Russian literature has gone to seed and nearly perished'. Leonid Leonov regretted that Stalin had curtly refused Roosevelt's request that the collective farms be disbanded to alleviate food shortages; he also regretted that the USSR was alienating the Allies by its curt tone in discussing the future of Poland, the Baltic States, and the Ukraine.[9]

Several voices indicated chaos and acute shortages. L. V. Soloviev, war correspondent and author of the play *Field Marshal Katuzov*, reflected on the catastrophic of food and disarray among a collectivized peasantry reluctant to work: 'Without the Americans' help we would have given up the ghost long ago.' Fyodor Gladkov, author of the novel *Cement*, a prototype for socialist realism was quoted: 'Just think, twenty-five years of Soviet power, and even before the war people were going around in rags, starving.'[10]

A subsequent secret report (31 October 1944) by State Security Commissar V. N. Merkulov to A. Zhdanov indicated that many of the writers criticised in the July 1953 report had been summoned by the Central Committee, but on the whole remained defiant or scornful of official literature, of the chaotic censorship, of being required to write to order. But here again the later report provides no sources or references, so one is left in the dark about the circumstances in which writers made the quoted declarations. Chukovsky again: 'With the fall of Nazi despotism, the world of democracy will come face to face with Soviet despotism. We will be waiting.' Konstantin Fedin is quoted: 'I sit in Peredelkino and entertain myself writing a novel that will never see the light of day if the current literary policy continues.... Can there be a discussion of realism when the writer is forced to depict what is wished for but does not exist?'[11] Several disaffected writers explained the new, stifling censorship in terms of the revival of the Party's self-confidence as the military tide turned.

In August 1945, the deputy head of the Central Committee's Agitprop submitted a scathing memo on the shortcomings of Soviet literature during the war years. Some had fallen silent in 1941-42 (Fedin among them). Some had written 'harmful' works lacking in ideals (Mikhail Zoshchenko, Chukvosky). Some had lauded commanders of the tsarist era. Some had depicted Russian fear in the face of the Germans: 'Motifs of suffering, death and the sense of doom'. Now some were demanding that Soviet symbolism replace realism, while others were demanding outright freedom of speech.[12] A year later a further memo from the same source criticised stories and poems which used the war as mere background, or told of individual soldier's attachments to bottles of beer or wine, or a frivolous attitude to girls.

Few Soviet novelists explored the sensitive period between the Nazi-Soviet Pact of August 1939 and Operation Barbarossa in June 1941. The present writer has been struck by the almost routine insistence of educated Russians that the Second World War began only with the German assault on the Soviet Union. Whatever earlier skirmishes may have occurred among the imperialist states, they evidently belonged to the 'phoney war.' This was indeed the impression imparted by Ilya Ehrenburg's novel *Padeniye Parizha* (*The Fall of Paris*), awarded a Stalin Prize in 1942.

Soviet fiction provides few examples of a critical attitude towards the Nazi-Soviet Pact – or of willingness to refer to that traumatic reversal beyond general platitudes directed against Western appeasement of Hitler. Largely unmentioned is fear of the Comintern and memories of the recent industrial action in pursuit of radical social demands associated with the time of the first (1936) Popular Front government in France. Not to be questioned by Soviet writers was the image sought by Stalin – for example in Spain and through the new Soviet constitution – of a USSR simply dedicated to democracy and the integrity of nations. One passage in Vasily Grossman's novel *For a Just Cause* (1952, revised 1954) does offer an oblique condemnation of the Pact. The leading academic protagonist, Shtrum, hears Ivan Ivanovich Maksimov, professor of biochemistry, recounting from first-hand experience what has happened to science in Austria and Czechoslovakia under Nazi ('fascist') occupation. Shtrum responds by advising Maksimov that it his duty to publish these dark observations. Someone else intervenes, speaking quietly 'in the tone normally reserved for addressing children': 'None of this is new, to print such recollections now would hardly serve our interest in protecting a policy of peace rather than impairing it.' Although the Pact itself passes unmentioned, the passage is typical of Grossman's ability to convey subversive points 'between the lines.'[13]

In *The First Circle*, Solzhenitsyn's coverage of the years 1939-1941 is fragmentary: 'Stalin had looked on with approval and malicious delight as Hitler had overrun Poland, France and Belgium, as his bombers had darkened the sky over England.' Yet Solzhenitsyn passes over the active measures taken by the Soviet state and military as a consequence of the Nazi-Soviet Pact—no mention of the Soviet seizure of eastern Poland, the annexation of the Baltic states by means of military occupation and phoney plebiscites, or the war of territorial expansion against Finland—all of which were motivated not only by fear of expanding German power but also in effect licensed by a series of territorial understandings with Hitler concerning 'spheres of influence,' starting with the secret additional protocol of the Pact.

Soviet novelists may have remained ignorant of the clause in the protocol granting to the USSR all Polish territory bounded by the rivers Narev, Vistula and San, while allocating to Russia western frontier posts in the suburbs of Warsaw on the eastern bank of the Vistula. In the event, Stalin held back from so naked an incursion into territory occupied by ethnic Poles, settling for a new frontier along the Bug on the pretext that he was coming to the rescue of Ukrainians and Byelorussians living under Polish rule – an exonerating perspective later stressed in Soviet school textbooks.[14] Both Soviet fiction and history writing bypass Stalin's ruthless massacre in March 1940 of an estimated four thousand Polish officers taken prisoner, shot and buried by the NKVD in Katyn Forest. Admittedly Moscow did not admit responsibility until 1989, when Gorbachev confirmed two other burial sites and the executions of some 25,700 Poles.

What of Stalin's responsibility for the military debacle of June 1941?—the failure to anticipate or adequately prepare for the German invasion, the forced retreats, the loss of huge territories and populations (some 70 million people came under Nazi rule).

Among Soviet writers Solzhenitsyn is unique in his mocking insistence that Stalin trusted Hitler, even though 'Distrust of people was the dominating characteristic of Joseph Djugashvili; it was his only philosophy of life.... In all his long, suspicion-ridden life he had trusted only one man... Adolf Hitler.' This was why—Solzhenitsyn adds in *The First Circle*—Stalin remained unperturbed despite the many warnings of an imminent German invasion.[15] 'Molotov had come back from Berlin [late 1940] thoroughly frightened; agents reported that Hitler was transferring his forces eastward; Hess flew to England, and Churchill had warned Stalin of an attack. Every jackdaw in the woods of Byelorussia and on the poplars of Galicia had shrieked war. Every peasant woman in every market place in Russia had prophesied war day in and day out. Only Stalin had remained unperturbed.' Churchill's intelligence warnings of a German attack were dismissed as a 'provocation.' In fact Stalin was far from 'unperturbed' by Germany's rapid domination of the Balkan states; his constant fear was an Anglo-German truce releasing German forces for an assault on Russia. As Isaac Deutscher points out, Stalin's extravagant professions of confidence in German intentions, made in May-June 1941, were desperate, indeed 'pathetic' attempts at public placation rather than signs of blind trust.[16]

Solzhenitsyn remained adamant: 'He had trusted Hitler.... The trust had very nearly cost him his own life. All the more reason never again to trust anyone...'[17]

In later years Stalin kept the history of the war under tight control. *The Great Patriotic War of the Soviet Union* consisted of Stalin's own writings and speeches. The first major statement on Soviet military unpreparedness appeared in *Voennaia Mysl'* (*Military Thought*) in 1955.[18] The 20th Congress of the CPSU accelerated discussion of this hitherto forbidden subject. In his secret speech to the Congress, Khrushchev confirmed that by 3 April 1941 Churchill's ambassador, Stafford Cripps, had warned Stalin of a German attack. In May, similar reports had come in from the Soviet embassy in Berlin. Khrushchev characterized war preparations as poor, equipment as old and in short supply. Even after the invasion began (claimed Khrushchev), Stalin ordered no return of fire because he believed it was a case of provocation by undisciplined units of the Wehrmacht. The situation was worsened by the purge and annihilation of military officers: the cadres with experience of Spain and the Far East had been almost completely liquidated. Following the German invasion Stalin did nothing, showed 'nervousness and hysteria,' never visited the front or any liberated city.[19]

The first fruit of revision among professional historians was a collective work edited by P.A. Zhilin, *Main Operations of the Great Patriotic War*, published by the Ministry of Defence in 1956. This displayed candour about the first phases of the war, backed by statistics.[20] What emerged in the late 1950s from historians like S. P. Platonov and A. M. Samsonov was well documented confirmation that Stalin's USSR had been disastrously unprepared. The notion of the glorious 'counter-offensive' (by which retreats emerged as a brilliant, well-planned strategy) was discarded.[21] A few novelists were now daring to move in this direction. Konstantin Simonov's novel, *Zhivyei myortvye* (1959)[22], appeared in the U.S. as *The Living and Dead* (1962), in Britain as *Victims and Heroes* (1963). The British publisher's blurb claimed this was the first novel to ask why 'when war with Hitler had been anticipated for years, he was able in 1941 to smash the Soviet forces...' According to the translator, Ainsztein, the novel asks a number of fundamental questions: 'How far were the mass executions and imprisonments of Red Army marshals, generals and officers in the years 1937-40 responsible for the German victories? How could Stalin, the man who distrusted everybody, allow Hitler to strike first? Why were millions of Soviet citizens allowed to fall into the hands of the Nazis to be murdered or turned into slaves when they could have fled east if warned in time? And what was the justification of the Ribbentrop-Molotov Pact if...it brought on them sufferings and losses unparalleled even in Russia's tragic and cruel history?'[23] One of Simonov's characters, experiencing the headlong retreat, angrily recalls a novel he had read about a future war in which fascist Germany would be smashed in three days by the Soviet Air Force. The author was Nikolay Shpanov and the novel was *The First Blow* (*Pervyi udar*). [24] Ainsztein was in effect proposing that Simonov had performed a historian's task at a time when the historians themselves were not free to expose the realities.

This was only partially true of *Victims and Heroes*. Simonov remained a Party writer capable of trimming and taking refuge in evasive abstraction. A character muses: 'Had we faced the truth after the Finnish War and, above all, drawn the conclusions that should have been drawn, everything might be different now.'[25] But what 'truth,' what 'conclusions' about the state of military preparedness or about the USSR's new habit of military expansion (Poland, the Baltic states, Finland, Moldovia)?

Simonov's character Serpelin is moved when in October 1941 Stalin addresses the nation with the Germans outside Moscow. Stalin had done 'a thing very few other people in his place would have dared to do – hold a parade when eighty German divisions were poised outside Moscow'.

A recurring theme in the work of Solzhenitsyn, fiction and non-fiction alike, is not only Stalin's military unpreparedness in June 1941, but also the outrageous treatment of Soviet citizens who through no fault of their own were taken prisoner, or forced to live in Nazi-occupied territory, or who were found wandering in bewildered isolation. Units which had been encircled and isolated but not captured in 1941 after heavy German tank assaults were arrested as soon as they broke out. 'And instead of being given a brotherly embrace on their return, such as every other army in the world would have given them...' they were held, deprived of rights, taken to screening centres for interrogation and painful confrontations. Some were restored to their former ranks, others were pronounced traitors to the Motherland under article 58-1b. Everyone was to blame except Stalin. Some fifty or so generals, mainly air force, had been incarcerated in Moscow prisons by the summer of 1941, among them Air Force Commander Smushkevich. According to Solzhenitsyn, those Muscovites who did not make good their escape after the authorities abandoned the city, were under suspicion of subverting Government authority (article 58-10) or of staying on to await the Germans (article 58-1a). These unfortunate innocents kept providing fodder for interrogators up to 1945.[26]

Solzhenitsyn's pursuit of Stalin is relentless: 'And with one slither of his greasy, stubby finger, the Great Strategist sent 120,000 of our young men... across the Strait of Kerch in December 1941 – senselessly, exclusively for the sake of a sensational New Year's communiqué – and he turned them all over to the Germans without a fight.'[27]

Solzhenitsyn's powerful short story, 'Incident at Krechetovka Station' (1963),[28] is set in October 1941 during a period of torrential rain that temporarily halted the German advance. Young Lieutenant Zotov, an ardent member of the Komsomol, finds himself frustratingly serving in the rear, in charge of transport arrangements at a small provincial station in the region of Voronezh, 300 miles south of Moscow, not far behind the shifting front line. Thousands of soldiers are pouring through Krechetovka station as they retreat eastwards. Was Moscow itself to be surrendered? To ask such a question was dangerous. Young Lieutenant Zotov's faith in Stalin has not been destroyed despite his anguish at the military setbacks.

The real subject of 'Incident at Krechetovka Station' is Stalinism as systematic paranoia, the handing over of an innocent man to the NKVD on mere suspicion. Lt. Zotov's phobia about spies, drilled into young Russians throughout the 1930s, leads him to hand over to the police a conscripted actor, Tveritinov, who is trying to rejoin his echelon. Zotov loves the theatre and feels intense admiration for this refined and cultivated man – yet finally takes the actor for a disguised White officer, a traitor. And why? Because Tveretinov had the indiscretion to ask him what Stalingrad had been called before it was debaptized. Only a clandestine White could ask such a question! Clearly the lieutenant's suspicion is culturally constructed out of systemic intolerance, particularly against the officer class – even though Zotov himself had come under suspicion when he volunteered to fight in Spain on his own initiative.

'Incident at Krechetovka Station' also uses its fictional license to introduce a long-term Solzhenitsyn theme, the causes of the poor military performance when Nazi Germany invaded. Blamed are the 1937-39 purges of the Red Army, the introduction of political commissars, Stalin's ineptitude as commander-in-chief. The airforce with a numerical superiority of five to one had been destroyed on the ground.[29] In *The First Circle*, Solzhenitsyn repeatedly comes back to the endemic, all-pervasive Soviet paranoia, to the guiltless Russians given huge sentences during the war—for example the fictional Potapov, a designer of the Dnieper dam, who refused to help the Germans reconstruct it. Here he sarcastically 'confesses':

'"Well, you see, I sold it to the Germans."

'"But it was blown up!"

'"So what? I sold it to them after it was blown up."'[30]

Civilian behaviour under the Nazi occupation remained a highly sensitive subject – witness the attack in 1947 on Aleksandr Fadeyev's novel, *Molodaia gvardiia* (*The Young Guard*), published in a first edition of 410,000 copies, lavishly praised and awarded a Stalin Prize the previous year. The attack was fierce despite Fadeyev's role as the long-serving First Secretary of the Writers' Union, a powerful post. Based on close observation of an episode in the Donets Basin, *The Young Guard* was now taken to task for failure to celebrate adequately the role of the Party in the military victory and for depicting panic during the German advance. Officially there had been no panic—the evacuations and retreats at the beginning of the war had an 'organized character.' Fadeyev had worked from local documents showing young people working independently to form resistance groups. The novel, which gave an impression of widespread chaos and showed the youth resistance cut off from the Party, thus failed to portray the exemplary and commanding role of the CPSU.[31] Attacks appeared in *Pravda* and

Kul'tura i zhizn.' An extensive revision of *The Young Guard* was demanded in an article, 'The Young Guard, on the State of Our Theatre.' The *New York Times* (29 December) announced: 'Soviet Novelist Retracts, Will Rewrite Novel. Fadeyev Bows to the Party, Will Make "Young Guard" Conform to Criticism.' Fadeyev thanked his detractors and rewrote the novel, which was republished in 1951. Later, following Fadeyev's suicide in 1956, Simonov recalled that it was well known to Fadeyev that Stalin had personally ordered the attack on his novel.

The setting of *The Young Guard* is July 1942, a full year after the Soviet armed forces suffered a series of crushing blows and ignominious retreats. Fadeyev does not inform his readers how many Soviet citizens had fallen under Nazi rule – an estimated at 70 million—nor does he investigate the reasons for the debacle. Early in the novel Fadeyev introduces the indirect monologue of a Soviet general, who braggingly concludes, despite the bitterness of massive defeat and retreat: 'Our soldier was worth more than the enemy soldier not only in the sense of moral superiority – what a comparison here! – but simply in the military sense. Our commanders are immeasurably superior not only in their political consciousness, but also in their military training...'32 So why the ignominious collapse? (Imagine a British officer making parallel claims on the beaches of Dunkirk as his men scramble for the boats.) No answer. At the end of *The Young Guard*, Fadeyev elevates the victory at Stalingrad into proof of Soviet economic, political and moral superiority.[33]

Most of the Ukraine has been in German hands since the autumn of 1941. Following the fall of Sevastopol a new retreat is under way in July 1942. In Fadeyev's novel, the regional institutions have moved from Vorochilovgrad and Stalino to Krasnodon, a coal mining town witnessing an endless flow of refugees—a typical Soviet industrial town, its new pits operating under the Coal Trust, its houses, hospitals, schools, and clubs testimony to the success of the five-year plans.[34] A group of Komsomol girls, including the novel's principal heroine, Ulya Gromova, emerge from the woods to find the road clogged with military and civilian evacuees. Worse, they are shocked to see the coal mines themselves being blown up to keep them out of German hands. Pit 1B is 'the pride of the Donetz basin.'[35]

The immediate issue for the families of Krasnodon is whether to stay and suffer occupation or to join the refugees. The majority of Party workers are being evacuated – Fadeyev does not explain why, although he does allow a female character, Elizaveta Alexeevna, to utter a bitter outburst against the so-called leaders who have fled, taking their furniture and goods in trucks, while ordinary people must remain behind: '"These dogs attach more value to their possessions than to us, the little people."' Fadeyev allows Elizaveta's friend, the heroic Communist Shulga, to castigate her for going too far in her condemnation – how many of our best have perished, Shulga asks, including 'the flower of our people, the Communists'."[36] The majority of Party workers are indeed evacuated. Only a chosen few stay behind to engage in partisan work. Protsenko, who is to lead the underground from the forest near a Cossack village, departs with his wife in his beat-up old Gazik 5-seater, the Soviet imitation of the 1930 Ford-A.

Chapter 12 provides an admirably detailed description of the confusion at a pontoon bridge across the Donets as citizens, soldiers, trucks all struggle to cross while under air and artillery attack. Nazi tanks appear across the open steppe. On 17 July, Voroshilovgrad falls. Members of the putative Young Guard like seventeen-year-old Sergei Tyulenin bury arms and ammunition. Fadeyev typically uses young Sergei as a springboard to extol Stalin and other Bolsheviks who escaped from tsarist prisons, heroes who flew across the North Pole or crossed floating ice – and on to Kirov, Stakhanov, uniquely Soviet prototypes (Sergei himself longs to become a pilot). His sister Nadia works as a nurse in the army hospital. She and others arrange for wounded soldiers to be hidden in private houses. The army doctor Fyodor Fyodorovich agrees with the plan and stays on disguised as a civilian doctor. [37] After the SS install themselves in the hospital, wounded Russian servicemen are taken out and shot in the woods. When Doctor Fyodor tries to intervene he is shot between the eyes by a brutal NCO of the SS.

The Nazis tramp all over Krasnodon in their grey uniforms and silvered eagle badges, destroying gardens, cutting down trees and jasmine which might provide cover for snipers, offending women by washing naked in the courtyards and by urinating in public, getting drunk, singing raucous songs. Young women are locked in wardrobes to keep them out of bestial hands. (Fadeyev keeps German sexual molestation in a low key, hard to ascertain whether out of respect for his female characters, or out of Soviet literature's dominant 'modesty,' or out of respect for the historical record. (Anatoly Kuznetsov's harrowing account of the occupation of Kiev in 1941, *Babyi Yar*, is even more reticent on the subject.) At Oleg's house, Marina enters with a bucket of water which she spills when she finds the German general's adjutant naked and coming at her with 'an impudent regard.'[38] Fadeyev's description of the Germans as crude and bestial, as pigs, in their personal habits, eating, belching and farting, washing themselves in public, drinking and singing, stops short of rape.

We follow in detail the build-up of the network of clandestine contacts. Fadeyev is also a keen chronicler of administrative and resistance structures. Secretaries of the Party's clandestine regional committees head the territorial areas. Special 'diversionary' groups answer sometimes at district level, sometimes at regional level, sometimes to the central clandestine apparatus for the Ukraine. Given the chaos prevailing at ground level, it all sounds a bit too neat or theoretical. The panoramic structure of the novel admits a huge number of 'characters,' many of whom do not outlive the page, and only a few of whom can develop truly individual qualities. The main purpose is to present types whose biographies within the Soviet system illustrate their integrity or treachery.

No mention is made of the collaboration of Ukrainian nationalists with the Nazis. Nationalist sentiment and separatism simply do not surface. 'Soviet power' is the only focus of loyalty for decent people like the peasant woman Marfa, whose husband is away at the front: '"Maybe our Papa will not come back, that he will fall in the field of battle, but we will know why. And when our Soviet power returns, it will serve as a father to my children"'.[39]

The great curse for those who remain in the town of Krasnodon (or anywhere occupied) is the requirement to register for work, which can lead on to deportation. Vividly described is the cursory medical examination of Valya Filatova, who is made to strip naked before being dubbed '*Tauglich*' (fit for service and therefore deportation). Fearing arrest if she doesn't, she has gone to join the queue of women registering at the work centre. Each female is keen to reverse the normal precedence of queues: you go before me. Once inside, Valya encounters a woman who teaches German in the town's schools, now helping as an interpreter for a brutal corporal.[40]

Although Russians who got separated from their military units during the retreat were notoriously treated with suspicion if they regained Soviet lines, Fadeyev minimises the paranoid aspect of NKVD-GRU behaviour. Indeed, these organs of state security are invisible. Constantly he describes a warm, emotional welcome for those who have escaped German captivity. We have the rather unlikely story of Lilya Ivanikhina, a surgeon's assistant and one of a group who escape from captivity in a camp in Germany by murdering the matron and walking all the way across occupied Poland and the Ukraine – although barely more than a year has elapsed since the war began. On her return, Lilya is immediately surrounded by joyful friends shocked by her physical condition; they recite from Lermontov's poem 'The Demon.'[41]

At the beginning of Part II, the youthful characters we have to come to know swear an oath of allegiance to the Young Guard. Here it becomes doubly apparent why Fadeyev was required to rewrite the novel, despite its Stalin Prize. Although the 1951 version frequently (but half-heartedly) mentions collaboration between the Young Guard and the Party, clearly this elite of about one hundred youths and girls who formed the Young Guard at Krasnodon had worked themselves up into a fervour of vanguard patriotism and boy-scout bonding whose mystical overtones were more apparent than the Marxist ones: 'I swear to avenge implacably our burnt-out, ruined towns and villages, the blood of our people, the martyrdom of our heroic miners. And if I violate this sacred oath under torture or through cowardice, may I be cursed for ever, me and my family, and may I be punished by the pitiless hand of my comrades.'[42]

In chapter 43, Vanya's blameless Ukrainian father is boiling with rage and resentment over his son's underground activities which put the entire family at risk – the Young Guard had just hanged the traitor Fomin from a lamppost—but which also result in more acute poverty. Twelve families with twenty-eight children between them are living in this communal house yet young Vanya is not working, bringing in no income, because he refuses to register and thus work for the Germans who – or so he reasons in the heat of an argument—wish to destroy his own brother, a soldier in the Red Army. The father remonstrates that due to all this idealism the family has not been able to find the fees for Vanya's brother and sister to finish their studies.

As the decisive battle of Stalingrad approaches, everyone gathers to hear Stalin's twenty-fifth anniversary speech, delivered in so measured a way that you can hear water being poured into his glass. Those who listen to the radio become aware of 'participating in something extraordinary and almost impossible' for a people humiliated, beaten, miserable. 'Thus spoke their hope and their vengeance.'[43] (In reality at that dire juncture, October 1942, Stalin had little to offer his captive people beyond the habit of disastrously over-ruling his generals.)

Evidently history cannot confirm beyond doubt how the Krasnodon Young Guard was betrayed, resulting in arrest, torture and horrible death. Fadeyev seems to attribute the betrayal to two silly, selfish, bad girls, Vyrikova and Lyadskaya, who are brought in for interrogation by the Germans, and who each accuse the other, weeping and wailing, while coughing up the names and addresses of school friends who turn out by almost accident to be the Young Guard.[44] The forensic process of detection and arrest remains cloudy. The final executions, the hurling of the young heroes and heroines down the shaft of Pit 5, are described in abbreviated, semi-documentary form, with gruesome detail kept to a minimum. Loads of coal are tossed down on their groaning bodies.

The date of writing the novel is given as '1943-45-51.' This formula may be taken as a smokescreen reflecting the reluctance of the Moscow editors of Editions du Progrès to signpost 1946 as the year that Fadeyev's novel was praised and garlanded – before being abruptly condemned a year later. The major question remains unanswered: was the Young Guard of Krasnodon motivated by loss of faith in the Party's capacity to lead effective resistance?

What of collaborators under the Nazi occupation? Where Soviet novelists acknowledge their existence, the flaw is invariably attributed to weakness of character and personal greed rather than to genuine nationalist sentiment opposed to Russian hegemony or collectivization – or commonly both. The myth of proletarian class consciousness transcending national and linguistic divisions within an expanding USSR has to be preserved as holy writ. Fadeyev's fictional Krasnodon has its share of traitors like Ivan Fomin, who hands over the Communist Matvei Shulga in order to ingratiate himself and to secure a job in the police. Fadeyev's traitors, collaborators, defectors are invariably doomed and damned to weakness of character by their social origins. The Bolsheviks Valko and Shulga, awaiting execution by the Germans, agree that infamous conduct has occurred at every historical juncture as the Bolsheviks fought their way through twenty-five years of continuous conflict. Says Valko, '"We Bolsheviks are used to death! The hangmen and gendarmes of the tsar killed us, the Cadets killed us in October, the whites killed us, the interventionists of all the countries of the world, the bandits of Makhno and Antonov, the kulaks shot us, and we are still living, thanks to the love of the people.'"[45]

Or take the case of Fadeyev's character Statsenko, a reliable, friendly worker for the Coal Trust, but secretly yearning for the idle life, praising foreign films he has never seen, adorning foreign fashion magazines displaying women in elegant attire or almost none. 'In secret' he envies 'ties and toothbrushes imported from abroad' – yet does not bother to learn foreign languages in order to study useful capitalist technical journals on coalmining. When the Germans arrive, Statsenko loses no time in presenting himself at the police station as a volunteer – and is immediately named Burgomeister by Bruckner, the Hauptwachtmeister, who contemptuously rewards him with a cigarette and a few squares of chocolate. [46]

Some citizens appear to flatter the Germans the better to prepare for resistance. When one of the young heroes, Oleg, visits his girlfriend Lena (also heroic) he is shocked to find her mother accepting sardines, chocolate, olive oil from a Nazi batman. Lena herself is in the parlour singing sweetly for the Germans, one of whom is playing the piano – yet Lena flatters the invaders the better to deceive them.[47] Another case of bogus collaboration, often at the bitter expense of harvesting the contempt of fellow-Russians, is the Communist Barakov, a combatant in the Finland war, who speaks excellent German and persuades the tall, thin Nazi Schweide to appoint him director of workshops by confiding him that he is one of the few representatives of the old, privileged classes still operating. Although in reality the son of a worker, Barakov pretends his father was director of a German company under the tsars. The Germans are taken in.[48]

Fadeyev's spectrum of human responses to brutal military occupation is largely echoed in another postwar Stalinist novel, Pavlenko's *Happiness*. While Pavlenko is fairly candid about the poor living conditions prevailing in the villages and kolkhozes, he, like Fadayev, is at pains to depict Soviet attitudes to citizens forcibly deported by the Germans as compassionate – though the florid girl Svetlana Chirikova, taken as a mistress by a German corporal, then pregnant by another before she was liberated, inspires Pavlenko's disgust even though she had had no choice in the matter. She 'lacked the courage' to disobey the German order and was sent to work in a shell factory. To Voropayev she cries, "'The baby! What will I do about the baby! How will I live?... Who will trust me?'" But Pavlenko is unforgiving in the familiar Stalinist mode: 'From now on a semi-animal existence was to be her lot for the rest of her life.'[49]

The more virtuous and politically conscious Komsomol Anya Stupina, volunteers to work in Germany because her girlfriends in the YCL have been commandeered to go, and because (she says) she hopes to take part in a future revolution in Germany. She returns home covered in shame. When Colonel Voropayev tells Stalin about the case of Stupina, Stalin responds wisely, "'She could rouse the people merely by her hatred of the Germans. If we direct that strength in the proper channel of course.'"[50] Instead of heading for the Gulag, the normal fate for those who returned from Germany, Stupina will be warmly accepted into Pioneer Sovkhoz, which will put her through college at its own expense after she leaves high school. She weeps tears of gratitude.[51]

By contrast, Lydia Chukovskaya's novella *Going Under* presents a bleak picture of Stalin's protracted punishment of citizens who fell under Nazi rule. Poor local women customarily do the chores and laundry at the Union of Writers' privileged retreat. From one of them, who is changing the bed linen, Chukovskaya's alter ego, Nina Sergeyevna, learns that because these people suffered eighteen months of German occupation they are now condemned to second-class status excluding higher education. The local librarian regularly withholds certain books as being 'not for villagers.' The servant girl is hostile and contemptuous of writers who know nothing about reality. The narrator allows herself the wider thought that whereas Russians conquered by Napoleon did not suffer reprisals, those suffering Hitler's occupation are still stigmatized, obliged to fill out forms for everything.

Solzhenitsyn, despite his obvious pride in his own war record as a front-line artillery officer, displays a striking ambivalence towards the German invaders. In *The First Circle*, after war breaks out, the peasant character Spiridon bolts with his family into the forest, waits for the front line to sweep past, then returns to his native village: 'The villagers were now told by the Germans they could help themselves to the land which had formerly belonged to the collective farm and work it on their own account.' Spiridon accordingly begins to sow and plough without any qualms of conscience, 'and scarcely bothered his head about how the war was going'. Always his first priority is the safety of his family and the land, not patriotism. Words like motherland, religion and socialism mean nothing to him.[52] Later, as the Germans retreat, he deserts a partisan detachment and joins a column of civilians heading west – the implication here can only be that these civilians wish to live under Nazi, rather than Bolshevik rule. The Germans send them by train to the Rhineland. By now undoubtedly a traitor—but by no means forfeiting Solzhenitsyn's sympathy—Spiridon and his sons work in a factory near Mainz, while his wife and daughter are taken on by a German farmer. Diligent doctors partially restore Spiridon's sight after he goes blind. 'He felt gratitude and respect for those German doctors.'[53]

Solzhenitsyn offers a coolly objective passage on the deadly subject of collaboration, narrated by a character called Viktor Kyubimichev, who finds himself in a German POW camp in 1942, 'to which the Red Cross, thanks to Stalin, was not admitted.' Some Soviet POWs become interpreters, others take on the role of guards. So many are dying even the gravediggers are on their last legs. Then some sign up to fight the Soviet regime, 'among them people who had been in the Komsomol.' The volunteers receive as much food as they can eat. Kyubimichev serves with the Vlasov army tracking down the French

Resistance in the Vosges, then fighting the Allies after the 1944 invasion. Returning to Russia, he 'slipped through the net' but was then imprisoned in Butyrki, finding himself heaped in willy-nilly with Russians who have served in the French Resistance. All receive the same ten-year sentence. 'Lyubimichev had thus been taught by the whole of his experience that nobody could ever possibly have any convictions – which was just as true of the people who had tried and condemned them.'[54]

Solzhenitsyn continues his indictment in his non-fictional *The Gulag Archipelago*. In 1945-46, 'a big wave of genuine, at-long-last, enemies of the Soviet government flowed into the Archipelago'—Vlasov men, Krasnov Cossacks, Muslims from the national units created by Hitler. Add to these at least a million fugitives returned to Stalin by the Western Allies – 'perfidiously,' in Solzhenitsyn's judgment. (This secret, he added, had been well kept by British and American governments, until Julius Epstein published an article in the *Sunday Oklahoman*, 21 January 1973).[55] At the end of the war the Motherland coaxed liberated prisoners home and snared them the moment they reached the frontier. Now, after twenty-seven years, the first honest account by a Russian of these crimes had appeared in samizdat, General P. G. Grigorenko's, 'A Letter to the Magazine "Problems of the History of the Communist Party of the Soviet Union",' 1968.[56]

Solzhenitsyn's uninhibited coverage of these off-limits topics points up the vast silences prevailing elsewhere in Soviet war fiction.

In Georgii Vladimov's novel *Faithful Ruslan*, Shabby Man, once an expert cabinet maker, had been taken prisoner by the Germans and automatically sent to the Gulag at the war's end. He talks sarcastically about the war of 1940 against the 'White Finns' in which he took part, and equates the 'White Finns' with 'the Finns pure and simple.' He drinks to the 'Big Amnesty' yet to come when they will open the gates of the cams. (Former prisoners of the Germans, automatically interned without trial, were merely 'amnestied' after 1956 without the positive rights awarded to prisoners who had been charged with a political offence, and who were now 'rehabilitated.' This status entitled them to housing and an appropriate job; by contrast an amnestied former POW like Shabby Man could only cling to hope and booze.)[57]

In his later novel, *The General and His Army* (*General i ego armii*), Vladimov boldly takes up the story of Vlasov's army, and the fraught issue of collaboration which Solzhenitsyn had confronted in *The First Circle*, *The Gulag Archipelago*, and in the early verse play *Feast of the Conquerors*.[58]

The ultimate liberation of Eastern Europe by the Red Army was celebrated in a self-congratulatory wave of novels, plays and films. In his Stalin prize-winning novel *Happiness* (1947) Pyotr Pavlenko portrays an utterly beneficent Red Army liberating subjugated Europe—no rapes, no brutalities, no looting. Pavlenko echoes the official line on every historical front: just as the Allies had treacherously delayed launching a second military front in France, so their performance on the battlefield did not amount to much: 'The British were capturing frightened Hitlerite generals in the backyards of the war and in prose and poetry were glorifying their "Monty" as if Montgomery's soldiers were the only ones on the battlefield. This hypocrisy did not offend [Colonel] Voropayev so much as disgust him...'[59]

Pavlenko sings from the standard hymn-sheet: Performance in war becomes the ultimate yardstick of social achievement. '"Lads, whoever was at Sevastopol and at Stalingrad has been everywhere!"'[60] After the fall of Berlin, the disabled veteran, Colonel Voropayev, addresses the collective farm workers: '"Socialism alone has won victory for all! The Soviet people have come to the forefront of humanity. For thirty years the most infamous lies were told about them.... Will those abroad even now doubt our strength, refuse to pay tribute to our glory? No!... Long live Stalin!"'[61]

More plausible is the depiction of defeated Austrians who have apparently never heard of fascism – their cringing, obsequious behaviour is experienced by the novel's heroine, Medical Lieutenant Colonel Aleksandra Ivanova Goreva, a surgeon, who spends less time at the operating table than in hurtling through Rumania and Hungary to Vienna, consorting with all classes. '"I have not met any fascists," she writes home to Voropayev. 'One would think there never had been any here.... Nobody knows anything about fascism.'"[62] She visits the grave of Beethoven and a monument to Johann Strauss, spoiled by '"Nude women listlessly rotating to the accompaniment of what looked like shepherd's pipes."' A dozy Austrian philosopher whom she mobilizes to help with a field dressing station raises her hackles by seeking to explain that Vienna is feminine, musical, capricious, a city of dances. Later she tells a crowd of anxious Viennese: '"You will live as you lived before the war. Austria will be a free country."' But she observes their distrust.[63] Here in bourgeois Vienna, Russian Bolsheviks can never be popular but in the working-class districts, '"There they kiss and hug our men and weep on their shoulders."' As for the bourgeoisie – what thieves! You capture a fine mansion and soon they turn up like carrion crows: '"Permit us, Herr Major, to take our things."' You capture another mansion and the same crowd arrive, wheedling and lying.

Goreva is thirty, tall and elegant, but she has aged since the battle for Budapest. Her face 'bore an almost physically palpable coating of despair which aged her fine, proud features.' She will look back on her experiences of liberated countries – 'how they flaunted their wretched humility towards the victors and were already putting out their hands for alms, dancing in cafés, singing in theatres, playing in beer halls, ready to serve the first-comer for a spoonful of egg powder or a pinch of tobacco.... But where was that Europe about which Herzen had written with such manly respect and which Turgenev had loved so tenderly? That Europe she had not seen.'[64]

At the opposite extreme is Solzhenitsyn's portrait of the Red Army as it finally advances into enemy territory. In *The First Circle*, Stalin's underling, the bloated Abakumov, embodies the hierarchical scale, according to rank, of looting from occupied Germany, particularly by SMERSH operating in the rear and stuffing trains with purloined goods.

Solzhenitsyn's character Lev Grigoryevich Rubin, a specialist in German philology who speaks German perfectly, down to dialects, had been arrested under Article 58 for his qualms about sending back captured Germans through the front lines with forged papers – and for speaking out against the slogan 'Blood for blood and death for death.' In his memoirs Lev Kopelev, the model for Solzhenitsyn's character Rubin, describes in detail the barbarous scenes he witnessed as the Red Army advanced into eastern Germany, his attempts to intervene—and how fellow-officers merely shrugged: 'What can you do? It's war; people become brutalized.' His superior, the broad-faced Zabashtansky, goes further: the Red Army soldier must hate the enemy, thirst for revenge, extermination, looting—everything belongs to the victorious soldier, even the women. Kopelev asks whether this means killing children. Zabashtansky answers that he and Kopelev would not do such a thing: 'But to be honest, if you like, let those who *will* do it also kill the little Fritzes in their frenzy until they've had enough – that's war, Comrade, and not philosophy or literature.'[65]

Soviet novelists, playwrights and film scenarists generally echoed the official Soviet line on the origins of the cold war, garnished in praise-poems to Stalin. Until 1946 historians and novelists remained in general faithful to the spirit of the wartime anti-fascist alliance, but thereafter Western leaders like Truman and Churchill were depicted as dire reactionaries who had sought a separate peace with Hitler. Even Solzhenitsyn's independent-minded fellow-prisoner at Marfino (the real name of Solzhenitsyn's 'Mavrino'), Lev Kopelev, grabbed every newspaper he could, convinced that Truman was pursuing an 'infamous' policy and accepting the official Soviet line on the wars in Greece and Indochina (with some justice!).[66]

Vasily Grossman and Solzhenitsyn figure prominently among the heretics. In his novel *Life and Fate*, Grossman prods the totalitarian theme into the ultra-sensitive territory of postwar politics and the Cold War, drawing direct lines of continuity between two systems of oppression. 'The great rising of the Warsaw ghetto, the uprisings in Treblinka and Sobibor; the vast partisan movement that flared up in dozens of countries enslaved by Hitler; the uprisings in Berlin in 1953, in Hungary in 1956, and in the labour camps of Siberia and the Far East after Stalin's death; the riots at this time in Poland, the number of factories that went on strike and the student protests that broke out in many cities against the suppression of freedom of thought; all these bear witness to the indestructibility of man's yearning for freedom.'[67] In this passage, Grossman resorts to direct authorial exposition, leaping clear of his fictional framework.

The original version of Solzhenitsyn's *The First Circle* began with an incident outrageous to Soviet sensibilities, reflecting Solzhenitsyn's pro-Western sympathies from the outset of the Cold War. A young Soviet diplomat, with the rank of counsellor in the Ministry of Foreign Affairs, Innokentii Volodin, makes an anonymous, clandestine call from a public telephone to the American embassy in Moscow. His intention? To warn the Americans of an imminent Soviet atomic espionage rendezvous in New York. The fictional setting is 1949 but composition began in 1955, so Solzhenitsyn very likely had in mind the case of Julius and Ethel Rosenberg, arrested in 1950 and executed in 1953. If, in terms of Solzhenitsyn's own allegiances, Volodin's act of treason amounted to a principled act of courage, this surely confirms that Solzhenitsyn's hostility to Soviet foreign policy marched in step with his detestation of the USSR as a murderous totalitarian force within its own borders.

Throughout *The First Circle* every reference to the West is either friendly or designed to ridicule postwar Soviet paranoia and propaganda campaigns. For example: 'So American magazines with diagrams and articles on the theory of "clipping", which in New York were openly sold on news-stands, were here numbered, tied with string, classified and sealed in fireproof safes for fear of American spies.'[68] The senior engineer working on the telephone scrambler at Mavrino uses the English word 'scrambler,' to the annoyance of officials like Abakumov. Solzhenitsyn takes the anti-Soviet view (through his characters) on a wide range of cold war issues, including the torture and bogus trial of László Rajk, the anti-Tito campaign, Americans allegedly dropping Colorado beetles from the air, and internal capitalist crises.

The postwar Party-line fiction issuing from the PCF presses in Paris included work by Louis Aragon, whose multi-volume novel, *Les Communistes* (1950-51), defended every zigzag of the Party line during the phoney war and the German invasion, while camouflaging the PCF's clandestine approach to the German occupation authorities in May-June 1940. Aragon provoked revulsion by eulogising Zhdanov's intimidating theses on art, literature and music as 'far-sighted' and 'profound.'[69] Communist writers gushed their tributes to Stalin on the occasion of his seventieth birthday in 1949, clapping in unison as doves of peace fluttered above the Velodrome d'Hiver.

André Stil, editor of *l'Humanité*, produced a three-volume novel, *Le Premier Choc*, taking as its theme the struggle of dockers in an Atlantic seaport against the American 'occupation.'[70] The Americans rape, dispossess peasants and small owners of their fields and houses, generate unemployment, incorporate ex-Nazis into their forces, and stock France with arms in preparation for a war against the USSR, all with the support and connivance of the French bourgeoisie and their hired hands, the police. (The East German film company DEFA was concurrently turning out movies depicting the depredations of American forces occupying West Germany.) Stil certainly knew his dockers and their dialect; his detailed and compassionate accounts of unemployment, poverty and suffering ring true. Certain scenes remain in the mind: Lucien and Georgette, humiliated by poverty, are forced to send their twelve-year-old daughter to Paris where a sympathetic teacher has offered to look after her. They watch the girl depart while the whole street looks on in sympathy. Through the docker Henri and his wife Paulette, both Communists, Stil provides the prototype of the positive hero and heroine. Secretary of the 'Dimitrov' cell, Henri is rarely behind on his reading of the Party's newspapers and cultural journals. The temper of Party life among the dockers is calculatingly depicted, private jealousies surface, and one docker complains at a section meeting that they have become obsessed by foreign affairs—'geography classes' – instead of focusing on the 'dog's life' they lead at home. (The inter-connection of domestic and foreign affairs is then patiently explained to him.) In the second and third volumes the artistic quality suffers as Stil abandons his pages to journalistic polemic and the Party blueprint. Translated into Russian and the languages of Eastern Europe, *Le Premier Choc* was awarded a Stalin Prize.

Meanwhile socialist realist production novels eulogising Stalin, the Party, the working class, clattered from Soviet presses. An excellent example of the genre is Vsevolod Kochetov's, *The Zhurbins* (1952): 'The mighty Party – once a mere handful of people grouped around Lenin – had come a long way...its great ideas had flooded like an ocean over the country, and indeed across its frontiers... millions of people, mutually educating and renewing each other. The party was leading them on and on, scooping out a channel through which that ocean could flow ever on into the future.'[71] Kochetov tells how at a young age he was 'itching to take part in this huge refashioning of the Soviet villages'. At the age of twenty, he served as director of a state farm before becoming a reporter on the *Leningradskaia Pravda*. He served as a war correspondent throughout the 900 days of the Nazi siege of Leningrad: 'I saw the Soviet man in his full gigantic stature.'

The plot of *The Zhurbins* hinges on a Government decree calling for the rapid expansion of the Soviet merchant fleet, and for ships of high quality and durability. The Zhurbin family, three generations, embodies the shipbuilding tradition as well as the best in Soviet man. In the course of the novel, we learn that American Liberty Ships were constructed too hastily – though adequate for short-term wartime needs, just as capitalism has inhibited the full realisation of British shipbuilding skills. The nominal Stalinist value system is constantly spelled out: science, education, good exam results, individual initiative, Stakhanovite prowess, Stalin prizes, technology, courage, experience, patriotism, pride in the history of Communism, peace, athletics, gymnastics, fishermen who are real men, Soviet woman taking on tough jobs (like Zina in the shipyards), respect for age, authority, and seniority right up to the Council of Ministers – not forgetting resourcefulness, self-help, honour, sexual shyness and modesty (author and characters alike).

The general literary technique is that of the Bildungsroman, a large, interlocking set of narratives exploring the Zhurbins in their plenitude. The non-conditional 'would' (plus verb) is used hundreds of times to indicate typification and the desired norms. A lot of the narrative takes the form of explicit dialogue which leaves nothing to the imagination. How does the Party function? Everything is discussed democratically and thought through, 'and everybody is appointed to his own special job. The Party Committee goes to the people in person and explains everything. The Party Organizer rolls up his sleeves and gets busy'. Old Matvei praises Stakhanovites. "'What does Comrade Stalin say here in this book? The Stakhanovite breaks down the old standards and works in a new way.'" Old Matvei reflects: 'And the man who's not a Stakhanovite is not a Communist either.' When Victor Zhurbin wins a Stalin Prize, third class, for his drawings and mathematical calculations, all rejoice – family, friends, colleagues, neighbours.

Meanwhile fine women are working in the shipyard. 'And among them were mother heroines – mothers of ten children or more – and women who had seen Stalin in the Kremlin; women who, like Semyonova, had served at the front; women who had been in Siberia, in the Caucasus, in Central Asia, and on Sakhalin; women who had gone to sea in fishing boats with their fathers, served as soldiers in the Civil War, worked in the coal fields, helped to build the Dnieper Hydroelectric Station.'[72]

18

The Tragic Case of Vasily Grossman

Vasily[1] Grossman (1905-1964) has become, since the late Gorbachev era war and the collapse of the Soviet Union, an iconic figure in late 'Cold War studies' of the anti-Soviet variety. Less well known in the West during his lifetime, and never a *cause célèbre* like Pasternak or Solzhenitsyn, he is now celebrated as a major Soviet insider who went over to Western totalitarian theory. Frank Ellis (1994) opens his study of Grossman by describing the at-long-last publication of *Life and Fate* and *Everything Flows* in the Soviet Union in the late 1980s as 'an unprecedented volte-face even by the standards of *glasnost'*.'[2]

Three years passed between first submission of the manuscript of *For a Just Cause* to the journal *Novyi mir* and the start of serialisation following the replacement of Simonov as editor by Aleksandr Tvardovsky.[3] Supported by Tvardovsky and Fadeyev, the novel was initially hailed as a Soviet *War and Peace* – but this kiss of life soon turned into a storm of condemnation in a manner normally associated with intervention by Stalin in person. The novel was now attacked for failing to show the sources of the mass heroism of the Soviet people, their immortal deeds, etc.[4]

Grossman had made his name as a decorated Patriotic War correspondent, reporting not only the Battle of Stalingrad but the Battle of Berlin for *Krasnaia zvezda* (*Red Star*) and *Znamia* (*Banner*). *Red Star* alone published forty pieces.[5] His *povest'* (story) *The People are Immortal* was published in London in 1943 as well as Moscow. The writer Viktor Nekrasov, who fought at Stalingrad, remembers how 'the papers with Grossman's and Ehrenburg's articles were read and re-read by us until they were in tatters'.[6] With Ehrenburg the most popular journalist and publicist of the time, he was a master of observation and naturalistic detail. What Western books Vasily Grossman was able to read we do not know – he never left the USSR in peacetime.

And he was a Jew.[7] His mother, Ekaterina Savelievna Grossman, a school-teacher, died at the hands of the Germans, having stayed behind in Berdichev to look after a sick niece. Found in his papers was a letter he had written to his mother nine years after she died: 'I have tried...hundreds of times, to imagine how you died, how you walked to meet your death.... I tried to imagine the person who killed you. He was the last person to see you. I know you were thinking about me...during all that time.'[8] Grossman was one of the first reporters to reach the Nazi death camp at Treblinka in 1944. In the journal *Znamya* (*Banner*) he published 'The Hell of Treblinka,' said to be the first journalistic account of a Nazi death camp in any language.[9] As a leading member of the Jewish Antifascist Committee, he took part in the compilation and editing of a *Black Book*, on which Ehrenburg and he began work in 1943, a documentation of the Hitlerian extermination. Ehrenburg recalls that the book was ready and in print by the beginning of 1944, then frozen and finally destroyed at the end of 1948 when the Jewish Antifascist Committee was dissolved.

It is this experience, closely followed by the anti-cosmopolitan campaign and the agony of getting *For a Just Cause* into print, which provides the clue to Grossman's authorship of *Life and Fate*. The key is his bitter encounter with Stalinist anti-Semitism from the end of the war to Stalin's death. Discovered in Grossman's archive is a diary providing a painstaking account of the vicissitudes of *For a Just Cause*, beginning on 2 August 1949, the day he submitted the manuscript to *Novyi mir*, and concluding on 26 October 1954, when the book version appeared in print: a seemingly endless cycle of writing, discussion and rewriting. As a result there are twelve different versions of *For a Just Cause* in the Central Archives. Ellis comments: 'No ordinary Soviet novel was ever subjected to such a bureaucratic pummelling before and after it was published.' Fluctuations within the editorial board of *Novyi mir* accounted for much of the prevarication. Mikhail Sholokhov, firmly against publication, wrote to Tvardovsky: 'Whom have you entrusted to write about Stalingrad? Are you in your right mind? I am against it.' This led to the jettisoning of the original title, which was to have been *Stalingrad*.

During the months when *For a Just Cause* was appearing in *Novyi mir*, the military college of the supreme tribunal of the USSR sat in secret and condemned thirty-two members of the Jewish Antifascist Committee to death.[10] The Jewish theme is tactically absent from the novel—apart from a conversation between Himmler and Hitler in which the former counsels a secret extermination of the Jews while the latter reproaches him for cowardice. Despite his caution, Grossman now came under attack as a Jewish nationalist and a reactionary idealist after a new wave of anti-Semitism was launched at the time of the Prague Zionist trial and weeks later in January 1953 at the time of the 'Doctors' Plot.' *Pravda* (13 February 1953), published an indictment of Grossman's novel by Mikhail Bubennov. A month had passed since the first communiqué revealing 'the assassins in white gowns.' A rival of Grossman as a war novelist, and one of the fiercest anti-Semites, Bubennov, claimed that Grossman had failed to create a single character worthy of the heroes of Stalingrad – only feeble, inexpressive silhouettes. He had failed to show the leading role of the Party or the heroism of the workers. The Shtrum family in the novel were dismissed as insipid. Grossman's errors were not new; this was an idealist writer, reactionary, dépassé. Several members of the editorial board including Tvardovsky and Fedin now hastened to apologize for having failed to detect the ideological and artistic faults of the novel. From February to May 1953, *Izvestia, Literaturnaia gazeta, Kommunist* and other organs published articles and notes resuming Bubennov's accusations, often in a form even more gross. Fadeyev promptly disavowed his protégé after Stalin died, savaging the novel in *Pravda* – though having previously promoted it. Grossman wrote to the Union of Writers recognising his errors.[11]

Remarkably, in 1954 *For a Just Cause* was published in book form and acclaimed. This edition of the novel was substantially the same as in the flayed *Novyi mir* edition.[12] Fadeyev came out in support. Ehrenburg recalled that after the rehabilitation of the Jewish doctors accused of plotting to assassinate Party leaders, Fadeyev 'came to me without ringing the bell, sat down on my bed and said: "Don't be too hard on me... I was frightened"'. Ehrenburg asked him why he had published the piece after Stalin's death. '"I thought the worst was still to come," he replied.'[13] At the end of 1955, for his fiftieth birthday, Grossman received the Banner of Labour. The Secretariat of the Writers' Union congratulated him. In 1958, appeared a thick collection of novellas, stories, essays from the 1930s and 1940s. The late 1950s was a time of apparent success for Grossman[14]—yet all the while he was composing the devastatingly heretical *Life and Fate.*

Two extracts extract from *Life and Fate* had appeared in *Literaturnaia gazeta* on 2 April and 26 August, and one more in *Vechernaia Moskva* (14 September 1960).[15] The editor-in-chief of *Znamia*, Vadim Kozhevnikov, sent the manuscript to the cultural section of the Central Committee without informing Grossman. After almost a year, *Znamia* returned the manuscript, calling it 'anti-Soviet.' Soon afterwards, on 14 February 1961, three officers of the KGB descended on Grossman's flat in Lomonovskiy Prospect with a warrant, seized the manuscript and notes during a search lasting ninety minutes, raided his typists, even took the copies held by *Znamia* and *Novyi mir*. Rough drafts, typewriter ribbons and carbon paper were all taken. By chance, the first draft of the even more deadly *Everything Flows* (see below) was left untouched. Two copies of *Life and Fate* survived, one in the possession of his friend Vladimir Lakshin.[16]

Grossman wrote to Khrushchev to protest the seizure of his novel. Mikhail Suslov, party secretary for ideology, summoned him on 23 July 1962 to a meeting which lasted three hours.[17] Suslov admitted to not having read *Life and Fate* but told Grossman that it could not be published for 250-300 years. Suslov had borrowed this verdict from advisers; they all agreed that publication would be far more damaging to Soviet interests than that of *Doctor Zhivago*. Suslov compared *Life and Fate* to an atom bomb. (It has been claimed that Grossman was the first Soviet writer to attribute to Lenin initial responsibility for the evils of Soviet society.) Suslov refused Grossman's request that the manuscript be returned to him.[18]

This was what 'liberalism' and 'thaw' could mean under Khrushchev. Grossman died of stomach cancer on 14 September 1964, aged fifty-nine. Ehrenburg's memoirs recall how bitter was Grossman's funeral, but all the surviving war correspondents of *Red Star* did turn out. Prior to the Gorbachev era, Simon Markish knew of only one reference to *Life and Fate* in Soviet literature.[19] At the end of 1974, Lakshin approached Vladimir Voinovich, a leading Soviet dissident writer, and gave him a copy to read. Assisted by Andrei Sakharov and Elena Bonner, Voinovich brought a microfilm to the West. The French edition received huge reviews and sold over 150,000 copies, despite a cover price reflecting its 800 pages.[20] The translator Robert Chandler's attention was first drawn to the novel by the émigré Soviet art expert, Igor Golomstok, who had been presenting it on the BBC's Russian Service.[21] 'Probably no great novel of the last sixty years is so untouched by the influence of Modernism,' comments Chandler.[22]

The literary genre of *Life and Fate* is that of photographic realism embracing a vast spectrum of settings: a German concentration camp; the dugouts and headquarters of the German Sixth Army at the battle of Stalingrad; Jews being transported to the extermination camps of Auschwitz and Dachau; a Soviet Physics Institute – and a labour camp. Grossman recognises that in 1942-1943 not only the fates of the occupied countries of Europe and the prisoners of war were at stake, but also the tragic destiny of the Kalmyks, the Crimean Tartars, the Balkars and the Chechens 'who were to be deported to Siberia and Kazakhstan, who were to lose the right to remember their history or teach their own children to speak their mother-tongue.' The phrases 'were to be,' 'were to lose,' draws attention to the narrator's future vantage point, the anti-Semitic terror of 1949-53: 'At stake also was the fate of Jewish actors, writers whose execution was to precede the sinister trial of Professor Vovsi and the Jewish doctors.... Stalin was to raise over their heads the very sword of annihilation he had wrested from the hands of Hitler.'[23] (Such was the prevailing terror that Grossman himself had felt constrained to sign a document calling for the punishment of the innocent doctors.)

Vasily Grossman's fiction not only presents characters of courage and principle but also argues the general case for judging individuals by their behaviour rather than by their social origins. The university scientist Shtrum reflects how questions about social origin had always seemed to him natural and moral, if only because the Russian revolution was a social one—but now the Nazis had arrived, imposing a parallel racism, insisting that some nations are inherently superior to others. Shtrum concludes that it amounts to the same thing, a blind obliviousness to the individual qualities of the victim. In Grossman's *For a Just Cause* the Bolshevik Abarchuk, a member of a faculty committee dealing with admissions ('the faculty Robespierre'), takes pleasure in expelling students who do not meet his class criteria, the stereotypes which have supplanted individual judgment in his head. Grossman depicts a devoted Communist tipping over the edge of his own certainties into a kind of social racism, obsessively severe with students found driving up to the Livorno restaurant in jackets and cravats, or girl students caught wearing a cross on their chest.[24] By the time of *Life and Fate*, Abarchuk has fallen victim to the policies he has pursued. Now interned, an empty vessel turned upside down, he is fearful and vulnerable to his fellow-prisoners.[25]

John Bayley described Grossman's method as 'indeed socialist realism, used with a wholly Tolstoyan truth and honesty'. But Bayley found a yawning gap in *Life and Fate*, characters without the time or inclination to be conscious of themselves. The Shaposhnikov family do not have the unifying function exercised by the Rostovs in *War and Peace*. Bayley further complained that 'extended scenes or dialogues, like those between fighter pilots, tank men and other heroic figures, sound all wrong, although in a manner the reader is quite used to'. Bayley pondered the possible influence of 'Kipling's version of the way professionals talk at their work...not for each other's benefit, but for the reader.' In addition, the fates of characters seemed arbitrary, 'who was killed where, who starved, drowned, was shot, gassed or relapsed into anonymous existence'. By the same paradox that operates in *Doctor Zhivago*, the random arbitrariness of coincidence and destiny, puts the author too much to the fore as 'an all-powerful instrument of fate rather than an artist'.[26]

19

Commentary: Collectivization

The collectivization of agriculture, launched by Stalin in the late 1920s, involved an immense mobilization of activists and idealists in a spirit of fierce and unforgiving class struggle. The result was hailed by the Party as an immense victory for socialism but the human devastation was appalling. Few writers dared say so. Koestler, traversing the USSR as a German correspondent, did not divulge what he witnessed in the Ukraine. Rather more surfaces in Victor Serge's novel, *The Case of Comrade Tulayev*, written from exile. The Kurgansk Regional Party Secretary Artyem Makeyev is accorded a long section called 'To Build is to Perish.' Makeyev has been up to his neck in collectivization:

'So began the black years. First expropriated, then deported, some seven per cent of the farmers left the region in cattle cars amid the cries, tears and curses of urchins and dishevelled women and old men mad with rage. Fields lay fallow, cattle disappeared, people ate the oil cake intended for the stock, there was no more sugar or gasoline... everywhere pilfering, collusion, sickness; in vain did Security decimate the [agricultural] bureaus...' Here Comrade Tulayev is introduced as the figure of authority insisting on draconian measures, new purges of the kolkhozes, detested even by Makeyev. At one point Makeyev voices opposition to Tulayev's policies, only to renounce his errors, grovel, and be reappointed as regional secretary.[1]

The major literary depiction of collectivization belonged to Mikhail Sholokhov, born in 1905 and the most internationally celebrated of Soviet novelists. His epic talent emerged with *And Quiet Flows the Don* (*Tikhy Don*—also *The Quiet Don*), which appeared in four volumes in 1928, 1929, 1933, and 1940. The subject is the Cossack communities of the Don region before and during the Revolution. To what extent Sholokhov wrote from personal observation and to what extent he borrowed from other writers has remained a subject for intense debate.

In 1932, before producing volume 3 of *The Quiet Don*, Sholokohov turned his pen to the ongoing collectivization of agriculture in the Don region. The first part of *Virgin Soil Upturned* (*Podniatnaia tselina*), published in *Novyi mir*, describes collectivization in the village of Gremyachy Log. The project is liquidation of the kulaks, confiscation by force of their properties. (Resistance and bloody uprisings took place in the Ukraine, North Caucasus, the Don region, Siberia, the Volga region.) Alarmed by the scale of resistance, Stalin published two warnings, 'Dizzy with Success' (*Pravda*, 2 March 1930) and 'Reply to Kolkhoz comrades' (*Pravda*, 3 April). The chastening, indeed shattering impact, of Stalin's intervention on the more zealous comrades is vividly described by Sholokhov, skilfully deploying a novelist's license. But he never takes us behind the closed doors in Moscow; he does not introduce real figures like Karl Bauman, head of the Rural Department of the Moscow Committee responsible for implementation of the extremist policy towards kulaks and much violence in the years 1929-30. In 1931, Bauman was demoted and moved to other work.[2]

Western attention, mainly hostile, suspected Sholokhov of sacrificing his integrity, his fine sense of the complexity of human allegiances, to political expediency and Party pressure. And why (it was asked) was the sequel to *Virgin Soil Upturned*, announced as *Harvest on the Don*, withheld from publication? In 1936 the editors of *Novyi mir* announced that the manuscript of had been returned to the author for revision. Why did *Harvest on the Don* not begin to appear until 1955 – the onset of Khrushchev's Thaw—and why was publication again interrupted? Not until 12 February 1960 did the concluding chapters of *Harvest on the Don* appear in *Pravda*.

In the final version, the Communist hero of collectivization, Davydov, and a colleague die one night when they break into the house of a kolkhoz property manager who is hiding two counter-revolutionary plotters. The novel ends with the exposure of a wide counter-revolutionary conspiracy in the Don region, the arrest of the conspirators, and their trial. Harrison Salisbury's 'Sholokhov Hero Dies a New Death' (*New York Times*, 18 February 1960) reported the rumour that Sholokhov had originally ended the novel with Davydov dying in prison during the purges of the mid-thirties. In this version, Davydov, a courageous Party worker who is assigned to head a collective farm in the turbulent days of 1930, combats intrigue, opposition, plots until his arrest. He commits suicide in prison.

But it has to be borne in mind that no such version appeared under Sholokhov's name. When Khrushchev visited Sholokhov in Veshenskaya Stanitsa and invited the writer to accompany him on his official visit to the United States in 1959, the Western press speculated that Sholokhov had been persuaded to change the ending and save Davydov from death in prison. While in the U.S. with Khrushchev, Sholokhov dismissed American journalists' questions about his difficulties over *Harvest on the Don* as 'mad fantasy.'[3]

If Davydov had been imprisoned during the purges of the late thirties this would self-evidently have carried the time-span of *Harvest on the Don* beyond the year 1930. The published text bears evidence of chronological confusion and hasty re-writing. Late in the novel, on page 355, the counter-revolution-ary Liatievsky says to his colleague Polovtsiev: 'Don't forget it's 1930 now,' i.e., set in the same year as its predecessor, *Virgin Soil Upturned*. On the other hand, on page 208 Davidov says to the chairman of a collective farm, 'I'm not Litvinov, and you're not Chamberlain, and there's no point in our being diplomatic with each other. Was the hay carted off by your orders?' Such a remark would be inconceivable in 1930—Chamberlain succeeded Baldwin as British prime minister in 1937, and Litvonov did not become well known as commissar for foreign affairs until the Munich era. The most likely hypothesis is that Sholokohov's first draft had carried the novel through to 1937-8, but the story line was later revised and the ending altered under Party pressure. Sholokhov agreed to have Davydov shot by counter-revolutionaries at a much earlier date, in 1930; the 'Chamberlain-Litvinov' remark became an unamended anachronism overlooked by author, editors and printers.

Circumstantial evidence is found in a confidential report to Stalin by V. P. Stavsky (16 September 1937), following a visit to Sholokhov's home in the village of Veshensk. In essence the great writer complained he could not write while his close colleagues in the District Party including its secretary, Lugavoi, were being arrested, imprisoned, tortured and interrogated without a break for five to ten days. 'If Lugavoi is guilty then so am I!' One of those imprisoned, Logachev, had been 'broken under torture, he gave false testimonies against many honest Communists, including me, and even accused himself.' And why was he being shadowed by the NKVD? Stalin brought Sholokhov to Moscow for a fraternal conversation. Lugavoi was released but others were not. In subsequent letters to Stalin, recently discovered in the archives, Sholokhov spoke the prevailing language about 'enemies of the people...a diabolically conspiratorial group of enemies' determined to rout Bolshevik cadres – but Sholokhov was in essence though not by name pointing the finger at the NKVD. As for the still unfinished *Harvest on the Don*, Sholokhov pointed out to Stalin that due to the prevailing hysteria and persecution, 'last year's crop was scarcely harvested, a huge quantity of grain rotted in the field, the seed wasn't preserved, and the ploughing wasn't finished for the spring sowing'.[4] All in all it is more than likely that in the original draft of *Harvest on the Don* Davydov was investigating sabotage of the harvest only to be arrested. Novelists tend to gravitate towards their own painful experiences.

Conceding that the local Communist leaders in *Virgin Soil Upturned* are 'vividly drawn by Sholokhov,' including Davidov, Makar Nagulnov, a hero of the Civil War who dreams of world revolution, and the chairman of the village Soviet Andrei Razmetnov, the émigré critic Vera Alexandrova nevertheless discerned an underlying lack of enthusiasm for collectivization: 'Sholokhov was the first writer to convey the truly tragic quality of the radical change that was being wrought in the life of the peasants. True, he also made use of the current clichés about the intrigues of Whites and kulaks, but he succeeded in raising an edge of the curtain over the thoughts and feelings of rank-and-file peasant Cossacks, and showed that the poor peasants were also frequently afraid of joining the collective farms and supported the Cossacks.' Alexandrova distinguishes between two Sholokhovs— 'the artist' and 'the Communist.' 'In his portraits of the Cossacks, Sholokhov succeeded best with those of the opponents of collectivization.... Sholokhov the artist understands the organic character of the peasant resistance to collectivization. Sholokhov the Communist attempts to explain this resistance by the rigidity of peasant psyche and the peasantry's natural reaction to the errors and "excesses" of the local authorities.'[5]

The dissident historian Roy Medvedev praised *Virgin Soil Upturned* as a truthful account of the deportation of kulak families of Gremyachy Log. Medvedev set Sholokhov's novel in the context of other collectivization literature, including the frightful episodes documented in Fyodor Panferov's novel *Brusski*. He also cited one of the passages of 'dekulakization' in an unpublished short novel by an author whose name he gave, protectively, as A. M---n, who had taken part in the collectivization drive as a brigade member 1930, involving deportations of even poor peasants who refused to join collectives. The scene from this manuscript novel – '*K viashchei slave gospodne*'—depicts Brigade leader Morgunov's horror after bursting into a house to discover how utterly poor was this 'class enemy':

'Terent'ev trembled and wept. "What kind of kulaks are we? What for? What did I do?"' The answer comes: '"Nothing! You're a kulak, a *podkulachnik!* You're against the kolkhoz. You don't want to join and you're disrupting the work."' [6]

In Aleksandr Fadeyev's *The Young Guard* (1947, 1951), collectivization is described in orthodox Stalinist terms, following an unwavering social determinism. The character Fomin, for example, is originally from the Vormezh region, where he flourished as a peasant of considerable wealth, though he pretended to support the Revolution. To obtain his brothers' lands, he denounced them. When collectivization arrived in 1930, Fomin's estate (including three farms and a dozen horses) was confiscated and he was sentenced to exile, but before the sentence could be carried out he had murdered the chairman of the village Soviet and the secretary of the party committee. He and his wife then fled and obtained forged identity papers at Rostov, before settling in the Donbass. He duly welcomed the Germans and betrayed the heroic Communist Shulga, who now lies beaten and bloody in a Nazi cell.[7]

In his early fiction, Vasily Grossman had adopted the orthodox attitude of revulsion towards the kulaks, strikingly similar in imagery to Fadeyev's. In the wartime novella (*povest'*), *The People Are Immortal*, Grossman allows himself a leering villain in the shape of old Kotenko, now sixty-five, observing the flight of the village Soviet, happily awaiting the coming of the Germans, whitewashing his house in their honour, and baiting the chairman of the collective farm. '"You are getting ready to travel, eh? Chairman of the collective farm," said Kotenko in a jeering tone."' We are given Kotenko's history – the natural history of his greed. 'Once, about forty years ago, he had gone to visit an uncle of his who had been a rich Estonian kulak. He had never forgotten the huge cattle yard, the steam mill, the master of the house himself...a rich, powerful muzhik. And from that moment Kotenko had dreamt of...beautiful russet cows, flocks of sheep, hundreds of enormous pinkish hogs...dozens of strong, subservient farm labourers...' By 1915, the ruthless Kotenko owned 162 acres. 'The Revolution had taken all this away from him... He waited, biding his time and hoping.' To add to his bitterness his sons had volunteered to fight for the Reds. In Kotenko's case, then, it is not in the great forced collectivization drive of 1929-30 that he loses his land; it is not clear why he had not recovered some of his property under NEP. He is consumed by envy of the old woman Cherednichenko: 'Kotenko saw that the honours which he had wanted to acquire under Tsarist rule had been acquired by her in a life of labour after the Revolution. She was taken to town in a car and made speeches in a theatre.' When her picture appears in the paper he is infuriated by her 'wise, stern eyes, and in his imagination she was laughing at him'. As the Germans approach he makes calculations: 'The collective farm stables were built on my land, which means that they'll be my stables' – likewise the orchard of cherry and apple trees, and the bee hives.[8]

Several years after *The People Are Immortal* appeared, Grossman's novel *For a Just Cause* pursues a similar perspective by introducing a remarkably similar old kulak, Pukhov, a relic of tsarist times who blames the kolkhoz for every misfortune. Governments have always given peasants a hard time (reflects Pukhov), and under the tsars there was hunger but it was better than now.[9] The collective farmer, Vavilov, who will die a hero at Stalingrad, answers Pukhov: the more the people help the state, the more the state will help the people.[10] Elderly women join in on Vavilov's side: we are now treated as people, they say, our children grow up into big people – that was not so under the tsar. In Part 1, chapter 60, Grossman again treats with disgust and hatred those kulaks who survived, nostalgic for tsars, lamenting the fate of brethren who perished, and now happy under German occupation.[11] *For a Just Cause* appears to condemn the Ukrainian kulaks, seen as base collaborators with the Nazi occupation yet deprived of the terrible historical experience which fashioned their outlook. In Part I, the reader encounters elegies for the happy life before the war, for the kolkhoz system, the organizing role of the Party, Stalin's genius as commander. Two panegyrics to Stalin in the serialized (periodical) version are not found in the published book. Given what we now know of Grossman's actual convictions at the time, these eulogies make difficult reading: 'Stalin knew what millions of Soviet citizens had experienced in the course of this year. He had shared with them the bitterness of the days and weeks of retreat... Throughout this war he was consumed by anger against the wretches who swamped Soviet territory in blood. He experienced also the grief and pity of soldiers who had lost their mother, their fiancée, their sisters... The organizer of the powerful Soviet war industry knew the hatred in the hearts of teachers, pupils, professors, students... His anger was shared by the workers and engineers who completed the hydro-electric station on the Dniepr...' (and more of the same).[12]

Grossman's depiction of kulaks and praise for collectivization in his early works is at variance with the damning perspective conveyed in *Life and Fate* and *Everything Flows*. In this, Grossman's final work, Ivan Grigorievich's partner, Anna Sergeevna, dies of lung cancer – but not before she confesses her involvement as a young party activist of twenty-two in collectivization and how the physical violence was preceded by a campaign in print, on the radio and in propaganda films against these bloodsucking exploiters. Anna Sergeevna was indoctrinated to believe that kulaks burn grain and kill children: 'I was bewitched and it seemed that everything, all the trouble came from the kulaks, that if they were destroyed, then a time of happiness would immediately arrive for the peasantry.'

'And who made up the lists? A troika—three people. Dim-witted, unenlight-ened people determined on their own who was to live and who was to die.' There were bribes, jealousies, whole families were driven from their homes. 'The eyes of the Party activists were glassy, like the eyes of cats.' 'It was so easy to do a man in: you wrote a denunciation; you did not even have to sign it. All you had to say was that he had paid people to work for him as hired hands, or that he had owned three cows.'[13] Driven out, the kulak families were transported by train then scattered in the Siberian taiga. The next decree required that the peasants of the Ukraine, the Don and the Kuban be put to death by starvation, along with their children, however young. The instructions were to take away the entire seed fund. Grain was searched for as if it were bombs and machine guns. The outcome was crying children, swollen stomachs, schools closed, people with faces like clay clinging to walls, legs swollen like pillows, children's heads lolling like heavy balls on thin necks, skin like yellow gauze stretched across skeleton bodies. Faces like those of dead birds, with sharp beaks—Grossman uses numerous painful similes.

The collectivization teams brought in new settlers but the stink in the houses of the dead was too great. 'The dead men and women still lay there, some on the floor and some in their beds.' The bodies fell apart as they were dragged out.[14] Grossman attacks Maxim Gorky, once his mentor and patron. Surely Gorky must have known the truth about collectivization?[15]

In Solzhenitsyn's intensely moving short story, *Matrena's Home*, the wife of the kolkhoz chairman haughtily sweeps into Matrena's, mice-infested, cockroach-infested *isba* without knocking, and demands that she help with spreading manure on the neighbouring collective farm – even though Matrena will not be paid for the work and must provide her own pitchfork. After the woman marches out 'with a swish of her stiff skirt,' Matrena fumes: .'..the way that place is run it's a wonder they ever get any work done – the women stand around leaning on their shovels just waiting till the factory hooter blows at twelve. And they waste time arguing about the hours they've worked, who's on and who's off.'[16]

The First Circle despatches several of its characters back to the terrors of collectivization. The philologist Lev Rubin had volunteered as a keen Communist to join the collectivization drive, which he thought of as an extension of the Civil War. 'It had all seemed so much a matter of course – digging up pits where grain had been hidden, seeing to it that none of the peasants could grind flour, bake bread or even draw water from their wells.' But he had now come to realise what a terrible thing he had done. 'He would have given anything to say it had never happened.'[17] In his memoirs Lev Kopelev (the model for Rubin) recalls that he did not immediately lose his Bolshevik faith as a result of the horrors he witnessed during collectivization: 'Nor did I curse those who had sent me to take away the peasants' grain in the winter, and in the spring to persuade the barely walking, skeleton-thin or sickly-swollen people to go into the fields in order to "fulfil the Bolshevik sowing plan in shock-worker style" '.[18]

The saga of the prisoner Spiridon in *The First Circle* illuminates the arbitrary cruelties not only of collectivization but of the whole thirty years of torment in the countryside. Spiridon talks with frankness to Nerzhin, relating the life story of a peasant aged seventeen at the time of the revolution. As usual Solzhenitsyn intervenes: 'Although it was the poor peasants who were the backbone of the new regime, people did not want to stay poor, but to get rich, and good workers – like Spiridon – were very keen to improve their lot. A fashionable word in those days was "intensive cultivator": it applied to people who farmed their land well, by using their brains, without the help of hired labour.' Given every encouragement in terms of loans, seeds, etc., Spiridon and his wife Martha went from strength to strength, 'the money piled up,' and they began to think about building a brick house. A Civil War hero, he joined the Party and was elected to the local soviet. But suddenly all the intensive cultivators were denounced as kulaks. Temporarily reprieved by the wheel of fortune, Spiridon found himself serving as a commissar for collectivization, herding people into the kolkhozes. 'He began to carry an ugly-looking revolver at his hip, evicted people from their houses and sent them off under police guard.... He took no account of whether they were kulaks or not, but went by the lists that had been provided.' Unable to prevent the peasants slaughtering their cattle, he sought refuge in drink and the wheel turned again. Stripped of his commissar's rank, hands tied behind his back, he was imprisoned, sentenced to ten years on a charge of economic counter-revolution, and sent to work on the White Sea Canal, then the Moscow-Volga canal. He remains a prisoner at Mavrino as he reminisces.

20

Pasternak: *Doctor Zhivago*

Towards the close of his seventy years, the gentle, mildly reclusive lyric poet and translator Boris Pasternak, having narrowly survived under Stalin, produced a novel—written between 1946 and 1955—whose suppression was to deal the severest blow to Soviet cultural prestige since the Second World War. Only the later suppression of Solzhenitsyn's work could equal it in negative impact.

Boris Pasternak was always an endearing figure in the West to those who knew him and his poetry: a handsome dreamer, warm, affectionate, sincere, a little 'unworldly,' wise in the ways of Shakespeare and Goethe (by translating whom he made a living.) His father, Leonid, a painter of the impressionist school, knew Tolstoy and illustrated his works. Boris's parents and two sisters emigrated in 1921, the latter settling in Oxford, but Boris (born in 1890) remained in Russia, a convert to Christianity, influenced by neo-Kantianism when he studied in Marburg, and by the Russian artistic, religious and philosophical revival of the early twentieth century.[1] Pasternak survived the purge era as a reluctant fellow-traveller, an internal émigré whose closest friends (Osip Mandelstam, Anna Akhmatova, for example) were either executed or silenced. The canons of socialist realism, the campaigns against 'formalism,' repelled him; Isaiah Berlin recalled that of modern Western writers Pasternak 'loved Proust most of all'—and was also 'steeped in *Ulysses*.'[2]

Although he remained married, Pasternak had fallen in love with Olga Ivinskaya, probably the model for his heroine Lara (Larissa Guishar) in *Doctor Zhivago*. He first met Ivinskaya in 1946, in the offices of *Novyi mir*, where she was working. Vivacious and twenty years younger than he, she was made to suffer for their close affair when she was arrested, then sent to a labour camp from October 1949 to 1953. Her interrogators, including the state security minister Viktor Abakumov, insisted that Pasternak was an English spy—he (like Anna Akhmatova) had received a visit from Isaiah Berlin after the war and perhaps other members of the British embassy. Ivinskaya was sentenced without trial to five years in the camps, apparently on the pretext that she was guilty of embezzlement at the editorial offices of the journal *Ogonek* (*Little Flame*, a popular, illustrated weekly magazine.) In prison, she bore Pasternak a stillborn son.[3] The poet Mikhail Lukonin scornfully reported to the Writers' Union that Pasternak valued and appreciated his recognition by foreign degenerates: 'He has always been selected by our enemies to be counterposed to us. He has spent his entire life in our poetry as a swine beneath an oak tree.'[4]

During the post-Stalin 'thaw' the editorial board of *Novyi mir* had been sitting on the manuscript of *Doctor Zhivago* for months, monitoring the shifting balance of power in the Kremlin. Forced to declare themselves by the news that *Doctor Zhivago* had reached the Italian publisher Giangiacomo Feltrinelli, five members of the editorial board wrote a private letter to Pasternak in September 1956, setting out their reasons for rejecting the novel.[5] They regarded Pasternak's fictional hero, Yury Zhivago, not as 'the acme of the spirit of the Russian intelligentsia' but as its 'slough.' 'Under cover of superficial sophistication and morality, a character arises of an essentially immoral man who refuses to do his duty by the people and who is interested only in his own rights, including the alleged privilege of a superman to betray with impunity.'[6] The letter of rejection does not mention a passage at the close of *Doctor Zhivago*, which reads like a deliberate challenge to the Zhdanovite establishment: 'Although the enlightenment and liberation which had been expected to come after the war had not come with victory, a presage of freedom was in the air throughout these post-war years, and it was their only historical meaning.'[7]

Furious efforts were made to prevent publication abroad. Alexei Surkov, secretary of the Writers' Union, travelled to Italy in an effort to persuade Giangiacomo Feltrinelli to drop the novel. Asked by Gerd Ruge why the masses could not be trusted to form their own opinions, Surkov replied, 'The masses are the masses and they will always be led by somebody.' Surkov further reflected, 'I came from Communism to literature, not the other way round. I am first foremost a Communist. Intervention by the Party in literature does not worry me. Somebody is always interfering.'[8] *Doctor Zhivago* sold 46,000 copies in Italy within a year. By January 1959, 300,000 copies had reportedly been sold in France. Publication in the U.S. took place in September 1958; 50,000 copies were sold within weeks. Pasternak's novel was an alternative selection of the Book of the Month Club.[9] But not until the award of the Nobel Prize, announced on 23 October 1958, was the full fury of the Soviet Party unleashed. Pasternak sent a telegram of acceptance to Stockholm: 'Immensely thankful, touched, proud, astonished, abashed. Pasternak.' In 'A Provocative Sally of International Reaction,' *Literaturnaya gazeta* (25 October) described the Nobel award as 'an intensification of the cold war against the Soviet Union...and against the idea of all-conquering socialism.' Pasternak's novel provided only 'the life story of a malicious philistine, an enemy of the Revolution'. The following day *Pravda* published 'Reactionary Uproar over a Literary Weed' by the veteran hatchet-man, the venomous David Zaslavsky: 'The snake is wriggling at our feet. It is irresistibly drawn downward to its native swamps where it enjoys the odours of rot and decay...warm and comfortable in the poetical dungwaters of lyrical manure.'[10] On 27 October the presidium of the Writers' Union expelled Pasternak, alleging (perhaps correctly) that he wanted the world to believe that the Revolution had been neither inevitable nor necessary. On 31 October, some eight hundred Moscow writers requested the government to 'deprive the traitor B. Pasternak of Soviet citizenship' and proposed that this 'cosmopolitan' (the anti-Semitic term was deliberately revived) be deported.[11] Greatly alarmed, Pasternak sent a new telegram of retraction to Stockholm: 'Considering the meaning this [Nobel] award has been given in the society to which I belong, I must reject this undeserved prize presented to me.'[12] But no one believed that his repudiation was genuine. Tributes from distinguished Western writers, including previous Nobel laureates, poured in. François Mauriac declared that '*Doctor Zhivago* is the most important novel of our age.' According to Albert Camus it was 'the best choice that could have been made.' Edmund Wilson and T. S. Eliot added their voices. A group of British authors, including Bertrand Russell, J. B. Priestley and Greene, all normally friendly to the USSR, appealed to the Union of Soviet Writers, insisting that *Doctor Zhivago* was 'not a political document.'[13] International PEN sent a telegram demanding 'proper conditions for free literary creation.'

Pasternak was now persuaded, partly by Ivinskaya, to write a pleading, abject letter to Khrushchev rejecting exile. 'I am tied to Russia by birth, by my life and work.' This letter was broadcast on Moscow Radio and published in *Pravda* on 1 November. But this was not enough. Pasternak signed a further letter of abject repentance, published on 6 November, recalling that *Novyi mir* had warned him that his novel might be taken as an attack on the October Revolution. 'I did not appreciate this and I regret it now.' He also now 'realised' that the award of the Nobel Prize had been a political move. Repeatedly insisting that this statement was not made under pressure, Pasternak spoke of his radiant faith in the Soviet future and of his pride in the age he lived in. (Solzhenitsyn, then a physics teacher at Ryazan, was shocked by these letters of recantation; he, like the cellist Rostropovich, thought they signalled defeat.) In her memoirs, Ivinskaya apologised for her part in concocting the two letters, which should never have been sent.[14]

Yury Zhivago takes his philosophy more or less complete from his uncle Vedenyapin,[15] an author who treats history as another universe, built by man with the help of time and memory in answer to the challenge of death.[16] History as we now know it began with Christ and the Gospels. 'That is why people write symphonies and why they discover mathematical infinity and electromagnetic waves.... You can't make such discoveries without spiritual equipment, and for this, everything necessary has been given us in the Gospels.'[17]

Pasternak accords Yury Zhivago a privileged social background, although his father has vanished and 'blown the family millions to the four winds' while 'wenching and carousing in Siberia.' Yury could remember a time in his child-hood when there were Zhivago factories, a Zhivago bank, a Zhivago bun, a large Zhivago park in Moscow. 'Suddenly it all vanished. They became poor.'[18] The profligate father sets up a second family which he duly abandons like the first. Eventually he commits suicide by jumping from a train.

Yury belongs to a generation too young to know much about the 1905 revo-lution yet harbouring a rather idealized vision of 'the revolution' in the sense understood by the students, followers of the poet Aleksandr Blok. Yury recog-nises the revolutions of 1917 as no longer the model idealized by the students in 1905, but 'born of the war, bloody, pitiless, elemental, the soldier's revolution, led by the professionals, the Bolsheviks.'[19] Initially (we are told) Yury admires the freshness and vitality of the Revolution, the ruthless destruction of the old order, as a product of the creative spirit, but he is soon disillusioned.

The contrasting foil to Zhivago is Pavel Antipov, who adopts the pseudonym Strelnikov when he becomes a partisan commander during the Civil War. As Hosking comments, 'He is the romantic, ascetic kind of Socialist Realist hero seen in the light of the narrator's Christian personalist philosophy.' Such char-acters are destined to be destroyed by the 'pock-marked Caligulas' devoted to power for its own sake, the hard men whose 'boastful dead eternity of bronze monuments and marble columns' preceded the Christian era. At the end of *Doctor Zhivago*, one of Yury's friends, Gordon, resumes Pasternak's Greece-Rome dichotomy: 'This has happened several times in the course of history. A thing which had been conceived in a lofty, ideal manner becomes coarse and material. Thus Rome came out of Greece and the Russian Revolution came out of the Russian enlightenment.' Gordon quotes Blok's line, 'We the children of Russia's terrible years'—adding that what Blok had meant 'figuratively, meta-phorically' had since become real children, real crowds of orphans wandering the face of Russia.[20]

One of the most illuminating political critiques of the novel was Isaac Deutscher's. A leading historian of the Soviet Union, with a keen eye for liter-ary structures, the interplay between fiction and reality, Deutscher remained devoted to the aspirations and achievements of the Revolution in the time of Lenin and Trotsky. His main charge against Pasternak, therefore, was his failure to distinguish between the early years of the Revolution and Stalinism. Deutscher complained that only the most attentive reader would grasp that the main story ends in 1922. Pasternak was accused of projecting 'the horrors of the Stalin era' back into 'the early and earliest phases of Bolshevik rule'. During the Civil War Zhivago and Lara are already revolted by the tyranny of the monolithic regime 'which in fact was not formed until a decade later'.[21]

Deutscher cites for example a passage in which Lara is clearly describing in specific detail the time of the Civil War. This kind of regime, she comments, '"goes through certain regular stages. In the first stage, it's the triumph of reason, of the spirit of criticism, of the fight against prejudice and so on. Then comes the second stage. The accent is all on the dark forces, the false sympathisers, the hangers-on. There is more and more suspicion – informers, intrigues, hatreds.'" Deutscher complains that what Lara (Pasternak) is describing fits only the Stalinist regime which came later. In fact, Lara is describing the Civil War era under Lenin when she reports: "'The local revolutionary tribunal has had two new members transferred to it from Khodatskoye – two old political convicts from among the workers, Tiverzin and Antipov. They both know me perfectly well, in fact one of them is quite simply my father-in-law. And yet it's only since their arrival, in fact, that I've really begun to tremble for Katya's and my life.'"[22] She tells Zhivago (and he wholeheartedly agrees): "'I can still remember a time when we all accepted the peaceful outlook of the last century. It was taken for granted that you listened to reason.... And then there was the jump from this calm, innocent, measured way of living to blood and tears, to mass insanity...'" (As a historical overview of the Lenin era, this was close to the one ultimately adopted by Solzhenitsyn.)

For Deutscher the most striking negative characteristic of the novel was its 'archaism, the archaism of the idea and of the artistic style alike.' It was 'a parable about a vanished generation.' A broad, pantheistic Christianity remains the hope and refuge, quasi-fatalistic and rejecting the attempt to remould human society. For Deutscher the first years of the Revolution were a time of 'bold intellectual and artistic experimentation.' (Ilya Ehrenburg recalled how during the May Day celebrations of 1918 'Moscow was decorated all over with Futurist and Suprematist paintings.')[23] Yet after Lenin dispersed the democratically elected Constituent Assembly through the barrel of a gun, alienating Gorky by suppressing non-conforming voices, fierce intolerance became institutionalized in Lenin's lifetime.

Deutscher compares Pasternak unfavourably to Tolstoy, because 'Tolstoy takes the characters of *War and Peace* straight into the centre of the great events of their time. He throws them right into the stream of history...' By damaging contrast, 'Pasternak places his characters in the backwoods and backwaters. They do not participate in any single important event; nor do they even witness any such event.... He runs away from history, just as all the time his chief characters flee from the scourge of revolution.'[24] Deutscher lists the events, the 'stream of history' ignored by Pasternak: the treaty of Brest-Litovsk, the move of Lenin's government to Moscow, the uprising of the Socialist Revolutionaries, etc., etc. It is indeed the case that Pasternak's novel mentions Lenin only once, Trotsky, Stalin and other leading Bolsheviks not at all. His characters know them not. This may have been caution on Pasternak's part, but he also grasped what life meant for ordinary Russians spread across the chaotic vastness of Siberia. Was it food and firewood or a faraway figure called Lenin? Was it the hellish conditions on trains caught in snowdrifts and beset by bandits or the terms of the Treaty of Brest-Litovsk? It is a paradox that Deutscher, a Marxist, saw History with a capital 'H' much as conservative historians had always done: great men, great battles, great 'events.' He wrote biographies of Trotsky and Stalin much as traditional historians had written about Caesar, Wellington, Napoleon, Washington – the top-down view which normally indicates a degree of psychological association between the historian and his subject. What did the Marxist Deutscher mean by 'backwoods and backwaters'?

The feminine condition, for example? One of Pasternak's major achievements was to illuminate the sex-war within both imperial war and revolutionary war. When Lara falls on her knees before her husband Antipov, begging him not to volunteer and desert his family, she echoes the prayer of almost every woman. The killing fields and the great causes which foster them have always been first and foremost the remote, uncontrollable province of men, male egos, male honour, male claims on history. Pasternak's sensitivity to the female condition is remarkable; Lara is a magnificent figure in literary terms, a beguiling, resilient and principled woman pitched into turmoil. She argues with Yury Zhivago about the wider issues as an equal. Despairing of being allowed to visit her husband Antipiv/Strelnikov in his military headquarters, she cries out, 'What do wives matter to them at a time like this? The workers of the world, the remaking of the universe, that's something! But what's a wife?' [25] Historians like Deutscher, fixated by politics, 'events,' and the great-man syndrome, contemptuous of 'backwoods and backwaters,' may ignore the malnutrition on the home front, the shattered hospitals struggling without electricity to put together the broken limbs of bombed children. Pasternak does no damage to real history if his fictional hero takes no part in the storming of the Winter Palace, is never elected to a soviet, never meets Lenin, is never privileged to hear an oration from Trotsky – and may never have heard of either. What Pasternak's 'reactionary' novel records is local 'history,' the lottery of rape and murder, hunger, destitution – and incomprehension: what is going on? Why is all this chaos and killing happening? Lenin? *Kto*? Who? For Deutscher this lack of correct perspective is inexcusable; like his hero Trotsky, he wants what he calls a *histoire politique*.

One strength of Pasternak's novel is to show how Russia's vast terrain, wrapped in snow drifts, turns 'history book history' into local chaos and dark rumour. There are endless queues for uncertain trains. Passengers had to board the train half a mile down the line because the platforms were filthy, and the tracks in front of the platforms unusable because of dirt and ice. Confronted by chaos and expropriation, the middle classes, the Zhivagos, did not necessarily care much about sophisticated distinctions between Bolsheviks, Mensheviks and SRs.

Deutscher complains that 'the author does not manage to set up any real contrast or counter-balance to Zhivago'. Pasternak keeps speaking for Zhivago and on his behalf rather than allowing the character to reveal himself, in the modern manner, through his actions and relationships. 'Not only the author sings his hero's praises—nearly all the characters do the same. Nearly all adore Yury, approve his ideas, echo his deep reflections, and nod their heads at whatever he says.'[26] Isaac Deutscher was not alone in this view. Even Pasternak's friends and defenders, Soviet and foreign, regretted the absence of effective characterisation and the lack of a more rigorous narrative structure. Ilya Ehrenburg commented that too many passages in *Doctor Zhivago* are 'devoted to what the author has not seen or heard'. Even Pasternak's friend, Anna Akhmatova, in conversation with Lydia Chukovskaya, complained that the characters 'lack vitality, they are contrived.' In her view, Zhivago himself was neither a 'Zhivago' (a play on the adjective *zhivoy*, meaning 'alive') nor a genuine doctor of medicine. Chukovskaya sadly agreed: 'The main figures aren't alive; they're made of cardboard, and the most cardboardy of the lot is Doctor Zhivago himself.' Nadezhda Mandelstam was scathing. Aleksandr Gladkov, an unstinting admirer of Pasternak's poetry, felt he would have done better to write a memoir of his times. Everything novelistic in *Doctor Zhivago* was weak. The characters were mere mouthpieces of the author; their dialogue consisted either of naïve expressions of Pasternak's own views, or else of 'maladroit impersonations.'[27] Pasternak's admiring biographer Ronald Hingley found no excuse for the 'thinness of the characterisation.' The narrative technique was 'certainly uneven and at its worst irritating' with its 'inept handling of exposition.' But, added Hingley, 'who can doubt its status as a masterpiece?' More recently Donald Rayfield has written, 'Like Alexander Blok, he [Pasternak] was a lyric poet whose prose logic is often unfathomable and perhaps absent.... Pasternak's fogginess makes *Doctor Zhivago*, for me at least, a novel whose internal monologue and dialogue are incompetent, betraying a total deafness to any collocutor or any alien psyche.'[28]

Pavel Antipov/Strelnikov, husband of Lara, is obviously Pasternak's main attempt at creating a radical antithesis to Yury, a man of education and sensitive conscience capable of spreading terror in the name of revolution. The author refers to Antipov's 'fanaticism,' his 'unbridled revolutionary fervour,' but the analysis of motivation is fragile, contradictory; this 'fanaticism,' we are told, was 'neither borrowed nor accidental, but his own, deliberately fostered by him and developed by the circumstances of his life.'[29] Yet Pasternak fails to cope with the fact that Antipov's 'circumstances' noticeably overlap those of Zhivago himself: although the son of a Bolshevik railway worker who suffered imprisonment, he too is an intellectual, a university-educated provincial school teacher with an arts degree, then self-taught in science and mathematics (a modest reversal of Yury's decision to study medicine while writing poetry). In a strained effort to separate these two main male characters in terms of social class, Pasternak has Antipov address Yury: 'You grew up quite differently. There was the world of the suburbs, of the railways, of the slums and tenements. Dirt, hunger, overcrowding, the degradation of the worker as a human being, the degradation of women. And there was the world of the mothers' darlings, of smart students and rich merchants' sons; the world of impunity, of brazen, insolent vice...'[30] Yet Yury's wealthy father, as we have seen, had vanished and 'blown the family millions to the four winds' while 'wenching and carousing in Siberia.'

One feels that Pasternak cannot decide whether Antipov becomes a ruthless revolutionary for social or personal reasons – or both – and this neat distinction is in any case dubious. Exempted from conscription into the tsar's army, Antipov enlists as a volunteer, is commissioned and sent to the front, captured, and rumoured to be dead. (Lara ventures to the front as a nurse in search of her husband, which is where Yury falls in love with her.) Why does this patriotic volunteer Antipov metamorphose himself into a Red commander capable of punishing whole villages – burning Lower Kelmes, held guilty of withholding food, of suppressing mutinies, acting as investigator and sentencer ('enforced his sentences with speed, harshness and resolution')? The name he adopts, 'Strel'nikov,' means 'Shooter' and he was nicknamed 'Razstrel'nikov,' the Executioner. 'He took it calmly, he was disturbed by nothing.' 'He had an unusual power of clear and logical reasoning, and he was endowed with great moral purity and sense of justice; he was ardent and honourable. But to the task of a scientist breaking new ground, his mind would have failed to bring an intuition for the incalculable: the capacity for those unexpected discoveries which shatter the barren harmony of empty foresight.'[31] This authorial exposition more resembles a blueprint than a man – and there is more of the same to follow: 'Filled with the loftiest aspirations from his childhood, he [Antipov] had looked upon the world as a vast arena where everyone competed for perfection, keeping scrupulously to the rules. `When he found that this was not a true picture, it did not occur to him that his conception of the world order might be oversimplified. He nursed his grievances and with them the ambition to judge between life and the dark forces which distort it, and to be life's champion and avenger.'[32] But what 'grievances'?

Yury tells a fascinated Lara of an encounter with her husband Antipov. 'He ought to have repelled me. We had actually passed through the country where he had brought death and destruction... It's a good thing when a man is different from your image of him. It shows he isn't a type. If he were, it would be the end of him as man.'[33] But a moment later Yury reverts to his central theoretical conviction: 'Revolutionaries who take the law into their own hands are horrifying, not as criminals, but as machines that have got out of control, like a run-away train. Strelnikov is as mad as the rest, but he has been driven mad by life and suffering, not by books.'[34]

By 'life and suffering'? Antipov/Strelnikov will tell Yury at their last, fatal, encounter: 'To win her [Lara] back after three years of marriage I went to the war...' But 'back' from what? After all, Lara had wanted him at home and begged him not to leave. Antipov explains to Yury that after news of the Revolution reached him while a prisoner of the Germans, he plunged into it under an assumed name 'to pay back in full all her [Lara's] wrongs, all that she had suffered, to wash her mind clean of these memories...'[35] This simply does not does not add up. Pasternak's 'social' explanation of Antipov's radicalism founders out of the mouth of his own fictional portrait. Further, Zhivago's judgment, 'mad as the rest' fits ill with Antipov controlled, indeed civilized, behaviour whenever we are brought close to him.

When Antipov sums up history (to Yury) he sounds rather like Yury and rather like Pasternak – who unfortunately can deploy only one educated voice to distribute among his conflicting characters. Yury reflects: 'But revolutions are made by fanatical men of action with one-track minds.... They overturn the old order in a few hours or days; the whole upheaval takes a few weeks or at most years, but for decades thereafter, for centuries, the spirit of narrowness which led to the upheaval is worshipped as holy.'[36] Yet Antipov's overview sounds uncannily similar: 'So you see, the whole of this nineteenth century – its revolutions in Paris, its generations of Russian emigrants starting with Herzen, its assassination of tsars...the whole of this new system of ideas with its novelty, the swiftness of its conclusions, its irony and its pitiless remedies invented in the name of pity – all of this was absorbed into Lenin...to fall upon the old world as retribution for its deeds... Russia, bursting into flames like a light of redemption for all the sorrows and misfortunes of mankind. But why do I tell you this? To you it must be so much empty noise.'[37] No, it sounds uncannily like Yury himself.

Deutscher pursues his prosecution. If, he wants to know, Zhivago had accepted military conscription by the tsar and enforced separation from his family so meekly, so uncomplainingly, why did he feel so outraged and violated in his human dignity when Red partisans pressed him into similar service, using the rough-and-ready method of kidnap because 'they had not yet had the time to build up a military machine which would mobilise doctors and others in a "civilised" manner'? 'Unintentionally, Pasternak portrays his hero, the sensitive poet and moralist, as the epitome of callousness and egotism.... The egotism is physical as well as intellectual... Here is [Goncharov's character] Oblomov in revolt against the inhumanity of a revolution that has dragged him out of bed.'[38] Is it so contemptible to be outraged when kidnapped and drafted into service as a doctor by Red partisans, having earlier accepted tsarist conscription as falling on every shoulder? All of Europe marched to war in 1914; the universal acceptance of conscription had as much to do with male obligation, duty, avoidance of shame, as with rampant patriotism. Pasternak makes a rather frail attempt to convey Yury's state of mind when the Tsar and the Grand Duke Nicolas visit his unit in the Carpathian mountains. 'The Tsar, smiling and ill at ease, looked older and more tired than his image on his coins and medals...' Yury felt was sorry for the Tsar, yet 'horrified to think that this diffident reserve and shyness were the essential attributes of the oppressor, that such weakness could kill or pardon, bind or loose'.[39] Here, as in other passages, Pasternak is hesitantly distancing himself from the old order without embracing the new. In a later episode, after Zhivago has escaped with his family from the terror of poverty-stricken Moscow, the cooperatist Kostoyed explains that the Russian peasant had first imagined the revolution was the fulfilment of the ancient dream of working on his own land: 'Instead of that, he found he had only exchanged the old oppression of the tsarist state for the new, much harsher yoke of the revolutionary super-state.'[40]

According to Andrei Sinyavsky—whose hour of punishment was to come a few years after Pasternak's – Soviet critics were especially indignant that Zhivago, forcibly recruited by the Red partisans, and obliged to hold a rifle during a battle, purposely fires wide of the target.'I still remember the livid rage of Soviet writer-officer Konstantin Simonov: better that Zhivago-Pasternak had been with the Whites[41] and shooting Reds than that uncertainty—loyalty to neither camp—that traitorous uncertainty.' This is one of the most interesting episodes in the novel. Coming under fire, the captive medical officer Zhivago throws himself to the ground next to the Bolshevik unit's telephonist. He is now close enough to the Whites to see their youthful faces. 'All his sympathies were on the side of those heroic children who were meeting death. With all his heart he wished them success. They belonged to families who were probably akin to him in spirit, in education, moral discipline and values.' When the telephonist is hit and lies still, Yury takes his rifle and cartridge belt and starts shooting, aiming at the branches of an old tree. By unhappy chance he hits three of the 'enemy.'

An amulet hangs by a silk cord from the dead telephonist's neck. Inside it Yury finds a disintegrating sheet of paper on which is written excerpts from the ninetieth psalm. The traditional Church Slavonic has been transcribed into Russian, the words condensed and partly misunderstood. Believed to be a miraculous protection against bullets, such texts were worn as talismans. Pasternak adds: 'Decades later prisoners were to sew it into their clothes and mutter its words in jail when they were summoned at night for interrogations.' The dead telephonist fighting for the partisans is accorded no distinctive features or qualities. By contrast, the White Guardsman whom Yury believes he has killed is superior in every way: 'The boy's handsome face bore the marks of innocence and all-forgiving suffering.' It turns out that he is carrying not only a cross but the same ninetieth psalm—'this time printed in full in its genuine Slavonic text'.[42] Better still he is alive. Zhivago nurses him back to health before releasing him, even though the prisoner makes it clear that he intends to return to Kolchak's army and continue fighting the Reds.

The main story ends in 1921 or 1922 as a prematurely aged Zhivago returns to Moscow having survived partisans, wolves, and the loss not only of his family (his wife Tonya and his children, the younger of whom he has never seen, have been granted exile abroad), but also the loss of his beloved Lara, now forced for her daughter's sake to accept the protection of the old predator Victor Komarovsky – he who had taken advantage of the young Larissa Guishar when her widowed mother was dependent on him.

There are two epilogues. The first is set in 1929, when Zhivago dies in Moscow. By chance Lara returns at the moment his body is awaiting cremation.

By now a woman clouded in grief, she is befriended by Yury's intelligent and admiring half-brother Yevgraf, who solicits her help in sorting Yury's effects, poems, papers. It is Yevgraf who enlightens Lara as to her husband's fate: how Antipov-Strelnikov had finally come in search of her and their daughter Katya in Siberia, only to find them gone with Komarovsky, Zhivago lingering alone in the house; how Pavel had confessed his eternal love for his wife—before killing himself in the snow.

Lara's turbulent emotions as she listens to Yevgrav then kisses Yury's cold forehead in his coffin are deeply moving, the more so that Pasternak does not tell us exactly what had happened when Lara lost her daughter Katya during a period of illness and unconsciousness. Alone in the world with her vast pain, Lara still entertains desperate hopes of tracing Katya. After a few days in Kamerger Street, she disappears: 'One day Lara went out and did not come back. She must have been arrested in the street, as so often happened in those days, and she died or vanished somewhere, forgotten as a nameless number on a list which was afterwards mislaid, in one of the innumerable mixed or women's concentration camps of the north.'[43] This is a painful passage but the phrase 'She must have' presents problems: how can an author be uncertain about the last years of his character? Presumably the uncertainty is intended to indicate how little Russians knew at the time about the fate of relatives and friends—but elsewhere Pasternak resorts to narrative uncertainty less excusably. When first seen after his gruelling escape from the partisans, Yury is depicted as being without his fur coat: 'His fur coat must have been taken from him on the road, or perhaps he had bartered it for food.'[44] A further instance occurs during the second Epilogue: 'On a quiet summer evening in Moscow, five or ten years later, Gordon and Dudorov were again together...turning the pages of a book of Yury's writings which Yevgraf had compiled.' If Pasternak can be certain of this conversation why the doubt about when it took place?

Pasternak's history tapestry of Russia at peace, then embroiled in imperial war, revolution and civil war, is magnificent in an epic Russian tradition. An admirer of Blok and the symbolists, devoted to Christ, he nevertheless does not aspire to rise *au dessus de la mêlée*. His grim details of life and death come as thick and fast as in Zola or Gorky. He does not scorn naturalism. Using Yury Zhivago as his surrogate, he lets loose volley after volley of vibrating loathing and rejection of the revolution. No professional historian could have ventured into this minefield. Fiction provided Pasternak with the easel and brush to consign the entire Bolshevik enterprise to hell while insisting on the moral supremacy of the individual conscience—a hero capable of saying no, however disastrous the consequences.[45] For Pasternak, already twenty-seven years old in 1917, the Revolution always remained the aberrant intruder, the alien invasion. The young poet Yevgeny Yevtushenko, whom Pasternak had befriended, concluded that 'Pasternak considered many events of our Soviet life as if he viewed them from the other bank of the river of time...'[46]

Isaac Deutscher regretted the ban on the novel within the USSR but concluded optimistically: 'Pasternak's personal freedom and well-being have so far remained undisturbed.... And perhaps in ten years' time another *affaire Pasternak* will also be impossible, because by then the fears and the superstitions of Stalinism will have been dispelled.'[47] Yet at the time Deutscher made these comments Pasternak had not only expelled from the Writers' Union but was regularly harassed, ostracised, vilified. When he died on 30 May 1960, at the age of seventy, he was accorded a four-line announcement in *Literature and Life*, but no other Soviet obituary. Foreign correspondents attended the funeral but the Writers' Union sent no representative. Eight years after Pasternak's Nobel Prize, Sinyavsky and Daniel were to be sentenced to hard labour for what they had written and published abroad; a further four years on and Solzhenitsyn was expelled from the Writers' Union; four years after that he was expelled from the USSR.

Not until 1 January 1987 did an article appear in *Literaturnaia gazeta* calling for a revised evaluation of *Doctor Zhivago* inside Russia. The Writers' Union announced that it had repealed its resolution expelling Pasternak and approved the impending publication of the novel. Instalments began in *Novyi mir* early in 1988 and were still appearing throughout 1990.[48]

21

Chukovskaya: Honour among Women

Lydia Korneevna Chukovskaya[1] (1907-1996) was born in St Petersburg, the daughter of a renowned critic, translator and writer of children's verse, Kornei Ivanovich Chukovsky. The circle of family acquaintances included Blok, Mayakovsky, Gorky and the painter Ilya Repin. Having studied at the Literature Department of the Petrograd-Leningrad Institute for the History of the Arts, until 1930 she worked as an editor under Samuil Marshak in the Children's Literary section (Detizdat) of the Leningrad State Publishing House. She lost her job when her section was shut down. Most of her co-workers are said to have been arrested.

In August 1937 her second husband, the physicist Matvey Bronshtein, was arrested. The following year he was executed. No one informed her. These grim experiences provide the raw material for her remarkable novella or *povest,' Sof'ya Petrovna*. It was at this time that she entered into a friendship with Anna Akhmatova, whose son was also being held. Akhmatova had stopped writing down her new poems for fear of the NKVD; Chukovskaya saved many of them by committing them to memory. In *The Akhmatova Journals* (*vol. 1, 1938-41*), Chukovskaya recalls that she fled Leningrad twice, in February 1938 and in May 1941: 'The first flight saved me from the camps. As I fled, I knew what I was running from and why. The second flight, as it later turned out, saved me from two deaths at one and the same time: the camps and...the blockade.'[2]

In February 1938, she had presented herself at 'a little wooden window on Shpalernaya Street.' There, 'doubled up, I said: "Bronshteyn, Matvey Petrovich," and held out some money – replied to me from above in a deep voice: "Gone!" and a man, whose face was too high for the visitor to see, pushed my hand with the money away with his elbow and stomach.'[3] She went to the Prosecutor's Office at Liteyny Prospekt, where she spent two or three nights on the steps. 'To my question he replied that I could find out what decision had been made at the Military Prosecutor's Office in Moscow.' She took the Red Arrow to Moscow that night. On arrival, she received a coded phone message from Leningrad to indicate that the KGB had raided the flat at Five Corners (flat 4, Zagorodny Prospekt, 11) where she and her husband Matvey had lived, and where since his arrest she had continued to live with her daughter Lyusha and nanny Ida. They had come for her at one in the morning, at which moment she was standing in the corridor of the train as it left Leningrad. On arrival at the Military Prosecutor's Office in Pushkin Street, Moscow, she heard the standard formula, "'Bronshteyn, Matvey Petrovich? Ten years without right of correspondence and confiscation of property.'" She already knew that such a sentence meant arrest and the camps for the wife, but she did not yet know what 'ten years without right of correspondence' really signified – that the man, in this case her husband Bronshtein, had been shot.

One day a policeman came to the flat at Five Corners and took nanny Ida to the police station. She returned twenty-four hours later 'on the verge of a nervous breakdown.' They had taken Ida to the Big House and interrogated her for six hours. 'They questioned her about me and my friends. Who came round? What did we talk about? Did we talk loudly or in a whisper? What kind of documents was I keeping and where? Crying, Ida told me that the interrogator had given her the code name "Petrova", and, as she was leaving, he had instructed her: "On Tuesday, Petrova, you will take the girl to school and on the way back you'll meet me at the tram stop. You will tell me who came to see your employer in the last few days." Of course I had no choice but to go along and do it.' Ida was asked: 'Does your employer tell anyone that her husband was not guilty of anything? Does she keep his photograph on her desk? What does she want her little girl to be when she grows up?' Only subsequently did Chukovskaya learn that families of 'enemies of the people' were supposed to be nurturing their children as future 'avengers.' She kept Akhmatova away by telling her that the flat was being redecorated. Later, after Chukovskaya fled then returned, the KGB became more threatening to Ida in their search for the 'document.' The 'document' was in fact the novella *Sof'ya Petrovna*, written during the winter of 1939-40, partly in the Dom tvorchestva (Creative House) at the Imperial residence outside Leningrad formerly known as Tsarskoe Selo (where one can visit Pushkin's schoolroom, with the original desks). The narrative strategy is highly skilled. When she read the secret manuscript of *Sof'ya Petrovna* to Akhmatova, the poet wept: 'This is very good. Every word is true.'

Chukovskaya invited eight friends to a reading. A ninth turned up uninvited. He was not a traitor but he did talk too much and by 1940 the NKVD in the Big House had heard about it, called it the 'document about '37,' and interrogated people who knew her. She placed her only copy, written in lilac ink, in a thick school exercise book with pages numbered by her eight-year-old daughter Elena (Lyusha), in 'reliable hands.' She had been searched three times and had her belongings confiscated.

On 10 May 1941, she went to live in Moscow with Ida and Lyusha in her father's new flat. She underwent a serious operation. The friend to whom she had entrusted the copybook containing *Sof'ya Petrovna* remained in Leningrad, was not drafted for medical reasons, and died of hunger during the siege. The day before his death he gave the copybook to his sister with an instruction: 'Give it back [to her] if you both survive.' Not until 1957 did Chukovskaya receive official notification about her husband's death and rehabilitation. Evidently Bronshtein had survived six months in prison before he was tried and shot on the same day, 18 February 1938. Physicists who joined efforts to free him included S. I. Vavilov, A. F. Ioffe, I. E. Tamm and the writers Samuil Marshak and Kornei Chukovsky, her father.[4]

'Even now thirty years after the Ezhov [Yezhov] Terror, as I write these lines [in 1965-66] the authorities will still not tolerate any mention of '37. They fear memory. This is what it is like now.'[5]

The eponymous heroine of Chukovskaya's *Sof'ya Petrovna*,[6] is a widow, Sof'ya Petrovna Lipatova, supervising the typing pool 'in one of the big Leningrad publishing houses.' She is often the first person to read a new work of Soviet literature: 'and although she found Soviet stories and novels boring, there was such a lot about battles and tractors and factory workshops and hardly anything about love – she couldn't help being flattered.'[7]

It is a time of denunciations – the purges have begun. The snake in the office is Zoya Viktorovna, who wears a 'triumphant expression' after being security screened and assigned to type out secret Party documents. Through sheer malice she engineers the dismissal of Sof'ya Petrovna's earnest young friend, Natasha Frolenko, despite five years' service. Lethal prejudice is justified in terms of social background. Timofeev, the Party organizer at the publishing house, addresses a staff meeting: 'And who is this Frolenko? She is – the daughter of a colonel, the proprietor, under the old regime, of a so-called estate.'[8] Sof'ya Petrovna bravely rises in Natasha's defence, insisting on correcting the false charge against her, based on a single typing error:

'She wrote not Red [Army] but Rad [Army] simply because on the typewriter – as every typist knows – the letter a is near the letter e. Comrade Timofeev said she wrote Rat [Army], but she didn't, she wrote Rad...' (Obviously such a passage requires adjustments in translation – 'Rad' is not an English word just as 'Krysnaia' is not a Russian word in the original.

Without her basic decency, the capacity to reject the Kafkaesque absurdities of universal accusation, the fictional Sof'ya Petrovna would not have captured Chukovskaya's literary imagination. Nevertheless, Chukovskaya identifies less with her protagonist than with her predicament. She endows Sof'ya Petrovna with distinct limitations of outlook and understanding – a mentality 'typical' of a conscientious, conforming Soviet citizen confronted by a monolithic state whose rectitude and wisdom is echoed by every institution: schools, the press, the unions, radio, every economic enterprise, the judicial and penal system, cinema, the arts, every cultural organ. Sof'ya Petrovna is never found reading a book, or even a newspaper, merely learning to perform her work loyally and bear the death of her husband and the loss of most of her apartment stoically, with dignity. At a staff meeting she is 'rather bored' when the director, Zakharov, makes a speech about the rise to power of the German fascists and the burning of the Reichstag – before driving away in his Ford car. Soon Zakharov himself will be 'unmasked' and arrested.

Chukovskaya piles on details of her heroine's triviality of mind. On her free days she likes to switch on the radio, to hear that Perfumery Store No.4 had received a consignment of scent and eau-de-cologne, or that a new operetta was soon to have its première. She enjoyed foreign novels from the library with titles like *The Green Hat*, or *Hearts of Three*.[9] Politically she is not much interested but perfectly conformist. The trial of Kamenev and Zinoviev had 'made a great impression' on her, though she did not follow the details. 'There was more and more talk all over the place about fascist spies, and terrorists, and arrests.... Just imagine, these scoundrels wanted to murder our beloved Stalin. It was they, it now appeared, who had murdered Kirov. They caused explosions in the mines and derailed trains. And there was scarcely an establishment in which they hadn't placed their henchmen.'[10]

Why does Sof'ya Petrovna refuse (or fail) to feel hostility towards the Bolshevik regime, even if only on class grounds? 'The only thing Sof'ya Petrovna did regret very much, especially now that Kolya was grown up, was her old flat. Other people had been put into it a long time ago, during the famine years.' Her late husband's consulting room had been taken over by the family of a militia man, the dining room was occupied by a book keeper's family, while Sof'ya and Kolya were left with Kolya's old nursery. Kolya would nowadays explain to his mother 'the revolutionary significance of the confiscation of bourgeois flats'.[11] Perhaps she wishes to share the values that her son is learning at school and in the Komsomol. She would hate to earn his contempt.

Now Kolya's face appears on the front page of *Pravda*: 'Industrial enthusiast, Komsomol NIKOLAI LIPATOV, who has invented a method for the manufacture of Fellow's cog-wheel cutters at the Urals Engineering Works.' As the new year 1936-37 approaches, shattering news of Kolya's arrest is brought from Sverdlovsk by his Jewish friend Alik Finkelstein. Sof'ya Petrovna's first reaction is predictably 'it must be a mistake' – her son has surely been mistaken for some namesake who is a real Trotsykist, a fascist hireling, a wrecker. Then it crosses her mind that Alik's impertinent attitude towards authority may have got Kolya into trouble. Alik, wonderfully loyal to Kolya and supportive of Sof'ya Petrovna, becomes the voice of luminary scepticism, his eyes bright behind his Jewish spectacles. All those people now in prison, he asks, are they any more guilty than Kolya is? 'All those mothers standing in queues somehow look awfully much like Sof'ya Petrovna.' She reproaches him: doesn't he read the papers? '"Uh! The papers..." said Alik, going out.'[12]

Alik is duly arrested after losing his job because unwilling to dissociate himself from Kolya.

Even after her own son's arrest, Sof'ya Petrovna keeps her distance from other women queuing day and night outside the prison; she imagines what it must be like to be one of 'them,' the wife or mother of real spies, saboteurs, murderers. This confidence in the integrity and reliability of the State is doubtless rooted in the desire for stability in everyday life.[13] The traditional hegemony of the state in Russian history is another factor, the yearning for firm authority, a strong man, a tsar. But politically correct attitudes are now no defence. The issue is whether Sof'ya Petrovna's nightmare will ultimately open her eyes.

Are Sof'ya Petrovna's prejudices to some extent the author's? The villains seem invariably to suffer from physical deformities, the mark of Cain. The Party organizer at work, Timofeev, walks with a limp and has no dress sense. The militantly conformist chairwoman of the trade union organisation, Anna Grigor'evna, is fat, has dirty nails, and delivers her speech in a hysterical voice. Tsvetkov, the public prosecutor who ultimately informs Sof'ya Petrovna that her son has been sentenced, is hunchbacked and, with his hirsute hands and fingers, resembles an ape. She thinks, 'If he wanted to scratch behind his ear – he'd no doubt use his foot.' He is on the telephone when he informs her that Kolya has been sentenced to ten years in a distant camp. She sits, heart thumping, waiting for him to come off the telephone. She asks what her son was found guilty of. She is told, 'Your son has confessed to his crimes. The investigation is in possession of his signature. He was a terrorist and took part in terrorist activities. Understand?'[14]

One day Sof'ya Petrovna reads a denunciation of herself in the office wall newspaper: 'It is known that Comrade Lipatova constantly favoured [Natalia] Frolenko, procured her overtime work, went to the cinema with her, and so on.' The anonymous attack, signed X, ends, 'Up with the banner of Bolshevik vigilance, in accordance with the teachings of our beloved leader, the genius of mankind [*genial'nyi vozhd' narodov*], Comrade Stalin!'[15] She resigns from her precious job, her anchor. When she looks for work again she is always asked, fatally, 'Have you anyone who's been repressed?' Eventually she is saved from starvation by Koltsov's article in *Pravda* denouncing slanderers and opportunists harming honest Soviet citizens for nothing (in effect the same tactic as Stalin's 'Dizzy with Success' in 1930, warning against excesses committed in the course of collectivization). She is taken on to the staff of a library.

Now the Party organizer Timofveev is arrested, he who unmasked the wreckers in the publishing house.

Although the proud and disillusioned wife of the arrested director of the publishing house is herself to be deported with her child to Kazakhstan, when Sof'ya Petrovna runs into her on the street and asks where her husband, the director, has been sent, she replies 'in a loud, sharp voice,' attracting everyone's attention: '"How on earth should I know. As if they told you where!"' Sof'ya

Petrovna asks the woman how she will trace her husband when he is released in ten years' time.

"'And do you imagine,' asked the director's wife, "that any of them" – and she gestured at the crowd of women with the "travel vouchers" – "know where their husbands are?"' When Sof'ya Petrovna declares that her own son Kolya will not be deported because he is innocent and was arrested by mistake, the director's wife bursts out laughing: "'Ha! ha! ha! By mistake!" And suddenly her eyes filled with tears. "Here, you know, everything's by mistake..."' ['*Tut, znaete li, vse po oshibke*'].[16]

Sof'ya Petrovna dutifully writes her appeal to Stalin, marking the envelope 'Personal and Private.' The receipt slip comes back signed eryan. Now some prisoners are being let out. In an affecting passage she loses her sense of reality, informing one acquaintance after another that her son is coming home. 'You know what? Kolya's been released. A letter. I've only just got it... Registered.' The desperate woman hopes subconsciously that her fantasy will give birth to the reality.

Finally Sof'ya Petrovna receives a letter on rough pink paper from Kolya, delivered to her door by an unknown hand. Kolya cannot reveal where he is: 'Mother, you are my only hope. My sentence was based on the evidence given by Pashka Gusev – you remember, a boy in my class? Pashka Gusev declared that he had persuaded me to join a terrorist organization. And I had to confess, too...the investigator Rudnev beat and kicked me, and now I'm deaf in one ear. I've written lots of appeals since I've been here, but have never had an answer. You must write yourself, saying you are my old mother, and put the facts before them. You know yourself that I never set eyes on Pashka Grusev after I left school...'[17]

She shows the letter to a friend, Nina Kiparisova, whose husband, Kolya's godfather, was arrested some time ago and deported for fifteen years. Nina Kiparisova, herself now due for deportation, has sold everything. She leads Sof'ya Petrovna into the bathroom because the telephone is bugged. After reading Kolya's letter she begs her not to write the appeal he requests: it won't help him, she cannot show anyone his letter because of its reference to the investigator beating him, she will only draw attention to the fact that she herself has not yet been deported. Sof'ya Petrovna goes home and burns her son's letter.

In the later novella, *Going Under* (*Spusk pod vodu*, first published in Russian in Paris in 1972), Nina Sergeyevna is clearly modelled on Chukovskaya herself: a writer from Leningrad who has lost her husband, Alyosha, in the 1937 purge and who is tormented by his fate. Whereas Sof'ya Petrovna is 'she' and does not shape the narrative of which she is the heroine, by contrast Nina Sergeyevna controls the narrative through the first person 'I' – and without any hint of the ironic distancing used, for example, by J. D. Salinger in *The Catcher in the Rye* when assigning the narration to his cool schoolboy protagonist Holden Caulfield, thus creating an 'I' who is both 'I' and 'he.'

The time is February 1949. Nina Sergeyevna has granted herself a month away from her daughter in a writers' residence. Her tastes (poetry, Pasternak) and her sense of honour and decency as the anti-cosmopolitan campaign unfolds, are precisely Chukovskaya's. *Going Under* is more 'personal,' intimate, and introspective than *Sof'ya Petrovna*. The heroine is haunted by terrible memories and confused, nighttime dreams of what happened in Leningrad after they took her husband, whom she has never seen again.

She arrives by car at the Writers' House (established by the Union of Writers under Stalin's benign patronage) in the company of a stranger, the unknown writer with whom she will become involved, Nikolai Aleksandrovich Bilibin. Nina Sergeyevna works hard in the morning, then takes walks in the birch woods, preferably alone, threading along paths cleared of snow. She cherishes solitude, and is initially disconcerted by the company she is forced to keep—no doubt a cross-section of Soviet literary life. It was again a bad time. It is remarkable how many hot baths Nina Sergeyevna takes – or *tells us* she takes—as if she is constantly trying to scrub herself clean of a polluted environment. In the guest room they are playing cards and chess, flirting, reading newspapers and listening to the radio extolling Stalin. Although we are a few years ahead of the uproar over *Doctor Zhivago*, in *Going Under* Pasternak is under attack in *Literaturnaia gazeta:* '…shunning the great achievements of the people, [he] preferred to rummage about in his own soul.' Pasternak is accused of writing incomprehensibly.[18] Nina Sergeyevna defends him to her fellow-guests despite the dangers.[19]

The purges of the late 1930s were not professedly anti-Semitic, although numerous Jewish politicians, intellectuals and writers figured among the victims. By contrast, the official 'anti-cosmopolitan' campaign of Stalin's years nakedly traded on endemic Russian anti-Semitism. Whereas Chukovskaya's heroine Sof'ya Petrovna is portrayed as being very mildly anti-Semitic (her ambivalent feelings about Kolya's Jewish friend Alik are buried under her innate decency and kindness), Nina Sergeyevna is fiercely anti-anti-Semitic – no doubt the war had reinforced Chukovakaya's own horror of anti-Semitism, as it did with another Leningrader, Dmitri Shostakovich. That the Power which had conquered the Nazis should pursue Jews not only by purges of the theatrical and literary professions, but also by means of executions and gangsterland 'accidents' (the case of Mikhoels for example) – was outrageous.

In *Going Under*, the manageress of the Writers' House, Lyudmilla Pavlovna, attributes all her difficulties to 'those Jews' and their cosmopolitan plots, so the honest people have to suffer. Here Chukovskaya lets fly: 'How could one rid her poor mind of this garbage? This was why the press and radio spewed up their insistent, stupid lies. For this was not the old, spontaneous anti-Semitism nor the anti-Semitism which was brought to us again from fascist Germany during the war, when one would hear in queues the words: "the Jews don't go short"... This time it was a madness deliberately organized, planned and spread, with a carefully thought-out purpose.'[20]

Another guest staying at the Writers' House, the Jewish writer Veksler, shows Nina Sergeyevna his war poems, which will appear in Yiddish in *Emes*, in Russian in *Novyi mir* and *Znamya*. (The publishing house Emes, specializing in Yiddish literature, was closed down in November 1948.) Veksler had fought the Germans right here at Bykovo, and shows her the spot where his friend Lieutenant Koptyaev died. 'I come here every day.'

Meanwhile, in the guest room Sergei Dimitreyevich Sablin, a staff writer for *Literaturnaia gazeta*, is explaining that the case against cosmopolitan theatre critics has been grossly exaggerated. 'There are real Marxists, genuine connoisseurs.... I don't see anything vicious in their articles. Zelenin, Samoilov... they're knowledgeable, talented people. And it's they who have taken the blow. It's disgusting!' Later Nina Sergeyevna will read in *Literaturnaia gazeta* a report of this same Sablin's speech to the paper's staff meeting, thanking the Party press for opening his eyes to the cosmopolitan threat. She reads on down an adjoining column: 'worthless ideas,' 'shoddy tendencies,' 'raise the standard,' 'inveterate,' 'double-dealer.' She hates the hyphens, 'the clichés turning somersaults in emptiness.'[21]

In *Going Under*, Chukovskaya keeps to fictional characters, but her account of the poisonous anti-Semitism rampant among intellectuals certainly reflects the cowardly behaviour of celebrated authors such as Aleksandr Fadeyev and Konstantin Simonov. A Politburo resolution of 8 February 1949 disbanded associations of Jewish writers and banned miscellanies written in Yiddish. On 9 March all the Jewish 'unpatriotic critics' were expelled from the Party and the Jewish theatre was shut down. The Jewish Anti-Fascist Committee, allowed prominence during the war, was accused of being a nest of spies working for American, British and Israeli intelligence. Fadeyev wrote a letter (21 September 1949) denouncing two Jewish colleagues, several times introducing the emotive phrase 'slither out of,' plus 'his cosmopolitan friends' and 'close contact with bourgeois Jewish nationalists of the Jewish theatre.' As for the young Simonov, conspicuously lacking the honour and truthfulness he demanded of American journalists in his play *The Russian Question* (1947), he had hastened to publish a vile article, 'The Tasks Before Soviet Drama and Dramatic Criticism,' (*Pravda*, 28 February, 1949). Here Simonov attacked 'the anti-patriots and the bourgeois cosmopolitans with their imitators who knowingly imitate them.' He listed a number of critics by name, mainly Jews, castigating their 'criminal activities' in important editorial posts: 'Cosmopolitanism in art is the endeavour to cut away the national roots and national pride...to remove our culture and sell us into slavery to American imperialism. Cosmopolitanism in art is the endeavour to replace Gorky by Sartre, Tolstoy by the pornographer [Henry] Miller, to replace classical art, which ennobles mankind, by stupefying Hollywood concoctions.'[22] Simonov later admitted in *Novyi mir* (December 1956) that he and other writers had lacked the courage to resist the anti-cosmopolitan campaign. In short, Simonov was no Harry Smith (hero of *The Russian Question*).[23]

One day, Nina Sergeyevna finds herself listening to an anti-Semitic conversation involving Pyotr Ivanovich Klokov, in charge of book reviews for one of the Moscow journals, and the same Sergei Dimitrievich Sablin of *Literaturnaia gazeta*. Klokov runs down the Jewish critic Zelenin by anecdote, citing his suspect love for Flaubert and Stendhal, and how he had dared over cards to attribute Tolstoy's psychologism to French influences. There is 'a whole trade union of them,' declares Klokov, mentioning a Jewish colleague called Landau: 'I went on leave and he published Meerovich. And Meerovich used to praise...what was his name? Mikhoels, do you remember?' Here Chukovskaya resumes her habit of endowing immoral characters with horrible physical characteristics and bad taste in clothes: Klokov was 'a puny figure with a dull, lumpy, shiny face, wearing fashionable patent-leather shoes and a bow-tie. I took an immediate dislike to him...the way he told off the waitress, Liza, because the soup was not hot enough, the way he gave a little hitch to his trousers to keep the crease in place and the way he said "Here's to your health" every time he emptied his glass.'

The novella cuts forward to February 1949. They come to the Writers' House at dawn to arrest the gallant Jewish writer Veksler, the war hero, who has humbly presented his newly typed pages to Nina Sergeyevna while falling in love with her. Hearing unaccustomed sounds and footfalls at this early hour, Nina Sergeyevna pulls back her curtain and sees four blurred figures hurrying into a car, three of them 'them.' In the morning, at breakfast, everyone knows what has happened, but it is business as usual – once more, as in Leningrad twelve years earlier, everyone keeps his head down. There are informers everywhere. *Sauve qui peut.*

The manageress of the Writers' House, Lyudmilla Pavlovna, is found crying in the woods while lugging a heavy parcel. She had sent it to her younger sister living in Vladimir, a woman who had survived the camps after her husband was arrested in 1937, and now twelve years later the sister had been arrested again and the parcel returned 'addressee unknown.' Vladimir was a town full of former prisoners who were not allowed to live in Moscow, but recently all the former prisoners had been re-arrested, the 'second-timers.' (Anna Akhmatova's son was among them.)

The writer Bilibin, also a guest at the Writers' House, smooth and over-courteous, has in fact been a prisoner in a concentration camp, a mine. Walking through the woods, he describes to Nina Sergeyevna how the prisoners worked with old-fashioned picks, nine or ten levels down, twelve hours a day, allowed only 400 grams of bread, half that if they did not fulfil their norm. Bilibin is the first ex-prisoner that Nina Sergeyevna has ever met—she holds her breath as he talks because he is transporting her into Alyosha's real fate. 'He was the first messenger from there! I wanted to hurry him, to jog his arm.' Bilibin describes the life of the camp, the deformed children, abscess and diarrhoea from hunger, people poisoning themselves because unable to distinguish mushrooms from toadstools.

She asks Bilibin whether he knows where such special camps, 'without right of correspondence,' are situated. His reply is brief, evasive. 'Either he didn't want to talk any more or perhaps he had noticed someone else nearby.' Later, lying ill in bed, he finally confides what ten years without right of correspondence really meant – the formula was used at police or prison windows to prevent howling and crying in the queue of women. No such sentence (or camps) existed. She begins to imagine Alyosha being shot. Bilibin opens his eyes, reads her thoughts: '"It's done all of a sudden. Whilst being led from one place to another. In the back of the neck."'[24]

She and Bilibin are on hand-touching terms when he decides to present her with the typewritten manuscript of a short story he has written. The colour of the ribbon is lilac. What she reads, horrified, is a paradigm of socialist realism. She summarises Bilibin's short story in a couple of pages: Gangs of miners are in competition. Victory over the fascists has led to a big rise in productivity. The miner Peter returns from the front but cannot come to terms with the fact that his wife, Fedosya, had matured ideologically and professionally like millions of Soviet women. She is now an engineer introducing modern coal-cutting machinery. 'The clever machine cut, loaded and did the transport work all by itself. They had worked like granddad for long enough!' Peter, who prefers to use the traditional pick, is jealous of the chief engineer (although his jealousy is misplaced, indeed Fedosya will be the first to unmask the chief engineer's wrecking activities). Their frail five-year-old son runs away, falling and stumbling in a blizzard, to tell the Party official that his father is beating his mother. 'Daddy, don't you touch my Mum or I shall write to comrade Stalin.' Peter asks Fedosya for forgiveness. 'His fingers trembled as he rolled a piece of paper to make a cigarette. '"Forgive the old fool. I've been led astray."'

Nina Sergeievna closes the manuscript and sits for a long time gazing at the neat folder: 'Fedosya's Victory. A Tale by Nikolai Bilibin.' She reflects: 'Up till now I had often experienced grief in my life. But this was the first time that I felt shame. My feeling of shame was so strong that time came to a stop.' When Bilibin enters the room she motions him to sit down and launches straight in: '"You're a coward," I said. "No, worse, you're a false witness." He started to get up. "You're a liar. You're pretentious, you're an old woman."' Couldn't Bilibin earn a living some better way? Nina Sergeievna's little love affair with Bilibin is over! Later she feels regrets. He is ill, after all. She sees him from a distance, on a lonely walk, taking some grains of nytroglycerine. She feels his pain, wishes he would put his hat on. '"Forgive me!" I wanted to say. "I didn't have the right to judge you; least of all I, for no [camp] dogs ever threw themselves on me and I've never seen the wooden tag on the leg of a dead man... Forgive me! You wouldn't wish to go back there: to felling trees, to the mines.... The story you wrote is your weak shield.... And how else can you earn money as a sick man?"'

But she merely pulls the ends of her coat over her knees. 'He was going out of my life.'[25]

By 1957, *Sof'ya Petrovna* was in circulation in samizdat. After the 22nd Party Congress heralded further liberalisation, she offered it to the publisher Sovtesky pisatel.' A contract was drawn up and in January 1963 she was paid 60 per cent of the agreed royalty. But in May 1963, she was told it could not be published because 'ideologically flawed.' Sovetsky pisatel' brazenly withheld the unpaid 40 per cent pf the advance. Chukovskaya's suit was not heard until ten years later, on 24 April 1974 in the People's Court of the Sverdlosk district of Moscow. The publisher's defence to the court was shamelessly frank:

> Citizen judges...we have no need today of this novel. The novel records the ugly phenomena of the time of the 'cult of personality.'... Since the publication of the Solzhenitsyn novel *One Day in the Life of Ivan Denisovich*, we have received a stream of manuscripts on this theme. But these manuscripts are being returned to their authors...we received instructions that for us, communists, there is no need, and above all no advantage, in simply criticizing this period.... It is not necessary to irritate old wounds and pour salt into them. Chukovskaya's work, because of its ideological thrust, cannot see the light of day anyway...[26]

Although the court awarded her the unpaid 40 per cent of the advance, it was no coincidence that the case came before the People's Court shortly after she was expelled from the Writers' Union and thus deprived of the right to earn a living.

Like her father, Lydia Chukovskaya was devoted to Pasternak and his poetry (all three are buried in close proximity at Peredelkino). Her increasingly public championing of the literary pariahs, Pasternak, Daniel, Sinyavsky, Solzhenitsyn, Sakharov, effectively ended her own career as a published writer within the Soviet Union.[27] From 1967, her books were removed from library shelves and she could no longer be mentioned in print. Her pariah status was reinforced by the publication of her work in the West, beginning with *Sof'ya Petrovna* (Paris, New York, 1965-66). A 1,500-word open letter to Mikhail Sholokhov, who had called for stiffer sentences on Sinyavsky and Daniel, was addressed to the editors of the main Soviet newspapers. 'Your shameful speech,' she addressed Sholokhov, 'will not be forgotten by history. Literature will take its own vengeance.... It has condemned you to the worst sentence to which an artist can be condemned—creative sterility.'[28] On 19 November 1966, the *New York Times* published the text.

Solzhenitsyn, too, became a friend. To his indispensable helper Elena Tsezarevna Chukovskaya (Lyusha), daughter of Lydia, Solzhenitsyn devoted a whole chapter in *Invisible Allies*. Granddaughter of Kornei Chukovsky, Elena was the most indefatigable of Solzhenitsyn's helpers and typists. 'From the end of 1965 (when she was thirty-three) for a period of almost five years, Lyusha Chukovskaya stood in the eye of the storm, at the heart of the vortex that engulfed me.'

'She was my chief of staff—or, rather, my whole staff rolled into one (as the KGB, alas, gradually came to understand full well).'[29] In 1968, her mother Lydia wrote to *Literaturnaia gazeta* in defense of Solzhenitsyn. The following year she sent a telegram to the Writers' Union protesting his expulsion. In September 1973, she sent abroad her polemic in defence of Solzhenitsyn and Andrei Sakharov, 'The Anger of the People' (*Gnev naroda*), to be published and broadcast in the West.[30] Chukovskaya declared that the campaigns of hatred against Pasternak, Solzhenitsyn and Sakharov were continuing the work of Stalin.[31]

In 1974 she herself was expelled from the Writers' Union.[32] *A Case of Expulsion* (*Protsess iskyuchenia*), published in Paris in 1979, lays out the censures and rebukes available to the Union of Writers, prior to expulsion: 'caution,' 'severe caution,' 'public reprimand,' 'rebuke,' 'rebuke recorded in writing,' 'severe rebuke recorded in writing.'[33] On 28 December 1973 she had been summoned to appear in the office of Yu. F. Strekhnin, a Union secretary, on the second floor of the Writers' Club. Strekhnin explained that Chukovskaya's colleagues in the Children and Youth Literature section had recommended her expulsion two weeks earlier. The written charges read out to her followed a remarkably uniform pattern or formula, all starting with the warning that she could no longer be allowed to shelter behind the memory of her revered father, Kornei Chukovsky, recently deceased in 1969; and that she was only interested in promoting herself in the West. None of her friends and admirers were allowed to speak on her behalf.[34]

She was summoned to attend a meeting of the board of the Moscow writers' organization on 9 January 1974. About two dozen people were present. A guard at the door had barred her friends, members of the Union, from attending. Chukovskaya, then in her late sixties and with very poor eyesight, had to stand by the window to read the depositions given to her, then walk back to see who was speaking and take down their name. The meeting amounted to a trial in camera without legal representation. Held against her was her support for Daniel and Sinyavsky, her letter to Sholokhov, her letters in support of Solzhenitsyn, Galaskov, Ginzburg and other dissidents, and the publication abroad of her two novellas. Almost all the speakers at the 9 January indictment were inveterate Stalinists. Each one professed eternal admiration for the works of her father, deploring the disgrace brought to his name by his daughter.

Solzhenitsyn was waiting for her when she returned home, keen to find out what had happened, amazed and indignant that no colleague had put in an appearance on her behalf. She was taken aback by the intensity of his questioning, his ability to concentrate his own 'I' on the 'I' of another: 'It was as if he pulled some lever inside himself – a switch – switching on his full attention, which he could then switch off again whenever he wanted.' Barely more than a month was to pass before he was arrested and bundled out of his country.[35]

Welcoming *The Gulag Archipelago*, Chukovskaya understood Solzhenitsyn's vital contribution to history-writing: 'Solzhenitsyn, a living tradition, a living legend, has once more run the blockade of silence. He has reinvested the deeds of the past with reality, restored names to a multitude of victims and sufferers, and, most importantly, he has re-endowed events with their true weight and instructive meaning.' In a statement dated 8 February 1974, she compared the significance of *The Gulag Archipelago* (1973) to Stalin's death. 'Solzhenitsyn has been declared a traitor in our newspapers.' What he had betrayed was not his country or his people but GULag, the Main Administration of Corrective-Labour Camps. 'Drawing on concrete facts, testimonies, and biographies, he has recounted a history which every person has a duty to know by heart, but a history the very *memory* of which the regime for incomprehensible reasons tries to suppress and to *betray*. Who then is guilty of betrayal?'[36]

Chukovskaya's annotated journal, the three-volume *Zapiski ob Anne Akhmatovoi*, brought her the State Prize for Literature in 1995, a year before her death (three decades after Akhmatova's).[37]

22

Commentary: Purge and Terror

By autumn 1937, Russians were expecting a nationwide amnesty to celebrate the twentieth anniversary of the Revolution. Instead, a succession of crushing blows were dealt to the upper ranks of the party, the government, the military command, the NKVD-GPU – and to the wider populace.

During a period of terror society becomes a snake garden of informants and whisperers. While historians and political scientists have tended to explore the systemic dimensions of totalitarian terror, Western and Soviet novelists alike almost invariably presented it as a testing ground for personal courage and integrity. Terror divides citizens according to their innate decency and sense of honour. False accusations pour in from neighbours greedy for apartments, colleagues seeking professional advantage, family members paying off personal scores—anyone shallow enough to exploit the organized hysteria of the police state. Ancestry and social background, as well as more far-ranging versions of 'guilt by association,' often substitute for hard evidence.

Lydia Chukovskaya's novella, *Sof'ya Petrovna*, conveys a unique insight into the terror which struck Leningrad in the late 1930s. A major virtue of *Sof'ya Petrovna* resides in Chukovskaya's determination to place her heroine in partial denial of the wider reality threatening her. While Kafka's Joseph K. represents the supreme literary achievement concerning a fictional protagonist who does not know – cannot know—the source of the prevailing terror, we may think that Joseph K.'s ignorance is so plausible because there is no ultimate truth to be known. This holds true for the terrorized Leningrad of 1937; even Chukovskaya, like her friend and mentor Anna Akhmatova, could not know who was calling the tune, or how many victims were shot, what 'ten years without right of correspondence' really meant, or how many citizens had been sent to camps. Naively absorbing the state's propaganda, when Sof'ya Petrovna's own son is arrested she imagines herself to be the only 'innocent' woman in the queue waiting outside the Big House because her son alone is the victim of a 'mistake'—whereas all the other women are the wives or mothers of saboteurs,

211

criminals, enemies. Almost every other woman in the queue harbours parallel illusions – each one can smell the guilt all around her.

Chukovskaya – likewise Solzhenitsyn in *Cancer Ward*—pays close attention to conflicts among close neighbours, between the long-suffering heroine and the woman who wants to drive her out of the communal kitchen with false stories and nasty innuendos about women relatives of 'enemies of the people' (as a man must surely be if arrested). Sof'ya Petrovna must share her kitchen with, among others, a spiteful nurse who accuses her of stealing her kitchen oil and sneers: 'If one member of the family's in prison – the rest are capable of anything. It's not for nothing you get put in prison.'[1]

Sof'ya Petrovna's beloved son Kolya is kind and charming, respectful and abstemious – he does not drink or smoke, and writes to her regularly, reassuringly, from Sverdlovsk, mostly about his factory and the growth of the Stakhanovite movement, enthusing about worm-gears and milling cutters.[2] Kolya is an orthodox Komsomol who uses stock phrases, recites Mayakovsky by heart, and even defends the Komsomol's refusal to grant membership to his mother's victimized young friend from the typing pool, Natasha Frolenko, on the ground that she comes from a bourgeois, landowning family – even though he himself is the son of an eminent physician and a mother whose school (gymnasium) was attended by aristocrats. His verdict on the exile of Sof'ya Petrovna's old school friend, Madam Nezhentseva, on the grounds of her class background and her overheard remark that everything was cheaper in the old days, is as cruel as the accusations leading eventually to his own arrest while working in Sverdlovsk. Leningrad, he tells his mother, has to be purged of unreliable elements.

Well, he is still young! He is of the 'Stalin' generation which grew up full of pride in the new Soviet society, indoctrinated to have absolute faith in the Party! Don't we forgive him his lack of maturity? Solzhenitsyn (a member of Kolya's generation) was to make this very point in *The Gulag Archipelago*: 'Along that same asphalt ribbon on which the Black Marias scurry at night, a tribe of youngsters strides by day with banners, flowers and gay, untroubled songs.' He recalls his third year at university in the fall of 1938. 'We young men of the Komsomol were summoned before the District Komsomol Committee not once but twice' – and urged to apply for admission to an NKVD school. 'How could we know anything about these arrests and why should we think about them?...we loved forming up, we loved marches.'[3]

After her son's arrest our heroine begins a new life of pacing the winter streets beside the frozen expanse of the Neva; a life of waiting and standing in queues. She learns that you must turn up the previous night, at about eleven or midnight, to put your name on the list, then appear every two hours for a roll-call, shivering with cold between three and six in the morning. You must go to the prosecutor's office on the first day of the week, 'and there they received everyone, and not in alphabetical order – whereas on Shpalernaya Street the days for "L" were on the 7th and 20th.' She also learns that the families of those who had been arrested are eventually deported from Leningrad. On Chaikovsky Street information is given out by a red-faced old man with a bushy moustache like a cat's, at the prosecutor's office by a young lady with a peaky nose and crinkly waved hair; on Chaikovsky Street you have to show your passport, but on Shpalernaya Street – not.[4] On Chaikovsky Street, the old man with the moustache looks at her passport, tells her that 'Lipatov, Nikolai' is being investigated – then the automatic shutter drops with a bang and a bell rings, meaning 'Next!' This is the totalitarian state at work.

Chukovskaya was a young member of the Soviet intellectual circle hounded and decimated during the years 1937-40, and personally friendly with its leading victims, notably Akhmatova. The Oxford philosopher Isaiah Berlin had left Russia in 1920, aged eleven. In the autumn of 1945, he paid his first visit as an adult, accredited to the British Embassy on a diplomatic passport. He made a beeline for the great Akhmatova in Leningrad. In *Personal Impressions* (1980), Berlin recalls visiting her apartment in Fontanny Dom, at 34 Fontanka, a former palace. At thirty-six, Berlin was twenty years Akhmatova's junior and had apparently never read a word she'd written. They talked through the night and shared a dish of boiled potatoes.[5] Tears filled her eyes when Berlin asked after the fate of her friend Osip Mandelstam. She read her *Requiem* to him from a manuscript, broke off and spoke of the years 1937-38 when both her second husband, Punin, and her son Lev Gumilyov had been arrested and sent to camps.[6] In a stanza of *Poem Without a Hero*, written rapidly after Isaiah Berlin departed, she chose him as her 'Guest from the Future.'

Berlin's report (23 March 1946), sent from the British Embassy in Washington, was clearly influenced by what he had been told in Russia by Akhmatova, Pasternak and Chukovsky: 'Then came the great debacle which to every Soviet writer and artist is a kind of St Bartholomew's Eve...and which is scarcely ever today spoken of other than in a nervous whisper. The government...struck at all supposedly 'doubtful' elements, and innumerable innocent and harmless with a thoroughness to which the Spanish Inquisition and the Counter-Reformation alone offer remote parallels. The great purges and trials of 1937 and 1938 altered the literary and artistic scene beyond all recognition.' Isaiah Berlin's list of victims included Mandelstam, Meyerhold, Babel, Pilnyak. 'Not a trace of any of these writers and artists has been sighted by the outside world.'[7]

Shortly after these lines were written, the notorious Party resolution on literature of 14 August 1946 – which took the form of an attack on two Leningrad journals – reflected an emboldened stiffening of Party policy since the turn of the military tide against Germany in 1943. A. A. Zhdanov, Party boss of Leningrad, produced a report on the journals *Zvezda* and *Leningrad*. *Zvezda* had imprudently published *The Adventures of a Monkey*, by the popular satirist Mikhail Zoshchenko, portraying (Zhdanov claimed) Soviet people as lazy, stupid and crude—'the venom of bestial enmity towards the Soviet order.' In fact, Stalin had been angered by what was in essence a tale for children describing the escape of a female ape from the zoo of a city under bombardment. Finding nothing to eat and the citizens standing in absurd lines for food, the ape gets her bunch of carrots by apelike means. Stalin's ire against the long-term offender Zoshchenko led to a Central Committee resolution accusing the satirist of 'slanderously presenting Soviet people as primitive, uncultured and stupid.'[8] Only 'the scum of the literary world' could write such works, declared Zhdanov, while blasting the literary group known as the Serapion Brothers, to which Zoshchenko had belonged in the 1920s, for 'philistinism, superficiality and lack of political belief'.

Zhdanov moved on to attack Akhmatova, 'with her petty, narrow personal life, her paltry experiences, and her religiously mystical eroticism.'[9] The Leningrad literary journals were accused of encouraging her to poison the minds of the young. 'What has this poetry in common with the interests of our state and people? Nothing whatever.' The journal *Leningrad* was held guilty of 'kowtowing to the contemporary bourgeois culture of the West' and was closed down by decree of the Central Committee. Akhmatova was duly expelled from the Writers' Union and the new book of poems she had promised to send to Isaiah Berlin was pulped.

A Jewish writer who did survive the purges was Vasily Grossman. In his final, fragmentary work of fiction, *Everything Flows*, Grossman returns to the terror culminating in the 1937 purge, which destroyed the generation of the Revolution and Civil War, 'the fathers of the Soviet state who were at the same time its children.' The prisons they had built swallowed them. They could not understand what was happening. 'They were all mixed up together. One Party secretary might find himself on a cell bunk next to the Party secretary who had exposed him as an enemy of the people and replaced him...' 'And inside the thick walls of the Lubyanka or the Butyrki there was the unending crackle of pistol and rifle fire—nine grams in the chest or the back of the head of those thousands of tens of thousands of innocents who had been denounced...'[10]

The second Epilogue of Pasternak's *Doctor Zhivago* takes place in the summer of 1943, in the form of an encounter between Yury Zhivago's childhood friends, Gordon and Dudorov. Having sent Zhivago's lover Lara into oblivion in 1929, 'perhaps' lost in the Gulag, Pasternak briefly grasps the nettle of the Stalinist 1930s: collectivization, purge, the Gulag. Dudorov has been, as he recalls, a political prisoner pre-war: 'We were told: "Here you are. This is your camp." – An open snow-field with a post in the middle and a notice on its saying: "GULAG 92. Y.N.90" – that's all there was.' Dudorov continues his story: 'For a long time we didn't know there was a war. They kept it from us. And then suddenly came the offer. You could volunteer for front-line service in a punitive battalion, and if you came out alive you were free.' Dudorov did not hesitate.

Gordon, too, had been a political prisoner; he comments that for himself and many others the war came as an omen of deliverance, a purifying storm. '"I think that collectivization was a mistake, a failure, and because that couldn't be admitted, every means of intimidation had to be used to make people forget how to think and judge for themselves, to force them to see what wasn't there, and to maintain the contrary of what their eyes told them. Hence the unexampled harshness of the Yezhov terror, and the promulgation of a constitution which was never intended to be applied, and the holding of elections not based on a free vote."'

Dudorov agrees about the outbreak of war; its real horrors were 'a blessing compared with the inhuman power of the lie...'[11]

Konstantin Simonov was by contrast an 'official writer,' sometimes an apparatchik, sometimes posing awkward questions. In his novel *Victims and Heroes*, Simonov introduces an officer called Serpelin. Tall, thin, balding, holding the Order of the Red Banner and the Twenty Years of the Workers' and Peasants' Red Army medal, Serpelin '...was the kind of man on whom it was enough to lay one's eyes only once to know and remember him as long as one lives.' When he was suddenly arrested in 1937, his accusers quoted as evidence of guilt the fact that he was studying German and that German Army manuals had been found in his home. As for the direct reason for his arrest, this was revealed to be the warnings he had given in his lectures of the dangers inherent in the tactical doctrines adopted by Hitler's Wehrmacht – warnings that were unfashionable at the time.[12]

Serpelin, we learn, had twice been interrogated by the head of the NKVD, Yezhov himself. For six months three interrogators took turns to make him sign a confession. He was sentenced to ten years' hard labour without trial. He was innocent! But others were not! Simonov in effect upholds the view that the purges would have been justified if not grossly misdirected towards the 'innocent.' Simonov's character Shmakov had worked in the Cheka. 'Shmakov stopped himself just in time from saying [to Serpilin], "My dear comrade, you and I have lately been all too ready to suspect people and all too often too dilatory in realizing that our suspicions were unfounded.' But that did not mean there were no genuine suspects, far from it. Although wrongly indicted and imprisoned, Serpilin remains fiercely intolerant of any deviation from the Party line. 'During his four years of imprisonment [Serpelin] had never once blamed the Soviet system for what had happened to him: he regarded the whole matter as a monstrous misunderstanding, as a mistake, as an act of imbecility. Communism was and remained to him a sacred and untarnished cause.'[13] 'Six months later he beat up a fellow prisoner, a man with whom he had fought side by side in the Civil War and who had later become a Trotskyite... [and] confided in Serpilin that in his opinion the Party had degenerated and the Revolution had been betrayed.'[14] This ultimate blindfold was the one behind which the relatively liberal writer Konstantin Simonov continually protected his career.

Solzhenitsyn allowed himself no such illusions. In *The First Circle*, the author describes the routine at the Lubyanka, where he himself was held in 1945, and where the fictional Innokentii Volodin will be taken under arrest at the end of the novel: the famous worn steps to the landing half-way between the fifth and sixth floors, there a passage connecting the main building to the interrogation block 'and every prisoner for the past thirty years and more had walked that passage – Cadets, SR's. Anarchists, Monarchists, Octobrists. Mensheviks, Bolsheviks...Bukharin, Rykov, Tukhachevsky...world-famous scientists and half-fledged poets...' Each prisoner had signed the thick Register of Destinies, writing his name through a slot in a tin plate so that he shouldn't see the other signatures. When relatives arrive for the half-hour visit, prisoner and visitor are not permitted to touch or kiss. Here Solzhenitsyn introduces a marvellous metaphorical image. 'These meetings were rather like those scenes depicted on ancient Greek steles, showing both the deceased and the living people who had erected the monument to him. The steles always had a thin line dividing the other world from this. The living looked fondly at the dead, while the dead man looked towards Hades with eyes that were neither happy nor sad but somehow blank – the look of someone who knew too much.'[15]

Outside the prisons the secret police are as ubiquitous as within. Solzhenitsyn introduces the case of Musa, a quite ordinary resident of a university hostel, 'an excessively fat girl whose coarse features and spectacles made her look older than her thirty years'. Polite and conscientious, Musa has been confronted by two plainclothes policemen who detained her for several hours, talked about patriotism, and proposed that she 'help' them by way of regular meetings and reports. If she refused she would not be allowed to finish her thesis. 'How could she write about the elements of Hamlet and Don Quixote in the human character, knowing all the time that she was an informer (*donoschitsa*, fem. of *donoschik*), that she had an agent's cover-name...a name suitable for a dog – and that she had to supply information on these girls, or on her professor.'[16]

A theme relentlessly pursued by Solzhenitsyn is the real fate of Leningrad's citizens. In *Cancer Ward*, Oleg Kostoglotov is talking to the ageing hospital orderly Elizaveta Anatolyevna, herself a former camp inmate, with a taste for French fiction. Her husband has been arrested for the second time in 1949, and is allowed only two letters a year. It turns out that she and Oleg had lived in neighbouring streets in Leningrad before the war. She recalls that 'they' deported a quarter of the city.

'"Everyone talks about the Siege," she said. "They write poems about it. That's allowed. But they behave as if nothing ever happened before the Siege."'[17] She recalls how some years before the great purges they had deported all the minor nobility from Leningrad, and the population thought nothing of it, taking the opportunity to buy their pianos cheap. She tells of a family with grown-up children, both keen Komsomol members: when the entire family was listed for deportation the children were invited to renounce their parents as socially harmful elements and to have no more communication with them. Solzhenitsyn indirectly comments on his own role as historical truth-teller when he has

Elizaveta Anatolyevna recall with bitterness her daughter shedding tears for Tolstoy's heroine Anna Karenina. 'How about us?' she asks in an anguished whisper. 'How about millions whose lives were destroyed or maimed by police arbitrariness? Where can I read about us? In a hundred years?'

Solzhenitsyn's cancer patient Shulubin, an academic, had not been arrested during the purges. He tells Kostoglotov: '"You haven't had to do much lying, do you understand? At least you haven't had to stoop so low – you should appreciate that! You people were arrested, but we were herded into meetings to "expose" you. They executed people like you, but they made us stand up and applaud the verdicts as they were announced. And not just applaud, they made us demand the firing squad, *demand* it!"'[18] As Solzhenitsyn deposits this self-pitying monologue into Shulubin's mouth, one is struck by the uncanny replication of Vasily Grossman's comprehensive indictment of the informers in *Life and Fate* and *Everything Flows*. Solzhenitsyn, his ear always close to the ground, must have known of the 'arrest' of Grossman's typescripts but how can he have read them? Two major intelligences had arrived at almost identical conclusions, wrapped in semi-protective fictional form. Both had been driven to polemic, putting too much into the lines and too little between the lines to have any hope of getting past the censorship.

Solzhenitsyn uses Shulubin to open up the whole question of the gullibility of the average citizen, the broad public, during the purges of the 1930s. '"Sud-denly all the professors and all the engineers turn out to be wreckers, and he believes it! The best civil-war divisional commanders turn out to be German and Japanese spies, and he believes it! The whole of Lenin's Old Guard are shown up as vile renegades, and he believes it! His own friends and acquaintances are unmasked as enemies of the people, and he believes it! Millions of Russian soldiers turn out to have betrayed their country, and he believes it all!... But can there really be a whole nation of fools? No, you'll have to forgive me. The people are intelligent enough, it's simply that they wanted to live."'

Oleg Kostoglotov responds, '"In my view the traitors were those who wrote denunciations or stood up as witnesses. There are millions of them too. One can reckon on one informer for every, let's say, two or three prisoners, right? That means there *are* millions."'[19]

Shulubin: '"I saved myself only because I bowed low and kept silent. I kept silent for twenty-five years...for my wife's sake, then for my children's sake, then for the sake of my own sinful body."'

In *Cancer Ward*, Pavel and Kapitolina (Kapa) Rusanov are the embodiment of the new class, closely linked to the state and jealous of their newfound bour-geois privileges. Before the war, Rusanov had denounced a friendly neighbour, an engineer who liked to exercise with weights on their communal balcony. Hoping to extend his own family's living quarters by fourteen square metres, Rusanov had denounced Rodichev by letter, accusing him of speaking privately in favour of the recently liquidated Industrial Party and of intending to get a group of saboteurs together. Now, eighteen years later, the Rusanovs are shocked to hear that the engineer has been rehabilitated and released from the Gulag. Will he come in search of revenge?

'What if they all start coming back?' Kapa Rusanova wails. Rusanov agrees: 'What *right* have they to let these people out now? Have they no pity? How dare they cause such traumas?'[20] In retrospect, Rusanov's daughter Avietta is not short of conventional euphemisms to cover the situation: 'A man who "sends a signal" is being politically conscious and progressive, he's motivated by the best intentions towards society... Normally a man is guided by his class instinct, and that never lets him down.' (Here Solzhenitsyn moves into the typical sardonic version of indirect narrative): 'In that excellent and honourable time, the years 1937 and 1938, the social atmosphere was noticeably cleansed and it became easier to breathe. The liars and slanderers, those who had been too bold in their criticism, the clever-dick intellectuals, all of them disappeared, shut up or lay low... Now times had changed, things were bewildering, unhealthy...'

In *The Gulag Archipelago*, Solzhenitsyn cites parallel cases from the era of terror, for example the plumber who regularly turned off the loudspeaker in his room every time the endless letters to Stalin were being read out on state radio. (Levitan, the announcer, used to read these letters hour after hour in 'rolling tones, with great expression.') A neighbour duly denounced the plumber.[21] Another case, more bizarre: 'A streetcar motorwoman of Krasnodar was returning on foot late at night from the car depot; on the outskirts of the city, to her misfortune, she passed some people working to free a truck that had gotten stuck. It turned out to be full of corpses – hands and legs stuck out from beneath canvas. They wrote down her name – she had seen too much—and next day she was arrested. The interrogator asked her what she had seen. She told him truthfully. (Darwinian selection!) Anti-Soviet Agitation – ten years.'[22]

23

The Iron Fist: The Trial of
Daniel and Sinyavsky

In 1965, Yuli Daniel and Andrei Sinyavsky (both born in 1925) became the first writers to suffer imprisonment since the death of Stalin. Each writer had been leading a double life, one above board, one covert. The trial resulted in a virtually unanimous international condemnation of Soviet cultural policy. Even Western Communists felt moved to protest.

Yuli Daniel was a severely wounded veteran of the Great Patriotic War – and Jewish. Known mainly as a verse translator, he was also the author of several anonymous prose stories written under the pseudonym Nikolai Arzhak and published in the West, notably, *This is Moscow Speaking* (*Govorit Moskva*), written in 1960-1961. Within the USSR he was known mainly as a verse translator; his one attempt to publish an original work had been unsuccessful. Of his four stories published abroad, the only one to have appeared in English was *This is Moscow Speaking*, described by Max Hayward as 'fantastic realism' and as 'a macabre fable very much along the lines of the Italian film, *The Tenth Victim.*' All four were freely used by the prosecutor.[1]

Teacher, critic and scholar, Andrei Sinyavsky worked as a staff member of the Gorky Institute of World Literature in Moscow and had recently published under his own name a study of Russian poetry, 1917-1920. A pallbearer at Pasternak's funeral, Sinyavsky had written the introduction to the largest Soviet collection of Pasternak's poems, published in 1965. Clearly the publication of *Doctor Zhivago* in the West had opened Sinyavsky's thoughts to sending his own manuscripts abroad. Using the pseudonym Abram Tertz, he had smuggled two manuscripts to the West in the baggage—as it transpired later—of Mme Hélène Pelletier née Zamoyska, the daughter of a former French naval attaché in Moscow.[2] *The Trial Begins* is a novel, *On Socialist Realism* a polemical essay. Two intellectual magazines, the Polish-language *Kultura* in Paris and *Il Tempo Presente* in Rome, had published both of Tertz's texts as complementary works. The American translations, by George Dennis, first appeared in *Dissent* (edited by Irving Howe), and was subsequently published in book form by Pantheon (1960).

In the satirical novella *The Trial Begins* (London, 1960), written pseudonymously and published only in the West, Tertz pokes fun at the icons of socialist realism by way of passing allusions – for example at 'The Young Guard' (the title of a novel by Fadeyev). We are told that 'the revolutionary Rakhmetov suppressed all his personal feelings. So did Pavel Korchagin' – the former being the ascetic hero of Chernyshevsky's nineteenth-century novel, *What is to be Done?*, the model for the ideal, self-sacrificing Soviet hero of Nikolai Ostrovsky's celebrated novel, *How the Steel was Tempered*, considered a model for socialist realism. This mockery of grimly dedicated asceticism does not add up to much. Indeed much of Tertz's satire is strained, as when he grafts 'brave new world' scientific fantasies into Soviet minds. 'Now, it is well known that the human embryo, at some early stage of its development, had much in common with the fish. Why should the country waste its potential fish reserves. In the Splendid Future, the fishlike embryo would be turned to good account. Carefully extracted from the womb...' And so on: turned into sardines, sprats, all 'strictly in keeping with Marxism.'[3]

Two plain clothes men patrol the empty streets. '"Look, Vitya," said Tolya, 'isn't it time the sewage system was made to do some real work? Think of all the secret material that gets flushed away without the least control! Plans, surveys, love letters, drafts of literary works, and sometimes even finished copies!"' Tolya wants to put a special dragnet, or a sieve, underneath each house, instructing the porters to extract all papers that have writing on them. Vitya agrees – he has heard that writer called Gogol burnt '"one his poems in his stove, it was called *Dead Scowls*. And to this very day, nobody knows what was in it."' Vitya has admired H. G. Wells's *Time Machine* and is interested in a new discovery called a psychoscope which detects what people think about and feel and projects its findings on a screen at the District Psychoscopic Point.[4]

Tertz presents a character called Karlinsky, a friend of Prosecutor Globov. Karlinsky has discovered the private diaries of Globov's errant son, Seryozha, and warns the boy's stepmother that Seryozha is on a slippery path: '"Revolution, party-maximalism, democracy in peasant-shirt sleeves, vintage 1920s...' The stepmother agrees that spies and saboteurs had to be destroyed mercilessly, 'as was being done by Beria.' 'She shuddered with disgust as a newspaper cartoon came into her mind: Trotsky, or Tito, or some such mercenary killer, pictured as a long-tailed rat and surrounded by his hangers-on, sat enthroned upon a hill of human bones.' Again: 'Spies and sharks, gangsters and Samurai, coiled like dragons, bloated like frogs, grinning from posters, caricatures and evil Japanese prints – the enemy reached out, encircled, spread his net.'

The character Yury possesses a German wireless set through which he can pick up BBC transmissions. He enjoys hopping up and down the ether from one end of the world to the other, the stations shouting each other down like market women. Tuning in to Radio Free Europe, he is rebuffed by the angry roar of the jammers. 'A rattle of machine-guns and artillery, loud enough to split the ear drums, swept American jazz, Paris commercials and Radio Free Europe and wiped them out.'[5]

Tertz turns his attention to the prevailing anti-Semitism. Trial proceedings set in motion against the Jewish gynaecologist Rabinovich, accused of performing an illegal abortion, assume a surreal, phantasmagoric form. Prosecutor Globov announces that enemies are threatening the nation from every side. The Interrogator Skromnykh entertains Globov and tells him of a large-scale plot by medical doctors. 'And all of them you know, chaps with long noses...cosmopolitans!' (It will turn out that the doctors are rehabilitated but Rabinovich is overlooked and still languishes in a camp three years later.)

In an introductory essay to *On Socialist Realism*, the Polish émigré Czesław Miłosz emphasized that Abram Tertz was far from a lone voice in the USSR. 'There is a good deal of evidence to show that his views are shared by a large proportion of the intellectuals, particularly among the younger generation.... Where this anonymous Russian differs from his fellow writers is the boldness with which he goes to the heart of the matter.' Meanwhile, in Communist Eastern Europe, Miłosz noted, 'such arguments as we find in this essay are, at least unofficially, as plain as daylight to everyone'. Miłosz went rather further than Tertz himself when he claimed that, 'Socrealism is directly responsible for the deaths of millions of men and women, for it is based on the glorification of the state by the writer and artist...and to scorn the sufferings of the individual. It is thus an effective anaesthetic.' Prophetically, Miłosz observed that Tertz 'is a Russian, and is guilty of lèse-majesté in criticising his own civilization'. National pride was the cornerstone of Soviet policy. 'Though they [the Soviet people] cannot eat the moon, it bears the emblem of the hammer and sickle. Collective glory...has been acquired by ruthless indifference to human life.'[6]

There is an uncertainty of tone in Tertz's *On Socialist Realism*; the bitter irony and sarcasm is not always sure of its audience, or when to show its head and when not. Tertz converts Marxism into ironic abstractions derived from Western thought and religious-messianic analogies alien to the standard Soviet vocabulary. But an underlying anger prevails: 'So that prisons should vanish forever, we built new prisons. So that all frontiers should fall, we surrounded ourselves with a Chinese Wall. So that work should become a rest and a pleasure, we introduced forced labor. So that not one drop of blood be shed any more, we killed and killed. In the name of the Purpose we turned to the means that our enemies used: we glorified Imperial Russia, we wrote lies in *Pravda* [Truth], we set a new Tsar on the now empty throne, we introduced officers' epaulettes and tortures... Sometimes we felt that only one final sacrifice was needed for the triumph of Communism—the renunciation of Communism. O Lord, O Lord—pardon us our sins.'[7]

Tertz describes the typical Soviet novel as a 'monstrous salad' of Dostoyevskian torment, Chekhovian sadness, family life in the mode of Tolstoy, while shouting platitudes from the press. 'It is semi-classical demi-art of a none too socialist demi-realism.' Tertz mocked the chauvinism of Soviet literature, producing one devastating quotation after another. For example, V. Il'enkov's novel, *The Great Highway*, which appeared in 1949 and won a Stalin Prize, declared: 'Russia took its own road—that of unanimity.... For thousands of years men suffered from differences of opinion. But now we, Soviet men and women, for the first time agree with each other, talk one language that we all understand, and think identically about the main things in life. It is this unanimity that makes us strong and superior to all other people in the world, who are internally torn and socially isolated through their differences of opinion.'

Tertz flashes an ironical rejoinder: 'Those of us who suffer from superfluous differences of thought we punish severely by excluding them from life and literature.' His own hope of redemption lay in the 'destructive laughter' which he calls—again ironically—'the chronic disease of Russian culture from Pushkin to Blok.' Here he quotes from Blok's *Irony* (1908): 'Irony is the faithful companion of unbelief and doubt; it vanishes as soon as there appears a faith that does not tolerate sacrilege...'[8]

Sinyavsky/Tertz set forth his own credo: 'Right now I put my hope in a phantasmagoric art, with hypotheses instead of a Purpose, an art in which the grotesque will replace realistic descriptions of ordinary life. Such an art would correspond best to the spirit of our time. May the fantastic imagery of Hoffmann and Dostoevski, of Goya, Chagall and Mayakovski (the most socialist realist of all)...teach us how to be truthful with the aid of the absurd and the fantastic.'[9] This, of course, was treated with respect by Western critics—although not by the author of *One Day in the Life of Ivan Denisovich*, whose soberly unfantastical style offered a more straightforward depiction of the truth and appealed to large audiences both in Russia and the West.

The detention of Andrei Sinyavsky and Yuli Daniel on 13 September 1965 was first revealed in Rome on 9 October by Vigorelli, secretary general of the Community of European Writers. Not until 13 January 1966, when Brezhnev made the final decision to go ahead with the trial, was the Soviet public made aware of the detention of Daniel and Sinyavsky. The Party leaders had been acutely anxious and hesitant about pressing ahead. Brezhnev had driven to the country villa of Konstantin Fedin, seventy-six-year-old head of the Writers' Union, to seek his advice. Fedin, who had been lampooned in one of Sinyavsky's short stories as being without talent and bearing a pathological hatred for all great writers, strongly urged Brezhnev to make an example of Sinyavsky and Daniel.[10] Sinyavsky/Tertz had gone out of his way, in his essay *On Socialist Realism*, to discomfort the powerful Fedin (a neighbour of Pasternak who had vetoed *Doctor Zhivago*, along with other members of the *Novyi mir* editorial board). Using the ironic term 'superfluous hero' to describe any individual capable of doubt, soul-searching and an individual conscience, Sinyavsky wrote: 'In *The Towns and the Years* Fedin purged his heart of the last drop of pity for the superfluous hero, formerly so enchanting.' Sinyavsky also quoted Fedin's *An Extraordinary Year*, published in 1949: 'There is nothing in the world more disgusting than fence-sitters...' Sinyavsky commented: 'Thus did the hero of nineteenth-century Russian literature perish ingloriously.'[11]

Only three of Sinyavsky's works figured in the indictment: *The Trial Begins*, *On Socialist Realism* and his third novel, *Lyubimov*, published in New York as *The Makepeace Experiment* (1965). Other titles were mentioned during the trial and used in evidence.[12] On 13 January 1966, *Izvestiia* published a diatribe by Dmitri Eremin, describing Daniel and Sinyavsky as 'were-wolves' and 'renegades' guilty of 'high treason,' and warning that no leniency would be shown despite foreign protests. 'Shielding behind the pen-names of Abram Tertz and Nikolai Arzhak, the two have for several years been sending...abroad their dirty lampoons on their own country, the party, and the Soviet system...hatred of our system, vile mockery of everything that is most dear to the fatherland and its people.... With morbid sensuality they both root about in sexual and psychological "problems"... Both spatter on to paper everything that is most vile and filthy.' Quotations of a sexual nature followed. And why did Sinyavsky, 'Russian by birth,' choose a pseudonym, Abram Tertz, which suggested he was Jewish? 'Sinyavsky was trying to create the impression that anti-Semitism exists in our country...a squalid provocation.' Eremin complained that even Chekhov did not escape 'their' vitriol. 'Can you imagine what they [*sic*: who?] wrote about Anton Pavlovich Chekhov, the outstanding Russian humanist who arouses men's better feelings by his mastery?' A mangled quote followed: '... just to take that Chekhov by his tubercular beard and push him nose-first into his own consumptive spittle.'

After Chekhov came Lenin. 'Into what bottomless bog of abomination must a so-called man of letters sink to cast a slur with his hooligan pen on the name [Lenin] we hold sacred! It is impossible to reproduce here the relevant quotations: so malicious is this scrawl, so disgraceful and filthy.' And more: 'They are not just moral perverts but active helpers of those who are stoking up the furnace of international tension, who would like to turn the cold war into a hot war, and who have still not relinquished their delirious dream of raising their hand against the Soviet Union.'[13]

Clearly the verdict had preceded the trial.[14] From the West came protests thick and furious. The *New York Times* (16 January) responded with an editorial, 'Soviet McCarthyism,' denouncing the 'vicious invective' in *Izvestiia*. 'The attack will provoke curiosity and a desire to read their forbidden prose, just as happened in the case of *Dr Zhivago*.' The *Guardian*'s response, by Victor Zorza, was headlined 'Russia prepares the ground for a Stalinist show trial.' *Le Monde* reported the standard flood of indignant letters demanding 'strict punishment' which surfaced in the pages of *Izvestiia*. Edward Crankshaw found the style of the attack on Daniel and Sinyavsky reminiscent of Vyshinsky's rhetoric in March 1938 at the trial of Bukharin: 'The graves of the hateful traitors and spies who are selling their country to the enemy will grow over with weeds and thistles...' Crankshaw predicted that 'Stalinists in the Soviet Union are preparing the biggest field day since the master died nearly sixteen [sic] years ago.'[15]

The trial took place from the 10th to the 13th of February before the Supreme Court of the RSFSR – but Western correspondents were excluded. Both Sinyavsky and Daniel were charged under the notorious Article 70 of the Criminal Code of the Russian Federation: 'Agitation or propaganda carried out with the purpose of subverting or weakening the Soviet regime...as well as the dissemination or production or harbouring for the said purposes of literature of similar content, are punishable...' [by a term of imprisonment from six months to seven years].[16] This was the first public trial in Soviet history in which the charges were overtly based on literary works. Commenting on the pleas of Not Guilty, *The Times* noted that such pleas were 'unprecedented in political trials of this kind in Russia.' (Under Stalin death by firing squad or exile to the Gulag had generally followed an unreported summary 'trial' by an NKVD triad far from public view.) In 1964, Joseph Brodsky had been put on trial and sentenced in Leningrad nominally for 'parasitism' – a euphemism for the actual offence, his poetry.

Two members of the Union of Writers acted as prosecutors: Zoya Kedrina, a sixty-year-old literary critic, and Arkadi Vasiliev, fifty-nine, a novelist. Vasiliev told the court that Sinyavsky had received 'two jackets, two sweaters, a nylon shirt and something else' from French friends. Kedrina, who worked in the Institute of World Literature, where Sinyavsky himself was employed before his arrest, focused on one story by Daniel/Arzhak, 'This is Moscow Speaking'—sometimes translated as 'Moscow Calling'—a fantasy about a day of permissible murder established by the Soviet government. She offered a more complete survey of Sinyavsky/Tertz's *The Trial Begins*, his essay *On Socialist Realism*, a collection of stories called *Fantastic Tales*, and a novel, *Lyubimov*, about a one-man revolution against communism in a small Russian town. Kedrina accused Tertz of writing pornography. The *New York Times* responded by quoting the critic Marc Slonim: 'Tertz's use of irony, his allusive style, his intellectual subtlety and his inner freedom are so refreshing and challenging that one cannot hesitate to rate him as the most significant Soviet writer of the sixties.' (One certainly could hesitate—this was the decade in which Solzhenitsyn had made his appearance.)[17]

Testifying in his own defence, Sinyavsky made the painful claim that 'I am not a political writer. No writer expresses his political views through his writings. An artistic work does not express political views.' Equally disingenuously, he also attempted to dissociate himself from Western values. Communism was the supreme goal. 'But the actual ways and means are not always in keeping with this goal.' His father had been arrested in 1951 and released only after Khrushchev's speech to the 20th Congress in 1956, dying soon afterwards. He also recalled what had happened to Akhmatova and Zoshchenko—hence his own secrecy. The judge, Lev Smirnov, chief justice of the RSFSR, intervened: 'What have Zoshchenko and Ahkmatova got to do with it? Those were different times, but you still go on hiding things.' Clearly these were not 'different times.'[18] 'You wrote about thought-readers and filters under toilets,' Judge Smirnov rebuked Yuli Daniel. 'In other words, someone made a decision about the installation of such devices. That is the sort of thing covered by Article 70—slander. Doesn't this malign our people, our society, our system?' The judge further commented, 'That's not the only passage where you besmirch the bright name of Lenin.'

Sinyavsky was sentenced to seven years 'corrective labour,' Daniel to five years. Noting the indignation of leading Western writers, including W. H. Auden, William Styron, Hannah Arendt and International PEN,[19] a New York Times editorial (17 February) commented, 'What emerges most vividly from this barbaric episode is the continued insecurity of those who now rule in Moscow.' The Russians possessed H-bombs and could send robots to the moon, 'But they still dread any expression of fundamental dissent and they still do not trust their people.'

Unlike the Pasternak affair, the trial of Sinyavsky and Daniel precipitated serious rifts between the USSR and the Western Communist parties, already beset by splits between liberal Euro-Communists and neo-Stalinists. On 15 February, the London Daily Worker quoted the misgivings expressed by John Gollan, general secretary of the CPBG . The heavy sentences, the barring of foreign observers, the Soviet press attacks in advance of the trial, the Tass versions of what went on in court—all this had caused great concern to friends of the Soviet Union. In New York, the Worker, although critical of Daniel and Sinyavsky, commented that 'many Americans will find it difficult to understand the need for the severity of the sentences'.[20] The Italian Communist daily, L'Unità, was critical of the trial and sentences; the Scandinavian Communist parties condemned them outright. Even the French party, notorious for its rearguard neo-Stalinism, buckled under the strain. On 16 February, l'Humanité published a declaration by Aragon: to send the two writers to prison and forced labour simply because of the books they published, 'c'est faire du délit d'opinion un crime d'opinion' ('délit' meaning a mere 'misdemeanour' as distinct from a 'crime.') A month later a three-day meeting of the PCF's Central Committee produced an eighteen-page resolution, presented by Aragon, affirming freedom of expression and freedom of religion. 'The experimental requirements of literature and art cannot be denied or shackled without gravely affecting the development of culture and the human spirit itself.'[21]

Only gradually did news of widespread disquiet among leading Soviet writers begin to surface. Forty writers had issued a protest against the sentences, including Konstantin Paustovsky, Yevtushenko (currently touring Australia), Andrei Voznesensky, Bella Ahkmadulina and Vassili Aksyonov. From Moscow, Henry Shapiro reported in the Guardian (19 March), that the trial judge,

Lev Smirnov, had been invited to explain himself to a meeting of the Union of Writers. 'Rapid-fire questions, many of which were hostile and embarrassing to the guest speaker, followed from the floor. Smirnov (a Soviet judge at the Nuremberg trials), admitted to the meeting that a prominent Russian writer (whom he did not name) had formally appealed to the court to allow him to defend Sinyavsky and Daniel.' (This was Konstantin Paustovsky.)

By the summer of 1966, international attention focused on the deteriorating physical condition of the two writers in captivity. The *New York Times* (27 June) reported that both were ill after four months in separate labour camps, set some twenty miles apart in the Mordovian Republic, 200-300 miles east of Moscow. 'Mr. Sinyavsky is said to have developed boils and other skin irritations. The huskier Mr. Daniel, according to the informants, found early this month that his prescribed work at a lathe was reviving a World War II muscle wound in his right arm. Pleading inability to continue, he was reported to have been confined to a single room for two weeks as punishment and his food rations were cut back.' On 18 August, the London *Times* cited testimony from Yuli Daniel's wife Larissa that her husband had been put on one hot meal a day, instead of three, for a period of twenty-five days after refusing hard labour assignments. She had been allowed to visit him twice.[22]

Not until November did the full text of a protest signed by sixty-three Soviet writers reach the West, after it came into the possession of the Polish-language magazine *Kultura*, published in Paris. It emerged that the first protest had taken the form of a letter addressed to the Presidiums of the 23rd Soviet Congress, the Supreme Soviet of the USSR and the Supreme Soviet of the RFSFR. 'We beg you, therefore, to release Andrei Sinyavsky and Yuli Daniel on our surety.' The petition argued that, 'Neither learning nor art can exist if neither paradoxical ideas can be expressed nor hyperbolic images used as an artistic device... Sinyavsky and Daniel are gifted men who should be given the chance to make up for their lack of political prudence and tact.' Heading the signatories was Kornei Chukovsky, the ninety-year-old grand old man of Soviet literature, who received an honorary degree at Oxford in 1965 and was a close friend of Pasternak. Ilya Ehrenburg and Bella Akhmadulina also signed. A *New York Times* editorial (20 November) described the petition as 'at once an act of moral courage and an indication that dissent is no longer a capital offence in the Soviet Union'. A second document surfaced in the shape of a 1,500- word open letter by Lydia Chukovskaya to Mikhail Sholokhov, who had called for stiffer sentences on Sinyavsky and Daniel. 'Your shameful speech,' she addressed Sholokhov, 'will not be forgotten by history. Literature will take its own vengeance... It has condemned you to the worst sentence to which an artist can be condemned—creative sterility.'[23]

Graham Greene, a four-time visitor to Moscow and held in high regard there, took up the sword some months after Daniel and Sinyavsky were condemned and imprisoned. 'Like many other English writers I have royalties awaiting me in the Soviet Union, where most of my books have been published. I have written to the Secretary of the Union of Writers in Moscow that all sums due to me on these books should be paid over to Mrs Sinyavsky and Mrs Daniel...' Declaring himself not anti-Soviet, he added, 'If I had to choose between life in the Soviet Union and life in the United States of America, I would certainly chose the Soviet Union...'[24] After three months he received a negative response from Moscow citing legal reasons. He wrote to Aleksandr Chakovsky, editor of *Literaturnaia gazeta* and a member of the Supreme Soviet, proposing a deed of attorney at the Russian Embassy in Paris as the legal basis for donating his royalties to the two wives. Chakovsky replied, 'My dear Greene, 'It goes without saying that I remember our encounters quite well, and those are very pleasant memories indeed.... The fact is we do not see eye to eye with regard to the matter raised in your letter.' Greene reported this to a PEN meeting on 28 March 1968: 'One must say that no bell tolls in Mr Chakovsky's ears: no thought that when we defend others we are defending ourselves.'[25]

24

Foreign Affairs: The Menace of Kafka

As in other realms of art and culture, Cold War literary competition was rooted in the shared values of the Enlightenment, a common heritage transcending nations and languages. The Russians not only proclaimed the rapid defeat of illiteracy within the USSR but the inherent seriousness of their approach to international literature. The war of statistics included the number of foreign novels published in translation – but *which* novels? According to Melville J. Ruggles, writing in *Slavic Review*, 'The America that the Russian knows from the American literature available to him is a land of Simon Legree, the coonskin cap, the heroic sled dog, the sharecropper, the sweatshop, the dispirited, the defeated, and depraved, the frivolous, the bloated billionaire, the regimented traveler in space.'[1]

Leading a delegation of eight Soviet writers and journalists to the U.S. in August 1959, Aleksandr Chakovsky, the conservative editor of *Inostranaia Literatura* (*Foreign Literature*, founded in 1955), complained that Soviet novels were published in America only when 'they take some political angle unfavourable to us'—he cited *Doctor Zhivago* and Vladimir Dudintsev's *Not By Bread Alone*.[2] Chakovsky had a point, although Sholokhov was the obvious exception, an icon of Soviet culture and widely read in the West. A year later, interviewed by *Soviet Literature* (a magazine bringing Soviet writing to foreign readers in several languages), was asked to name some of the most important foreign works published in *Inostranaia literatura* during the past five years. Chakovsky was happy to oblige. An unsigned article in the London journal, *Soviet Survey* (No 14, 1957) responded sceptically about the Soviet habit of selective anthologising: 'The occasional translation of an entire novel by Mauriac or Greene (e.g., *The Quiet American*) does not signify a departure from the criterion of political usefulness, since the works chosen are invariably of a kind calculated to deepen the Soviet public suspicion of all things Western.'[3]

The partisan nature of Soviet literary policy came under frequent attack in the West. In April 1956, L. R. Lewitter, Fellow of Christ's College, Cambridge, wrote to the *Manchester Guardian* about the teaching of 'Eng. Lit.' in the Soviet Union. The Faculties of Philology had produced a syllabus for students of foreign literatures covering the period 1871-1917. Lewitter quoted the section relating to England: 'The decay and crisis of the British Empire at the turn of the century. The crisis of English bourgeois culture.... Aestheticism: the work of O. Wilde. R. Kipling, the leader of the aggressive-imperialist decadent movement in English literature. Anglo-Saxon chauvinism and advocacy of colonial expansion in the works of Kipling.... The work of Conan Doyle, the figure of Sherlock Holmes, the faithful guardian of the English bourgeoisie. The negative influence of Fabian and Labour ideas on English literature.... The problem of conflict in the work of Galsworthy. His critical attitude towards bourgeois England abandoned during the First World War and the revolutionary upsurge after 1917. The decline of realist tendencies in Galsworthy's post-war work.... The intensification of decadent-aestheticist elements in Galsworthy's work in the thirties...'[4]

As the American National Exhibition of 1959 opened in Moscow, Max Frankel reported in the *New York Times* (25 July)that the Russians had insisted on the removal of more than one hundred titles (the majority of them non-fiction). In November 1959, the British Council organized the first British book exhibition at the Lenin Library, Moscow. Thirty volumes were removed from four thousand 'by mutual agreement.' Although these, too, were predominantly non-fiction, they included Aldous Huxley's novel *Brave New World*, Lawrence Brander's *George Orwell* and Joyce Cary's *Art and Reality*. Scornful comments about the British Council's abject capitulation to Soviet bullying came from the historians Alan Bullock and Hugh Trevor-Roper, Regius Professor at Oxford. According to Trevor-Roper, the Council had 'effectively become an agent of the Russian censorship in eliminating from its presentation of British culture all living British ideas or standards of objectivity.'[5]

Writing in *Literatura i zhizn* (Literature and Life),[6] Raisa Orlova took as her subject those American authors worthy of translation but hitherto neglected in the USSR, among them Thomas Wolfe, Scott Fitzgerald and William Faulkner (a selection of whose short stories had already been translated). The best of the plays of Tennessee Williams, 'that highly controversial but definitely interesting dramatist,' (in Orlova's words) still awaited a Soviet publisher and a Soviet theatre producer. She also supported the claims of Norman Mailer's *The Naked and the Dead* and James Jones's *From Here to Eternity*. At this juncture, however, she changed tack and rose to the defence of Soviet translation policy: 'We cannot agree with the universal contempt that American critics have for the American literature of social protest of the 1930s. We cannot agree with the oblivion surrounding the works of Dreiser...with the conspiracy of silence which surrounds the writers associated with the American Communist Party... Not a single big magazine or newspaper found space for even a passing mention of Carl Marzani's novel *Survivor*, although this is one of the best and most topical novels. We are publishing this book...'[7] 'It would also be true to say' (Orlova continued) 'that Mitchell Wilson's novels are more popular here than in his own country... Wilson is moved by the same problems that move many Soviet people...the same, organic interconnection between the personal, intimate life and their creative work.' Orlova's initially innovative article gradually retreated to the established territory of the 'real' and worthy America. According to Orlova, when the American critic Alfred Kazin visited Moscow in August 1959 and talked with the editors of *Foreign Literature*, he relegated the work of socially involved novelists like Hemingway, Steinbeck and Caldwell to the 'yesterday' of American literature. Orlova was incensed.

The battle for history continued to dominate fictional canons. Invited to Leningrad in July 1960, the British writer Colin Wilson asked his Soviet guide if he could visit Dostoyevsky's residence. The great novelist had been, after all, the tsar's prisoner in the Peter and Paul Fortress. 'Unfortunately, [the Soviet guide] said, that was impossible; Dostoyevsky had lived and written in so many houses that we would have to travel all over Leningrad. Anyway, he felt that Dostoyevsky was greatly overrated in the West...[he] had gone insane and become a mystical reactionary. His later work was worthless.' (In 1960, the present Dostoyevsky Museum, housed in his last residence close to the Kuznechniy market, did not exist. His impoverished descendants, who lived in complete obscurity in Leningrad, received no royalties from sales of his books.)

In 1948, at the height of Stalin's freeze, the critic Vladimir Yermilov had delivered a lecture, 'Against Reactionary Ideas in the Works of Dostoyevsky.' The *Great Soviet Encyclopaedia* noted that Gorky had struggled against Dostoyevsky's reactionary philosophy—particularly *The Double*, an early work, and *The Demons* (also known as *The Possessed*), published in 1871. By 1955, however, in a more liberal climate, Yermilov was scheduled to publish a critical biography to accompany the publication of the complete fiction, in ten volumes, beginning February 1956, to mark the seventy-fifth anniversary of Dostoyevsky's death. Yermilov now depicted Dostoyevsky as a writer who protested against insult and humiliation, but who remained hostile to any 'positive' (progressive) solution.[8] An editorial in the *New York Times* ('Dostoyevsky Back in Soviet Favor,' 23 October 1955) asked mockingly: 'But one wonders what desk-bound Soviet god it is that...can turn the Pushkin faucet on with one hand and the Tolstoy faucet off with the other?'

Khrushchev's memoirs discuss the literary 'thaw' with characteristic frankness, evasion and chronological imprecision. 'We were scared—really scared. We were afraid the thaw might unleash a flood, which we wouldn't be able to control and which would drown us. How could it drown us? It could have overflowed the banks of the Soviet riverbed and formed a tidal wave which would have washed away all the barriers and retaining walls of our society.'[9] To appease a powerful conservative faction, Khrushchev felt obliged, periodically, to play the cop who halts traffic with his right hand while waving it through with his left. This was never more apparent than in the years 1962-1963, when the oscillations of Soviet literary policy, and the bitter struggle between conservatives, led by Vsevolod Kochetov, chief editor of the literary journal *Oktyabr*, and liberals, headed by Aleksandr Tvardovsky, chief editor of *Novyi mir*, offered the Western press a bumper harvest of headlines throughout 1963:

'Soviet Liberal Writers Suffer a reverse.' (*The Times*, 12 February)

'Communistes et Progressistes aux Prises chez les Ecrivains de la capitale.' (*Le Monde*, 17 April)

'Liberal Soviet Writers Gaining In a Fight for Free Expression.' (*New York Times*, 26 November)

'Leading Russian Writer Attacks Soviet Leaders,' ran the *Sunday Times* headline (9 December) over a story by Ronald Hingley. After a visit to Italy, the writer Victor Nekrasov, whose novel *Frontline Stalingrad* had won a Stalin prize in 1947, had published a provocative report in *Novyi mir*, quoting Italian Communists as severely critical of Soviet policies. Why, he had been asked, had Camus, Faulkner and Kafka not been translated into Russian? Nekrasov offered some questions of his own: why did the USSR throw away good roubles on *Oklahoma*, *The Count of Monte Cristo* and the like instead of going for *La Dolce Vita*, *The Bridge Over the River Kwai* and Orson Welles's *Citizen Kane*? Nekrasov described a number of Soviet follies including the arrest of an Italian publisher for taking snapshots of Kiev market place, and the inclusion of secret police watchdogs in Soviet tourist groups travelling abroad. When published in book form, Nekrasov's memoir, *On Both Sides of the Ocean*, landed him in hot water. Khrushchev told the March 1963 writers' plenum, held in the Kremlin's Sverdlov Hall, that trips by Soviet writers to foreign countries had too often 'proved to be against our country's interests'. Nekrasov refused to recant at a meeting held in his home town, Kiev on 9 April. On 18 June, Khrushchev demanded that he be expelled from the Party. An editorial in the *New York Times* (5 July) regretted this 'bitter violence reminiscent of the days of Stalin'.

Ilya Ehrenburg's memoirs, *People*, *Years*, *Life* had begun to appear in the August 1960 issue of *Novyi mir*. At the same plenum in the Sverdlov Hall, Khrushchev assailed Ehrenburg for the 'gross ideological mistake' of defending the formalists of the 1920s. Ehrenburg's admiration for modernist artists and writers, both Russian and foreign, could be tolerated, but closer to the bone was his 'theory of silence,' whereby many people had known of Stalin's abuses of power but clenched their teeth. This theory, declared the Party's culture chief, Ilyichev, 'casts a shadow on the Soviet people who were enthusiastically building socialism and who believed in the correctness of Stalin's actions'. He quoted back to Ehrenburg his own words, spoken in 1951, eulogising Stalin: 'He helped me, as all of us, to write much of what I have written, and he will help me to write what I am dreaming about.' Western commentators took obvious pleasure in the attacks on Ehrenburg, Robert Conquest virtually speaking for them all: 'Khrushchev implies that [Ehrenburg] was a coward to have kept "silent" when Sholokhov and "other courageous Communists" had complained about injustices. Moreover, unlike others, [Ehrenburg] had not been arrested: the implication was that he had managed to trim his sails to the wind.'[10]

In August 1963, one hundred writers from East and West came together in Leningrad under the auspices of UNESCO and the Community of European Writers (COMES). The agenda was explosive—to discuss the modern novel. The exchanges were as integral to the cold war as the Cuban missile crisis less than a year earlier. Here for the first time since 1945 realists and modernists, Communists and social democrats, engaged in open debate within the borders of the Soviet Union.

The 1963 Leningrad convention got off to a fractious start when Ivan Anisimov and Konstantin Fedin contemptuously dismissed Proust, Joyce, Kafka, Musil and Beckett as carriers of decadence 'not acceptable to us and not worth adopting by the writer who strives by his creative work to take a part in changing the present-day world.' 'If Soviet novelists were to follow the intuitivism of Proust,' said Fedin, 'it would then be logical to resurrect some of our homegrown modernists as well.' This remark was quoted approvingly in *Literaturnaya gazeta* (8 August). Leonid Leonov made a speech in which he seemed to hold the Western writers present at the conference responsible for every vulgarity and absurdity of Western commercial culture, a branch of 'hell.' Switching the attack to modernism, he declared: 'Original thinkers, originators of ideas, do not waste the strength that has been granted them in cogitations which, when everything is considered, are sterile: what is life, what is the sun, what is man for?'[11] Konstantin Simonov likened a writer's responsibility to that of the airplane pilot, admonishing his audience that neither writer nor pilot has the right 'to be himself at the expense of others.'

At this Alain Robbe-Grillet burst out that literature 'is not a means of transport.' The Czechoslovak writer Jiri Hajek had damned the *nouveau roman* as a product of 'social and ethical nihilism'; Robbe-Grillet replied that literature was not 'a means which the writer puts at the service of some cause'. The author of *Jalousie* won no Soviet plaudits when he claimed that the literary forms adopted by socialist realist writers were in essence those of the world they were fighting. 'The writer by definition does not know what he is doing.' Roger Caillois protested against the classification of Joyce, Proust and Kafka as decadents. Agreeing, Nathalie Sarraute described the meeting as 'a dialogue of the deaf'.[12] When the young essayist, poet and critic Hans Magnus Enzensberger remarked that contemporary German writers like Günter Grass and Uwe Johnson had fashioned new literary methods of portraying the Nazi experience and its legacy, this elicited 'noisy approval' among the younger Soviet writers like Vasily Aksyonov.[13]

Making his first public appearance since the attacks on him in March by Khrushchev and Party Culture Secretary Ilyichev, Ilya Ehrenburg applied his skills as a mediator. The writer might be a pilot but the test pilot was as important

as any other. As for Kafka and Joyce, he chided Soviet writers for attacking foreign authors they had not read. Joyce was 'a writer for writers,' he said, adding:
'We need have no fear of experiment.' However: 'The successful work of art
firmly establishes human solidarity and brings people closer together.' (When
Ehrenburg died in 1968 there were hardly any official representatives at his
funeral, but several hundred young people of the sixteen to twenty generation
turned up to register appreciation.)[14]

The newly famous Aleksandr Solzhenitsyn was urged by his editor Tvardovsky him to attend the COMES conference 'in the interests of Soviet literature'
– but also to fly the flag of *Novyi mir.* As Solzhenitsyn later put it, 'It would
be quite impossible to say what I thought, and...to go there like a pet monkey
would be shameful.' He added: 'And I was supposed to sit in a symposium,
bound and gagged, listening to forty mouths chorusing, "The novel is dead!"
"The novel is obsolete!" "There can be no more novels!"'[15] He had read Dos
Passos and Hemingway with admiration, but no doubt his relative ignorance of
the foreign writers taking part in the conference – and of their admired models
like Joyce and Kafka— only deepened his reluctance to take part.

Although Franz Kafka's work began to appear in Poland after the upheaval
of 1956, it remained unpublished and virtually unmentionable in the USSR.
Kafka[16] was dangerous not merely for his oblique yet unforgettable parables
about the stifling embrace of the faceless State, regulations obsessively enforced
but never explained (or even acknowledged), but also because of his pervasive
pessimism, his implicit message that the individual citizen is incapable of
regaining his liberty. Victor Nekrasov described the author's discomfort when
he and other Russian writers (Vera Panova, Daniel Granin) had been forced to
admit to Alberto Moravia that they had never heard of Kafka.[17] Several years
later *Le Figaro littéraire* (4-10 June 1964) published a conversation between
Günter Grass and Konstantin Simonov, during which the Soviet writer admitted
that he had not read Kafka's *The Castle.*

Why was Kafka (dead since 1924) to become so crucial and emblematic a
figure in Cold War cultural dialogue, the godhead of revisionism? Kafka did
not consciously sign up to any literary movement; his was an intensely political imagination which fastidiously recoiled from every political party and
every partisan packaging of man's condition and destiny. The 'message' in
The Trial and in the allegorical story, *The Metamorphosis*, nowhere surfaces
translucently. Kafka is the incarnation of ambiguity. These qualities appealed
to Marxists in revolt against the Party-led, prescriptive, formulaic literature
of Soviet socialist realism. Kafka's depictions of an oppressively bureaucratic
regime, which frustrates human reason by means of arcane mysteries, secretiveness, rules closed to scrutiny, had obvious attractions for the anti-Stalinist
revisionists.

The debate about Kafka was a debate about current politics conducted in
other terms.

Perhaps the most influential denigrator of Kafka among Marxist literary critics was the Hungarian guru, Georg Lukács. Formed in the Central European Hegelian-Marxist culture whose primary intellectual language was German, Lukács's *Theory of the Novel* described a series of timeless literary 'forms' which correspond to the expression of specific human attitudes. He presented the novel as the form in which man appears as neither completely alienated nor fully liberated. Later, in *History and Class Consciousness*, this scheme is modified, while further works on the historical novel and nineteenth-century bourgeois realism bring us back to the rejection of modernism (Dostoyevsky, Proust, Joyce, Freud, Kafka) as symptoms of decadence, despair, helplessness, art-for-art's sake in the age of monopoly capitalism and global imperialism.

Lukács had been sent to Berlin by the Party in 1931 at the height of the Comintern's assault on 'social-fascism' (i.e., social democracy). He detected 'forerunners of fascism' in virtually every literary and artistic movement which deviated from the straight road of 'progressive humanism.' Even in himself!—in 1934 he told the philosophical section of the Communist Academy in Moscow that his *History and Class Consciousness* (1923) was fatally 'idealist' and objectively fascist because 'The front of idealism is the front of Fascist counter-revolution and its accomplices, the Social Fascists.' In 1938, Lukács published 'Marx und das Problem des ideolischen Verfalls' in *Internationale Literatur-Deutsche Blätter*—an outspoken condemnation of creeping 'formalism' then prevalent among progressive writers, including Dos Passos, Ehrenburg and Brecht. Every departure from the nineteenth-century 'critical realist' heritage in fiction and drama was condemned. Brecht's *Journals* refer to the 'Moscow Hungarian clique,' who had established a special status on the German left.[18] After the war (which Lukács spent as a pedagogue in the Soviet Union), his attacks on Sartrean existentialism, formalism, and bourgeois decadence closely mirrored Stalinist orthodoxy. Both *The Meaning of Contemporary Realism* and *The Destruction of Reason* traded in crude correlations between modernism and late capitalist imperialism.[19] Pamphlets like *Fortschritt und Reaktion in der deutschen Literatur* and *Deutsche Literatur während des Imperialismus* helped to guide Soviet-zone criticism at a time when German Communists were wrestling with national guilt. Scholastic and dogmatic, Lukács set up a register of aesthetic forms he found 'objectively progressive' and able to contribute to the re-education of the German people.

Terming Lukács a 'disaster,' George Lichtheim concluded, 'Instead of a genuine critique of modernity in all its forms (including its "ideological reflex" in literary modernism), there is a blind commitment to the simplified Leninist version.'[20]

After participating in the short-lived Nagy government during the Hungarian Revolution, Lukács was arrested, taken to Rumania, and shut up in a castle where he and his fellow-prisoners were treated sometimes like felons and sometimes like guests of honour. After a few days of this, Lukács is supposed to have said, 'So Kafka was a realist after all!'

Addressing the 1962 World Peace Congress in Moscow, Sartre commented that the hostility to Kafka prevalent in the socialist countries only made it easier for the West to exploit him for Cold War purposes. He likened Kafka to a cartload of dynamite standing between east and west, which each side tries to wheel into the other's camp hoping it will explode there. But by this time one could buy paperback editions of Kafka's main works in Belgrade or Zagreb. He was also popular in Poland and Hungary. When Hans Mayer lectured on Kafka and others at Budapest University in 1962, the hall was packed. In 1948, Mayer had settled in East Germany, at a time when Ernst Bloch, Brecht, Arnold Zweig, Heinrich Mann, and others were doing the same. Mayer stayed for fifteen years. His gifted pupil Wilhelm Girnus became a party apparatchik who hated modernism and Brecht (and who told the present writer in 1965 that *Doctor Zhivago* was not worth the paper it would consume if published in the USSR). Believing that new developments in literature can no more be ignored than cybernetics or nuclear physics, Hans Mayer finally left the University of Leipzig for West Germany. 'It is impossible to lead a healthy literary life in Warsaw, Moscow, or Leipzig, without knowing about Joyce and Kafka, Beckett and Ionesco, Brecht and Dürrenmatt, *et al.*' Girnus tried to persuade him to return; following Mayer's refusal, Girnus lead a raid on his flat and confiscated fifty boxes of his books.[21]

In May 1963, Eduard Goldstücker,[22] of the German Institute of the Charles University, Prague, organized a Kafka conference in Liblice, which can be seen in retrospect as a stepping stone to the Prague Spring five years later. The East Germans turned up but failed to report the conference in their press. Reacting to the notion that Kafka and the conference itself were swallows heralding a new spring, the GDR's Alfred Kurella leapt to his feet to announce that he saw only bats coming out at nightfall. The Austrian Marxist Ernst Fischer asked mockingly, 'Are you going to give Kafka a permit to stay?' Fischer had recently offered his own revisionist vindication of Kafka in *Sinn und Form* (no. 4, 1962). In a sharp written riposte to Fischer, the East German hardliner Werner Mittenzwei contrasted Brecht's noble commitment to man mastering his own destiny with Kafka's passive view of man as a helpless victim.[23]

Two Czech writers attending the Leningrad Symposium of European Writers made effective 'Kafka' interventions supported again by Sartre, who commented that Kafka 'wrote slim books which are only concerned with specific, petit-bourgeois problems. But if one reads them in depth one discovers that totality which a *modern* new novel must always aspire to attain. The totality is what the writer and his readers have in common.' Describing Kafka as 'an undoubted realist,' Hans Magnus Enzensberger reported that he repeatedly found himself in the situations depicted by Kafka. But the liberals encountered stiff conservative resistance from East Germans like Hans Koch. The Russians now made tentative overtures towards a dialogue. *Novyi mir* published a passage from *The Trial*, 'Before the Court of Justice.' The January 1964, number of *Inostrannaya literatura* followed up with 'The Metamorphosis' and 'In the Penal Colony,' accompanied by a thoughtful commentary from Yevgenia Knipovich. After recommending that the Soviet reader should get acquainted with Kafka's work before judging it, the critic Tamara Motyleva offered some cautionary words of her own: in both *The Trial* and *The Castle*, 'man is helpless in his clash with the inaccessible Untruth, with irrational Evil...the forces hostile to man acquire in Kafka mystical, hyperbolized dimensions; they are surrounded by a cloud of ill-omened secrecy, which makes them invulnerable—such is the incomprehensibly cruel law in the allegory ['Before the Court of Justice'].'[24]

These esoteric debates reinforce the view of international Communism as a movement of, by and for 'schoolmasters of the soul,' a system of cross-referential, scholastic signalling, whereby a verdict on a short story by Kafka might herald the appearance of tanks in the streets of a foreign capital. Under a closed yet intensely culture-conscious political system, literary debate provided a partially metaphorical language for genuine political discussion – and 'the struggle for history.'

(In December 1966, the Russians surprisingly removed the lid from one of their own modernists, Mikhail Bulgakov, whose *The Master and Margarita* suddenly surfaced twenty-six years after the author's death. *Le Monde* (December 30) called it 'the literary event of the year.')

In Soviet and East German circles, Kafka was also held symptomatic of, if not responsible for, the dangerous, revisionist backsliding of the French Party culminating in its outspoken condemnation of the trial of Daniel and Sinyavsky in 1966. Faced with a steady erosion of its membership and electoral base, by the early 1960s elements within the PCF were desperate to humanise and indeed Europeanise its image. The pages of Roger Garaudy's *D'un réalisme sans rivages* (1963) reflected the ambivalence of French revisionist criticism. Did it matter—asked the leading Party ideologue, himself a member of the Political Bureau—what Kafka's subjective political attitudes had been? Working in an insurance office in the years before the First World War, Kafka had witnessed workers' accidents, death and mutilation, processed through an impersonal bureaucratic system. The Bolshevik Revolution and demonstrations in Prague (said Garaudy) had failed to convince Kafka that all such attempts to build a better world were not at root religious self-deceptions. Yet works of literary genius may transcend the author's conscious opinions. (This was the neo-Marxist theory promoted by the influential critic, Lucien Goldmann.) In his preface to Garaudy's *D'un réalisme sans rivages*, Louis Aragon added that our knowledge of reality is often enhanced by artists who did not regard themselves as realist: Matisse, Joyce and Jarry, for example. Aragon described the Party's attitude to Kafka as 'years of errors.'[25] The normally orthodox PCF cultural journal, *La Nouvelle critique*, opened its pages to a series of Kafka meditations. In '*Que faire de Kafka?*' André Gisselbrecht blamed Lukács for banishing Kafka from the realist canon; Kafka's work amounted to the *témoignage bouleversant* of a victim of inhuman capitalism.[26]

Revisionists like Gisselbrecht were eager to welcome on board the major modernists—Joyce, Faulkner and Moravia. It was now 'discovered' that the artists who had rallied to the Bolshevik Revolution almost all adhered to avant-garde movements: Mayakovsky (futurism), Brecht (expressionism), Aragon and Eluard (surrealism), Blok (symbolism), Hans Eisler (through the serial revolution of Schoenberg), Shostakovich (via Mahler), Kurt Weill and Paul Dessau (through jazz and Hindemith). Lenin's scathing remarks about the 'various 'isms' were out of fashion.[27] Revisionist rhetoric occasionally verged on the fatuous: 'We ought not,' concluded Ernst Fischer, 'to abandon Proust, nor Joyce, nor Beckett and even less Kafka to the bourgeois world. If we permit it then they can be used against us. If we do not permit it, these writers will not help the bourgeois world, they will help us.'[28]

Lukács was not to be moved. Questioned about the Aragon-Garaudy thesis of a 'realism without frontiers,' he confirmed that disoriented modernist writing which renounced a three-dimensional portraiture of man could not be realist. Joyce was of purely experimental interest and Beckett was negative. Lukács continued to champion 'bourgeois-progressive' novelists like Thomas Mann while belittling the fashionable nonconformist writers at work in postwar West Germany who—in effect—upheld 'the régime.'[29]

In 1968, fear and loathing of Dubček was to be rapidly translated into the more long-standing fear and loathing of Kafka. At the twentieth anniversary of the reopening of the German National Theatre in Weimar, Dr Klaus Gysi, the East German minister of culture, bitterly attacked Kafka's advocates Eduard Goldstücker and Ernst Fischer, the Austrian revisionist whose works were banned in East Germany. 'Such reverence for Kafka,' Dr Gysi declared, had been 'the ideological origin of all the theories and tendencies of the "third way to socialism" in that country [Czechoslovakia], especially the non-recognition of the power of the working class and its leading role...' Gysi contrasted the sublimity and nobility of Goethe's hero Faust with the absurdity and indignity of Gregor Samsa, Kafka's hero in *Metamorphosis*, who wakes one morning from uneasy dreams to find himself changed into a monstrous insect.[30]

The embittered reaction of 1968 continued into the Brezhnev era and the years of Husak's political and cultural clampdown in Czechoslovakia. In 1975 appeared in Moscow a fiercely orthodox collection of essays defending 'Marxist-Leninist' aesthetics on a 'broad front' against a pestilence of deviationists: 'revisionists of various shades,' 'professional anti-Communists,' Gleb Struve, Herbert Marcuse, Daniel Bell, with special attention to the 'renegade' Roger Garaudy's attempt to build bridges with modernism, *Pour un réalisme sans rivages*, and the art criticism of Ernst Fischer. This defence of rigid orthodoxy was the work of Aleksandr Dymshits, previously chief cultural officer of the Soviet Military Administration (SMAD) in occupied Germany after the war, later chief editor of the script division of the Gorky Film Studio. Georg Lukács was praised for his *Die russische Realismus in der Weltliteratur* (Berlin 1952), but sadly taken to task for his final essays lauding Aleksandr Solzhenitsyn, widely publicized in the West.[31]

Night descended in Czechoslovakia. In some respects (but not all), the work of Milan Kundera – much influenced by Kafka—epitomised the voice of Czech liberalism associated with the Prague Spring. Born in 1929 in Brno, the son of a well-known pianist, Kundera enrolled in the Czechoslovak CP immediately after the war. Expelled from the Party after the Prague coup of 1948 when a student, he underwent hard times before prospering as lecturer and writer during the 1960s, when his students were associated with the Czech New Wave in film.

The Joke (1967), his first novel, is sectioned out between several narrating characters, including the hero Ludvik Jahn. Their stories interlock across the first two decades of Communist rule. Ludvik, a Moravian Slovak, a 'good' Communist and an official in the League of Students, is an exemplar of 'the generation of 1948'—except for an independent streak which allows him to throw everything away in a single, frivolous postcard sent to a serious young woman, Marketa. 'Optimism is the opium of the people!' he writes. 'The healthy atmosphere stinks! Long live Trotsky! Ludvik.'[32] A distressed Marketa shows the card to the comrades. Ludvik defends himself before the tribunal as having written the offending postcard in haste, without thought. 'At least we know what is hiding inside you,' he is told.[33] He is duly expelled not only from the party but also from the university.

Vividly depicted is the Party mentality, interrogations, admonitions and reprimands, the group against the individual, careerism in the university, the self-righteous cruelty of youth. 'We were bewitched by history, intoxicated at having jumped on its back and being able to feel it beneath us. Admittedly, in most cases this did develop into an ugly lust for power...' Kostka, a Christian, advises Ludvik that socialism may have its roots in rationalism and scepticism but the prevailing ethos since 1948 has been that of religious zealotry and 'great collective faith,' which is now giving way to irony and cynicism, 'without enthusiasm or ideals.'[34]

One result of Kundera's modernism is that the characters in The Joke generally manage to sound like each other, or like Kundera, who on this showing is incapable of physical or verbal characterisation. The novel's separate voices are too discursive and too little dramatic. Perhaps more disturbing, Kundera's attitude to women comes as something of a shock. Whatever virtue and courage his fictional heroes may display in the face of Communist conformism, is pretty well cancelled out by their male chauvinism, often violent. In The Joke, the hero Ludvik hits a deeply disturbed young woman, Lucie, because he refuses to sleep with him. Proudly he tells of a scene with Helena, a radio journalist and wife of Pavel Zemanek, who had engineered his expulsion from the party after the postcard episode. Now it is time for revenge—Helena must undress for him: 'I am not dragging out the individual details of the scene from any predilection for the process of female undressing, but because I took careful note of each of these details.' He then gives her a sound beating: 'hoisting myself slightly over her I beat her on her arms and flanks and breasts...' The ellipses are Kundera's. He goes to the bathroom 'to savour the rare delight of sudden solitude...I felt myself the victor'. When he returns to the room Helena says, 'Come here, darling.'—which he hears 'with embarrassment and distaste.' Sobbing, she declares she is in love with him. He now sees her 'as a body which had been *stripped*—stripped of the allurement which till then had blurred over all the faults of age (corpulence, sagging, over-ripeness)...' This metamorphosis is evidently accelerated because she was now 'without a husband or any links binding her to a husband.'[35]

In part 2 of Kundera's *The Book of Laughter and Forgetting* (1982), a character called Karel encounters Eva, 'a light-hearted man-chaser.' Soon Karel is commanding her to strip. '"Shut up and strip," he barked out at her.' Lacking any rock music, she has to do so to Bach. She grabs herself between the legs. The year is 1972, Bobby Fischer has just won the world chess championship in Iceland. Soon the serious Communist Marketa is drawn into the homespun little orgies, clinically described – another revenge.

The Book of Laughter and Forgetting offers another version of the essentially autobiographical, history-bound novel, yet far from conventional realism. The book has been likened to a chamber of echoes, multiplied and distorted as the familiar becomes alien through a succession of tragic public events. Kundera recalls how in June 1950 the former Socialist deputy Milada Horakova was hanged with Zavis Kalandra, a Czech surrealist and friend of André Breton and the French Communist poet Paul Eluard. Breton called on Eluard to join him in trying to save their friend: 'But Eluard was too busy dancing in the gigantic ring encircling Paris, Moscow, Warsaw, Prague, Sofia and Athens... and all the Communist parties of the world; too busy reciting his beautiful poems about joy and brotherhood.'[36] Instead Eluard produced 'Le Visage de la Paix,' ironically quoted by Kundera. Seventeen years later Kalandra was rehabilitated.

A novel in seven parts, *The Book of Laughter and Forgetting* presents seemingly disparate characters who turn out to be linked together by travesties of fate. Kundera joins himself to his character Mirek. After the Russian invasion of 1968, 'No one was allowed to hire me.' Invited to write a horoscope for an illustrated weekly for young people, his recall then merges with that of Ludvik Jahn in *The Joke*: 'I too once danced in a ring. It was in the spring of 1948.... Then one day I said something I would better have left unsaid. I was expelled from the Party and had to leave the circle.'[37] We find Mirek in 1971, three years after crushing of the Prague Spring by Soviet armed intervention, insisting that free speech is legal but forced to work on a building site. Arriving home, he finds the police ransacking his apartment. After a year of investigatory custody he is put on trial and sentenced to six years. His eighteen-year-old son gets two years, and a dozen friends are given terms of one to six years. The young woman who had hired Kundera to write an astrology column is fired after a police interrogation: 'The people who have emigrated (there are a hundred and twenty thousand of them) and the people who have been silenced and removed from their jobs (there are half a million of them) are fading like a procession moving off into the mist.'[38]

In Book Four we are with a young woman, Tamina, and her husband – the couple had left Czechoslovakia illegally, while on a group tour of Yugoslavia. The husband then fell ill and died. As time passes, Tamina would dearly love to recover the notebooks she left behind with her mother-in-law in Czechoslovakia: memory is infinitely precious now, her past is shrinking, blurring, she wants life. She knows she cannot go back, despite the amnesty, because her husband's colleagues, who had publicly slandered him after he left, in order to save their jobs, are still in place.

Kundera explains: 'This entire book is a novel in the form of variations... It is a novel about Tamina, and whenever Tamina is absent, it is a novel for Tamina... all the other stories are variations on her story and come together in her life as in a mirror. It is a novel about laughter and forgetting, about forgetting and Prague and the angels.'[39] The theme of memory and forgetting leads Kundera back to his recurring debt to Kafka: 'Gottwald, Clementis and all the others did not know about Kafka, and Kafka knew that they did not know. Prague in his novels is a city without memory. It has even forgotten its name. Nobody there remembers anything, nobody recalls anything. Even Josef K. does not seem to know anything about his previous life.' Again: 'If Kafka is the prophet of a world without memory, Gustav Husak is its creator...*the president of forgetting*. The Russians brought him to power in 1969. Not since 1861 has the history of the Czech people experienced such a massacre of culture and thought... Husak dismissed some hundred and forty-five Czech historians from universities and research institutes.'[40]

One of them was Kundera's almost blind friend Milan Hubl, who came to visit him one day in 1971 in his tiny apartment on Bartolomejska Street. Hubl told him that the first step in liquidating a people is to erase its memory. Six months later Hubl was imprisoned. Kundera's books were removed from the libraries. In 1975 he settled in France. Following publication of *The Book of Laughter and Forgetting*, the Husak government revoked his citizenship.

The dissident playwright Václav Havel (who stayed to face the music and imprisonment) expressed scepticism about Kundera's solidarity with persecuted colleagues like Hubl. Havel comments that Kundera's own position resembled that of his character Tomás in *The Unbearable Lightness of Being*—when Tomás's son asks him to sign a petition in support of political prisoners, he refuses on the ground that the petition won't help the prisoners, merely gratify the signatories, whom he likens to parasites feeding off the prisoners' misery. (This kind of casuistical evasion is mercilessly explored in Havel's third 'Vanek' play, *Protest*.) In Havel's view the actual petition circulated on behalf of Jaroslav

Sabata, Milan Hübl and others under arrest had been 'the first significant act of solidarity of the Husák era.' When the prisoners eventually were freed, 'they all said that the petition had given them a great deal of satisfaction.' It was also the start of a stiffening of 'people's civic backbones.'[41]

The Unbearable Lightness of Being later enjoyed international success. Havel liked it—but: 'I don't want to do Kundera an injustice, but I can't avoid feeling that his notion of a Europe pillaged by Asia, his image of the spiritual graveyard, his idea that amnesia rules history and that history is an inexhaustible source of cruel jokes, all this lends support to the notion that nothing has changed in Czechoslovakia since the beginning of the 1970s...'[42] Kundera's intellectual development following his exile was in its fashion as scandalous as Solzhenitsyn's, although quite different in orientation. Kundera wrote in the *New York Times*: 'Faced with the eternity of the Russian night, I had experienced the violent end of Western culture...based on the individual and his reason, on pluralism of thought and on tolerance.... That was the grand farewell.' Replying, the exiled Leningrad poet Joseph Brodsky called this 'pure histrionics,' pointing out that the barbarism suffered by Czechoslovakia as recently as 1938 had come from the West. Brodsky insisted that Western values invariably recovered (more or less Vaclav Havel's point); Kundera, he said, wanted to be 'more European than the Europeans themselves'.[43]

Although his own fiction is replete with political references, Kundera now objected to the politicising of fiction (therefore of life itself)—and found Orwell's *Nineteen Eighty-Four* to be 'political thought disguised as a novel.' He admired Orwell's outlook as lucid and just but deformed by its fictional disguise. The situations and the characters belonged to poster platitude. The unfortunate influence of the novel resides in its 'implacable reduction of a reality to its purely political aspect and in the reductions of politics to propaganda.' Kundera concluded, 'Thus Orwell's novel, despite its intentions, makes itself part of the totalitarian spirit, the spirit of propaganda.'[44]

Western emphasis on politically dissident fiction and drama from the Soviet bloc irritated him. In October 1977 he told his exiled compatriot George Theiner: 'If you cannot view the art that comes to you from Prague, Budapest, or Warsaw in any other way than by means of this wretched political code, you murder it, no less brutally than the worst of the Stalinist dogmatists. And you are quite unable to hear its true voice. The importance of this art does not lie in the fact that it pillories this or that political regime but that, on the strength of social and human experience of a kind people here in the West cannot even imagine, it offers new testimony about mankind.'[45]

He chastised Czech friends who speak of 'forty lost years' or 'forty years of communist horror.' Had they forgotten their work, vacations, friendships, loves, the films of Forman, the books of Hrabal, the little nonconformist theatres, the jokes mocking power? Kundera accused them of having *orwellisé* their memories.[46]

In October 2008, a Czech research group, the Institute for the Study of Totalitarian regimes, posted an allegation against Kundera, namely that as a result of his tip-off to the Prague police, in 1950 they arrested a Czech deserter who had returned to the country as a spy for Western intelligence, along with others involved. The basis for the allegation is apparently the discovery of a police document from the time. In response Kundera issued an adamant denial, calling the accusations 'pure lies.'[47]

25

Germany Doubly Divided:
Christa Wolf and Uwe Johnson

Divided Germany was the heartland of the cold war. Not only did West and East Germany embody mutually hostile systems of government, capitalism and state socialism competing for skilled labour, but through the city of Berlin ran the frontier between America's Europe and Soviet Europe. The West Berlin city administration, set up to amalgamate the three Western sectors, and its charismatic Social Democratic mayors Ernst Reuther and Willy Brandt, posed a continuous challenge to the impoverished Soviet sector of the city, from the crisis of the Berlin blockade (1948-49) to the crisis of the Berlin wall, a physical barrier to free movement imposed by Ulbricht's German Democratic Republic on 13 August 1961 with the authorisation of Moscow (Khrushchev). Up to that time more than 2.6 million of the GDR's 17 million inhabitants had chosen to leave. In August 1961 alone, 47,000 made the move.

Christa Wolf's much translated prize-winning novel *Der geteilte Himmel* (*Divided Heaven*), was published by Mitteldeutscher Verlag, Halle, in 1963 and awarded the GDR's Heinrich Mann prize, followed by the National Prize third class.[1] Her biographer describes it accurately enough as 'a love story from the time of the Wall.' It caused great excitement, was praised by Kurt Hager in the Central Committee, and was regarded as fulfilling the Party's Bitterfeld programme – artists go to the workers. On the other hand, conservatives complained about its unusual, irritatingly 'modern' style including frequent flashbacks, its 'subjective atmosphere,' and about figures who were not 'typical' (i.e., did not display the customary, stereotyped profiles). Christa Wolfe's local paper, the Halle *Freiheit*, flaying the author for weak class consciousness, employed against her the vocabulary she herself had absorbed during ten years as a student and book editor: 'typical, twisted, decadent view of life – *typische, verquere, dekadente, Lebensauffassung.*' To a Western reader such strictures must seem astonishing, given the relative orthodoxy of the novel's content and literary style. One of the most penetrating criticisms came from Hans Sachs, head of Mitteldeutscher Verlag, the book's own publishing house. While defending Wolf against diehard attacks, he was critical of the strangely inactive attitude of the heroine Rita when she made her final decision to remain in the GDR. By viewing Rita's decision as mainly a matter of individual integrity, Wolf (said Sachs) played down 'the clarity of the national question.' He felt in retrospect that his publishing house had failed to give Wolf 'appropriate advice' (*entsprechende Hinweise*) on this vital question.[2]

Reactions in the Bundesrepublik to this new novel from 'the zone' were generally favourable – an improvement on the usual black-and-white stuff from the GDR. But Walter Osten wrote in *Stuttgarter Zeitung* (7 November 1963) that despite its literary quality *Divided Heaven* was 'made-for-a-purpose Wall literature [*zweckgebundene Mauer-Literatur*]. Osten also saw it as an almost programmatic 'Soviet zone national literature.'[3]

Christa Wolf, née Ihlenfeld in 1929, came from an East Prussian middle-class Protestant family. Her father Otto joined the Nazi Party (NSDAP) in 1933 and was to be found in uniform on the Polish border on 1 September 1939. On 29 January 1945, the sixteen-year-old Christa and her family fled west from an area of East Prussia assigned to Poland by the advancing Russians. Settling in Mecklenburg, she joined the Party (SED) in February 1949, when twenty. Having studied literature at Jena and Lepizig (1949-53), she worked for the Writers' Union (1953-59) and as a publishing editor for Neues Leben. It was in the 1950s that she gained her long-term mindset and anti-fascism. Contact with authors returning from the emigration generation was inspirational—Willi Bredel, F. C. Weiskopf and Anna Seghers among them. They, like Brecht, represented a kind of utopian vision of German spiritual renewal which was later supplanted by 'real existent socialism.'

In 1959, she moved to Halle where, under the influence of Bitterfeld movement, she worked in a factory until 1962, at the same time acting as a freelance editor for Mitteldeutscher Verlag. Ministry of State Security (Stasi) records found in 1993 show that she acted as an informant (*Inoffizieller Mitarbeiter*) for the secret police for almost five years from March 1959, but the Stasi found her too reluctant, too reticent.[4] Interviewed by *Die Zeit* (29 September 2005), she did not deny that she had written reports for the Stasi but did not explain why: 'I've honestly attempted to confront this episode from my past.'

Divided Heaven reaches its climax at the time of the building of the Wall, separating Rita from her lover Manfred for ever. Yet the Wall itself is scarcely mentioned by Wolfe; Kennedy, Khrushchev, Ulbricht likewise lie beyond our vision; the conflicting nature of the two political systems is mentioned but never discussed. Every 'touchy' subject is evaded – indeed the novel is in effect ultimately about what it refuses to confront. The author is whispering in the wings of discretion. The ubiquitous informer system run by the Stasi, with which she herself half-heartedly collaborated never surfaces. We are not told what East

Germans hear on West German Radio – except that it is propaganda. We do get references to individual defectors to the West but we are not told why the Wall was built – because over three million people had moved to West Berlin and West Germany since the war, many of them skilled cadres, an unsustainable leeching when taken alongside the massive economic reparations extracted by the Soviet Union, the burden of which fell on Russia's client German state alone.

Divided Heaven does very briefly mention how one of its main characters had been arrested by Soviet troops, sent to the Siberian mines for three years, then to an antifascist school before returning home; but what the novel never alludes to is the devastating experience of Red Army looting, rape, sometimes murder in the eastern districts where Wolf herself was brought up.

Despite accusations of modernism in the GDR, *Divided Heaven* is written in a strictly realist idiom apart from variations in the time sequence covering the two years 1959-61. The author is the traditional hidden god who can account for all her characters' thoughts and actions. In that sense the format is as naively manipulative as the content. The heroine Rita's sentiments are poured over her like sauce on a pudding – she can never surprise her creator and is incapable of any negative characteristic. The tone is always solemn; flickers of humour are confined to descriptions of Manfred's parents. Although the greater part of the novel is told in extended flashback, this is a familiar device and raises no complications about memory and consciousness. Doubt never crosses the threshold; no gap is allowed between the storytelling and the 'reality.' When Wolf's narrative points of view wobble, it is down to amateurishness not design.

At the outset (August 1961) we find Rita Seidel in a sanatorium convalescing from a nervous breakdown (*Zusammenbruch*) which coincided with a dangerous accident in the wagon workshop where she, a trainee teacher, works part time. The rest of the novel explains why a healthy and normally cheerful young woman, indeed a model citizen of the new socialist Germany, suffered this breakdown. During her recovery the events of the previous two years are recapitulated. Working as an office assistant in a small village, Rita meets Manfred, a man of thirty, ten years her senior, and a skilled chemist. Selected for a teacher training course in Manfred's home town (Halle/Saale), Rita finds herself living under the same roof as his parents, whom he despises and treats abominably, his contempt occasionally loathsome: 'My father is a typical German,' says Manfred. 'He lost an eye in the First World War, so that he didn't have to fight in the second. And he's still doing the same sort of thing – giving up an eye and hanging on to his life.' Clearly Wolf herself shares some of Manfred's contempt for his parents, the bourgeois Herrfurths. The father had worked as a buyer in a shoe factory and joined the SA; Manfred remembered, from the age of four, his father standing in front of a mirror to admire the new uniform. Manfred was made to join the Hitler Youth after the war started. Frau Elfriede Herrfurth slims on a rigid salad diet, does the daily exercises prescribed by a West German radio programme, despises her husband Ulrich, who has opportunistically joined the SED. Manfred tells Rita: 'He never had any convictions of his own and he didn't have anything special on his conscience.' The mother had kept the family from starving by organising a black market in a time of desperate scarcity.[5]

So much for the anti-fascist theme. But what about life and work in the socialist zone? Rita joins a twelve-man brigade at the wagon works and begins to identify with the brigade leader Metternagel, who comes to exemplify the noble desire to build socialism. Her lover Manfred meanwhile remains sceptical about the economic system prevailing in the GDR. On the personal front, the issue of 'love,' the central narrative consciousness so much belongs to Rita that we enter Manfred's point of view uneasily, not least when Rita discovers that this 'cold, offhand young man longed for warmth and intimacy'. 'Manfred, who had some experience of women and love, understood more clearly than Rita what was special about their love.'[6] This switch of viewpoint reads awkwardly because one wants to ask the author, 'How do you know what Manfred understood?' Sex is never described and barely alluded to – the couple simply spend nights together under the roof of Manfred's despised but devoted parents.

Divided Heaven owes an obvious debt to the Soviet production novel, indeed Wolf herself, as already mentioned, had chosen to do time in a Halle factory. Rita's protracted and detailed encounter with a railway wagon shop struggling to improve its performance (more window frames per hour, etc.), and Wolf's diligent research into production technique, raw materials, foreign suppliers, etc., almost puts the novel into the dreaded 'girl meets tractor' category. Rita's interests alternate between such universal values as love, dancing and harmony on the one hand, and socialist values – mainly learned from male persons whom she overhears discussing crises about shortages of spare parts. Through Rita's gaze we evaluate the leading figures in the production team ('brigade') and their quarrels, jealousies, intrigues. The 'negative' features are deliberately played up (again in the familiar Soviet style), particularly backward attitudes towards personal productivity, the need for exceptional hard work, the bitter reality that the most dedicated leaders are often punished for their virtues. Rita gets to like Rolf Meternagel, a family man almost fifty, who has suffered a 'retrogressive development.' A skilled carpenter before the war, then wounded several times and more than once the sole survivor in battle, he tells Rita how he became a POW. 'After that I was put to tree-felling and building barracks, a long way East.' He joined the SED on his release, slaved to better his skills while neglecting his young family, but swam out of his depth: 'He learned to use bigger and bigger words and to understand them less and less.... He even learned to shout at people when he could think of no answer to give them.' Then he was caught out in a bad mistake and was demoted to foreman in the railway wagon works. A second mistake occurred when he was diddled about the wages he paid out. Rita listens: 'A cold breath was clouding her mirror on the world.' Despite socialism, 'she was entering a region where only results counted, not good will...'[7] Meternegel is shown confronting the brigade, including the ever-sneering ex-Wehrmacht officer Kohn, to persuade them to fix ten wagon window frames per shift instead of eight. He tells them: 'Abnormal is crawling, swindling and tagging along. We've been doing that long enough.' He wants them to sign a pledge. None does so. But consciences are awakened: 'Gradually, however, one or two of them began to feel they ought to put their backs into their job.' Wolf does not explain why the workers are offered no bonus incentives. We may smile when we read that Rita's 'biggest day was perhaps the one in which they celebrated the five thousandth wagon built since the war.' The occasion (20 April 1960) was marked by speeches and a band, after which the members of the brigade retired to the local beer hall.

East-West competition is the long-running backcloth. 'West German newspapers wrote about the "once flourishing Mildner Wagon Factory now facing ruin – a mixture of truth, half-truths and downright lies".' Wolf comes to the seminal issue of defections to the West. Great is the humiliation and disgust when the ex-director of the factory is heard over Western radio, sending greetings from 'the happier part of Germany.' The next day his speech is relayed over the Mildner works loudspeaker system, each sentence interrupted by the voice of a Party agitator: '"Comrades! Colleagues! That is the voice of a traitor to our works, to our state, to us all!"'[8]

Another production hero, Ernst Wendland, thirty-two years of age, delivers a speech about the shortage of raw materials, semi-finished parts and labour. He provides exact figures on the number of mechanics, carpenters and welders needed. Wendland tells Rita – most of the men like to confide in her—how he was picked up carrying a pistol by Red Army men: '"Well, I spent the next three years in the mines in Siberia.... Over there they sent me to the Anti-Fascist School....When I got back home I went and joined the Free German Youth at once."'[9]

Rita's lover Manfred is sceptical about the use of all these works meetings; can they turn bad managers into good ones or persuade workers to stop thinking about their own pockets? Manfred displays cynicism at a drinks party, 'a long monologue about history being based on indifference, ending up with a remark about people all being cut to the same pattern.' But will Manfred defect? We shall see.

Wolf allows herself many negative touches about rigid bureaucratic mentalities, as incarnated by a know-all trainee teacher called Mangold, previously a department head in a town council. When this a harsh and cocky Party man hears that Rita's friend Sigrid, left entirely alone by her defecting parents, has been sitting on her secret in miserable loneliness, and that Rita, too, has kept silent out of loyalty, Mangold flies into oratory (here Wolf uses indirect speech very effectively): 'So she had known about it. A fine conspiracy. A worker deserts our state, our republic. His daughter deceives this same state. And her friend, who also draws a stipend from this state, conspires with her. This will have serious consequences. His voice droned on and on about the Party line – like a Catholic talking about the immaculate conception.'[10] The positive character Schwarzenbach, of the teachers' training college, tells Rita how he has criticised dogmatism in the teachers' journal; 'The thing to do was to convince them socialism was right, not to make yes-men of them.'[11]

Manfred, meanwhile, belongs to a research institute and is working on a complex formula for dyeing clothing, a spinning jenny to be used in a synthetic fibre factory. After the invention developed by Manfred is not accepted by the Technical Department (*Planungsbehörden*), and his friend Martin Jung loses his research job, Manfred's despondency turns to bitterness and anger. He fails to return from a Chemistry Congress in West Berlin. Rita does not hear from him for eleven weeks. 'They've offered me chances which I can't possibly miss,' he writes.

The international atmosphere is tense – people fear that war is imminent. Now living alone and confiding her intention to no one, Rita eventually makes a two-hour train journey to Berlin in pursuit of Manfred. An affable fellow-passenger (is he a spy?) asks her where her fiancé is living in Berlin. She lies and chooses an East Berlin district: in Pankow, she says. On arrival she buys an S-Bahn ticket for Zoologishcher Garten, uncertain whether she can pay for a return ticket in East German currency (she can: 40 pfennig). Crossing the sector boundary by the S-Bahn, she encounters the fellow-passenger who had been keen to question her; he gives her a wry smile.

Our heroine feels a stranger in this capitalist city with its gaudy Kurfürstendamm; equally serious, she finds in Manfred another kind of estrangement. 'For the first time in her life she wished she were somewhere else...she had got herself in a situation which went against the grain.'[12] Though she loves him his values are no longer hers. Later, when recovering from her nervous breakdown in Halle, she will ask an older friend whether he has ever been in West Berlin—though she does not name it, using the more alienated term 'dort' (there): 'It's like being in a foreign country, familiar, yet horrible.' She had felt ashamed of herself (*sich selbst zu schaden*).[13] A year or so after *Divided Heaven* came out, the present writer, visiting East Berlin and the GDR, was struck by the over-policed, over-regulated, over-sloganed, austere atmosphere to be found in Communist cities worldwide –Huge portraits of Walter Ulbricht dominated major street intersections. I was assured that 'Comrade Ulbricht himself has warned against any cult of personality' – an Orwellian touch that had escaped Orwell.

Rita and Manfred are together for half a day in West Berlin. He promises her the pleasures of the Rhine and other West German beauty spots, and speaks disparagingly of the GDR: 'Those senseless difficulties. Those exaggerated hymns of self-praise when some little thing happens to work out. Those self-flagellations. I'm getting a job now where other people are paid specially to get rid of all those obstructions.' Wolf imparts wisdom to a saddened Rita: 'She knew now that he had simply given up the struggle. He had not gone away out of protest, but had just given up. This going to the West was not a new experiment but the end of all experiments...' Manfred confirms Rita's saddened view of him: 'The fact is that man's not made to be socialist. If you force him into it he twists and turns until he's back where he belongs – at the best filled trough.'[14] She returns home, distraught, a week before the Wall goes up. The following Sunday, 13 August, 'I went to the works as soon as I heard the news. It was queer to see so many people there on a Sunday.'[15] The closure of the border and the erection of the concrete wall is 'the news.'

Later Wolf allows herself a daring passage when Manfred writes to his friend and fellow scientist Martin Jung (who has not defected): 'I'm not one of those who make pilgrimages to the Wall just for the thrill of it, but I still listen to your radio...it's hardly possible that you don't feel some horror at what human nature is capable of after what came out at the last Moscow Party Congress' (a reference to Khrushchev's last major push for de-Stalinisation, the 22nd Party Congress). Manfred adds that the basic fact of history everywhere is individual misfortune and anxiety ('...*wenn der Bodensatz der Geschichte überall das Unglück und die Angst des einzelnen ist.*')[16]

Forty years later, Wolf commented on her most famous novel: 'I can't say it corresponds to my idea of literature at its best.' What she called 'my brand of realism,' or 'subjective authenticity,' emerged with the story 'Juninachmittag' ('Afternoon in June'), which did not (she recalled) correspond to the 'vulgar realism that was being propagated.' Indeed the highly contentious sequel, *The Quest for Christa T.* (*Nachdenken über Christa T.*, 1969) is marked not only by a dramatic stylistic departure but by a new emphasis on the heroine's restless quest for self-fulfilment from her own inner resources. An acceptable novel in the GDR was one in which 'our state, our republic' provided a hero or heroine's third dimension. By contrast, Christa T. already possesses her own third dimension – a restless probing of life's possibilities for a woman. In *Divided Heaven* the 'production novel' resides outside of Rita although she takes part in it; the proto-feminist heroine Christa T. is larger than the world she shares and observes. One report to the publisher rejected the manuscript, complaining that Christa T. seemed to have died not only of leukaemia but 'out of a kind of necessity, an inner compulsion, her yearning for love and spiritual vulnerability frustrated by the society in which she lived'. The second report praised the masterly prose but regretted the fundamental social isolation of the heroine which rendered impossible every 'humanistic activity.' In December 1968, the long-delayed publication in the GDR was again interrupted and the book came under attack in the Central Committee.[17] As a result Rowohlt Verlag's edition inspired a minor cult in West Germany.

At the end of the 1950s – and gathering pace in the 1960s—came a cultural rebellion in the Federal Republic of Germany against the intellectual stagnation of the Adenauer era with its 'economic miracle' or *Wirtschaftswunder.*

During the 1950s what Hans Meyer called '*der totale Ideologieverdacht*' (total suspicion of ideology) had prevailed. Max Frisch's *Andorra* was premiered in 1961, followed by a wave of plays dealing with the Holocaust, Nazism and its successor state, the Federal Republic. A new wave of writers, Günter Grass, Heinrich Böll, Rolf Hochhuth and Peter Weiss among them, emphasised the challenge of national guilt and denial: consciousness, memory and repression.[18] More to come – the student uprisings, the indictment of a whole generation, were about to be played out on the streets during the climactic months of 1967-68. However, a distinguished critic, Hans Magnus Enzensberger, himself a member of Gruppe 47, conveyed scepticism in the neo-conspiratorial terms of the New Left: 'Literature was supposed to take the place of a void in the Federal Republic – the absence of a genuine political life...opposition could be repressed into book reviews; revolutions in poetry were the substitute for the non-occurrence of revolutions in the social structure...'[19]

Uwe Johnson's itinerary offers a classic contrast to that of Christa Wolf, the more so in that both shared a strikingly common background. Johnson (born in Pomerania in 1934) belonged, like Wolf, to a German refugee family which fled in fear from the east to Mecklenburg before the advancing Red Army. Wolf's father had joined the Nazi Party in 1933 and was to be found in uniform on the Polish border on 1 September 1939. Johnson's parents were likewise convinced Nazis. His father, a farmer who joined the NSDAP, made the mistake of returning after the war to the Heimat in Poland (as it had now become); identified as a Nazi, he died in a Soviet camp in the Ukraine. Uwe Johnson began to show his own colours when, a student at the University of Rostock, he refused to deliver an assigned speech assailing the Christian Youth organization known as the Young Congregation. He was expelled from the university. In 1956, Johnson's mother and sister compounded his pariah status when they fled to West Germany. Even so, he was able to study literature at the Karl Marx University in Leipzig under two outstanding Marxist 'liberals,' Ernst Bloch and Hans Mayer, each destined to part company with the GDR. Johnson perfected his English, worked as a translator, absorbed and embraced the tenets of modernism and the *nouveau roman*, indeed early post-modernism, and began to write fiction utterly unacceptable, both in form and content, in the GDR. In 1956 he submitted his first novel, *Ingrid Babendererde*, to four East German publishers, earning four rejections. 'Author needs a brainwashing,' one of them reported. The heroine leaves for the West after taking a moral stand against the treatment of the Junge Gemeinde, target of an official smear campaign from April 1953. Yet the West German editor Siegfried Unselde, of Suhrkampf Verlag, turned the same novel down because, among other reasons, he perceived too much loyalty to communism in the text.[20]

So ideologically unacceptable was Johnson's second novel, *Speculations about Jacob* (*Mutmassungen über Jakob*, 1959), that the author rapidly followed the book to the West after it was accepted by Suhrkampf. Not only is one of the principal characters an insidious, serpentine Stasi agent who wreaks a trail of destruction, but certain passages detail the depredations of the invading Red Army in 1945 with an objectivity as unacceptable in the GDR as Christ's possible sexuality would have been in Counter-Reformation Europe. Rumours circulate of a woman raped by a Soviet soldier in the woods; and of how 'a wild, embittered band in their conquered zone of Germany roamed about beating and shooting and getting drunk...in the surprisingly belted blouses of their uniforms... eggs were still being handed over at gunpoint to individual marauding Soviet soldiers...'[21] In Christa Wolf's *Divided Heaven* there is no mention of the East Berlin workers' uprising of 1953, suppressed with the support of Soviet tanks. By contrast, in Johnson's *Speculations About Jacob* one of the characters is overheard talking about the Stasi agent Rohlfs: 'I'm sure he's not one of those who tore the buttons off their lapels three years ago, and sneaked through the back doors while the labourers were out in the street and the hooligans set fire to the pavilions of enlightenment and nobody knew what it would come to. I'd like to think he was strutting about with the same lordly airs and his party button...'[22] This presages a more taxing examination of individual performances during the 1953 uprising in Johnson's next novel, *The Third Book About Achim*.

Two years after Wolf's *Divided Heaven*, Johnson produced his own 'Wall' novel, his own tale of star-crossed lovers wrenched apart at the political frontier – but a tale told primarily from the opposite side of the Wall. Johnson's *Two Views* (*Zwei Ansichten*, 1965) is less aggressively post-modernist in form than his previous fiction, *Speculations About Jacob* and *The Third Book About Achim*, less concerned to construct a complex, polyphonic narrative to convey a relativity of experiences and viewpoints. Whereas Wolf remains fully 'in charge' of both her creations, the virtuous Rita and the fatally flawed Manfred, Johnson's hero and heroine[23] occupy largely separate narratives whose literary styles subtly embody not only two contrasting personalities but also the ethos of the two Germanies.

Our West German Romeo, Dietbert, twenty-five years old at the fatal moment of 13 August 1961, incarnates city-slicker values in a superficial, unattractive way – an astute reversal of Wolf's pedestrian equation of political virtue with timeless good character. A 'plumpish, tall fellow,' Dietbert has come through military service as a playboy of hedonistic, selfish impulses who can scarcely remember all his conquests. Riordan calls him 'a paradigm of cynicism who is as dishonest with himself as with others'.[24] Dietbert likes to move about the city asking roundabout questions while wearing a movie actor's poker face—'handled himself like the sort of guy nobody is going to make a fool of'.[25] As an opportunistic photographer, Dietbert makes a lot of money and falls in love with a red sports car adroitly acquired after a road accident. This phallic car – frequently described as his 'red thing' (*rotes Ding*)—no sooner arrives with Dietbert in West Berlin than it is stolen right outside his hotel by knaves cleverer than himself. Despite consequent existential anguish, he remains semi-serious about his East Berlin hospital nurse Beate – although 'From the few days spent with her he didn't known her much better than all the girls he had slept with during the past five years.... He did not know very much more than his memory had preserved, mostly glimpses, distributions of light...'[26] In photographic terms, Beate properly belongs to his reels of negatives. The prose style of the Dietbert narrative resonates with 'sixties cool' and the *distantation* of the nouveau roman, of Jean-Luc Godard and Antonioni's *Blow Up*. Dietbert reaches Hamburg by plane. Why Hamburg? Apart from the bars, jukeboxes and dancing, no particular reason: 'He was here to think quietly under the bright light, he wouldn't be fooled. The purpose of his visit to this city was to laugh softly along with others in the conversation that surrounded him.'[27]

The hospital nurse Beate works in the rigid, impoverished, spy-ridden setting of East Berlin. She shares, as it happens, a seminal fate similar to Johnson's – a Nazi officer father arrested by the Russians and not heard from again. But in Beate's case she is penalised for her origins when denied access to university preparatory classes and to the medical career she aspired to. Her many virtues – including loyalty, unselfishness, stoicism – mirror Dietbert's shallow vices. She loves her mother, who is living in Potsdam, and cares about her three brothers. The younger one makes her position difficult by settling in Munich in an engineering school. As a result, the Stasi are on to her and she loses her apartment; when she mails his birth certificate pasted into the cover of a picture book about East Berlin's zoo, she runs the risk of being arrested as an accomplice to his escape—or 'kidnapping/trafficking/ smuggling' in official East German parlance. (East German television, whether the nightly news programme 'Aktuelle Kamera,' or crime serials like 'Blaulicht,' constantly manipulated the semantics of border-flight, preferring *Abwegung* (enticement), *Menschenhandel* (people-smuggling), and *Kopfläger* (head-hunters). In the long-running 'Blaulicht' the open border constituted a source of flagrant criminality featuring cigar-smoking racketeers and cynical teenagers wearing 'Real American jeans!... Original Texas. Made in USA.' American spymasters were depicted as imposing loyalty tests in the form of tasks assigned, notably smuggling precious works of art.[28]

At work Beate is demoted, treated poorly and given menial tasks. East Berlin is running short of basic supplies including medicines, with the East mark set at one fifth of the value of the West mark. When visiting relatives in the Western sector of the city, Beate has long made a habit of furtively picking up cosmetics, Nescafé, anything she can hide under her dress: 'She also got out and casually took from the toe of her shoe the notes and prescriptions which the doctors at her institution had wordlessly laid on the nurses' table, and obtained the Western medicines, each time from a different pharmacy, with a slight uneasiness at the nape of her neck, for such imports also were forbidden...' She has become accustomed to lying to people connected with the East German state, 'people recognizable by vocabulary, manner of posing questions, insignia, uniforms and a certain tie-up between expression and behaviour which you did not see until you adjusted to it'.[29] This chilling collective portrait is of course nowhere to be found in Christa Wolf.

Beate has no hesitation about conversing with Western-sector citizens. She is said to be 'indifferent to politics' but now, locked in by the Wall, 'she felt cheated, deceived, deluded. The feeling was like that of an insult one cannot return...'[30] Dietbert, too, 'felt personally offended by the confinement of Beate in her Berlin; he had a private anger against the forbidden zones, minefields, lines of sentries, obstacle ditches, glaring lights, barbed wire, walled-up windows, shooting orders and threats of punishment for attempts to cross'.[31] It is this shared sentiment of confinement which now unites Beate and Dietbert – although they can no longer communicate directly, since telephone calls from the West are automatically refused by Beate's hospital switchboard. East Berlin is a city under siege yet also a city which has laid siege to itself.

Unlike Wolfe's flimsy sketch of Rita's brief visit to Manfred, Johnson describes life in the two Berlins both before and after the Wall,[32] providing not only an absorbing guide to the city's topography but also a vivid description of the bold photographs Dietbert takes of the Wall, its watchtowers and Volkspolizei sentries, the cement block and layered concrete slabs, the tracery of barbed wire, guards on three-level watchtowers with dogs prowling the field of fire. Dietbert's camera-haul includes a refugee shot in the boundary canal, another who plunged to his death from a roof, the cloud of tear gas used to drive the photographers away.[33]

To say that Dietbert is determined to get Beate out of East Berlin would be to wrap him in too fine a cloth. One evening, he writes her a letter in a drunken stupor but leaves it lying on the bar. It is delivered to Beate by a member of the escape group. Dietbert visits a man said to be a tunnel digger – an encounter skilfully sketched – before making contact with a clandestine student escape organization. 'She doesn't know any languages, she knows Russian', he says of Beate. The student rep already knows of her: 'We'll make her number four hundred and fifty, the anniversary number.' Although her own escape will be a slow, protracted process, Beate will hasten to repay the debt by running risky missions on behalf of West Berlin students in Brandenberg. She will eventually escape on false papers, pretending to be an Austrian tourist in transit, travelling from West Berlin to the Baltic coast by train, to Copenhagen by ferry, to Hamburg then back to West Berlin by air – hundreds of miles to end up a few blocks from where she started.[34]

Compared with his two earlier novels, *Two Views* is very much more accessible to the reader, less formalistic and 'experimental,' but Johnson does introduce a new trick of the trade late in the story. Initially the 'two views' appear to be the work of the standard omniscient author/narrator standing outside the story. A clue arrives when the word 'I' surfaces almost surreptitiously, indicating that the narrative has in fact been the work of someone with a role inside the story. Johnson introduces the 'I' (*ich-Erzähler*) at the moment when Dieter is knocked down by a bus in a minor street accident. 'I helped him up'—it seems playful, perfunctory. The nameless 'I' figure also has contact with Beate when she receives her false identification papers and is seeking accommodation. It is this person who has presented us with two narratives based on what Dietrich and Beate have told him. Johnson maintained that, 'The form has exclusively the function of bringing the story undamaged into the world.'

Johnson's biographer Bernd Neumann points to a number of influences on the novel. Romeo and Juliet come to mind, with the two German states standing in for the warring Montagues and Capulets – except that it is the love of Romeo and Juliet which precipitates their separation whereas the 'love' of Dietrich and Beate is largely a protest against, and an obsession fostered by— the Wall. Neumann mentions the currently influential exemplars of the nouveau roman, Alain Robbe-Grillet and Michel Butor, as reflected in the succession of instantaneous 'moments' recorded (*Momentaufnahmen*) by Johnson. Johnson was also impressed by Bernard Larsson's book, *Die ganze Stadt Berlin. Politische Photos*, which appeared in 1964, with a foreword written by Butor, while Johnson was at work on his novel. Larsson played up the dramatically contrasting images provided by the divided city, the sparkling ads of the consumer paradise and the stern agitprop slogans of the workers' state. As Neumann says, the title of *Two Views* refers both to the optical and the ideological, Berlin as photo-journalism, Berlin as Cold War politics.[35]

Johnson had much to say about history-through-literature, about fiction's ability to focus on the individual life and to avoid tossing away 'a pile of people in a single sentence.' He saw this focus on individuals as an antidote to ideological packaging, citing Aristotle in support of the view that 'the narration that invents is more useful than history writing, because fiction has the essence (of human life) in view and not merely the particulars'.[36]

Part 4

Solzhenitsyn

26

One Day in the
Life of Ivan Denisovich

Shortly before publication of *One Day in the Life of Ivan Denisovich* cata-pulted him into the international limelight, Aleksandr Solzhenitsyn (1918-2008) was introduced to Anna Akhmatova. She is said to have asked this unknown young writer whether he realized he would be the most famous man on earth within a month. Solzhenitsyn knew by heart Akhmatova's *Poem Without a Hero*, partly a distillation of memory, partly a meditation on history, partly a poetical statement on Russia's destiny – but never published in full in the Soviet Union. Akhmatova, Nadezhda Mandelstam, Pasternak remained inwardly free – though outwardly shackled—because their pre-revolutionary heritage offered them an alternative frame of intellectual and emotional reference, largely immunizing them to the 'Soviet temptation.' Solzhenitsyn by contrast, born one year after the Revolution, had lived his life within Bolshevik Russia, was part of it, originally admired Lenin, and became the Soviet Union's most influential convert.

After their meeting, Akhmatova described Solzhenitsyn to Chukovskaya as 'a bearer of light. Fresh, sharp, young, and happy. We've forgotten that such people exist. Eyes like precious stones. And stern: he listens to what he is saying.'[1]

Solzhenitsyn's life and writing offer unrivalled insight into the interaction of history and literature. With Solzhenitsyn recent history runs without stutter into current events, even into the immediate future. The writer himself becomes not only a witness to history, an impassioned interpreter, he also causes the KGB and the Party's Presidium to regularly bite their fingernails about an un-fortunate incident at his dacha; or how to trace his hidden manuscripts; or the likely reach of his most recent interview with a foreign journalist—and what he may do next. In these years he was a restlessly experimental writer engaged in a rich variety of literary forms: prose and verse, drama and the novel, short story and epic invention, polemic and open letter, personal memoir and essay, 'history' as art, 'art' as history. But Solzhenitsyn had as little time for modernism or post-modernism in the arts as for flabby liberalism. They were off the same rotting tree.

Solzhenitsyn's career affords an extended opportunity to test the hypothesis that Russian writers alchemize recent history into fiction under censorship and repression. But any monist causal link here is complicated by the fact that he continued to write fiction after he was exiled into freedom, while his major ventures into non-fiction like *The Gulag Archipelago* and *The Oak and the Calf*[2]—as well as the open letters and manifestoes—were already well under way, at full throttle, before his expulsion in 1974. The indirect fictional voice having been stifled by censorship, the literary avenues 'between the lines' having been blocked off, the writer responded by resorting increasingly to more urgent forms of expression, direct argument and exhortation, at the top of his voice—while covertly distributing further long manuscripts in conditions of oppressive surveillance.

When did Solzhenitsyn lose faith in Lenin's work and legacy? Lukács stresses that in *The First Circle* and *Cancer Ward*, no character wants to restore the old regime or capitalism. Lukács is gratified by Nerzhin's admiration for Lenin. But the Medvedev brothers, Roy and Zhores, both attested that when *One Day in the Life of Ivan Denisovich* brought Solzhenitsyn acclaim at home and abroad, the writer remained strongly attached to Lenin. In other words, he still held that the revolution had gone wrong after Lenin's incapacitating illness, as with the Jacobin terror, Thermidor and Napoleon in France. The Medvedevs were adamant that in 1963-64 Solzhenitsyn had set his heart on the Lenin Prize for *One Day* and was bitterly disappointed when he did not get it. Even so, according to Lev Kopelev, whom Solzhenitsyn came to know well as a prisoner at Marfino, as early as their time in this special prison (June 1947 to May 1949), Solzhenitsyn 'hated Stalin and had come to doubt Lenin'[3] According to a report to the Central Committee by the KGB's chairman, V. Semichastny, following a raid on a house where copies of *The First Circle* had been seized, during Solzhenitsyn's KGB-bugged conversations with his confidant V. L. Teush, the writer had expressed his detestation of Lenin, citing a new study by the American author Louis Fischer, *The Life of Lenin*.[4]

Unlike Akhmatova and Pasternak, Solzhenitsyn was a convert from the Soviet creed. Akhmatova, who relished his energy but was not so keen on the crude, heavy, plebeian elements in his art, described him as a 'Soviet man.'[5] Olga Carlisle, whose father had smuggled the microfilm of *The First Circle* out of Russia, met Solzhenitsyn by pre-arrangement at a friend's house; walking her home to the Leningradskaya Hotel, he explained his situation and aims in an 'intense, high-pitched voice'; this was not the 'lyrical Russian' she had heard from Pasternak or other members of the old intelligentsia, this was 'Soviet Russian, robust, staccato, with a modern vernacular unfamiliar to me, now and then an ancient folk proverb from the depths of rural Russia, and occasional prison camp terms...'[6]

Solzhenitsyn belonged to the new technological class fostered by Stalin and thousands of institutes of learning in the 1930s. On the evidence he was widely read, phenomenally so, despite ten years in captivity, much of it as a prisoner of the Gulag. He was determined to get hold of everything, including foreign works, relevant to his ongoing research. Fluent in German, capable in English, he knew where to look, go, and find. According to one commentator, Solzhenitsyn's view of history stands in contradiction to the empirical school of Western historians who try to approach their source material objectively, divesting themselves of prejudices as far as possible. He resembles Soviet historians in his unashamed bias, his willingness to read into his sources what he wants to see, his desire not merely to establish the truth about the past, but to use it for social engineering in the present and future. He was rightly described by Alain Besançon as an "inverted Communist". To use Isaiah Berlin's term, Solzenhitsyn is a "'hedgehog": someone who relates everything to a monological central vision...'[7] Nevertheless, he is arguably the best – and certainly the most widely read—historian that Soviet Russia produced.[8]

Aleksandr Solzhenitsyn was born in 1918, in the Caucasus, six months after the death of his father, who had served as an artillery officer in the First World War. Aleksandr entered Rostov University's Faculty of Mathematics and Physics in 1936, later transferring his studies to the correspondence department of the Moscow Institute of History, Philosophy and Literature. Conscripted in October 1941, he was first enlisted as a driver in a transport unit due to poor health. Transferred to an artillery school, he graduated from an abridged course in November 1942, then served as a reconnaissance artillery battery commander at the front until February 1945, winning two decorations and rising to the rank of captain.

His progress towards the world's headlines began in February 1945, when he was arrested in East Prussia while on active service, after the interception of letters to a school friend containing unfavourable comments about Stalin. 'Drafts of stories and ideas, found in my field bag, served as additional material for the charge.' He was transported to the Lubyanka prison, even though he had been awarded the Order of the Fatherland War, class two, and the Order of the Red Star. The charge was that from 1940 until the day of his arrest he had conducted anti-Soviet propaganda among his friends and undertaken steps to establish an anti-Soviet organization. In his diary and letters to a friend, N. D. Vitkevich, he had denigrated both Stalin and the air of unreality prevailing in Soviet literature. Under article 58 of the Criminal Code of the RSFSR, a sentence of eight years in corrective labour camps was handed down on 7 July 1945 by decree of the Special Board of the NKVD.

Due to his skills as a mathematician, however, he was transferred a year later to the MVD-MGB prison research institute in Marfino, near Moscow. This experience became the basis for his novel, *The First Circle*. In May 1950, his relatively privileged existence ended and he was sent to labour camps in north-

ern Kazakhstan, where he worked as a bricklayer and foundry worker. Out of
these years was to come his first published novella, *One Day in the Life of Ivan
Denisovich* (1962). In March 1953, having served his full eight-year term, he
was condemned to 'perpetual exile' in a remote Kazakh settlement, where he
taught maths and physics in the local school. His intensive treatment for stomach
cancer in a Tashkent oncological hospital was also to be turned to good account
in *Cancer Ward*. On 6 February 1956 the Military Collegium of the Supreme
Court, a three-man panel, examined the Protest of the Chief Military Prosecutor
against his original sentence. Released from exile in the summer of that year, he
moved to Vladimir province in Central Russia, where he continued his career as
a school teacher. In February 1957, he was judicially rehabilitated. At this time
he was writing in secret, showing his manuscripts to few other people. 'In 1961,
following the 22nd Party Congress and Tvardovsky's speech there, I decided to
let it out: to submit *One Day in the Life of Ivan Denisovich*.'[9]

Solzhenitsyn's ground-breaking novella[10] was published in December 1962
through the efforts of the liberal editor of *Novyi mir*, Aleksandr Tvardovsky, who
set about harvesting a dossier of laudatory opinions from leading writers. Kornei
Chukovsky, to whom he showed the manuscript, called it 'a literary miracle.'
He particularly admired the pure and traditional prose style, an admixture of
camp slang, a style which did not draw attention to itself but seemed as natural
as breathing. The author had not taken the easy path of facile indignation: 'In
this lies his greatest achievement: nowhere does he express his passionate rage.
He is not a polemicist but a historian.'[11] Here, clearly was history presented
as a fictional narrative in the naturalist tradition virtually without comment
or generalization. Tvardovsky managed to leapfrog the entire Soviet literary
bureaucracy. Having won the crucial support of Khrushchev's son-in-law,
Adzhubei, the novella was then submitted to Khrushchev himself through his
chef de cabinet, Vladimir Lebedev, who read it aloud to the boss. Six years
had passed since Khrushchev launched the anti-Stalin campaign in his secret
speech to the Twentieth Congress of the CPSU. Since that time many prisoners
had been released from the camps and many victims had received certificates
of formal rehabilitation.

A limited number of proofs of *One Day* were printed for submission to top
brass. Encountering almost unanimous opposition to the novella in the Presidium
(Mikoyan was an exception), Khrushchev hectored his colleagues, reminding
them that 'there's a Stalinist in all of us'. This was in October 1962. At a second
meeting he again failed to obtain their approval and announced that he was
interpreting silence as consent to a book he found revelatory and wonderfully
written.[12] No work of fiction – no book! – had ever been sanctioned at so high a
level, but *One Day* was to come back to haunt Khrushchev during his remaining
two years in office, until he cursed the day he had set eyes on it.

Had the same 'facts' about a typical Soviet Gulag camp appeared on
Khrushchev's desk in the form of an academic thesis written by a historian,

it certainly would not have survived ten minutes' scrutiny by his secretary Lebedev. Nor would Tvardovsky have felt able to promote it. As a work of fiction, *One Day* could simply evade the causes of the Gulag system, avoid attributions of responsibility and finger-pointing. The camp was simply – but unbearably – there.

Novyi mir's normal print run was 100,000 copies. On the day of publication the Moscow kiosks were sold out by the end of the morning. One Moscow bookshop with an allotment of ten copies had 1,200 subscriptions by the end of the day.[13] Copies were borrowed and reborrowed. People read it over each other's shoulders. In January 1963 a cheap mass edition of 750,000 was issued. By the time of the March 1963 plenum on literature, Khrushchev had become alarmed. Magazines and publishing houses, he complained, had been flooded with manuscripts about exile, prisons, and camps. 'I repeat once again this is very dangerous theme, and difficult material to deal with.... This "spicy" stuff will, like carrion, attract huge fat flies, and all kinds of bourgeois scum will crawl from abroad.'[14]

The novella's hero, Shukhov, can be taken as a portrait of the Russian common man: resilient, stubborn, hardy, jack of all trades, cunning, kindhearted. Why is he here? Before 1949 you got eight or ten years, after 1949 twenty-five years. Shukhov himself had confessed to high treason to avoid being shot. Captured in February 1942 after his whole army was surrounded on the North-Western front, he had escaped from the Germans – only to be arrested on regaining the Soviet lines and accused of carrying out a mission for German intelligence: 'What sort of mission neither Shukhov nor the interrogator could say.' This theme – the injustices inflicted by a paranoid regime on citizens for whose captivity Stalin was responsible – runs throughout Solzhenitsyn's work.

Solzhenitsyn himself had totally shared the life and conditions of other zeks in the camps. He was not a metropolitan intellectual; he lived under Shukhov's skin; he knew how to re-lay a mud floor every week after it turned to dust; how to attend to every detail of daily survival; his ear revelled in the cadences of the vernacular and camp slang. There are occasional cultural conversations. One prisoner calls Eisenstein's film *Ivan the Terrible* (*Ivan Grozny*) a justification for political tyranny, the director himself an ass-kisser obeying a vicious dog's order. We can assume this was Solzhenitsyn's own verdict.

Probably no historian – even given perfect conditions for research and free publication; even armed with social and medical statistics unknown to the novelist – could have universalized the concentration camp experience so authentically and in so few pages. *One Day* has a conventional third-person narrative, although the author rarely ventures a yard or a heart-beat from the mindset and point of view of Ivan Denisovich Shukhov. This intimacy is reinforced by frequent adoption of the proverbial 'you' form, as if the man were talking to himself. Nothing unusual happens on this particular day. The prisoners are roused from their sawdust mattresses at five by reveille, and have ninety minutes to themselves before work begins. Two hundred men occupy one hut. Bugs abound, as does theft. Food rations are always below weight. Prisoners must address guards and officials as 'citizen chief.' Galoshes are made from scraps of motor tyres. The colloquial style is replete with swear words, obscenities. In the cold mess hall most prisoners keep their hats on, picking out putrid little fish from under cabbage leaves. Bones are spat out on to the table. Ten minutes are allowed for breakfast, five for dinner, five for supper. Magara, a Chinese oatmeal, sets into solid lumps when cold.

Survival requires free enterprise, small jobs to earn a rouble and buy tobacco. Be friendly with those who receive parcels, although the parcels are despoiled by the guards. Shukhov wears rags tied round his feet under his boots; he conceals his bread supply inside his mattress. He craves tobacco and freedom; he thinks about tobacco but dare not think about freedom. A zek's day is punctuated by roll calls, inspections. Anyone wearing too many undershirts is punished. The brutal security chief, Lt Volkovoi, carries a whip and uses it. Prisoners may be sent for ten days to terrible punishment cells for trivial offences—many do not survive the ordeal. The time-setting is 1951.

A prisoner is entitled to receive two letters a year. His wife writes to tell Shukhov about life on the kolkhoz; the young have left for the towns or the peat fields; half the kolkhozniks had not come back after the war, and those who did lived there but earned their money outside. 'The real work in the kolkhoz was done by the same women who'd been there since the start, in 1930.' She hopes Ivan Denisovich will become a carpet painter when released because no real money can be gained from farming. Shukhov himself would rather be a plumber or carpenter. The prisoners are currently working on a new power station surrounded by guard towers. The methods and tools employed are described in detail, likewise work charts, strategies for slacking, the chain of authorities, tricks for wangling a second helping of food. It is one long battle of wits. Rations depend on the productivity of each work team. The guard lieutenants receive bonuses proportionate to the productivity of the teams they supervise.

At the end of the working day each column of prisoners is anxious to get back to camp before the others, to be first to the washhouse, first to the food. They think of the camp as 'home.' Privileged prisoners like the barber and bookkeeper, who are 'in' with the authorities, go to the front of the food queue. Everyone requires a tip: the barber, the letter office, the bath attendant all expect a coin in the palm. The escort guards allow a certain amount of pilfering of firewood from the building site for the prisoners' stoves since they get a kickback. The warders are poorly paid and conduct a black market in grain, filched from the prisoners' daily rations. Ivan Denisovich is far from being a fighter. His motto is 'groan and bend your back; if you fight them, they'll break you'.

As Hosking puts it, 'In the furnace of the camp, as on the Calvinist day of judgement, all the hierarchies of this world are rendered meaningless...'[15] For example, Fetyukov, previously a factory director, is now a meek fellow, always begging favours. A key figure is the prisoner chosen as brigade leader. It is he who deals with the Commandant's aides, the Production Planning Section, the work supervisors and engineers. 'You could cheat anyone you liked in the camp, but not Tyurin. That way you'd stay alive.'[16] Team leader Tyurin had been in the Red Army in the 1930s, a first-class machine gunner, until they discovered his father was a kulak. (This is another perennial Solzhenitsyn theme, the brutal injustice of collectivization – but it remains peripheral, since he had no direct personal experience of it.) Tyurin was cashiered from the Red Army in 1930: '"I got home late one night and entered by the back garden. Father had already been deported, and mother and the kids were waiting for a transport. A telegram had come about me and the Village Soviet were already after me. We put out the light and sat trembling against the wall under the window, because activists were going round the village peering in at the windows. I left again the same night and took my kid brother with me..."'[17]

Fourteen months after *Novyi mir* scored its greatest coup, the publication of *One Day*, it came out with a work of fiction portraying collectivization as a highly coercive operation. Sergei Zalygin's *By the Irtysh (Na Irtyshe)* makes it clear that 'dekulakization' was directed against any peasant who refused to obey orders. The Stalinist official Koryakin brands Chauzov, the hero, a 'kulak' and exiles him from the village not because he is rich, but because he refuses to endorse an order to give up personal grain to meet the target of the kolkhoz sowing plan. Zalygin's novel is said to have had a major impact on the intelligentsia.[18] In *The Gulag Archipelago*, Solzhenitsyn praises 'S. Zalygin's novel' (without providing its title) and its character Chauzov.[19]

Ivan Denisovich himself is heir to a Christian peasant tradition, half destroyed. He was one of those Russians 'who didn't even remember which hand you cross yourself with'. He prays briefly and desperately when he fears his precious piece of metal is going to be discovered in a search, but normally 'all these prayers are like the complaints we send to higher-ups – either they don't get there or they come back to you marked "Rejected".'[20]

Such is Solzhenitsyn's flair for indirect narration and indirect introspection that it often feels as if Shukhov himself is himself telling the story—though he is technically a third-person figure in a landscape. The author takes his narrative stance very close to Ivan Denisovich, at times letting the two voices merge. The style, sometimes called *erlebte Rede*, was much used in the nineteenth century to illuminate mental and psychological processes, but it was absolutely central to Solzhenitsyn's literary strategy, and extensively used by Vladimov, Voinovich and Trifonov, to gain vividness, the sense of personal values being at stake. Hosking comments: 'The Russian language is unusually well adapted to this function, through its variety of impersonal and infinitive constructions, its ability to dispense with a verb in the present tense, and above all the absence of any differentiated sequence of tenses for indirect speech. All this means that direct and indirect speech are often indistinguishable from one another, and for quite long passages it remains ambiguous who is speaking.'

Solzhenitsyn draws on the powerful underground stream of folklore and popular language, which had virtually disappeared during the imperial period of Stalinism:

'Every man for himself' or 'he who can devours his neighbour,' *Kto kogo smozhet, tot togo i glozhet.*'

'How can a warm man understand a cold one?' *Teplyi zyabologo razve kogda poimët'*

'The belly is an ungrateful bastard, doesn't remember past services,' *Bryukho – zlodei, starogo dobra ne pommit.* [21]

Hosking comments that in the longer passages the language often takes on the character of folk narration, with the rhythms, repetitions, parallelisms and word inversions of the *skazka* (fairy tale).

One Day in the Life of Ivan Denisovitch inevitably aroused keen interest in the West—this was the first sanctioned description of the fight for survival in the Gulag (the Russian acronym for the Chief Administration of Corrective Labour Camps) – and therefore the first sanctioned admission of the Gulag's long-denied existence.[22] Michel Tatu hailed *Une journée d'Ivan Denissovitch* in *Le Monde* (23 November 1962) as wonderfully written, restrained, sober, magisterial. Here was a universe stranded on the margins of the USSR and of history, a degradation comparable to that inflicted by the Nazis. For prisoners released since Stalin's death, said Tatu, Solzhenitsyn's novel arrived as a second liberation. At both the 20th and 22nd Congresses of the Party, Khrushchev's emphasis had been on rehabilitating leading figures of the Party, State and Army; the mass purge remained in the shadows, the word 'camp' was not heard. The editors of *Le Monde* had a further point to make—French Communists had always denied the existence of Soviet forced labour camps for political prisoners.

Like all Soviet works unprotected by international copyright, *One Day* was up for grabs in the West as soon as publishers laid hands on it. At least three rival editions rapidly appeared in English, two in German, but the only payments the author received were from Sweden and Norway.[23]

27

The First Circle

In a lecture delivered at Yale, Hannah Arendt maintained that *The First Circle* ought to be required reading for students of totalitarianism.[1] By coincidence, Solzhenitsyn's fictional time-frame, 1949, also witnessed the publication of Orwell's dystopia. But whereas Orwell was portraying a future nightmare, a warning, Solzhenitsyn was already Big Brother's prisoner. The title of *The First Circle* is an allusion to Dante's most privileged, least fiery, circle of hell. After a period of hard labour in the Gulag, Solzhenitsyn himself had temporarily enjoyed the soft conditions permitted for the scientific *sharashka* at Marfino.

The First Circle encompasses a broad swathe of Soviet society. The privileged 'first circle' of prisoners selected from the camps are put to work under civilized conditions: philologists, mathematicians, chemists, radio engineers, telephone engineers, artists, translators, book binders, architects, designers and 'even a geologist who got in by mistake' are working in teams on several urgent projects: a walkie-talkie radio, a scrambler telephone designed for Stalin's personal use, and a voice decoder capable of revealing the identity of a caller by detailed acoustic analysis. Solzhenitsyn's prisoners at Mavrino suffer the bitter irony of being forced to entrap others, although some of those assigned to this task suffer from residual party loyalty.

The principal characters among the prisoners at Mavrino are Gleb Nerzhin (based on Solzhenitsyn), Lev Rubin (based on Lev Kopelev) and slightly to one side Dmitri Sologdin (based on Dmitri Panin). In their free time, Mavrino's elite prisoners passionately debate all the great issues of Soviet history. Rubin is a Leninist, Sologdin a Christian and militant anti-Communist. The Socratic Nerzhin is portrayed as oscillating between them (rather as Solzhenitsyn had done), but gradually moving closer to Sologdin. The message was that man should believe his eyes but not his ears, listen to his moral instinct and conscience. In an entertaining episode,[2] Rubin leads Nerzhin and others in a spoof trial of Prince Igor, hero of Russian legend, accusing him of treason, of surrendering to the Polovtsian Khan, Konchak. At the end of this witty mock-up of a Soviet trial, the prisoner Kagan comes up with a new and dastardly punishment, article 20, section 'a'—'stat'ia 20-ia, punkt "a".' This consists of a spiritual castration, expulsion from the USSR, left to rot in the West: 'ob'iavit' vragrom trudissh-chikhsia i izgnat' predelov CCCP. Post' tam, na Zapade, khot' nodokhnet!' The ultimate irony resides in the fact that was precisely the fate which was to befall Solzhenitsyn himself in 1974.

The action dimension of the novel is a race against time: will Mavrino develop the telephone scrambler in time to mollify Stalin; will the prisoner-technicians develop the voice decoder in time to identify an unknown person (in reality the conscience-stricken diplomat Innokentii Volodin) whose subversive telephone call has been recorded? We observe the diplomat and his privileged milieu during the three days while his fate is sealed by technical experiments beyond his horizon (but not beyond ours, the readers). This suspense aspect of the 'true novel' is secondary to the history-painting and it is doubtful whether any reader would stay with the full span of The First Circle to find out 'what happens next.' Plot based on character interaction is more or less absent. The fascination lies in each episode, each character, each brilliantly evoked segment of history.

For Solzhenitsyn a good man is invariably one who takes a step—brave, defiant, principled—beyond mere interior opposition to the regime. Leading characters in The First Circle experience moments of critical decision: Nerzhin will not collaborate in technical work designed to benefit Stalin; the prisoner Bobynin defiantly refuses to help Minister of State Abakumov speed up work on the scrambler for Stalin's telephone. Bobynin reflects that 'they' had al-ready deprived him of his freedom: 'What more can you do to me? Take me off this special project? You'd be the loser.' Less noble and more 'Brechtian' is Sologdin, an engineer for fourteen years, a prisoner for twelve of them; hav-ing made advances on the acoustical experiment, he then destroys his notes because he fears that if he presents the drawing to the colonel in its final shape, he might be transferred to the Gulag camps, with somebody else's signature on his design.[3]

It has been argued that unlike the convicts in Dostoyevsky's House of the Dead, Solzhenitsyn's 'zeks' are innocent of any crime, indeed they end up in the camps because they are innocent. In other words, Article 58 could mean anything other than what it said it meant. According to Terrence Des Pres, The First Circle is an inventory of the victimization of innocence: Gerasimovich for 'intent to commit treason,' Kagan for 'failure to inform,' Dyrsin for 'a denunciation cooked up by some neighbours who wanted his apartment and afterwards got it.'[4] But Rubin (Kopelev) is not mentioned here because his case (outspoken opposition to Soviet looting and rape in Germany) does not quite fit, and Nerzhin (Solzhenitsyn) is not mentioned because the cause of his arrest is deliberately kept in the shadows.

In fact, at the time of his arrest in East Prussia in February 1945, Solzhenitsyn himself had committed substantial 'thought crime' by way of letters, poems and plays. He was far from 'innocent'; reading the poems and plays he wrote during the war, his later detractors were not wrong when they insisted that Solzhenitsyn had already been a serious opponent of the regime at the time of his arrest, at the age of twenty-seven, and not merely as a result of his embittering experiences in the Gulag. In this respect the fictional character Gleb Vikentich Nerzhin does not convey the full truth about Solzhenitsyn. We learn the circumstances of his arrest by inverted means – how his wife Nadya did not know what had become of him until she eventually received a letter from a prison. But if the Socratic Nerzhin – he likes to ask questions – is a mathematician who committed a crime, a thought crime, or a non-crime, the nature of it remains hazy. We know he is secretly compiling notes on how history purified became the gulag, we know that he refuses to work on the special voice-detection project, but we do not know why he was arrested in February 1945. Why did Solzhenitsyn not graft his own offence – writing subversively about Stalin and the Soviet system while still in uniform – on to the fictional hero Nerzhin?

By the time Nerzhin is released, if he ever is, his wife Nadya will perhaps be too old to have children, almost a voluntary member of the tragic generation of Soviet women condemned by history, politics, war, death to live in a condition of emotional deprivation and acute hardship. Now thirty-seven, Nadya fears she will be 'an old woman' in three years time. The couple had enjoyed only one year living together, working and taking final exams, before war broke out. From Krsanaya Presnya transit prison Nerzhin had written, 'My darling, You've waited for me through four years of war – don't curse me but it was all for nothing, because you must now wait for ten more years.' He had urged her to free herself and marry someone else. Her family and friends despise her for not doing so. *Sauve qui peut.* Through Nadya's experience we learn that prisons never allowed a wife to be informed of a permitted visit by the confidential channel of 'post restante,' but always insisted on sending a postcard to her address. 'Not only did the MGB file the wife's address, it tried to reduce the number of women willing to receive such postcards – by letting their neighbours know they were "enemies of the people", by flushing them out, isolating them, surrounding them with hostility.'[5]

Prisoners' wives are lucky to see their husbands once a year. The women visiting the prisoners of Mavrino are likely to have aged prematurely. In the course of a rare visit to her husband she spills out her anguish: 'I'm at the end of my tether. I won't last another month. I might as well die. The neighbours treat me like dirt – they've thrown my trunk out of the hall and pulled down a shelf I put on the wall.... I've stopped going to see my sisters and my Aunt Zhenya – they all jeer at me and they say they've never heard of such a fool. They keep telling me to divorce you and remarry.'[6] In short, the prisoner Nerzhin is fortunate as compared to his wife, the nominally 'free' citizen Nadya. 'Nobody pushes you around,' she tells him, 'but I've been sacked, I've got nothing to live on, I won't get a job anywhere. I can't go on.' Yet she remains stubbornly faithful to her man.

A haggard woman clutches Nadya by the sleeve and expresses one of Solzhenitsyn's dominant perspectives, that things were never so bad under the tsars. Standing in for the author, the haggard woman compares the good fortune of the womenfolk of the Decembrist rebels of 1825, allowed to follow their men into Siberian exile (often in good carriages, accompanied by servants and wardrobes). She asks, 'Did they have to hide the fact that they were married as though it were an infectious disease, simply to avoid losing their jobs, simply in order not to lose their only income of five hundred roubles a month... Did they have to hear other people whispering they were traitors to their country every time they went to the communal tap for water?'[7]

Strikingly depicted are the lives of the MVD and MGB personnel and the military scientists in charge of the prison camp at Mavrino, reaching up to the state hierarchy, the Party, the government, Minister of State Security Abakumov, Stalin. Almost the whole of Soviet society was connected by what Michael Scammell calls 'the silken threads of Solzhenitsyn's narrative and portrayed as a single web, in which it was sufficient for one strand to be jerked for the whole net to be set swaying.'[8]

Both SMERSH and the Ministry are portrayed as completely unscrupulous, engaged in constant frame-ups. Abakumov 'had arrested and condemned millions'. Formerly head of SMERSH personnel, a poorly educated but physically formidable brute, he is suspicious of all subordinates, whom he terrorises. Solzhenitsyn later returned to Abakumov in his non-fiction masterpiece, *The Gulag Archipelago*, revealing that Abakumov personally practised torture, for example, in 1948 on Aleksandrov, former head of the Arts Section of VOKS, 'who has a broken spinal column which tilts to one side, and who cannot control his tear ducts and thus cannot stop crying...'[9] The account here of the 'Doctors' Plot' – which occurred some three years after the November 1949 time-frame of *The First Circle*—and of Abakumov's arrest under Stalin makes fascinating reading.[10]

The First Circle fits Solzhenitsyn's preferred genre, the 'polyphonic novel,' associated with Dostoyevsky: 'The way I interpret polyphony, each character, as soon as the plot touches him, becomes the main hero. That way, the author is responsible for, say, thirty-five heroes and doesn't give preference to any of them.'[11] But of course he does privilege his inner circle and he is reluctant to examine his authorial relationship to his leading characters. What is at issue here is not so much literal correspondences between fiction and reality, who is who, but the adventures of the author's own voice weaving in and out of his characters' words and thoughts – normally with the brash confidence of a queue-jumper.

Victor Ehrlich describes Solzhenitsyn as 'a novelist so sturdily and expansively old-fashioned, so steeped in the nineteenth-century realistic tradition, so unselfconscious about the "point of view"' as to suddenly inset into a section reconstructing Rubin's past largely in his own terms an exterior remark like:

"He was all-in-all a tragic figure."'[12] Other examples abound: 'Posterity can never have any conception of what travelling was like in those days, especially travelling to Moscow.' Or: '...the power of the secret denunciation in our country is such that the lady was dismissed and she left in tears.'[13]

Solzhenitsyn's expository method often uncannily echoes Vasily Grossman's 'Prisoners are generally inclined to exaggerate the number of people "inside"; when the actual prison population was no more than twelve or fifteen million, for instance, they were convinced that there were no more men left outside.'[14]

One of his naturalistic techniques is to run unattributed dialogue down the page, as when at the start of chapter 2 the new arrivals at Mavrino encounter the resident prisoners. Unattributed dialogue may work on the stage of a theatre, where voices are embodied in flesh, but it becomes difficult to follow in print. Naturalism becomes strained when a nameless voice from among the Mavrino prisoners declares: 'I was in Auschwitz. The terrible thing was: they took people straight from the station to the gas chamber, with a band playing.'[15] Solzhenitsyn frequently loads information into the dialogue, normally a feature of sub-genres such as thrillers and detective stories. A prisoner explains: 'They're new camps, Special Camps. They were only set up last year, in 'forty-eight. There was a directive to tighten up on security in the rear.' (In reality people who refer to 'last year' rarely add, conveniently, which year it was.)

Negatives of a certain type tend to impart an excessively godlike authority to a fictional narrative. This is because while a positive ('he noticed') allows the authorial voice to merge intimately with the character's own consciousness, a negative ('he did not notice') unsnaps the lock: 'In the Ministry waiting-room Pryanchikov was still so overwhelmed by his impressions that he failed to notice even the tables and chairs.' A fictional character like Pryanchikov who fails to notice something stands before his creator like a truant before his headmaster.

It has become apparent that from his mid-twenties, before his arrest in Germany on the basis of private correspondence belittling Stalin, Solzhenitsyn was the most lucid and unrelenting opponent of the whole Communist system. When did that anti-Soviet sentiment dawn? Surely we may interpret the prisoner Gleb Nerzhin as standing in for the author himself in reporting that he was only in the tenth grade at school 'when he pushed his way to the newspaper kiosk on a December morning and read that Kirov had been murdered, and suddenly felt, in a flash, that the murderer was none other than Stalin – because only Stalin stood to gain by it. In the midst of the jostling crowd of grown-ups, who did not understand this simple truth, he felt desperately lonely.' The arrests of the Old Bolsheviks followed, inexplicably confessing in court, heaping abuse on themselves. 'It was so excessive, so crude, so far-fetched that you had to be stone-deaf not to hear the sound of the lies.' Yet Russian writers 'lauded the tyrant with cloying panegyrics, composers vied to lay their sycophantic hymns of praise at his feet.'[16]

Assuming that Nerzhin stands in for Solzhenitsyn, the question remains: when did these thoughts take possession of Solzhenitsyn? When sixteen years old, reading of Kirov's murder? Or later, when witnessing the shambolic rout of the Red Army in 1941? During the war and the advance into Germany, as the cult of the Generalissimo flourished? We may take note of an apparently contradictory passage in *The Gulag Archipelago* where Solzhenitsyn describes the police state and the Blue Caps in his student days: 'Along that same asphalt ribbon on which the Black Marias scurry at night, a tribe of youngsters strides by day with banners, flowers and gay, untroubled songs.'[17] He was among them, the new generation. He recalls his third year at university in the fall of 1938: 'We young men of the Komsomol were summoned before the District Komsomol Committee not once but twice' – and urged to apply for admission to an NKVD school. 'How could we know anything about these arrests and why should we think about them? ...Twenty-year-olds, we marched in the ranks of those born the year the Revolution took place, and because we were the same age as the Revolution, the brightest of futures lay ahead.' The NKVD school offered special rations and double or triple pay—'we loved forming up, we loved marches.'[18]

Passages in *The First Circle* reveal a nostalgia for pre-revolutionary Russia, an era which Solzhenitsyn (unlike Pasternak and his hero Zhivago) never experienced. For example, the errant diplomat Innokentii Volodin learns much about the charms and passions of the old society when he discovers his late mother's diaries and letters. One description 'went straight to his heart' (and presumably to Solzhenitsyn's), 'of a white June night in Petersburg, when his mother, as an enthusiastic teenage girl, went with a crowd, all equally carried away, all crying for joy, as they met the Moscow Arts Theatre troupe at Petersburg station.... He knew of no such theatre company today...no one would weep for joy.' Volodin's mother had collected issues of the daily theatre paper, the *Spectator*, and the *Cinema News*, magazines illustrated by paintings and sculptures now unknown ('not a trace of them at the Tretyakov Gallery!'), the names of European writers of whom Innokentii had never heard, 'dozens of publishers, all vanished and forgotten as though the earth had swallowed them up' with names like Scorpion, Halcyon, Northern Lights, The Common Good.[19]

It is after reading through his late mother's notebooks, that Volodin is prompted to make the fatal intercepted call from a street telephone kiosk to warn his mother's doctor that he will be dangerously compromised if he fulfils a promise to hand over a new medicine to a French colleague. As Hosking puts it, 'The morality of another generation, though repudiated and indeed crushed, retains odd traces of its power even to the present.'

The errant diplomat is rapidly arrested after acoustic identification of his fatal telephone call to his family doctor, and in the closing chapters is shown enduring the humiliating reception procedures in the Lubyanka as a prelude to interrogation. Once inside he is stripped, his mouth and anus and nostrils and ears are examined. Solzhenitsyn has no inhibition about direct exposition: 'The proud young diplomat who had walked with such an independent air down the gangways of international airports and glanced with such vague, *blasé* eyes at the busy daytime glitter of Europe's capitals around him, was now a dropping, raw-boned, naked man with a half-shaved head.'[20]

So what is Solzhenitsyn's overarching view of history? Like Camus, he rejects the metaphysical capital letters—History or Progress – which enslave men by demanding they march in step towards an ultimate goal under power-hungry dictators and totalitarian regimes which benefit only the prophets (until they fall) and the rulers (also dispensable). Solzhenitsyn renounces all ultimate goals; he prefers the 'eternal moment,' regardless of epoch, in which each individual is tested by eternal values. He evidently believed that only through a truthful re-examination of Russia's past would her people be able to recognize, and repent of, their sins and build a decent future.

The original version of *The First Circle*, ninety-six chapters, was begun in 1955 in Kok-Terek, South Kazakhstan, and completed in 1957 in Miltsevo, in the Vladimir region. It was written in miniscule handwriting on onion-skin paper with no margins. From 1962 Solzhenitsyn worked on a fourth, definitive version. This contained the message from Volodin to the U.S. Embassy about atomic espionage. In 1964 he produced a fifth version in eighty-seven chapters and offered it to Tvardovsky's *Novyi mir*, which had published *One Day*. In this version Volodin's utterly out-of-bounds atomic warning was changed to the relatively anodyne medical one. Tvardovsky wanted the long biographical chapter about Stalin removed on grounds of evidence: Stalin's collaboration with the tsarist police was impossible to prove. No one could be sure of the details of Djugashvili's life in a Georgian theological seminary in the 1890s. In subsequent discussions with the editorial board at *Novyi mir* (all of them liberals in Soviet terms), Vladimir Lakshin complained that the didactic passages in the Stalin chapters were like jagged rocks breaking the smooth surface. Aleksandr Dementiev complained that the propaganda passages bordered on pamphleteering. According to Dementiev, the novel as a whole called the Bolshevik revolution into question. He was right. Solzhenitsyn continued to mask his purpose and to claim the novel was not directed against the Soviet system, or Leninism, only against the Stalin personality cult.

Then the KGB struck. Solzhenitsyn had found a kindred spirit, V. L. Teush, a former colleague on the teaching staff of Ryazan's high school and Solzhenitsyn's only confidant in the city—one of very few people who had been allowed to read everything he had written. Over Aleksandr Tardovsky's protests, Solzhenitsyn had removed all four manuscripts of *The First Circle* then in the keeping of *Novyi mir*, fearing a KGB raid on the magazine's safe; three of the manuscripts he had deposited with Teush. 'I was out of my mind,' he later recalled.[21] The KGB raided Teush's house and seized the lot in September 1965.

A painter and journalist of Russian ancestry, in her late thirties, Olga Carlisle was introduced to Solzhenitsyn during her fourth visit to the USSR in April

1967. Escorting her back to her hotel on an icy night, Solzhenitsyn charged her to see to the Western publication of *The First Circle*: he told her that the book was 'my life,' the one that mattered and which would hit the Soviet leadership hardest; it would 'stun public opinion throughout the world. Let the true nature of these scoundrels be known'. He urged her to utmost secrecy.[22] Flying back to Europe, she contacted her father Vadim Andreyev in Paris and took possession of the Solzhenitsyn microfilms he earlier had carried out of Russia. In this way the truncated, eighty-seven-chapter version of *The First Circle* reached America.[23]

Only the previous year Solzhenitsyn had refused to sign an appeal against the prison sentences inflicted on Daniel and Sinyavsky. Sinyavsky's wife, Maria Rozanova, had approached him through an intermediary, and received back a message that he could not sign because he 'disapproved of writers who sought fame abroad'. Given Solzhenitsyn's own conduct in the years lying immediately ahead, when foreign fame fell to his own name, it was hardly an admirable response. Later, in his memoir *The Oak and the Calf*, he refers to the 'literary schizophrenia' of Daniel and Sinyavsky, and confirms his disapproval of their publishing in the West. Yet in the same memoir he takes Tvardovsky to task for believing that 'work published abroad was irretrievably lost, and its author disgraced.'[24]

28

Commentary: Stalin and Lenin in Soviet Fiction

Stalin had Lenin's remains embalmed and placed on show in Moscow's Red Square for the benefit of pilgrims. The practice of carrying in procession huge portraits of Lenin and other leaders—like *khorugvi* (church banners)—persisted.[1] By the early 1930s, the Stalin cult was a firmly established aspect of Party ideology. In November 1936, *Pravda* described Stalin as the 'genius of the new world, the wisest man of the epoch, the great leader of Communism.' The anniversary number of 7 November mentioned Stalin's name eighty-eight times and the adjective 'Stalinist' fifteen times. (Lenin got only fifty-four mentions.)[2] George S. Counts documented the abasements of the Soviet intelligentsia to the personality cult at the time (as it happened) that Orwell was writing *Nineteen Eighty-Four*.

—October 1946: 'Dear Joseph Vissarionovich! The members of the Third Session of the Academy of Medical Sciences of the USSR send you, great captain of all victories, their ardent greetings and deep gratitude for your unceasing concern for the growth and development of Soviet science.'

—October 1946 again: 'We, professors, instructors and directors of the higher educational institutions of Moscow...send you, our dear leader and teacher, our flaming greetings.'[3]

In Vsevolod Kochetov's novel, *The Zhurbins*, every worthy Party man carries the example of Lenin-Stalin (invariably twinned in a single breath to the exclusion of all other revolutionary leaders, airbrushed from history). 'And what do Vladimir Ilyich [Lenin] and Joseph Vissarionovich [Stalin] tell us about indulgence? It's slackness they tell us.... We must learn from Lenin and Stalin how to live, how to work, and how to behave...'[4] Which means modestly: Old Matvei recalls: "'Why, it's a well-known fact that when Vladimir Ilyich went into a barber's shop once everyone there got up and asked him to have his turn."' Old Matvei again: "'Why Joseph Vissarionovich himself, if he needs to go anywhere, rings up the garage and asks first how they are for petrol...'" A younger man, Ivan Stepanovich, becomes irritated: "'You're talking rubbish! Joseph Vissarionovich with such colossal work to do and asking about petrol! And anyhow we've got all the petrol we need.'"[5]

Stalin rises above all known mortals. 'They spoke of Stalin, who saw everything and knew everything, whether it happened in Kuznetsk, in the Urals, in the Donbas, in Saratov or on the Lada.' A few lines down: "'Comrade Stalin is the friend of every inventor, every Soviet man.'" Indeed Stalin is the friend of working people in all countries. The story is told how a Soviet ship was lying off the Chilean port of Coronel, 'where the miners get silicosis in their lungs from the coal dust'. At night, the Soviet sailors see lights in the hills moving like glow worms, miners lamps forming the word 'Stalin.'[6]

Recalling the Revolution and its leaders, Kochetov mentions only Lenin and Stalin. Grandad Old Matvei had been serving on the *Aurora*: 'That was when I heard Lenin speak. He and Comrade Stalin gave us the order: smash the capitalists and those Provisional fellows, this is our great day! So we let 'em have it without our for'ard guns...' Later the Party mobilized the lads for the labour front. "'We rolled up our sleeves on the rebuilding. Then all kinds of riffraff – they call 'em Trotskyites...tried to chuck a spanner in the works. 'It's no use wasting your time rebuilding,' they said; 'we're going to catch it anyway. They've crushed the revolution in Germany, and in Bulgaria, and we'll go under too, Soviet power won't last.'"

Even normally astute foreign writers succumbed to the cult. In Malraux's *Days of Hope*, during a conversation in Madrid between Scali and Garcia it is suggested that the ubiquitous portraits of Stalin in Russia should be attributed to the popular passion for signs and badges, not to Stalin's vanity. 'If, for instance, we are always being told, there are too many pictures of Stalin in Russia, it's not because that ogre Stalin, squatting in a corner of the Kremlin, has decreed it should be so.'[7] Can Malraux really have fallen for the same myth as the novelist Lion Feuchtwanger in his notorious report, *Moscow 1937*? When lecturing in America, Malraux declared Stalin to be the prototype of the admirable democratic leader, tactfully adding Roosevelt and the French premier, Léon Blum, to this illustrious company.

But in *The Case of Comrade Tulyaev*, Victor Serge offers a more sceptical portrait of Stalin, 'the Chief.' One scene uncannily anticipates Solzhenitsyn's description in *The First Circle* of the monthly audience of Minister of State Security Abakumov with Stalin. Serge's doomed High Commissar for Security, Erchov (clearly based on Yezhov), is summoned to the General Secretariat and kept waiting in an ante-room for thirty-five minutes:

—'Everyone in that Secretariat knew that he was counting the minutes.'

—'At last the tall doors opened to him, he saw the Chief at his desk, before his telephones – solitary, greying, his head bowed.... The Chief did not raise his head, did not hold out his hand to Erchov, did not ask him to sit down. To maintain his dignity, the High Commissar advanced to the edge of the table and opened his brief case.'

Erchov had been appointed not only High Commissar for Security but also People's Commissar for Internal Affairs, an unprecedented elevation. The Chief had urged him "'to go easy with personnel, keeping the past in mind yet never failing in vigilance, to put a stop to abuses.'"

—"Men have been executed whom I loved, whom I trusted, men precious to the Party and the State!" he exclaimed bitterly. "Yet the Political Bureau cannot possibly review every sentence! It's up to you," he concluded. "You have my entire confidence.'"

In this scene Stalin is endowed with a '...kindly smile, in which the russet eyes and the bushy moustache joined...made you love him, believe in him, praise him as he was praised in the press and in official speeches, but sincerely, warmly'.[8] Or so Erchov feels.

In another passage Stalin complains bitterly to a long-standing colleague, the honest Kondratiev:

—'Everyone lies and lies and lies! From top to bottom they lie, it's diabolical.... The statistics lie, of course.... The plans lie...our most expert economists lie.... To remake the hopeless human animal will take centuries.'[9]

Partly because Stalin rarely went anywhere, beyond his office and the podium of Red Square, novelists were almost obsessed by his sinister solitude – a man, a pipe, a desk – and his relentless suspicion, the quest for signs of treason in his russet eyes. On the day of his arrival back from Spain Kondratiev is received by Stalin:

—'The room was so huge that at first Kondratiev thought it empty; but behind the table at the far end of it, in the whitest, most desert, most solitary corner of that closed and naked solitude, someone rose, laid down a fountain pen, emerged from emptiness...' Determined to speak only the truth, Kondratiev tells the Chief that it had been a mistake to unload so many old model planes on Spain. "'Our B 104 is inferior to the Messerschmitt, outclassed in speed.'" Stalin does not deny it but resorts to the standard formula: "'The maker was sabotaging.'" Kondratiev hesitates, convinced that the disappearance of the Aviation Experiment Centre's best engineers had resulted in poorer aviation products. The Chief repeats: "'He was sabotaging. It has been proved. He confessed it.'"[10]

When Kondratiev bravely tells Stalin he was wrong to liquidate Nicolai Ivanovich Bukharin, Stalin again responds mechanically: "'He was a traitor. He admitted it...'" adding, "'I'll wipe out every one of them, tirelessly, mercilessly.... I do what must be done. Like a machine.'" He adds: 'We have had too many traitors...conscious or unconscious...no time to go into the psychology of it....I'm no novelist.'"[11]

Virtually every day the traffic of central Moscow was disrupted as Stalin travelled from his dacha outside the city to the Kremlin, his cavalcade sweeping down narrow Arbat Street, roaring through Arbat Square, and on down Kalinin

Street. Plainclothesmen were so thick on Arbat Street, reported Harrison Salisbury, that they frequently pushed the shoppers off the sidewalk.[12] Orwell may not have known every detail but he had the big picture in mind when writing *Nineteen Eighty-Four*. He observed how in France the postwar cult projected Stalin as leader of nation and party; as father-figure and spiritual symbol; as the sublime expert in all fields of scholarship including genetics. Jean-Richard Bloch, who had broadcast to France from Moscow throughout the war, wrote of 'this man who, not once since he took the responsibility of power, had flattered or lied or committed a fundamental error.'

In Sinyavsky/Tertz's *The Trial Begins*, Prosecutor Globov takes his son Seryozha to Red Square to watch the military parade. But the main reviewing stand is a long way off and the boy cannot see it properly. '"He's smiling," said his father who, by some miracle, always knew.'" Another man confirms it: '"Yes, he's smiling, and he just waved like this."' A bony woman with an opera glass joins in as bombers fly overhead in close formation: '"He's looking up at the sky, our bright-eyed eagle! He's looking at his fledgelings!"' Seryozha feels embarrassed by his own indifference. 'To his shame, he still could not make out, among the blobs on the grandstand, the One whose proud name intoxicated all the rest like wine.'[13]

In *The Historical Novel*, Lukács sought to establish that in the classical historical novel the 'world-historical personage' (Cromwell, Napoleon) appears only as a minor character compositionally, described mainly from the outside, in action, without internal development. He is depicted because his decisions make history and have an impact on other characters. As examples of this genre Lukács cited Walter's Scott's renditions of Elizabeth I, Mary Stuart, and Cromwell. In Pushkin's *The Captain's Daughter* (influenced by Scott), Pugachev and Catherine the Great fall into the same category.[14] There is however no reason why real historical characters should not be depicted 'internally,' alongside fictitious ones; no reason why a novelist should not adopt a dual approach, biographical and psychological—as indeed Solzhenitsyn does with the figure of Stalin in *The First Circle*. Of course, a psychological portrait of a major figure has to be controlled by, if not utterly subordinated to, what is already know about him and his actions. The fact that the real Stalin had been systemically responsible for Solzhenitsyn's imprisonment obviously places Solzhenitsyn in a different category of historical portraitist from Scott, Pushkin, Hugo, or Tolstoy.

In *The First Circle*, the time is November 1949: Stalin is discovered at night in his fortified, window-less workroom in the Kremlin, reading the latest adulatory biography in which he is predictably depicted as a military strategist of genius, etc. etc. Three days have passed since worldwide celebrations of his seventieth birthday. Megalomaniac—and wishing to record a lasting contribution to Thought—he has now chosen to make a decisive intervention in the field of linguistics.

We eavesdrop on his thoughts. Stalin is both observed from without and 'overheard' from within. What Solzhenitsyn provides is not a full-scale interior monologue (Molly Bloom's climactic reverie at the end of Joyce's *Ulysses* is a classic example). Modernist interior monologues like Molly's trade on uncontrolled streams of consciousness, the fragmentation of the self; by contrast, Solzhenitsyn is writing within the realist tradition, and Stalin's inner voice always follows a coherent, logical progression which stands in for direct exposition by the author. The tyrant lost in night-time reverie obligingly opens a succession of windows into his stinking soul.[15] What is more, Stalin's consciousness obligingly covers the entire terrain of Soviet history for our benefit, even though (we are told) old age is bringing unwelcome visitors like memory loss, extreme fatigue, confusion, despondency.

Alexander Schmemann contrasts Solzhenitsyn's internal historical portrait of Stalin with Tolstoy's externalized Napoleon.[16] Lukács's interpretive emphasis is different when he claims that Solzhenitsyn's depiction of Stalin never dwells on petty psychological factors, 'whether of an accusing or excusing character,' but concentrates the inner monologue on the central questions of Stalin's historical existence – as when Stalin ponders what Lenin may have meant when he said, 'Any cook should be able to run the country.' But in reality Solzhenitsyn's 'inward' Stalin, extolled by the admiring Schmemann, is largely an implant from outside, from the author's external perspective, which amounts to pretty much the same thing as Lukács's 'central questions of Stalin's historical existence.' For example, Solzhenitsyn's Stalin here reflects on the past: 'The October Revolution was also an adventure, but it succeeded, so well and good. It succeeded. Fine. Lenin can be given full marks for that. What will happen in the future is uncertain, but it's all right now. Commissar of nationalities? Fine, so be it. Compose a constitution. Fine, so be it.' From this interior monologue Solzhenitsyn abruptly switches to authorial narration. 'Stalin got used to it.'[17]

Solzhenitsyn's failing is an inability to keep his own voice (and anger) out of the frame. Sarcasm constantly intrudes like a scalpel, puncturing the illusion that we are resident in Stalin's head. At almost every paragraph a new hagiographical phrase is mockingly tossed at the reader – Great Helmsman, Father of the Peoples of East and West, Leader of All Progressive Mankind, the Great Generalissimo, the Greatest Strategist in History, etc. Solzhenitsyn invents some honorific titles of his own: 'the Policeman's Best Friend,' for example. The sculptor-author is constantly throwing stones at the portrait.

Solzhenitsyn's Stalin blames everyone but himself: 'Communism would have come about much sooner if it had not been for...all those soulless bureaucrats... swollen-headed Party bigwigs.... The unwillingness of youth to go out and work in the backwoods. The wastage of grain during harvest. The embezzlement. The pilfering. The swindling. Sabotage in the labour camps. Leniency by the police. Corruption in housing. The rampant black market.' There was still a lot wrong with the people—why had the population retreated in 1941 rather than stood firm and died?

A characteristic of Solzhenitsyn's prose is its rapid, often seamless, alternation between inner and exterior narratives. Here, for example, Stalin in 1949 is enraged by the thought of Tito's defiant stand: 'To think of the trials Stalin had successfully organized, the number of enemies he had forced to grovel and confess to the vilest crimes – and now look how they had bungled the Kostov trial.' [The Bulgarian Communist Kostov had repudiated his confession of Titoism in open court.] 'He had to die, anyway, so he might at least have died in a way that did the Party some good!'[18]

Frequently the author's sarcasm is presented as Stalin's actual state of mind: 'All his best ideas came to him between midnight and four o'clock in the morning – how to welsh on the state lottery, for instance, by paying premium winners in new bonds instead of cash; how to introduce prison sentences for absenteeism; how to lengthen the working day and the working week...how to abolish the Third International; how to deport whole peoples to Siberia.' Yet 'welsh' belongs to Solzhenitsyn not to the self-justificatory Stalin.

A similar problem arises when Solzhenitsyn is explaining in sardonic terms that Stalin never visited the collective farms: 'In general the situation on the collective farms was very good, as he had seen from the film *Kuban Cossacks* and from Babyevsky's novel *The Knight of the Golden Star*.' And: 'The film-makers and the novelists had actually been to the collective farms.... Stalin himself, too, had talked to collective farmers at various congresses.'[19] But whose voice are we really hearing?

In another case, the attempt to render Stalin's interior point-of-view is drastically subverted by authorial interventions signalled by brackets ( ): 'He seemed to remember that one of the Right Oppositionists (there had never been any such thing as "Right Opposition", but it had suited Stalin to lump a number of his enemies together and deal with them all at one blow) had warned that this problem would arise.' Here the entry into Stalin's mind—'He seemed to remember'—is immediately cancelled by the authorial 'there had never been' and 'it suited Stalin to lump.'

In another passage, Solzhenitsyn depicts a Shakespearean Stalin, a haunted Macbeth, but here again we encounter an uneasy relationship between the internal and external narrative voices: 'Why was it that the people he liquidated had always managed to be right about something? Despite himself, Stalin was swayed by their ideas and kept a wary ear cocked for their voices from beyond the grave.'[20] The phrase 'despite himself' tends to separate the all-knowing author from his character; even more so the use of the name Stalin.

Stalin's chief secretary Poskryobyshev puts in an appearance. We are told that he has 'the soul of an officer's batman'—Solzhenitsyn clearly yearns to put the boot into the man's slimy gut.

Once a month, when summoned by Stalin in the middle of the night, Minister of State Abakumov quails, never knowing whether to stand, sit, squat or crouch in the presence of those deadly yellow eyes. If Stalin's loses his temper, or swears, or 'pokes you with something heavy or sharp,' or treads on your toe, or blows hot ash out of his pipe in your face, this means the danger is only temporary, it's going to be all right; death comes with his silences and 'the puckering of his lower eyelids.' Every monthly visit could be Abakumov's last night on earth.

A problematical passage concerns the process of ongoing postwar purge: 'One of the most attractive features of Abakumov's state security reports, and the main reason why Stalin liked them, was his invariable discovery of some sinister, widely ramified group of spies and traitors.' On each occasion a new gang had been put out of action. Stalin asks him 'thoughtfully': 'Do we still have cases involving charges of terrorism?' (Surely the supreme architect and orchestrator of bogus allegations would know?)

'Abakumov heaved a bitter sigh. "I would be glad if I could tell you that there were no more such cases. But there are. We come across them in all sorts of stinking holes."'

Stalin closes one eye; the other eye registers pleasure. 'So you're doing your stuff,' he says. Stalin is pleased enough to invite Abakumov to sit down.[21]

This exchange raises the problem of the novelist as history-teller. There is no evidential basis for any such conversation. It does not begin to resolve the great puzzle of *how* Stalin and his most powerful subordinates operated the terror. Most if not all treason and sabotage charges during Stalin's thirty-year reign as General Secretary of the Party had been authorized by the Boss. Nothing more poignantly illustrates this surreal use of power than the arrests of close relatives of leading Party figures like Molotov and Khrushchev. History offers no obvious precedent or parallel: would Hitler have arrested Goebbels's wife while retaining Goebbels in his post as propaganda supremo? Solzhenitsyn's rendition of Stalin's conversation with Abakumov does not venture into this problematic terrain.

Solzhenitsyn's rendering of the fictional conversation between Stalin and Abakumov is surprisingly abstract, devoid of the specific international tensions of 1949. Solzhenitsyn seems unwilling to admit, anywhere in his work, that the United States, armed with atomic weapons and a formidable propaganda apparatus, posed a fundamental challenge not only to Soviet hegemony in Eastern Europe but to the survival of the Soviet system. Here was an enemy capable of incorporating a rearmed Germany in the Western Alliance. In that respect, the chauvinism of Stalin's anti-cosmopolitan campaign did have its rationale, just as a series of trials in Eastern Europe served as a warning against association with British Intelligence, the Labour Party, and other social democrats.

At one juncture, Stalin addresses Abakumov in Mephistophelean terms: 'There will be plenty of work for you to do, Abakumov.... We shall take the same measures that we took in thirty-seven. Before a great war there has to be a great purge.' A couple of acrid, pipe-stinking breaths later he adds: 'Just wait until we really get started – then you'll see. And when it comes to war we'll force the pace even harder. That means more power to the security services. Budgets, salaries – I won't stint you!'[22] This passage relies on the dubious proposition that in November 1949 Stalin (having recently ended the Berlin blockade) was planning a world war and didn't mind his subordinates knowing it.

Alone with Stalin, Abakumov pleads for the restoration of the death penalty. Solzhenitsyn finds Stalin in firm agreement. 'For two years now he had bitterly regretted giving way to his momentary impulse to show off to the West. In abolishing the death penalty he had betrayed his own principles...' Now he slides into leering Shakespearean villainy: 'his eyes narrowed cunningly' as he asked Abakumov: '"Aren't you afraid, though, that you might be one of the first to be shot?"' Stalin ponders his strategy for Terror: '...first lash the executioners into a fury of activity, then disown them at the critical moment and punish them for an excess of zeal.'[23] Critics have noted that the portrait of Stalin bears a close resemblance to Satan in Canto XXXIV of Dante's *Inferno*.[24] Stalin is portrayed not only as an epigone of the Grand Inquisitor in Dostoyevsky's *The Brothers Karamazov*, but also as a product of spiritual crossbreeding with other Dostoyevsky's 'mangods' and 'devils' found in *The Devils* and *Crime and Punishment*.[25]

Chapter 21 begins with the familiar (usually self-defeating) sarcasm: 'The Immortal One, his imagination aroused, paced firmly up and down his study.' A page later he is 'the Greatest of the Great': 'Yes, but suppose...of course he had no equals, but suppose – up there, above the clouds...?'[26] Solzhenitsyn reports that the former seminarian, Djugashvili-Stalin, had been gratified in recent years to be mentioned in the church's prayers as the 'Leader Elect of God,' which was why he had maintained the cathedral and monastery at Zagorsk out of Kremlin funds. He always went to the outer door to greet 'his tame, infirm old Patriarch.'[27] Solzhenitsyn's Stalin feels drawn again to the religion of his seminary youth – repetition, ritual, obedience, dogma.

Puzzling out his pathfinding article on linguistics, Stalin writes: 'Language is created in order to...' 'The superstructure is created by the base in order to...' Here the author breaks off to comment: '...poring low over the paper, he did not see the angel of medieval teleology smiling over his shoulder.' Once again the negative separates author and character. On top of that, the instrumental teleology of a Marxist takes care of the phrase 'in order to.' This brings us to a valid complaint by Rosalind Marsh: 'Solzhenitsyn also fails to discuss...what made Stalin a Marxist, and why he became a Bolshevik follower of Lenin when most Georgian Marxists were choosing Menshevism. Solzhenitsyn does not refer to Stalin's love of books, or mention any intellectual influences which could have inspired him to become a Marxist... [Solzhenitsyn's] main purpose is to demonstrate Stalin's total lack of ideas and principles. All Stalin's actions are ascribed to personal ambition and the idea-less lust for power.'[28]

Like Isaac Don Levine in *Stalin's Great Secret* (New York, 1956), Solzhenitsyn suggests that Stalin stopped being an agent of the tsarist Okhrana only after being elected to the Bolshevik Central Committee in Prague in 1912. Solzhenitsyn believes that only his guilt about this and a haunting fear of discovery could account for Stalin's conduct in the 1930s: eradication of documents, falsification of records, execution of people who knew too much. Stalin's secret was 'almost revealed in 1937.'[29]

According to the historian Roy Medvedev, Solzhenitsyn spoke the truth when he accused Stalin of launching mass repressions, deportations, torture, and faked trials long before Hitler came to power – and continuing them after the defeat of fascism. Medvedev also endorsed Solzhenitsyn's overview of the tsarist punitive regime run by the Okhrana as a relative holiday camp, both in terms of the number of prisoners and the quality of life.[30] Indeed, Solzhenitsyn frequently distinguishes between the savagery of the Soviet penal system, and the relatively short penal sentences and clement prison conditions prevailing under the tsars. In *The First Circle*, he interrupts/subverts Stalin's monologue with typical sarcasm: 'the Tsarist regime knew how to stick on ruthless sentences – four years, it's terrifying to relate.'[31]

The sarcasm aside, Rosalind Marsh may be too logical when she comments that Solzhenitsyn's 'insinuation that no one feared arrest in Tsarist times is not only a highly debatable point, but also inadvertently undermines his own argument that the short sentences meted out to [the young] Stalin prove his complicity with the [Tsarist] secret police.'[32] On the other hand Solzhenitsyn was ready to use artistic means to prove historical hypotheses about which he had no proof (as he admitted elsewhere): 'I tried by psychological and factual arguments to prove the hypothesis that Stalin had collaborated with the Tsarist secret police.' And: 'My view was that Stalin should reap the harvest of his secretiveness. He had lived mysteriously – so now anyone was entitled to write about him as he thought fit.'[33]

In volume 2 of *Cancer Ward*, we come to the second anniversary of Stalin's death (5 March 1955). Ill in hospital, the bureaucrat Rusanov searches newspapers in vain for a portrait within a black border, but finds only an article, 'Stalin and some problems of Communist construction.' Rusanov's indignation is conveyed in narrated monologue: '"What about the military victories? What about the philosophical genius? What about the giant of the sciences? What about the entire people's love for him?"' Solzhenitsyn then intervenes authorially: 'It was this ingratitude that wounded Rusanov most of all, as though his own great services, his own irreproachable record, were what they were spitting on and trampling underfoot. If the Glory that resounds in Eternity could be muffled out and cut short after only two years, if the Most Beloved, the Most Wise, the One whom all your superiors and superiors' superiors obeyed, could be overturned and hushed up within twenty-four months—then what remained?'[34] Once again the momentum of sarcasm carries Solzhenitsyn beyond a plausible character-portrait or a plausible interior landscape of the villain of the piece, Rusanov. The mind of the monster becomes a cipher for the author's anger.

Finally an amusing anecdote found in Solzhenitsyn's *The Gulag Archipelago*. At a Party conference in Moscow province, when the district secretary called for an ovation for Stalin, no one in the hall dared be the first to stop. 'Their goose was cooked! They couldn't stop now till they collapsed with heart attacks!'[35]

Following Solzhenitsyn's incensed excavations of the mental universe of Stalin and the Stalinists, Anatoly Rybakov created a more clinical portrait of Stalin's inexorable domination of his Party colleagues during the 1930s. Rybakov's novel *Children of the Arbat* (*Deti Arbata*) focuses on Stalin's relations with his greatest potential rival, Kirov, shortly before the Leningrad supremo's still unresolved assassination in 1934, an event exploited by Stalin, whether he himself planned it or not, to unleash a wave of terror. Rybakov convincingly exposes Stalin's resentments of Kirov's popularity, but stops short of accusing Stalin of the assassination. The evidence available to a Soviet novelist at work in the early 1960s was lean, although the research undertaken by the historian Roy Medvedev may have been known to Rybakov.

Children of the Arbat refers to a group of young Muscovites, friends and fellow-students, who grew up in the relatively sophisticated Arbat district of Moscow during the hard and socially tumultuous years of the early 1930s. To be more precise, *Children of the Arbat* is set in the period September 1933-December 1934, the interval between the first Five Year Plan and the beginning of the major purges following the assassination of Kirov. Through these 'children' we experience the ideological tensions created by the agony of forced growth and breakneck industrialization. But Rybakov's novel is most remarkable for its extended portrait of a younger Stalin, still consolidating his absolute power, and for its replication of many of Solzhenitsyn's insights and literary techniques. Yet a direct literary debt cannot be proved. Rybakov's novel was completed and announced for Soviet publication in 1966 (well before Solzhenitsyn's *The First Circle* had been published in the West), but remained suppressed until 1987. Rybakov chose not to circulate the book in samizdat or send it abroad or otherwise join the circle of outright dissident writers.[36] *Children of the Arbat* aroused considerable interest when eventually published in instalments in the journal *Druzhba narodov*.[37]

Rybakov has Stalin summon Kirov from his bailiwick, Leningrad. Urging Kirov to purge Zinoviev's followers in that city—'an undestroyed bastion of opposition'—Stalin embarks on a diatribe against inner party factions and enemies, all biding their time—Zinoviev, Kamenev, Bukharin—all more cunning than Trotsky.[38] Stalin does not conceal that he wants to transfer Kirov to Moscow, away from his power base in Leningrad; Kirov replies that having begun the reconstruction of Leningrad, he would like to complete the job. Stalin complains that Kirov is the only member of the Politburo who flouts its rules about proper security protection (i.e., playing for popularity, at ease with the population). Stalin thinks: '[Kirov] had not won the Leningraders over to the Party's side, they had won him over to their side...'[39]

Rybakov assigns chapter 16 to Kirov's PV but he does not emerge as a distinctive personality, merely as a straightforward man who understands Stalin's game: 'He realized that Stalin wanted to reshape history not only in order to extol himself but to justify the harshness of his past, present and future actions.'

After land reform and the nationalities question, Rybakov's conducted tour of Stalin's mindset passes through Russian history from Ivan the Terrible and his *oprichnina* (terror) to Peter the Great. In his *Brief History of Russia*, the dean of post-1917 Soviet historians, Pokrovsky, had condemned Tsar Peter's treatment of his wife as well as the torture and murder of his own son – and for own his death from syphilis. Stalin is incensed:

'And that's all Pokrovsky could see in Peter [the Great]! And this rubbish came from the "head of a school of history"! How could Pokrovsky have overlooked the fact that Tsar Peter had transformed Russia! That was where the dogmatic interpretation of Marxism could lead—to the denial of the role of the exceptional individual in history! And this primitive sociologist Pokrovsky was the man Lenin had advanced to the front rank of historians, praising his *Brief History of Russia*, 'a pathetic piece of work that presented all Russia's historical figures as men of no talent, nonentities.'[40] But Kirov stands his ground, describing the recent campaign against Pokrovsky as intolerable. '"Pokrovsky wrote his book in 1920 and it was the first attempt to throw light on Russian history from the Marxist-Leninist point of view. And he wrote it as a book for the masses on Lenin's orders."'

'"See?" Stalin grinned. "And you say you're no good at history."'[41]

Rybakov has Stalin pursue recent Bolshevik history into a storm of personal resentments. Here Rybakov like Solzhenitsyn makes use of indirect monologue. The Civil War had not been won by Trotsky or the military experts but by tens of thousands of Party cadres. 'He [Stalin] represented those cadres, and therefore their role in the Civil War was his role, and his role was the Party's role. These and there alone were the principles on which history and the history of the Party must be based.'[42] Obsessed by the need to rewrite history, Stalin has set the faithful Andrei Zhdanov to work on an updated history of the CPSU. 'We have to take the writing of history into our own hands,' he tells Kirov.

Stalin feels particularly threatened by certain senior members of the Party currently publishing their often damaging memoirs. For example, Lenin's widow Krupskaya had recently written: 'After October, people began to come to the fore who had not taken a chance to show themselves earlier because of the circumstances of the old underground... Among them was Comrade Stalin.'[43] This infuriates Stalin. Rybakov's Stalin may appear petty when he raises with his enforced guest Kirov the question of a pamphlet published by Abel Enukidze, a veteran member of the Central Committee. Enukidze has caused offence by remarking that Lenin had given instructions that the illegal party press known as 'Nina' should be known only to three named people, one of them Enukidze himself. Stalin needs to convince Kirov that one of the other 'three named people,' Ketskhoreli, had not concealed the existence of 'Nina' from him, Stalin. (This cannot be checked out since Ketskhoreli is conveniently dead.) Over Kirov's protests, Stalin insists that Enukidze's agenda is 'to prove that the present leadership of the Central Committee is not the direct successors to Lenin, that before the Revolution Lenin did not rely on the current leader-ship...did not trust the present leadership.'[44]

What may seem to us the downright triviality of Stalin's jealous approach to the re-rewriting of contemporary history in fact reflects the Bolsheviks' intense need to view their own actions within a validating Marxist-Leninist text. So many of the major disputes within the European social democratic movement since Marx's time had taken the form of published polemics high in erudition! Lenin himself had continued with his compulsive polemics after taking power, not merely to influence foreign comrades but, seminally, because theory for a Marxist is the validation of action.

Stalin remains haunted by Lenin's repudiation of him in the so-called 'will' which he has taken care to suppress, but which is well known to the entire cadre of Old Bolsheviks. 'Kirov recognized with bitterness that the Party had made a grave error is not taking Lenin's advice and removing Stalin as general secre-tary.'[45] In short – and here is one clue to the purges and trials of the 1930s – any of Lenin's surviving colleagues is the enemy because his or her memory may come back to haunt or challenge Stalin's ongoing claim to godlike status.

Stalin arrives at a public meeting to discuss the reconstruction of Moscow. Everyone rises and applauds his appearance. While listening to the debate he sketches and doodles ancient ruined churches in Ateni, a village near Gori where his father the cobbler had had customers. From this Rybakov leads us into Stalin's childhood memories by way of indirect monologue: 'Lenin had understood the importance of sculpture when he had ordered the creation of monumental propaganda. But Lenin had understood it too narrowly...' Stalin is determined to incorporate the classical heritage:

'Skyscrapers built on classical lines, that was the style of the future.'

'He paused once more. He knew that what he was saying was already well known, but he also knew that his audience took words as revelation because it was he who was uttering them.'[46]

After the meeting to discuss the reconstruction of Moscow Stalin returns to his study and watches Chaplin's *City Lights*. 'He loved Chaplin, who reminded him of his father, the only person he ever held dear.'

The conducted tour of Stalin's biography and beliefs progresses: 'The Rus-sians are a coarse nation, they're not like the Georgians. Because of his withered arm, nobody had ever picked on him at school or in the seminary. That was merely ingrained Georgian good manners.' This leads on to: 'The people's coarse instincts could be restrained only by a powerful regime, by a dictatorship.'

Social progress requires fear and strong authority: 'If a few million people had to perish in the process, history would forgive Comrade Stalin.... All the great rulers had been harsh.' But Machiavelli had been wrong to advise the ruler to base his power on fear alone; both love and fear should co-exist.[47]

At this stage (probably 1933) Stalin entertains perhaps rather too clear a plan for dealing with the Old Bolsheviks who finally came to grief three years later. Employing hindsight, Rybakov extrapolates Stalin's intentions before he launched the great purge with a degree of certainty not available to historians: 'He would not send Zinoviev and Kamenev into exile abroad: they were going to serve as the first foundation stones of the bastion of fear he must build in order to defend the nation and the country. And they would be followed by their allies. Bukharin was one.... He had secretly run to Kamenev and had said he would prefer to see Zinoviev and Kamenev in place of Stalin in the Politburo... There was no room in politics for pity.' A quote from Lenin – but we are not given the source, the novelist requires no footnotes —is invariably at hand to bring comfort to Stalin: 'Soviet socialist centralism in no way contradicts individual leadership and dictatorship...a dictator who can sometimes do more on his own...can sometimes embody the will of the class.' And further: 'To agree to place the dictatorship of the masses in general in opposition to the dictatorship of the leaders is ridiculous, absurd, stupid.'[48]

Now Stalin is vacationing on the Black Sea. He is found sitting with his face to the sun in a wicker armchair on the veranda of his dacha in Sochi. Again the frontier between authorial narration and Stalin's claim on his own thoughts is hazy as he conveniently reflects on a wide variety of literary figures. 'Once upon a time, Stalin had flirted with writing poetry' (authorial narrative). And 'The greatest of all Russian writers was Pushkin' (indirect monologue).[49] 'He'd been struck by Boris Godunov in his youth, and by the image of Otrepyev the pretender in particular: 'the unfrocked monk, the fugitive novice, and only twenty years old.... Small of stature, broad of chest, one arm shorter than the other, his hair light brown' (indirect monologue).

Here Rybakov yields a retreat into authorial uncertainty: 'Stalin had perhaps read Pushkin in the Seminary, as he was included in the curriculum...' This 'perhaps' is repeated: 'Perhaps it floated unrecognized into his mind, when he met Sofya Leonerdovna Petrovskaya, a Polish aristocrat in Baku?'[50] In orthodox history writing the word 'perhaps' presents no problems because uncertainty is one of the tools of the trade, but in a work of realist fiction, characterized by passages of authorial omniscience, only characters can get away with doubts.

'Reverie' may be the right term for Rybakov's method of portraying Stalin—though 'reverie' is a floating state of mind far from the novelist's need to condense, as found in the following passage: 'To be a revolutionary was a matter of character, of making a protest against one's oppression. It was the assertion of one's own personality. Five times he'd been arrested and exiled. He'd escaped from exile, he'd hidden, he'd starved, gone without sleep – what was it all for? Was it for the peasants who knew nothing except their own dung...[or] for the sake of the "proletariat" – those blinkered workhorses, dirty, ignorant, and dim-witted?'

Stalin swats a bee (we are in a novel after all) before revolving his sour thoughts back to the sins of Kirov: 'He [Kirov] had spoken at the Politburo against the execution of Ryutin, and against those of Smirnov, Talmachev, and Eismont. And he'd carried other Politburo members with him. Even Molotov and Voroshilov had wavered. Only Lazar Kaganovich had been unequivocally in favour of shooting them all.'[51]

In a sequence starting with chapter 10, Stalin suffers toothache and requires immediate attention. He wears a plate. With only five of his own yellow-stained teeth remaining in his upper jaw, he rages against being a toothless 'old man' (he is fifty-five although this is not stated). Dr Lipman of the Kremlin Hospital, Moscow, is brought by plane to Sochi, 'a handsome, good-natured Jew less than forty years old.' Stalin resents the way these dentists give themselves a self-important air and turn their profession into an enigmatic mystery. But Lipman is frank, talkative. Stalin is torn between pain, impatience for a quick dental fix, desire for a gold tooth, a determination to dominate the dentist, worry that awe and fear may make the practitioner's hand shake, admiration for Lipman's frankness about the virtues of plastic plates compared to heavy metal ones. Stalin respects this dentist's independence of mind, his ability to stand up to him – but he always, invariably, suspects that he is being deceived—and indeed he is, a new denture having been ordered from Berlin behind his back. At the end of the course of treatment, after Lipman has departed, Stalin casually deprives him of his job in the Kremlin hospital, partly because Stalin learns from the extrovert Kirov that he and Lipman have been enjoying the reserved beach at Sochi together, relaxing, swimming and chatting. Stalin has not wanted his guests, Kirov and Zhdanov, to know about his dental treatment. Someone must be punished and the dentist is a Jew, after all. But Lipman (he orders) he must not be 'touched.'

Anatoly Rybakov's *Children of the Arbat* ends with the exiled young hero, Sasha, reading of Kirov's assassination. The newspapers are adamant that the assassin was dispatched by enemies of the working class, yet 'the identity of the assailant has yet to be established.'[52]

While fictional condemnation of Stalin was relatively common (yet never published), few novelists took the risk of extending the verdict back to Lenin. To do so was to call into question the Revolution itself. Pasternak's Yury Zhivago does so implicitly, though Lenin himself is mentioned only once in the entire novel when Antipov admiringly presents him as the culmination of a full century's revolutionary struggles and 'pitiless remedies invented in the name of pity – all of this was absorbed into Lenin...to fall upon the old world as retribution for its deeds... Russia, bursting into flames like a light of redemption for all the sorrows and misfortunes of mankind.'

We first encounter a drastic reappraisal of Lenin and his work in Grossman's last, fragmentary work of fiction, *Everything Flows*. The embittered Grossman takes the decisive step of repudiating the Revolution of 1917 and the first generation of Bolshevik leaders under Lenin: 'The Bolshevik generation of the Civil War did not believe in freedom of the individual, freedom of speech, freedom of the press.... Like Lenin, it regarded as nonsense, as nothing, those freedoms of which many revolutionary workers and intellectuals had dreamed.'[53] The state became an end in itself, a grim tyrant.

For Grossman, the highest order of life is individual freedom. 'Do you know what these elections [of 1917] to the Constituent Assembly meant for Russia? In a thousand-year period Russia was free for a little longer than six months.'[54] Lenin (who gave the order to disperse the Constituent Assembly because it lacked a Bolshevik majority) is depicted as possessing a range of endearing qualities, but: 'The history of the state had no use for Lenin's rapt listening to the "Appassionata", nor his love of *War and Peace*, nor his democratic modesty...nor his chats with peasant children, nor his kindness to pets...'[55] Absolutely intolerant of political democracy, Lenin displayed 'contempt for and disregard of human suffering, subservience to abstract theories, the determination to annihilate not merely enemies but those comrades who deviated even slightly from complete acceptance of the particular abstraction in question.' Like a surgeon, 'his soul is really his knife.'[56] Thirst for power, implacable cruelty, a kindly smile. For a century Russia had absorbed, drunk down the idea of freedom evolved by Western philosophers (Grossman frequently uses the term 'Western')—but the slave foundation within Russia opted for Lenin. Grossman concluded that fascination with Byzantine culture and ascetic Christian meekness had the same source in Russia as 'Leninist passion, fanaticism and intolerance.'[57]

Grossman's reflections on Lenin essentially belong to historical reflection. Not until the publication in the West of the exiled Solzhenitsyn's *Lenin in Zürich* (1976), did a novelist of the Soviet era put Lenin under the microscope of close-up portraiture. Here is a work of fiction which breaks the 'rules' of Lukács's model of the classical historical novel, whereby the 'world-historical personage' (Cromwell, Napoleon) should appear only as a minor character compositionally, described mainly from the outside, in action, without internal development. But in *Lenin in Zurich*, Solzhenitsyn's Vladimir Ilyich Lenin is the epicentre of the earthquake, dominating every page, every thought, every repressed desire.

This book is in artistic terms the most perfect product of the long-term project among Russian writers to excavate the truth of history through the imaginative license of fiction. Solzhenitsyn's majestically achieves fluid shifts of focus and points of view, relishing his ability to operate inside and outside a famous man almost simultaneously. This short, tightly disciplined, narrative—as if composed in reaction to the epic dimensions of *August 1914* – evokes the contained focus of a Giotto triptych, but free of stasis. Wrongly overshadowed by earlier works set in more recent times, according to the author *Lenin in Zurich* stands as 'fragments of an epic,' unified by Lenin's personality and the setting, Zurich. Here is history as a novel, the novel as history. In an interview with the BBC, Solzhenitsyn expanded on his approach: 'I have to use the artist's vision, because a historian uses only documentary material, much of which has been lost...the artist can see farther and deeper, thanks to the force of perception in the artist's vision. I am not writing a novel.'[58]

Lenin is discovered during the First World War when living in exile in Switzerland, cut off from events in Russia, struggling to stay in touch, and leading the small, minority faction of the Second Socialist International which not only opposed the war but called for its transformation into a revolutionary civil war. No one listened, the workers of Europe went to war: 'There were moments when it seemed that there would be no one left, that the whole Bolshevik Party would consist of himself, a couple of women, and a dozen third-raters and washouts...'[59] Lenin foresees the entirely welcome defeat and dismemberment of the Russian empire. Later, in 1916, he fears that Germany and Russia will make a separate peace. He has lost hope in the Russian peasantry and people: 'The game was lost. There would be no revolution in Russia.'[60]

Now free to pursue research in Zürich, Solzhenitsyn came across what his preface calls 'much important additional material.' What fascinates Solzhenitsyn is Lenin's personality, the psychic roots of his ruthlessness. Short-tempered with his Swiss and Russian Social Democratic colleagues, intolerant of others' opinions, incapable of friendship, Lenin was addicted to plotting and scheming. *Lenin in Zurich* takes delight in inserting a furious vocabulary under Lenin's gleaming cranium: filthy blackguards, base betrayal, scoundrelly intriguer and political prostitute, superficial, philistine minds, criminal, depraved, useless, spineless—and here we not only enter Lenin's head but listen to a million imitative Bolshevik voices of the short twentieth century.[61]

Though the narrative is virtually synonymous with the inner voice of Lenin himself, the author keeps this voice at a distance and normally avoids the pronoun 'I' – yet occasionally deep feeling breaks the rule: 'Hanecki didn't abandon me in my time of trouble.' The general narrative pattern is an alternation of 'he' and the more intimate 'you' (used in the context of tasks, mistakes, lessons of life). Lenin's devotion to the common people is conditional on their support and obedience: he has nothing but loathing for 'obscene outbursts of mob fury' and the 'ignorant rabble.' Likewise his devotion to individual comrades is conditional: his closest collaborators keep changing: they can be discarded, dismissed, forgotten, anathematized when expedient. There can be no friendship transcending political, class and material ties.[62] The exception is his increasingly elusive mistress Inessa Armand.

Solzhenitsyn systematically undermines the hagiographical Soviet image of Lenin. He has Lenin stumble across the realisation that he is capable of anything except real action, making things happen. What he habitually does in crises is to head for (say) London to write a philosophical work 300 pages long which 'no one has ever read' –works like *What Is to Be Done?*, *Two Tactics*, *Empirio-Criticism,*, *Imperialism* (all titles here shortened).[63] Solzhenitsyn depicts the two-faced Russian Jew, A. L. Helphand-Parvus, with his 'fat, fleshy, bulldog head,' visiting Lenin in Switzerland and chiding him for not giving effective support to the strikes arranged by Parvus in January 1916 in the Putilov works and elsewhere. 'What are you waiting for, Vladimir Ilyich? Why don't you give the signal?' Parvus is working for the Germans.

Solzhenitsyn portrays Lenin and the exiled Bolsheviks as completely caught by surprise, dumbstruck, by the Revolution of February 1917. 'He no longer knew where he should go. He stood still. Only two hours ago, at lunchtime, everything had been so clear: he had known that he must split the Swedish Party, known what he must read, write and do for this purpose.' But dumbstruck not for long: it is urgent time to negotiate with Berlin for his rapid return to Russia in a sealed armoured train, courtesy of the Hohenzollern monarchy. What a joyful prospect! 'Lenin's slit eyes twinkled merrily.' 'Radek grinned and bobbed up and down as though there were splinters in the chair. Lenin too bounced happily in his seat.'[64]

A businessman called Sklarz acting on behalf of Parvus brings Lenin all necessary papers from the German General Staff authorizing transit to Russia—documents 'with their Gothic flourishes, with the German eagle stamped all over them.' It's only twelve days since the tsar abdicated, but Lenin begins to worry that such a deal with the Germans could not remain secret, the threads would be relentlessly unravelled until they led back to Parvus: '...you would be daubed with the same mud, and the rudder of revolution wrested from your hands' (he tells himself). Solzhenitsyn conscientiously cites his sources, relying on Western historians who insisted that Helphand-Parvus had channelled German money to the Bolsheviks and thus helped to bring about the October putsch in Petrograd.[65]

Elsewhere Solzhenitsyn delivered his overall verdict on the man Lenin: 'The author of these lines, who in his day landed in jail precisely because of his hatred of Stalin, whom he reproached with his departure from Lenin, must now admit that he cannot find, point to, or prove any substantial deviations.'[66] Lenin's crimes (as he explained in a separate essay) included seizing land originally given to the peasants and taking it into state ownership under the Land Code of 1922. Factories promised to the workers had been on the contrary rapidly brought under central administration; trade unions were forced to serve the state; military force was used to crush border nations, Transcaucasia, Central Asia, the Baltic States; concentration camps appeared during the years 1918-21; the Cheka engaged in summary executions; the church suffered savage destruction and plundering in 1922; bestial cruelties were perpetrated in the Solovki (the popular name for the Solovetsky Islands in the White Sea).

Solzhenitsyn granted that Stalin did depart from Lenin in one major respect, the ruthless treatment of his own party ('though he was only following the general law of revolutions.') 'But close study of our modern history shows that there never was any such thing as Stalinism (either as a doctrine, or as a path of national life, or as a state system).' [67] Stalinism was simply Bolshevism.

29

From *Cancer Ward* to *The Gulag Archipelago*

The original Russian edition of *Cancer Ward*, entitled *Rakovyi korpus*, was published in Paris by the YMCA Press (Part 1, 1968, Part 2, 1969) and in London in May 1968. *Cancer Ward* has been likened to Thomas Mann's *The Magic Mountain*. The Soviet cancer hospital itself is both a reality – Solzhenitsyn himself had been treated and cured in one soon after his release from the Gulag – and a metaphor. As with Mann's tuberculosis retreat in the Swiss mountains, a single factor of fate—serious illness, often deadly—brings about the convergence of Solzhenitsyn's characters, but here the parallel ends. Thomas Mann's patients belong by definition to the European upper class who can afford expensive treatment; by contrast, Solzhenitsyn's cancer patients are all Soviet citizens, many of them bitterly divided not only by the Soviet class structure but also by the unbearable pains and penalties of a recent history still ongoing. These enmities also divide some of the privileged patients from the medical staff.

The setting allows Solzhenitsyn to explore the fractures and wounds of recent history by means of two literary strategies. Each main character brings his or her personal biography to the cancer ward; and they have time to talk, discuss, argue, to give offence and take offence. The author's personal experience as a cancer patient, and his ability to absorb medical knowledge, endows the novel with the expertise, the true-to-life dimension, considered essential by naturalist and realist novelists. But is *Cancer Ward* a 'novel'? Although it is populated by fictional characters within an invented narrative, when referring to both *The First Circle* and *Cancer Ward*, Solzhenitsyn usually described only the former as 'the novel.' The two volumes of *Cancer Ward* more resemble a historian's notebook adroitly fictionalized within an extended metaphor.

Received into a hospital in Tashkent in 1954, after he had been released from the camps and sent into 'permanent exile,' Solzhenistyn's health was saved by the skill and devotion of the medical staff. The fictional hero of *Cancer Ward*, Oleg Filimonovich Kostoglotov (meaning 'bone chewer'), has suffered cruelly.

His grandmother and mother had died in the siege of Leningrad; his sister, a nurse, was killed by a shell. But here Solzhenitsyn departs from the standard Soviet pieties; Kostoglotov tells the cancer-ward nurse Zoya not to blame the Leningrad blockade on Hitler alone: "'Those who drew their salaries for decades without seeing how Leningrad was geographically isolated and that this would affect its defence. Those who failed to foresee how heavy the bombardments would be and never thought of stocking up provisions below ground.'"[1]

Thirty-four years of age, Kostoglotov is largely self-taught and scoffs at education—but is alert to anything. He'd done one year in geophysics in 1938, then served in the Red Army as acting platoon commander with rank of senior sergeant, from Yelets to Frankfurt-on-Oder. "'I tried to spread democracy in the army, that is I answered my superiors back. That's why I wasn't sent on an officers' course in 1939, but stayed in the ranks.'" He resented this acutely—all his friends were commissioned. Kostoglotov tells his fellow-inmate Shulubin that he 'believed' "'Right up to the war against Finland".' After one incomplete year studying geodesy in 1946-47, he got seven years in a labour camp because he had been a member of a group of first-year students, male and female, who talked politics, criticized Stalin, and expressed dissatisfactions. They were arrested just before second term exams. He was never formally sentenced, just exiled by order under Article 58 of the Penal Code, paragraph 10, which dealt with individual 'anti-Soviet agitation.' In one camp, he met a teacher of classical philology and ancient literature at Leningrad University, and tried to learn Latin from him in freezing weather without pencil or paper. When the teacher took off his glove and drew Latin words in the snow, the chief of camp security interrogated them. Kostoglotov is currently living in administrative exile in Ush-Terek under Article 11, in perpetuity. This means he can never return home. His wage as an assistant surveyor is 350 roubles a month. Even though himself from central Russia, and ignorant of the Uzbek language, he by now thinks of Ush-Terek as home. He is suffering from cancer. Jealously he guards, from staff and patients alike, the secret of his status as an ex-zek condemned to exile.

Shulubin confides to Kostoglotov that the only basis for socialism in Russia, "'with our repentances, confessions and revolts, our Dostoevsky, Tolstoy and Kropotkin"'—is ethical socialism. "'We have to show the world a society in which all relationships, fundamental principles and laws flow directly from ethics, and from them *alone*.'"[2] Socialism must be *nravstvennyi*, based on love rather than hate. But when Shulubin is sceptical about democratizing actually-existing socialism, it is not clear (Lukács noted) what Solzhenitsyn himself thinks.[3] This passage and the issue of 'ethical socialism' was to become a major motif of indignation among officials of the Writers' Union determined to suppress *Cancer Ward*. Yet the portrait of Soviet life in the novel is far from wholly negative. Idealism, heroism, self-sacrifice are much in evidence, particularly among the hospital's medical staff, notably Dr Vera Kornilyevna Gangart, a radiotherapist about thirty years old. Chief Doctor Donsova is another heroine; she soon forgets all her most successful cases of treatment but will always remember the handful of poor devils who have fallen under the wheels. She is without a trace of careerism and the patients regard her with unshakable respect.

Solzhenitsyn wrote to Tvardovsky and *Novyi mir*: 'I cannot allow *Cancer Ward* to repeat the dismal career of my novel [*The First Circle*]: first there was an indefinite period of waiting, during which the author was repeatedly asked by the editors not to show it to anyone else; and then the novel was both lost to me and to those who should have read it...'[4] A discussion of *Cancer Ward* took place, after delays, at the Central Writers Club in Moscow, on 17 November 1966. Even those in support of the book were uncomfortable about the hateful portrait of Rusanov, while the passages describing his daughter's attitudes were widely criticized as farcical and exaggerated.[5] By March 1967, the entire editorial board of *Novyi mir* had read Part 2, and Tvardovsky told Solzhenitsyn it was 'three times better' than part 1 – but he had little hope of publishing it during the coming year.

In May 1967, Solzhenitsyn sent a challenging statement to the Fourth Congress of Soviet Writers, convening to celebrate the fiftieth anniversary of the Revolution. Diligently he typed out some 250 copies and posted them to individual delegates: 'I ask the Congress to discuss the no longer endurable oppression to which censorship has subjected our literature from decade to decade, and which the Writers' Union cannot tolerate in the future.' He added that censorship was not provided for in the constitution and was therefore illegal. The Writers' Union should become in practice what it was in theory, a defender of its members who were subjected to 'slander and unjust persecution.' The Union's history of subordination, he added, had led to 'sorrowful' results, the surrender of more than six hundred wholly innocent writers to execution or imprisonment. He called on delegates to the Congress to elect a new leadership which would have 'no historical need' to share responsibility for this tragic past. He himself sought redress on eight issues, from confiscation of his manuscripts to prohibition of his public readings. 'No one can bar truth's course, and for its progress I am prepared to accept even death. But perhaps repeated lessons will teach us, at last, not to arrest a writer's pen during his lifetime.'[6]

No mention of Solzhenitsyn's manifesto was heard from the platform of the Writers Congress. Signed appeals for a public reading and discussion reached the union's presidium, but to no avail. The text was published in *Le Monde* on 31 May immediately after the end of the Congress. On an almost unanimous vote, the text was read aloud to the delegates of the Congress of Czechoslovak Writers in June 1967. As was widely reported in the West, huge applause followed. The Stalinist Jiri Hendrych stormed from the hall shouting, 'You have lost everything, absolutely everything.'

Indeed by now the boat was thoroughly burned. On 22 September, Solzhenitsyn was personally grilled by some thirty of the forty-two provincial secretaries of the Writers' Union.[7] Tvardovsky argued that the secretariat of the Union must make the decision whether to go ahead with publication of *Cancer Ward* – he himself recommended publication 'with certain emendations.' The seventy-five-year-old First Secretary of the Writers' Union, Konstantin Fedin, chaired the meeting, which lasted five hours, and led the attack.

The dominant question repeatedly hurled at Solzhenitsyn concerned his attitude towards publication of his most recent manifesto-letter of 12 September, addressed to all forty-two secretaries of the Writers' Union. Fedin was obsessed by Solzhenitsyn's recent challenge to the Soviet power structure: 'You must begin by protesting against the vile ends for which your name is used by our enemies in the West.'[8] In reply, Solzhenitsyn promised to explain his attitude towards 'bourgeois propaganda' only when the text of his letter was published and discussed in the Soviet Union.

Konstantin Simonov intervened in support of *Cancer Ward*: 'I do not accept the novel *In* [sic] *The First Circle* and I am against its publication. But I vote for the publication of *Cancer Ward.... We must also deny the lies that are being spread about Solzhenitsyn.'[9] Simonov had good reason to dislike *The First Circle*, where he was coldly portrayed as the fashionable writer Galakhov, who had first made his name as a war correspondent from the 'Third Echelon.' In *The First Circle*, Solzhenitsyn comments that the distance between even the bravest correspondent who dashed to the front line and the actual combatants (who could not dash out again a day later) was 'as great as between a prince who ploughs and a peasant at his plough.' The soldier was rooted, with nowhere to go from the face of death, whereas the winged journalist would soon be back in his Moscow flat.[10]

The majority of the Writers' Union provincial secretaries present on 22 September were hostile. Kozhevnikov: '*Cancer Ward* evokes revulsion with its excessive naturalism, its piling up of all manner of horrors. All the same, its main themes are not medical but social and that is the unacceptable part.' Baruzdin: '*Cancer Ward* is an antihumanitarian work. The end of the story leads to the conclusion that that "a different road should have been taken".' Petrus Brovka: 'In Byelorussia there are also many people who were imprisoned.... Yet they realized that it was not the people, not the Party, and not the Soviet system that were responsible for illegal acts.... Yes, you feel the pain of your land, perhaps too keenly. But you don't feel its joys. *Cancer Ward* is too gloomy and should not be printed.' Kerbabayev (a Turkman): 'Everyone is a former prisoner, everything is gloomy, there is not a single word of warmth. It is utterly nauseating to read.... And then there is the remark: "Ninety-nine weep while one laughs": how are we to understand this? Does this refer to the Soviet Union?...' Novichenko: 'All who once suffered are set up in judgment over society, and that is insulting. Rusanov is a loathsome type, accurately portrayed. But it is intolerable that instead of representing a particular type he becomes the vehicle and spokesman of Soviet official society at large.' Yashen proposed Solzhenitsyn's expulsion from the Writers' Union. 'As for the siege of Leningrad, he now blames "others too" besides Hitler. Whom? It's unclear. Is it Beria? Or today's splendid leaders? He should speak out plainly.'[11]

Alexey Surkov (first secretary of the Writers' Union at the time of the Pasternak crisis) warned the meeting that Solzhenitsyn's works were more dangerous than *Doctor Zhivago*: 'Pasternak was a man divorced from life, whereas Solzhenitsyn has a bold, militant, ideological temperament, a man with an idea.' Surkov added: 'We represent the first revolution in the history of mankind that has kept unchanged its original slogans and banners. "Moral socialism" is philistine socialism.'[12]

Solzhenitsyn explained to the meeting – perhaps somewhat disingenuously—that the real subject of his open letter was not so much censorship as 'the fortunes of our great literature, which once conquered and captivated the world but which has now lost its standing. In the West, they say the novel is dead, and we gesticulate and deliver speeches saying that it is not dead. But rather than make speeches we should publish novels—such novels as would make them blink as if from a brilliant light, and then the "new novel" [*nouveau roman*] would sing small and the "neo-avant gardists" would subside.'[13] But the old beavers and badgers seated in judgment on him knew that it was politics, the reinterpretation of history, not artistic styles, that set in motion real blinking either side of the iron curtain. Senior literary bureaucrats like Fedin and Surkov cared only about Solzhenitsyn's outrageous challenge to the Party's authority.

Surkov: 'You should state whether you dissociate yourself from the role ascribed to you in the West—that of leader of a political opposition in the USSR.'

Solzhenitsyn: 'Aleksei Aleksandrovich, it makes me quite sick to hear such a thing—and from you all of all people. Literary man and leader of the political opposition: are the two compatible?'[14] (Yes! Here was the first Soviet writer to exploit openly and unapologetically the media resources of the Cold War with the clear aim of bringing down the curtain on Bolshevism.) Speaking at length, he complained that Soviet newspaper editors 'are ganging together to weave a circle of lies about me. They never publish my letters of denial.... They are now claiming that I was a prisoner of war and that I collaborated with the Germans.... It's a farce.'

The playwright Alexander Korneichuk reminded Solzhenitsyn that he was not the only person to have served time in the camps. 'In our past there was not only injustice, there was heroism too. You don't seem to have noticed that. You must speak out openly and attack Western propaganda.' Korneichuk then tossed American thermonuclear weapons into the argument. 'Do you realize that a colossal, worldwide battle is being fought under very difficult conditions? We cannot stand aloof. With our works, we defend our government, our Party, our people... We know that you have suffered a great deal but you are not the only one.... Our past consists not of acts of lawlessness alone; there were also acts of heroism—but for these you had no eyes.... When were you imprisoned? Not in 1937. In 1937 we went through a great deal, but nothing stopped us!... you must speak up in public and hit out at Western propaganda.'

This is a revealing intervention, naked before the mirrors.[15] Soviet ideology was suffocated by the hegemonic notion of 'us.' The visionary, internationalist doctrine of Karl Marx, open to the oppressed of the whole world, had become a generation of Russian males demanding loyalty to their own memories and medals—and their flag. We won the war. We made history and we will write the history of that history.

Shortly after the September 1967 meeting, Fedin is said to have visited Brezhnev, advising that *Cancer Ward* be banned. In January 1968, Tvardovsky finally abandoned plans to publish. The KGB was now developing a new tactic, blocking publication within the USSR by putting manuscripts in the hands of Russian émigré publishers. In April, *Novyi mir* received a telegram from the editors of *Grani* in Frankfurt am Main: 'We hereby inform you that the Committee for State Security [KGB], through the medium of Victor Louis, has sent a further copy of *Cancer Ward* to the West, so as to block publication in *Novyi mir*. We have therefore decided to publish this work immediately.'[16] Solzhenitsyn's letter of 18 April 1968 to the Secretariat of the Writers' Union and to all members of the Union, to *Novyi mir*, and to *Literaturnaya gazeta*, protested against the stated intention of *Grani* to publish *Cancer Ward*, and denounced the KGB agent Victor Louis for taking the manuscript abroad. The letter duly appeared in the U.S. Information Agency's *Problems of Communism* (July-August 1968). Translated editions rapidly appeared in the West. 'Writer "more dangerous than Pasternak",' announced *The Times* on 20 August.

Even Tvardovsky, who wanted to publish *Cancer Ward*, could not travel the whole distance traversed by Solzhenitsyn. Nobody could. Writing in *Novyi mir* (1, 1965), Tvardovsky had referred to Stalinism as 'a notorious period in the life of our country...it was paralysing the genuine human memory about the events through which we lived... The reader badly needs the full truth about life; he is sickened by evasiveness and hypocrisy.'[17] But this was as far as Tvardovsky would go; although a liberal and a fine editor, he remained a Party potentate, loyally subscribing to Leninism (*'po leninskomu puti'*) and the party spirit.'[18] He told Solzhenitsyn that he was 'not used to riding a streetcar without a ticket.' Their relationship broke down acrimoniously.

Solzhenitsyn's perhaps inevitable expulsion from the Writers' Union took place in 1969, following his refusal to disown publication of *The First Circle* and *Cancer Ward* in the West.

In October 1970 – as in 1958—the Swedish Academy raised the political roof by awarding the Nobel Prize for Literature to a Russian writer whose work was effectively suppressed in his own country. The strongest backing came from France, where fifty of the most illustrious intellectuals appealed to the Nobel Prize Committee in July to honour Solzhenitsyn for the 'entirety of his work'—that is, both published and unpublished in Russia. On 17 October, *Komsomolskaya pravda* hinted that the best solution for this 'morbidly conceived man' was 'to turn him out into the free world,' but the Soviet press avoided the hysteria of 1958, and there were no mass meetings or denunciations.

Meanwhile the Western Communist press, dismayed by the trial and imprisonment of Daniel and Sinyavsky, had become increasingly critical of Soviet cultural authoritarianism. Beginning with *L'Unita*, leading Communist papers came out in support of Solzhenitsyn's Nobel Prize —*l'Humanité* in France, *Volkstimme* in Austria, *Land og Folk* in the Netherlands, *Kansan Uutist* in Finland, *Borba* in Yugoslavia, *Politika* in Sweden, the *Morning Star* in Britain. *Les Lettres françaises* (France's equivalent to *Literaturnaia gazeta*) declared that 'the choice of Alexander Solzhenitsyn justifies the existence of the Nobel Prize for Literature.' As a consequence, all these newspapers were been confiscated by the Glavlit controller and prevented from going on sale. A document, dated 13 October and entitled 'Report of the Chief Directorate for the Preservation of Government Secrets in the Press (Glavlit) of the USSR Council of Ministers,' and signed by P. Romanov, reported to the Central Committee on the disarray among Western Communists on the issue of Solzhenitsyn. In a 'Top Secret' special file memo dated 20 November, Andropov, head of the KGB, returned to the question of whether to allow Solzhenitsyn out of the country—or back in if he chose to travel to Stockholm to receive the Nobel Prize.[19]

On 10 December, Solzhenitsyn listened to the ceremony in Stockholm on the Swedish radio's Russian service. A moment of silence marked the point at which the king would have presented him with his prize insignia. The king then stood to lead the applause. A message from the laureate himself was read out. He could not overlook 'the portentous coincidence of the Nobel Prize presentation with Human Rights Day.... So at this festive table let us not forget that political prisoners are on hunger strike today to defend their infringed or completely trampled rights".' But the final sentence had been excised in Sweden—there was no mention of 'this festive table.' A long attack followed in *Pravda* (17 December), describing Solzhenitsyn as 'a spiritual inner émigré, hostile and alien to the entire life of the Soviet people.' The article revealed a fever of paranoid xenophobia: 'As we see, the affairs of the adversaries of communism are in such a sorry state that to squeeze out any anti-Sovietism they have to resort to the services of criminal elements, an assortment of renegades, parasites, rascals and swindlers, and even people in whom psychiatrists take an interest...rogues and schizophrenics.'[20]

A year later, Solzhenitsyn physically challenged the Soviet state in the only circumstance where the muscle was his: by choosing to attend Tvardovsky's funeral, the lying in state at the House of Writers; by sitting in the front row with the widow and children; by making the sign of the cross over the open coffin and by kissing the dead man before the coffin was nailed up. It was Solzhenitsyn's living presence rather than Tvardovsky in his casket that attracted the entire Moscow corps of foreign correspondents—photographers gave offence by standing with their backs to the casket and firing off flashbulbs point-blank at Solzhenitsyn, who was scribbling notes.[21]

Olga Carlisle recalls Kornei Chukovsky, then eighty-five, telling her how he had witnessed local toughs in the pay of the police trying to intimidate Solzhenitsyn, while he was staying in the Chukovsky dacha at Peredelkino: "'It's worse when he's home in Ryazan. At least here I'm 'Grandfather Kornei.' That has some effect on these scoundrels. There – *chort*! [devil!] All hell breaks loose! *Chort, chort*!'" Solzhenitsyn himself had told Olga Carlisle much the same. 'They spied on him, threw stones at his house, tried to terrify him and his family. They were restless.'[22]

Highly publicised in the West was an incident which took place in August 1971. Solzhenitsyn fell ill in Moscow and asked a friend, Aleksandr Gorlov, to fetch a spare part for his car from the cottage made available to him by the great cellist Rostropovich. When Gorlov, a young scientist about to defend his doctoral dissertation, arrived at the supposedly empty cottage, he heard voices and found ten men in plain clothes inside. On the command of the senior officer, 'to the woods with him and silence him,' Gorlov was knocked to the ground, dragged face down into the woods and beaten viciously. Neighbours came running. One of the beaters then showed a red KGB card and the neighbours let them pass. His face torn to ribbons, Gorlov was taken to the local police station, where Captain Ivanov of the KGB demanded that he sign an oath of secrecy. Gorlov was warned: 'If Solzhenitsyn finds out what took place at the dacha, it's all over with you. Your career will go no further. You will not be able to defend any dissertation. This will affect your family and children and, if necessary, we will put you in prison.' Gorlov refused. Solzhenitsyn responded to the event very much as the KGB had feared—with an open letter to Andropov, demanding 'public identification of all the robbers, their punishment as criminals and an equally public explanation of this incident.... Otherwise I can only believe that you, Chairman of the KGB, sent them.' This letter was handed by friends to Western correspondents in Moscow and made world headlines.[23] Andropov submitted a cynical memorandum on the Gorlov incident to the Politburo, admitting that it was the KGB which had been staking out Solzhenitsyn's dacha: Sounding like a SMERSH villain in a James Bond film Andropov concluded: 'Solzhenitsyn will be informed that the participation of the KGB in this incident is a figment of his imagination.... In order to neutralise the negative consequence we consider it advisable to have the USSR Ministry of Internal Affairs contact the police to confirm the "robbery" version of events.'[24]

Never had a writer been so embattled. He threw out polemics, notably against the Russian Orthodox Church which he accused of spineless subservience ('Lenten Letter to the Patriarch (Pimen),' and the State, which he accused of mindless tyranny ('Letter to the Soviet Leaders'). This was no timid Pasternak

– and Brezhnev's regime could no longer resort to repression on the Stalin model. As the archives reveal, the Praesidium (Brezhnev, Kosygin, Andropov, etc.) felt tormented by legal restraints when confronted by an onslaught which captivated the Western media and put KGB harassment under the spotlight. Michael Scammell was able to publish from the Moscow archives an astonishing memorandum (undated but no later than 7 October 1971) submitted to the Presidium by N. Shchelokov, minister of internal affairs, 'On the Solzhenitsyn Question.' Here the entire official Soviet position is undermined if not abandoned: 'Objectively, Solzhenitsyn has talent. He is a literary phenomenon.... It would be extremely useful to have his pen serving the interests of the people.' The minister then wrote a phrase that Brezhnev underlined: *In resolving the Solzhenitsyn question we must analyze past mistakes made in dealing with people in the arts.* *Cancer Ward* (continued Shchelokov) was written from 'the very same ideological position as *One Day in the Life of Ivan Denisovich*. In the first instance he was received into the Writers' Union. In the second instance, he was removed from the Writers' Union.' So far so good, but here the devious mind of an interior minister surfaced. 'Solzhenitsyn's works could have been published in the Soviet Union after painstaking editing. One way or another, even without the author's consent, works such as these can be edited down and published so that subsequently they can be hushed up.' Hushed up? Did Shchelekov seriously believe Solzhenitsyn would have tolerated such treatment in silence? 'The author [continued the minister] must not be forced to seek publication abroad... *In the Solzhenitsyn business we are repeating the same glaring errors that we committed with regard to Boris Pasternak.* [Here again Brezhnev underlined the passage.] *Doctor Zhivago* should have been "edited down" and published here in this country. In that case, there would certainly have been no interest in the book in the West.' Shchelokov actually imagined that, given friendly treatment, Solzhenitsyn would arrive in Sweden and 'speak the following phrases: "I have no differences with the Soviet authorities. I have no differences with the Party. I am a Soviet writer. I am proud of what is happening in the country. I have differences with my literary colleagues. These are professional differences. They have always existed and always will, as long as there is literature".'

On 7 October 1971, the Secretariat of the Central Committee met to discuss Minister Shchelekov's memorandum. Mikhail Suslov set the tone immediately by ignoring everything in the memo except the question of where Solzhenitsyn should be allowed to live.[25]

August 1914 [26] is the first part, or 'Knot' (which he defined as a historical turning point) of *The Red Wheel*, the story of how the wheel of history brought Russia to the Communist revolution.[27] As Michael Scammell says, Solzhenitsyn's choice of subject and period was part of his long term task to restore the living memory and condensed experience of the nation. Like Pasternak in *Doctor Zhivago*, he was suggesting that pre-revolutionary Russia did indeed briefly enjoy the opportunity of a third way – neither the tsar nor the Bolshevik Revolution. *August 1914* has been described as a total reconstruction of Russian society on the eve of a great upheaval, a searching inquiry into the causes of disintegration.[28] The test of good character and bad is willingness to undertake military service – yes, even in the service of the imperial tsars. Among men of draft age the dubious characters avoid conscription or serve unwillingly, or have contempt for the colours, or run under fire. Among regular officers the contemptible ones are those whose first thought is to promote their careers. Among women and girls the silly ones mock patriotic demonstrations and try to deter sons and schoolmates from joining up. Mary McCarthy commented that for Solzhenitsyn, 'It is not a question of approving of the war; few of the good do, and to the more educated and wiser among them the war is a tragedy that will set progressive forces in Russia back ten years, twenty, a generation. Rather, it is a question of being willing to take one's part in the tragedy or not. The central ethic of the novel is one of sharing, and the characters are judged by whether, in their souls, they are sharers or hoarders.'[29]

A wide variety of literary devices are employed, including cinematic sequences, montages of revolutionary newspaper headlines, adverts, street posters, proverbs printed in bold capitals, brief chapters of historical summary and exegesis. Some of this collage is borrowed from Dos Passos's *1919*, read by Solzhenitsyn in the Lubyanka prison immediately after the war. His newspaper montages reflected fascination with the vitality and vulgarity of a free(er) press, which he first encountered when going through his mother's papers and clippings after her death. In this respect, Solzhenitsyn was by diligent research catching up with the pre-1917 values absorbed by Pasternak as a young man. Michael Scammell was among those irritated by 'an excess of historical documentation tricked out with the dubious experimentalism of the twenties.'[30]

Real characters rub shoulders with fictional ones and it is not always easy to distinguish between them. Mary McCarthy found *August 1914* 'a difficult book. The geography is unfamiliar; the logistics are bewildering to anyone but a military specialist; and the chronology is not easy to follow since the scene keeps shifting and many events overlap.' Nina Khrushcheva, senior fellow at the World Policy Institute in the New School for Social Research, New York, complains that the novel is very hard to read, with its abundance of characters and their separate, unlinked, parallel destinies, the only connection being Russia in the years 1914-1916. Solzhenitsyn's desire to recover an authentic Russian language results (she says) in clotted passages.[31]

The novel's attitude to the intelligentsia, to liberals and social democrats, is largely negative. The principled and intelligent patriotism of Colonel Georgi Vorotyntsev provides the thread, or spine, of the novel. The majority of those characters we are invited to admire in *August 1914* are officers who belong to the gentry or property-owning class. Yes, there are also admirable artisan and peasant figures: 'those trusting bearded men, those friendly eyes, those placid, selfless faces.' Mary McCarthy complained that Solzhenitsyn does not offer a single proletarian character. 'From a Soviet point of view, the amount of favourable space allotted to individuals of the officer class is utterly disproportionate.'32 In this respect, also, Solzhenitsyn's narrative resembled Pasternak's. As the KGB propaganda machine was not slow to point out, Solzhenitsyn's own father had been a lieutenant in the tsarist army and a Tolstoyan.

The most controversial aspect of *August 1914* was its underlying political philosophy. Here is a corrosive portrait of a corrupt, cowardly and criminally inept ruling class including the tsar and his entourage. Yet Solzhenitsyn also depicted a buoyant and flourishing pre-revolutionary Russia capable of evolutionary progress. Then there were his pro-German sentiments, in evidence throughout his work but here set in the context of a great war between Russia and Germany.

In March 1971 he wrote to the editors of seven Soviet publishing houses offering them *August 1914*. In May, Solzhenitsyn passed a copy to the émigré YMCA Press in Paris. The novel did not strengthen the cohesion of what might be called the 'family' among his devoted readers and followers. On the contrary, it split their ranks. He himself attributed to *August 1914* 'the schism among my readers, the steady loss of supporters, with more leaving me than remaining behind.... In my first work I was concealing my features from the police censorship – but by the same token from the public at large. With each subsequent step I inevitably revealed more of myself: the time had come to speak more precisely, to go even deeper. And in doing so, I should inevitably lose the reading public, lose my contemporaries in the hope of winning posterity. It was painful, though, to lose support among even those closest to me.'33 By November 1972, *August 1914* was number 2 on the American best-seller lists, a minor compensation.

'And if freedom does not dawn on my country for a long time to come, then the very reading and handling of this book will be very dangerous...'34 [Solzhenitsyn on his *Gulag Archipelago*.] Should we leave this work out of account because avowedly a work of history, of non-fiction? By instinct Solzhenitsyn is always what we may call 'a historian by other means.' As Geoffrey Hosking puts it: *Gulag* is history, memoir, autobiography, anthropology 'but behind it all is the controlling intelligence and sensibility of the novelist...that is, in the Russian sense, where the categories of social commentator, theologian and prophet are also implied'.

Solzhenitsyn called *The Gulag Archipelago* a 'monument of solidarity with all the martyrs and the dead of 1918 to 1956.' He took the grim story back to its origins under Lenin, digging names out of old newspapers, forgotten documents, testaments, eye-witness accounts. 'And then [as Edward Crankshaw put it] on through the modest but vicious trials of the 1920s, a cortège of ghosts; the engineers, wreckers all, wave after wave of them; the "churchmen"—the survivors, actual or alleged, from the historical revolutionary parties—all caught for a moment in the limelight to be crushed and thrown down into outer darkness. And so on to the first grand climax, which was the deliberate extermination of the Russian peasantry as a coherent class. And on to Stalin's apogee and what came to be known as the Great Terror of the 1930s.' Solzhenitsyn, added Crankshaw, 'set himself the task, single-handed and working in the most difficult conditions, of raising a memorial, a cenotaph, to the millions who suffered and died to build the world's first socialist country—or to sustain a handful of men in power.'[35]

In his preface, Solzhenitsyn writes, 'I would not be so bold as to try to write the history of the Archipelago. I have never had the chance to read the documents. And, in fact, will anyone ever have the chance to read them?'[36] After publication of *One Day*, he had become the chronicler to whom former prisoners entrusted their experiences; in his own words 'the trusted archivist of the camp world to whom everyone brought their truth.' He evolved a form of literary investigation, 'a way of handling factual (not transformed) real-life material in such a way that the facts and fragments, linked by artistic means, yielded a general idea that was convincing and in no way inferior to that produced by a scientific investigation'.[37] Many of his 227 informants insisted on anonymity. There were secret meetings, confidential letters, hushed conversations. The gathering and sorting of the materials was a collective effort yet inspired by this one man of extraordinary will.

His original plan had been to publish *The Gulag Archipelago* in 1969 shortly after he completed it. But he kept putting it off in the light of other calculations. From the moment that a copy got out of Russia in June 1971, he 'was really ready at last to do battle and to perish'. In September 1973 the KGB confiscated a copy after raiding the Leningrad home of his devoted typist Elizaveta Voronyanskaya. After five days and nights of interrogation, she revealed that another copy had been buried in the garden of a dacha at Luga. (She died soon afterwards, perhaps by suicide.) In December 1973, the first of the two volumes was published in Paris, creating shock waves throughout the Communist parties of Europe. 'What a burden I had shed. Secretly, surreptitiously, I had carried it and brought it safely to its destination! And now it was no longer on my back, but set where all could see it – that unwieldly stone, that great petrified tear.'[38]

Solzhenitsyn's expulsion from the Soviet Union had been in the pipeline and lodged in the low brow of the Presidium for more than two years before it happened. He travelled from Peredelkino to Moscow on 11 February 1974, then read aloud a passage from the third volume of *Gulag* to correspondents of the *New York Times* and the KGB. That evening he heard himself on foreign radio. On the 13th the KGB poured into his apartment, 'eight of them altogether.' He was taken to the Lefortovo prison, where he was charged under Article 64—treason. He was to be expelled from the USSR, and his citizenship revoked, under a decree of the Presidium of the Supreme Soviet dated 12 February (the previous day), on the basis of Article 7 of the USSR law of 19 August 1938. A doctor accompanied him in the car to Sheremetevo Airport. Seven plain clothes men boarded the plane with him, plus the doctor. He had no idea where he was going. Only on landing did he see 'Frankfurt am Main' on the airport building.[39]

'The Path of Treason' appeared in *Pravda* on 14 January. 'Solzhenitsyn is worthy of the fate he has so diligently pursued – that of a traitor, from whom every Soviet workingman and every honest person on earth cannot but turn away in anger and disgust.'[40] Solzhenitsyn's name was not mentioned in the eight volumes of the *Short Literary Encylopedia*, 1962-1975.[41]

Exiled, he fell out, bitterly, with erstwhile allies including the Medvedev brothers, Roy and Zhores, Andrei Sakharov, and further down the line Lydia Chukovskaya, all appalled by his reincarnation as an arch-conservative, dedicated exponent of the Cold War and supporter of the Vietnam war. He chastised an American judge for finding in favour of Daniel Ellsberg, author of the *Pentagon Papers*, against the U.S. government; he let fly at flabby liberalism during a Harvard commencement speech ('A World Split Apart'), so delighting Andropov and the KGB that they privately ran videos of the event and chortled over the growing condemnation of Solzhenitsyn in the Western press. He was damned for messianism, Judaeophobia, contempt for liberal values and spineless democracy. He never apologised or retreated: 'The writer's ultimate task is to restore the memory of his murdered people... They murdered my people and destroyed its memory. And I'm dragging it into the light of day all on my own. Of course, there are hundreds like me back there who could drag it out, too. Well, it didn't fall to them; it fell to me.'[42]

30

Commentary: Bureaucracy, the New Class and Double Standards

The privileges enjoyed by the 'new class' in communist Russia figured prominently in Cold War fiction. In Orwell's *Nineteen Eighty-Four* members of the Inner Party enjoy a luxurious lifestyle, including servants. When Winston visits O'Brien in a 'huge block of flats,' he is struck by 'the richness and spaciousness of everything, the unfamiliar smells of good food and good tobacco...the white-jacketed servants.'[1] Power is evidently a means as well as an end in itself.

Although this kind of indictment was most associated with dissident Soviet writers, it can be found in discreet form in a novel awarded a Stalin Prize, Fadeyev's *The Young Guard*. Komsomol Stakhovich, who denies having deserted the partisans in battle, offers his Young Guard interrogators a full and indeed credible report of terrible enemy fire and of his special ability to survive by swimming on his back with only his nose exposed. Fadeyev wheels in the man's social background to explain his less-than-perfect behaviour. 'He was not an arriviste or a man who sought only personal profit'—but he grew up in the new Soviet class. Stakhovich belongs to those who find themselves from childhood among highly placed people, and who become spoiled by imitating certain exterior aspects of their seniors' authority, not yet mature enough to appreciate the raison d'être of popular power and that people possessing must merit it by their work and character.[2] All this may seem a rather contrived explanation why Stakhovich did what so many others did, lose their nerve under fire and make an escape, but it indirectly confirms the documents unearthed since the fall of Soviet power showing popular resentment about privileges enjoyed by Stalin's new elite in the 1930s.

Party privileges emerged soon after the October Revolution, according to Pasternak's *Doctor Zhivago*. During the ensuing months of anarchy, meals for Moscow's masses consisted of 'boiled millet and fish soup made of herring heads, followed by the rest of the herring as a second course; there was also gruel made by boiling wheat or rye. This was to be the staple food of the majority for a long time to come.' But privilege soon resurfaces: when Yury is invited to treat members of the government who have fallen ill, he is paid in the highest currency, chits on the first of the newly introduced closed-consumer shops. Here one brings pillow cases and other suitable 'containers' to carry away flour, cereals, macaroni, sugar, fats, soap, matches and paper packets containing Caucasian cheese – all unavailable to the ordinary people.[3]

In Grossman's *Life and Fate*, Krymov is arrested, interrogated in the Lubyanka, and accused of fantastical collusion with Trotsky, the Germans, etc. Krymov's interrogator ignores him for long periods, sharpens pencils, writes letters, waiting for Krymov to offer a confession. The interrogator (the new class) telephones his wife: '"At the special store? Goose—that's fine. But they should have given it you on your first coupon. Sergey's wife rang the department. She got a leg of lamb on her first coupon.... How's the gas been today? And don't forget the suit.... Don't miss me too much. Did you dream about me? What did I look like? In my underpants again? Pity! Well, I'll teach you a thing or two when I get home."'[4]

Sinyavsky/Tertz's depiction of the new class in *The Trial Begins* is derisive. Prosecutor Globov is a model of self-esteeming hypocrisy: 'With these two hands I've ploughed the soil and I've sent people to their death...' His colleague, Interrogator Skromnykh, entertains members of the new class at home—witty, home-loving men, who enjoy fishing or cooking or making toys for their children. They like to talk about their summer holidays at the Crimean seaside. A lieutenant colonel announces he is buying a car, a Probyeda (Victory) but cannot make up his mind between beige and grey. Some guests object that beige is common. Toast follows toast. 'The table was like a battlefield: wine dribbling like blood, pies squelchy like a military road on a wet autumn day; splintered skeletons of herrings; ash and cigarette butts; red and rusty stains.'[5]

Ilya Ehrenburg's novel *The Thaw*, first published in the magazine *Znamya* in May 1954, soon lent its name to the period of post-Stalin liberalisation and self-scrutiny. Set in an ordinary Russian town, its central characters include Zhuravilov, a factory director who has neglected the workers' interests in his eagerness to fulfil the plan. Central to Ehrenburg's purpose is an ambitious artist and portrait painter: 'Volodya dreamed of fame, of money, he always knew which were the "shock" themes, what artists had been rewarded and who had been told off.' Some ten pages later, Volodya reflects to himself: 'Everybody trims his sails, manoeuvres, lies, only some are smarter at it, some less smart.'[6] Ehrenburg was not bold enough to confront the 'unmentionables': the purges, the Gulag, Stalin's monomania. The theme of managerial greed and selfish ambition was in any case not new – several stage plays had addressed the issue. Nevertheless, Sholokhov fiercely attacked *The Thaw* during the Soviet Writers Congress of 1954.

Vladimir Dudintsev's novel, *Not By Bread Alone*, enjoyed a temporary and politically driven notoriety somewhat beyond its literary merit. Published in serial form by *Novyi mir* (August-October 1956), the magazine's print-run of 140,000 copies rapidly sold out. A discussion held at the Writers' House in Moscow was packed to overflowing, 'and young people climbed stepladders and poked their heads in through the windows.' Dismissing the novel as a 'failure,' *Izvestiia* and expressed fears about the 'unhealthy agitation' surrounding it. *Kommunist* complained that Dudintsev had 'lost his sense of perspective, got into a panic and exaggerated the danger, presenting bureaucracy in our conditions as an impenetrable brick wall.'[7]

In essence, Dudintsev turns the literary conventions of socialist realism against bureaucratic corruption according to a familiar formula which Katerina Clark calls the 'master plot,'[8] constantly justifying the hero's lonely stand in terms of improving socialist production and putting an end to the squandering of public money on second-rate techniques. Historical progress in the master plot occurs through the working out of the spontaneity/consciousness dialectic. Consciousness involves both individual and political activities which are controlled, disciplined, and guided. Spontaneity, by contrast, is sporadic, uncoordinated, even anarchic – yet required in certain circumstances.[9] This tension serves as one of the energising contradictions of socialist realism.

Not By Bread Alone takes place in the years 1946 to 1949 (when the inventor-hero faces trial), then moves on to 1954. The inventor-hero, Dmitri Alexeyvich Lapotkin, is the victim of a scientific bureaucracy hobbled by greed, jealousy, pride and ambition. Dudintsev provides the standard furniture of the socialist realist living room: a principled hero, described as a 'visionary who lives not by bread alone,' who has proved himself under fire and been wounded (Red Star); the schoolteacher Nadia, a heroine self-sacrificingly loyal to him; her husband Drozdov, a scheming bureaucrat of the new class who causes his wife physical disgust until she leaves him for Lopatkin. It is devotion to a communist future rather than personal ambition which inspires Lopatkin to continue work on his spurned blueprint for producing pipes more efficiently, despite bitter discouragement by the establishment.

Lopatkin's description of the spirit of Communism may remind us of the Holy Ghost: 'Then I suddenly understood that communism is not a construction thought out by the philosophers, but a force which has existed for a long time and which is covertly training cadres for a future society. This force has already entered me.' By contrast the villainous manager of the *kombinat*, Drozdov, glibly misuses such catchphrases as 'duty of the State' and 'collective' – when in cynical mood he puckers his yellow face up into innumerable wrinkles of amusement. In one passage bureaucratic indifference under attack is said by an elderly professor to be a survival from capitalist times.[10]

The deputy district prosecutor, Comrade Titov, who summons Lopatkin, turns out to be a woman with lustreless eyes who chain smokes. Lopatkin chides her for believing the bureaucratic scientists who have accused him: 'And yet all these scientists, Avdiyev, Fundator, Volovik, Tepikin, are still riding along on the technical methods of the day before yesterday. Like the silkworm, they spin cocoons for themselves out of their own spittle!' And is it not these same bureaucrats now persecuting him who are responsible for the Soviet economy's failure to produce a small car capable of rivalling the foreign models?'[11]

Suddenly the Minister agrees to receive Lopatkin with a display of affability. The year is 1947. Lopatkin speaks out bravely. The hero of a six-year-long struggle for a state-of-the-art pipe casting machine, he accuses Drozdov of stealing and putting into production one of his own earlier blueprints for pipe-casting machinery. The character Shutikov remarks, 'They built themselves a sort of Scythian fortress, surrounded by a wall, divided the duties up between themselves, and now live according to Malthus, limiting fresh births.'[12] The dispute goes before a military court. Lopatkin is sentenced to a spell of eight years in a reformatory labour camp. One member of the panel, a major, submits a dissenting opinion: 'The matter is one of principle. I cannot be a blind instrument, particularly in a case like this.' Lopatkin's response is worthy of Solzhenitsyn's *The First Circle*: 'Whoever has learned to think can never be completely deprived of freedom.'[13] Later a sympathetic character speaks for Dudintsev (and certainly not for Solzhenitsyn) when he tells Lopatkin: 'A genuine party man cannot tolerate an injustice. He can sense it, however carefully it is hidden. And he cannot tolerate it!'[14]

The bureaucrats then discover an over-expenditure of cast iron amounting to sixty thousand tons. Released, Lopatkin is at last taken on to the payroll. Now head of the designing office, he is jokingly encouraged to buy himself a Pobeda, a weekend cottage, and a television set – but humour is not his forte: '"Man lives not by bread alone, if he is honest," Lopatkin's voice rang out in the silence.' Colleagues tease him that if one of his new subordinates were to think up a better invention than his own he would surely claim it or suppress it. Lopatkin indignantly denies it.

An anonymous critic in the London-based *Soviet Survey* (Winter 1956-1957) summed up Dudintsev's achievement: 'He has indicted Soviet society by challenging the official picture of human (not industrial) relations. It is his devastating account of dishonesty and distrust at all levels, even among close friends and relatives, that has got beneath the skin of the official reviewers.' And more in the same vein.[15] Katerina Clark comments that Lopatkin 'recapitulates the pattern of the Stakhanovite, who, it will be recalled, did not have to be a Party member.' He meets the exigencies of the Heroic Code, scorning material comfort and standing firm before mockers. He survives a prison term with his faith intact. He allows himself only two recreations, physical exercise and classical music. Clark points to the 'great irony of Soviet culture, the fact that in many ways "dissident" and "orthodox" values form...different forces locked in a dialectical relationship within the one system, each feeding on the other.'

One notes Dudintsev's binary insistence on the existence of an absolute truth and its opposition to error, rather than on complexity. Promethean symbolism, the myth of the martyred expert, offers a higher order of knowledge available only to an elite. Clark concludes, 'Paradoxically, then, during the 1956 thaw the one novel that is most "dissident" more closely resembles Stalinist fiction than any of the more "conformist" writings of that year.'[16]

Solzhenitsyn's short story, *For the Good of the Cause*, published by *Novyi mir* in 1963, is set in the early 1950s, but this seems to have been driven by the demands of expediency, a tactical move in the light of Khrushchev's anti-Stalin campaign (to which, of course, the writer owed the publication of *One Day in the Life of Ivan Denisovich*). *For the Good of the Cause* carries the immediacy of an extended contemporary newspaper report, and readers' excited responses – whether enthusiastic praise or fierce criticism – indicated that the issues raised remained alive and well in the sixties.

In a provincial city idealistic young volunteers join hands to build a modernised technical school. Staff and pupils alike donate voluntary labour in a genuine collective bonding of mutual trust and affection. The old premises are inadequate, the pupils cannot be accommodated, the authorities are bureaucratically delaying new buildings. So the 'education workers' take the matter into their own hands.

Suddenly a state commission appears, inspects the old, inadequate, premises cursorily and superficially, discovers them to be 'quite in order' for the existing technical school, and assigns the new building – though built by the volunteers—to a research institution favoured by Moscow. An injustice not to be tolerated!

A notable feature of the critical disputes following publication of *For the Good of the Cause* was the extent to which the story itself was treated by critics as if 'reality' rather than mere fictional invention. Writing in *Literaturnaya gazeta* (31 August 1963), Yuri Barabash describes the initial situation in the story as if it were a here-and-now reality in Ryazan or Minsk. On the other hand, R.N. Seliverstov asked: 'Can that atmosphere of passivity and helplessness described by Solzhenitsyn exist today in any community? I don't think so. At least not in any of the educational communities with whose life I am acquainted.' Solzhenitsyn's story, he went on, 'seems rather to evoke echoes of life the day before yesterday.... Genuine justice, fought for and won by the Party and our whole people – and not abstract "justice" – runs through our life today and is triumphant!'[17] Seliverstov uses the word 'today' three times.

When Tvardovsky, editor of *Novyi mir*, staged his counter-attack (October 1963) on behalf of *For the Good of the Cause*, the correspondents he quoted in support of Solzhenitsyn said in effect: 'The author of the story is right. In reality, petty bureaucrats—and there are still plenty of them, and quite unreformed ones—in our country...frequently conceal their bureaucratic desires and actions by imaginary "considerations of state"...' The liberal Tvardovsky also resorted to the old Stalinist tactic of wheeling in a letter to support Solzhenitsyn's story signed by 'V. SHEINIS, Lathe operator in the Kirov factory, shock-worker of Communist labour, [and] R. TSIMERINOV, T-crane operator.' From Hungary, the dean of Marxist literary critics, Lukács, praised Solzhenitsyn's story in typically convoluted terms: 'Here the gauntlet is thrown down by the sectarians before the friends of progressive literature – namely the claim that the enthusiasm of the masses for reconstruction work during the era of the "personality cult" should be described "independently" of that cult – is boldly taken up.'[18]

But Solzhenitsyn's story nowhere refers to the 'era of the personality cult.' His target is less-than-human Communist bureaucracy – now as then.

In *The First Circle*, Solzhenitsyn explores the outlook and lifestyle of Innokentii Volodin's privileged bureaucratic milieu – the point being that Volodin found within himself the integrity to take a fatal risk despite his privilege. The authorial voice is nakedly expository: 'They belonged to that circle of society where such a thing as walking or taking the Metro is unknown...where there is never any worry about furnishing a flat.... They held that "you only live once". Not a breath of the sorrow of the world fanned the cheeks of Innokentii and [his wife] Datoma.' The couple even avoid having children because of the inconvenience. When Innokentii is posted to Paris, Datoma ('Dottie') sends home case after case of dresses, hats, shoes.

We enter the home of the prosecutor Makarygin. He boasts an antique pedestal desk but rarely puts pen to paper. 'The inkstand on it was in the latest fashion, with a nearly two-foot high model of the Kremlin Spassky Tower, complete with clock and star.' On the shelves, inside the glazed bookcases, can be found the *Large Soviet Encylopaedia* ('the wrong one, with enemies of the people in it') and the *Small Encyclopaedia* ('also wrong and also containing names of enemies'). We are told that the prosecutor rarely opened his law books because all of them had been effectively replaced by directives, most of them secret, known only by code numbers (083 or 0050).[19] At one point the prosecutor's daughter chides her father for his Communist pretensions: 'Oh! Come off it, father! You don't belong to the working class. You were a worker once for two years and you've been a prosecutor for thirty.... You live off the fat of the land!'[20]

In another scene the arrogance of the prevailing class system is exposed in a flash: '"Hey, you!" the foreman shouted curtly. The woman stopped her washing. Moving aside to leave the room to pass her in single file, she did not raise her head from her bucket and floor-cloth.

'The general walked past.

'The foreman walked past.

'Rustling her flounced perfumed skirt and almost brushing the charwoman's face with it, the general's wife walked past... Clara [the general's daughter] was transfixed by her look of burning contempt.'[21] Could it be worse in the capitalist West? In one episode the lights have fused in an elite Moscow flat. Solzhenitsyn lists the occupations of those present: a diplomat, a writer, a critic, a civil servant, an actor, a frontier guard, a law student. None volunteers to mend the fuse – it's not their kind of work.

In *Cancer Ward*, Solzhenitsyn introduces a character who was to cause dissension, indeed uproar, among the audiences which heard the author give readings from this fictional documentary in 1966, and among the literary apparatchiks who were granted confidential access to *Novyi mir*'s printed proofs of the work. Solzhenitsyn brings to the cancer ward the embodiment of the new class, Pavel Nicolayevich Rusanov, admitted to Wing 13 with a tumour on the right side of his neck. Currently expecting promotion as a result of economic reorganization at republic and province level, Rusanov arrives in a little blue Moskvich, escorted by his devoted wife and adult son. Recoiling from the populist bustle within Wing 13, he feels demeaned to find himself in a public hospital. Are there no VIP wards? He manages to bypass the waiting room, the public bath and the required change of clothing: "'Perhaps the doctors would come to our house? We'd pay them.'"

His wife Kapitolina (Kapa) is cut from the same cloth. She wears two silver-fox furs, hectors the staff, and announces how important her husband is. She wants to pay for private nursing; when this is rejected by the hospital she tries to bribe a nurse and is rebuffed. As for Kapitolina, 'She'd been a worker in the same macaroni factory where he'd started work in the dough-kneading shop. But even before their marriage he had risen to membership of the factory trade union committee and was working on safety arrangements. Then through his membership of the Young Communist League he'd been posted to reinforce the Soviet trade organisation, and a year later he was made director of the factory's secondary school. During all these years...their proletarian sympathies did not change. On festive occasions...the Rusanovs would recall their days in the factory and break into loud renderings of old workers' songs.' But now: 'Kapa, with her broad figure, her two silver-fox furs, her large handbag the size of a briefcase and her shopping bag full of provisions, was taking up at least three places on the bench in the warmest corner of the hall.' Rusanov complains: "'If only there was a separate lavatory I could use! The lavatories here are terrible. There are no cubicles. Everyone can see you!'" Solzhenitsyn adds in brackets: '(To use a public bath or lavatory inevitably subverts one's authority. In his office Rusanov went to another floor to avoid having to use the general staff lavatory.)'

The couple discuss urgent repairs and improvements to their flat. The vexing problem is the workmen, assigned by state warrant and paid by the state, who would inevitably 'extort' more money from prosperous clients like the Rusanovs. Did he himself ever ask for tips? 'And why were these unscrupulous workers, ten a penny as they were, such money-grubbers?'[22] The couple fear that their layabout, playboy son Lavrik 'might well be led up the garden path by some ordinary weaver girl from the textile factory.' A colleague's daughter had narrowly avoided the disaster of marrying a fellow-student, a country boy

whose mother was an ordinary collective farmer. Imagine them having influential guests to dinner with the mother-in-law sitting there in a white headscarf
and without a passport!

Lavrik was named after Lavrenti Beria. "'Give him the same name as the
Minister,' they'd said, "Stalin's staunch brother-in-arms. Let him be like him
in every way." But for more than a year now you had had to be very careful
about saying the words "Lavrenti Pavlovich" aloud. All right, let's suppose
Beria was a double-dealer, a bourgeois nationalist and a seeker after power.
Very well, put him on trial and shoot him behind closed doors, but why tell the
ordinary people anything about it? Why shake their faith? Why create doubt
in their minds?'[23] For twenty years Rusanov has worked in personnel records
administration. This gives him intimate knowledge and power. He enjoys making
people worry and sweat: "'Everyone is guilty of something or has something to
conceal.'" Any member of staff summoned to Rusanov's office has to wait in
a dark little cubicle no more than three feet across, no light or air, 'and he felt
the full weight of his nothingness compared with the importance of the man
whose office he was about to enter.'[24]

Rusanov now avoids public transport whenever possible—people push-
ing you, insults, dirty overalls, you can get oil or lime all over your coat:
'The worst thing was their inveterate habit of clapping you familiarly on the
shoulder and asking you to pass a ticket or some change along the car.' So
the Rusanovs used office cars and taxis, and now had their own. Ordinary
railway carriages were out of the question; they travelled only in reserved
compartments or 'soft class.' When they holidayed in rest homes it was only
those 'where it was arranged for the beach and the walks to be fenced off
from the general public.'[25]

A story told by the cancer patient known as 'the professor,' who has had an
operation on his larynx, again exemplifies the greed of the new rich. Someone
called 'Sashik' Yemelyan has built a big house stuffed with tables, statues,
pianos, mirrors, bowls, pictures purloined from conquered Europe. Another
pillar of society, a general, occupies a house with ten rooms, two cars and his
own man to stoke the boiler. A patient recalls a recent newspaper story 'about
a man who built himself a villa with government funds. Then it all came out.
And you know what happened? He confessed he'd made a "mistake", handed
the place over to a children's home, and all he got was an official reprimand.
He wasn't even expelled from the Party.'[26]

Utopian dreams of equality are now pie-in-the-sky. In *Cancer Ward*, the
professor argues that "'Socialism provides for differentiation in the wage-
structure".'

"'To hell with your differentiation," Kostoglotov raged, as pig-headed as
ever.

"You think that while we're working towards communism the privileges some
have over others ought to be increased, do you?" "It makes no difference," he

adds, 'if you had ten proletarian grandfathers, if you're not a worker yourself you're no proletarian.'"

'Beseeching him to have mercy on his stricken larynx, he [the professor] whispered a few reasonable sentences about people making different contributions to the national product and the need to distinguish between those who washed hospital floors and the men in charge of the health service.'[27] But earlier the cancer patient Shulubin has quoted Lenin's April [1917] Theses: '"No official should receive a salary higher than the average pay of a good worker." That's what they began the revolution with.' Shulubin describes the life of a collective farm girl working in the chicken house steaming stale sprats in an open vat. '"She works without a break. In summer her working day lasts from three in the morning till twilight. When she's thirty she looks fifty."'[28] Solzhenitsyn hammers at the theme of social inequality. Kostoglotov recalls his time in the army: '"I was in for seven years, as a sergeant. It was called the Workers' and Peasants' Army then. The section commander got twenty roubles a month, but the platoon commander got six hundred. And at the front they gave the officers special rations: biscuits and butter and tinned food. Who's got the bourgeois mentality?"'[29]

In Solzhenitsyn's fiction contented fatcats of the Soviet new class are the ones who take refuge from personal responsibility behind a theory of contaminating class origins, equivalent to original sin. In *Cancer Ward*, the 'professor' spreads his hands while explaining these unfortunate deviations from good Communist morality as a survival of the pre-revolutionary bourgeois mentality. The bureaucrat Rusanov concurs: '"If you dig deep into such cases you'll always find a bourgeois social origin." The young geologist Vadim agrees.

Solzhenitsyn's alter ego, Kostoglotov, reacts angrily:

'"Why, it's human greed, that's what it is, not bourgeois mentality. There were greedy people *before* the bourgeoisie and there'll be greedy people *after* the bourgeoisie."'

Kostoglotov adds rudely that their heads are stuffed with nonsense about social origins: '"That's not Marxism. It's racism."'[30]

Vasily Grossman, as we have seen, had come to much the same conclusion.

In general Western critics damned the Soviet system when it did permit publication of a critical novel, or performance of a stage play – exposed at last!—and damned the same system when it practised censorship. Much overlooked was the fact that the Union of Writers expected of its members an actively critical function operating within broadly preordained boundaries. The Soviet writer was expected to expose laziness, male chauvinism, failure to take responsibility, suspicion of new techniques, greed among factory managers and their wives, arrogance, insensitivity. Western critical attention tended to switch elastically from the critical content of published novels and plays to the issue of censorship and party control when publication or performance was refused. The rules were conveniently changed when the focus was on Western literature. Commentators took pride in the open society's patronage of its critics (the Angry Young Men and the Beats, for example), while interpreting 'angry' fiction, drama and poetry as more indicative of creative vitality than of genuine social crisis.

Soviet commentators, by contrast, seized on the 'angry' movement as reflecting – albeit in 'petit-bourgeois' form—the insoluble contradictions of capitalism. Western liberty of expression was rarely mentioned or explained in terms of an 'upsurge of democratic voices' which the 'monopolists' were powerless to suppress. Although the 'liberal mask' of monopoly capitalism was perpetually on the verge of capitulating to 'naked fascism,' somehow it never quite did.

Double standards featured prominently in the literary commentaries of the encyclopaedically well-informed but relentlessly hostile Sovietologist Robert Conquest. Conquest was inclined to accept all dark portraits of Soviet society – and added a few of his own; he also tended to emphasise the official attacks on dissident Soviet literature, rather than the liberal dimension implicit in the fact of publication. His adroit and frequent use of the word 'censured'—instead of 'criticised' – carried the odour of 'censored.' For example:

'Another poem much censured was the twenty-three-year-old Yevtushenko's "Zima Station". He describes squalor as well as happiness in his home village in Siberia.... Another story in *Literary Moscow*, "The Levers", by Yashin, depicts the brutalization of human beings as soon as they act solely as instruments of the Party. Yet another, "Visit to the Home Town", exposes the faults of the collective farm system. *Literary Gazette* described the whole thing, during the Moscow debate, by the now stereotyped phrase, "unhealthy agitation".'

Conquest continued in this vein: 'Another Soviet novel of this Thaw, *The Difficult Campaign*, by Lyubov Kabo, shows the children of a Soviet secondary school turning against various things in Soviet life: the way events are reported in the press, which one of the children calls "lies"; the chauvinism which imposes words like "City bread" and "Southern nuts" for the usual "French bread" and "American nuts"; the system of Stalin Prizes and the generally false picture given in Soviet literature.'[31]

In Conquest's commentaries the positive fact of publication is less important than 'censure' by orthodox critics. He emphasised the indignant official reactions to literary portraits of Party and Komsomol officials as 'hidebound bureaucrats.' In April 1958, *Molodoi Kommunist* complained that the figure of the Party activist now 'migrates from book to book, from play to play, from film to film, and always wearing the same silly mask of a bureaucrat, a colourless, stupid person.' If this was true, surely a symptom of progress? But no, Conquest usually found more significance in the complaints of the conservatives, not least the neo-Stalinist Surkov, 'the Party's literary chief.'

31

Vladimov: *Faithful Ruslan*

Born in Kharkov in 1931, Georgii Nikolaievich Volosevich assumed the penname 'Vladimov.' His father had been killed at the front during the war; his mother was imprisoned during the final surge of Stalin's terror in 1952. Georgii used to visit her in a camp near Leningrad and afterwards heard her stories. They were also preparing a case against Vladimov himself, but Stalin's death cut it short. After graduating from Leningrad University law school in 1953, he joined the staff of *Novyi mir*, in whose pages he acutely reviewed J. D. Salinger's *Catcher in the Rye*. Then came a seminal encounter: the essayist N. Melnikov, a *Novyi mir* author, arriving from Temirtau, where there had formerly been a camp, told Vladimov about some unfortunate camp guard dogs left to the will of fate, so emaciated they had to stand sideways to be seen; whenever a column or demonstration passed them they closed in on it by Pavlovian reflex and attacked anyone who straggled out of line.

'And I realised – there was my hero!' In the years 1963-65, Vladimov wrote a short story, 'The Dogs,' describing how a peaceful May Day demonstration was attacked and broken up by a pack of former prison camp guard dogs, who mistook it for a ragged column of prisoners. Obviously inspired by *One Day in the Life of Ivan Denisovich*, and hopeful that the new liberalism would work in favour of 'The Dogs', he offered his story to publishers including Tvardovsky, but in vain. The version which circulated in samizdat was the original one (it was widely assumed that Solzhenitsyn was the author), and soon the history of a dog became an oral legend, a stray plot to which a dozen people wrote variations (Vladimov later recalled). Vladimov then rewrote 'The Dogs' in 1965 but the second version did not get distributed in samizdat, the market was glutted. 'And again I put the manuscript away, right at the farthest corner of my desk, with no hope of coming back to it in the future.'

Solzhenitsyn records that after his open letter to the Writers' Union in 1967 he received a letter of support with one hundred signatures: 'And to crown all, there was a valiant, uncompromising letter from Georgii Vladimov, who went much

317

further than I had in his hymn to samizdat.' Interviewed by AP and *Le Monde*, on 28 August 1973, Solzhenitsyn listed Vladimov (and Voinovich) among thirteen writers 'who represent the core of contemporary Russian prose as I view it.'[1] That was praise indeed from a great writer who grudgingly dispensed it.

Not until July 1969 did Tvardovsky find it possible to publish another Vladimov story, 'Three Minutes Silence'[2] – but 'The Dogs' was considered to be beyond the pale. Vladimov's masterpiece, *Faithful Ruslan* (*Vernyi Ruslan*), was rewritten in 1974 after the émigré publisher *Possev* requested publication rights. *Vernyi Ruslan* occupied a complete issue of *Grani* (Frankfurt-am-Main) in 1975, with Vladimov's authorship acknowledged for the first time. Possev published the novella in book form. 'I was describing the camps closing down, and how the end of a terrible epoch had come – whereas that epoch was still continuing and gathering strength again.'[3] *Faithful Ruslan* was never printed in the USSR.

Andrei Sinyavsky had been living in France since 1973, where he edited the magazine *Syntaxis*. Still writing under the pseudonym Abram Tertz, in January 1980 he praised *Faithful Ruslan* in the *New York Review of Books*: 'The labor camps have disappeared, plowed over and hidden under the ground, yet they go on giving birth...strange to say, almost the only fertile soil for literature today.' Sinyavsky described Vladimov's guard dog Ruslan as the ideal Soviet hero, the 'knight of communism seeking to serve not from fear but from conscience... the golden mean, the honourable communist of whom so few are now left,' belonging to both the people and the Party. He lives (Sinyavsky continued) only to preserve order, which means that the marching columns of prisoners hold to their predetermined formation. 'In Ruslan's golden eyes the entire world is a camp. If he could (if only he could!) he would convert the entire world into the ideal condition of a camp.'[4] (In fact Sinyavsky's *The Trial Begins* contains a poignant scene in Moscow immediately following Stalin's death: 'Dogs who have lost their masters stray about the earth and sniff the air in anguish.... They wait, they are for ever waiting, gazing, longing: 'Come and feed me! Come and kick me! Beat me as much as you like...' The dogs don't want freedom, they want a Master.[5]

Robert Porter points to a key element in the canine tradition of literature: the thoughtful dog comments on human conduct from the outside, but from inside as well, since his own nature and mentality is fashioned through successive genera-tions by man.[6] (Jack London's severe stories of wolves and dogs were widely admired in the Soviet Union.) In 'The Colloquy of the Dogs,' Cervantes enlists the all-knowing gaze of dogs to depict and dismember the human condition as found in Spain c. 1600. Cervantes and Vladimov share the ability to portray the low life of tooth and claw, of animal survival in the face of human cruelty and indifference, but what Cervantes offers is essentially a conceit, detached in spirit, a flourish of highly formalized composition, beginning when Berganza and Cipión find themselves unaccountably endowed not only with human speech but with classical and biblical culture in addition to syntactical mastery of the Spanish language. What makes Vladimov's Ruslan so affecting (and modern) is that the dog struggles for understanding within the imaginative limitations of his species. Unlike Cervantes, the author is not smiling *de haut en bas*, not at all. Gogol is a more likely influence, but his *Diary of a Madman* shares a feature in common with Cervantes's 'colloquy': in both cases the dogs are overheard by a man feverish or insane. By contrast Vladimov's Ruslan is totally 'his own dog.' Another possible influence, Mikhail Bulgakov's *The Heart of a Dog*, is a tall tale, a verbose, facetious and undisciplined farce, about a Frankensteinian mutation: the dog Sharik, picked up on the street when starving, is turned into a rather uncouth and obstreperous man by means of surgery.

Vladimov's guard dog Ruslan is a genuinely tragic figure whose life experience painfully mirrors that of his country. (The name 'Ruslan' is rich in connotations of folklore and Russian national sentiment: Glinka's opera *Ruslan and Lyudmilla* is based on Pushkin's narrative poem (*poema.*)

Robert Porter points out that Vladimov's dog Ruslan is a true Stalinist because lacking any sense of the accidental or fortuitous – everything must occur on purpose, within a permanent war zone of the mind. If he passes a bakery which tempts him with its smell, then 'a secret, hateful enemy' must have put it there. The Stalin connection is even more pronounced in the original Russian text, given that the word for 'master' (*khozyain*) can also be translated as 'the boss' (as Stalin was widely known). Porter singles out the key word in the Russian text as 'divine' (*bozhestvennyy*): Ruslan sees the 'divine face' and hears the 'divine voice' of the Master (who in fact is an ordinary corporal).[7]

The literary form used by Vladimov had evidently mutated. Originally a satire, with the canine commentator as the central narrative device, in the final version Ruslan is on the contrary the subject of varying measures of authorial empathy and commentary. Commenting on Ruslan's fear and loathing of the moon, Vladimov not only turns Ruslan from subject to object, but tosses in a weight of human knowledge: 'In this sense Ruslan was a perfectly ordinary dog. The legitimate descendant of that primeval Dog who was driven by fear of darkness and hatred of moonlight towards the fire inside Man's cave and forced to exchange his freedom for loyalty.'

But on other occasions Vladimov employs the engaging device of planting in Ruslan's head perceptions which lend a canine odour to a human joke: he sees the statues of Lenin and Stalin, 'men the colour of an aluminium feeding bowl' and 'obviously acting.'[8]

Vladimov's moral awareness has been likened to Orwell's in *Animal Farm*. In both Vladimov's gulag camp and Orwell's Manor Farm, the dogs serve the rulers and oppress the masses – human prisoners in Vladimov's scenario, humble animals in Orwell's. The dog is intelligent but trained to work in a fierce pack at its masters' bidding. But whereas Orwell keeps his narrative at a distance from this pack, Vladimov studies its training and performance in detail, focussing on one canine oppressor totally at the service of the masters, and exploring how master and dog coexist in this animal's head.

Faithful Ruslan takes place during the winter of 1956-57, following the Twentieth Congress of the CPSU and Khrushchev's traumatic denunciation of Stalin. (An estimated eight million prisoners were released, and an estimated six million who had died were rehabilitated.) Whereas *One Day in the Life of Ivan Denisovich* describes a concentration camp from the perspective of one prisoner, with major naturalistic emphasis on the prisoners' daily routine, their food, outlook, habits, desires and vivid vernacular, their jokes, slang and obscenities, in ·*Faithful Ruslan* the perspective is almost wholly that of the guards (the Masters), and their dogs. The prisoners are seen only in long shot, at a distance, as an irritating and inferior rabble without any intelligible perspective of their own.

A concentration camp somewhere in Siberia has just been emptied of its prisoners. They have gone. There will be no further need for guards and no further need for guard dogs. The guards, the beloved 'Masters,' are about to shoot the redundant canines, however loyal. Ruslan's alert, golden eyes do not at first register the awful truth. Ruslan has been trained, indoctrinated, to serve the Service, to take up an alert, reactive position beside his Master's left leg. The supreme, almost orgasmic joy for Ruslan and his fellow guard dogs was to hear the command 'Get!' (*Fas*). 'The greatest reward for service was the Service (*Sluzhba*) itself.' The camp is the only world he knows and he supposes that its rules, disciplines, hierarchies, rewards and punishments apply, or should apply, everywhere and for ever.

On this fateful morning the Master comes as usual to collect Ruslan while the dog is feeding. The Master contemptuously lets a lighted cigarette butt fall into Ruslan's bowl – something which has never happened before. The dog senses this is a deliberate gesture, but he does nothing to show that he is surprised or upset. As Ruslan emerges from his kennel he is astonished to discover that the prisoners' (*lagerniki*) snow-covered huts now stand empty. The gates hang wide open in both the inner and outer fences. The watchtower has been partly dismantled. There is an eerie silence in the camp. Ruslan has seen Masters shoot their dogs – particularly when a dog stops understanding what is happening, as he himself has stopped understanding this morning. When Ruslan – a Caucasian sheepdog or Kavkazkaya ovcharka, according to Michael Glenny (Vladimov's gifted translator)—affectionately rubs his shoulder against the Master's leg, he does not receive the usual reassuring pat. When the Master draws his revolver, Ruslan understands that his own time has come. He shivers, yawns, masters himself and stands to await his fate. 'When the worst happens, an animal always takes it standing up.'

What saves him is an approaching tractor carrying a huge railway freight car and a number of free workers lacking respect for the camp guards. The driver calls cheekily, 'Hi there, soldier! What are you looking so miserable for? Sorry to finish your spell in the Service, are you?' Spotting that the Master is planning to shoot Ruslan, the worker suggests retraining the dog. The Master is forced to answer: 'Not this one. All the dogs that could be taught new tricks have been retrained already.' The Master turns back to him: 'Still here, you stupid brute? I thought I told you to get lost.'[9]

Ruslan leaves the camp, exiled, and makes his way to the local town station on the Trans-Siberian railway, where new shipments of prisoners had regularly arrived. 'He had finally realized why he had been sent away: he was meant to be there, on the platform, when the red lantern was lit and the trainload of escaped prisoners would slowly steam into the siding.' About twenty other abandoned guard dogs with the same idea have gathered on the platform.

The temptation to implant human reasoning in Ruslan's head creates problems. We are told that Ruslan had been mated by the Masters with a bitch called Alma: 'Ruslan never found out whether anything came from that spell of service...' Animals, surely, do not make that connection? And there are dubious conversations between dogs. The brutal dog Djulbars addresses Ruslan, who has discovered him working sycophantically for an ex-prisoner: '"Why get so neurotic? We've got to live, old man. Think I like having to creep to that decrepit old fool?... This isn't the camp, you know, where you got your rations and that was that."' The incorruptible Ruslan berates him: '"Have you given up the Service for this?"'[10]

Comes the occasion when Ruslan traces his former Master to a café where he is drinking with a former prisoner, the Shabby Man (*Potërtyi*). Ruslan is reminded how all the beloved Masters smell of rifle oil, tobacco, and 'strong, well-scrubbed youth.' The Master explains to Shabby Man that prisoners are prisoners forever, even if temporarily released, because what they have done is written down in a notebook. These dossiers are subject to 'perpetual preservation' (*vechnoye khraneniye*)—like the bugs and butterflies kids collect. As for the other customers in the café, 'Don't worry, we'll get them too, if need be. There's plenty about them in the records.' Ruslan, too, has a camp dossier, full of negatives: Ruslan 'was not,' 'did not take part in,' 'did not have.'[11] 'If the government thought you ought to be punished, that means there was a reason for it,' Ruslan's Master tells Shabby Man. 'They don't punish people for nothing.' Waiting for the Master to acknowledge his presence in the café, Ruslan has some further un-canine thoughts. All masters' faces were in some respects alike. 'Faces like this could only belong to the most superior breed of bipeds, to the most intelligent, priceless and select race, but he had always been curious to know one thing about them: were these faces purposely selected for the Service or was it the Service itself that made them look as they did?'[12]

But now the Master torments Ruslan, earning the indignation of the other customers in the café when he forces the dog to eat a sandwich with mustard inside – agony! The other customers are depicted as decent, sensible people while the Master, stinking of vodka and with trembling hands, is a fanatic.

Ruslan allows Shabby Man to adopt him, reassuring himself that he is really guarding Shabby Man until he is returned to the camp as a prisoner. Shabby Man is living with a large and portly lady, Stiura, who has many men; among them Ruslan scents the smell of the Chief Master, 'Comr'd Cap'n P'mission Tspeak.' Shabby Man is waiting for a letter and takes Ruslan regularly to the poste restante, but nothing comes. Can Shabby Man now return to his family? Will they want him to rise from the dead? His daughter would not have got into university if she had acknowledged that her father had been a prisoner since 1946. 'A convict's a convict; they'd never understand that I wasn't jailed for anything I did wrong.'

A train finally arrives, disgorging a new wave of strangers, cheerful, laughing people carrying suitcases, trunks, backpacks and emitting a wave of stupefying smells. Believing the Service has returned, the overjoyed Ruslan jumps up and licks faces, but in reality these are civilians who have come to build a cellulose fibre factory on the site of the old prison camp. They form a column – as the prisoners used to do. Ruslan takes up position on the right-hand side near the head of the column. Other guard dogs converge on the column from alleyways and yards, tongues hanging out. Some of the newcomers play guitars, accordions, some dance (Ruslan has never had dealings with women and ignores them.)

This brings us to the true story originally told by Melnikov to Vladimov, which inspired 'The Dog.' Presently the former guard dogs begin to attack and bite people who step out of line. Ruslan gets into intense fights with some strong and angry men. Kicked and beaten, most of the dogs retreat, but Ruslan is resolved to maintain order until the masters arrive. His back is broken in the struggle; he crawls back to the station to die. Now he remembers – quite impossibly!—how as one of a litter of puppies he was chosen by the Master, who drowned the others, his siblings, while his bitch mother offered no resistance. 'What kind of pact existed between her and the Master? There must have been some grim truth that she knew...' This truth was revealed today when the humans attacked the dogs: 'Never, never was the hatred stifled in the hearts of these dimwits.'

As he dies Ruslan imagines himself happily back in service to the Service: 'Get him, Ruslan! Get! Fas.'

Although the publication of *Faithful Ruslan* in the West in 1974-75 brought no dire consequences to the author, in 1977 Vladimov was refused an exit visa after the Norwegian publisher of *Ruslan* invited the author to the Frankfurt Book Fair. Responding with a scathing letter to the Executive Board of the Writers' Union, pouring scorn on servile bureaucrats managing literature under orders from the Party,[13] he sent back his Union membership card and announced that he had joined Amnesty International, an illegal organization in the Soviet Union (he became chairman of the Moscow branch). Prominent in support of human rights activists like Orlov, Ginzburg, and Shcharansky during their trials in 1978, in November 1980 Vladimov was summoned to Lefortovo prison and interrogated, following which he suffered a heart attack, although only forty-nine. In January 1981, he issued an open letter to 'The Released American Diplomats' (held in Iran) calling on them to support other hostages, notably Sakharov, internally exiled to Gorky. In February 1982, the KGB carried out a search of his flat lasting a full day. His wife was detained in the Lyubyanka for four hours.

In Vladimov's satirical short story, 'Pay No Attention Maestro,'[14] the KGB's young agent Fatface invades Sasha's family home in order to set up surveillance of a neighbouring celebrity writer (clearly Vladimov himself, but off-stage throughout the story). Fatface takes a keen interest in Sasha's shelves, finding *Faithful Ruslan*, Voinovich's fantasy *Chonkin*, Lipkin's *Freedom*, one or two things by Berdyaev, Zinoviev's *The Yawning Heights*, the latest Aksyonov, Fazil Iskander in an uncensored edition. Fatface tells Sasha, 'Besides, take it from me, some stages in our history need to be forgotten. Remembering them can only be a hindrance. They're of no use for understanding our present position.' The female agent of the pair tells her KGB colleague that she adores the cabaret star and poet Vystosky: 'It's just that I feel a total sexual attraction for him.' The agents spend time making provocative and facetious telephone calls to leading dissidents or their families: 'It's Academician Sakharov here. What am I ringing for? Well, to say how amazed I am by your husband's outrageous behaviour...'[15]

In 'Pay No Attention, Maestro,' the writer under KGB observation has been thrown out of the Writers' Union and belongs to the 'fourth generation,' as it is called. He used to be published (like Vladimov himself) in *Novyi mir* and now is visited every three months by a local policeman who asks what money he is living on, implicitly threatening him with breach of the parasitism laws. The KGB is monitoring by audio-cassette the progress of the writer's new book. The story then pitches into cruel farce as the occupants of the flat call in the local militia on the grounds that the couple claiming to be KGB agents may be thieves or spies, since they engage in anti-Soviet jokes and talk about Italian leather goods, etc. Angry militiamen arrive, shove the KGB couple up against the wall and slap the girl's buttocks. Later the KGB couple start having sex in Sasha's room. They explain that 'ideology' is the reason for their operations, the objective being to keep the writer under surveillance 'all his life' (an echo of the 'perpetual preservation' of dossiers in *Faithful Ruslan*). Vladimov mocks the minute attention the KGB are paying to the daily activities and habits of dissident writers, photographing their arrivals and departures, their exchanges of signed books, building up files about habits, weaknesses, medication, what sort of women are preferred, drinking habits, whether mentioned on foreign radio stations, the movement of manuscripts.

When published in the West in 1983, Vladimov's satire enraged the KGB: as he put it, they went 'completely bestial' (*ozvereli*), broke into his flat a second time and took the typewriters. In May 1983, he and his family were allowed to emigrate. From 1984 to 1986 Vladimov was chief editor of *Grani*, but acrimony led to his resignation. Even in the late Gorbachev era of *perestroika*, *Literaturnaia gazeta* published two uncompromising attacks on him in January and September 1987, depicting him as a mercenary of the CIA who had been expelled from the Writers' Union. A familiar anti-Semitism surfaced during these attacks: 'Volosevich was his father's name, Zeifman his mother's, but the little son liked neither of these, and when he started out on the path of a writer he called himself Vladimov...'[16]

Part 5

The American Novel and the New Politics

32

Commentary: Fiction, the New Journalism, and the Postmodern

In *The New Journalism* (1975), Tom Wolfe signalled a recent and significant shift from fiction to direct reportage. Yet the leading novelists of the mid-century had far from turned their backs on pressing social issues – witness the fiction of Greene, Bellow, Roth, Mailer, Patrick White, Malamud, Gordimer, Styron, Baldwin, Capote. What advanced the thrust of the new journalism was a growing feeling that reality was constantly outstripping invention; real life was often larger than imagined life. When *Esquire* put out a collection of its best work from the sixties, it omitted fiction entirely. Harold Hayes, the magazine's editor, explained that events during that period 'seemed to move too swiftly to allow the osmotic process of art to keep abreast'.[1]

According to Wolfe, the novel was losing ground to the new journalism mainly because it had wilfully abandoned the terrain demanded by the public – vivid realism. Novelists had made 'a disastrous miscalculation' over the past twenty years about the indispensability of realism. 'The introduction of realism into literature by people like Richardson, Fielding, and Smollett was like the introduction of electricity into machine technology. It was *not* just another device. It raised the state of the art to a new magnitude. The effect of realism on the emotions was something that had never been conceived of before.' In Wolfe's view, the New Journalism took off (in book form) not because the reading public was tired of fiction-as-invention, of made-up stories, of the 'imagination' – but because the modernist novel had lost its way, and forgotten the basic electricity.[2]

Under the influence of the Depression (he continued), the American novel had experienced its greatest phase of social realism. Only after the Second World War did the 'European mythic vogue' arrive and gradually impose its canon. By the time of writing (said Wolfe) almost all serious American novelists were university educated and looking to such models as Beckett, Pinter,

Kafka, Hesse, Borges, Zamyatin. The upshot has been fictional characters with no specific history, no background or specific class or even nationality, acting out their fates in timeless, elemental terrain, speaking, if they spoke at all, in short, mechanical sentences, responding to inexplicable forces and dreads. Wolfe calls these writers the 'neo-Fabulists.'

The new journalism was practised as extensively by proven novelists and essayists as by professional reporters, for example Truman Capote, James Baldwin, Norman Mailer, Tom Wolfe, Susan Sontag, and Mary McCarthy. The new style of reporter-centred journalism borrowed heavily from the techniques of realist fiction. Dwight Macdonald discerned in Tom Wolfe and others a new 'parajournalism,' a 'bastard form, having it both ways, exploiting the factual authority of journalism and the atmospheric license of fiction.' Even so, throughout the sixties and seventies writers like Mailer and E. L. Doctorow sought to straddle the frontiers between fiction, journalism and history, addressing Cold War contests while commanding large audiences.

However one defines 'postmodernism,' one thing is clear: the traditional, humanistic claims of literature and art to truth and value were now under challenge from within the academy. Traditionally writers (whether 'romantic,' 'realist' or 'modernist') had had faith in the constitutive power of the imagination and the intellect,[3] but such faith was out of fashion.

Irving Howe's essay, 'Mass Society and Postmodern Fiction' (1959)[4] was published a year before Harry Levin used the same concept of the postmodern to designate an 'anti-intellectual undercurrent' threatening the humanism and enlightenment characteristic of modernism. Postmodernism took off with a vengeance in the 1960s. As one commentator puts it, 'Since then the notion of postmodernism has become key to almost any attempt to capture the specific and unique qualities of contemporary activities in art and architecture, in dance and music, in literature and theory.'[5] (But whatever assault postmodernism might initially seek to inflict on such articles of faith, in the end they had to be recuperated in one form or another short of everyone going out of business.)

In the lapel buttonhole of this challenge was pinned a flamboyant denial that language could ever meaningfully convey anything – outside of itself. 'All writing, all composition, is construction,' declared the much-quoted Robert Scholes, 'We do not imitate the world, we construct versions of it. There is no mimesis, only poesis. No recording, only constructing.'[6] In the jargon, no 'signifier' could refer to a non-linguistic reality. To believe otherwise – as on the whole the naïve world had hitherto done – was to fall into the error of what Jacques Derrida called 'logocentricity.' Stock market shares in esoteric jargon shot up. Here, for example, is a sub-heading formulated by a lively exponent of postmodernism, Marcel Cornis-Pope: 'Relocating Postmodern Innovation: Contemporary Culture's Critical Interloctutor or Incommensurate "Other".'[7]

Obviously this new, outspoken challenge to language's capacity to tell us anything beyond itself and its own constructions would surely drive a wedge between the new criticism and political commitment. Strangely, it didn't. Uncle Sam, for example, took a beating in texts admired by postmodernists – as if the words 'Uncle Sam' could, after all, actually signify something beyond the words themselves. Likewise a fictional 'Richard Nixon' could denote a real version. In theory, postmodernist critics held that history lacked pattern and rationally intelligible meaning because history was nothing other than historiography and therefore mere strings of words. Consequently (they said) literature could do nothing but expose its own inability to invest history with an ordering, shaping imaginative coherence.[8] Scholes again: 'Now we know that fiction is about other fiction, is criticism in fact, or metafiction. And we know that criticism is about the impossibility of anything being about life, really, or even about fiction, or finally about anything. Criticism has taken the very idea of "aboutness" away from us. It has taught us that language is tautological...'[9] But evidently not when used by Scholes! And evidently criticism left intact one privileged 'about' – namely 'about criticism.' Obviously the temptation is there to dismiss all this as pure Ubu Roi nonsense, an aberrant craze; such a temptation is scarcely diminished by the discovery that when the postmodernists or advocates of 'surfiction' discussed politically congenial fiction, novels which ruptured the hegemonic white male consensus of 'Amerika,' then strangely criticism recovered its capacity – and literature's capacity—to talk 'about' politics and history. External 'referentiality' swept back through the nursery window whenever Peter Pan presented himself as Che Guevara. American revisionist culture gravitated towards the grim profile of 'Amerika' as the later, post-Kennedy Cold War diversified into new channels of political concern—fear of the bomb, the Vietnam War, space wars – as well as reconsideration of Allied bombing during World War II, including Hiroshima.

A major difficulty besetting postmodernist criticism was the definition of 'literature.' While some voices might claim that all language, every kind of discourse including journalism, is incapable of rendering an external or pre-existing reality,[10] others held that literature differs from 'everyday language' by its 'unwillingness to claim innocence' about the possibility of 'unmediated expression.'[11] By this approach 'literature' must be, surely, a particular highbrow genre willing to 'problematize itself,' built out of 'self-deconstructive' language calling attention to its own fictiveness. This contrasts with language which assumes a naïve confidence in its own (mythical) ontological authority: 'No language is purely mimetic or referential,' writes J. Hillis Miller, 'not even the most utilitarian speech. The specifically literary form of language, however... calls attention to this fact, while at the same time allowing for its own inevitable misreading as a "mirroring of reality".'[12] But this word 'literary' – is it conveniently granted immunity from the mimetic frailty of language in general, is it gold-plated in hard meaning? Is 'popular literature' a contradiction in terms? More serious perhaps, does the long heritage of world literature since the Greeks, and the entire realist-naturalist heritage, cease to fit the name 'literature' because it failed to 'allow' for its own inevitable misreading?

But, as said, postmodernism tends to forget its more extreme theories when convenient. Cornis-Pope, for example, addresses American postmodernist novelists as if it were theoretically possible not only to write fiction *about* a real cold war but actually to affect it: 'Pynchon's and Coover's novels have created significant rifts in the Cold War ideologies, inserting in them the other's retrieved perspective'[13] ('the other' as used here is a post-Sartrean term referring to an alienated entity like the poor, the blacks, the reds). When Cornis-Pope gets going on 'otherness' and 'alterity,' one detects that the vocabulary is in pursuit of a New Left outlook: 'Coover's protagonists seek out these excluded "others" because they function as expanded mirrors for the self, promising the experience of lost alterity.'[14] At the same time, Cornis-Pope exemplifies the post-1960 tendency to view 'the Cold War' as essentially an internal American growth or tumour, with the Russians scarcely accorded walk-on parts: 'Coover's novel foregrounds the confrontational narratives of the Cold War,' writes Cornis-Pope, 'tracing their origin back to a Manichean collective ideology embodied in Uncle Sam – the novel's official reflector and "tyrant Other".'[15] Indeed on page 8 of *The Public Burning* Uncle Sam declares, 'I tell you, we want elbow-room – the continent – the whole continent – and nothin' but the continent.' As for Communism, the great force of 'alterity,' it turns out to be no more than 'the ungraspable Phantom,' 'made of nothing solid.'[16] We therefore have a school of politically dissident postmodern novelists challenging (as one critic puts it) 'hegemonic values – technocratic, bureaucratic, militaristic, business-oriented,' and challenging 'the polarizing imagination inherited from the Age of Reason and the hypercompetitive animus of capitalism.'[17]

As Cornis-Pope tells it, 'postmodern theories and practices played a catalytic role' in the 'breakup of the Cold War structure' right through to the *Glasnost* era. He asks why 'innovative fiction' (a favourite term) 'has often been misconstrued as a self-indulgent formalism rather than as a meaningful response to a historical and literary crisis.' A large part of the answer, surely, must reside in critical claims that fiction is essentially about itself, its own development, its own gymnastics, and that the postmodern novel must steer clear of 'the factuality of history.'[18] Authentic fiction writers of our day evidently 'believe that reality as such does not exist, or exists only in its fictionalized version.'[19] One must at least tentatively agree with the late-Marxist critics who reject postmodernism as a version of recent history fragmented, fabricated, imploded and depleted. Cornis-Pope blames these negative verdicts on 'our guilty conscience about artistic innovation.'[20]

All this said, a new wave of post-sixties American fiction, including political fiction, faced exceptionally sharp choices of genre and style, each hard to reconcile with the other, from Tom Wolfe and the new journalists who revered 'realism' to the new fabulists developing a fiction rooted in myth, fable, fantasy and 'magical' language: Kurt Vonnegut, Jr., Robert Coover, Thomas Pynchon, Donald Barthelme, and John Barth. The novelist – often an academic—was beginning to play the role of critic to his or her own novel – a practice much abetted by changing critical practice in the university literature faculties. Fiction inspired by self-referral appealed to a younger generation of American critics and students impressed by the structuralist and semiotic theories of Lucien Goldmann, Roland Barthes, Jacques Derrida. Metafiction was now favoured by departments of comparative literature, cultural studies, and media studies. A novel which deconstructs itself is doubly deconstructable – a feast for critics armoured in theory. The New Criticism tradition of an inverted, self-referring literature had passed from conservative into radical hands; from those who loved the Old South or Olde England to those who wanted the planet swept clean of multinational conglomerates.

33

Mailer: *The Armies of the Night*

At the age of seventeen, Norman Mailer had discovered what he called 'my naturalist heritage'—Dos Passos, James T. Farrell's *Studs Lonigan* trilogy and John Steinbeck's *The Grapes of Wrath.*[1] The impact of Hemingway, too, pervades Mailer's first published novel, the best-selling *The Naked and the Dead* (1948). The subsequent novella, *Barbary Shore* (1951), marks a deliberate break with epic muscularity, opting for Kafka rather than Hemingway. Here the versatile Mailer offers an allegory on the age of suspicion, the great fear taking hold of America at the time of the Korean War and the Congressional Inquisition. He had joined the Henry Wallace campaign and taken part in the Waldorf conference, but a significant shift occurred in his political and literary outlook, partly due to the influence of his Polish-born friend, Jean Malaquais, translator of *The Naked and the Dead* as *Les Nus et les Morts*. Malaquais's neo-Trotskyist orientation surfaces clearly in *Barbary Shore*.

Compact, claustrophobic and elliptical, the novel also registers a debt to Kafka, Beckett and the absurd. Mailer opts for a first-person narrative, a form generally indicating a shift from the objective to the psychological and, often, to the 'outsider' or 'marginal' character. 'Probably I was in the war,' begins the voice of Mikey Lovett, signalling not only a personal identity crisis but also, by inference, a historical identity crisis as well: whose war had it been? Clamped together in the same Brooklyn boarding house, each locked into his own secret history, are Lovett (before the war, a dedicated militant of a Trotskyist organization, dreaming of the Petrograd revolution); McLeod, who works in a department store as a window dresser, has a mania about neatness, reads a lot, and will reveal that he joined the CP when twenty-one and left it when forty, four years previously; thirdly, Hollingsworth, the soft, mild, nervous inhabitant of a messy room, who works as a clerk on Wall Street (but does he?), is a snob and yearns for dirty books. When he asks McLeod if he is a Bolshevist and if his allegiance is to a foreign power, McLeod replies "'on the whole, yes".' Hollingsworth makes a list of McLeod's 'admissions' – such as being an atheist, blowing up churches, being against free enterprise and Wall Street, advocating the murder of the president and Congress using poison, supporting the rise of colored people.[2]

Lovett, who works in unskilled jobs and wants to write a novel, indignantly denounces Soviet purges, the Pact, the perversion of socialism. McLeod answers, "'What a stinking two-penny left deviationist you are.... Have you any idea how many revolutionaries have to be devoured to improve the lot of a common man one bloody inch?'" McLeod admits he was once a Balkan Communist involved in arrests, murders, betrayal; he also reveals he found he could recover his passport if he went to work as an informer for the organization Hollingsworth works for. Lovett suspects that McLeod still works for the Party, otherwise why didn't they dispose of him? The narrative yields to longer and longer monologues in a general climate of paranoia.[3]

According to Norman Podhoretz, *Barbary Shore* was a flop both with the broad public and with highbrows: 'By 1951 the modernism of *Barbary Shore* was beginning to seem as dated as the naturalism of *The Naked and the Dead*.... Trotskyism, too, seemed old hat by 1951.' Invited by *Partisan Review* in 1952 to take part in the influential symposium 'our country and our culture,' Mailer accused Hemingway, Dos Passos, Faulkner, Farrell, and Steinbeck of travelling from alienation to 'varying degrees of acceptance, if not outright proselytizing for the American Century.'[4] But he himself was already in the grip of a quite different conversion – he later explained that every time he tried to think about Marxism he found himself thinking about sex and murder: 'My conscious intelligence, as I've indicated, became obsessed by the Russian revolution. But my unconscious was much more interested in other matters: murder, suicide, orgy, psychosis, all the themes I discussed in *Advertisements* [*for Myself*].'[5]

His repudiation of all 'ideological' thinking in favour of existentialism (Hip) coincided with a marked shift from fiction to journalism. In 'The White Negro' (1956), which first appeared in Irving Howe's journal, *Dissent*, Mailer argued that Marxism had failed in application because its roots were in the 'scientific narcissism we inherited from the nineteenth century,' 'the rational mania that consciousness could stifle instinct.' The liberated individual, the hipster, must reject all taboos, must give absolute priority to the Self over society.[6] The hipster's demand for immediate gratification would, he predicted, carry the future.

The ensuing decade, the sixties, witnessed a cosmic shift of intellectual emphasis from the individual's needs to collective urgencies, from psycho-solutions to mass action. While a novelist-reporter like Mailer, a pioneer of the ego-laden 'new journalism,' author of 'The White Negro' (1959) and *The Presidential Papers* (1963), could still earn big money from commercial publishing, he had to keep pace with an insurgent generation of students bent on collective action against the Vietnam War, inspired by guerrilla insurrections in Latin America and Asia against the *pax americana*. Caught in the stresses of overt generation conflict, young Mailer would find himself no longer young. In *The Armies of the Night* (1968) a student from California addresses the over-thirties through a megaphone: 'You want to come along with us, that's okay, that's your thing, but we've got our thing, and we're going to do it alone whether you come with us or not.'[7]

Out of these concerns came a semi-fictional grappling with the most urgent political question of the time. Using a version of the parodic vernacular, the novella *Why Are We in Vietnam?* (1967) sets hardhat America among rugged Texans, the hot rodders, hunters, cattlemen, oil riggers, insurance agents and their inevitable sexual hang-ups. In hot-fanned, semi-Beat, half-hippie prose with perhaps a debt to William Burroughs, he sprays out his puns (Norloins for New Orleans). Enter eighteen-year-old D.J., a hipster into McLuhan, electronics, the media. His father Rusty, a big corporation executive, belongs to a joke-list of Texan clubs, causes, associations and is humorously endowed with all of the standard right-wing prejudices and concomitant fears, generational, regional, racial, sexual. Father and son go hunting in Alaska. Big Luke, a professional hunter and leader of the expedition, also enlists amphibious planes and heli-copters – known as 'Mr Cop Turd' – which set the wealthy hunters 200 yards downwind from a grizzly. The bear charges, things go dangerously wrong. At the end of the allegory, D.J. (part Huck Finn, part Holden Caulfield, disciple of Burroughs, rating himself the quickest cerebral gun since McLuhan) announces that he and his friend Tex are off 'to see the wizard in Vietnam.'

Mailer comments in *The Armies of the Night* that 'the true war party in America was in all the small towns, even as the peace parties had to collect in the cities and suburbs.'[8] His next port of call was these peace parties, engaged in besieging the Pentagon in the fall of 1967. *The Armies of the Night* – a phrase taken from Matthew Arnold's poem 'Dover Beach'—carries the arresting sub-title: 'History as a Novel. The Novel as History'—but the book (Pulitzer prize, National Book Award) is not exactly history and by no means a novel, though the spirit of Cervantes's Don Quixote often surfaces as Mailer, Chomsky, Ginsberg, Lowell, Macdonald, Goodman and other knights of the intellect sign statements implicating themselves legally in aiding and abetting draft resistance.[9]

Military police are barring access to the Pentagon. Mailer darts past an MP and begins to run: 'It was his dark pinstripe suit, his vest, the maroon and blue regimental tie, the part in his hair, the barrel chest, the early paunch – he must have looked like a banker himself, a banker gone ape!' By insistent demand, he gets himself arrested but does not relish the physical fury of the moment and shouts, 'Take your hands off me, can't you see? I'm not resisting arrest.'[10] The event, as he explains, was somehow mixed up with making an extended portrait for BBC television; in short, for making history on-camera. Appearing before the commissioner, he pleaded nolo contendere and was given a heavier than usual sentence because he was a responsible citizen and an influential writer.

'The New Left,' he concluded, 'was drawing its political aesthetic from Cuba...you created the revolution first and learned from it, learned of what your revolution might consist and where it might go out of the ultimate truth of the way it presented itself to your experience.' Even so, the World War II veteran was worried by what he saw of the fancy-dress hippies: 'They were close to being assembled from all the intersections between history and the comic book, between legend and television, the Biblical archetypes and the movies.' They had 'promiscuously, wantonly, heedlessly...gorged on LSD and consumed God knows what essential marrows of history...' And yet (he reported) 'Mailer's final allegiance' was with the hippie villains against the 'corporation-land villains who were destroying the promise of the present in their self-righteousness and greed and secret lust (often unknown to themselves) for some sexo-technological variety of neo-fascism.'[11] *The Armies of the Night* provides masterly reporting, but novels were the least favoured literary category for this unbookish generation. Movies yes, theatre yes, street theatre, carnival, commedia dell'arte, all immediate, tactile, sensual, communal, here-and-now—but novels were cold between the hands, odourless, designed for elderly and middle-aged book club subscribers, to be read in a state of torpor.

Mailer ends with a rhetorical metaphor: he sees America as a pregnant woman about to give birth either to 'the most fearsome totalitarianism the world has ever known' or to a 'babe of a new world brave and tender, artful and wild.'[12] What followed rapidly was Lyndon Johnson's capitulation to unpopularity, the hectic street scenes described in Mailer's *Miami and the Siege of Chicago* (1968), the election of Nixon as president, continuation of the war, the shooting of student protestors at Kent State University by National Guardsmen, no doubt kindred spirits to the phalanxes of blank-eyed military police described in *The Armies of the Night*.

34

Fiction and the Rosenbergs:
E. L. Doctorow and Robert Coover

Out of the major concerns of the Cold War came a novel which reconfirmed the potentialities of political fiction in an era when the postmodern was already pressing its claims on modernism. This was E. L. Doctorow's *The Book of Daniel* (1971).[1] Lecturing at Harvard after the turn of the millennium, Doctorow offered a credo: 'I believe so completely in fiction that I regard it as a mega-discipline, one that incorporates all others, blurs the genres, whips together facts and imagination, and at its best reasserts the authority of the single unaffiliated mind to render the world.'[2]

The literary structure of the novel is complex but never baffling. It purports to be written in 1967-68 by its eponymous hero, Daniel Isaacson, eldest child of Paul and Rochelle Isaacson, executed for espionage in 1954. Doctorow originally embarked on the novel using a third-person narrative and the past tense, but after 150 pages he began again: 'it turned out Daniel was talking and he was sitting in the library at Columbia University and then I had my book.'[3] That was exactly right in terms of form and content—the voice of Daniel, the agonised orphan of the fifties, reporting through the freewheeling, iconoclastic tones of the sixties. In critical terms, the subject of the story thus doubles as the subject of the telling; the two 'I's' are not necessarily identical. From the first line Daniel subverts homology by referring to himself sometimes as 'Daniel Lewin' (the surname comes from his foster parents), and sometimes as 'I.'

Although young Daniel cannot plausibly shoulder the cargo of historical information and research which Doctorow means to unload, the author seeks to persuade the reader that by the age of five Daniel has stored up a prodigious archive of observation for future reference: 'Of the war I remember some tin cans flattened for a "scrap drive". The idea that bacon fat could be turned into bullets.... I remember thick arrows with shanks stamped on maps in the newspapers and magazines. I remember the Four Freedoms. I remember what ration stamps looked like, and the stickers A, B or C on the windows of automobiles.' (This 'scrapbook' effect – picture album history—presages the listings in Doctorow's novel *Ragtime*.) Though only five at the time, Daniel remembers the words of listed songs, including the Red Army Chorus singing 'Meadowland' on a 78rpm album, FDR riding up the Grand Concourse in an open car 'without a hat although the day was chill.' The history novelist may be anxious to convey how different things had been 'then': he crowds his canvas with genre detail, idioms of speech, clothes, housing, furnishings, tools of the trade, prices, food, means of transport, popular music, prevalent diseases, available medicine – all period stuff. Ideally the observant Daniel would have been eight or ten in 1945, but the Rosenberg chronology and the imperatives of the Cold War timetable ruled out any gerrymandering – although the narrative suffers from chronological inconsistencies and anachronisms which do not appear to be deliberate.[4]

Doctorow takes us out of the Rosenbergs in order to lead us back into them; he changes their names, their key dates, their children, their New York address, and maybe their tastes in clothes, in order to give himself space in which to render faithfully their passions, commitments, and motives as Jews, New Yorkers, leftists and would-be honorary heroes of the Soviet Union. He creates a son and a daughter (the Isaacsons) instead of two sons (the Rosenbergs). He creates a daughter who commits suicide (Susan Isaacson) instead of two sons who did not. Clearly he had the living Greenglasses within his sights when he chose to replace David Greenglass, Ethel Rosenberg's brother, with the fictional family dentist Mindish in the role of nemesis.

Daniel is aware of course that his family is history, that his parents were electrocuted because of the Cold War, the Red Scare, fear of Soviet Russia, and clearly he has never quite made up his mind about their innocence. Highly self-righteous and combative, Paul and Rochelle Isaacson had never indicated to their young children Daniel and Susan what they had done, beyond the fact that they had done nothing wrong – or simply nothing. Whether responding to the young Daniel's questions, or whether overheard by him in conversation, Paul and Rochelle simply present themselves as victims of the witch hunts and of the family dentist Mindish's lies, his meanness, envy and lust. Discussing Doctorow's work in 1994, the literary critic James Wood remarked that the Rosenbergs 'were convicted on no evidence for treason in 1951 and electrocuted.' Such utterances raise the possibility that the novel could well lead the unbriefed reader to that conclusion: 'convicted on no evidence.'[5]

Daniel Isaacson describes his mother: 'Rochelle had a profound distaste for the common man. Her life was a matter of taking pains to distinguish herself from her neighbors.' 'My parents associated with interesting people. That was her phrase.... They were not doomed by their shabby apartment buildings. They were not imprisoned by their miserable wages. They were not conditioned to accept slavery. Their minds were free. They had ideas. They met and discussed and contributed money to a dream future.' 'So if they walked around nude or shopped for the best meat at the lowest price, or joined the Party, it was to know the truth, to be up on it.... They rushed after self-esteem. If you could recognize a Humphrey Bogart movie for the cheap trash it was, you had culture.'[6]

Daniel recalls his father Paul Isaacson – owner of a radio repair shop like Julius Rosenberg, and endowed with the same long legs and skinny frame : 'He'd find me reading the back of the cereal box at breakfast, and break the ad down and show what it appealed to.... There were foods one didn't eat, like bananas, because they were the fruit of some notorious exploitation. There were companies we boycotted because of their politics or labor history.... He didn't like General Motors because they were owned by Du Pont, and Du Pont had cartel agreements with I. G. Farben of Nazi Germany.' Further: 'Whatever he did had such personal force that it seemed offensive. Like sticking his tongue out to examine it in the mirror.... He didn't keep his razor clean. He left blotches of gloppy shaving cream in the sink.... He left towels wadded up. You knew he'd been there.... Even his breathing was noisy. Bending over those radios.... Smoking one of those cigars that didn't go with his face, he studied his son like a psychologist through a pane of glass.'[7]

It is the year 1967. Daniel Isaacson, his nineteen-year-old wife Phyllis, and their baby son are living in two rooms on 115th Street between Broadway and Riverside Drive. Daniel is working on a dissertation at Columbia for Dr Sukenick, a history professor, based on a wide variety of sources, voices, legal documents, stories, invented scenes, reordered conversations, newspaper articles, excerpts from history books, notes, self-admonitions. Daniel belongs to the New Left culture and addresses people as 'man.' He is often very explicit about sex; liberal use of 'fuck' or 'fucking' is a mark of liberation.

When the novel opens Daniel has recently suffered his younger sister Susan's withering scorn because he does not entirely go along with her plan to invest their trust funds in an Isaacson Peace Foundation. Daniel recoils from the publicity, the loss of the shelter afforded by the adopted name Lewin; he also senses that the Isaacson Case means little or nothing to the youth culture of the sixties. Distraught, desperate to mobilize young radical opinion in support of her parents' innocence (in effect, to undo the trauma of her awful childhood), Susan Isaacson tears into Daniel, calls him a 'piece of shit,' and reminds him that 'My mother and father were murdered.' Sororial dismissal follows: 'Go back to the stacks, Daniel. The world needs another graduate student...jerk off behind a book.'[8] This is followed by a brief, cruel letter of total rejection and by her attempted suicide with a razor in the toilet of a Howard Johnson's. Daniel and the Lewins find her incarcerated in a hospital mental unit. 'They're still fucking us,' she says. 'Goodbye, Daniel. You get the picture.'

The boy Daniel belongs to the 1940s and early 1950s, but the adult Daniel, whose voice prevails, is a product of one of the most abrupt and influential cultural changes in American history. The general patriotic assumptions, the respect for presidents, generals, and the FBI, which had prevailed in the Norman Rockwell fifties, had been subverted with remarkable rapidity by iconoclastic scepticism, disgust at war, contempt for authority: now was the hour of Roy Lichtenstein and Andy Warhol. Daniel Isaacson takes J. D. Salinger's celebrated novel, *Catcher in the Rye* (1951), to be a bridge between the two cultures, the seed of subversion; the poetry and performance of Allen Ginsberg is another bridge.

Daniel visits a prominent hippie-Digger, Artie Sternlicht. When Susan got to know Artie she told him she had a politically undeveloped brother. 'She made it sound like undescended testicles,' Artie tells Daniel, adding: 'You want to know what was wrong with the old American Communists? They were into the system. They wore ties. They held down jobs. They put people up for President. They thought politics is something you do at a meeting. When they got busted they called it tyranny. They were Russian tit suckers. Russia! Who's free in Russia? All the Russians want is steel up everyone's ass. Where's the Revolution in Russia?' Artie continues over a joint: 'The American Communist Party set the Left back fifty years. I think they worked for the FBI. That's the only explanation. They were conspiratorial. They were invented by J. Edgar Hoover. They were his greatest invention.'[9] And more: 'Your folks [the Isaacsons but really the Rosenbergs] didn't know shit. The way they handled themselves at their trial was pathetic. I mean they played it by their rules. The government's rules. You know what I mean? Instead of standing up and saying fuck you, do what you want, I can't get an honest trial anyway with you fuckers – they made motions, they pleaded innocent, they spoke only when spoken to, they played the game.'

The fictional Artie Sternlicht doubtless owes something to the Yippies Abbie Hoffman and Jerry Rubin, who wrote: 'The 1950s were the turning point in the history of Amerika. Those who grew up before the 1950s live today in the mental world of Nazism, concentration camps, economic depression and Communist dreams Stalinized.... Kids who grew up in the post-1950s live in a world of supermarkets, color TV, commercial, guerrilla war, international media, psychedelics, rock'n'roll and moon walks.... This generation gap is the widest in history. The pre-1950s generation have nothing to teach the post-1950s.'[10] Rubin's *Do It!* was published a year before Doctorow's novel.

For Julius and Ethel Rosenberg, Stalin's Russia was indeed the future. For the New Left generation—who identified the peasant-guerrilla communism of Cuba and Vietnam as virgin springs of popular insurrection free of Soviet bureaucratism and elaborately braided epaulettes—Russian communism was old hat. The New Left was libertarian, theatrical, flamboyant, putting performance above perfected philosophy; it did not trust curricula or exams; unlike the Old Left it did not believe in hierarchy or the economic necessity of personal competition. The Old Left held street rallies and marches but it did not occupy university buildings or attempt to levitate the Pentagon. Even Commies who committed espionage were respectable, law-abiding citizens who wore hats, believed in curricula and exams, fostered respect for parents and deplored narcotics. Life was a ladder. The Party knew best.

Doctorow inevitably reflected modernist doubt about 'real history' and the relationship of text to 'message.' *The Book of Daniel* offers three endings: 'For my third ending, I had hoped to discuss some of the questions posed by this narrative. However, just a moment ago, when I was sitting here writing the last page, someone came though announcing that the library is closed.'[11] Daniel is interrupted by a student who insists that the Columbia University Library is closed because all students have been liberated.

Can the novelist be faulted for having walked past the real subjects presented by journalists, polemicists and lawyers examining the Rosenberg case (albeit without access to the closed Rosenberg files held by the Department of Justice)? Did the Rosenbergs fail to confront their own guilt or did they continue to lie in the service of the Cause? And what about the accusations of corruption directed by their supporters at the state and everyone involved in the prosecution? Daniel is nagged by doubt about his parents' innocence, but his doubts are largely resolved by the euphoric cleansing power of New Left ideology. By and large, Doctorow does not offer the reader a license to disagree with his fictional narrator Daniel.

Dissident Soviet novelists had no choice but to speak into the void left by Soviet historians. By contrast, the American novelist cheerfully cites revisionist historians (W. A. Williams, D. Horowitz, etc.) on general responsibility for the Cold War – yet there are no acknowledgments of real commentaries on the actual Rosenbergs, only fictitious books on the 'Isaacson case': 'Two support the verdict and the sentence, two support the verdict but not the sentence, which they find harsh, and two deny the justice either of the sentence or the verdict.'[12]

'Jack Fein,' a veteran reporter for the *New York Times*, writes a reassessment piece to mark the tenth anniversary of the execution. Talking to Daniel in a luncheonette, Fein seems to represent Doctorow's point of view: his conclusion is that the Isaacsons had been up to something, maybe worth a five-year sentence, but not atomic espionage:'I don't know – your parents and Mindish had to have been into some goddam thing. They acted guilty. They were little neighbourhood commies probably with some kind of third-rate operation that wasn't of use to anyone except maybe it made them feel important.' Fein goes on: 'The case against them was nothing. Talking Tom's word as a convicted spy wasn't worth shit.' ('Talking Tom' is the fictional Thomas Flemming, who fits the real figure of Harry Gold in the Rosenberg trial, but Gold's evidence, as it turns out, was substantially correct.) Jack Fein continues: 'Even before the execution, when the heat was on to commute the sentence, they [the U.S. government] dropped these hints about evidence they had and couldn't use in the interest of national security.... There's a report all right, and the reason it's classified is because it favors the defense. Shit, between the FBI and the CP your folks never had a chance.' But Fein goes on to contradict himself: 'I don't believe either that the U.S. Attorney, and the Judge, and the Justice Department and the President of the United States conspired against them.... In this country people don't get picked out of a hat to be put on trial for their lives.' But if the government really did withhold evidence 'classified because it favors the defense,' then the government did indeed conspire, and monstrously.[13]

Fein is confused because Doctorow could not reconcile the contrary strands of probability. Another stab at the truth of the matter is attempted in a conversation between Daniel and his foster-father and guardian, Robert Lewin, whose view of Soviet atomic science so closely resembles Jack Fein's that we may not be entirely out of order in attributing it to Doctorow: 'In those days, this was years before the sputnik thing, it was necessary to downgrade the Russians' science. People who knew something about these things didn't make that mistake.... And when they got it [when the Russians got the bomb] the only alternative to admitting our bankruptcy of leadership and national vision was to find conspiracies.... Well, if you're the Bureau you have on hand a resource of files, especially of known left-wing activists. That is what you go to first, your own files.'[14]

This is the moderate voice of conspiracy theory. It is less stridently accusatory and conspiratorial than the books vindicating the Rosenbergs by William Reuben or John Wexley, but it ends up in the same bag: conspiracy to pervert the truth. At every juncture Lewin is mistaken. He does not mention the crucial Fuchs case in England.[15] Without the atomic physicist Klaus Fuchs's confession the trail might never have led to Rosenberg, yet Fuchs is mentioned only once in the entire novel but not named. The Soviet spy ring in Canada also passes unremarked. In Lewin's purblind wisdom, the Russians simply did not need to engage in espionage. They had the required science. People like Lewin prided themselves on their ability to see through the lies foisted on the brainwashed public by the government, the press barons, big business, etc. Daniel's studies as a Columbia student tend to confirm this outlook: 'We may tentatively define Cold War as a condition of incipient bomb-falling hostility by which the United States proposed to apply such pressure upon Soviet Russia that its government would collapse and the power of the Bolsheviks be destroyed. Citations available from Kennan (also known as Mr. X), Acheson, Dulles.'[16]

Later in the narrative, Daniel seems to entertain the theory of 'the other couple' sometimes aired in the Rosenberg case – that Mindish/Greenglass named the Isaacsons/Rosenbergs in order to protect another Communist couple thought to be working under cover, thus diverting the FBI away from people of real value. When, in a brilliantly imagined scene, Daniel finally catches up with Mindish's daughter Linda in a house off the Pacific Coast Highway, she makes mincemeat of the 'other couple' theory. We may infer that she is sincere about the guilt of the Isaacsons and how they landed her father in jail because she furiously stubs out her cigarette and says 'Oh my God, oh my God,' and stands up and smooths her blouse and skirt: 'Papa didn't tell the half of it. They [your parents the Isaacsons] were into all sorts of things that never came up at the trial. They had their hooks into space research and missiles and germ warfare – everything. Your parents were the head of a whole network. They ran the show. They planned things and they paid people off. Lasers – years before anybody heard of lasers. Everything.'[17] The remarkable aspect of Linda's declaration is that, in the light of our current knowledge, it combines a plausible account of Julius Rosenberg's actual behaviour and outstretched fingers ('they ran the show') with a fantastical description of the pies hidden in the larder ('germ warfare, lasers').

Yet not so fantastical! Here fact is wilder than fiction. Julius Rosenberg's brazen theft of the highly secret proximity fuse, a state-of-the-art antiaircraft device, from Emerson Radio and Phonograph, the Eighth Avenue electronic manufacturer where he was employed, can be causally linked to the Russians' ability to bring down the U-2 spy-pilot Gary Powers in 1960 without destroying him or his plane. It is said that Soviet SA-2 missiles so equipped brought down a total of six U-2s. Rosenberg set aside a defective fuse and methodically replaced the parts over the course of months, until he had built a working model which he smuggled out of the factory in a delivery van in December 1944, relying on Christmas holiday torpor at the gate. Feklisov, Rosenberg's NKVD handler at that time, reports that the stolen fuse was examined by Soviet experts 'and, based on their conclusions, the Council of Ministers created by emergency decree a special laboratory and factory to produce these devices.'[18]

As it later turned out, the evidence that the FBI (and the National Security Agency and the Atomic Energy Commission as well) possessed but could not use was real enough: the Venona intercepts, released to the public in 1995, are damning to the Rosenbergs.

Paul Levine holds that Doctorow's guiding theme is found in Leslie Fiedler's essay 'Afterthoughts on the Rosenbergs,'[19] which appeared in *Encounter* soon after the couple were executed. Fiedler regarded the guilt of the couple as an 'open-and-shut case' but said his own concern was with the symbolic Rosenbergs who supplanted the real Rosenbergs with their 'painfully pretentious style' which, he held, was the 'literary equivalent' of their cynical and manipulative politics. Their prison letters, for example, consist of intimacies which should never have been published and lay sermons which should never have passed between husband and wife.[20] In 'The "Idealism" of Julius and Ethel Rosenberg', [*Commentary*, November 1953] Robert Warshow held that Ethel Rosenberg's references in her prison letters to high culture, to Arturo Toscanini, or to popular culture, the Brooklyn Dodgers, revealed a life filled with what Warshow repeatedly called the 'second-hand': '...almost nothing really belonged to [the Rosenbergs], not even their own experience; they filled their lives with the second-hand, never so much as suspecting that anything else was possible.'[21] This was partly a tussle about authentic Jewish experience of America (Fiedler and

Warshow, like Doctorow himself and Daniel himself, were Jews, though Fiedler was now a Catholic.) In the McCarthy era powerful mainstream Jewish bodies, including the Anti-Defamation League and the American Jewish Congress, had spared no effort to denounce Reds and equate the Jewish image with American-ism; *The Book of Daniel* may be taken as the author's affirmation of a shared cultural heritage with East Side radicals like the Rosenbergs.

Unresolved is why Doctorow/Daniel should so thoroughly embrace the revisionist theses on the origins of the Cold War, while adopting a view of the Soviet Union and the American Communist Party which would not be out of place in the pages of *Commentary, Partisan Review, New Leader*, or *Encounter.*[22] David A. Shannon's scathing study, *The Decline of American Communism* (1959) is quoted uncritically: '[Shannon] shows us the immense contribution made by the American Communist Party to its own destruction after the war. They had all the haughty, shrewd instincts of a successful suicide. It is no wonder in this club of ideologues of the working class, self-designed martyrs, Stalinist tuning forks, sentimentalists, visionaries, misfits, hysterics, fantasists, and dreamers of justice – no wonder that a myth would spring out of their awe for someone truly potent.'[23] And yet Doctorow rejects what he (or Daniel) calls 'the premises of the cold war.' American anti-Communism, its state agencies like the FBI, and its media propaganda are viewed as wholly contaminated by false agendas.

Late in the novel arrives a section called 'TRUE HISTORY OF THE COLD WAR: A RAGA,' no doubt indebted to Dos Passos's 'documentary inlay.' The author's selected history passages and the cited authorities operate as a kind of Brechtian 'alienation' effect and as a fictional equivalent to Piscator's 'parliamentary the-atre.' On offer is a collage of familiar revisionist positions adopted by the new wave of historians challenging the rectitude and rationality of postwar American policy. They go largely unevaluated. We are told: 'Diplomacy in the formulation of Truman, Byrnes and Vandenberg, is seen not as a means to create condi-tions of peaceful postwar détente with the Soviets, but as a means of jamming an American world down Russia's throat. The historian W. A. Williams's *The Tragedy of American Diplomacy* is more than once the Gospel: the hardliners under Molotov take over in Moscow about the time Henry Wallace is fired from the Truman cabinet...'[24] Generally, it looks as if it was devious, Machiavellian Truman administration which goaded Stalin into behaving like Stalin. Daniel Isaacson's overview anticipates a memoir published in 1975 by the Rosenbergs' sons, Michael and Robert Meeropol, fully endorsing Julius Rosenberg's letter to his attorney, 10 November 1952: 'There had to be a Rosenberg case because there had to be an intensification of the hysteria in America to make the Korean War acceptable to the American people.... And there had to be a dagger thrust in the heart of the left to tell them that you are no longer gonna give [?get?] five years for a Smith Act prosecution or one year for Contempt of Court, but we're gonna kill ya!'[25]

The fictional son, Daniel, doodles in capitals: A MESSAGE OF CONSOLATION TO GREEK BROTHERS IN THEIR PRISON CAMPS. AND TO MY HAITIAN BROTHERS AND NICARAGUAN BROTHERS AND DOMINICAN BROTHERS AND SOUTH AFRICAN BROTHERS AND SPANISH BROTHERS AND TO MY BROTHERS IN SOUTH VIETNAM, ALL IN THEIR PRISON CAMPS: YOU ARE IN THE FREE WORLD![26]

The novelist and academic Robert Coover[27] became interested in the Rosenberg case after reading John Wexley's elaborate proof of their utter innocence. He read *The Book of Daniel* in the autumn of 1972, found it powerful, and commented that he had a difficult time separating his own perception from Doctorow's. But Coover's *The Public Burning* (1977) was a very different kind of bravura fiction, marginally indebted to America's expressionist masterwork, Dos Passos's sprawling *USA*. The method of composition calls to mind Dos Passos's scissors-and-paste approach; the third-person narratives are indebted to 'The Camera Eye' newsreels of *USA*. More immediately Coover's extended plunge into postmodernism, with its pyrotechnic displays and impenetrable mazes of the subconscious, echoes Thomas Pynchon's *Gravity's Rainbow* (1973), 760 large, close-packed pages—find your way if you can.

Whereas Doctorow displays an intense, almost old-fashioned, interest in his characters, offering his reader the pleasures of evocation, empathy and concern, *The Public Burning* more resembles a monument to itself. The verbal ferocity of the novel was the product of a full decade of rage directed against Uncle Sam by playwrights, theatre directors, painters, sculptors, and 'alternative' filmmakers engaged in an orgy of lampoon and scatology at the expense of the nation's oafish statesmen and generals—unwrapping the stinking cheese of the conservative subconscious. Once the Vietnam dragon was up on the hoof, the subtle nuances of the East Coast critical idiom, often psychoanalytic (as exemplified by the cartoonist and playwright Jules Feiffer) fell short of requirements. In this respect *The Public Burning* was innovative in terms of literary form but not in motivating spirit.

Coover's central historical setting is both real and fantastical—the execution of the Rosenbergs in Times Square rather than in Sing Sing prison. The novel consists of twenty-eight chapters narrated alternately by (1) an anonymous third-person narrator lacking any distinct fictional identity, presumptively the author himself, and (2) by Richard Nixon. (At the time of the Rosenbergs' execution Nixon was vice president to Eisenhower, and in point of fact never had anything to do with the Rosenberg case, though a vigorous witch-hunter who had pursued Alger Hiss.) The authorial narrator absorbs newspapers, public speeches, sermons, film and theatre scripts, random elements, an almanac, assembled tongue-in-cheek to provide a conspiratorial theory of America's history.

A powerful ongoing motif involves the intervention of the heartland of fabulous America, showbiz. The novel opens with a glimpse of the construction of an electric chair atop a stage in the middle of Times Square—part of the preparations for the grand finale of an elaborate, televised execution pageant featuring high school marching bands, a middleweight title bout, and a performance by the Mormon Tabernacle Choir.[28] Coover is fascinated by America's movie and TV mega-stars, its favourite cartoons, its Hollywood moguls. Walt Disney is appointed animator of the Times Square 'burning' alongside the anti-Communist zealot, Cecil B. DeMille, he of *The Ten Commandments*. What is America if not a theatre stage, a big top, a musical that never closes?

It is hoped that a fierce public exorcism right now might flush the Phantom from his underground cells, force him to materialize, show himself plainly in the honest electrical glow of an all-American night-on-the-town. The Phantom is International Communism, the omnipresent Devil, eternal foe of Liberty, and right now incarnated by the mesh of deceit spun by a humble Jewish couple, parents of two, from the Lower East Side, the Rosenbergs. *The Public Burning* treats with relentless derision the religious dimension of official American ideology, and what J. Edgar Hoover, Cecil B. DeMille and Legion commanders liked to call 'our Judeo-Christian heritage.' Long passages parody the Bible-punching rhetoric of 'God Save America' and of the Covenant.

Were the Rosenbergs guilty as charged? For Coover this is obviously a question of supreme interest, with particular ramifications for the novelist in portraying Julius and Ethel's behaviour after their imprisonment, including their attitudinizing prison correspondence rapidly presented to the world. Even after the trial, the U.S. government clearly wanted to know more, was uncertain about the degree of Ethel's involvement, and was prepared to grant a stay of execution, and almost certainly clemency, if they capitulated and confessed, incriminating others in the spy ring. Ethel's recorded admiration for St Joan (in Bernard Shaw's play), her willingness to face the stake, the burning pyres, endows this humble Lower East Side mother calls up the question: did she have information to confess, or was she the innocent victim of a frame-up against which she had no defence? Shortly before the execution in Sing Sing, Attorney General Brownell despatched James V. Bennett, federal director of the Bureau of Prisons, to the death cells to find out whether Julius – and subsequently Ethel – would now cooperate with the government. If they did, 'they have a basis to recommend clemency.' Whether or not she trusted Bennett and the U.S. government, Ethel could have succumbed to a mother's instincts to be restored to her anguished sons even if it meant life imprisonment for her husband.

Coover's portrait of the couple has a surprising amount in common with the hostile projections of Cold War liberal commentators like Leslie Fiedler, who wrote of the Rosenbergs 'peering slyly out from behind the Fifth Amendment.' Here is Coover: 'Julius and Ethel take the stand and say it isn't so. When they're asked if they're Communists, though, they duck behind the Fifth Amendment.'[29] On the other hand, his analysis of the trial seems to draw heavily on an influential revisionist work, which ran to several editions, by Walter and Miriam Schneir, *Invitation to an Inquest* (1964). The Schneirs argued in great detail that the

Rosenbergs were victims of a frame-up by the FBI. When later interviewed,[30] Coover's offered an overview not dissimilar to the one expressed by the fictional *New York Times* reporter, Fine, in Doctorow's *Book of Daniel*: 'If you read the trial record...you pretty much have to conclude that the Rosenbergs were innocent of the charges against them.' But, he added, 'they were responsible for protecting others, or believed themselves to be.' The Rosenbergs were consumed by role-playing (as in the *Death House Letters*). In *The Public Burning*, this conclusion is shared by Richard Nixon and the anonymous narrator, who reports that Ethel, during one of her prison conversations with Julius, 'repeated her wish to see Arthur Miller's *The Crucible*, currently playing at the Martin Beck Theater. She had heard that the audience applauds when a character says toward the end that he'd rather burn in hell than become a stool pigeon.'[31] Julius and Ethel became absorbed by role-playing and image-projection, by hyperbole, indignation, political cliché, abstraction. 'I was a good student,' Julius wrote to Ethel, 'but more, I absorbed quite naturally the culture of my people, their struggle for freedom from slavery in Egypt.' And again: 'Our upbringing, the full meaning of our lives, based on a true amalgamation of our American and Jewish heritage, which to us means freedom, culture and human decency, has made us the people we are. All the filth, lies and slander of this grotesque frame-up will not in any way deter us...'

Comments Coover's 'Nixon': 'With such grandstanding, who would not find them guilty?'[32]

Nixon himself knows all about grandstanding. In a fantastical scene, the vice president of the U.S. visits Ethel Rosenberg in prison on the eve of her execution, arriving at Sing Sing in disguise, wearing an upside-down moustache. When Ethel urges him to take off his pants in order to sexually possess her, he is full of reluctance and regressive fear. 'I cried, Damn it, I was doing my best! I seemed to hear my mother getting me ready for school. You're going to be late!'[33] Feminists have looked askance at this scene. In 'The Suffering Body: Ethel Rosenberg in the Hands of the Writers,' Carol Hurd Green argues that in both Doctorow and Coover 'the physical body of Ethel Rosenberg is transformed into a representation of a ferocious will, unnatural in her pride and determination, stronger than a woman has any right to be.' In her poem 'For Ethel Rosenberg,' with obvious disgust Adrienne Rich incorporates and italicizes Coover's words 'sizzling half-strapped whipped like a sail' and 'rigid of will.' On the other hand, Virginia Carmichael describes his 'masculist' style as 'purposeful...an outrageous parody of the hegemonic American Manifest Destiny Man's World in the formative stages of the cold war: a racist, classist, sexist, hierarchical, exploitative, aggressive, violent, and obscene world.'[34]

Ethel Rosenberg emerges from the archival revelations of the 1990s as a knowing accessory but a more marginal case than Julius. According to the Venona intercepts, on 27 November 1944 a Soviet official in New York, Kvasnikov, reported (intercepted) to Pavel Fitin in Moscow that Ethel Rosenberg was twenty-nine and married for five years, a member of the CP since 1938. 'Sufficiently well developed politically. Knows about her husband's work and the role of METRE and NIL [codes]. In view of delicate health [she] does not work. Is characterized positively and as a devoted person.'[35] Her devotion is confirmed by one particular document from the Moscow archives. In setting up a meeting with Julius for 15 December 1945, his Soviet handler Feklisov laid down that Ethel Rosenberg was to visit their local East Side drugstore to indicate that it was safe to go ahead with the meeting. The Moscow document (File 40694) describes the sequel: 'That afternoon, Feklisov left his home and checked for surveillance. He went first to the Brooklyn maternity hospital where his wife was awaiting the birth of their child; he then spent time in a Turkish bath.... Finally, Feklisov entered the drugstore at 11 P.M. and noticed Ethel making a purchase. After spotting the Russian, Ethel left.' He followed her home and the ensuing conversation in the kitchen with Julius was described in a report to Moscow.[36]

Or take the desperate situation in May-June 1950, when the FBI was closing in shortly before the arrest of Greenglass and the first FBI interrogation of Rosenberg. The Moscow archives again show Ethel fully in the frame: 'Kirilov' [Boris Krotov], their Soviet handler in New York, agreed that Julius must not visit David Greenglass again. Moscow advised that Ethel should visit her brother David and take back all but $1,000 of the money ($4,000) previously given him for his escape to Mexico.[37] In his memoirs Feklisov, is on dubious ground when he now claims that Ethel knew that Julius worked for Soviet intelligence but 'had never participated in his covert activities. The best proof is that she was never given a code name in secret cables...' That may indeed be why the FBI remained uncertain, up to the moment of Ethel's death, of the extent of her involvement – as was revealed by one of the Justice Department's questions to be put to Julius were he to opt for a last-minute confession on the day of execution: 'Was your wife cognizant of your activities?'[38] The FBI was not sure because the crucial KGB files revealing Ethel's intermediary roles in 1945 and 1950 are discovered not in the Venona cables intercepted by U.S. intelligence but in the KGB Moscow archives researched fully fifty years later by Professor Allen Weinstein.[39]

Coover's commentators and admirers broadly divide between literary critics primarily interested in his radically experimental, postmodernist, format; and the 'politicals' primarily interested in *The Public Burning* as a demolition of the Uncle Sam Cold War culture(s) prevailing in the 1950s. Molly Hite (1993) describes Uncle Sam's speeches as 'malapropistic collages of foundational American myths.' Hite's target is political: Cold War liberalism, its phoney definition of the free Self, and its claim to be non-ideological. As she sees it, Coover focused on the execution of the Rosenbergs 'as a defining moment in the formation of cold war consciousness and on the anticommunist rhetoric surrounding their trial and deaths as emblematic of the ways in which conventionally good people convince themselves to countenance conventionally inconceivable acts.'[40]

The critical history of *The Public Burning*, across two decades, illuminates the late-century's conversion to metafiction and its cousin deconstruction. Frequently quoting Kenneth Burke's *Rhetoric of Religion*, Virginia Carmichael describes Coover as 'a Burkean critical fiction writer, the writer who most consistently practises Burke's strategy of "perspectives by incongruity" or acategorical juxtapositions to unsettle the "natural", mythic (often the same thing), and rational categories that structure systems of knowledge, power, social relationships, and common sense...'[41] Readable or not, this kind of criticism turns literature into an adjunct of criticism; the novelist-as-critic becomes the primary 'signifier.' Terry Eagleton has noted the absence of a clear division for post-stucturalism between 'criticism' and 'creation'; he further warns against writing which 'turns in on itself in a profound act of narcissism...'[42]

Thomas LeClair comments that Coover like Barth, Pynchon and Heller, devises imitative forms 'to defamiliarize important subjects, to break through the moderating haze of conventional wisdom and media Knowledge.'[43] Larry McCaffery (1982) compares Coover's technique to Joyce's *Ulysses*. By means of language men can arrange and rearrange the random elements of existence into historically significant events. 'Thus all the major characters – the Rosenbergs, Uncle Sam, Nixon, the Phantom, react to the prospect of randomness in the same way: they storify it, creating soothing possible fictions that they can feel comfortable with.'[44]

According to Heinz Ickstadt, *The Public Burning* is 'the logical application of postmodern epistemology to the public domain of the historically recorded.' Even more than *Gravity's Rainbow*, it is '*the* postmodern novel of politics par excellence.' Unlike Doctorow, says Ickstadt, 'Coover is not interested in the individual psychology, the injustice suffered, the character destroyed by a vindictive and bigoted society (the concerns of the realistic novel) but in the structure of "fictions that make us".' This is a quote from Coover himself in 'The State of Fiction.' According to Ikcstadt, fabulation not only makes and shapes the record but the events themselves—witness the ritualistic Congressional Hearings of the era.[45]

The Grove Press reissue of the novel in 1998 led the journal *Critique* to devote its fall 2000 issue to the event. In an editorial declaration, '*The Public Burning*. Coover's Fiery Masterpiece on Center Stage Again,' the editors claimed it to be 'perhaps the most complete replenishment of the language since Whitman and (in a different way) Mark Twain.... No writer since Melville has dived so deeply and fearlessly into the collective American dream as Coover has in this novel.'[46] Coover's friend, fellow-academic and fellow-novelist, William H. Gass, scripted an introduction to the 1998 paperback edition. In accounting for the novel's style, Gass mentions 'the fierce satirical images of Felicien Rops, George Grosz, of Hogarth and Daumier.'[47] Gass emphasises 'the insistent and successful orality of Coover's prose...an entire nation's mendacity is given rhythm by its political marches, by the brasses of its big bands, through its swoony hymn singing...'

Gass calls the Rosenberg trial a 'show trial.' It is certainly the case that trial judge Irving Kaufman and the press joined in a campaign of hysteria, and the death sentence was the result of improper collusion between Kaufman and the Justice Department. Yet the accusations were never substantially correct in any of the 'show trials' staged in the Soviet Union and Eastern Europe from the early 1930s to the early 1950s. The Rosenbergs did not confess, they were not subjected to physical torture, they denied everything.

Conclusion

In his retrospective on the great age of the political novel, *Politics and the Novel* (1955), Irving Howe put forward the proposition that political fiction tends to prosper in the soil of civil turmoil: 'Neither conservative stasis nor social democratic moderation...are [sic] able to inspire first-rate novels dealing with political themes.... Political fiction requires wrenching conflicts, a drama of words and often blood, roused states of being...'[1] True! In the United States and Western Europe, the 'political' novel, the urgent, morally committed depiction of recent struggles in the public domain, flourished spontaneously in the 1930s and 1940s, the years scarred by economic depression, fascism, the Spanish Civil War, the rise of Stalinism, and the devastation of Europe during the Second World War. The thirties and forties – the crisis years—arguably produced the greatest political fiction and playwriting we have known. The novel rode escort to contemporary history.

The Spanish Civil War provided Malraux, Hemingway, Orwell and Dos Passos with a theatre of high emotion and bloodshed. Ruthless oppression and grotesque show trials fathered Koestler's *Darkness at Noon.* First-hand experience of Stalinist persecution, including internal exile and near-starvation, inspired Victor Serge's *The Case of Comrade Tulyaev.* Sartre's trilogy, *Roads to Freedom*, was hewn out of a succession of disasters: Spain, appeasement, the abandonment of Czechoslovakia, war, occupation, imprisonment. Indeed Sartre's postwar plays like *Dirty Hands* are saturated with violence. The inspiration for Orwell's *Animal Farm* was the Nazi-Soviet Pact and the convergence of two vast totalitarian systems smashing the life out of Europe. Given the ongoing oppression in Eastern Europe's 'Popular Democracies'—more show trials, more idolatry, more Newsspeak—Orwell needed only the added despondency of a dire personal illness to produce *Nineteen Eighty-Four.* Simone de Beauvoir's *The Mandarins*, set in a Paris now at peace and recovering its poise, yet anticipates fear of a third world war. Koestler's *The Age of Longing* was inspired by the forked tongue of Stalinist realities and progressive illusions about the beast at the gate.

The literary mode of political novels in these years was predominantly 'realist' – although Malraux wrote with the zeal and zip of an expressionistic film director. Hemingway's realism verges on the picaresque. Like most of his colleagues, he carries a journalist's ear and eye, grafting documentary realia into his tightly tensioned tale. The invisible, omniscient, god-author is generally favoured by this generation. The point of view is normally shared between characters, almost promiscuously in Malraux, with more measure in Hemingway, freely in Sartre (who believed that characters must be given their 'freedom'). The second volume of Sartre's trilogy, charting the collapse of Europe at the time of Munich, borrows from the streams of consciousness, cross-cutting and cinematic behaviourism of Dos Passos's *USA*. The point of view alternates rapidly. Koestler's *Darkness at Noon* stays rigorously with the imprisoned Rubashov, veering away only at the time of his execution. De Beauvoir's *The Mandarins* distributes camera angles in the orthodox manner, although she chooses to alternate her heroine between 'I' and 'she,' in an attempt to see herself as others do. Orwell's omniscient narrator in *Animal Farm* tends to empathise with kindly characters like the carthorses Boxer and Clover, while viewing the enemy, the pigs, by their estranging utterances and actions. In *Nineteen Eighty-Four* we are pretty well with Winston Smith throughout, our point of view confined to his.

Any objective study of the major political novelists whom Howe held to represent the genre at its most vital and 'unblocked,' the writers of the Spanish Civil War and the ensuing 'god that failed' era, must discover a literature of disenchantment pitching into despair. The liberational visions of twentieth-century socialism disintegrated. Fascist victories and blitzkriegs in Spain or France were psychologically bearable, leaving humanistic values in tact; in Malraux's *Days of Wrath* and *Days of Hope* the Left sustains its solidarity against the fascist enemy, the *fons et origo* of cruelty and obscurantism. In the cant of the time, the defeated volunteers could console themselves that they had been fighting 'for Spain.'

But Malraux's perspective was to alter; by 1945 he was a zealous anti-Communist, warning America about Russia's Asiatic designs. What lacerated the souls of these writers was self-betrayal on the Left. Internecine conflicts within the Popular Front surface as the dominant theme in Orwell, Koestler, Dos Passos, Hemingway, Serge, Sartre, de Beauvoir. In Orwell's *Homage to Catalonia* and Dos Passos's *Adventures of a Young Man*, the Republican camp is tearing itself apart and Stalinism presents as imminent a threat to liberty as fascism. Koestler's early ideals, like those of Dos Passos, were twisted, tortured beyond repair. Sartre's 'Roads to Freedom' lead anywhere but to authentic freedom; the Germans are almost frozen figures in a frieze, dead-eyed bystanders to the drama of betrayal within the Left. De Beauvoir faithfully chronicles the debilitating quarrels ensuing from the Left Bank's inability to distinguish the Marxist claims from the horrific realities of a slave state. Orwell finally proposed a vision of the totalitarian future as the endless thud of a boot into a human face. So many works ostensibly written under the shadow of Hitler turned out to be written under the shadow of Stalin.

By mid-century, with the return of peace and an American-led prosperity, the heyday of *une littérature engagée* was over. The word 'progressive' was in bad odour. The derogatory term 'fellow-traveller' was in vogue. The god had failed, the slave labourers had emerged in their millions, the writers and intellectuals were shedding their illusions (while, of course, embracing others). With 'Soviet democracy' exposed as 'the totalitarian temptation,' the political novel fell into disrepute in the West. The dominant literary creed of the era was 'no politics.'

Yet the Soviet novel followed the opposite trajectory during the 1950s; it became genuinely interesting as Stalinism made a partial retreat. By and large revisionist Soviet fiction, the dissident works applauded in the West, took the form of retrospectives on ghastly traumas within the Soviet Union: collectivisation, the pain of industrialisation, the purges, the terror, the trials, the catastrophe of June 1941 and the epic victory which followed. Stalin's defeat, Stalin's victory.

For two decades the figure of Stalin – particularly his imagined mindset, his stream of consciousness –fascinated novelists, Soviet and Western, admirers and detractors alike. In Malraux, he remains a name and a field of energy; in Koestler, he remains off-screen but ever ominously observant; Orwell turns him into a giant boar, then into a televisual ogre, Big Brother; Serge allows us to glimpse him at close quarters, but briefly, as he hurries past, on foot, in a cloud of pipe smoke. Leaving aside the adulatory portraits of Stalin in Soviet fiction by Pavlenko, Chakovsky and their ilk, the two most intimate, sustained – and punishing – fictional descriptions of Stalin are those by Solzhenitsyn and Rybakov.

All major pathways of dissidence (whether via Pasternak, Grossman, Chukovskaya or Vladimov) seem to lead to the monumental figure of Aleksandr Solzhenitsyn. Conspicuous among his qualities was the capacity to thrive under official displeasure, even persecution. His almost military strategies for combating censorship, for coping with the caution of his editor Tvardovsky, for facing up to ostracism and expulsion by the Writers' Union, for shrugging off demands that he publicly repudiate European editions of his work and the plaudits of the Western press – this protracted guerrilla campaign by Russia's greatest twentieth-century writer amounted to a work of art in itself. Of necessity Solzhenitsyn had to play cat-and-mouse with the Party, the Writers' Union, Glavlit, the magazine editors, even with the secret policemen shadowing him. He led the way in showing how each incident of harassment and surveillance could be stored and recorded for play-back to the West – to the BBC, Deutsche Welle, the *New York Times*, the Scandinavians. Works of fiction and 'open letters' were duplicated, passed to friends through samizdat, and spirited abroad on microfilm in overcoat linings or via diplomatic bags. Indeed his description of Stalin at work by night might be applied to Solzhenitsyn himself: 'Stalin continued to write with that special concentration and seriousness which is appropriate when every word becomes history the very moment it flows from his pen.'[2]

Most of the Russians under consideration in these pages were influenced by Tolstoy (Grossman in particular, Pasternak to an extent), some by Chekhov (Grossman again and Chukovskaya). In Russian realism fictional characters are normally granted clear definition and literary autonomy. The omniscient narrator presides over their apparent independence. Dialogue, reflection, action are the essential ingredients. The narrative point of view is rarely thrown into doubt, likewise the feasibility of mimesis – language is that famous clear mirror. In general Soviet novelists were keen on naturalistic descriptions – the hardness of nature, the poverty of men – and on colloquial dialogue—though cautious when common speech reaches obscenity. Only in the 1960s did a new generation of subversive writers emerge, Sinyavsky-Tertz and Daniel among them, taking their cue from Kafka, or surrealism, the absurd, and Western modernism in general.

The more orthodox (in literary terms) opponents of the regime tended to favour indirect monologue. Solzhenitsyn is the greatest exponent. It's both a tone of voice and a loose, freewheeling syntactical structure hard to translate or emulate. It skips, it jumps, it catches itself in mid-stride. By means of indirect monologue the author harnesses himself on to his character while harnessing the character on to the author. It is a kind of grafting. The character's thoughts – and what he says—tend to come unannounced, like an aside, a murmur or mutter. This technique is particularly obvious (and occasionally hazardous) when the chosen character is a real person – Stalin or Lenin.

Howe's *Politics and the Novel* appeared during a short-lived 'time out,' the apex of the Manichean Cold War culture, when the Western academy had discovered that political commitment within the text is virtually incompatible with the genuine art of imaginative fiction. Social 'messages' were anathema. Exceptions were conveniently made for the civic courage or liberal vision of a Pasternak, a Solzhenitsyn, an Akhmatova – in short, Soviet dissidents were granted a special license to confuse art with justice. One notable writer who missed the 'time out' of the Marshall Plan era was Graham Greene, whose *The Quiet American* belongs to the mid-fifties. Greene did not exactly part company with the prevailing pessimism of the god-that-failed novel; he found nothing hugely to admire in the Vietminh; but what he did was to fire up the latent theme of anti-Americanism. As the u.s. moved to fill the power vacuum left by the disintegrating British and French empires, Greene can be regarded as a godfather to the cynicism which pervaded literature and the arts after Johnson succeeded Kennedy. All the more influential because of his constant commercial success –*Time* magazine could not ignore him—it was Greene who began pointing the finger in the unfashionable direction before the sixties became the Sixties.

A further factor reinforced literature's self-imposed political purdah in the era when the CIA-funded magazine *Encounter* presented a political 'front half' vigorously committed to the cold war and a literary 'back half' consistently aloof from such concerns. Western university faculties of history, government, and political science achieved in the 1950s an unprecedented degree of self-confidence. From lands devastated by Nazism and Communism arrived émigré scholars with first-hand knowledge of totalitarianism; at the same time the Cold War brought military subsidies on an unprecedented scale to specialized institutes in America. Among the scholars and intellectuals[3] associated with the Congress for Cultural Freedom, one finds a remarkable galaxy of talents displaying common values – notably the designation of 'totalitarianism' as a description fitting both the Hitler and Stalin regimes, the importance of social psychology, and the advocacy of convergence politics at the expense of traditional working-class socialist values. The terms left and right were pronounced redundant, consensus at the centre held the key. The 'end of ideology' was nigh, 'ideology' being equated with messianic visions, dogmatic versions of history, state-driven blueprints for a redeemed future, whether Leninist or Hitlerian, whether Marxist or national-racist. The fifties consensus in the West, which accepted the democratic-capitalist model, based on negotiated social progress and class-conciliation, as the only viable norm, was evidently not 'ideological'—but in reality it too was underpinned by values and ethical choices. Ideology is as often implicit as explicit – even Jane Austen had an implicit ideology, taking the British class structure, the monarchical system and the existence of a convenient servant class for granted.

Back to the fifties: the political scientists now commanded the terrain. Following Orwell, Sartre, Camus and Koestler, further literary contributions to the Cold War consensus appeared superfluous, a confusion of genres. An Isaiah Berlin was worth a platoon of novelists.

By the time that Western political fiction did stage a comeback, the prevailing consensus of the 1950s had fractured. Indeed, it was in ruins. The revisionist counter-culture celebrated the lost arcadias of the utopian tradition with enchantment. But more: the counter-culture also tended to regard fictional realism as a mechanism for political deception and psychic oppression. The deception inflicted by the omniscient author was painfully obvious. The same process had become visible in Eastern Europe. Under the scrutiny of Brecht and the post-Marxists, realism had lost its innocence. Uwe Johnson could not write like Christa Wolf. Havel and Kundera emerged from the Prague Spring, representing reality by way of alternative codes of imaginative writing. Although the Union of Soviet Writers continued to draw a line in the shifting sand, in practice Soviet writing, like Soviet painting, became modestly 'experimental.'

In the West a new generation of the avant-garde took a torch to realism. New academic vocabularies rapidly evolved, leaving previous generations baffled. The prefix 'post' was much in evidence as each new critical theory somersaulted its predecessor. Post-structuralists and postmodernists were turning faculty corridors into shooting galleries. Language, or literary language, inevitably defeated attempts to employ it to describe or record an external reality. Language could never accurately stand in for anything outside itself –although the language the postmodernists were using to explain this fatal blockage was somehow exempt from the rule it propounded—as when the proverbial philosopher tells us 'Nothing I say can be true.' Electronic innovations reinforced the visual image as the vital medium of 'access.'

Above all criticism was now paramount. Once the valet of the novelist, opening windows into the writer's meaning, intentions, style and techniques, the critic now announced the rules, subjecting the writer to merciless, laboratorial scrutiny.

Obviously if this climate of discussion had prevailed from the thirties through the fifties, much of the realist political fiction discussed in these pages could not have seen the seen the light of day. From the mid-sixties on, not many novelists attempted to pursue the old realism through the barbed wire of the counter-culture. Mailer and DeLillo did make that attempt, each in his own gifted fashion, supported by readers who liked to know where they were. The case of Doctorow's *The Book of Daniel* is exceptional. Here we find a basically realist novelist of the left adopting strategies which owe much to modernism and rather less to postmodernism, while addressing a subject residing at the heart of the Cold War conscience, the Rosenbergs. Shortly thereafter Robert Coover approached the same subject in *The Public Burning*, but in a radically disjunctured form, offering a feast to postmodernist criticism and launching a cult largely confined to faculties. Meanwhile political fiction resurfaced in excellent shape in the colonial and post-colonial terrain of Africa and Latin America, inspired by violent confrontations and what Irving Howe called 'roused states of being.' Still believing that novelists can say what they mean, and mean what they say.

Notes and References

Abbreviations used in the main text and the reference notes: BBC, British Broadcasting Corporation; *DT, Daily Telegraph* (London); *DW, Daily Worker* (London & NY); *IHT, International Herald Tribune*; *LNC, La Nouvelle critique*; *LLF, Les Lettres françaises*; *LG, Literaturnaia gazeta*; *LM, Le Monde*; *LNC, La Nouvelle Critique*; *LTM, Les Temps modernes*; *LRB, London Review of Books*; *MG, Manchester Guardian*; *MN, Moscow News*; *NLR, New Left Review* (London); *NM, Novyi mir*; *NR, New Republic*; *NRF, Nouvelle Revue française*; *NS, New Statesman*; *NYRB, New York Review of Books*; *NYT, New York Times*; *PR, Partisan Review*; *SL, Soviet Literature*; *SN, Soviet News*; *SR, Saturday Review*; *ST, Sunday Times* (London); *TLS, Times Literary Supplement*

1. Commentary: The Spanish Labyrinth

1. Orwell (2001), 351-52.
2. Koestler (1956), 328.
3. In Hemingway's case some twenty-eight syndicated newspaper articles for the North American News Agency; Dos Passos had earlier contributed some sixteen articles about Spain to magazines in the years 1917-1922. Fishkin, 159-69.
4. Cate, 263.
5. Cate, 260.

2. Malraux: *Days of Hope*

1. See 'Enquête sur le Communisme et les jeunes,' *Esprit* (Feb. 1946).
2. Léon Trotsky, La Révolution étranglée,' and André Malraux, 'Réponse à Trotsky,' *NRF* (1 Apr. 1931, no. 211), 488-500, 501-7.
3. Malraux (1936), 5.
4. Ibid., 7.
5. Howe (1957), 206.
6. Lacouture, 238.
7. Cate, 270-1.
8. Cate, 235; Lacouture, 263-65.
9. Lacouture, 45.
10. L'Escadrille España was in existence from August to November 1936, with thirty-two members, of whom twenty-two were French and five Italian, with seventeen pilots and no known breakdown of political affiliation. It was replaced by L'Escadrille André Malraux (Nov. 1936 to Feb. 1937), with forty-two members of whom thirty-three were French. Here a political breakdown is available from Thornberry: eleven Communists, seventeen Antifascists, the rest socialist, anarcho-syndicalists, with three mercenaries and three 'adventurers.' Thornberry, 214.
11. Malraux, *L'Espoir*, 756. Malraux, *Days of Hope (DH)*, 1968 ed., 329.
12. *DH*, 1968 ed., 164.
13. *DH*, 1968 ed., 177.
14. Todd, 280. See Malraux (1939).
15. Thornberry provides a list of characters with real persons attached, as if the correlation was intended by Malraux to be exact. See Thornberry. 218 However, the earlier biography by Lacouture mentions these correspondences with caution. Lacouture, 274-75.
16. *DH*, 1968 ed., 208.
17. *DH*, 1968 ed., 221.
18. The reader will encounter in these pages a plethora of terms and acronyms denoting Soviet state security organs enjoying powers of investigation, arrest, interrogation and incarceration: principally the Cheka (1917-1922), the NKVD (People's Commissariat for Internal Affairs, 1922-1946), OGPU/GPU ((Joint) State Political Directorate, 1922-1946), MGB (Ministry for State Security, 1946-1951), and latterly the KGB (Committee for State Security, 1954-1991). State security organs were frequently reorganized,

merged, replaced; for this reason the security set-up under Stalin from 1922 to 1953 was more complex than the rudimentary indications given here.

19. Todd, 237-38, ref. 52, citing in general 'les rapports de Marty qui figurant dans les dossiers du Comintern.'
20. *DH*, 1938 ed. 202.
21. Ibid., 389.
22. Ibid., 113-17.
23. Deutscher (1963). Other sponsors of Malraux's American tour included the American League Against War and Fascism, American Friends of Spanish Democracy, the Committee for Medical Aid to Spain.
24. Howe (1957), 213.
25. *DH*, 1938 ed., 166-67.
26. Cate, 263.
27. All cited by Thornberry, 186-87.
28. Ibid., 191.
29. *PR*, Winter 1938-39, 126-27.
30. GPU, also known as OGPU, 'State Political Department,' the Soviet political police.
31. Thornberry, 193.
32. In 1945 at the Ciné Max Linder, Paris, and the Academy Cinema, London. It reached The Fifth Avenue Cinema and the Fifty-Fifth Street Playhouse, New York, in Jan. 1947.

3. Hemingway: *For Whom the Bell Tolls*

1. Hemingway (1899-1961) was a decorated veteran of the First World War (Italian front) and subsequently a member of the 1920s expatriate community in Paris. A sportsman, adventurer, fisherman and admirer of physical and spiritual courage, notably bull-fighting, his early prose style (*A Farewell to Arms*, *The Sun Also Rises*) was distinguished by economy and understatement. In 1953 he was awarded a Pulitzer Prize for *The Old Man and the Sea*, and the Nobel Prize the following year. In 1961 he committed suicide by a gunshot to the head.
2. Greene, *Spectator*, 7 March 1941, printed in Meyers, 343.
3. Cited by Meyers, 319.
4. Baker, Carlos, 223-24.
5. Ibid., 238.
6. Josephs, 238-39.
7. Orwell (2001), 147.
8. Schorer, *Kenyon Review*, winter 1941, in Meyers, 341.
9. Hemingway (1941), 185.
10. Payne, 168.
11. Quoted in Meyers, 327.
12. Hemingway (1941), 12.
13. Ibid., 158-59.
14. Ibid., 350.
15. Ibid., 226.
16. Moorehead, 164.
17. Hemingway (1941), 235.
18. Ibid., 237.
19. Macdonald's review is in Meyers, 330.
20. Hemingway (1941), 238, 398-99.
21. Moorehead, 152-3, 179.
22. Davison (1996), 84.
23. Hemingway (1941), 395.
24. Baker, Carlos, 240, 261.
25. Calvino, 19.
26. Hemingway (1941), 305.
27. Baker, Carlos, 245.
28. Ibid., 242-43.

4. Dos Passos: Betrayal

1. Charley Anderson of Detroit, a major character in *The Big Money*, had been documented by Dos Passos working as a journalist. In the *New Republic* he first wrote about Ivy Lee, father of modern PR, on whom he based the only fictional character to span all three volumes of *USA*, J. Ward Moorehouse. Fishkin, 168-69.
2. Dos Passos (1966), 131.
3. *Villages are the Heart of Spain*, 14, cited by Rosen 95.
4. Dos Passos (1939), 211.
5. Ibid., 228.
6. Ibid., 263.
7. Wilson, *NR* (28 Oct. 1940), in Meyers, 321.
8. Cowley cited by Maine, 205-7.
9. Sillen cited by Maine, 210.
10. Farrell cited by Maine, 217-20.
11. Dos Passos, 'The Failure of Marxism,' *Life* (XXIV, 19 January 1948), 96-108; Dos Passos (1956), 236,237; Dos Passos (1959), x; *SR* (24 May 1952).

5. Orwell: *Homage to Catalonia*

1. Orwell (2001), 353. The updated edition of *Homage to Catalonia* referred to is the one found in *Orwell in Spain*, with editorial notes by Peter Davison.
2. Orwell was born Eric Blair in India in 1903, the son of a colonial civil servant. Educated at Eton, he joined the Indian Imperial Police in Burma (see his novel *Burmese* Days). He adopted his pseudonym when about to publish *Down and Out in Paris and London*. Subsequently *The Road to Wigan Pier*, a Left Book Club publication, recounted his experiences among the miners of the North during the depression. A committed socialist opposed to totalitarianism, he was to achieve international fame with two works of fiction, *Animal Farm* and *Nineteen Eighty-Four*. His collected journalism is equally admired if not equally widely read. He died of tuberculosis in 1950, at the age of forty-seven.
3. Orwell (2001), 34.
4. Ibid, 183.
5. Ibid., 183-4.
6. Stansky & Abrahams, 194.
7. Orwell (2001), 98-100.
8. Ibid., 100.
9. Ibid., 187, 215.
10. Ibid., 219.
11. Ibid., 186.
12. Ibid., 91.
13. Ibid., 196.
14. Cited in Ibid., 199-200.
15. Ibid., 203-06.
16. Ibid., 199, 205-7.
17. Serge (1951), 127.
18. Ibid., 151-52; Stansky & Abrahams, 223.
19. Koestler (1938), 20, 36.
20. Orwell (2001), 349.
21. Ibid., 350, 353.
22. Malraux, *DH*, 1938 ed., 163.
23. Orwell (2001), 132.
24. Ibid., 153, 163.
25. Ibid., 158-60.
26. Crick, 339.
27. Stansky & Abrahams, 225.
28. Pritchett, 734.
29. Ibid., 736.
30. Davison (2001), 84-85.

31. C. Hitchens, Letters, *LRB* (3 Feb. 2000, vol. 22, no. 3), 5
32. Crick, 363.
33. Davison (2001), 234.

6. Koestler: Sentence of Death

1. Arthur Koestler (1905-83) was born in Budapest of Jewish parents. In 1922 he entered the University of Vienna, then worked with the militant Zionist Vladimir Jabotinsky. Koestler left for the Palestine in 1926 without completing his degree, working as a farm labourer, then as a Jerusalem-based correspondent for German newspapers. In 1930 he became science editor of *Vossische Zeitung* and foreign editor of *B.Z. am Mittag*.
2. Koestler (1956), 62-63.
3. Ibid., 96.
4. Ibid., 90-107.
5. Ibid., 107.
6. Ibid., 206-7.
7. Ibid., 315.
8. Koestler (1938), 33-34.
9. Koestler (1956), 349.
10. Ibid., 328-30.
11. Koestler (1938), 38, 48.
12. Ibid., 44.
13. Ibid., 45, 122.
14. Ibid., 281.
15. Ibid., 285-7.
16. Koestler (1956), 359.
17. Ibid., 349, 360.
18. Koestler (1938), 366.
19. Ibid., 380-83.
20. Koestler (1956), 367.
21. Koestler (1938), 178.
22. Orwell, *CE* (vol. 3, 1943-45), 273.
23. Koestler (1956), 387-89.

7. Commentary: The Soviet Trials

1. Cited by Hitchens, 44.
2. Grossman (1985), 775, 786.

8. Koestler: *Darkness at Noon*

1. Koestler, 'The Initiates' in Crossman, 62.
2. Ibid., 62 & Koestler (1956), 386-87.
3. See Google, 'Eva Weissberg,' 'Letters about Polyani, Koestler, and Eva Zeisel,' 'www.missouriwestern.edu/orgs/polyani...
4. Solzhenitsyn (1974), 409, 412, 414-15.
5. Ibid., 130-31.
6. Rees, 115.
7. Koestler (1941), 89.
8. Ibid., 78.
9. Sturgess, 266.
10. Koestler (1941), 83 quoted by Sturgess 278.
11. Koestler (1941), 94.
12. Ibid., 103.
13. Ibid., 210, 218.
14. Ibid., 211.
15. Ibid., 183-84.
16. Ibid., 214-16.

17. Ibid., 224.
18. Koestler stresses that when he wrote *Darkness at Noon* he had not read General Walter Krivitisky's similar analysis in *I Was Stalin's Agent*. Koestler (1956), 398.
19. Koestler (1941), 226-229.
20. All Union Communist Party (Bolshevik) Central Committee, 4 December 1937. Document 167.
21. Levene, 61.
22. Rees, 119.
23. Fyvel, 150-154. Orwell was literary editor of *Tribune* from 1943 to 1945. Koestler wrote several articles for him, published simultaneously in the *NYT* Sunday Magazine.
24. Orwell, *CE* (vol. 3), 272.
25. The novel is given as written July 1942 to July 1943.
26. Orwell, *CE* (vol. 3) 270-282.

9. Serge: *The Case of Comrade Tulayev*

1. Many of Serge's manuscripts taken from him or stolen in 1936 have not been found.
2 Serge (1963), 274.
3 Serge (1951), 137, 146.
4 Serge lists his disagreements with Trotsky in *Memoirs of a Revolutionary*, 349. Serge saw no virtue in founding a Fourth International.
5 See Peter Sedgwick's comments in 'Victor Serge and the RPF,' in his edition of *Memoirs of a Revolutionary*, 383. See also Weissman xii, 257n.
6 Serge (1951), 294.
7 Ibid., 34.
8 Ibid., 27.
9 Ibid., 46.
10 Ibid., 40-41.
11 Ibid., 170.
12 Ibid., 169, 174-75.
13 Ibid., 175.
14 Ibid., 164-55.
15 Ibid., 212-13.
16 Ibid., 217-18.
17 Ibid., 221.
18 Weissman, 167.
19 Serge (1951), 178.
20 Ibid., 185, 193.
21 Ibid., 248-89.
22 Ibid., 249.
23 Ibid., 251.
24 Ibid., 260.
25 Serge's biographer Susan Weissman writes: 'Koestler's view is monolithic, falling entirely in line with the stance adopted by the cold warriors that equates Marxism, Leninism, Bolsheviks and Stalinism.' She adds that *Darkness at Noon* 'is a pure statement of Stalinist thinking.' Weissman, 200n, 203.

10. Orwell: from Big Pig to Big Brother

1. Orwell, *CE* (vol. 1), 370.
2. Ibid. (vol. 4), 101.
3. Todd (1946), 421, 537.
4. De Beauvoir (1998).
5. Orwell, *CE* (vol. 4), 507.
6. Foreign Office minute of 21 Apr. 1951, in National Archive, FO 1110/383.
7. National Archive: FO1110/221.
8. Ibid.
9. Ibid. *Times* (London), 11 July 1996.

10. Orwell, *CE* (vol. 4.), 433-4. See Orwell's letters to his agent Leonard Moore, 21, 28 July 1949. Berg Collection. Fleay & Sanders, 511.
11. Orwell to Koestler, 20 Sept. 1947, Orwell, *CE*, (*vol.* 4), 433.
12. Gehring, 74-75.
13. 'If Orwell Were Alive Today,' in Podhoretz, 62, citing Orwell, 'In Defence of Comrade Zilliacus,' (1948), *CE* (vol. 4), 452.
14. Kazin (1984), 13.
15. Orwell, *CE* (vol. 4), 448.
16. Orwell (1949), 19.
17. Hitchens, 135.
18. Orwell (1949), 150. See Christopher Roper, 'Taming the Universal Machine,' in Chilton & Aubrey, 59.
19. Orwell (1949), 153.
20. Ibid., 160.
21. Huxley, 29.
22. Orwell (1949), 59.
23. Ibid., 58.
24. Ibid., 110-11.
25. Ibid., 220.
26. Ibid., 162.
27. Ibid., 211.
28. Orwell, 'James Burnham and the Managerial Revolution,' (1946), originally, 'Second Thoughts on James Burnham,' *CE* (vol. 4), 212, 210. When William Buckley launched *National Review*, Burnham contributed to it a regular column 'Third World War.' Orwell distrusted Burnham's grand theories but drew on them for his bleak tripolar militarized world in 1984. Hitchens, 67.
29. Gleason, 84.
30. National Archive: FO 1110/221.
31. *Observer*, 29 Jan. 1950, reprinted in Koestler (1955), 104.
32. Quoted by Chilton & Aubrey, 11.
33. Glenny (1984), 15-17.
34. Deutscher (1955), 44.
35. Ibid., 45-50.
36. Thompson (1974), 81-85. 'Inside Which Whale?' is a reprinted section from the longer essay, 'Outside the Whale.'
37. O'Brien, 31-35.
38. Rushdie, 'Outside the Whale,' 1984, cited by Hitchens, 27.
39. Kazin (1984), 16. Donoghue, 7.
40. Williams (1974), 4.
41. Williams (1979), 390, 395, 404.
42. Chilton & Aubrey, 7.
43. This statement was published in *Socialist Leader* (21 Aug. 1948) and *Peace News* (27 Aug.). Signatories included Orwell, Brockway, E. M. Forster, Harold Laski, Henry Moore and others.
44. National Archives, FO 1110/221.
45. Ninety-nine suspects, all dead, are laid out in volume 20 of the complete works. The editor has withheld thirty-six further names of the living for fear of libel.
46. Watson memo to Sheridan and Murray, Apr. 1949. National Archive, FO1110/189 PR1135.
47. Orwell, *CE* (vol. 4), 511-13.
48. Crick, 550, 445.
49. Orwell (1998), vol. 20, 241ff.

11. Commentary: Totalitarianism, Ideology, Power

1. See Orwell, 'Literature and Totalitarianism,' *CE* (vol. 2), 161-64.
2. Grossman (1985), 487.
3. Ibid., 215.

4. Grossman (1973), 218.
5. Markish, 154.
6. Grossman (1985), 213.
7. Ibid., 401.
8. Ibid.
9. Ehrlich, 23n.
10. Schmemann, 523.
11. Solzhenitsyn (1974), 173-74.
12. Orwell, *CE* (vol. 3), 273-75.
13. Orwell (1949), 220.
14. Kazin (1984), 16.
15. Pasternak, 174, 176.
16. Ibid., 177.
17. Ibid., 178.
18. Hosking, 118, quoting *Gulag* (vol. 1), 147.
19. Solzhenitsyn (1974), 150-51.
20. Hosking, 120, citing *Gulag* (vol. 2), 615-16
21. Grossman (1985), 579.
22. Ibid., 581.
23. Solzhenitsyn, *The First Circle*, 280-1.
24. Solzhenitsyn, *Cancer Ward*, vol. II, 171.

12. Sartre: History, Fiction and the Party

1. Jean-Paul Sartre (1905-1980), existentialist philosopher, novelist, playwright and essayist, was educated in Paris, attended the Ecole Normale Supérieur, and absorbed the work of modern German philosophers. His relationship with the PCF was protracted and tormented. Founder of *Les Temps modernes*, his work focused on the quest for authentic freedom and personal responsibility, both individual and collective. His later work strives to synthesis existentialism and an updated Marxism (*Critique de la Raison dialectique*).
2. De Beauvoir (1952), 40-41
3. De Beauvoir (1963), 34,
4. Sartre (1951), 107-8.
5. Ibid., 121.
6. '...kak sledstvie iakoby rokovoi i neodolimoi razobshchënnosti liudei.' *Bol'shaia sovetskaia Entsiklopediia*, 2nd ed., vol. 38, 1956, 122-3.
7. Sartre (1951), 107.
8. Sartre (1984), 222.
9. Sartre, *Iron in the Soul*, 225.
10. It could be translated 'Phoney Friendship' as in 'Drôle de guerre.'
11. Hayman, 255. See also Sartre (1984).
12. Sartre, *The Reprieve*, 79.
13. Sartre, *Iron in the Soul*, 15-25.
14. Ibid., 30.
15. Sartre (1950), 117, 119, 206.
16. De Beauvoir (1965), 263, 268.
17. Simone de Beauvoir (1908-1986) was a prolific novelist, essayist and autobiographer. A lifelong colleague of Sartre, she was associated with existentialism, postwar Left Bank radicalism, and wide-ranging reports from Mao's China and Castro's Cuba. She is perhaps best known for *The Second Sex*, a reference point for modern feminism.
18. Camus (London, 1953), 178.
19. Todd (1996), 571-2.
20. De Beauvoir (1965), 263, 268.
21. De Beauvoir (1963), 190.
22. Her letters to Algren, which now fill more than 500 printed pages, were acquired by Ohio State University at a public sale after his death in 1981. His own letters to de Beauvoir

passed into the care of her perennial companion Sylvie Le Bon (now Sylvie Le Bon Beauvoir).
23. On Koestler's relationship with Sartre's circle, see de Beauvoir (1965), 139-41.
24. De Beauvoir (1952), 111.
25. si on n'est pas entièrement avec moi on est très loin de moi.

13. Commentary: Soviet Forced Labour Camps

1. De Beauvoir (1965), 220.
2. Orwell, 'London Letter,' *PR* (12/4, Winter 1945), 323-24, quoted by Newsinger, 99.
3. Camus's novels are less reflective of the major Cold War issues than his plays. See Caute (2003), Ch. 11, 'Dirty Hands: The Political Theatre of Sartre and Camus.'
4. *Combat*, 7 Oct. 1944.
5. De Beauvoir (1965), 125-26.
6. Kanapa, 105.
7. Camus (Paris, 1953), 202.
8. De Beauvoir (1952), 372.
9. Ibid., 333-34.
10. Ibid., 374.
11. 'Ma conviction, c'est que ces camps ne sont pas exigés par le régime comme le soutient Peltov; ils sont lies à une certaine politique qu'on peut deplorer sans metre en question le regime lui-même.' Ibid., 374-75.
12. Sartre & Merleau-Ponty (1950), 1153-68.
13. Buber-Neumann, 5-8.
14. Ibid., 125.
15. Ibid., 323.
16. Hayman, 257.
17. See Rousset, *passim*.
18. *LLF*, 28 Dec. 1950.
19. *LM*, 24 Nov. 1962.
20. Bernard & Rosenthal, 413.
21. Lottman, 274.
22. Sartre & Merleau-Ponty (1950), 1153-68.
23. *LLF*, 19 Jan. 1950.

14. Koestler: The Little Flirts

1. Goodman, 39.
2. Hamilton 137, 199. Koestler (1956), 403-4.
3. And professor of philosophy at Lyons, the Sorbonne and the Collège de France. The text first appeared in *LTM* under the title 'Le Yogi et le prolétaire.'
4. Cited by Merleau-Ponty, 321.
5. Ibid., 68.
6. For his part, Merleau-Ponty had by the mid-1950s largely abandoned his dialectical illusions.
7. Saunders, 61. Cesarani, 305.
8. Crossman, 1-2, 10.
9. Cesarani, 352.
10. Hamilton, 129.
11. Cesarani, 290 quoting the Koestler Archive, Edinburgh University Library, MS2341/2. L'Herne, 240-47 refers to Pierre Debray-Ritzen (ed.), L'Herne, *Cahiers* No. 27, 'Arthur Koestler,' Paris, 1975.
12. Koestler (1955), 60-61.
13. Ibid., 62-64.
14. 'Political Neuroses,' in ibid., 226.
15. Ibid. 216-17.
16. Ibid., 227-28.
17. Koestler (1951), 105.

18. Ibid., 106-7.
19. Ibid., 225-26, 229-30.
20. Ibid., 431.
21. Ibid., 113.
22. Ibid., 116-17.
23. Ibid., 405.
24. Ibid., 154-55.
25. Levene, 123-24.
26. Goodman, 41-42.
27. Ibid., 58.
28. Koestler (1951), 273.
29. Ibid., 368.
30. Ibid., 266.
31. Crankshaw (1951), 237.
32. Kazin (1951), 398-400.

15. Commentary: Fellow-Travellers

1. Orwell, *CE* (vol. 1), 328.
2. Koestler (1955), 62-64.
3. Serge (1951), 285.
4. Solzhenitsyn *The First Circle*, 330-40.
5. Kundera (1984), 257-67.
6. Ibid., 248-51.

16. Greene: *The Quiet American*

1. Greene (1980), 165.
2. Norman Sherry's research indicates that the American was Leo Hochstetter, who worked under Robert Blum, head of an economic aid mission. Sherry, vol. 2, 418-19.
3. A headline in the *New Republic* (30 July 1951) announced, 'Vietnam *Has* a Third Force,' described as 'a hard nucleus of patriots who are fighting for a truly independent, libertarian Viet Nam.' Cited by Shelden, 398.
4. Greene (1980), 163-64.
5. Ibid., 189.
6. Greene (1955), 65.
7. Ibid., 146-51.
8. Quoted in Sherry, vol. 2, 479-80. In his reference section Sherry does not date the article, which he takes from a reprint translated from the French, but the bibliography in volume 3 indicates 'Indo-China: France's Crown of Thorns,' *PM*, 12 July 1952.
9. On Greene's own opium habit in Saigon and Hanoi, see Sherry, vol.2, 372.
10. Greene (1955), 16.
11. Ibid., 85.
12. Ibid., 57, 74-75.
13. Ibid., 140, 156, 162.
14. Ibid., 95.
15. Ibid., 93.
16. In a 14 Aug. 1956 interview. Greene (1989), 57.
17. Greene (1955), 35.
18. Cited by Sherry, vol. 3, 80.
19. Sherry, vol. 2, 401.
20. Greene (1955), 135.
21. Ibid., 58.
22. Greene (1980), 163-64.
23. Ibid., 164.
24. Sherry, vol. 2, 432.
25. Greene (1989), 56-57.
26. Sherry, vol. 2, 473.

27. *MG*, 25 Oct. 1956. An unsigned article in *Soviet Survey* (no. 9, 1956) reported on the Soviet critical reception of Greene's novel. A special discussion of the book arranged by the Writers' Union appeared in *Inostranaya literatura* (no. 7, 1956).
28. Laqueur & Lichtheim, 42-43.
29 . Sherry, vol. 2, 488-89.

17. Commentary: The Socialist Realist Novel from War to Cold War

1.   Marx & Engels, Book Review 1850, in *Literature and Art*, 35.
2.   Quoted by Polonsky, 228.
3.   Zhdanov, 19-47.
4.   *MN*, 7, 18 June 1947.
5.   Hosking, 101.
6.   Frankel, 10.
7.   Berlin (1980), 58-59.
8.   Sartre, *Iron in the Soul*, 30.
9.   Lyons, 356, 381, 382, 361.
10. Ibid., 363.
11. Ibid., 382, 383
12. Ibid., 395-97.
13. Grossman (956) 148-49. Vse eto ne novo, i takie vospominaniia vriad li seichas sleduet pechatat,' v nashikh interescakh ukrepliat' politiku mira, a ne rasschatyvat' ee.'
14. See I.V.Bekhin, *Istoriya SSSR* and P.M. Kuz'michev, *Noveishaya Istoriya*, both cited in Lyons.
15. Solzhenitsyn, *First Circle*, 109.
16. Deutscher (1949), 455.
17. Solzhenitsyn, *First Circle*, 109-10.
18. No. 3, 7-8.
19. *Anti-Stalin Campaign*, 44-55.
20. *Vazhneishie operatsii Velikoi Otechestvennoi voiny 1941-1945*. Gallagher in Keep, 224.
21. Gallagher in Keep, 229. See in general *Istorii mezhdunarodnykh otnoshenii i vnesheni politiki SSSR*, II (Moscow 1962). On Soviet historiographical policies on Stalin and the debacle of 1941, see Daglish (1969), 6-7. In 1965 the historian Aleksandr M. Nekrich published an officially licensed book, entitled *22 Iiunia 1941g.* (*June 22, 1941*), documenting and discussing Stalin's failure to prepare the country for the German attack. But following a heated discussion at the Party's Institute of Marxism-Leninism, Nekrich was expelled from the party in 1967 and his book withdrawn.
22. First published in *Znamya* (1959, nos. 4 & 10-12).
23. Ainsztein, introd. to Simonov (1962), np.
24. Ellis, 35.
25. Simonov (1962), 336.
26. Solzhenitsyn (1974), 79-80.
27. Ibid., 241.
28. 'Sluchai na stantsii Krechetkovka,' written in 1962, first published in *NM* (Jan. 1963), along with the story 'Matrena's Home' [or Place].
29. Scammell (1984), 115.
30. Solzhenitsyn, *First Circle*, 13-24.
31. Frankel, 94-97.
32. Fadeyev, 34.
33. Ibid., 481. All references are to this excellent French text.
34. Ibid., 36.
35. Ibid., 25.
36. Ibid., 84-85.
37. Ibid., 120-24.
38. Ibid., 223.
39. Ibid., 272.
40. Ibid., 290-93.

41. Ibid., 281-84.
42. Ibid., 337.
43. Ibid., 440-41.
44. Ibid., 534.
45. Ibid., 321.
46. Ibid., 250-55.
47. Ibid., 199-200.
48. Ibid., 212-13.
49. Pavlenko, 193.
50. Ibid., 352.
51. Ibid., 566.
52. Fadeyev, 397.
53. Ibid., 396, 398.
54. Ibid., 470-77.
55. Solzhenitsyn (1974), 85 n.45.
56. Ibid., 240.
57. See Michael Glenny, foreword to Vladimov (1979), 9-18.
58. See Ellis (2003).
59. Pavlenko, 455.
60. Ibid., 110-12.
61. Ibid., 471.
62. Ibid., 264.
63. Ibid., 408.
64. Ibid., 522-23.
65. Kopelev, 57-58.
66. Ibid., 193.
67. Grossman (1985), 216.
68. Solzhenitsyn, *The First Circle*, 55.
69. Aragon in *LLF*, 9 Sept. 1948.
70. *Au Château d'eau* (1951), *Le Coup du canon* (1952), *Paris avec nous* (1953).
71. Cited by Hosking, 18.
72. Kochetov, 463-65.

18. The Tragic Case of Vasily Grossman

1. The name is sometimes rendered 'Vasiliy' or 'Vasilii' but 'Vasily' follows the English-language translation of *Life and Fate*.
2. Ellis (1994), 1.
3. Ibid., 7-8. Ellis draws on Grossman's *Diary of the Manuscript's Passage* from A.G. Bocharov, *Vasily Grossman*, 1990, 164-176.
4. *Molodoi communist* (4, 1953), 127, cited by Ellis (1994), 75.
5. See Grossman (2005), reviewed by Andrey Kurkov, *Guardian Review*, 19 Nov. 2005; and by Anne Appelbaum, *NYRB*, (LIII/6), 6 Apr. 2006.
6. Chandler, np.
7. Vasily Grossman was born in 1905 in the Ukrainian town of Berdichev, one of the largest Jewish communities. A chemist-engineer by training, his first *récit*, fifteen pages long, 'In the Town of Berditchev' was published in *Literaturnaia gazeta*. Gorky read it and invited him to visit. His first novel, *Glückauf* (1934), was about the miners of the Donbass and falls into the category of production novels. See Markish (1983), 17-21. On Grossman's early years and career see also Ellis (1994), 1-5.
8. See Markish (1983), 75-76.
9. *Znamia* (11, 1944), cited ibid., 75.
10. Ibid., 89.
11. Ibid., 92-93.
12. For example A. Lektorski, 'Roman iskazhaiuchtchii obrazy sovetskikh liudei,' 'a novel distorting the portraits of Soviet people' *Kommunist* (3, 1953), 106-15. Or the editorial 'On romane V. Grossmana *Za pravoe delo*,' *Molodoi kommunist* (4, 1953), 127-28. Ellis reports six editions since serialisation in *NM*, from 1954 to 1989. Ellis (1994), 222.

13. Frankel, 12.
14. Markish (1983), 94.
15. Ellis (1994), 11.
16. See ibid, viii-ix.
17. Grossman wrote a long report of the discussion from memory, which after his death was deposited in the *spetskhran* of a state archive (TSGALI) where it lay untouched until 1988.
18. Ellis (1994), 13-16.
19. Markish (1983), 147. Markish in his reference notes uses a French notation i.e transcription of Grossman's Russian titles. Thus: *Life and Destiny* = *Vie et Destin* = *Jizn i soudba* = *JS* in its Russian-language version published by L'Age d'Homme in 1980. *VD* refers to its French translation, published by Julliard-L'Age d'Homme, 1983.
20. Markish (1986), 42.
21. Grossman (1985), 16 & Chandler, np.
22. Grossman (1985), 13.
23. Ibid., 647.
24. Grossman (1956), 122.
25. Ellis (1994), 177-78.
26. Bayley, 4.

19. Commentary: Collectivization

1. Serge (1951), 106, 107, 111.
2. Getty, 225 n12.
3. *NYT*, 26 Sept. 1959; Alexandrova (1962), 269.
4. Clark & Dobchenko, 336-342.
5. Alexandrova (1962), 259-60.
6. Medvedev, Roy, (1971), 211.
7. Fadeyev, 257-8.
8. Grossman (1943), 48-50.
9. Grossman (1956), 16. Obychno konchal tak: a boobshche vse by khorosho, tolko by ne kolkhozy.
10. Ibid., 16.
11. Markish (1983), 155.
12. *NM* (8, 1952), 129-30, and (9, 1952), 11-12.
13. Grossman (1973), 141-43.
14. Ibid., 139-166.
15. Ibid., 162-63.
16. Solzhenitsyn (1971), 23-24.
17. Solzihenitsyn, *The First Circle*, 416-17.
18. Kopelev, 12.

20. Pasternak: *Doctor Zhivago*

1. Hosking, 34
2. In 1956 Berlin brought him some Kafka but Pasternak took no interest and gave them to Akhmatova, 'who admired them intensely.' Berlin (200), 178.
3. Fleischman, 254-55.
4. Fleischman, 254.
5. Not until the novel was awarded the Nobel Prize did *NM's* liberal editor, the poet A. Tvardovsky, permit *LG* to publish the September 1956 letter to Pasternak, adding 'the disgust and contempt which we, like all Soviet writers, feel over Pasternak's present shameful and unpatriotic attitude.'
6. Hosking, 33.
7. Pasternak, 463.
8. Quoted Conquest (1961), 67-68.
9. *DT*, 25 Oct. 1958. *ST*, 9 Nov. 1958.
10. Conquest (1961), 90, 127, 131.

11. Fleischman, 295.
12. Hingley (1983), 241.
13. Conquest (1961), 49, 97.
14. Levi, 248. Hingley (1983), 245-46.
15. Hosking, 35.
16. Ibid., 34, Pasternak, 71 (66).
17. Hosking, 34-5, Pasternak, 17-18 (10).
18. Pasternak, 15.
19. Ibid., 148.
20. Ibid., 463.
21. Deutscher (1969), 261.
22. Pasternak, 366-67.
23. Deutscher (1969), 263; Ehrenburg, *Men, Years, Life*, vol. 1, 55.
24. Deutscher (1969), 253.
25. Pasternak, 273.
26. Deutscher (1969), 258-59.
27. These comments are found in Hingley (1983), 224-25.
28. *TLS*, 2 July 1999, 13.
29. Pasternak, 225.
30. Ibid., 418.
31. Ibid., 226.
32. Ibid., 227.
33. Ibid., 268.
34. Ibid., 268.
35. Ibid., 413.
36. Ibid., 406.
37. Ibid., 413.
38. Deutscher (1969), 256-257.
39. Pasternak, 115.
40. Ibid., 202.
41. Sinyavsky (1990), 138.
42. Pasternak, 301-3.
43. Ibid., 449.
44. Ibid.. 340.
45. Gifford, 27.
46. Yevtushenko (1963), 117-19, discusses Pasternak.
47. Deutscher (1969), 266.
48. Fleischman, 314.

21. Chukovskaya: Honour among Women

1. By Library of Congress transliteration, her name should be rendered Lidiia Chukovskaia, but here we use the version found in Western translations of her work.
2. Chukovskaya (1994), 3.
3. Ibid., 3. The translation here is awkward.
4. Ibid., 247.
5. Ibid., 181.
6. In 1965 the Pyat' Kontinentov publishing house in Paris put out what she called a 'distorted version' under the title of *Opustelyi Dom* (*The Deserted House*), a phrase taken from Akhmatova's *Rekviem*, the series of poems on the Yezhov terror. Characters' names were changed, including 'Olga' for the heroine Sof'ya. Translations from this version appeared in English, French, German and other languages. This 'distorted version' carries an author's preface, in which she reports that after the siege of Leningrad, 'The people keeping the manuscript perished, but the manuscript itself survived. 'The version approved by Chukovskaya was published in New York in Russian as *Sof'ya Petrovna* (*Novyi zhurnal* [83, 84]). Not until 1988 did it appear within the USSR, in the Leningrad journal *Neva* (no. 2).

7.   Chukovskaya (1967), 10.
8.   Ibid., 77.
9.   Ibid., 26.
10. Ibid., 43.
11. Ibid., 21.
12. Ibid., 70-71.
13. Murray, introd. to Chukovskaya (1998), xiv.
14. Chukovskaya (1967), 89, 91.
15. Ibid., 95. Chukovskaya (1998), 74.
16. Chukovskaya (1967), 88. Chukovskaya (1998), 68.
17. Chukovskaya (1967), 121.
18. Chukovskaya (1972), 27.
19. Ibid., 64.
20. Ibid., 93.
21. Ibid., 91.
22. Fadeyev's letter is in Clark & Dobrenko, 471. See Simonov (1949), 183-8.
23. See Caute (2003), ch. 4.
24. Chukovskaya (1972), 69.
25. Ibid., 134-35.
26. Medvedev, Zhores (1974, *NYRB*).
27. In 1960 Chukovskaya published *V laboratorii redaktora*, on the art of editing, and in 1966 *Byloe i dumy Gertsena*, about Aleksandr Herzen.
28. *ST*, 13 Nov. 1966.
29. Solzhenitsyn (1997), 100.
30. Her povest,' *Spusk pod vodu*, came out in Paris in 1972. Further polemics, poems, memoirs followed, as well as the three volumes devoted to Akhmatova.
31. Garrard, 154.
32. The episode is described in her *Protsess isklyucheniya: Ocherk literaturnykh nravov* (Paris, 1979).
33. Garrard, 146 ref. 13, citing Chukovskaia, *Protsess isklyuchenia*, 51.
34. Garrard, 154-55.
35. Scammell (1984), 827-32.
36. The translator Alexis Klimoff notes the difficulty of rendering Chukovskaia's play on the various meanings of the word *predat'* (to betray). See Klimoff in Dunlop, 456-57.
37. *Zapiski ob Anne Akhmatovoi/Lidiia Chukovskaia*, redactor L.S. Erminal, (Kniga, Moskva, 1989) covers the years 1952-62. See also ref.2, above, *The Akhmatova Journals*.

22. Commentary: Purge and Terror

1.   Chukovaksya (1998) 62. Chukovskaya (1957), 81.
2.   Chukovskaya (1998), 21.
3.   Solzhenitsyn (1974), 7.
4.   Chukovskaya (1967), 66.
5.   Ignatieff (1997), 10.
6.   Dalos, 37, quoting Berlin's report to the Foreign Office on his Russian trip.
7.   Berlin (2000), 56.
8.   1946 Central Committee Resolution on Leningrad journals. Bilingual edition, Royal Oak Michigan, 1978.
9.   Akhmatova's first husband, the poet Nikolai Gumilyov, had been shot by the Cheka in 1921. Her second husband, the art historian Nikolai Punin, died in a camp. Her son, Lev Gumilyov, suffered arrest three times and spent a total of eighteen years in camps.
10. Grossman (1975), 182.
11. Pasternak, 452-53.
12. Simonov (1962), 119.
13. Ibid., 120.
14. Ibid., 120.
15. Solzhenitsyn, *First Circle*, 199.

16. *NM* (1990/3), 75, 80. *First Circle*, 267-68, 274.
17. Solzhenitsyn, *Cancer Ward*, vol. II, 218.
18. Lukács, 74-75, citing *Cancer Ward*, vol. II, 164.
19. *Cancer Ward*, vol. II, 166-67.
20. Ibid., vol. I, 222, 217.
21. Solzhenitsyn (1974), 74-75.
22. Ibid., 11.

23. The Iron Fist: The Trial of Daniel and Sinyavsky

1. Hayward, 15-18.
2. *LM*, 11 Feb. 1966.
3. Sinyavsky/Tertz, *The Trial Begins* (*Trial*), 32.
4. Ibid., 96.
5. Ibid., 85, 87, 79.
6. Milosz, in Sinyavsky/Tertz, *On Socialist Realism* (*SR*), 9, 10, 19.
7. Sinyavsky/Tertz, *SR*, 38.
8. Ibid., 52, 75.
9. Ibid., 94-95.
10. *S. Telegraph*, 28 July 1968.
11. Sinyavsky/Tertz, *SR*, 68,69.
12. Including *Fantastic Stories*, his collection of aphorisms, *Unguarded Thoughts*, the unfinished 'Essay in Self-Analysis' confiscated during the search of his apartment, and the short story 'Pkhentz,' recently published in the West in Polish and English.
13. Quoted in *Guardian*, 20 Jan. 1966.
14. Leonard Schapiro commented in the *Guardian* (22 Jan. 1966) that the President of the Supreme Court of the USSR, A. Gorkin, had in December 1964 published a directive on 'Socialist justice' in which, inter alia, he deplored the 'occasional' practice of some newspapers in publishing articles in guilt is taken for granted before the trial takes place.
15. *LM*, 19 Jan. 1966. *Guardian*, 20 Jan. 1966. *Observer*, 23 Jan. 1966.
16. *SN*, 11 Feb. 1966.
17. *NYT*, 23 Jan. 1966.
18. Sinyavsky/Tertz, *Trial*, 57, 98-101, 125.
19. By the mid-sixties International PEN had seventy-six centres in fifty-five countries. The Congress for Cultural Freedom had bent its energies since the 1950s to keep the Communists from achieving influence within PEN.
20. Quoted in *NYT*, 21 Feb. 1966.
21. *NYT*, 16 Mar. 1966.
22. For first-hand evidence, see Marchenko, 367-83.
23. *ST*, 13 Nov. 1966.
24. *Times* (London), 4 Sept. 1967.
25. Greene (1989), 144-45.

24. Foreign Affairs: The Menace of Kafka

1. Barghoorn (1964), 77, cites Melvin J. Ruggles, 'American Books in Soviet Publishing,' *Slavic Review* (XX/3, Oct. 1961), 431-432.
2. *NYT*, 12 Aug. 1959.
3. See Laqueur & Lichtheim, 58-60.
4. On the *Forsyte Saga* shown on Russian TV, see Daglish (1971), 63-64.
5. *Times* (London), 23, 24, 30 Nov. 1959; *DW* (London), 23 Nov. 1959.
6. Reported in *SN*, 15 Oct. 1959.
7. Carl Marzani was a Communist official in New York for whom Ethel Rosenberg worked during the war. He is said to have worked for Soviet intelligence agents.
8. Steiner, 320.
9. Khrushchev, 72-75.
10. Johnson, Priscilla, 170, 145. Conquest (1969), 134.

11. *LG.*, 8 Aug. 1963, quoted by P. Johnson, 65.
12. *L'Express*, 22 Aug. 1963, quoted by P. Johnson, 65.
13. The conference was reported at length in 'The Condition of the Novel' (see bibliog.), 19-39.
14. Werth, 205-9.
15. Scammell (1984), 477.
16. Franz Kafka (1883-1924) was born to a middle-class German speaking family in Prague. He composed his works in German. Deeply alienated by his relationship with his father, his fiction describes the struggle of alienated individuals to comprehend the rules of an impersonal, often bureaucratic, society riddled by persecution and reflexive cruelty. His major works (including *Metamorphosis*, *In the Penal Colony*, *The Trial* and *The Castle*) brought him to public attention only after his death, due to the efforts of his admiring literary executor, Max Brod. These works were banned in the totalitarian states. The over-used term 'Kafkaesque' denotes a regimented world lost to the logic of the absurd.
17. Nekrasov, 59-60.
18. Brecht (1993), 462-463.
19. On Lukács's distinction between realism and naturalism (Zola) see Jameson, 160-205.
20. Lichtheim, 74, 80.
21. Mayer & Bondy, 83-89.
22. Goldstücker, whose family had perished in Auschwitz, had been condemned to life imprisonment at the time of the Slansky trial in 1952. In 1962 he became Rector of Charles University. At the time of the Dubček government in 1968 he was Chairman of the Czechoslovak Writers' Union. He later took refuge in England. Kafka went with him.
23. Fischer & Mittenzwei, Reprinted in *LNC*, Apr. 1963, 81-92.
24. Quoted by Mallac, 66-67.
25. A year later Aragon published his *Entretiens avec Francis Crémieux*, in which he barely mentioned politics or socialism, confining himself to his happy encounters with surrealism, Joyce, Cummings, Shakespeare, Mallarmé, love, and narrative time. Evidently there were two Aragons—at least.
26. *LNC*, Mar. 1963, 73-79.
27. Gisselbrecht, 39-52.
28. 'Entretien à Prague sur la notion de "décadence", *LNC*, juin-juillet 1964, 73-84.
29. *LNC*, juin-juillet 1964, 61-66.
30. David Hotham, *Guardian*, 6 Sept. 1968.
31. Dymshits's essays were published in Moscow as *Nishcheta sovetologie i revizionizma – Poverty of Sovetology and Revisionism* (1975). *SL* (7, 1960), 203.
32. Kundera (1970), 30.
33. Kundera (1993), 266.
34. Kundera (1970), 221-22.
35. Ibid., 198-205.
36. Kundera (1982), 66.
37. Ibid., 59 65.
38. Ibid., 5.
39. Ibid., 165-166.
40. Ibid., 157-159.
41. Havel (1976), 175.
42. Havel (1990), 176.
43. Brodsky, 31.
44. Kundera (1993), 262-63.
45. *Guardian*, 12 Oct. 1977, 10, quoted by Hames, 142.
46. Kundera (1993), 263.
47. For fuller accounts see Boyd Tonkin, 'The unbearable betrayal of Milan Kundera, *The Independent* (London), 14 Oct. 2008, and 'Eleven Authors Rally in Defense of Milan Kundera' (4 Nov. 2008), www.pw.org/content/eleven_authors_rally_defense_milan_kundera.

25. Germany Doubly Divided: Wolf and Johnson

1. Other works include *Nachdenken uber Christa T* (*The Quest for Christa T*, 1968), *Kindersheitsmuster* (*Patterns of Childhood*, 1976), *Kassandra* (*Cassandra*, 1983). She was awarded the Georg Buchner Prize in 1980 and the Schiller Memorial prize in 1983.
2. Magenau, 140.
3. Ibid., 141.
4. See ibid., 96-108.
5. Wolf (1965), 49.
6. Ibid., 18-19.
7. Ibid., 62. 69, 65.
8. Ibid., 57.
9. Ibid., 111.
10. Ibid., 138.
11. Aber wir brauchen keine Nachplapperer, sondern Sozialisten.
12. Wolf (1985), 185.
13. Ibid., 190; Wolf (1963), 277.
14. Wolf (1965), 191, 195, 197.
15. Ibid., 198.
16. Ibid., 142; Wolf (1963), 211.
17. Magenau, 198-205.
18. Huyssen, 106.
19. Enzensberger, 86-87.
20. Baker, Gary, 27-28.
21. Johnson, Uwe (1963), 54.
22. Ibid., 128.
23. In the German original the lovers are endowed only with initials, 'young Herr B' and 'Krankenschwester D'; in the English translation they are accorded Christian names, Dietbert and Beate.
24. Riordan, 61.
25. Johnson, Uwe (1967), 119 .
26. Ibid., 26.
27. Ibid., 24.
28. I am indebted to Heather Gumbert, of Virginia Tech, for her paper, 'Narrating the Second Berlin Crisis in the GDR: Television before the Berlin Wall.'
29. Johnson (1967), 29-30.
30. Ibid., 35.
31. Ibid., 18. 'Er fühlte sich elbst gekränkt durch die Einsperrung der D. [Beate] in ihrem Berlin. er hatte eine private Wut auf die Sperrzone. Minenfelder. Postenketten. Hindernisgraben...' Johnson, *Zwei Ansichten*, 25, cited by Neumann, 527.
32. Johnson (1967), 37.
33. Ibid., 106, 108.
34. The novel is indebted to Sonja and Bernt Richter, who had assisted Johnson's escape (before the Wall) and to the flight of his fiancée Elisabeth Schmidt. See Neumann, 445.
35. See Neumann, 527-38.
36. Cited by Baker, Gary, 17, 18.

26. *One Day in the Life of Ivan Denisovich*

1. Scammell (1984), 440.
2. *Bolalsya telenok s dubom* – in full *The Calf Collided with the Oak*.
3. Marsh, 157 ref. 99, citing L. Kopelev, 'Solzhenitsyn na sharashke,' *Vremya i my* (Jerusalem, no. 40, 1979), 187.
4. Scammell (1984), 8.
5. Akhmatova quoted in *Survey* (24/1, Winter 1979), 134-35. See Marsh, 209, refs 30, 31.

6. Carlisle (1978), 15.
7. Marsh, 209, refs 30, 31, citing Alain Besançon, 'Solzhenitsyn at Harvard,' *Survey* (24/1 Winter 1979), 134.
8. It is hard to agree with Marsh when she describes Solzhenitsyn as 'a fiction writer who also has pretensions to being a serious historian of twentieth-century Russia.' Marsh, 142.
9. Solzhenitsyn's autobiographical sketch for the anthology *Nobel Prize Winners of 1970* (Stockholm, 1971), reprinted in Scammell (1984), 335-37.
10. *Odin den' Ivan Denisovicha.*
11. Scammell (1984), citing Chukovsky.
12. Burg & Feifer, 166-70.
13. Slonim, 363.
14. Johnson, Pricilla, 181.
15. Hosking, 43.
16. Ibid., 41, citing *One Day* (Bantam ed.), 66-67.
17. Hosking, 46, citing *One Day*, 45. According to Hosking, the *NM* text (11/62) on which the Bantam translation is based, is much shortened at this point, due either to censorship or self-censorship. The fuller text is found in the Sovteskii Pisatel' version, 1963, 77, on which Hosking's translation is based.
18. Brudny, 51.
19. Solzhenitsyn (1974), 56.
20. Hosking, 46. Solzhenitsyn, *One Day*, 15, 196.
21. Examples provided by Hosking, 44.
22. During 1964 and 1965 some factual reports about the camps appeared inside the USSR. Slonim, 364.
23. Burg & Feifer, 325. Solzhenitsyn (1980), 268.

27. *The First Circle*

1. Ehrlich, 23n. The original Russian title is *V Kruge pervom*, literally 'In The First Circle.'
2. Ch. 55 of the *NM* version, ch. 50 of the original English version.
3. Solzhenitsyn, *First Circle*, 462.
4. Terrence Des Pres, 'The Heroism of Survival,' in Dunlop, 52.
5. Solzhenitsyn, *First Circle*, 155.
6. Ibid., 228.
7. Ibid., 215-16.
8. Scammell (1984), 497.
9. Solzhenitsyn (1974), 126.
10. Ibid., 158-59.
11. Scammell (1984), 582.
12. Ehrlich, 17, citing *V kruge pervom*, Paris, YMCA Press, 1969, 477.
13. Solzhenitsyn, *First Circle*, 206, 262.
14. Ibid., 317.
15. Ibid., 66.
16. Ibid., 203.
17. Solzhenitsyn (1974), 7.
18. Ibid., 160-61.
19. Solzhenitsyn, *First Circle*, 346.
20. Ibid., 536.
21. Solzhenitsyn (1980), 102.
22. Thomas, 315, citing Olga Carlisle (1978), 16.
23. Solzhenitsyn later sharpened a sixth version and smuggled the microfilm out via the son of the Italian Communist writer Vittorio Strada. In 1968 the 87-chapter version was published in the West. His goose was cooked. The 1978 version, revised in exile, restores the text to its original form.
24. Scammell (1984), 557.

28. Commentary: Stalin and Lenin in Soviet Fiction

1.   Hingley (1978), 112.
2.   Schapiro, 406; Fischer, 58 .
3.   Counts, 151-6; Mead, 61.
4.   Kochetov, 217.
5.   Ibid., 218.
6.   Ibid., 349, 339, 351.
7.   Malraux (1968), 333.
8.   Serge (1951), 43.
9.   Ibid., 151.
10. Ibid., 153.
11. Ibid., 155.
12. Salisbury, 20.
13. Sinyavsky/Tertz, *Trial*, 76, 77.
14. Rosalind Marsh points out that this technique of external characterisation is also found in Victor Hugo's *Quàtre-Vingt Treize* (Marat, Danton, Robespierre), in Anatole France's novel of the French Revolution, *Les Dieux ont Soif*, and in Tolstoy's two novels *War and Peace* (Napoleon)and *Hadji Murat* (Tsar Nicholas I). Marsh, 3.
15. In his detailed study of literary technique in the Stalin chapters of Circle-87, Gary Kern distinguishes four voices: omniscient author; the character's indirect interior monologue; the ironic author; and the character's 'direct discourse.' G. Kern, 'Solzhenitsyn's Portrait of Stalin,' *Slavic Review*, 33, 1974, 1-22. Rosalind Marsh argues that the term 'narrated monologue' is preferable to Kern's 'indirect interior monologue' (which she holds to be 'confused' because it is not strictly 'indirect'). Marsh, 185-187, ref. 8.
16. Schmemann, 523.
17. Marsh, 187, ref. 9, citing Solzhenitsyn, *Sob. Soch.*, vol. 1, 133.
18. Solzhenitsyn (*First* Circle), 97.
19. Ibid., 99.
20. Ibid., 100.
21. Ibid., 108, 113.
22. Ibid., 116.
23. Ibid., 115.
24. Marsh, 150.
25. Marsh, 180, 182.
26. Solzhenitsyn, *First Circle*, 116.
27. Ibid., 118.
28. Marsh, 149.
29. Ibid., 153 refs 83 84, refers to A. Orlov, *The Secret History of Stalin's Crimes*, London, 1954, 240, and to A. Solzhenitsyn, *Sob. Soch.* vol. 1, 1978, 130.
30. Roy Medvedev in Dunlop, 465-66.
31. Marsh, 154, ref. 88, citing Solzhenitsyn, *Sob. Soch.*, vol. 1 (1978), 130.
32. Marsh, 154-55.
33. Ibid. 141, ref. 26. Solzhenitsyn (1980), 78. The sources available to him in the USSR when writing *The First Circle* included Stalin's writings, official and unofficial biographies, literary works of the cult period, Khrushchev's secret speech, Djilas's *Conversations with Stalin*. Marsh suggests that 'most probably' the manuscript of Roy Medvedev's *Let History Judge*, a work which contains psychological interpretations echoed in *The First Circle*, 'may well have exerted the most significant influence on Solzhenitsyn.'
34. Solzhenitsyn, *Cancer Ward*, vol. II, 22, 23.
35. Solzhenitsyn (1974), 69.
36. In all probability it was constantly revised during these sterile years; the English version gives the dates of composition as 1966-83, Moscow. This makes Solzhenitsyn's influence a distinct possibility.
37. Marsh, 81, ref. 86, citing *IHT*, 16 Mar. 1987.
38. Rybakov, 577-79.
39. Ibid., 350-351.

40. Ibid., 278-281.
41. Ibid., 566.
42. Ibid., 283.
43. Ibid., 567.
44. Ibid., 568-69.
45. Ibid., 632-37.
46. Ibid., 275.
47. Ibid., 345.
48. Ibid., 348.
49. Ibid., 496, 498.
50. Ibid., 498-99.
51. Ibid., 505.
52. Ibid., 685.
53. Grossman (1975), 192.
54. Ibid., 228.
55. Ibid., 198.
56. Ibid., 200.
57. Ibid., 212, 217.
58. Scammell (1984), 942.
59. Solzhenitsyn (1976), 22.
60. Ibid., 35, 88.
61. Twelve titles in Russian are cited, theses, essays, correspondence, nine of them taken from Lenin, *Sobranie Sochinenii*, 4th edition, and one from the 5th edition: *Pis'ma Lenina voennykh let, 1914-1917*, vols. 48, 49. Listed in Solzhenitsyn (1976), 222.
62. Solzhenitsyn (1976), 16, 21.
63. Ibid., 153, 91.
64. Ibid., 175, 218.
65. His sources included Werner Hahlweg, *Lenins Rückkehr nach Russland 1917*, which reproduces correspondence between Baron Romberg, German ambassador to Bern, and the Ministry of Foreign Affairs; Romberg to Zimmerman, Secretary of State to the Supreme High Command; Zimmerman's reply; Romberg to Imperial Chancellor Bethmann Hollweg. Solzhenitsyn also cites Z. A. B. Zeman and W. B. Scharlau, *The Merchant of Revolution*, London, 1965; Willi Gautschi, *Lenin als Emigrant in der Schweiz*, Köln, 1971; and Fritz N. Platten Jun.: *Von der Spiegelgasse in den Kreml. Volksrecht, 13iii-17iv.67.*
66. Solzhenitsyn (1975), 12.
67. Ibid., 12.

29. From *Cancer Ward* to *The Gulag Archipelago*

1. Solzhenitsyn, *Cancer* Ward, vol. I, 36.
2. Ibid, vol. II, 175.
3. Lukács, 75.
4. Scammell (1984), 568.
5. Ibid., 571.
6. Burg & Feifer, 245.
7. This highly confidential discussion appeared in transcript in the July-August 1968 issue of the US Information Agency's *Problems of Communism.*
8. Burg & Feifer, 261.
9. Ibid., 264.
10. Solzhenitsyn, *First Circle*, 377.
11. Solzhenitsyn (1980), 470-75.
12. Solzhenitsyn, *Cancer Ward*, vol. II, 473.
13. Solzhenitsyn (1980), 479.
14. Ibid., 480.
15. Ibid., 471-72.
16. Ibid., 483.
17. Quoted by Frankel, 143.

18. *NM* (1965, 11), 3-8, cited by Frankel 142-43.
19. Scammell (1995), 98.
20. Quoted by Zhores Medvedev, *Ten Years*, 148.
21. Scammell (1984), 748-49.
22. Carlisle (1978), 16, 65.
23. The text of Solzhenitsyn's letter to Andropov is in Scammell (1995), 159.
24. Ibid., 158-60. Aleksandr Gorlov was subsequently dismissed from his institute. He emigrated to the USA in 1975; YMCA Press, Paris, published his Russian-language report of the incident at the dacha.
25. Ibid., 161-164.
26. 1971, English translation 1972.
27. He coined the term 'knot' to describe three chronological stages of *August 1914* and the volumes planned to follow it.
28. Ehre, 'On August 1914,' in Dunlop, 352. There are 64 chapters, which comprise 35 episodes in direct narration, 2 flashbacks, 4 summaries, 3 montages of newspaper clippings.
29. Mary McCarthy, 'The Tolstoy Connection,' in Dunlop, 334-35.
30. Scammell (1984), 789.
31. Nina Khrushcheva, 'Russia's tarnished icon,' *Guardian*, 24 Apr. 1999.
32. Dunlop, 337.
33. Scammell (1984), 791.
34. Solzhenitsyn (1974), xii.
35. Crankshaw (1984), 216-17.
36. Solzhenitsyn (1974), x-xi.
37. Scammell (1984), 941.
38. Ibid., 824.
39. Solzhenitsyn (1980), 418-48.
40. 'Put' predatel'stva,' *Pravda*, 14 Jan. 1974.
41. Slonim, 375.
42. Scammell (1984), 981.

30. Commentary: Bureaucracy, the New Class and Double Standards

1. Orwell (1949), 169.
2. Fadeyev, 377.
3. Pasternak, 179, 192.
4. Grossman (1985), 779.
5. Sinyavsky/Tertz, *Trial*, 91.
6. Ehrenburg (1955), 41, 53.
7. Mehnert, 114; Conquest (1960), 153.
8. According to Katerina Clark there is an ideal model ('master plot') for the socialist realist novel. She lists a core group of exemplars including Gorky *(Mother* and *Kim Samgin)*, D. Furmanov's Chapaev, A. Serifomovich's *The Iron Flood*, F. Gladkov's *Cement*, Sholkhov's *Quiet Flows the Don* and *Virgin Soil Upturned*, A. Tolstoy's *The Road to Calvary* and *Peter the First*, N. Ostrovsky, *How the Steel was Tempered*, A. Fadeyev's *The Rout* and *The Young Guard*. Clark (1981), 4. Clark produces a longer list based on favourable references at official events, see Clark (1981), 262-63. She identifies six genres: the production novel; the historical novel; the novel about a worthy intellectual or inventor;—the novel of war or revolution; the villain or spy novel; novels about the West. All involve a road to consciousness and usually a task. Clark (1981), 255-58.
9. Clark (1981), 15.
10. Dudintsev, 174, 197, 212.
11. Ibid., 216.
12. Ibid., 250.
13. Ibid., 326; Clark (1981), 218.
14. Dudintsev, 385.
15. Reprinted in Laqueur & Lichtheim, 56.

16.   Clark (1981), 218-219.
17.   *LG*, 19 Oct. 1963, cited in Solzhenitsyn, '*For the Good of the Cause*', 114-15.
18   Lukács, 25.
19   Solzhenitsyn, *First Circle*, 367.
20   Ibid., 367.
21   Ibid, 240. *NM* (1990/3), 42.
22   Solzhenitsyn, *Cancer Ward*, vol. I, 210-11.
23   Ibid., vol. I, 214.
24   Ibid., 227.
25   Ibid., 228-29.
26   Ibid., vol. II, 130-31.
27   Ibid., 135-36.
28   Ibid., 103.
29   Ibid., 138.
30   Ibid., vol. II, 133.
31   Conquest (1960), 153-54.

31. Vladimov: *Faithful Ruslan*

1.   Solzhenitsyn (1980), 164, 521.
2.   *Tri minuty molchaniya*, Sovremennik, Moscow, 1976. Trans. by Michael Glenny (London, 1985).
3.   Quoted by Porter (1989), 147-49.
4.   Sinyavsky/Tertz (1989), 22-24.
5.   Sinyavsky/Tertz, *Trial*, 115-16.
6.   Porter (1989), 152.
7.   Ibid., 158-59.
8.   Ibid., 161.
9.   Vladimov (1979), 37.
10.   Ibid., 51, 54.
11.   Porter (1989), 157.
12.   Vladimov (1979), 65.
13.   An abridged version of this letter appeared in the *NYRB* (4 May 1978).
14.   Published as 'Ne obrashchayte vnimanyya, maestro,' by Possev, Frankfurt (1983).
15.   Vladimov (1983), 44.
16.   B. Ivanov, 'Otshchepentsy nachinayut i proigryvavyut,' *LG*, 14 Jan. 1987, 15. B. Ivanov, 'Yeshcho raz ob igrakh otshchepentsev,' *LG*, 30 Sept. 1987, 15, cited by Porter (1989), 169. Vladimov's novel *The General and His Army* (*General i ego armii*) boldly takes up the fraught story of Vlasov's army, and the issue of collaboration, which Solzhenitsyn had confronted in *The First Circle*, *The Gulag Archipelago*, and in the early verse play *Feast of the Conquerors*. See Ellis (2003), 33.

32. Commentary: Fiction, the New Journalism, and the Postmodern

1.   Weber (1980), 9.
2.   Wolfe, 49-50.
3.   See Graff, 32.
4.   Reprinted in Howe (1970).
5.   Huyssen, 161.
6.   Scholes, 233.
7.   Cornis-Pope, 11.
8.   Graff, 55, 208.
9.   Scholes, 233.
10.   Sukenick, *The Life Fiction* (1977) cited by Graff, 171; Federman, *Surfiction: Fiction Now and Tomorrow* (1975) cited by Graff, 60.
11.   Cited by Graff, 174.
12.   J. Hillis Miller, 'The Fiction of Realism' (1971), cited by Graff, 19, 242.

13. Cornis-Pope, xii.
14. Cornis-Pope, 53.
15. Cornis-Pope, 94.
16. Coover (1979), 336.
17. Paul Maltby, *Dissident Postmodernists: Barthelme, Coover, Pynchon* Philadelphia, 1991, 25, cited by Cornis-Pope, 5.
18. Cornis-Pope, xiii, 6.
19. Raymond Federman, *Surfiction: Fiction Now and Tomorrow*, 7, cited by Graff, 60.
20. See Cornis-Pope, 8, 10.

33. Mailer: *The Armies of the Night*

1. Asselineau,155, quoting Richard Foster, *Norman Mailer* (Minnesota, 1968), 10.
2. Mailer (1951), 59.
3. Ibid., 88, 199.
4. Podhoretz (1999), 182.
5. Schaub, 72.
6. Asselineau, 162.
7. Mailer (1968), 76.
8. Ibid., 154. Weber (1980), 86.
9. Mailer (1968), 286.
10. Ibid., 120, 128, 131.
11. Ibid., 91-93.
12. Ibid., 288; Weber (1980), 82.

34. Fiction and the Rosenbergs: E. L. Doctorow and Robert Coover

1. E. L. Doctorow (1931-) was born in New York City of Russian-Jewish descent. He graduated from Kenyon College, served in the army, and published his first novel, *Welcome to Hard Times* in 1960. After working as a publishing editor, he completed the novel that was to establish his reputation, *The Book of Daniel* while a visiting writer at UC, Irvine (he was to maintain close links with the academic world). Subsequent novels include the best-selling *Ragtime* and *World's Fair.*
2. Doctorow (2003), 51.
3. Doctorow (1983), 62; Levine, 40.
4. For example, when were the Isaacsons arrested and when did their trial take place? When their execution? (In the Rosenberg case the answers to these questions are 1950, 1951, 1953.) On several occasions the novel confuses 1951 with 1954.
5. James Wood, 'A Striking Approach to Radical History,' *The Guardian*, 4 June, 1994.
6. Doctorow (1971), 94, 95, 32.
7. Ibid., 34, 33.
8. Ibid., 81-82.
9. Ibid., 150.
10. Rubin, Jerry, 90-91.
11. Doctorow (1971), 302.
12. Ibid., 227.
13. Ibid., 214, 212.
14. Ibid., 221-22.
15. Klaus Fuchs was a German-born refugee physicist, British by naturalization, who had worked on the Manhattan Project 1944-45 and who occupied a senior post at the British atomic centre, Harwell, until his arrest and conviction.
16. Doctorow (1971), 225, 227, 232.
17. Ibid., 282.
18. Quoted by Tanenhaus, 41.
19. Fiedler, 51-52.
20. Ibid., 25, cited by Hite, 88.
21. Warshow, 76.
22. Doctorow (1971), 53-54.

23. Ibid., 278-92.
24. Ibid., 234-37.
25. Meeropol, 326.
26. Doctrow (1971), 236-37.
27. Robert Coover (1932-), a writer of fabulation and metafiction, was born in Iowa, graduated from Indiana (Slavic Studies) in 1955, then served in the US Navy. His first novel, *The Origin of the Brunists*, was followed by others including *The Universal Baseball Association, Inc* and a volume of short stories, *Pricksongs and Descants*. Winner of the 1987 Rea Award for the Short Story, and one of the founders of the Electronic Literature Organization, he is a professor in the Literary Arts program at Brown University.
28. Dee, passim. See also review of Grove paperback edition 1998, www.findarticles.com.
29. Coover (1977), 23.
30. Walsh, 334, cites Thomas Alden Bass, 'An Encounter with Robert Coover,' *Antioch Review* (40, 1982), 297.
31. Coover (1977), 99.
32. Ibid., 305-6, 311-12.
33. Ibid., 445.
34. Carmichael, 160-62.
35. No. 1657 VENONA files quoted by Weinstein, 333. See also Haynes & Klehr, 16.
36. Weinstein, 217, citing File 40594, vol. 7, 352-53.
37. Weinstein, 331, file 86192, vol. 1, 132
38. Radosh, 417.
39. Weinstein, 217, file 40594, vol. 7, 352-53.
40. Hite, 86.
41. Carmichael, 160-62.
42. Eagleton, 139-140.
43. LeClair, 5-6.
44. McCaffery, 85-87.
45. Ickstadt (1986).
46. Quoted by Evenson, 111.
47. Gass, xvi.

Conclusion

1. Howe (1957), 254.
2. Solzhenitsyn, *First Circle*, 107.
3. To list some of these figures may support the point: Adorno, Horkheimer, Arendt, Aron, Friedrich, Popper, Berlin, Schapiro, Lipset, Shils, Glazer, Hofstadter, Parsons, Macdonald, Wolfe, Howe, Hook, Niebuhr, Schlesinger, Beloff, Hughes, Moore, Bell, Kennan, Polyani, Mannheim, Talmon, Trevor-Roper.

Bibliography

Alexandrova, Vera, 'Soviet Literature since Stalin,' *Problems of Communism*, 4/3 (July-August 1954).
————, *Soviet Literature Under Stalin* (NY, 1962).
The Anti-Stalin Campaign and International Communism. A selection of documents (NY, 1956).
Arzhak, Nikolai (see Daniel, Yuli).
Asselineau, Roger, 'Norman Mailer's Quest among the Naked and the Dead,' in Bock & Wertheim.
Baker, Carlos, *Hemingway. The Writers as Artist* (Princeton, NJ, 1973).
Baker, Gary L., *Understanding Uwe Johnson,* Columbia (South Carolina, 1999).
Barghoorn, Frederick C., *Soviet Foreign Propaganda*, (Princeton, NJ, 1964).
Bayley, John, 'Off the Record,' *LRB*, 19 Sept. 1985.
Beauvoir, Simone de, *Les Mandarins* (Paris, 1952) [*The Mandarins*, trans. by Leonard M. Friedman (London, 1954)].
————, *La Force des Choses* (Paris 1963) [*Force of Circumstances*, trans. by Richard Howard (London, 1965)].
————, *Beloved Chicago Man. Letters to Nelson Algren, 1947-1964* (London, 1998).
Berlin, Isaiah, *Personal Impressions* (London, 1980).
————, 'The Arts in Russia Under Stalin,' *NYRB*, 4/16, 19 Oct. 2000.
Bernard, Théo & Rosenthal, Gérard, *Le Procès de la déportation sans jugement* (Paris, 1954).
Bock, Hedwig & Wertheim, Albert (eds.), *Essays on the Contemporary American Novel* (Munich, 1986).
Bol'shaia Sovetskaia Entsiklopediia, vtoroe izdanie, Moscow [date according to volume].
Tret' izdanie, (Moscow, date according to volume).
Brecht, Bertolt, *Journals 1934-1955*, trans. by Hugh Rorrison, ed. John Willett (London 1993).
Brodsky, Joseph, 'Why Milan Kundera is Wrong about Dostoyevsky,' *NYT,* 17 Feb. 1985.
Brudny, Yitzhak M., *Reinventing Russia. Russian Nationalism and the Soviet State, 1953-1991* (Cambridge, MA, 1998).
Burg, David & Feifer, George, *Solzhenitsyn. A Biography* (London, 1972).
Calvino, Italo, *The Path to the Spider's Nest,* trans. By Archibald Colquhoun, revised by Martin McLaughlin (London, 1998).
Camus, Albert, *Actuelles, I: Chroniques 1948-1953* (Paris, 1953).
————, *The Rebel* (London, 1953).
Carlisle, Olga, *Voices in the Snow. Encounters with Russian Writers* (London, 1963).
————, *Solzhenitsyn and the Secret Circle* (New York, 1978).
Carmichael, Virginia, *Framing History. The Rosenberg Story and the Cold War* (Minneapolis, MN, 1993).
Cate, Curtis, *André Malraux. A Biography* (London, 1995).
Caute, David, *The Dancer Defects: the Struggle for Cultural Supremacy During the Cold War* (Oxford & New York, 2003).
Cesarani, David, *Arthur Koestler. The Homeless Mind* (London, 1998).
Chandler, Robert, 'Vasily Grossman,' *Prospect* (London, Sept. 2006).

Chilton, Paul & Aubrey, Crispin (eds.), *Nineteen Eighty-Four in 1984* (London, 1983).
Chukovskaya, Lydia, *The Deserted House*, trans. by Alison B. Werth (London, 1967). [*Sof'ya Petrovna*, ed. with intro., notes and vocabulary by John Murray (Bristol, 1998)].
———, *Going Under*, trans. by Peter M. Weston (London, 1972).
———, *The Achmatova Journals*, trans. by Milena Michalski & Sylvia Rubashova. Poetry trans. by Peter Norman (London, 1994).
Clark, Katerina, *The Soviet Novel. History as Ritual* (Chicago, 1981).
Clark, Katerina & Dobrenko, Evgeny (eds), *Soviet Culture and Power. A History in Documents* (New Haven & London, 2007)
'Condition of the Novel: Conference of European Writers at Leningrad, Summer 1963,' *NLR* 29 (Jan.-Feb. 1965).
Conquest, *Robert, Common Sense about Russia* (London, 1960).
———, *Courage of Genius: the Pasternak Affair* (London, 1961).
———, *The Politics of Ideas in the USSR* (London, 1967).
Coover, Robert, *The Public Burning* (New York, 1977).
Cornis-Pope, Marcel, *Narrative Innovation and Cultural Rewriting in the Cold War and After* (New York, 2001).
Counts, George S. & Lodge, Nucia P., *The Country of the Blind. The Soviet System of Mind Control* (Boston, 1949).
Crankshaw, Edward, *Russia by Daylight* (London, 1951).
———, *Putting Up with the Russians 1947-1984* (London, 1984).
Crick, Bernard, *George Orwell. A Life* (London, 1980, 1982).
Crossman, Richard (ed.), *The God that Failed* (New York, Bantam edition, 1959).
Cruise O'Brien, Conor, *Writers and Politics* (New York, 1965).
Daglish, Robert, 'Moscow Diary,' *Anglo-Soviet Journal* (XXIX/3, May 1969).
———, 'Forsyte Saga shown on Russian TV,' *Anglo-Soviet Journal* (XXXII/1, Sept. 1971).
Dalos, György, *The Guest from the Future. Anna Akhmatova and Isaiah Berlin, with the collaboration of Andrea Dunai*, trans. by Anton Wood (London, 1998).
Daniel, Yuli (Nikolai Arzhak), *Govorit Moskva* (*This is Moscow Speaking*), clandestine publication, 1962.
Davison, Peter, *George Orwell: a Literary Life* (London, 1996).
———, Orwell in Spain, London, 2001. [See Orwell, George, Orwell in Spain, below].
Deutscher, Isaac, *Stalin. A Political Biography* (Oxford 1949).
———, 'The Mysticism of Cruelty,' in *Heretics and Renegades* (London, 1955).
———, *Heretics and Renegades, 2nd ed.* (London, 1969).
Doctorow, E. L., *The Book of Daniel* (New York, 1971).
———, *Essays and Conversations* (Princeton, NJ., 1983).
Donoghue, Denis, 'On Plain English,' *LRB*, 6/24, 20 Dec. 1984, 7.
Dos Passos, John, *Manhattan Transfer* (New York, 1926).
———, *USA* (1) *The Forty Second Parallel* (New York, 1930); (2) *Nineteen Nineteen* (New York, 1933); (3) *The Big Money* (New York, 1936).
———, *The Best Times* (New York, 1966).
———, *Adventures of a Young Man* (New York, 1939, Popular Library Edition).
———, "The Failure of Marxism," *Life*, XXIV, 19 Jan. 1948.
———, *The Theme is Freedom* (New York, 1956).
———, Foreword to William Buckley, *Up from Liberalism* (New York, 1959).
Dudintsev, Vladimir, *Not by Bread Alone*, trans. by Edith Bone (London, 1957).
Dunlop, John B., Haugh, Richard & Klimoff, Alexis, (eds.) *Aleksandr Solzhenitsyn. Critical Essays and Documentary Materials* (London, 1975).
Eagleton, Terry, *Literary Theory. An Introduction* (London, 1983).
Ehrenburg, Ilya, *The Thaw*, trans. by Manya Harari (London, 1955, 1961).
———, *Men, Years, Life*, trans. by Anna Bostock & Yvonne Kapp. Vol.2. First Years of Revolution, 1918-1921; Vol.3, 1921-41 (London, 1961-1966).
Ehrlich, Victor, 'The Writer as Witness,' in Dunlop and others (eds.).
Ellis, Frank, *Vasiliy Grossman. The Genesis and Evolution of a Russian Heretic* (Oxford/ Providence, RI, 1994).

————, 'The Russian War Novel of the 1990s: a Question of National Identity,' *Salisbury Review*, 22/1 (Autumn 2003).

Evenson, Brian, *Understanding Robert Coover* (Columbia, SC, 2003).

Fadeev (Fadeyev), Alexandre, *La Jeune Garde* [*The Young Guard*, *Molodaia Gvardiia*]), traduit de russe par Jean Champenois (Moscow, n.d.).

Fiedler, Leslie, *A Fiedler Reader* (New York, 1977).

Fischer, Louis, *Men and Politics* (New York, 1941).

Fishkin, Shelley Fisher, *From Fact to Fiction. Journalism and Imaginative Writing in America* (Baltimore, MD & London, 1985).

Fleay, C., & Sanders, M.., 'Looking into the Abyss: George Orwell at the BBC,' *JHC* (24), 1989.

Fleishmann, Lazar, *Boris Pasternak. The Poet and his Politics* (Cambridge, MA. 1990).

Frankel, Edith Rogovin, *Novy Mir. A Case Study in the Politics of Literature, 1952-1958* (Cambridge, 1981).

Fyvel, T.R., 'Arthur Koestler and George Orwell,' in Harold Harris (ed.).

Garaudy, Roger, *D'un réalisme sans rivages* (Paris, 1963).

Garrard, John & Carol, *Inside the Soviet Writers Union* (London & New York, 1990).

Gass, William H., Introduction to Robert Coover, *The Public Burning* (1998 ed. Grove Press, New York).

Gehring, Hansjörg, *Amerikanische Literaturpolitik in Deutschland 1945-53. Ein Aspekt des Re-Education Programms*, (Stuttgart, 1976).

Getty, J. Arch, *Origins of the Great Purges. The Soviet Communist Party Reconsidered, 1933-1938* (Cambridge, 1985).

Gifford, Henry, 'Indomitable Pasternak,' *NYRB*, 37/9, 31 May 1990.

Gisselbrecht, André, "Propositions pour une critique marxiste," *LNC* (Feb-March 64).

Gleason, Abbott, *Totalitarianism. The Inner History of the Cold War* (New York & Oxford, 1995).

Glenny, Michael (edit.), *Novy Mir. A Selection 1955-1967* (London, 1972).

————, 'Orwell's 1984 through Soviet eyes,' *Index on Censorship*, 13/4 (1984).

Goodman, Celia (edit.), *Living with Koestler. Mamaine Koestler's Letters 1945-1951* (London, 1985).

Graff, Gerald, *Literature Against Itself. Literary Ideas in Modern Society* (Chicago & London, 1979).

Greene, Graham, *The Quiet American* (London, 1955).

————, *Ways of Escape* (London, 1980).

————, *Yours etc. Letters to the press 1945-1989*, selected & introd. by Christopher Hawtree (London, 1989).

Grossman, Vasily, *Kolchugin's Youth*, a novel, trans, by Rosemary Edmonds (London, 1946).

————, *The People Immortal*, a novel (London, 1943).

————, *Za pravoe delo* [For a Just Cause] (Moscow, 1956).

————, *Forever Flowing* (*Everything Flows*), trans. by Thomas P. Witney (London, 1973).

————, *Life and Fate* (*Zhizn' i sudba*), trans. by Robert Chandler (London, 1985).

————, *A Writer at War: Vasily Grossman with the Red Army, 1941-1945*, trans. by Luba Vinogradova (London, 2005).

Hames, Peter, *The Czechoslovak New Wave* (Berkeley, 1985).

Hamilton, Iain, *Koestler. A Biography* (London, 1982).

Harris, Harold, (ed.), *Astride Two Cultures. Arthur Koestler at 70* (London, 1975).

Havel, Václav, *The Increased Difficulty of Concentration*, trans. Vera Blackwell (London & New York, 1976).

————, *Disturbing the Peace*, trans. Paul Wilson (London, 1990).

Hayman, Ronald, *Writing Against. A Biography of Sartre* (London, 1986).

Haynes, John Earl & Klehr, Harvey, *Venona: Decoding Soviet Espionage in America* (New Haven, 1999)

Hayward, Max (edit. & trans.), *On Trial. The Soviet State versus 'Abram Tertz' and 'Nikolai Arzhak,'* (New York, 1966).

Hemingway, Ernest, *For Whom the Bell Tolls* (New York, 1941).

————, *By-Line: Selected articles and despatches of four decades*, ed. by William White (London, 1968).

Hingley, Ronald, *Pasternak. A Biography* (London, 1983).

————, *The Russian Mind* (London, 1978).

Hitchens, Christopher, *Orwell's Victory* (London, 2002).

Hite, Molly, '"A Parody of Martyrdom": The Rosenbergs, Cold War Theology, and Robert Coover's *The Public Burning*', *Novel*, 27:1 (Fall, 1993).

Hosking, Geoffrey, *Beyond Socialist Realism. Soviet Fiction Since Ivan Denisovich* (London, 1980).

Howe, Irving, *Politics and the Novel* (New York, Meridian Books edition, 1957).

————, *The Decline of the New* (New York, 1970).

Huxley, Aldous, *Brave New World* (London, 1932).

Huyssen, Andreas, *After the Great Divide. Modernism, Mass Culture, Postmodernism* (Indiana, 1986).

Ickstadt, Heinz, 'Plotting to What End? Doctorow, Coover and the Intervention(s) of History,' in Antonia Sanchez Macarro (1991).

————, 'History, Fiction and the Designs of Robert Coover,' in Hedwig Beck and Albert Wertheim (eds.), *Essays on the Contemporary American Novel* (Munich, 1986).

Ignatieff, Michael, 'Isaiah Berlin (1909-1997), *NYRB*, 44/ 20, 18 Dec. 1997.

————, *Isaiah Berlin. A Life* (London, 1998).

Jameson, Fredric, *Marxism and Form Twentieth-Century Dialectical Theories of Literature* (Princeton, NJ, 1971).

Johnson, Priscilla, *Khrushchev and the Arts. The Politics of Soviet Culture 1962-1964* (Cambridge, MA, 1965).

Johnson, Uwe, *Speculations about Jacob,* trans. by Ursule Molinaro (London, 1963) [*Mutmassungen über Jakob,* (Frankfurt, 1959)].

————, *The Third Books about Achim* (London, 1968) [*Das dritte Buch über Achim* (Frankfurt, 1961)].

————, *Two Views* (London, 1967) [*Zwei Ansichten,* Frankfurt, 1965]).

Josephs, Allen, 'Hemingway's Spanish Sensibility,' in Donaldson (1996).

Kanapa, Jean, *L'Existentialisme n'est pas un humanisme* (Paris, 1947).

Kazin, Alfred, 'Ideology vs the Novel,' Commentary, 11/4 (April 1951).

————, 'Not One of Us,' *NYRB*, 14 June 1984.

Keep, J.H. *Contemporary History in the Soviet Mirror* (London, 1963).

Khrushchev, Nikita, *Khrushchev Remembers. The Last Testament. Memoirs*, vol.2, trans. & edit. by Strobe Talbott (London, 1974).

Kochetov, Vsevolod, *The Zhurbins* (Moscow, 1952).

Koestler, Arthur, *Spanish Testament* (London, 1938).

————, *Darkness at Noon* (London, 1941) [*Le Zéro et l'infini* (Paris, 1944)].

————, *The Yogi and the Commissar* (London, 1945).

————, *Arrival and Departure* (London, 1943).

————, *The Invisible Writing* (Boston, 1956).

————, *The Age of Longing* (London, 1951).

————, *The Trail of the Dinosaur and Other Essays* (London, 1955).

Kopelev, Lev, *The Education of a True Believer,* trans. by Anthony Austin (London, 1977).

Kundera, Milan, *The Joke,* trans. by David Hamblyn & Oliver Stallybrass (London, 1970).

————, *The Book of Laughter and Forgetting,* trans. by Michael Henry Heim (London, 1982) [*Le Livre du rire et de l'oubli* (Paris, 1979)].

————, *The Unbearable Lightness of Being,* trans by Henry Heim, London, 1984.

————, *Les testaments trahis* (Paris, 1993).

Kuznetsov, Anatoly, *Baby Yar*, trans. by Jacob Guralsky (New York, 1967).

Lacouture, Jean, *André Malraux*, trans. by Alan Sherdian (London, 1975).

Laqueur, Walter & Lichtheim, George (eds.), *The Soviet Cultural Scene 1956-1957* (London, 1958).

Lazareff, Helene & P., *L'URSS à l'heure Malenkov* (Paris, 1954) [*The Soviet Union after Stalin* (London, 1955)].

LeClair, Thomas, 'Robert Coover, *The Public Burning*, and the Art of Excess', *Critique*, 23/3 (Spring 1982).

Levene, Mark, *Arthur Koestler* (London, 1984).

Levi, Peter, *Boris Pasternak* (London, 1990).

Levine, Paul, *E,L. Doctorow* (London, 1985).

Lichtheim, George, 'On Lukács,' *Encounter,* XX/5, May 1963.

Lottman, Herbert R., *The Left Bank. Writers, Artists and Politics from the Popular Front to the Cold War* (London, 1982).

Lukács, Georg, *The Meaning of Contemporary Realism* (London, 1962).

——, *The Historical Novel,* trans. By Hannah Mitchell and Stanley Mitchell (London, 1963).

——, *Solzhenitsyn*, trans. by William David Graf (London 1970).

Lyons, Graham (ed.), *The Russian Version of the Second World War* (London, 1978).

Macarro, Antonia Sanchez (ed.), *Studies in American Literature* (Valencia, 1991).

Magenau, Jörg, *Christa Wolf. Eine Biographie* (Berlin, 2002).

Mailer, Norman, *Barbary Shore* (New York, 1951).

——, *Advertisements for Myself* (London, 1961).

——, *Why Are We in Vietnam?* A Novel (New York, 1967).

——, *The Armies of the Night. History as a Novel, the Novel as History* (New York, 1968).

Maine, Barry (ed.), *Dos Passos. The Critical Heritage* (London & New York, 1988).

Mallac, Guy de, 'Kafka in Russia,' *Russian Review*, 32/1 (January 1972).

Malraux, André, *Les Conquérants* (Paris, 1927).

——, *La Condition humaine* (Paris, 1933, 1946) [*Man's Estate*, trans. by Alastair Mac-Donald (London, 1948 (Penguin ed. 1961)].

——, *Le Temps du mépris* (Paris, 1935 [*Days of Wrath*, trans. by Haakon M. Chevalier (New York, 1936)].

——, *L'Espoir* (Paris, 1938, 1947) [*Days of Hope,* trans. by Stuart Gilbert & Alastair MacDonald (London, 1938, 1968)].

——, 'The Fascist Threat to Culture' (Cambridge, MA, 1937).

——, *Esquisse pour une psychologie du cinéma* (Paris, 1939).

Marchenko, Anatoly, *My Testimony*, trans. by Michael Scammell (London, 1969).

Markish, Simon, *Le Cas Grossman*, traduit du russe par Dominique Négrel (Paris, 1983) [*Primer Vassiliia Grossmana*].

——, 'A Russian Writer's Jewish Fate,' *Commentary,* 81/4 (1986).

Marsh, Rosalind, *Images of Dictatorship. Portraits of Stalin in literature* (London & New York, 1989).

Marx, Karl & Engels, Friedrich, *Marx and Engels on Literature and Art* (Bombay, 1956).

Mayer, Hans & Bondy, François, 'The Struggle for Kafka and Joyce,' *Encounter*, 22/5 (May 1964).

McCaffery, Larry, *The Metafictional Muse. The Works of Robert Coover, Donald Barthelme, and William H. Gass* (Pittsburgh, 1982).

Mead, Margaret, (ed.), *Soviet Attitudes toward Authority* (London, 1955).

Medvedev, Roy A., *Let History Judge. The Origins and Consequences of Stalinism* (New York, 1971, London, 1972).

——, 'On Solzhenitsyn's *The Gulag Archipelago,'* in Dunlop and others (ed.)

Medvedev, Zhores, *Ten Years after Ivan Denisovich*, trans. by Hilary Sternberg (London, 1974).

——, 'The Attack on Lydia Chukovskaya,' *NYRB 21/3*), 7 March 1974.

Meeropol, Robert & Michael, *We Are Your Sons* (Boston, 1975).

Mehnert, Klaus, *The Anatomy of Soviet Man*, trans. by Maurice Rosenbaum (London, 1961).

Merleau-Ponty, Maurice, *Humanisme et terreur* (Paris, 1947).

Meyers, Jeffrey (edit.), *Hemingway. The Critical Heritage* (London, 1982).

Moorehead, Caroline, *Martha Gellhorn. A Life* (London, 2003).

Nekrasov, Viktor, *On Both Sides of the Ocean. A Russian Writer's Travels in Italy and the United States*, trans. by Elias Kulukundis (London, 1964).

Neumann, Bernd, *Uwe Johnson* (Hamburg, 1994).

Newsinger, John, *Orwell's Politics* (London, 1999).

Oates, Joyce Carol, *You Must Remember This* (New York, 1987).

Orwell, George, *Homage to Catalonia* (London, 1938). Revised ed. in *Orwell in Spain* (London, 2001).

———, *Animal Farm* (London, 1945).

———, *Nineteen Eighty-Four* (London, 1949).

———, *Collected Essays, Journalism & Letters (CE),* edit. by Sonia Orwell & Ian Angus: vol. 1, 1920-1940; vol. 2, 1940-1943; vol. 3, 1943-1945; vol. 4, 1945-1950 (London, 1970).

———, *The Complete Works of George Orwell,* vol. 20, 1949-50, ed. by Peter Davison assisted by Ian Angus & Sheila Davison (London, 1998).

Pasternak, Boris, *Doctor Zhivago,* trans. by Max Hayward & Manya Harari (London, 1959).

Pavlenko, Pyotr, *Happiness. A Novel* (Moscow, 1947).

Payne, Stanley, *The Spanish Conflict, the Soviet Union and Communism* (New Haven & London, 2004).

Podhoretz, Norman, *The Bloody Cross Roads. Where Literature and Politics Meet* (New York, 1986).

———, *Ex-Friends* (New York, 1999).

Polonsky, V., 'Lenin's View of Art and Culture,' in Max Eastman (ed.), *Artists in Uniform* (London, 1934).

Porter, Robert, *Four Contemporary Russian Writers* (Oxford, 1989).

Pritchett, V. S., 'The Spanish Tragedy,' *NS* (15/375, 30 Apr. 1938).

Rees, Goronwy, 'Darkness at Noon and the "Grammatical Fiction"' in Harris (1975).

Riordan, Colin, *The Ethics of Narration. Uwe Johnson's Novels from 'Ingrid Babendererde' to 'Jahrestage'* (London, 1989).

Rosen, Robert C., *John Dos Passos. Politics and the Writer* (Lincoln, NE, 1981).

Rousset, David, *Police-State Methods in the Soviet Union,* trans. By Charles R. Joy (Boston, 1953).

Rubin, Jerry, *Do It!* (New York, Ballantine ed., 1970).

Rybakov, Anatoli, *Children of the Arbat,* trans. by Harold Shukman (London, 1988).

Salisbury, Harrison, E., *To Moscow and Beyond. A Reporter's Narrative* (London, 1960).

Sartre, Jean-Paul, *The Age of Reason,* trans, by Eric Sutton (London, Penguin ed., 1951) [*L'Age de raison* (Paris, 1945)].

———, *The Reprieve,* trans. by Eric Sutton (London, 1947, Penguin ed., 1986) [*Le Sursis* (Paris, 1945)].

———, *Iron in the Soul,* trans. By Gerard Hopkins (London, Penguin, 1986) [*La Mort dans l'âme,* Paris, 1949].

———, 'Drôle d'amitié,' *Les Temps modernes* (1949).

———, *What is Literature?*), trans. by Bernard Frechtman (London, 1950) [*Qu'est-ce que la littérature,* (Paris, 1947)].

———, (& Maurice Merleau-Ponty), 'Les jours de notre vie', *LTM,* January 1950.

———, *War Diaries. Notebooks from a Phoney War, 1939-40,* trans. by Quentin Hoare (London, 1984).

Saunders, Francis Stonor, *Who Paid the Piper? The CIA and the Cultural Cold War* (London, 1999). Published as *Cold War: The CIA and the World of Arts and Letters* (New York, 2000).

Scammell, Michael, *Solzhenitsyn: a biography* (New York, 1984).

———, *The Solzhenitsyn Files* (Chicago, 1995).

———, 'The Solzhenitsyn Archipelago,' *NYRB,* XLV/19, 3 Dec. 1998.

Schapiro, Leonard, *The Communist Party of the Soviet Union* (London, 1970).

Schaub, Thomas Hill, *American Fiction in the Cold War* (Madison, Wisconsin, 1991).

Schmemann, Alexander, 'Reflections on The Gulag Archipelago,' in Dunlop (1975).

Scholes, Robert, 'The Fictional Criticism of the Future,' *Triquarterly,* 34 (Fall 1955).

Schwarz, Wilhelm Johannes, *Der Erzähler Uwe Johnson* (Munich, 1970).

Serge, Victor, *The Case of Comrade Tulayev* , trans. by Willard R. Trask, (London, 1951).

———, *Memoirs of a Revolutionary, 1901-1941,* trans. & ed. by Peter Sedgwick (London, 1963).

Shelden, Michael, *Graham Greene: the Man Within* (London, 1999).

Sherry, Norman, *The Life of Graham Greene*: vol. 2, 1939-1955 (London, 1994); vol. 3, 1955-1991 (London 2004).

Sholokhov, Mikhail, *Virgin Soil Upturned*, trans. by Stephen Garry (London, 1935).

———, *Harvest on the Don*, trans. by H.C. Stevens (London, 1960).

Simonov, Konstantin, 'Plays, The Theatre, and Life,' *VOKS Bulletin*, 50 (1946).

———, 'The Tasks Before Soviet Drama and Dramatic Criticism,' *Soviet Studies*, 1/2 (Oct. 1949).

———, *Victims and Heroes*, trans. by R. Ainsztein (London, 1962).

Sinyavsky, Andrei (as Abram Tertz), *On Socialist Realism*, trans. by George Dennis (New York, 1960).

———, (as Abram Tertz) *The Trial Begins*, trans. by George Dennis (New York, 1960).

———, (as Abram Tertz), 'Beasts and Men,' *NYRB* (XXVI/21-22, 24 Jan. 1980).

———, *Soviet Civilization*, trans. by Joanne Turnbull (London, 1990).

Slonim, Marc, *Soviet Russian Literature: Writers and Problems* (New York, 1977).

Solzhenitsyn, Aleksandr. *One Day in the Life of Ivan Denisovich*, trans, by Ralph Parker (New York, Signet ed., 1963). [*Odin den' Ivan Denisovicha*].

———, 'An Incident at Krechetovka Station,' *NM* (Jan. 1963). [*Sluchi na stantsii Krechetovka*].

———, 'Matrena's Home,' *NM* (Jan. 1963). [*Matrenin dvor*].

———, *For the Good of the Cause*, trans, by David Floyd & Max Hayward (New York & London, 1970). [*NM*, July 1963].

———, *The First Circle*, trans. by Michael Guybon (London, 1968) [*V Kruge Pervom*].

———, *Cancer Ward*, Parts I & 2, trans. by Nicholas Bethell & David Burg (London, 1968) [*Rakovye Korpus*].

———, *Stories and Prose Poems,* trans. by Michael Glenny (London, 1971).

———, *The Gulag Archipelago 1918-1956*, vol. 1, trans. by Thomas P. Whitney (London, 1974) [*Arkhipelag GULag 1918-1956, opyt khudozhestvennogo issledovanii*].

———, 'As Breathing and Consciousness Return,' in Solzhenitsyn et al., *Under the Rubble* (London, 1975).

———, *Lenin in Zurich*, trans. By H.T. Willetts (London, 1976) [*Lenin v T Si urikhe: glavy*].

———, *The Oak and the Calf, Sketches of Literary Life in the Soviet Union*, trans. by Harry Willetts (London, 1980). [*Bolalsya telenok s dubom*].

———, *Invisible Allies*, trans. by Alexis Klimoff & Michael Nicholson (London, 1997).

Stansky, Peter and Abrahams, William, *Orwell: The Transformation* (London, 1979).

Steiner, George, 'Marxism and the Literary Critic,' in *Language and Silence* (New York, 1967).

Sturgess, Philip J.M., *Narrativity. Theory and Practice* (London, 1992).

Tanenhaus, Sam, 'Red Scare,' *NYRB*, 14 Jan. 1999.

Tertz, Abram (see Sinyavsky, Andrei).

Thomas, D.M., *Alexander Solzhenitsyn. A Century in his Life* (London, 1998).

Thompson, Edward P., 'Outside the Whale,' (1960) in *The Poverty of Theory & Other Essays* (London, 1978).

———, 'Inside Which Whale?' in *George Orwell. A Collection of Essays*, ed. by Raymond Williams (London, 1974).

Thornberry, Robert S., *André Malraux et L'Espagne* (Geneva, 1977).

Todd, Olivier, *Albert Camus. Une Vie* (Paris, 1996).

———, *André Malraux. Une Vie* (Paris, 2001).

Vargas Llosa, Mario, 'The Truth of Lies', in *Making Waves,* ed. & trans. by John King (London, 1996).

Vladimov, Georgii, *Faithful Ruslan. The Story of a Guard Dog*, trans. by Michael Glenny (London, 1979). [*Vernyi Ruslan. Istoriia karaul'noi sobaki*].

———, 'Pay No Attention Maestro,' *Literary Review* (London), 50 (May 1983).

———, *Sobranie sochoinenii v chetyrekh tomakh*. Tom pervyi (Moscow, 1998).

Walsh, Richard, 'Narrative Inscription, History and the Reader in Robert Coover's "The Public Burning",' *Studies in the Novel* (Univ. of North Texas), XXV/3, (Fall 1993).

Warshow, Robert, *The Immediate Experience* (New York, 1962, 1964).

Weber, Ronald, *The Literature of Fact: Literary Nonfiction in American Writing* (Athens, OH, 1980).

———, *Hemingway and the Art of Nonfiction* (London, 1990).

Weissman, Susan, *Victor Serge: the course is set on hope* (London, 2001).

Wellek, Rene & Warren, Austin, *Theory of Literature* (1942, Harvest Book ed., 1956).

Werth, Alexander, *Russia: Hopes and Fears* (London, 1969).

Willett, John (ed.), *Brecht on Theatre* (London, 1964).

Williams, Raymond (ed.), *George Orwell. A Collection of Critical Essays* (New Jersey, 1974).

Williams, Raymond, *Politics and Letters* (London, 1979, 1994).

Wolf, Christa, *Divided Heaven* (Berlin, 1965). [*Geteiligt Himmel* (Berlin, 1963)].

———, *The Quest for Christa T,* trans. by Christopher Middleton (London, 1971) [*Nachdenken über Christa T,* (Halle, 1968)].

———, *Ein Tag im Jahr* (Munich, 2002).

Wolfe, Tom, *The New Journalism* (London, 1975).

Yevtushenko, Yevgeni, *A Precocious Autobiography* (London, 1963).

Zhdanov, A. A., *On Literature, Music and Philosophy* (London, 1950).

Name Index

Subject Index

Press: *Arbeiter Illustrierte Zeitung* 50;
Berlin am Morgen 50; *Der Monat* 85,
125; Berlin (post-1945), 2, 84, 125,
245, 250, 254-6
German Federal Republic; 251-2; Gruppe; '47 252; Suhrkampf Verlag; 252
German Democratic Republic (GDR)
236, 245-8, 250-3, 373 (28); Berlin
uprising (1953), 166, 253; Berlin Wall
(1961), 245-55; Karl Marx University,
Leipzig, 252; Socialist Unity Party
(SED), 238, 246, 248; Stasi (Ministe-
rium für Staatssicherheit), 246, 253-4;
Press: *Freiheit* (Halle), 245; *Sinn und
Form,* 236
God that failed, 10, 33, 36, 47, 49, 69,
72, 89, 94, 97, 103, 112, 124, 125, 352

International relations: First World War,
33, 230, 237, 247, 261, 290; Treaty
of Brest-Litovsk, 1, 120, 189; Treaty
of Versailles, 107; Economic depression 1930s, 1, 11, 340, 351; Munich
Agreement (1938), 2, 54, 61, 85,
104, 106-7, 179, 352; Nazi-Soviet
Pact (1939), 3, 21, 54, 77, 104, 109,
120, 153, 351; Phoney war (drôle de
guerre), 108, 153, 167; Nazi invasion
of France, 77, 167; Nazi invasion of
the USSR (Barbarossa, 1941), 59, 153-
63, 271, 279, 353; Soviet-Finnish War
(1939-40), 59, 92, 156, 164; Soviet
incorporation of the Baltic states, 152,
154, 156; Second World War, 1, 2,
19, 21, 30, 104, 119, 122, 153, 185,
327, 329, 336, 351; Soviet conquest
of Germany (1945), 164-5, 247, 253;
Berlin blockade (1948-49), 94, 245,
282; Cold War, nature and origins,
95, 103, 119, 148, 166, 171, 186, 330,
344, 347-8, 354; Atomic weapons, 83,
87, 90, 113, 281; Atomic espionage,
167, 273, 337, 341-2; Korean War, 75,
333, 344; World Peace Congresses,
236; Hungarian Revolution, 166, 235;
Vietnam War (see also France, Indo
China), 5, 132, 135-9, 142, 305, 329,
334-5, 340, 345

Literature: Allegory, 2, 12, 69, 80, 83,
96-7, 150, 237, 333, 335; Cinema,

influence on literature, 12, 18, 30, 302,
352 *Storm over Asia,* 50; Expressionism, 10, 13, 30, 238, 345, 351;
Formalism, 2, 127, 185, 232, 235, 330;
Hero, heroine, role of, 3, 13, 14, 18,
21, 33, 60, 85-7, 90, 106, 108-9, 127-
8, 186, 190, 193, 195, 199-200, 202-4,
220, 238-9, 246-7, 249-53, 263, 265,
267 269, 294, 317-18; Hero, heroine
in socialist realist novels, 3, 150-2,
158-162, 165, 168-9, 171-2, 175, 178,
181-3, 188, 190, 220. 222-3, 309-
10; Indirect monologue (polyphony)
27, 158, 270, 285-7; Journalism and
the novel, 11, 30, 84, 91, 105, 111,
137, 354, 357 (1-3); New Journalism
(USA), 327-8; Modernism, 2, 5, 233,
235-6, 238-9, 247, 252-3, 260, 327-8,
334, 337, 341, 354, 356; Plays, playwrights, 1, 26, 103-5, 110, 149-50, 152,
164, 166, 204, 230, 241, 252, 269, 297,
308, 315-16; Poets, poetry, 15, 110,
127, 193, 195, 198, 203, 207, 214, 216,
219, 224, 240, 242, 252, 287, 316, 323;
Postmodernism, 5, 252-3, 328-9, 330-1,
337, 345, 348-9, 355-6; Realism (and
Critical Realism), 5, 30, 69, 72, 147-8,
150, 153, 174, 219-22, 235-40, 251,
327-8, 330, 349, 351, 354-6; Satire,
2, 83, 85, 123, 132, 213-14, 220, 319,
323; Socialist realism, 5, 103, 111, 148,
152, 175, 206, 234, 309, 349; Surrealism, 110, 238, 354, 372 (25); Symbolism, 153, 195, 238, 311

Marx, Karl, 14, 62, 80, 82, 83, 98, 128,
147-8, 235, 298; Marxism, Marxists,
14, 20, 27, 30-1, 37, 50, 62, 68, 72, 83,
91, 98, 103, 111, 124, 147-8, 150, 160,
189-90, 204, 220-1, 234-8, 252, 282-3,
285-6, 312, 315, 334, 352, 355

New Left revisionism, 5, 91, 330, 335,
339-41

PEN, 187, 225, 227, 371 (23-19)
Poland, 1, 29, 30, 152-4, 156 160, 166,
234, 236, 246, 252
Power and power hunger, 11, 12, 27, 43,
51, 65, 67, 80-2, 86-7, 89, 90, 97-100,
148, 160, 188, 232, 238-9, 272-3, 276,